Teach Yourself VISUALLY™

Google Workspace™

by Guy Hart-Davis

Teach Yourself VISUALLY™ Google Workspace™

Published simultaneously in Canada

Wiley publishes in a variety of print and electronic formats and by print-on-demand. Some material included with standard print versions of this book may not be included in e-books or in print-on-demand. If this book refers to media such as a CD or DVD that is not included in the version you purchased, you may download this material at booksupport.wiley.com. For more information about Wiley products, visit www.wiley.com.

Library of Congress Control Number: 2021932146

ISBN: 978-1-119-76327-7

ISBN: 978-1-119-76331-4 (ebk)

ISBN: 978-1-119-76332-1 (ebk)

Manufactured in the United States of America

Trademark Acknowledgments

Contact Us

For general information on our other products and services, please contact our Customer Care Department within the U.S. at 877-762-2974, outside the U.S. at 317-572-3993 or fax 317-572-4002.

For technical support please visit hub.wiley.com/community/support.

SKY10025934_033021

Sales | Contact Wiley at (877) 762-2974 or fax (317) 572-4002.

About the Author

Guy Hart-Davis is the author of more than 150 computer books, including *Teach Yourself VISUALLY iPhone 12, 12 Pro, and 12 Pro Max; Teach Yourself VISUALLY Chromebook;* and *Teach Yourself VISUALLY Word 2019*.

Author's Acknowledgments

My thanks go to the many people who turned my manuscript into the highly graphical book you are holding. In particular, I thank Devon Lewis for asking me to write the book; Lynn Northrup for keeping me on track; Liz Welch for skillfully editing the text; Doug Holland for reviewing the book for technical accuracy and contributing helpful suggestions; Rachel Fogelberg for proofreading the book minutely; and SPi Global for laying out the book.

How to Use This Book

Who This Book Is For

This book is for the reader who has never used this particular technology or software application. It is also for readers who want to expand their knowledge.

The Conventions in This Book

1 Steps

This book uses a step-by-step format to guide you easily through each task. **Numbered steps** are actions you must do; **bulleted steps** clarify a point, step, or optional feature; and **indented steps** give you the result.

2 Notes

Notes give additional information — special conditions that may occur during an operation, a situation that you want to avoid, or a cross-reference to a related area of the book.

3 Icons and Buttons

Icons and buttons show you exactly what you need to click to perform a step.

4 Tips

Tips offer additional information, including warnings and shortcuts.

5 Bold

Bold type shows command names, options, and text or numbers you must type.

6 Italics

Italic type introduces and defines a new term.

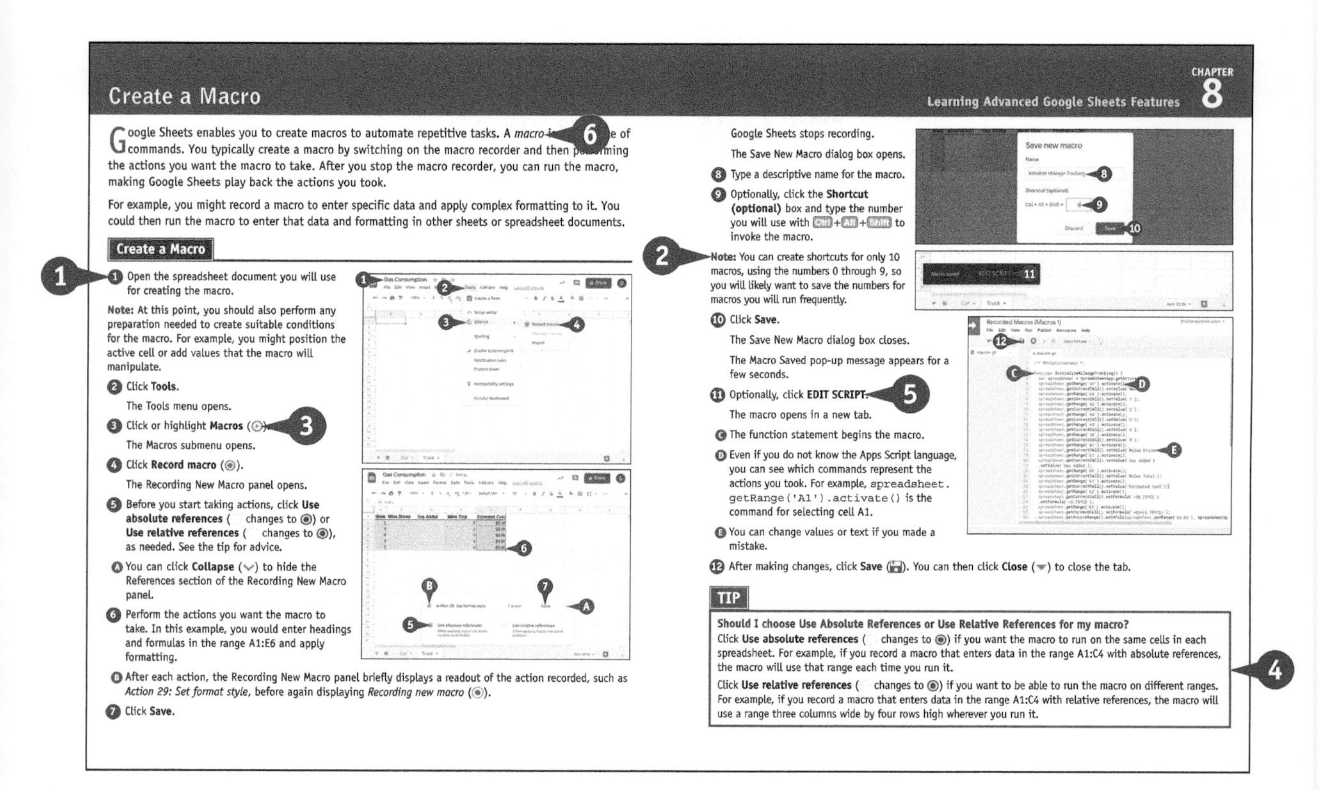

Create a Macro

Learning Advanced Google Sheets Features — CHAPTER 8

Google Sheets enables you to create macros to automate repetitive tasks. A *macro* is a sequence of commands. You typically create a macro by switching on the macro recorder and then performing the actions you want the macro to take. After you stop the macro recorder, you can run the macro, making Google Sheets play back the actions you took.

For example, you might record a macro to enter specific data and apply complex formatting to it. You could then run the macro to enter that data and formatting in other sheets or spreadsheet documents.

Create a Macro

1. Open the spreadsheet document you will use for creating the macro.

Note: At this point, you should also perform any preparation needed to create suitable conditions for the macro. For example, you might position the active cell or add values that the macro will manipulate.

2. Click **Tools**.
   The Tools menu opens.
3. Click or highlight **Macros** ( ).
   The Macros submenu opens.
4. Click **Record macro** ( ).
   The Recording New Macro panel opens.
5. Before you start taking actions, click **Use absolute references** (changes to) or **Use relative references** (changes to), as needed. See the tip for advice.
   - A You can click **Collapse** ( ) to hide the References section of the Recording New Macro panel.
6. Perform the actions you want the macro to take. In this example, you would enter headings and formulas in the range A1:E6 and apply formatting.
   - B After each action, the Recording New Macro panel briefly displays a readout of the action recorded, such as *Action 29: Set format style*, before again displaying *Recording new macro* ( ).
7. Click **Save**.
   Google Sheets stops recording.
   The Save New Macro dialog box opens.
8. Type a descriptive name for the macro.
9. Optionally, click the **Shortcut (optional)** box and type the number you will use with Ctrl + Alt + Shift to invoke the macro.

Note: You can create shortcuts for only 10 macros, using the numbers 0 through 9, so you will likely want to save the numbers for macros you will run frequently.

10. Click **Save**.
    The Save New Macro dialog box closes.
    The Macro Saved pop-up message appears for a few seconds.
11. Optionally, click **EDIT SCRIPT**.
    The macro opens in a new tab.
    - C The function statement begins the macro.
    - D Even if you do not know the Apps Script language, you can see which commands represent the actions you took. For example, `spreadsheet.getRange('A1').activate()` is the command for selecting cell A1.
    - E You can change values or text if you made a mistake.
12. After making changes, click **Save** ( ). You can then click **Close** ( ) to close the tab.

TIP

Should I choose Use Absolute References or Use Relative References for my macro?

Click **Use absolute references** (changes to) if you want the macro to run on the same cells in each spreadsheet. For example, if you record a macro that enters data in the range A1:C4 with absolute references, the macro will use that range each time you run it.

Click **Use relative references** (changes to) if you want to be able to run the macro on different ranges. For example, if you record a macro that enters data in the range A1:C4 with relative references, the macro will use a range three columns wide by four rows high wherever you run it.

Table of Contents

Chapter 1 Getting Started with Google Workspace

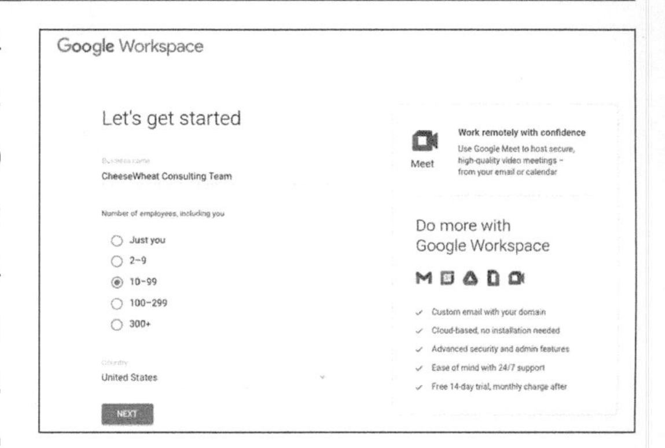

Chapter 2 Managing Files and Folders in Google Drive

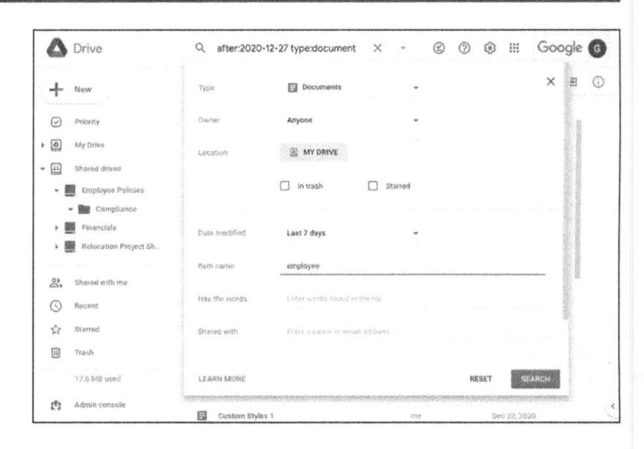

Chapter 3 Performing Common Tasks in Google Docs, Google Sheets, and Google Slides

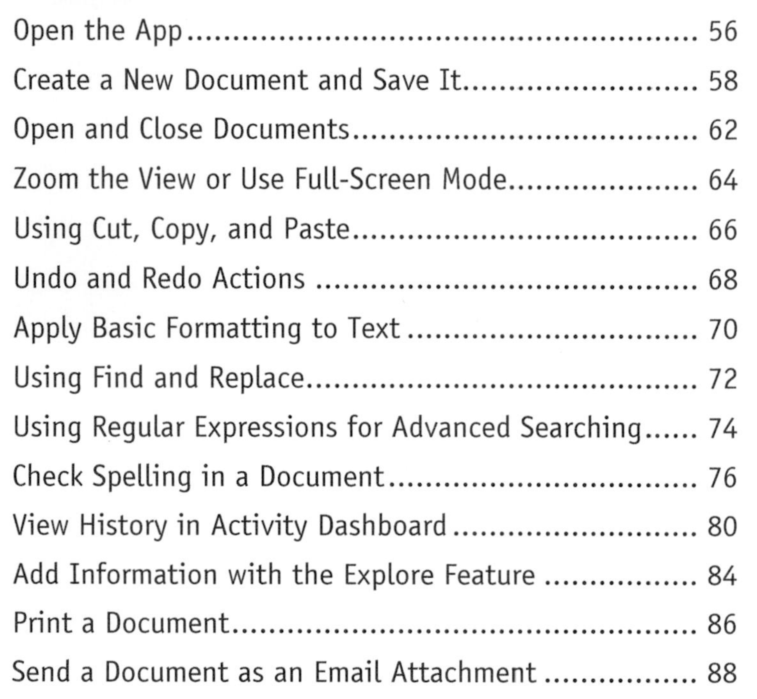

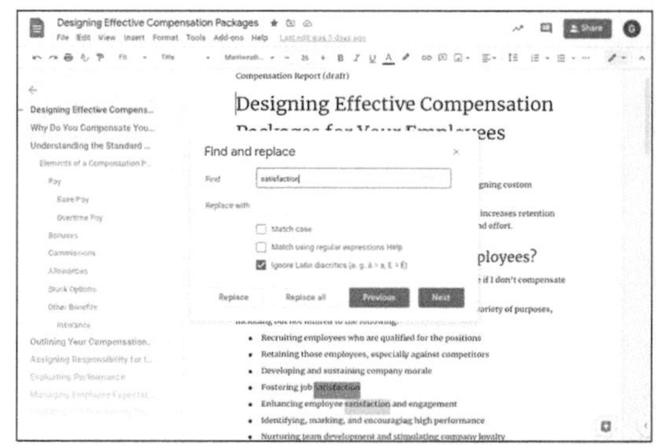

Chapter 4 Inserting Objects in Google Docs, Google Sheets, and Google Slides

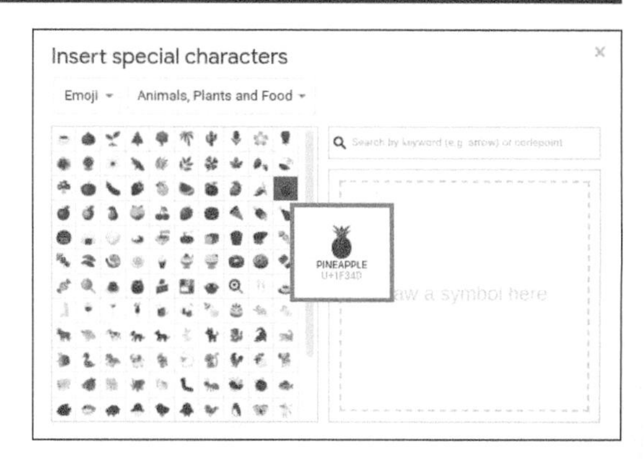

Table of Contents

Chapter 5 Working in Google Docs

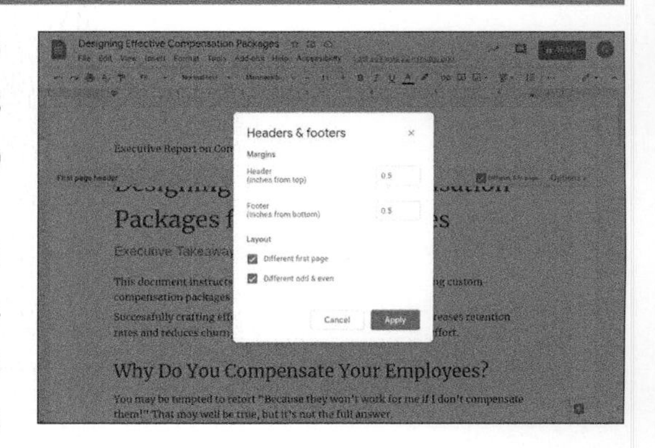

Chapter 6 Sharing and Collaborating on Files

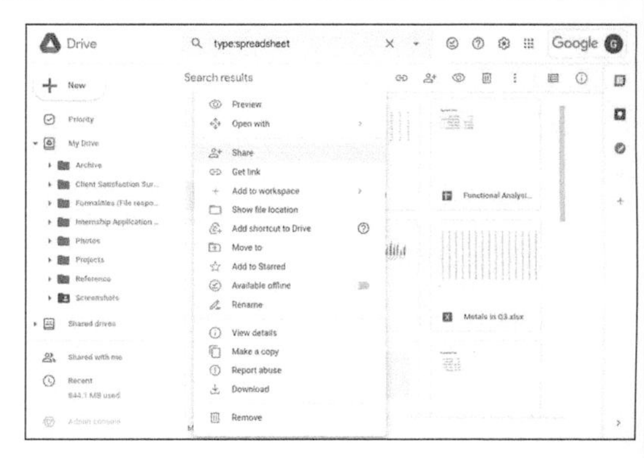

Chapter 7 Working in Google Sheets

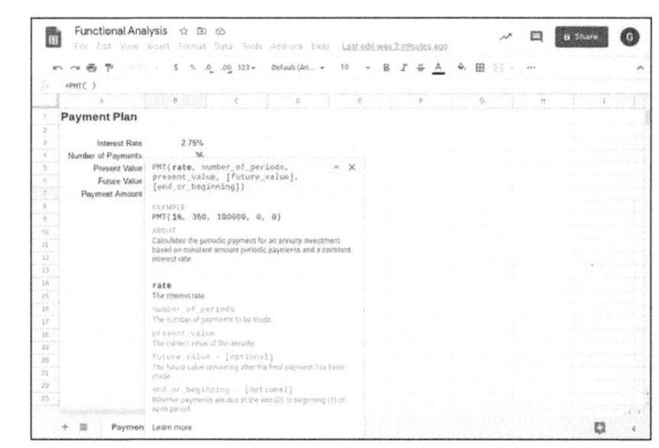

Chapter 8 Learning Advanced Google Sheets Features

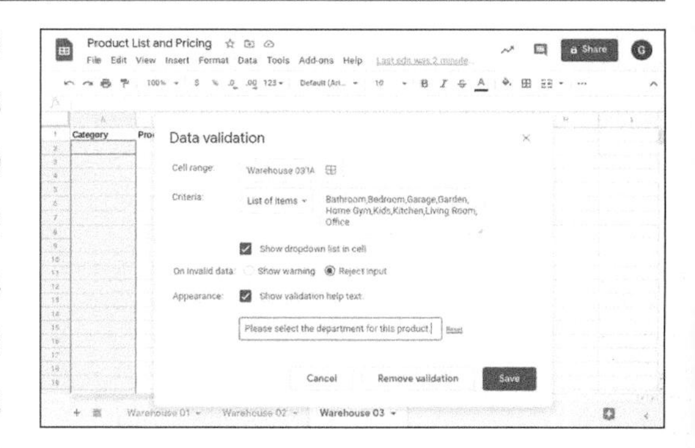

Table of Contents

Chapter 9 Working in Google Slides

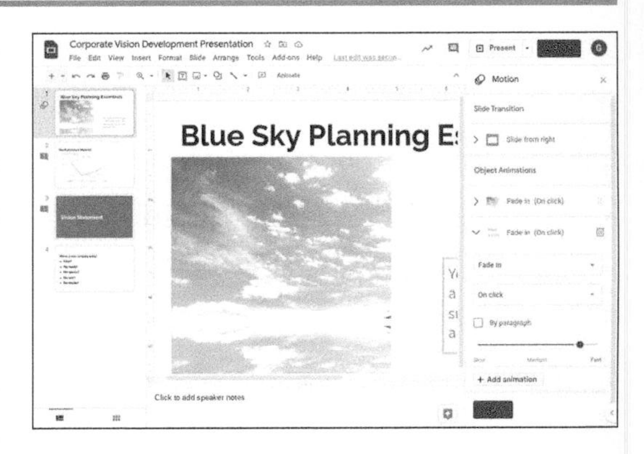

Chapter 10 Sending and Receiving Email

Table of Contents

Chapter 11 Organizing Your Life

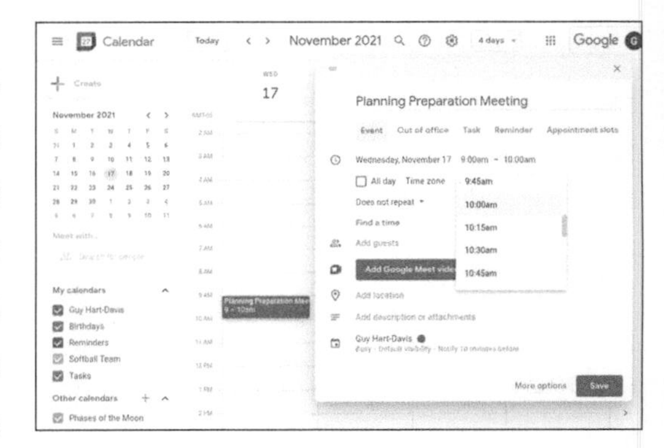

Chapter 12 Creating Forms with Google Forms

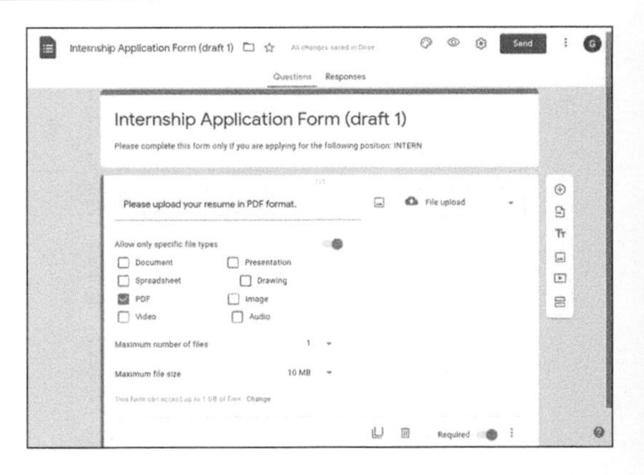

CHAPTER 1

Getting Started with Google Workspace

In this chapter, you learn what Google Workspace is, meet the suite's apps, and get an executive overview of the various account types available and how to sign up for Google Workspace. You then discover how to sign in, how to run apps, and how to configure your profile information and photo. You also learn about using Google Workspace on mobile devices.

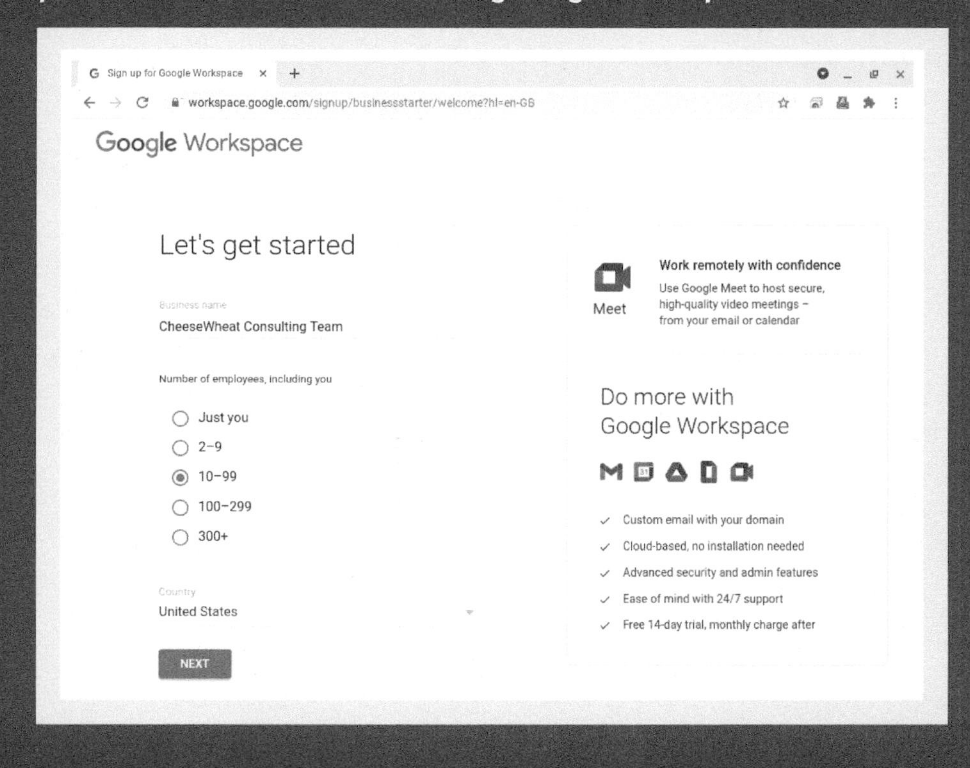

Understanding What Google Workspace Is

Google Workspace is a suite of web applications and services built on Google's client computing infrastructure. Google Workspace's apps include the Gmail email service; the Google Drive online storage service; the Google Docs, Google Sheets, and Google Slides productivity apps; the Google Keep notes app; the Google Forms app for designing forms, distributing them, and collecting their responses; and various communications apps, such as Google Meet and Google Chat.

Google launched the service as Google Apps for Your Domain in 2006, renamed it to G Suite in 2016, and rebranded it as Google Workspace in fall 2020.

Google Workspace Is a Business-Focused Service

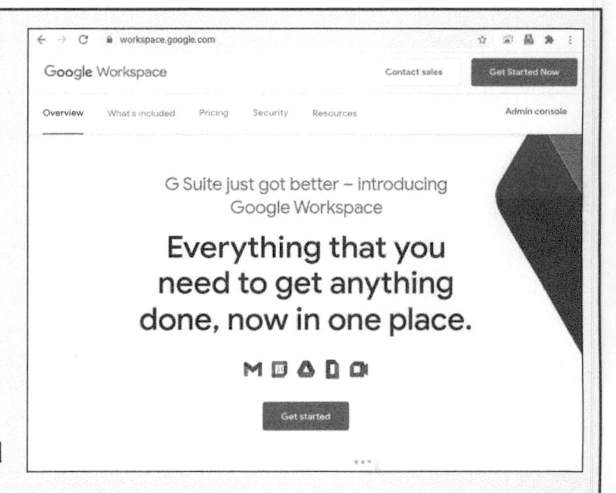

Google is universally known for the free services it provides to consumers in exchange for some of their personal information. For example, consumers can use the Google search engine, the Gmail email service, and the Google Hangouts chat and videoconferencing service for free.

By contrast, Google Workspace is a business-focused service with a monthly fee per user. Many of the apps and services included in Google Workspace are the same as those available to and widely used by individual consumers, but Google Workspace brings them together into a comprehensive suite that delivers extra features and enhanced capabilities. For example, Google Workspace enables an organization to use its own domain for email addresses, provides administrative tools for creating and managing user accounts, and offers larger amounts of storage on Google Drive.

Users Access Google Workspace via Google Accounts

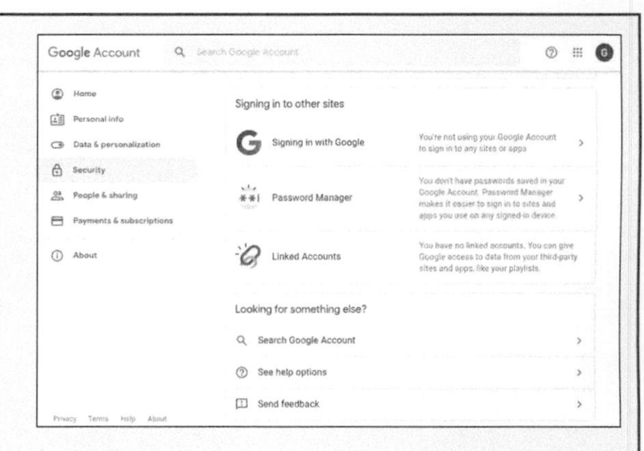

A Google Account is a single credential — a username and password pair — that gives you access to Google apps and services.

The Google Account acts as a key to both consumer accounts and Google Workspace accounts. The principal difference is that a consumer sets up their own Google Account and an administrator sets up a Google Account for each user in a Google Workspace organization.

The administrator retains centralized control of the Google Accounts in a Google Workspace organization and can configure many settings to control what the users can do. As a trivial example, the administrator can control whether or not users can change their profile photos and personal information.

Web-Based Apps Provide Easy Version Control and Updating

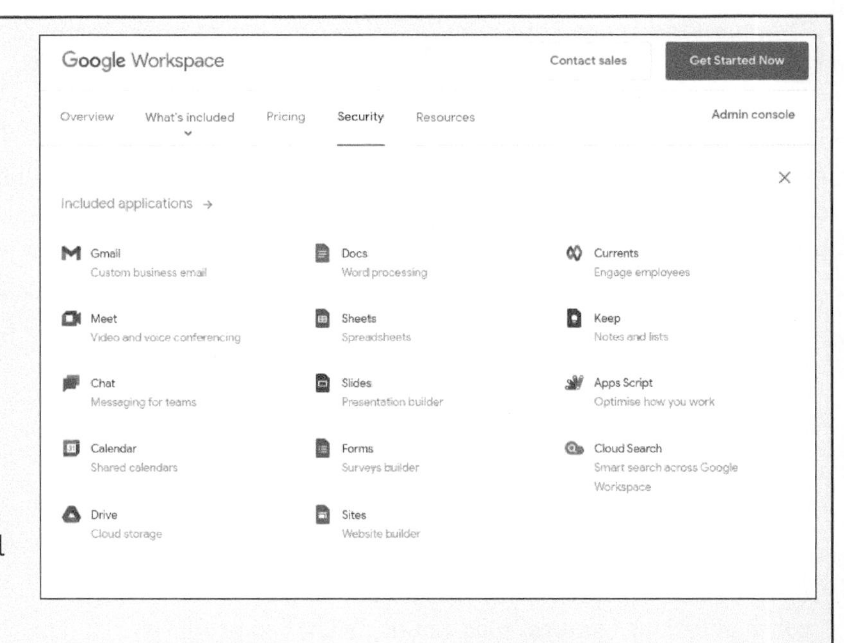

Like most Google apps, the Google Workspace apps are web based rather than being installed on users' computers. Web-based apps require an Internet connection but deliver substantial benefits for management, standardization, and updating: Each time the user accesses a web-based app, they get the current version of the app without having to worry about updating it; and because each user receives the same version of the app, app features and capabilities will be consistent for all users — as will any bugs.

Google provides mobile versions of many apps for Android phones and tablets and for iOS devices — the iPhone, the iPad, and the iPod touch. These mobile apps do require installation, but both Android and iOS can either automatically install updates or prompt users to install them, so keeping the mobile apps up to date is not usually a problem.

Users Can Easily Work on Different Devices

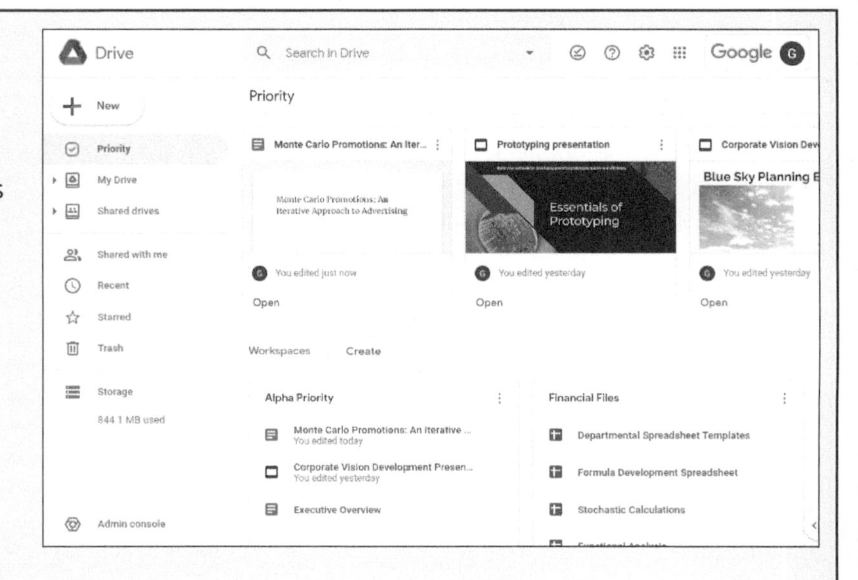

Because the Google Workspace apps are web based, and because the apps store their files in Google Drive, users can easily work on different devices without having to worry about synchronization. For example, a user might create a spreadsheet in the Google Sheets app when working at the office on a desktop computer, make some changes to the spreadsheet at home that evening using the Google Sheets app on an iPad, and then enter data in the spreadsheet on a laptop the next day while visiting clients.

Meet the Google Workspace Apps

Google Workspace contains a bewildering list of apps, many of which are available to all Google Account holders but some of which are available only to Google Workspace users.

This section introduces you to the most important apps, including the email app, Gmail; the storage app, Google Drive; the productivity apps, Google Docs, Google Sheets, and Google Slides; the communications apps, Google Chat and Google Meet; the note-taking app, Google Keep; and the form-design app, Google Forms.

Gmail

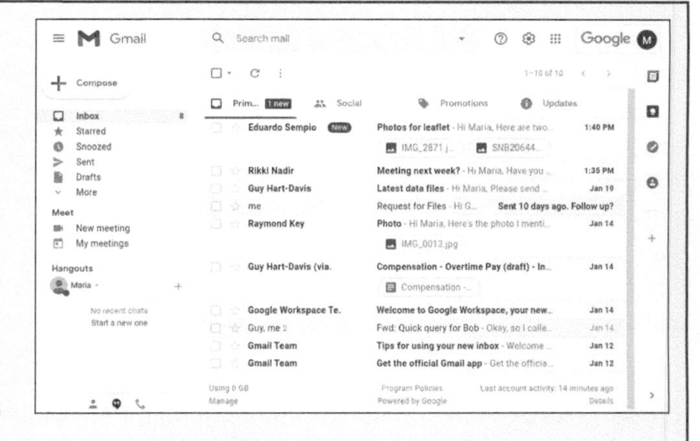

With an estimated 1.8 billion active users as of this writing, Google's Gmail service needs little introduction. Apart from enabling you to send and receive email messages on your Google Account, Gmail provides powerful search and filtering tools to help you access and manage your messages.

Gmail's tight integration with Google Workspace communications features, such as Google Chat and Google Meet, enables you to chat via text, voice, and video straight from your Inbox. Gmail also offers collaboration features that tie in to Google Drive and the productivity applications. For example, you can use Gmail to share files from Google Drive, and you can receive email notification of activity, such as comments, on your documents in the productivity applications.

Chapter 10 discusses Gmail.

Google Drive

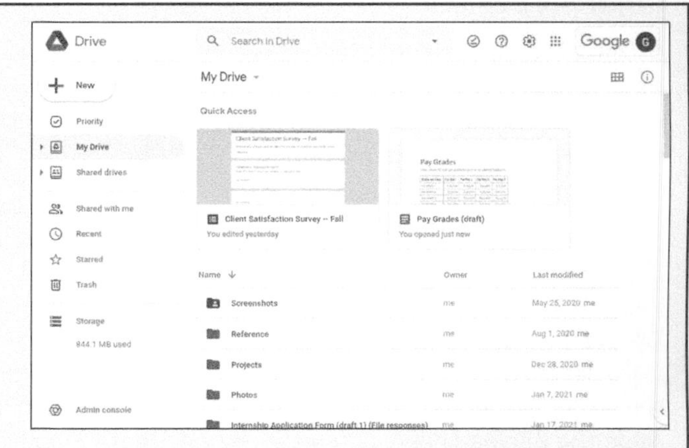

Google Drive is the online storage service for Google Account users, used both by consumers and by Google Workspace users. Google Drive serves as the storage backbone for Google Workspace apps: Each file or document you create or manipulate in the Google Workspace apps is stored in Google Drive, whether it is listed there or not.

Each consumer Google Account receives a certain amount of Google Drive space — as of this writing, 15 GB — which they can expand by paying a monthly or yearly fee. For business usage, the organization's Google Workspace administrator sets each user's amount of space by choosing a suitable plan.

Chapter 2 shows you how to manage files and folders in Google Drive, and Chapter 6 explains how to use Google Drive to share and collaborate on files.

Google Docs

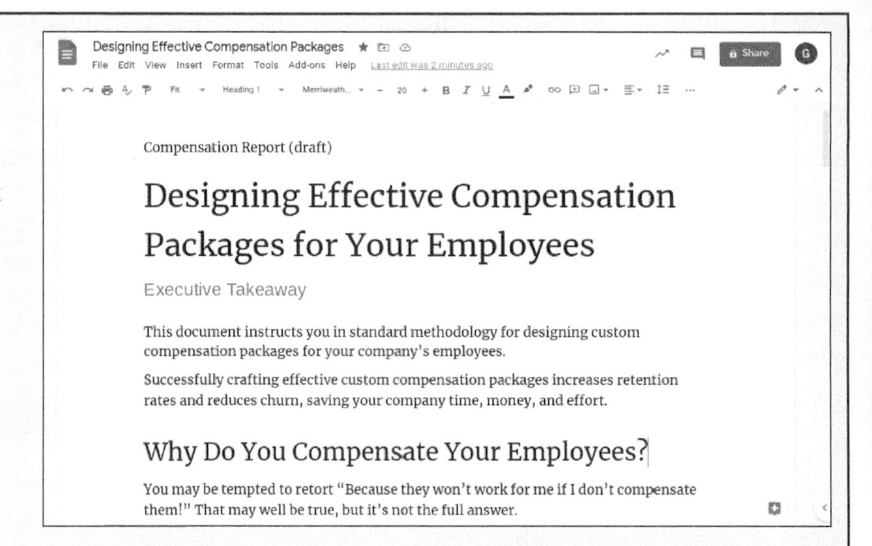

Google Docs enables you to create, edit, and collaborate on word processing documents. You can either create a new, blank document or get a jump-start by creating a document based on a template. Google Docs offers a wide range of formatting, including paragraph styles; the capability to include tables, images, and other graphical objects; and collaborative features such as change tracking and comments.

Google Docs can work with documents in the most widely used Microsoft Word formats. You can import a Word document and convert it to Google Docs format; open a Word document, edit it, and save your changes in Word format; or export a Google Docs document to a Microsoft Word file.

Chapter 3 covers common tasks in Google Docs, Google Sheets, and Google Slides. Chapter 4 explains how to insert objects in these three apps. Chapter 5 focuses on Google Docs–only features.

Google Sheets

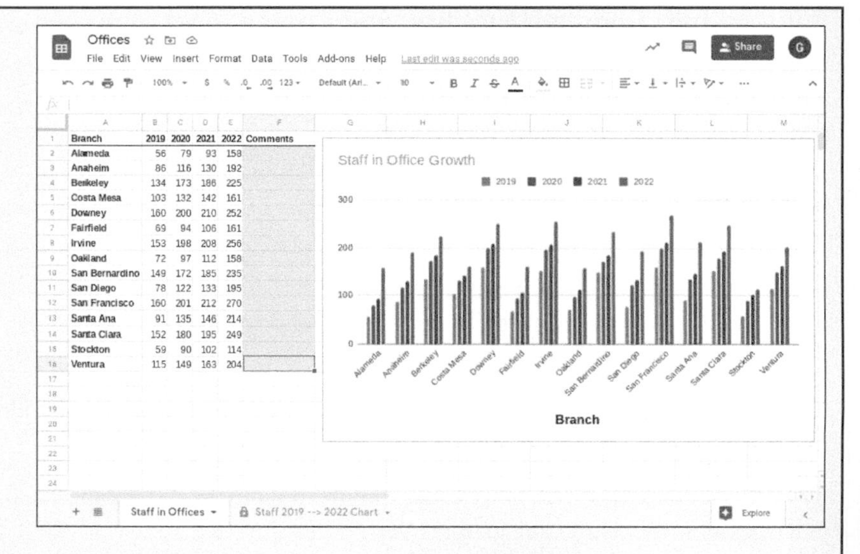

Branch	2019	2020	2021	2022	Comments
Alameda	56	79	93	158	
Anaheim	86	116	130	192	
Berkeley	134	173	186	225	
Costa Mesa	103	132	142	161	
Downey	160	200	210	252	
Fairfield	69	94	106	161	
Irvine	153	198	208	256	
Oakland	72	97	112	158	
San Bernardino	149	172	185	235	
San Diego	78	122	133	195	
San Francisco	160	201	212	270	
Santa Ana	91	135	146	214	
Santa Clara	152	180	195	249	
Stockton	59	90	102	114	
Ventura	115	149	163	204	

Google Sheets enables you to create spreadsheets in which to store and manipulate data. You can use either a single sheet or multiple sheets to organize and present your data, enhancing it with charts, images, or other graphical objects, as needed.

Google Sheets offers high compatibility with Microsoft Excel, the leading spreadsheet app. Google Sheets enables you to import an Excel workbook and convert it to Google Sheets format; open an Excel workbook, edit it, and save changes to the original workbook; or export a Google Sheets spreadsheet to an Excel workbook file.

Chapters 7 and 8 dig into using Google Sheets.

continued ▶

Google Docs, Google Sheets, and Google Slides let you collaborate with other people on creating and editing documents in real time, which can help get work finished faster.

Because the Google Workspace apps are web based and store their data on Google Drive, you can access the apps and work on your documents using almost any current or recent computer or device that has an Internet connection.

Google Slides

Google Slides is the presentation app included in Google Workspace. Google Slides enables you to create a new presentation either from scratch or by using a design template or a content template; include a wide array of content, such as diagrams, images, and video; and deliver the finished presentation to its audience.

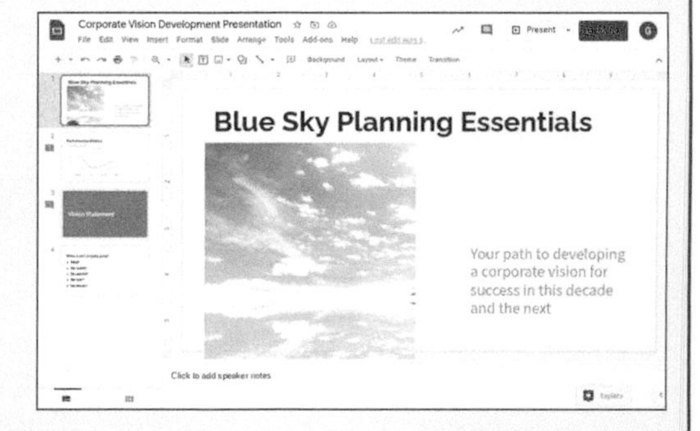

Google Slides can work with the main file formats for Microsoft PowerPoint, the market-leading presentation software. Google Slides can import a PowerPoint presentation and convert it to a Google Slides presentation; open a PowerPoint presentation, make changes to it, and save the changes back to the same presentation file; or export a Google Slides presentation to a PowerPoint presentation file.

Chapter 9 covers working in Google Slides.

Google Chat, Google Hangouts, and Google Meet

Google Workspace gives you access to several apps for chatting and conferencing online, including Google Chat, Google Hangouts, and Google Meet. The capabilities of the apps overlap considerably, which means you will need to determine which app is best suited for the type of communication you plan to use.

Google Chat is a chat app that includes features such as *rooms*, which enable you to get a group of people together for a chat, and *bots*, which help you assign tasks and schedule meetings. From Google Chat, you can also start a video meeting in Google Meet.

Google Hangouts is Google's all-in-one app for chat, audio calls, and video calls. Google Hangouts is available to anyone with a Google Account.

By contrast, Google Meet is available only to Google Workspace users. Google Meet is a business-grade videoconferencing app that enables you to pack up to 250 users into a single meeting. Google Meet also includes features that Google Hangouts does not, such as recording your videoconferences and taking polls; recording and polls are available in Google Workspaces editions except Business Starter Edition.

Chapter 11 briefly discusses Google Chat, Google Hangouts, and Google Meet.

Google Keep

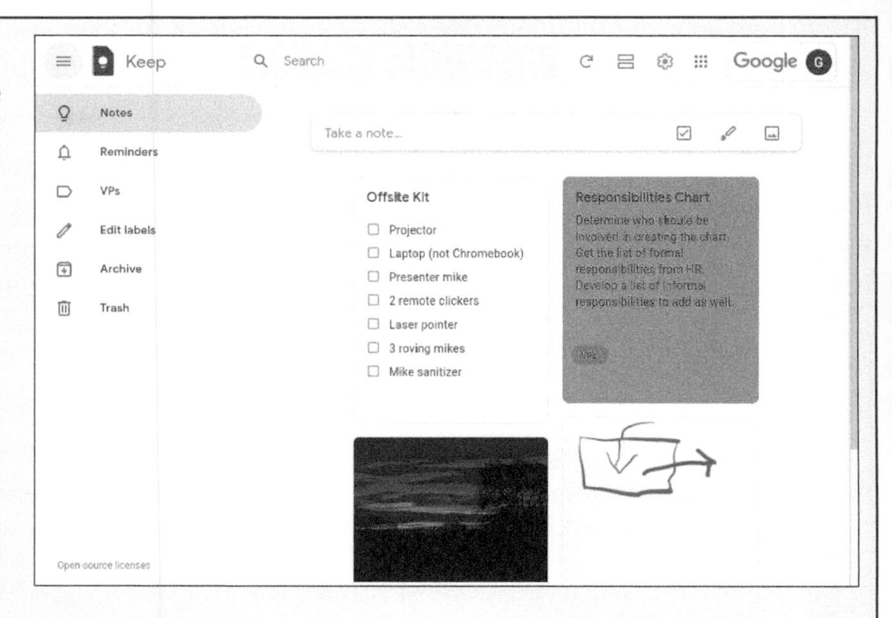

Google Keep is an app and service for taking and managing notes. You can create straightforward text notes, notes with images, notes with drawings, or lists of items. You can use labels to organize your notes into different categories, and you can turn a note into a reminder by adding an alarm to it.

When you need someone else to work on a note, you can add that person as a collaborator. If you need to create a document from a note, you can send the note to a Google Docs document in moments.

Chapter 11 shows you how to create notes using Google Keep.

Google Forms

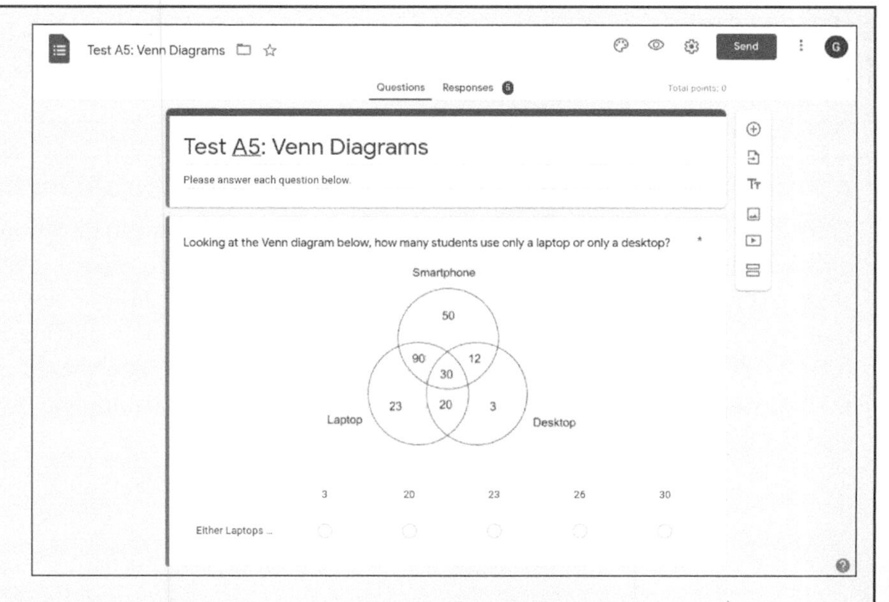

Google Forms enables you to create a wide variety of online forms, from a job application to an order form, and from a self-marking quiz to a registration form for an event. After creating the form, you can preview it and test it before sending it or otherwise sharing it with its respondents, the people whose answers you want.

When the respondents submit their responses, Google Forms collects the data automatically, letting you browse the data as a summary, by individual response, and by the responses to each question. You can also export the data to Google Sheets for your own custom analysis.

Chapter 12 explains how to use Google Forms.

Evaluate Google Workspace and Choose an Edition

If you are considering Google Workspace as a solution for your organization's needs, you will likely want to analyze how it stacks up against its main competitors, such as Microsoft 365 and LibreOffice. You should also determine whether your organization can safely and legally store all its data online.

Assuming you go for Google Workspace, you need to decide which version, or edition, to get and work out how much it will cost. As of this writing, Google offers four editions — three Business editions, with varying prices and features, and one Enterprise edition for larger organizations.

Compare Google Workspace with Its Main Competitors

As of this writing, Google Workspace has two main competitors: Microsoft 365 and LibreOffice.

Microsoft 365 is Microsoft's subscription-based plan for its Office productivity apps, cloud storage on OneDrive, collaboration with Microsoft Teams, and email and calendaring using the Outlook client and the Exchange Server software. Microsoft 365 is a full-featured offering that competes head to head with Google Workspace. For example, Microsoft Word competes with Google Docs, and Microsoft Teams takes on Google Meet, Google Chat, and some collaboration features of Google Drive. To learn more about Microsoft 365 and what it costs, go to www.microsoft365.com.

LibreOffice is a free office suite, the successor to the popular OpenOffice.org. LibreOffice includes apps that compete with those in Google Workspace; for example, LibreOffice Writer competes with Google Docs, and LibreOffice Calc competes with Google Sheets. However, LibreOffice does not offer features such as storage or conferencing, so it is not a direct competitor for Google Workspace. To learn more about LibreOffice and its capabilities, go to https://libreoffice.org.

Assess the Viability of Storing All Your Organization's Data Online

Before committing to Google Workspace, assess whether your organization can realistically store all its data online. This is pretty much a requirement for using Google Workspace, because the apps are designed to store their files on Google Drive, enabling them to be accessed from anywhere and making it easy to share them both with people inside your organization and with people outside it. But online storage can also increase security threats to your data. Beyond those threats, you should consider any compliance issues that storing the data online may raise; these issues vary by region and by business area, and you may well want to get legal input to make sure you understand them fully.

Assess the Viability of Storing All Your Organization's Data Online (continued)

Google Workspace enables an administrator to use its Data Regions Policy feature to choose the data region in which Google stores your organization's data. As of this writing, the choices are United States, Europe, or No Preference.

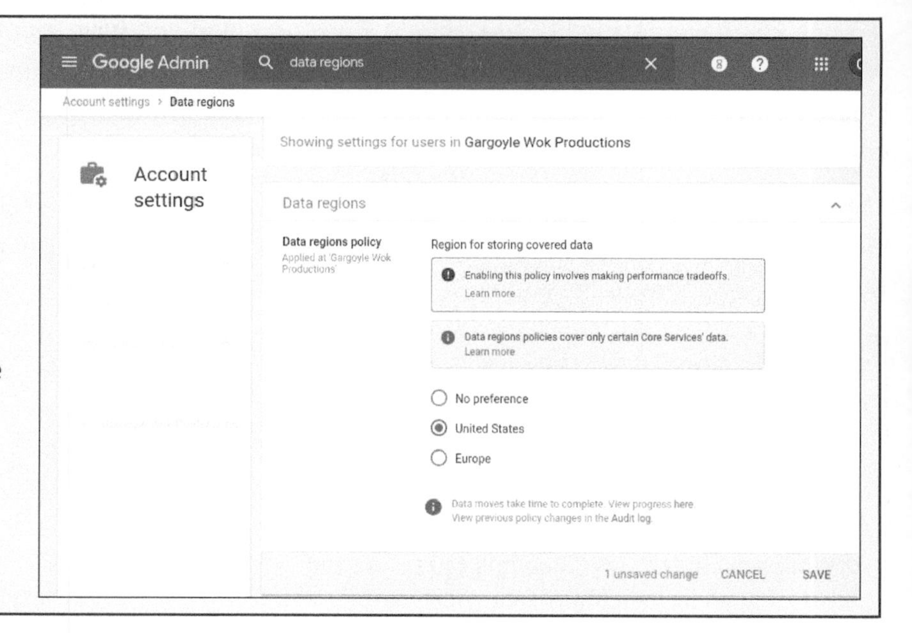

Choose an Edition of Google Workspace and Determine the Cost

Next, decide which version of Google Workspace will be best for your organization. Google offers four versions, which it calls *editions*: Business Starter Edition, Business Standard Edition, Business Plus Edition, and Enterprise Edition.

The first part of the decision — Business or Enterprise? — is easy. The three Business Editions have a maximum of 300 users. If your organization has more than 300 users, your only option is Enterprise Edition.

If your organization has 300 users or fewer, you can choose among the three Business editions. The following table shows the key differences.

Cost Per User	Storage Per User	Video Meetings Max	Meeting Recording	Shared Team Drives	Chat Outside Organization	Enhanced Security Features
$6/month	30 GB	100 people	No	No	No	No
$12/month	2 TB	150 people	Yes	Yes	Yes	No
$18/month	5 TB	250 people	Yes	Yes	Yes	Yes

Using this information, you can quickly determine which edition will work best for your organization. Although making the right choice the first time is ideal, it is not crucial, because Google enables you to switch between plans if necessary.

To find out the cost of Google Workspace Enterprise Edition, you will need to speak to Google's sales team. See the next section, "Sign Up for Google Workspace," for contact information.

Sign Up for Google Workspace

Once you have decided to use Google Workspace and you have identified the Google Workspace edition best suited to your organization, you are ready to sign up for the service. You can either sign up online, which is usually convenient and which offers a 14-day free trial for up to 10 users, or contact Google's sales team for personal attention.

The online sign-up form is lengthy but fairly straightforward. This section takes you through the sign-up process to the point at which you specify the domain to use, and tells you how to contact Google's sales team if necessary.

Go to the Google Workspace Website

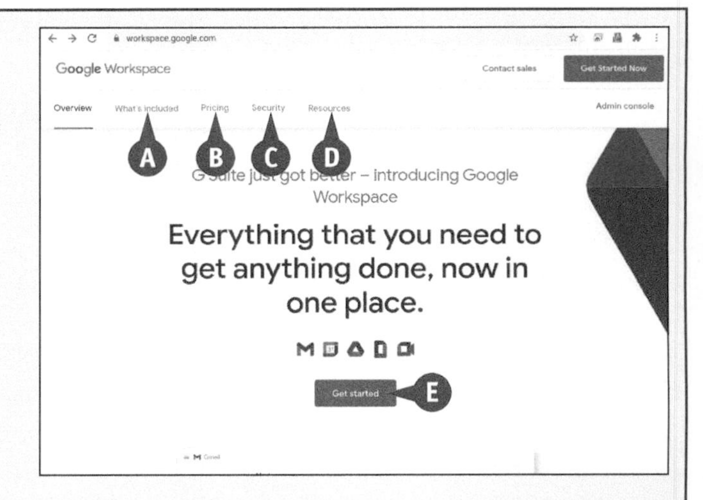

Open a browser window to https://workspace.google.com. This page opens to the Overview tab, but you can click other tabs to explore or review information:

- **What's included.** (A) Click this tab to see the list of apps included in Google Workspace.
- **Pricing.** (B) Click this tab to review the current pricing for the various Google Workspace plans.
- **Security.** (C) Click this tab to read summaries of the key security features Google Workspace offers.
- **Resources.** (D) Click this tab to view information resources related to Google Workspace, including FAQs, customer stories, and information on working remotely.

When you are ready to proceed, click **Get started** (E) to display the Let's Get Started Screen.

Enter Essential Information and Contact Details

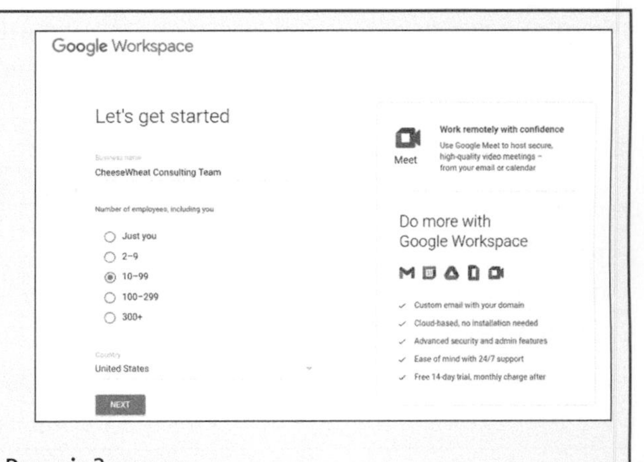

On the Let's Get Started screen, click **Business name** and type the name of your organization. Then go to the Number of Employees, Including You list and click **Just you** (◯ changes to ◉), **2–9** (◯ changes to ◉), **10–99** (◯ changes to ◉), **100–299** (◯ changes to ◉), or **300+** (◯ changes to ◉).

Click **Country** (▾), and then click your country. Then click **Next** to display the What's Your Contact Info? screen. On this screen, fill in your first name, last name, current email address, and business phone number, and then click **Next** to display the Does Your Business Have a Domain? screen.

Provide Your Existing Domain Name or Find a Suitable Domain Name

On the Does Your Business Have a Domain? screen, click **YES, I HAVE ONE THAT I CAN USE** if your organization has a domain name that you will use for your Google Workspace deployment. The What's Your Business's Domain Name? screen then appears, on which you provide the name.

If your organization does not have a domain name for your Google Workspace deployment, click **NO, I NEED ONE.** The Let's Find a Domain Name for Your Business screen then appears. Click **Search domain names**, type the domain you want to search for, and then press Enter or Return to search.

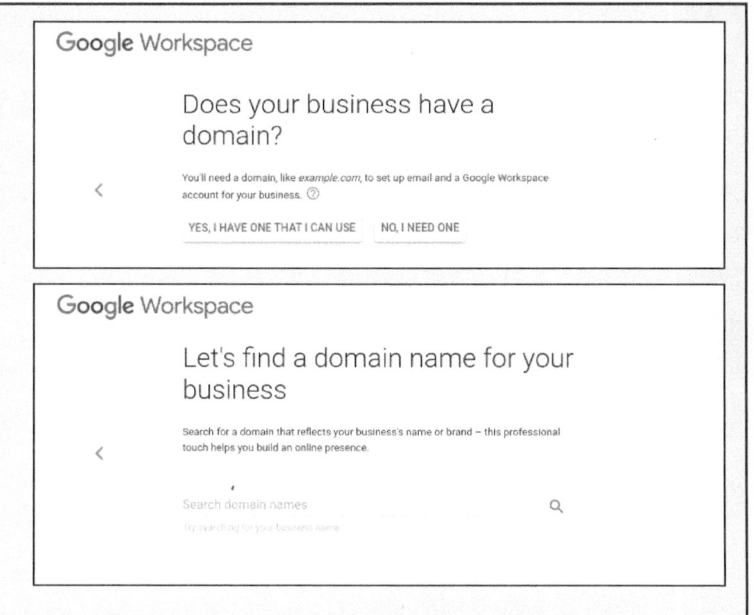

Once you have specified or chosen the domain name, follow the prompts to set up your Google Workspace user account and complete the sign-up routine.

Contact Google's Sales Team for Personal Attention

Signing up for Google Workspace online is fast and easy for many administrators, but if you have a large organization or complex needs, you may do better to contact Google's sales team and discuss those needs.

To contact Google's sales team, go to https://workspace.google.com/contact and click the I Want to Talk to Someone in Sales link. Click **Number of employees** (▾) to open the pop-up menu, and then click the appropriate number.

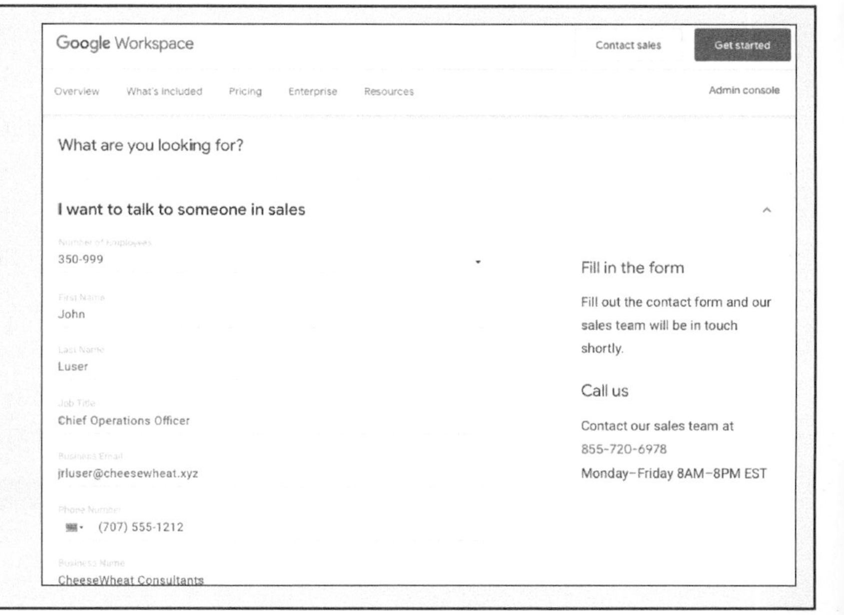

Sign In to Google Workspace

Once your organization's administrator has set up your Google Workspace account, you can sign in to the account. This section uses the Google website as an example for starting the sign-in process, but you can also sign in via the websites for individual Google Workspace apps, such as Google Drive or Gmail.

Depending on how your organization's administrator has configured Google Workspace, you may need to go through 2-Step Verification the first time you sign in on any computer or device. You can normally waive 2-Step Verification for future sign-ins on the same computer or device.

Sign In to Google Workspace

1. Open a browser tab to a Google site, such as www.google.com.
2. Click **Sign In**.

   The Sign In screen appears.

3. Click **Email or phone** and type the email address for your Google Workspace account.
4. Click **Next.**

   The Hi screen or Welcome screen appears.

5. Click **Enter your password** and type your password.

   Ⓐ You can click **Show password** (☐ changes to ☑) to display the characters of your password so you can verify you have typed them correctly.

6. Click **Next.**

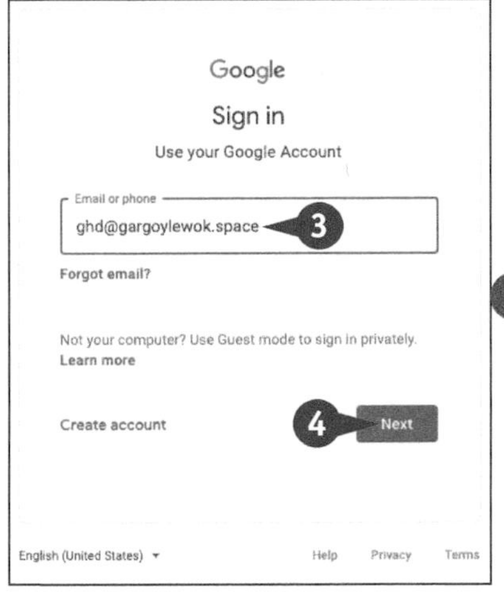

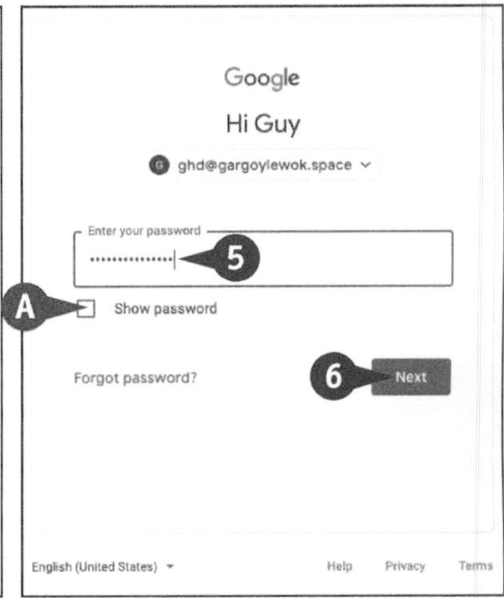

Depending on how your Google Workspace account is configured, the 2-Step Verification screen may appear.

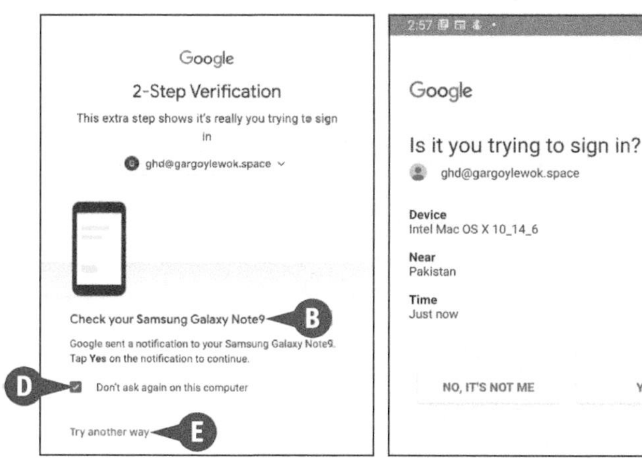

B If so, follow the prompts to confirm your identity.

C In this example, you would tap **YES** on the Is It You Trying to Sign In? screen on your phone to confirm that the sign-in attempt is legitimate.

D You may be able to select **Don't ask again on this computer** (☑) to exempt this computer from 2-Step Verification in the future.

E If your phone is not available or is incapacitated, you may be able to click **Try another way** to try another means of 2-Step Verification.

Once you pass 2-Step Verification, Google Workspace signs you in to your account.

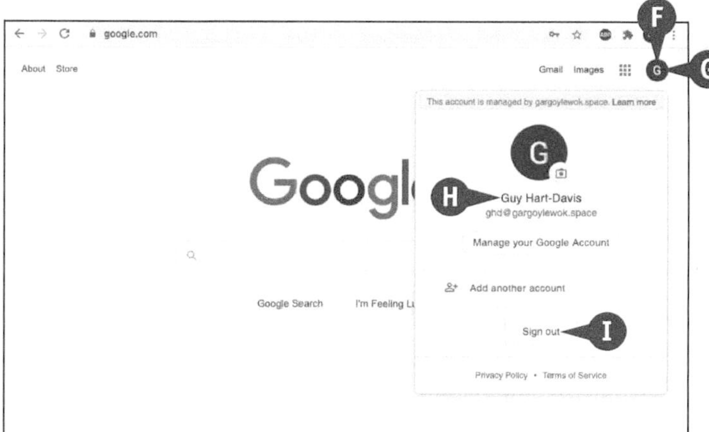

F Your account icon appears, indicating that you are signed in.

G You can click **Google Account** (such as M) to display the Google Account pop-up panel.

H You can see the account under which you are signed in.

I You can click **Sign out** to sign out of the account.

TIP

What means of 2-Step Verification are available?

Depending on how your organization's administrator has configured Google Workspace, you may be able to use the following second verification steps:

- A "Google prompt" on your mobile device, as shown in this section
- A one-time verification code generated by a hardware authentication device or by an authentication app, such as Google Authenticator, on your mobile device
- A numeric code sent via text message or voice call
- A hardware security key or the built-in security key on an Android phone or an iPhone
- A backup code generated ahead of time for when your mobile device will not be available or will have no signal

Run an App

Once you have logged in to your Google Workspace account, you can run the apps available to you, such as Google Docs, Google Sheets, or Google Forms. You can run an app in various ways, but usually the most convenient way is to use the Google Apps panel, which you can open from Google Drive, from Gmail, from the Google website, and from some other apps, such as Google Chat. On a Chromebook, you may prefer to use the Launcher.

Exactly which apps you can run depends on how your organization's administrator has configured Google Workspace for your account.

Run an App

Note: This example uses Google Drive as the starting point. You can also start from Gmail; from some other apps, such as Google Chat; or from the Google website, assuming you are logged in to your Google Workspace account.

1. Open a browser tab to drive.google.com.

Note: If the Choose an Account dialog box opens, click your account, and then follow the prompts to sign in.

Google Drive appears.

2. Click **Google Apps** (⋮⋮⋮).

The Google Apps panel opens.

3. Click the app you want to open. This example uses **Google Docs** (▤).

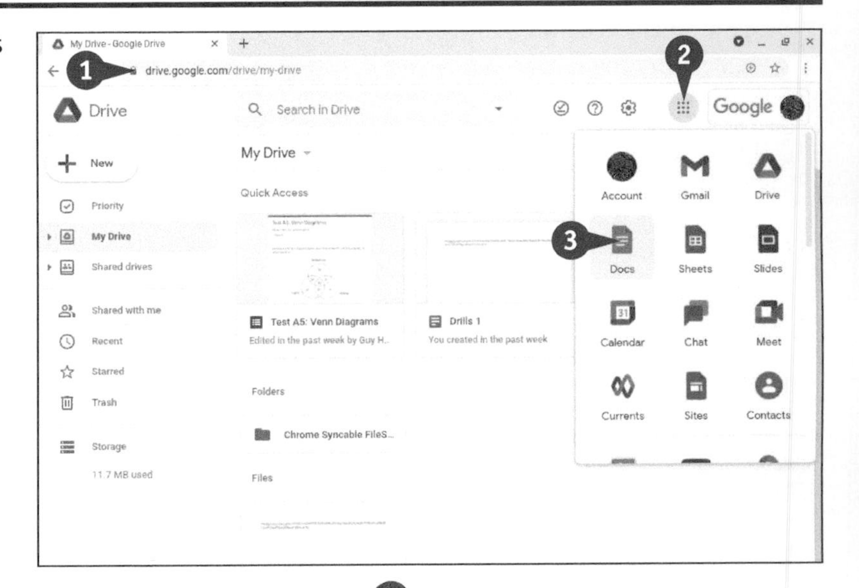

A. The app opens in a new tab in the same browser window.

The app's Start screen appears. The contents of the Start screen vary depending on the app, but the ones shown here are fairly typical.

B. You can start a new blank document or a document based on a template.

C. You can open a recent document.

4. Click **Blank** (+).

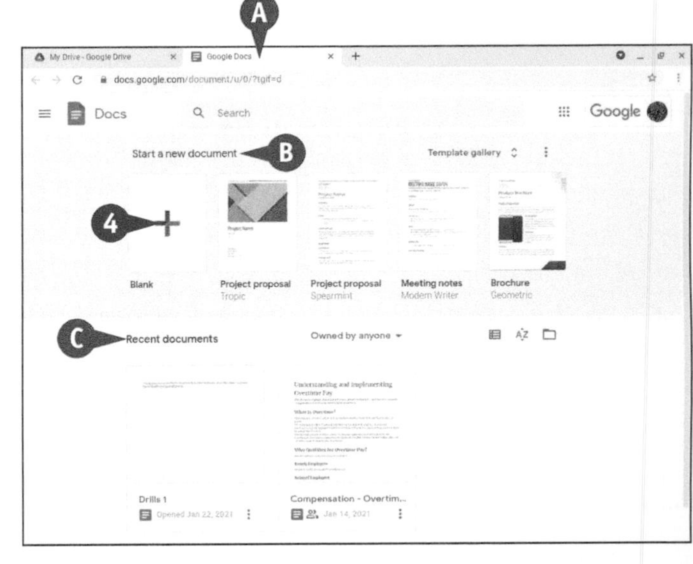

The app creates a new blank document.

5 Double-click **Untitled document**.

The text becomes selected.

6 Type the name under which you want to save the document, and then press Enter or Return.

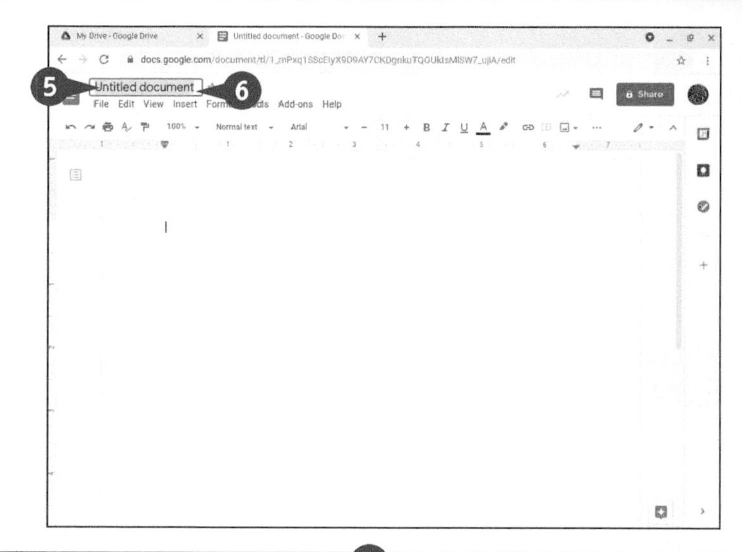

D The app saves the document under the name you entered.

E You can click in the document body and enter text.

7 When you finish working in the document, click **Close** (✕) on the tab containing the document.

The tab and the document close.

The previous tab appears. In this case, the Google Drive tab appears.

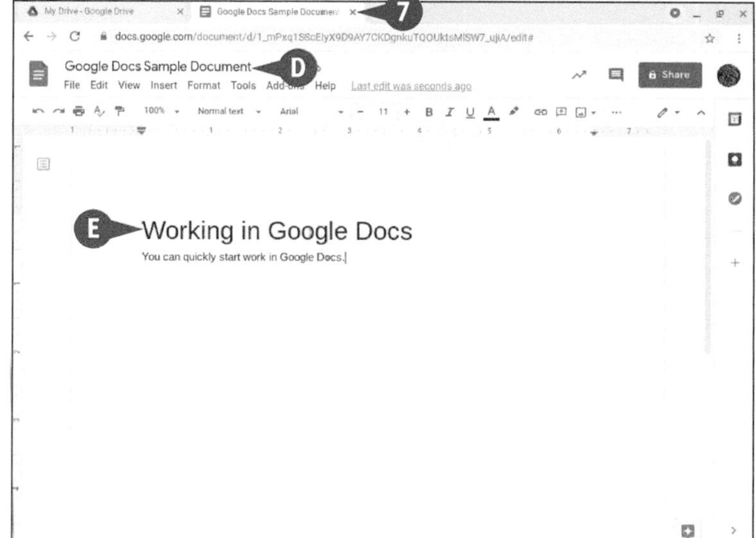

TIP

What other ways can I run a Google Workspace app?

In any browser, you can run an app by opening a tab to its web address. For example, you can go to **docs.google.com** to run Google Docs, **sheets.google.com** to run Google Sheets, or **forms.google.com** to run Google Forms. This method is occasionally useful.

From Google Drive, you can launch an app by creating a new document in it. Click **New** (+) to display the New pop-up menu, and then click the app, such as **Google Sheets** (⊞).

On a Chromebook, press Shift+click **Launcher** (○) to display the Launcher screen, and then click the app you want to launch.

Set Your Profile Information and Photo

Your Google Account includes profile information and a photo that may be available for your colleagues to view. The profile includes your name, gender, birthday, and work location. You should review your profile information and your photo to make sure they are accurate and present the information you want to share.

Depending on how your organization's administrator has configured Google Workspace, you may be able to edit only some profile information, or even none. If you cannot edit certain information, you may need to ask the administrator to edit it.

Set Your Profile Information and Photo

1 In Google Drive, or in any of the Google Workspace apps that display your Account icon, click **Google Account** (such as M).

The Google Account panel opens.

2 Click **Manage your Google Account.**

The Google Account screen opens in a new browser tab.

A The Google Account screen contains seven tabs: Home, Personal Info, Data & Personalization, Security, People & Sharing, Payments & Subscriptions, and About.

The Home tab appears at first.

Note: If the browser window is narrow, the tabs appear across the top of the screen without their icons.

3 Click **Personal info**.

The Personal Info screen appears.

4 Click **Add a photo to personalize your account.**

Note: You can click anywhere on the Photo row of the Basic Info table, including your account icon.

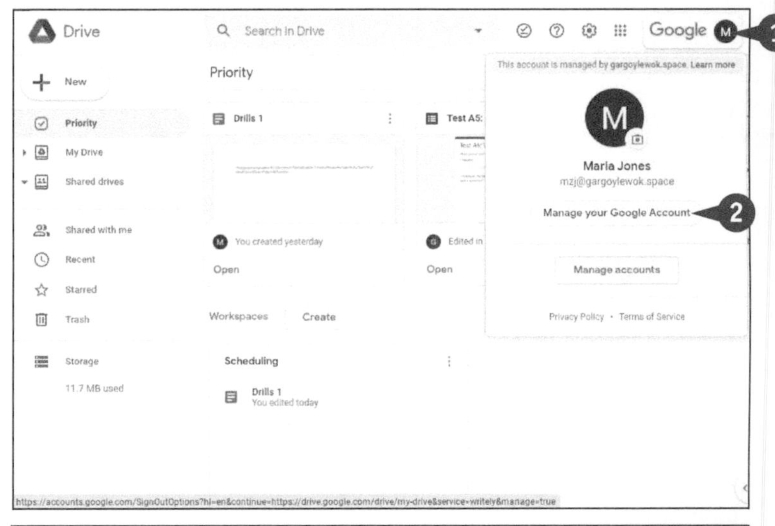

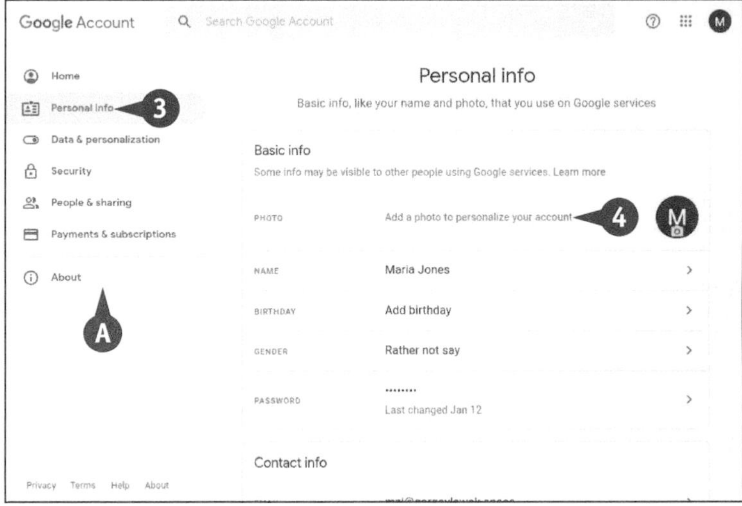

The Select Profile Photo dialog box opens.

B You can click **Your photos** and select an existing profile photo or a photo stored in Google Photos. Go to step **11**.

5 To upload a photo from your computer, click **Upload Photos**.

6 Click **Select a photo from your computer**, and then follow the prompts.

7 You can click **Left** (↶) or **Right** (↷) to rotate the photo 90°.

8 Select the area of the photo you want to use.

9 You can click **Add Caption** and type a caption.

10 Click **Set as profile photo.**

The photo appears on the Photo row.

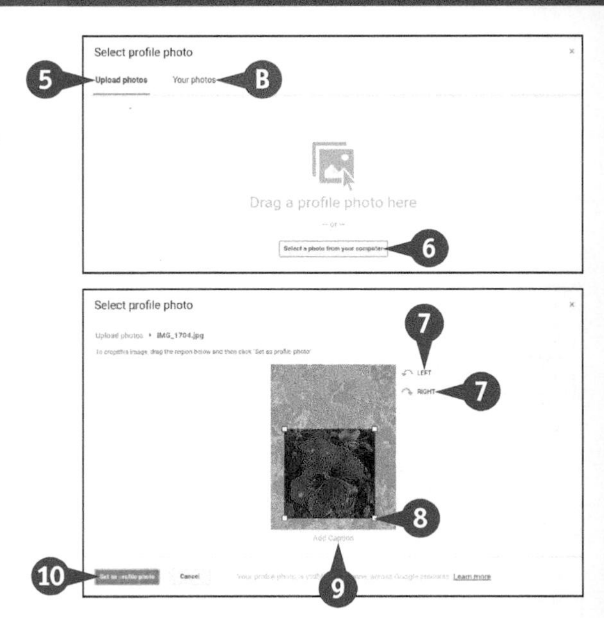

11 Click the next item you want to change, follow the prompts to change it and to decide who can see the change, and then click **Save**.

For example, click **Gender** to display the Gender screen. You can then click **Female** (○ changes to ◉), click **Male** (○ changes to ◉), click **Rather not say** (○ changes to ◉), or click **Add custom gender** (+) and specify a custom gender.

See the tip for information on your choices on sharing personal data.

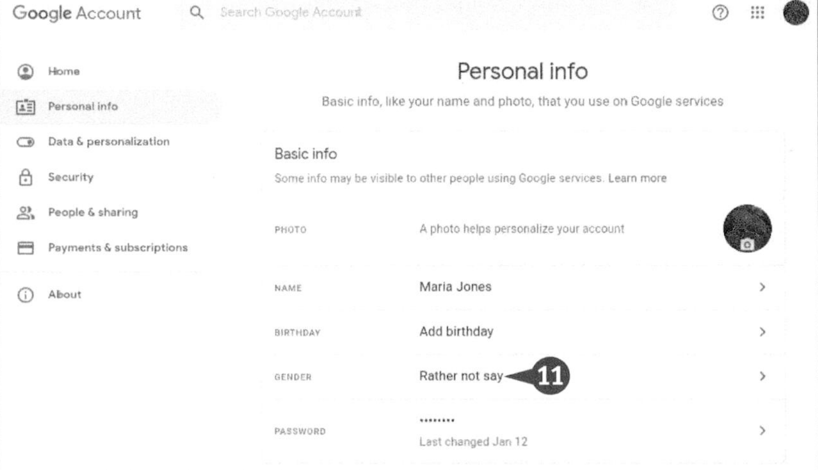

TIP

What are my choices for sharing my personal info?

The Google Account screens offer three choices for information such as your birthday and your gender. Click **Only you** (🔒) to prevent others from seeing the information. Click **Your organization** (🏢) to let people in your organization see the information but prevent anyone beyond the organization from seeing it. Click **Anyone** (👥) to allow anyone to view the information.

Using Google Workspace on Mobile Devices

Working on mobile devices, such as smartphones and tablets, is an integral part of many jobs, and Google Workspace gives you the tools to carry your work with you and carry it out wherever you are. Google provides versions of Google Docs, Google Sheets, Google Slides, and other apps for both Android and Apple's iOS, enabling you to create, edit, and share content on Android phones and tablets, iPhones, iPads, and the iPod touch. Google also provides Android and iOS versions of Gmail, Google Drive, and some other apps.

Install and Run a Google Workspace App on Android

To install a Google Workspace app on Android, tap **Play Store** (▶) on the Home screen or in the App Drawer to open the Play Store app. Tap **Search** and type your search term; this example uses **google docs**. Tap the appropriate search result (A) to display the list of matching apps. Identify the appropriate app, and then tap **Install** (B). When installation completes, you can run the app by tapping **Open** on the app's entry in the Play Store app or by tapping the app's icon, such as Google Docs (▤), in the App Drawer.

With the app open, follow the prompts to sign in and authenticate yourself. You can then browse your documents, and tap the document you want to open (C); alternatively, tap **New** (+; D) to start creating a new document in the app.

The app opens the document, and you can view and edit the document. In Google Docs, tap **Edit** (✎; E) to switch from viewing a document to editing it; the keyboard appears, and you can use it to enter text. Tap **Done** (✓) in the upper-left corner of the screen when you want to switch back to viewing the document.

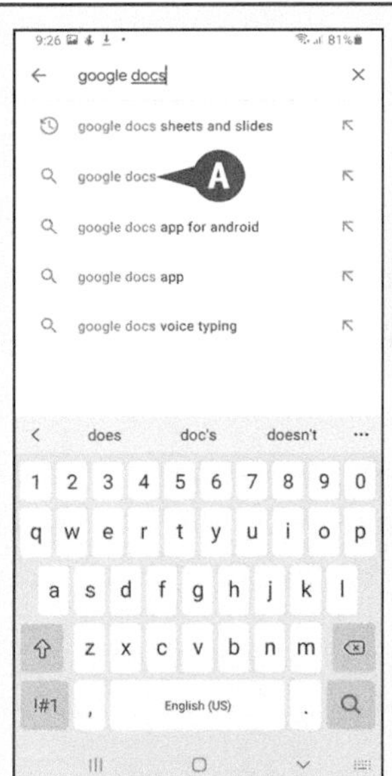

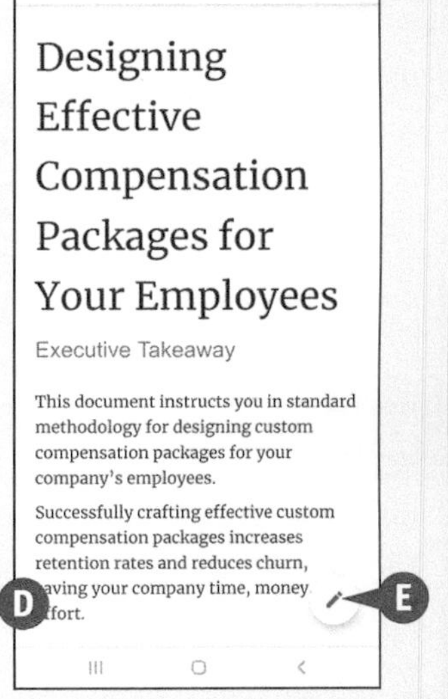

Install and Run a Google Workspace App on iOS

To install a Google Workspace app on iOS, such as the iPad used here, tap **App Store** (A) on the Home screen or in the App Library to open the App Store app. Tap **Search** (Q) to display the Search tab, and then type your search term (F); this example uses **google drive**. Look at the search results that appear, locate the Google Workspace app, and then tap **Get** (G). When the installation finishes, you can run the app by tapping **Open** on the app's entry in the App Store app or by tapping the app's icon, such as Google Drive (△), on the Home screen.

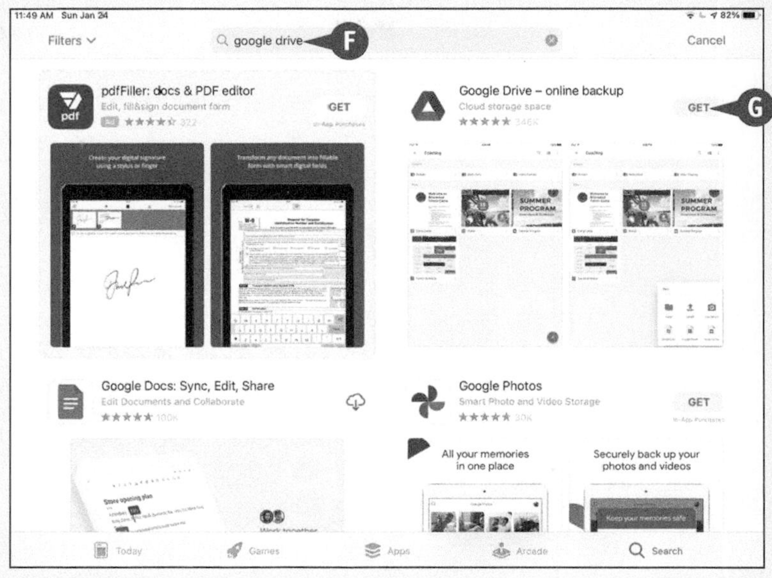

The first time you open the app, follow the prompts to sign in and authenticate yourself. After that, you can tap the appropriate icon on the navigation bar at the bottom of the screen to display the category you want to use: tap **Priority** (☑ changes to ☑, H) to display the Priority category, tap **Workspaces** (∴ changes to ∴, I) to display the Workspaces category, tap **Shared** (👥 changes to 👥, J) to display the Shared category, or tap **Files** (□ changes to ■, K) to display the Files category. You can then tap the file you want to open.

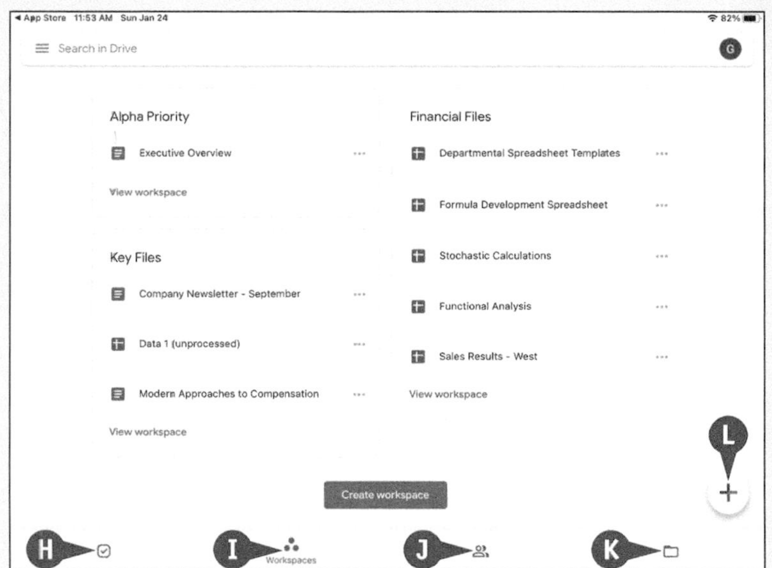

Alternatively, tap **New** (+, L) to start creating a new document in one of the apps.

CHAPTER 2

Managing Files and Folders in Google Drive

Your Google Account includes space on Google Drive, Google's online storage service. In this chapter, you first explore Google Drive, create folders, upload existing files and folders, and enable Offline Mode. You then learn essential operations, from opening, moving, and renaming files and folders to putting them in the Trash — and recovering them if necessary. You also learn how to work with Microsoft Office documents and streamline your work with workspaces.

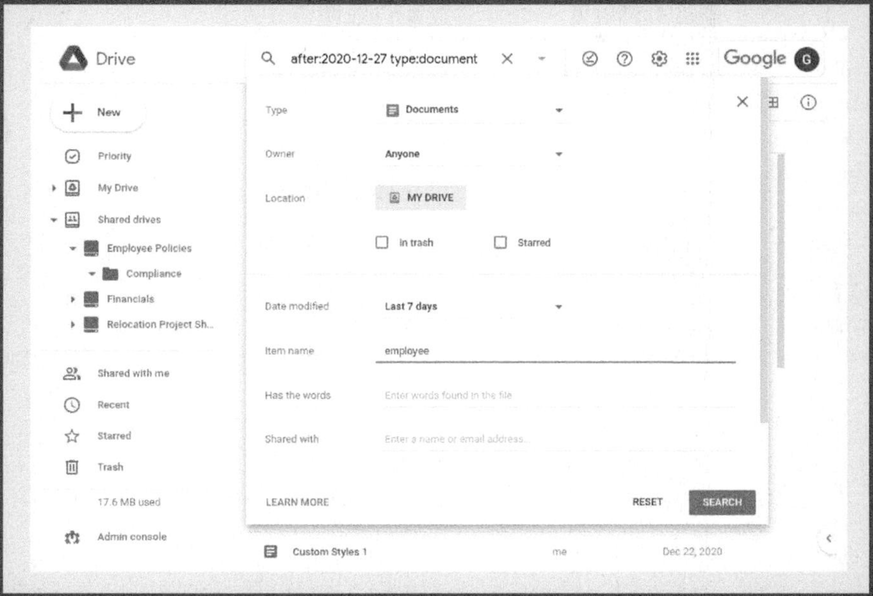

Open and Explore Google Drive

Google Drive is Google's online storage service used for personal accounts and Google Workspace accounts. Your Google Account includes an amount of storage provided using Google Drive; the amount varies depending on your service plan.

You can access your Google Drive storage through your web browser on your PC, Mac, or Chromebook; Chrome OS devices also have direct access to Google Drive through the Files app. On Android and iOS, the Google Workspace mobile apps can work directly with your Google Drive files — meaning you do not need to use a browser; you can also install the Google Drive app on your device.

Open and Explore Google Drive

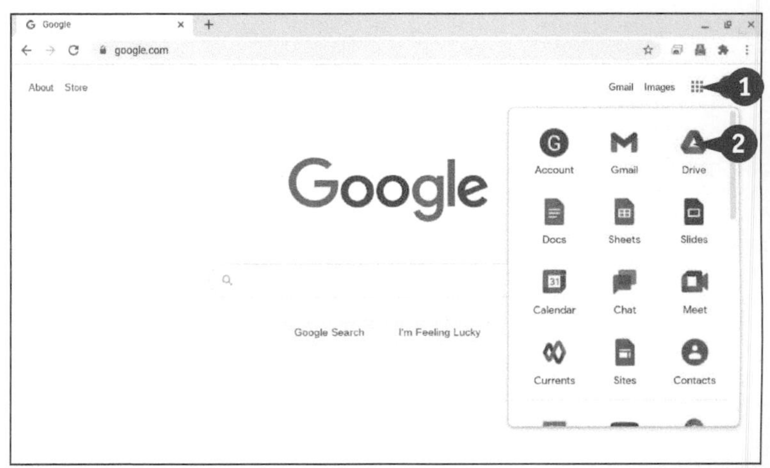

1 After signing in to your Google Workspace account, click **Google apps** (⁝⁝⁝).

The Google Apps panel opens.

2 Click **Drive** (△).

Note: If you open the Google Apps panel and click **Drive** (△) in a new tab, Google Drive opens in the same tab. But if you open the panel and click **Drive** (△) in a tab containing a Google app, Google Drive opens in a new tab.

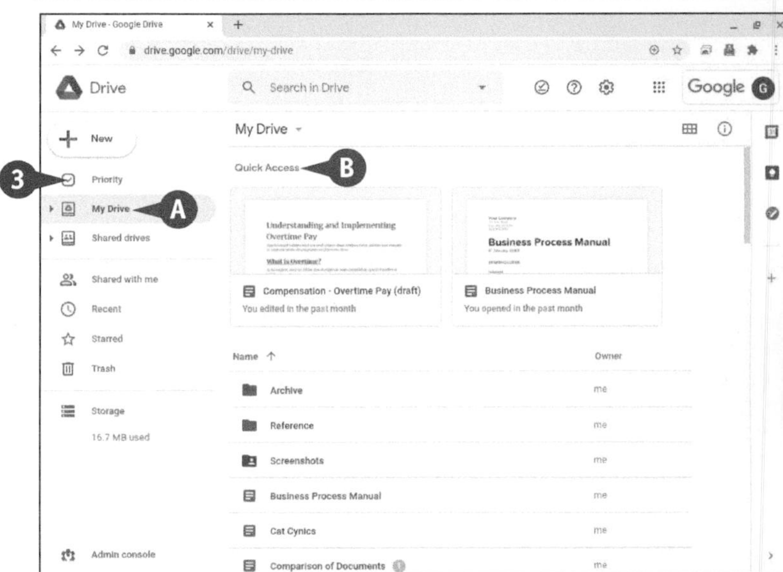

Google Drive opens.

A The My Drive category (▣) is selected at first.

B The Quick Access section provides links to files you have used recently.

3 Click **Priority** (☑).

The Priority category appears.

C The Priority section shows documents you can open.

D The Workspaces section shows different workspaces available to you.

E You can click **Create** to create a new workspace.

F Google Drive may suggest a workspace based on files you edit often. Click **Save**, which appears at the bottom of the Suggested Workspace box, if you want to save the workspace.

Note: See the section "Streamline Your Work with Workspaces," later in this chapter, for details on using workspaces.

4 Click **Shared drives** (▣).

The Shared Drives category appears.

G The Shared Drives list shows the shared drives available to you.

H You can click **Hidden shared drives** to display the Hidden Shared Drives list.

5 Click **Expand** (▸).

Note: You can double-click **Shared drives** (▣) to display the Shared Drives category and expand its contents to the level at which they were previously displayed.

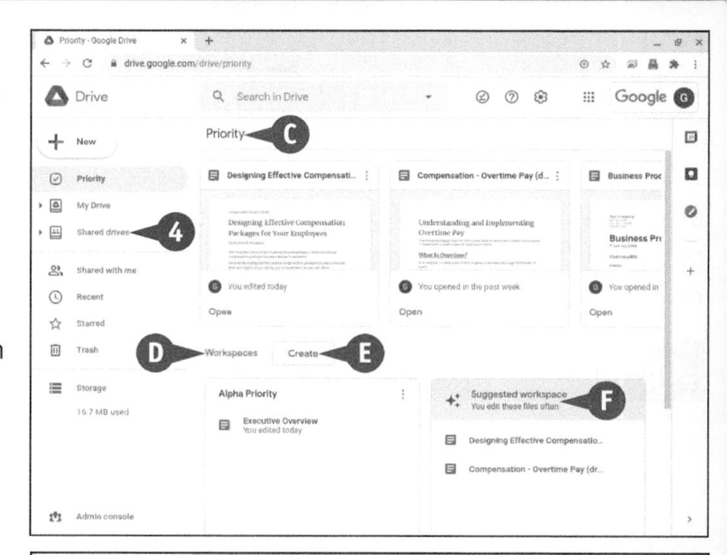

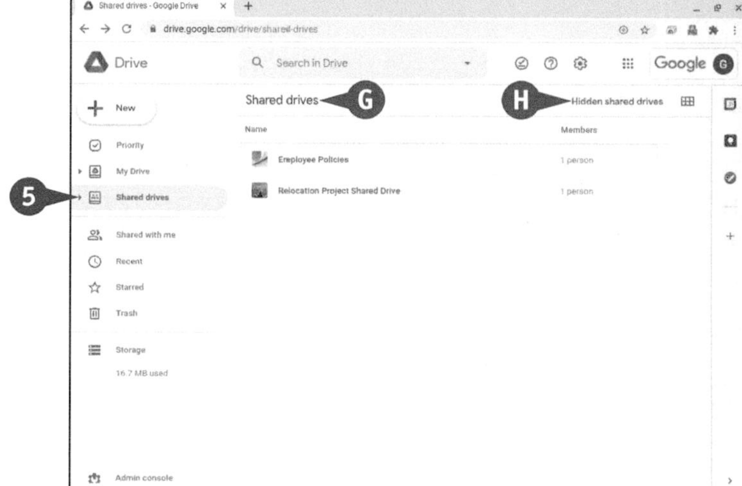

TIP

What uses my Google Drive storage space?

Any files you upload to Google Drive will use an amount of storage proportional to their size.

Files you have sent or received as attachments in Gmail also occupy Google Drive storage, even though you cannot access these files directly from Google Drive.

Documents stored in Google apps formats, such as documents in Google Docs format or presentations in Google Slides format, do not count against your storage usage. But if you export such a document to a non-Google format and save the exported document in Google Drive, it will count against your storage.

Any media files you store in Google Photos on the Original Quality setting will also use Google Drive storage.

continued ►

The Google Workspace apps are built on the Google Drive platform and automatically use Google Drive for storing files. Google Drive is the backbone for sharing and collaborating on Google Workspace documents with people both inside and outside your Google Workspace organization.

If you need to work with files on Google Drive as if they were on your Windows PC or Mac, you can use Google Drive for Desktop to integrate Google Drive into File Explorer on Windows or the Finder on macOS. See the section "Using Google Drive for Desktop" in Chapter 6, "Share and Collaborate on Files," for information on Google Drive for Desktop.

Open and Explore Google Drive (continued)

The shared drives appear.

6 Click **Expand** (▸).

Note: You can also double-click the shared drive (■) to expand its contents.

The top-level folders in the shared drive appear.

7 Click the appropriate folder.

I The folder's contents appear.

8 Click **Shared with me** ().

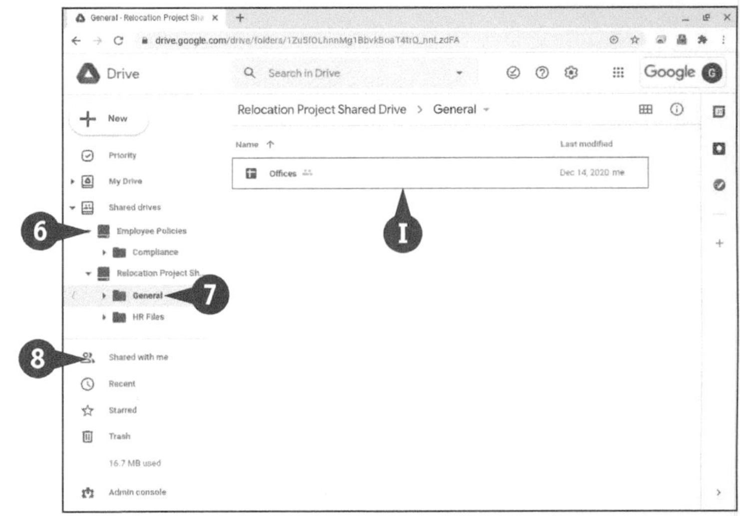

The Shared with Me category appears, showing folders and documents that others have shared with you.

J The Quick Access box gives quick access to files that have been shared with you recently and shared files that have been edited recently.

K You can right-click a file to display the contextual menu, which includes other actions you can take with the file — for example, renaming the file or downloading it.

L You can click **Add to Starred** (☆) to add the file to the Starred category — for example, because the file is important.

9 Click **Recent** ().

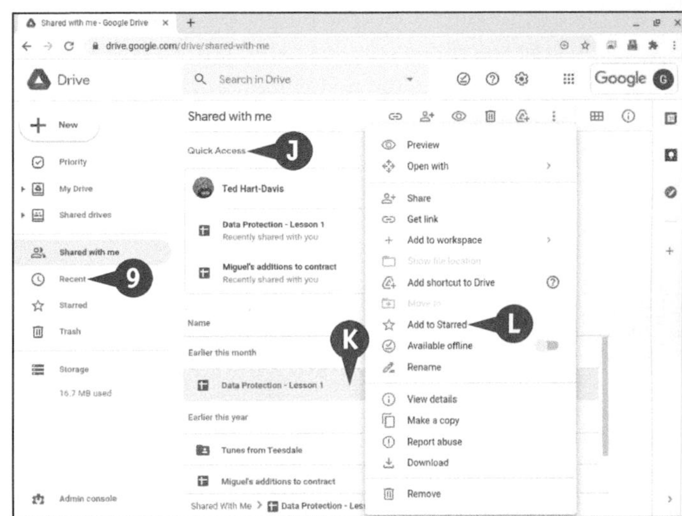

The Recent category appears, showing files that have been saved recently.

M The list of files is sorted by reverse data, starting with the Today section.

10 Click **Starred** (☆).

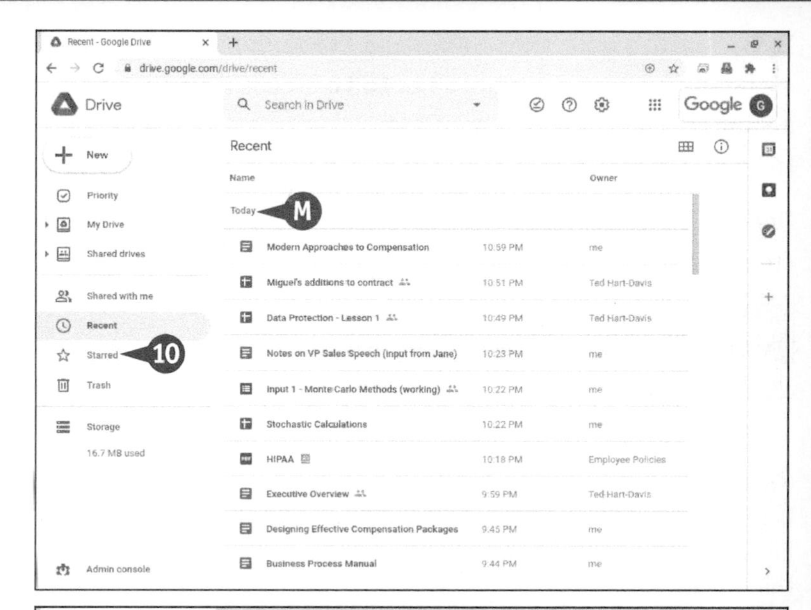

The Starred category appears, showing the files you have marked as Starred.

11 Double-click the file you want to open.

The file opens in the default app for that file type. For example, if you double-click a Google Docs document, it opens in the Google Docs app.

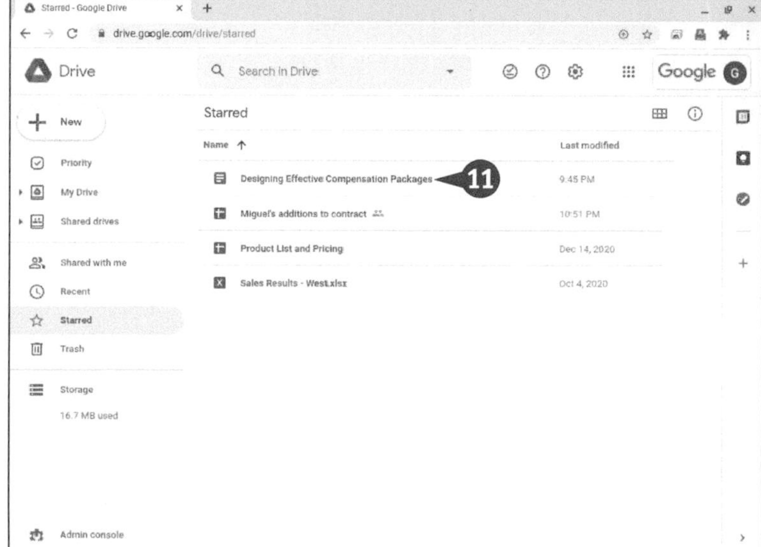

TIP

What does the Storage category on Google Drive do?

Click **Storage** (☰) to display the Storage category, which shows you a list of all the files you have stored on Google Drive and the amount of space each file is taking up. The list is sorted in descending order by default, so the largest files appear at the top, helping you see what is occupying most space.

Create a Folder and Add Files

To organize your files on Google Drive, you will likely want to create various folders and subfolders. For example, you might choose to create a folder for each major project and, inside that folder, a subfolder for each of the project's components. If needed, you could then create subfolders inside those subfolders.

Once you have created the folders you need, you can copy or move existing files into the folders or create new files in them.

Create a Folder and Add Files

1. In Google Drive, navigate to the category in which you want to create a folder.

Note: If you do not currently have Google Drive open, click **Google apps** (⁝⁝⁝) in a browser tab, and then click **Drive** (△) on the Google Apps panel.

A. For example, you might double-click **My Drive** (▣) to display the My Drive category and the folders it contains.

2. If you want to create the new folder inside an existing folder, click that folder.

   The folder's contents appear.

3. Click **New** (+).

   The New pop-up menu opens.

4. Click **Folder** (▣).

   The New Folder dialog box opens.

5. Type the name for the new folder.

6. Click **Create.**

   The New Folder dialog box closes.

   The *Working. . .* pop-up message appears briefly in the lower-left corner of the window while Google Drive creates the folder.

B. The new folder appears.

7. Double-click the new folder.

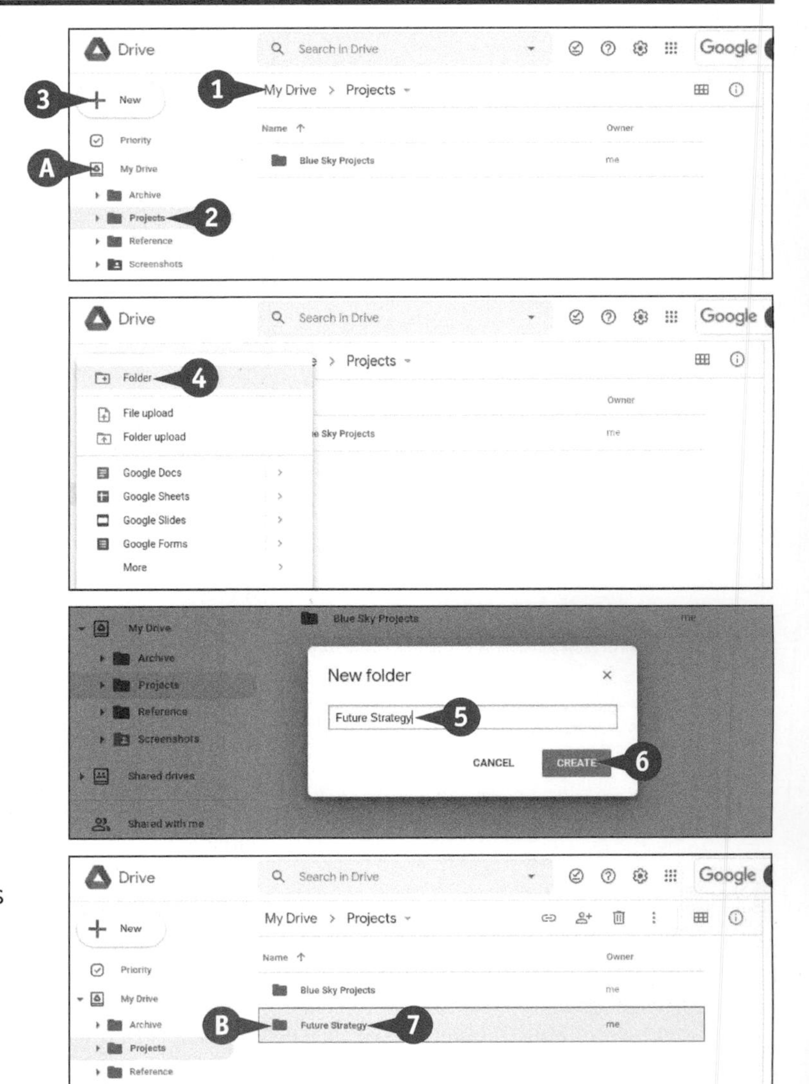

The folder opens.

C At first, the new folder has no contents and displays a prompt to drop files in it.

You can now add files or folders to the new folder.

8 For example, click a folder that contains files you want to move into the new folder.

This example uses the Reference folder.

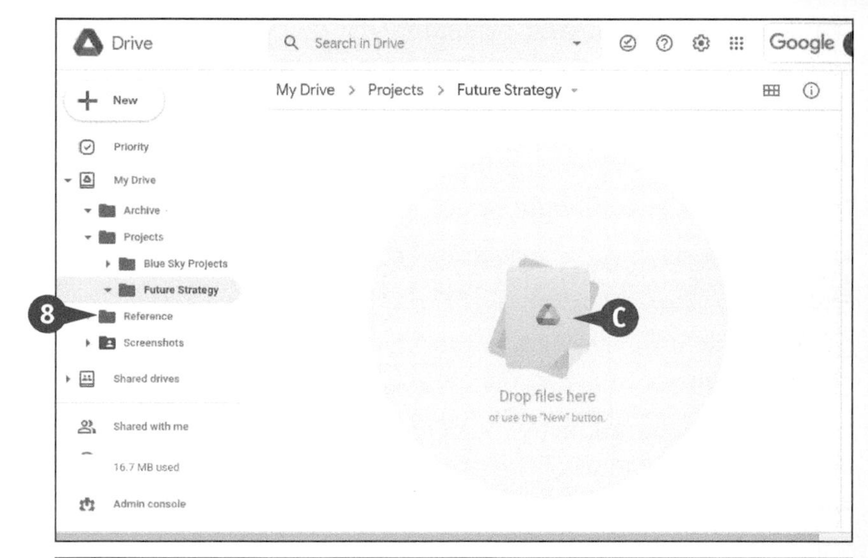

The contents of the folder appear.

9 Select the files you want to move to the new folder.

10 Drag the files to the folder.

Google Drive moves the files to the folder.

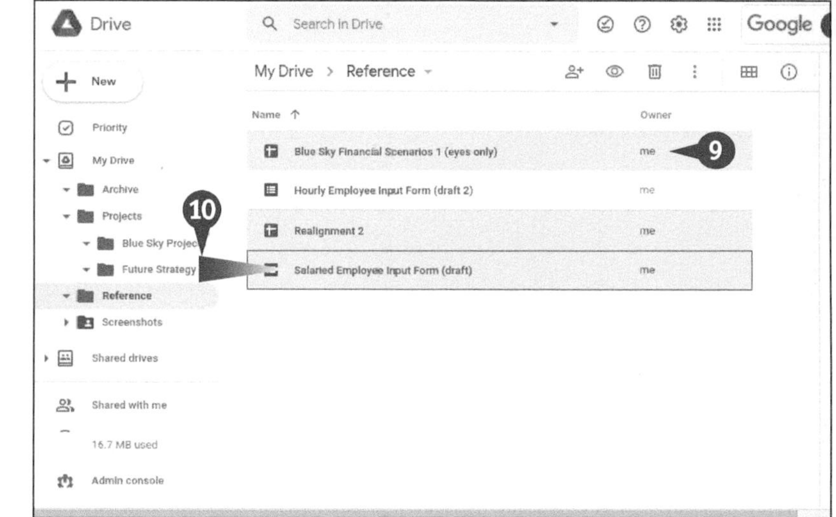

TIP

How many levels of subfolders can I create on Google Drive?

Exactly how many levels of subfolders you can create depends on which part of Google Drive you are using. For example, on a shared drive you can create up to 20 levels of subfolders. Generally speaking, using only a handful of levels of subfolders will produce a more navigable folder structure.

Upload a File to Google Drive

If you have files on your computer that you want to use in the Google Workspace apps, upload those files to Google Drive. Google Drive makes the uploading process easy by providing the File Upload command.

You can also upload an existing folder and its contents to Google Drive. See the next section, "Upload a Folder to Google Drive," for instructions.

Upload a File to Google Drive

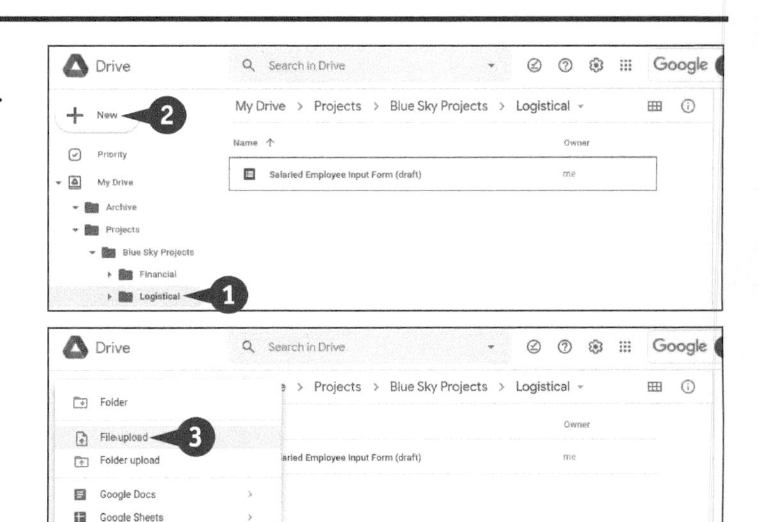

1 In Google Drive, navigate to the folder in which you want to store the file you upload.

Note: If you do not currently have Google Drive open, click **Google apps** (⋮⋮⋮) in a browser tab, and then click **Drive** (△) on the Google Apps panel.

2 Click **New** (+).

The New pop-up menu opens.

3 Click **File upload** (⇧).

A dialog box opens for selecting files.

For example, on Chrome OS, the Select One or More Files dialog box opens.

4 Navigate to the folder that contains the file or files.

5 Select the file or files.

6 Click **Open**.

The dialog box closes.

Google Drive uploads the file or files, displaying a progress readout while it does so.

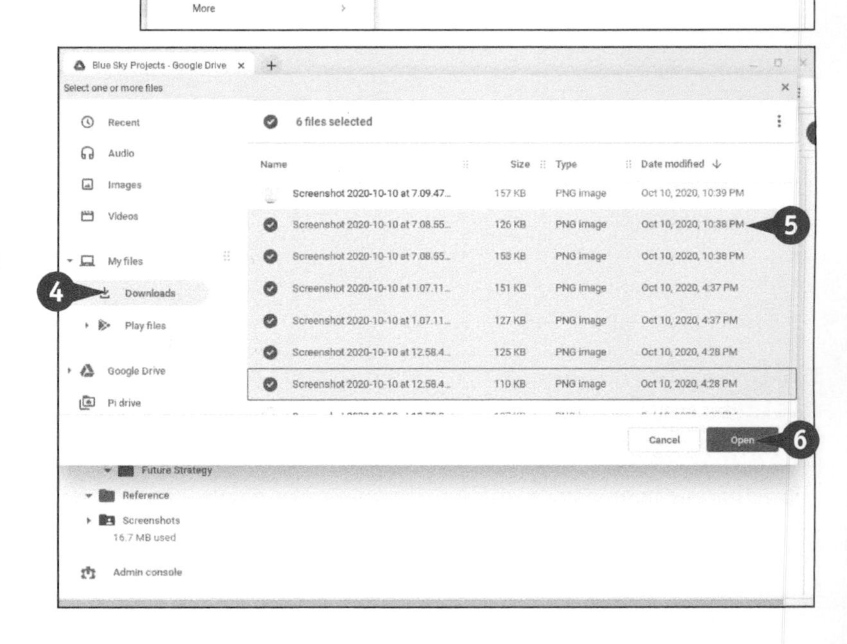

Upload a Folder to Google Drive

As well as enabling you to upload individual files, Google Drive lets you upload one or more folders, and the documents they contain, in a single operation. Uploading folders is usually a quicker way of getting your files into Google Drive and is convenient as long as you want to upload all the files in the folder.

Upload a Folder to Google Drive

1. In Google Drive, navigate to the folder in which you want to store the file you upload.

Note: If you do not currently have Google Drive open, click **Google apps** (⋮⋮⋮) in a browser tab, and then click **Drive** (▲) on the Google Apps panel.

2. Right-click open space in the folder.

   The contextual menu opens.

3. Click **Upload folder** (📁).

   A dialog box opens for selecting the folder you want to upload.

   For example, on Chrome OS, the Select a Folder to Upload dialog box opens.

4. Click the folder you want to upload.
5. Click **Upload**.

   The Upload Files to This Site? dialog box opens.

6. Read the warning.
7. Click **Upload** if you want to proceed.

   The Upload Files to This Site? dialog box closes.

   Google Drive uploads the folder, displaying a progress readout as it does so.

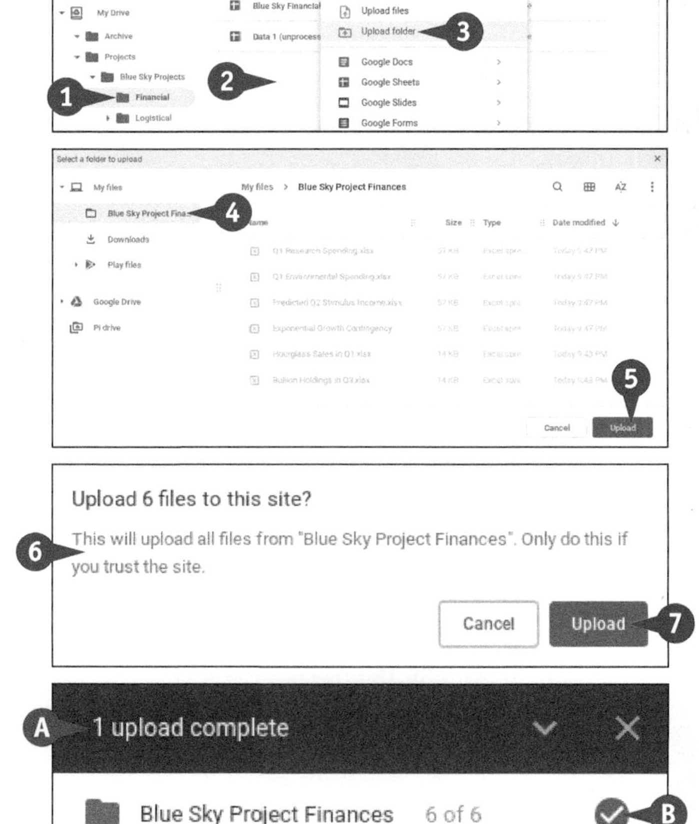

Ⓐ When the upload finishes, the Upload Complete message appears.

Ⓑ You can move the cursor over **Upload complete** (✔) to display Show File Location (📁 replaces ✔). Click **Show file location** (📁) to display the location that contains the uploaded folder.

Enable and Use Google Drive's Offline Mode

As an online storage site, Google Drive requires an Internet connection. But if you will need to work on your Google Docs, Google Sheets, or Google Slides files when you do not have an Internet connection, you can enable Google Drive's Offline Mode, which makes local copies of files. To use Offline Mode, you must use Google's Chrome browser app rather than any other browser.

With Offline Mode active, you can work on the files when your computer is offline. Once your computer connects to the Internet again, Google Drive synchronizes the local files with the online files.

Enable and Use Google Drive's Offline Mode

Enable Google Drive's Offline Mode

1. In Google Drive, click **Settings** (⚙).

   The Settings panel opens.

2. Click **Settings.**

   The Settings screen for Google Drive appears.

   The General category of settings appears at first.

3. In the Offline area, select **Create, open and edit your recent Google Docs, Sheets, and Slides files on this device while offline** (☑).

4. Click **Done.**

   The Settings screen for Google Drive closes.

   A pop-up message in the lower-left corner of the screen shows the readout *Setting up offline* while Chrome configures Offline Mode and downloads the files needed for it. The readout *Offline setup complete* appears when it finishes.

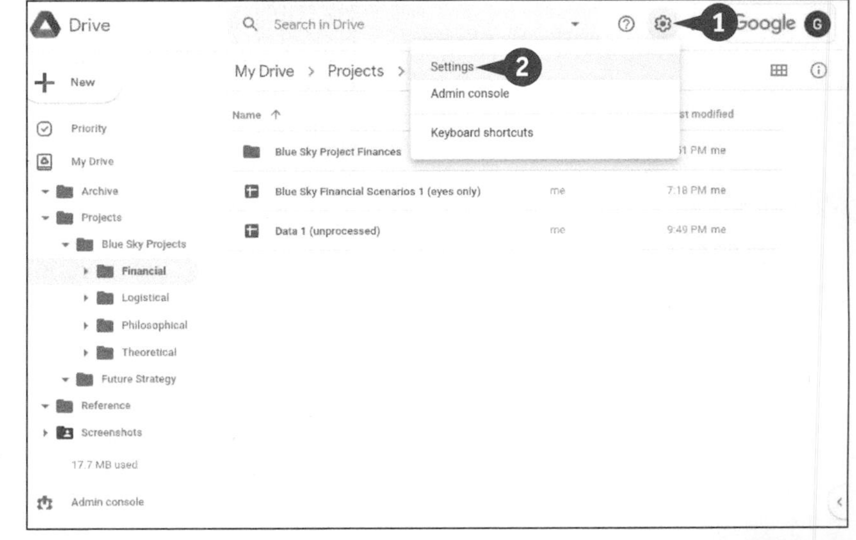

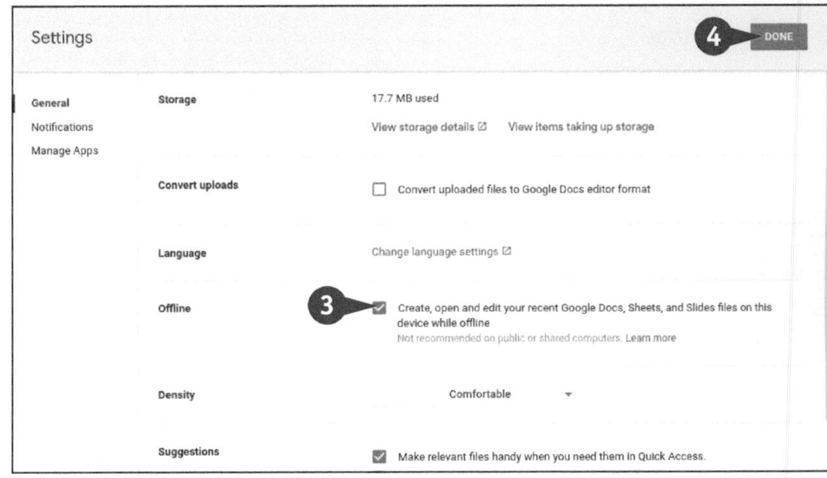

Make a File Available Offline

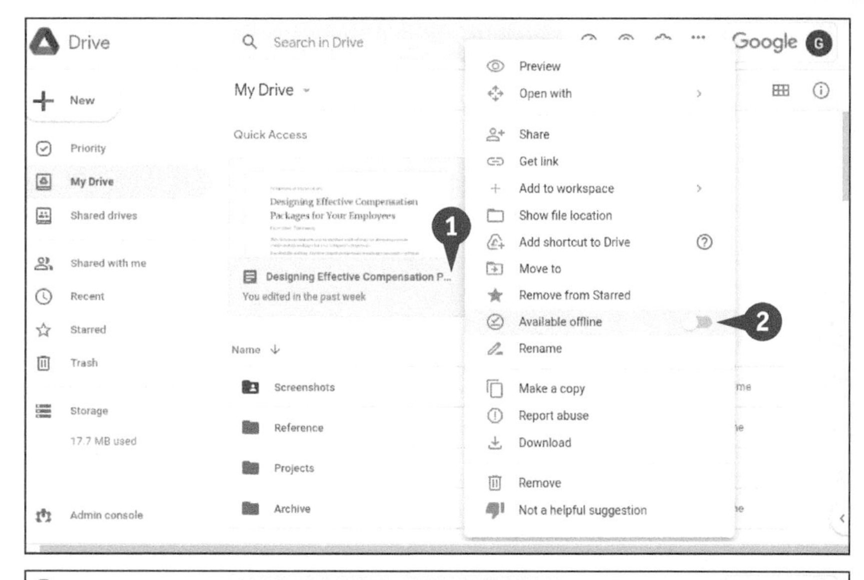

1. In Google Drive, right-click the file you want to make available offline.

   The contextual menu appears.

2. Click **Available offline** (changes to).

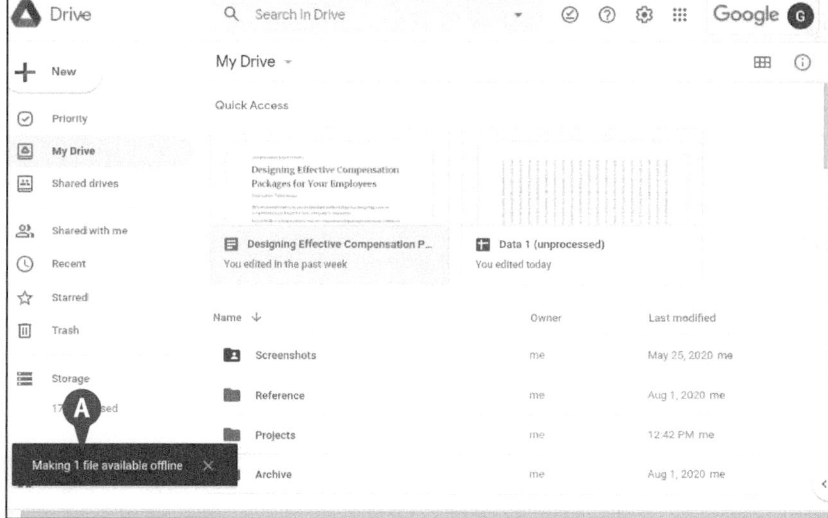

A. A confirmation message, such as *Making 1 file available offline*, appears briefly.

TIP

How do I make a Google Drive file available offline while I am editing it?

When you have a Google Docs, Google Sheets, or Google Slides file open for editing, you can make it available offline by clicking **File** to open the File menu and then clicking **Make available offline**. A readout such as *Document now available offline* appears in the lower-left corner of the window to confirm the change.

If you click **File** again, you will see the File menu displays a check mark next to the Make Available Offline command.

Open a File

To work with a file in an app, you open the file from the folder or location in which it is stored. You can open the file either from Google Drive or by using the Open command on the app's File menu.

Each file type has a default app associated with it. For example, the Google Sheets app is the default for the Google Sheets file type, as you would expect. When you double-click a file in Google Drive, the default app opens the file. To use a different app than the default, you can use the Open With command.

Open a File

Open a File from Google Drive

1. In Google Drive, navigate to the folder that contains the file you want to open.

2. Double-click the file you want to open.

   This example uses a Google Sheets spreadsheet file.

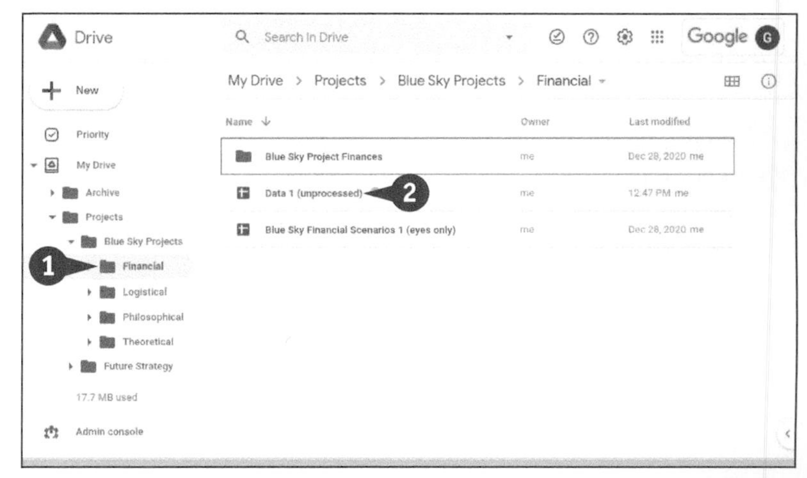

The file opens in the associated app.

Ⓐ In this example, the spreadsheet file opens in the Google Sheets app.

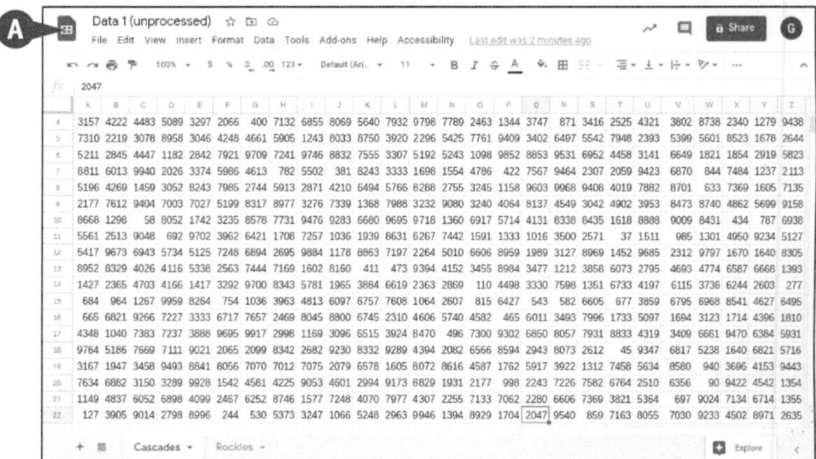

Open a File from Within an App

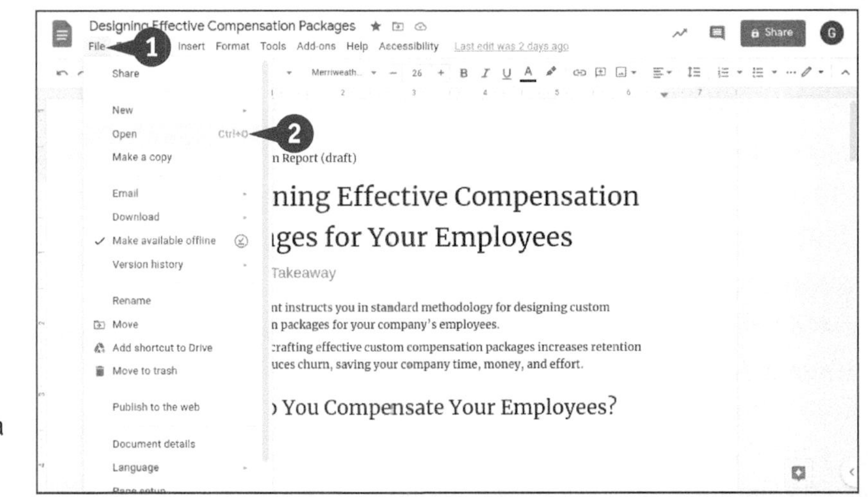

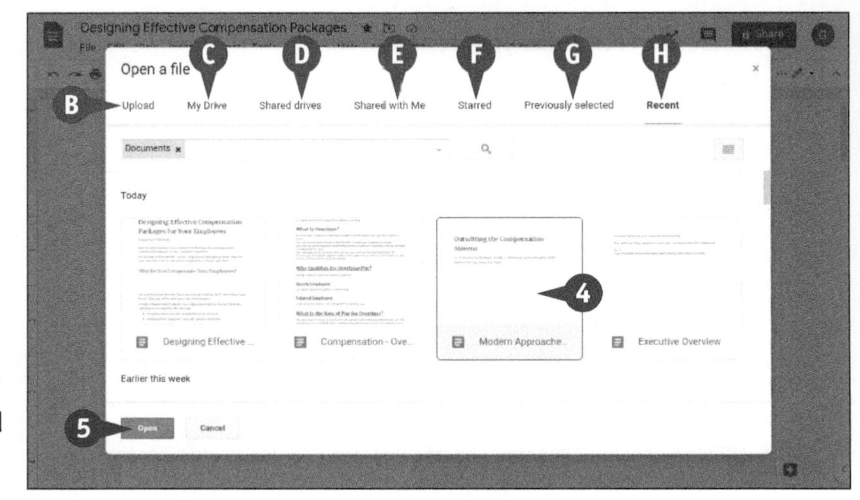

1. In the app, click **File**.

   The File menu opens.

2. Click **Open**.

   The Open a File dialog box appears.

3. On the tab bar, click the appropriate tab.

- B You can click **Upload** to upload a file from your computer.
- C You can click **My Drive** to display the My Drive category.
- D You can click **Shared drives** to display shared drives to which you have access.
- E You can click **Shared with Me** to display files that others have shared with you.
- F You can click **Starred** to display files you have marked with a star.
- G You can click **Previously selected** to display files you have previously selected.
- H You can click **Recent** to display files you have saved recently.

4. Click the file you want to open.
5. Click **Open**.

   The file opens in the app.

TIP

How do I open a file in a different app from the default app?
In a Google Drive tab, navigate to the folder that contains the file you want to open. Right-click the file, click or highlight **Open with** on the contextual menu, and then click the app you want to use.

Move a File or Folder

Google Drive enables you to move a file or a folder from one location to another. Moving is useful for keeping your files and folders logically organized and for giving others access to the files and folders they need.

You can move a file or folder either by clicking and dragging or by using the Move To command and the pop-up windows it produces. You can move a single file or folder at a time or move multiple items together, as needed.

Move a File or Folder

Move a File or Folder Using the Move To Command

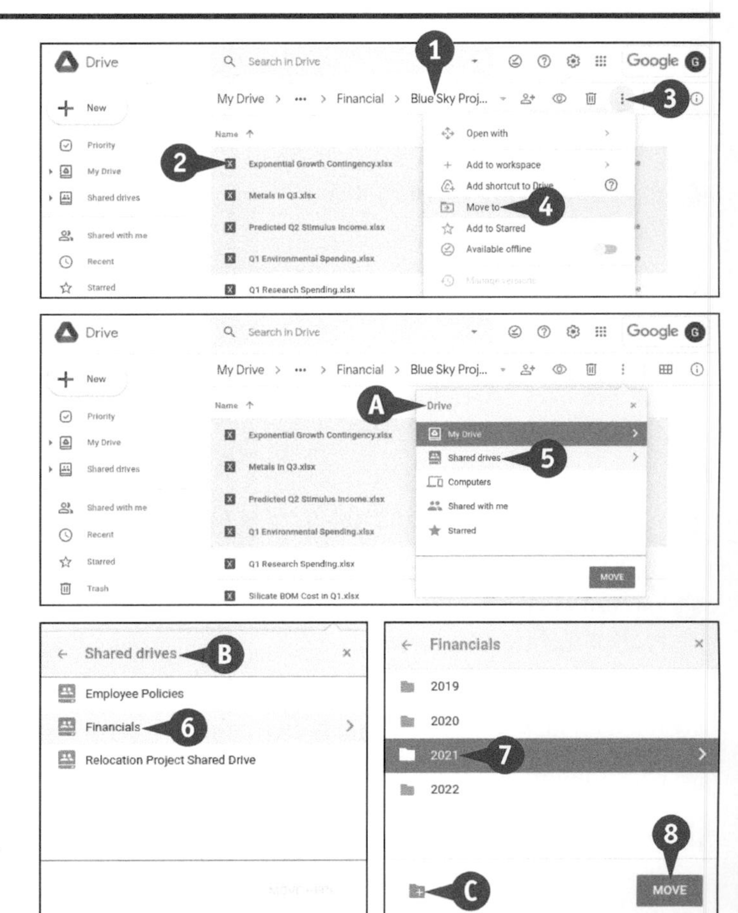

1. In Google Drive, navigate to the folder that contains the file or folder you want to move.
2. Select the item or items you want to move.
3. Click **More actions** (⋮).

   The menu opens.
4. Click **Move to** (📁).

   A pop-up window for navigating to the destination folder appears.

   A. The title bar shows the name of the location or folder at the top of the hierarchy shown.
5. Double-click the location or folder you want to open.

   In this example, you would double-click **Shared drives**.

   The pop-up window shows the hierarchy for the folder or location you double-clicked.

   B. The title bar shows the name of the folder or location you double-clicked.
6. Navigate further, as needed.

   In this example, you would double-click **Financials**.
7. When you reach the destination folder, click the folder to select it.

   C. You can click **New folder** (📁) to create a new folder in the current folder.
8. Click **Move**.

If you are moving the item or items to a shared drive, the Change Ownership to a Shared Drive? dialog box opens to make sure you understand the result of the move.

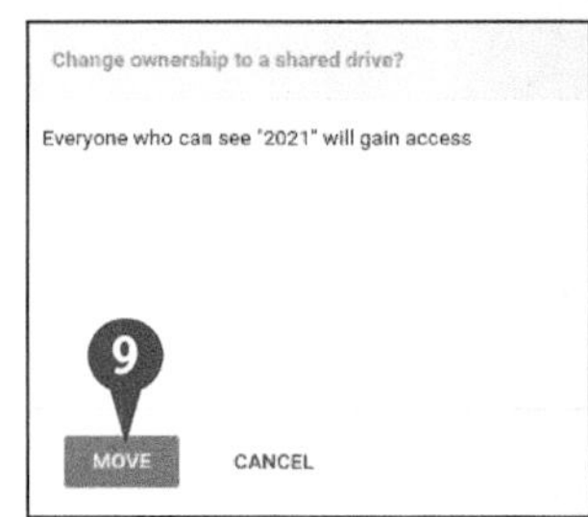

9 Click **Move**.

Google Drive moves the files.

D A pop-up message appears for a few seconds, confirming the details of the move.

E You can click **Undo** to undo the move.

Move a File or Folder Using Drag and Drop

1 In the sidebar, expand the destination location until you can see the destination folder.

For example, you might expand the Shared Drives location and a folder it contains.

2 Navigate to the location or folder that contains the file or folder you want to move.

3 Drag the file or folder to the destination folder.

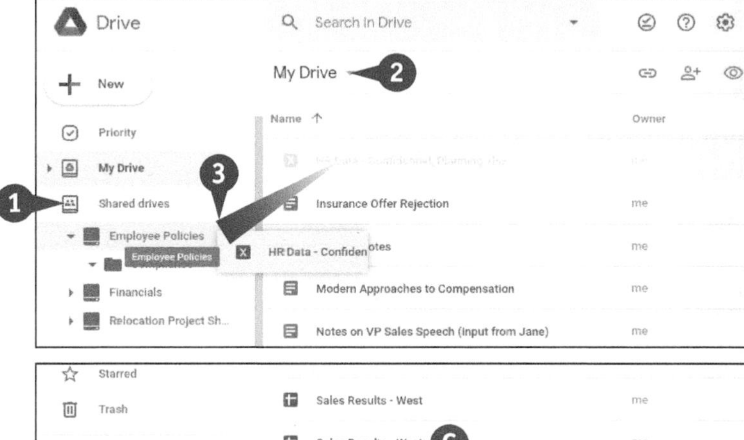

F A pop-up message appears for a few seconds, summarizing the Move operation.

G You can click **Undo** to undo the move.

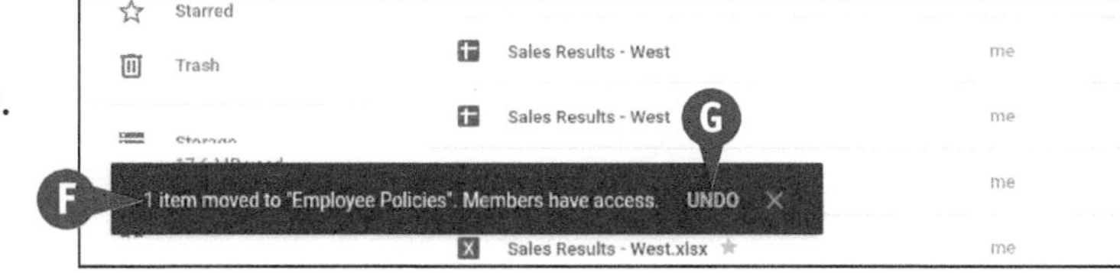

TIP

Is there another way to perform a Move operation?

Yes — you can start a Move operation from the contextual menu. Right-click the file or folder you want to move, or right-click the files or folders you have already selected, and then click **Move to** (icon) on the contextual menu.

When you do this, the Move To pop-up window at first shows the folder that currently contains the item or items rather than showing Google Drive as a whole. So if you want to move the item or items to a nearby folder, starting from the contextual menu may be more convenient than starting from the More Actions menu.

Copy a File

Most file managers make it easy to copy a file or a folder from one location to another, which is useful when you need to share a file or folder with other people or keep a copy of the file or folder safe from harm. By contrast, Google Drive discourages you from copying files within Google Drive itself, although it does enable you to duplicate a file or to download a file or folder. You can also create a shortcut to a file or folder, as explained in the following section.

Duplicate a File

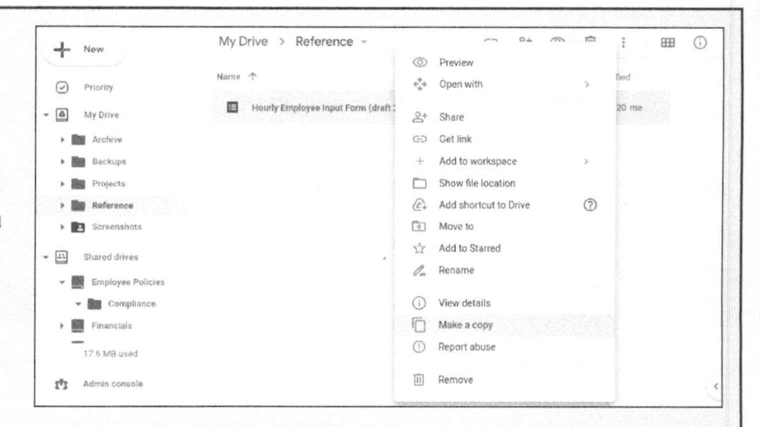

When you need to duplicate a file, use the Make a Copy command. Right-click the file, and then click **Make a copy** (⧉) on the contextual menu; you can also select the file, click **More actions** (⋮), and then click **Make a copy** (⧉). Google Drive creates a copy of the file in the same folder, assigning it the name *Copy of* and the original name. For example, the copy of a file named *Business Process Manual* receives the name *Copy of Business Process Manual.*

Once you have created the duplicate, you can move it to another folder, as explained in the previous section. You can also rename the duplicate file. Keep in mind that if you want the copy to have the same name as the original file, as would happen with a standard copy operation to a different location, you must first move the copy: You cannot give the copy the original file's name while both are in the same folder.

Download a File or Folder

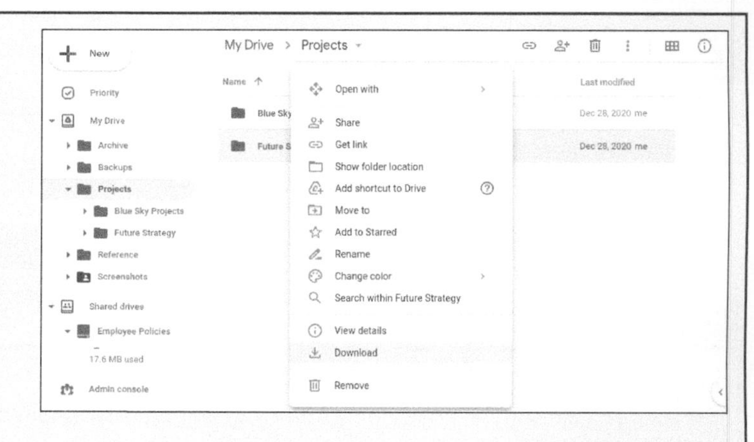

Another way of copying a file is to download it to your computer. Downloading works for folders as well, so it can be a handy way to keep spare copies of files or folders.

To download a file or folder, navigate to the location or folder that contains it, and then click to select the file or folder. You can also select multiple files or folders. Click **More actions** (⋮) to open the More Actions menu, and then click **Download** (⤓); you can also right-click a file or folder, or right-click selected files or folders, and then click **Download** (⤓) on the contextual menu.

Your browser places the downloaded item or items in the Downloads folder specified in its settings. You can then move the item or items to a different location, as needed.

Create a Shortcut to a File or Folder

Google Drive enables you to create shortcuts to files or folders. Creating shortcuts provides a quick way to access files and folders that you need to use frequently or ones that are deeply buried within subfolders.

The formal way to create a shortcut is to use the Add Shortcut to Drive command, which you can find on the More Actions menu and the contextual menu. The informal way is to hold down Ctrl while you drag a file to the folder in which you want to create the shortcut. On the Mac, hold down Option while you drag.

Create a Shortcut to a File or Folder

1. In Google Drive, navigate to the folder that contains the file or folder to which you want to create a shortcut.
2. Select the item for which you want to create the shortcut.
3. Click **More actions** (⋮).

   The More Actions menu opens.
4. Click **Add shortcut to Drive** ().

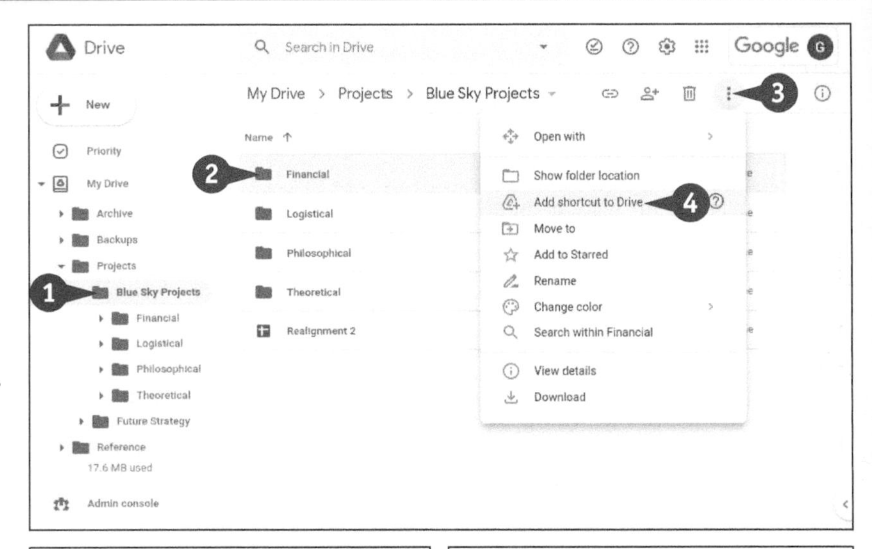

A pop-up window for specifying the location for the shortcut appears.

5. Navigate to the folder that contains the folder in which you want to place the shortcut.

   In this example, you would double-click **My Drive** () to display the folders it contains.
6. Click the destination folder.
7. Click **ADD SHORTCUT**.

   Google Drive creates the shortcut.

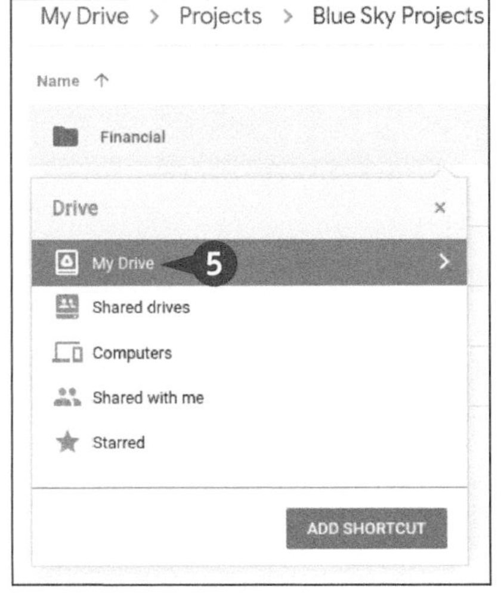

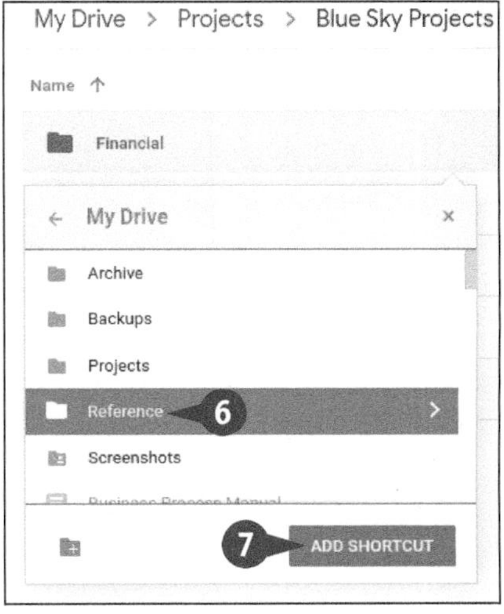

Rename a File or Folder

Google Drive enables you to rename any file or folder you have created. It is often helpful to rename files and folders to keep your Google Drive storage logically organized and to make it easy to find the files and folders you need.

You can begin the process of renaming a file or folder from either the More Actions menu or the contextual menu for a file or folder.

Rename a File or Folder

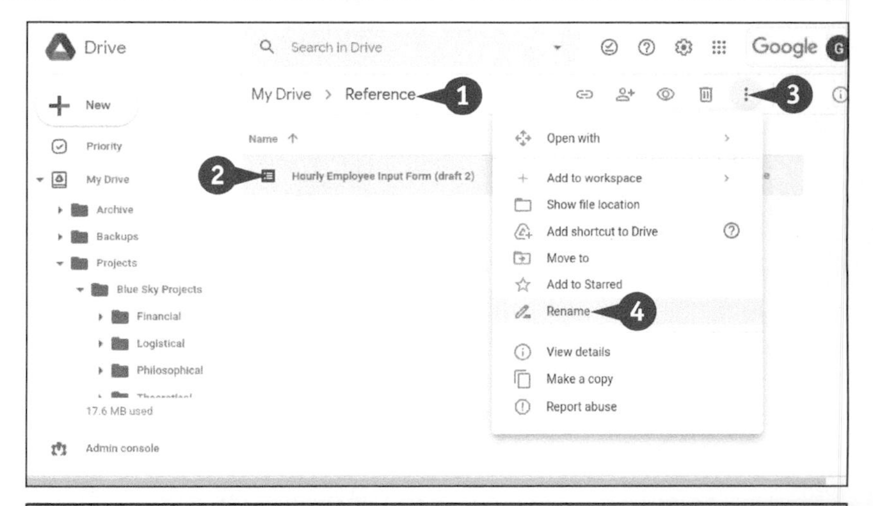

1. In Google Drive, navigate to the folder that contains the file or folder you want to rename.
2. Click the file or folder to select it.
3. Click **More actions** (⋮).

   The More Actions menu opens.
4. Click **Rename** (✎).

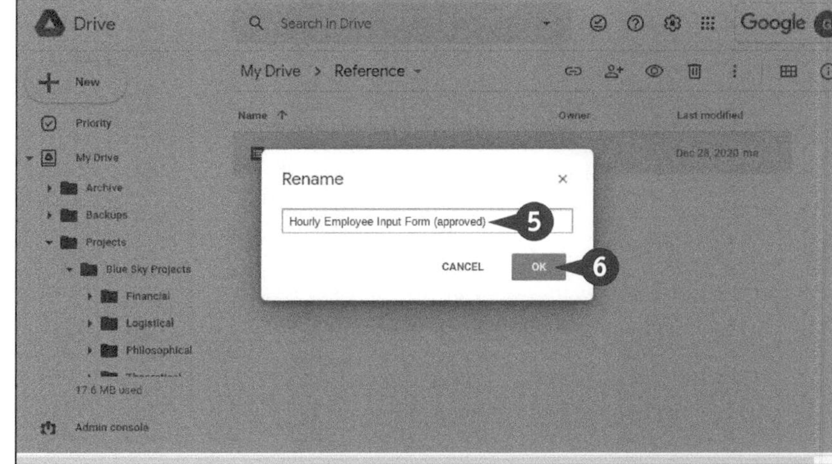

The Rename dialog box opens.

5. Type the new name, or edit the existing name, as appropriate.
6. Click **OK**.

   The Rename dialog box closes.

   The file or folder's new name appears.

View Info and Activity on a File or Folder

Google Drive stores a large amount of information about each file and the actions that users have taken with it. You can view this information by using the View Details command from either the More Actions menu or the contextual menu.

Using the View Details command opens a pane on the right side of the Google Drive window. The pane contains two tabs: the Details tab and the Activity tab. The Details tab includes the file type, size, location, creation and modification dates, and a preview. The Activity tab shows a summary of the actions taken with the file.

View Info and Activity on a File or Folder

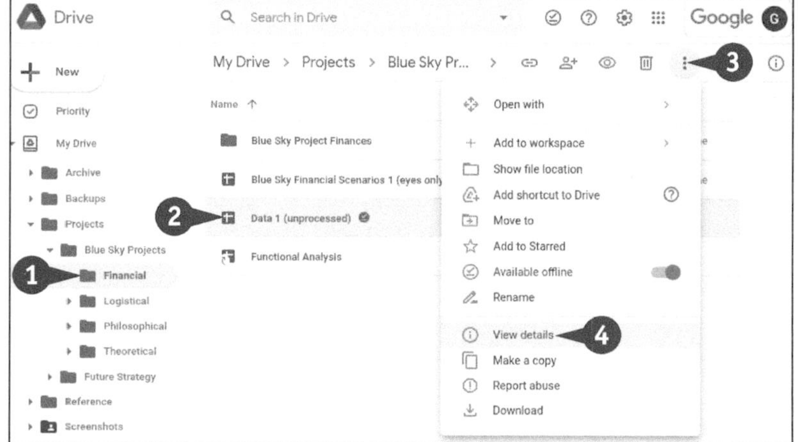

1. In Google Drive, navigate to the folder that contains the file for which you want to view info and activity.
2. Click the file or folder to select it.
3. Click **More actions** (⋮).

   The More Actions menu opens.
4. Click **View details** (ⓘ).

   The Information pane appears, showing the Details tab first.

   A. You can see whether or not the file is shared.

   B. You can see the file's type, such as Google Sheets.

   C. You can see the file's owner.

   D. You can see when the file was created, last opened, and last modified.

   E. Optionally, you can add a description.
5. Click **Activity**.

   The Activity tab appears.

   F. You can see actions taken with the file, such as editing it.
6. Click **Close** (✕).

   The Information pane closes.

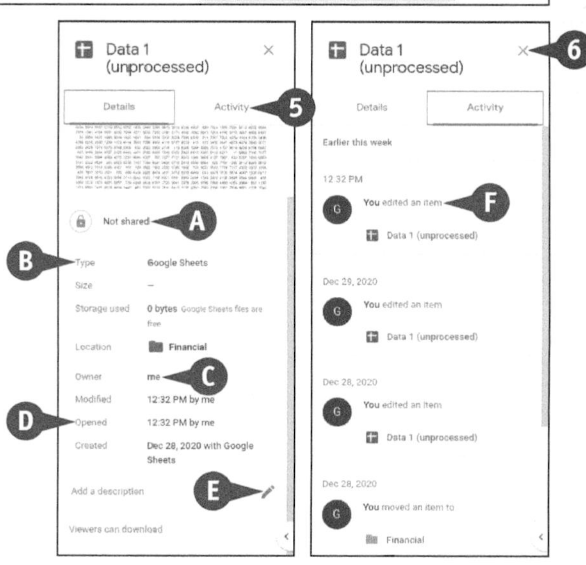

Search for a File or Folder

To locate a file or folder on Google Drive, you can search using the Search in Drive feature, which enables you to perform either simple or complex searches.

For a simple search, you type one or more search terms, and optionally choose the file type or location. For a complex search, you expand the Search in Drive box and specify further details of what you want to find. When the file or folder you want appears in the search results, you can click it to open it.

Search for a File or Folder

Perform a Simple Search

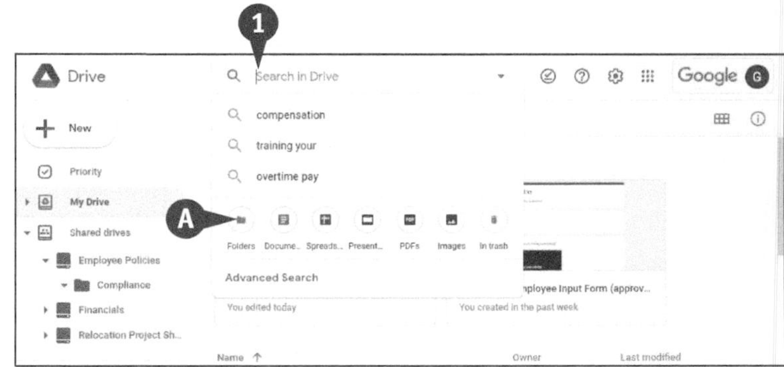

1. In Google Drive, click **Search in Drive**.

   The Search in Drive box becomes active.

   The Search in Drive panel opens.

   A. Optionally, click **Folders** ( ), **Documents** ( ), **Spreadsheets** ( ), **Presentations** ( ), **PDFs** ( ), **Images** ( ), or **In trash** ( ) to restrict the search.

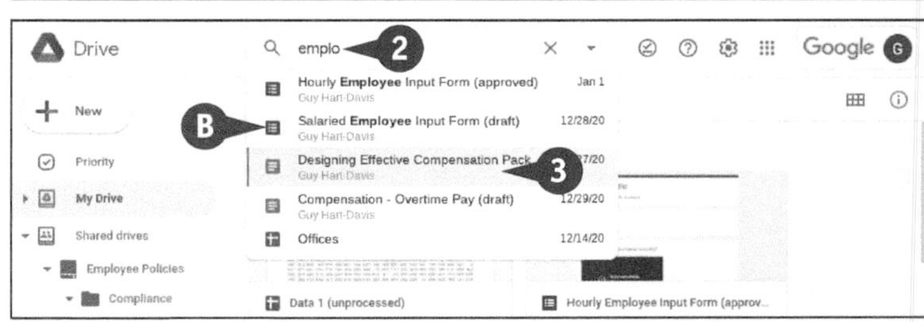

2. Start typing your first search term.

   B. Search results appear.

Note: If needed, type other search terms to refine the search.

3. Click the item you want to open.

Perform a Complex Search

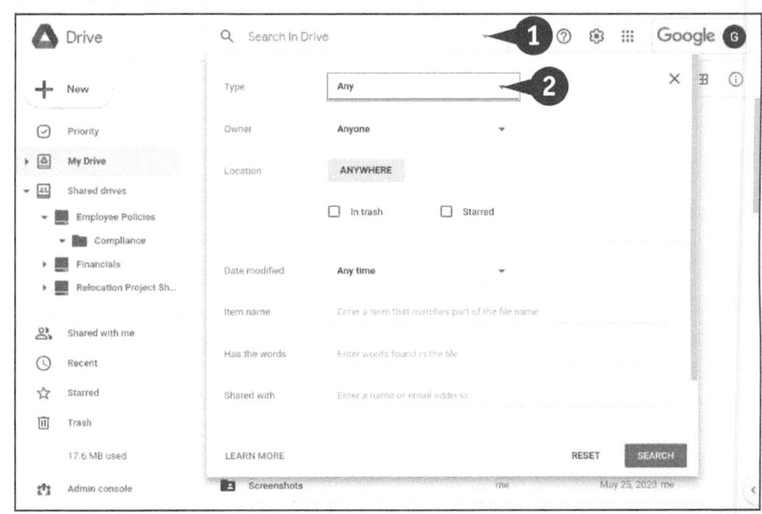

1. In Google Drive, click **Search in Drive** ( ).

   The Search in Drive dialog box opens.

2. To specify the item type, click **Type** ( ), and then click **Photos & images** ( ), **PDFs** ( ), **Documents** ( ), **Spreadsheets** ( ), **Presentations** ( ), **Forms** ( ), **Audio** ( ), **Videos** ( ), **Archive (zip)** ( ), **Drawings** ( ), **Shortcuts** ( ), **Folders** ( ), or **Sites** ( ), as needed. The default type is Any.

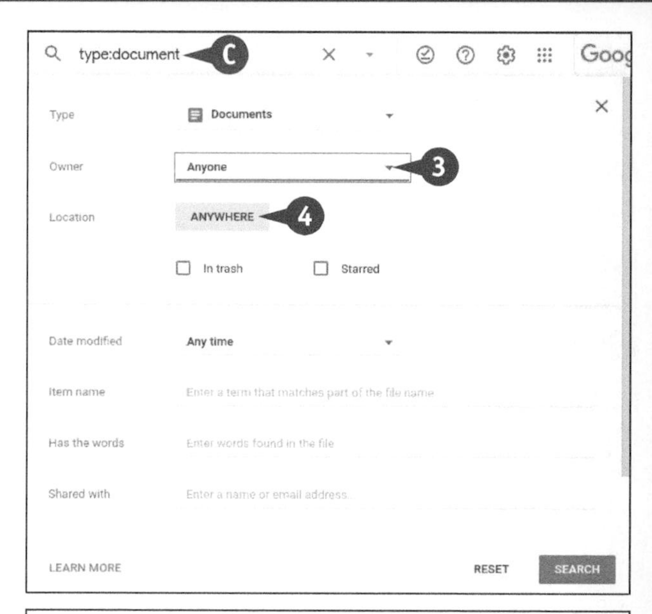

C The Search in Drive box shows the search parameters you have entered so far. In this example, *type:document* represents selecting Documents in the Type pop-up menu.

3 To specify the item's owner, click **Owner** (▾), and then click **Owned by me**, **Not owned by me**, or **Specific person**. If you click **Specific person**, type the person's name or email address. The default owner is Anyone.

4 To specify the location, click the Location button, which shows **ANYWHERE** by default; click the location, and then click **Select**.

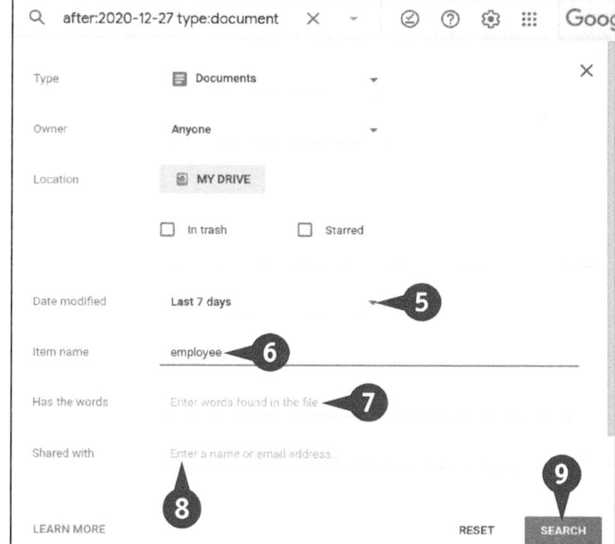

5 To restrict the search by time, click **Date modified** (▾), and then click **Today**, **Yesterday**, **Last 7 days**, **Last 30 days**, **Last 90 days**; or click **Custom** and specify start and end dates. The default is Any Time.

6 To search by file name, click **Item name** and type a term.

7 To search by contents, click **Has the words** and type a term.

8 To search by users with whom the item is shared, click **Shared with** and type a name or email address.

9 Click **Search**.

The Search in Drive dialog box closes.

Search results appear.

TIP

What do the In Trash setting and the Starred setting do?

You can select **In trash** (☑) to restrict the search to only items in the Trash. Similarly, you can select **Starred** (☑) to restrict the search to only items you have marked as starred.

Delete a File or Folder

When you no longer need a file or folder, you can delete it. To help you avoid getting rid of items accidentally, deleting an item moves it to the Trash rather than actually erasing it immediately. The item remains in the Trash for 30 days, during which time you can retrieve it if necessary; see the following section for instructions. After 30 days, Google Drive permanently deletes the item, and you can no longer retrieve it.

Delete a File or Folder

1. In Google Drive, navigate to the folder that contains the file or folder you want to delete.
2. Click the file or folder to select it.
3. Click **Remove** (🗑).

   The Move to Trash? dialog box opens.
4. Click **MOVE TO TRASH**.

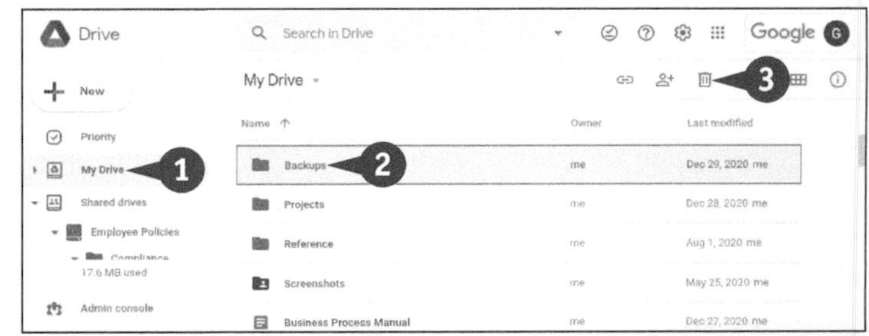

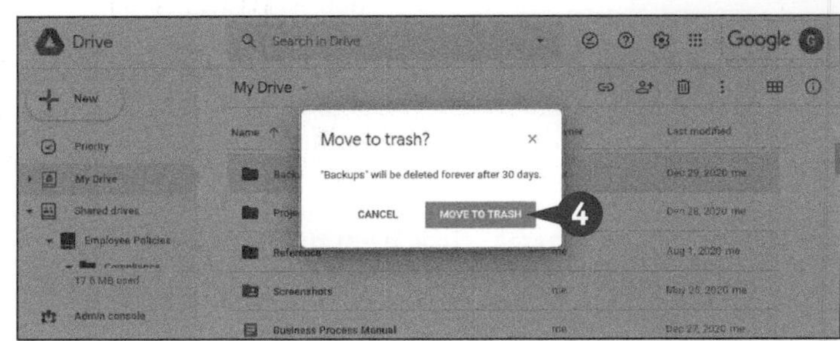

Ⓐ A pop-up message appears for a few seconds, summarizing the operation performed, such as *Folder moved to trash*.

Ⓑ You can click **UNDO** to retrieve the item from the Trash immediately.

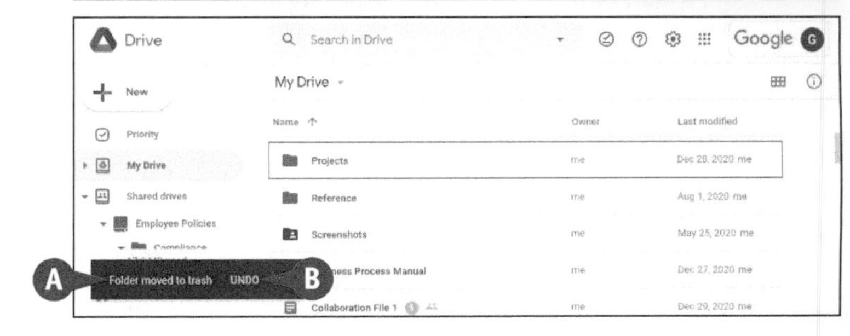

Recover a File from the Trash

When you select a file or folder and give the Remove command, Google Drive does not delete the item immediately but instead moves it to the Trash folder. Google Drive keeps the item in the Trash for 30 days before deleting it permanently. During this time, you can recover the item from the Trash if you need to.

You may sometimes want to get rid of items permanently without letting them fester in the Trash for 30 days. You can achieve this either by emptying the Trash or by issuing the Delete Forever command for an item in it.

Recover a File from the Trash

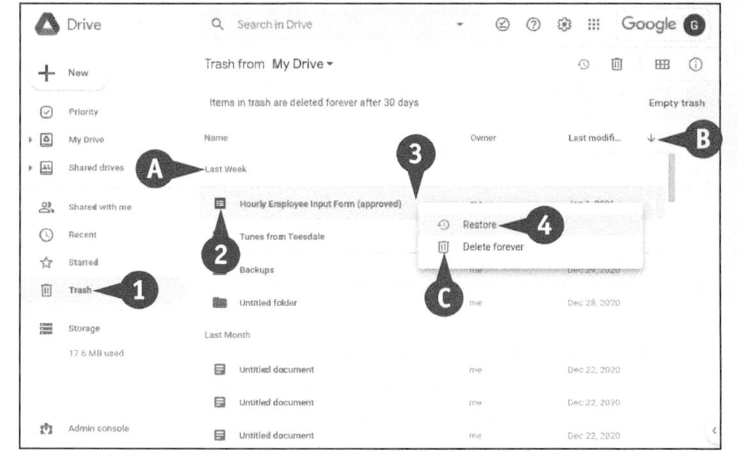

1. In Google Drive, click **Trash** (🗑).

   The Trash category appears.

   Ⓐ By default, the Trash sorts files in reverse order by Last Modified by Me, so items you deleted recently appear at the top of the list.

   Ⓑ You can click **Descending sort** (↓ changes to ↑) or **Ascending sort** (↑ changes to ↓) to reverse the sort direction.

2. Click the item or items you want to recover.
3. Right-click in the selection.

   The contextual menu opens.

4. Click **Restore** (⟲).

   Ⓒ You can click **Delete forever** (🗑) to delete the item forever.

   Ⓓ A pop-up message appears for a few seconds with the readout *Restored* and the item name.

   Ⓔ For a file, you can click **SHOW FILE LOCATION** to display the file's location — for example, so you can open the file.

   Ⓕ You can click **UNDO** to put the item back in the Trash immediately.

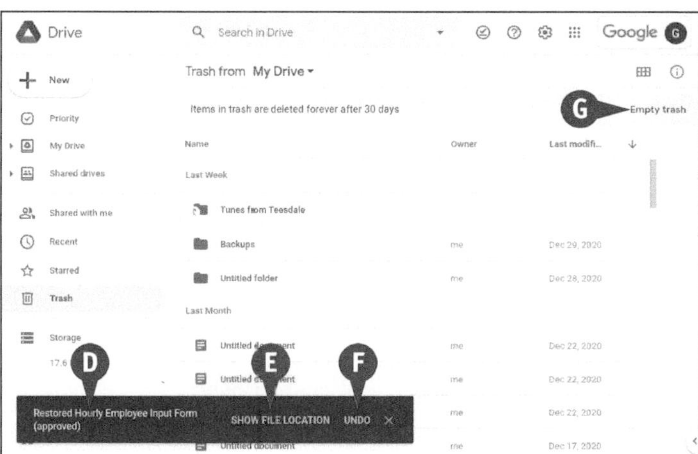

Ⓖ You can click **Empty trash** to get rid of all the files in the Trash permanently.

Work with Microsoft Office Documents

Google Workspace enables you to work with Microsoft Office documents. Google Docs can open, save, and convert Microsoft Word documents; Google Sheets can open, save, and convert Microsoft Excel workbooks; and Google Slides can open, save, and convert Microsoft PowerPoint presentations.

You can upload Microsoft Office documents to Google Drive, keeping the documents' file formats, using the method explained in the section "Upload a File to Google Drive," earlier in this chapter. You can then convert the documents to Google Docs, Google Sheets, or Google Slides format, as needed.

Work with Microsoft Office Documents

Open a Microsoft Office Document in a Google Workspace App

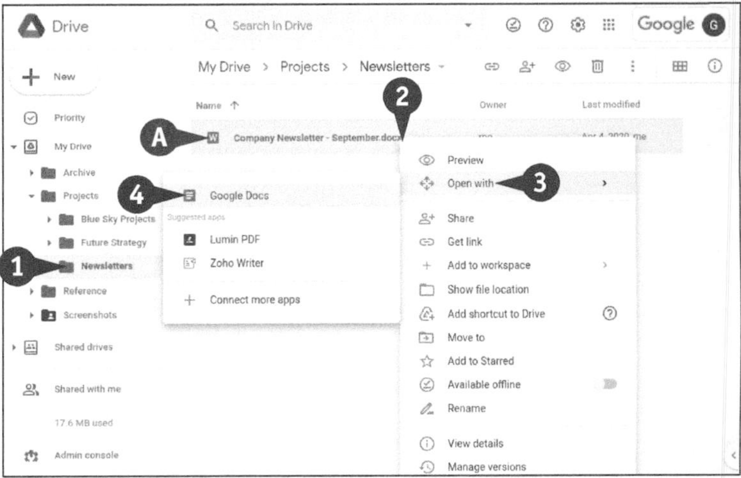

1. In Google Drive, navigate to the folder that contains the document.

   A The Word icon (W) indicates a Microsoft Word document.

2. Right-click the document.

   The contextual menu opens.

3. Click or highlight **Open with** (✥).

   The Open With submenu appears.

4. Click the appropriate Google Workspace app.

   In this example, you would click **Google Docs** (▤).

   The document opens in the app you specified.

   B The .DOCX file extension indicates that the document is in Microsoft Word format, which uses this file extension. See the tip for information on other Microsoft Office file extensions.

   You can now edit the document.

   The Google Workspace app — in this case, Google Docs — automatically saves changes you make, keeping the document in its Microsoft Office format.

Save a Microsoft Office Document in a Google Workspace Format

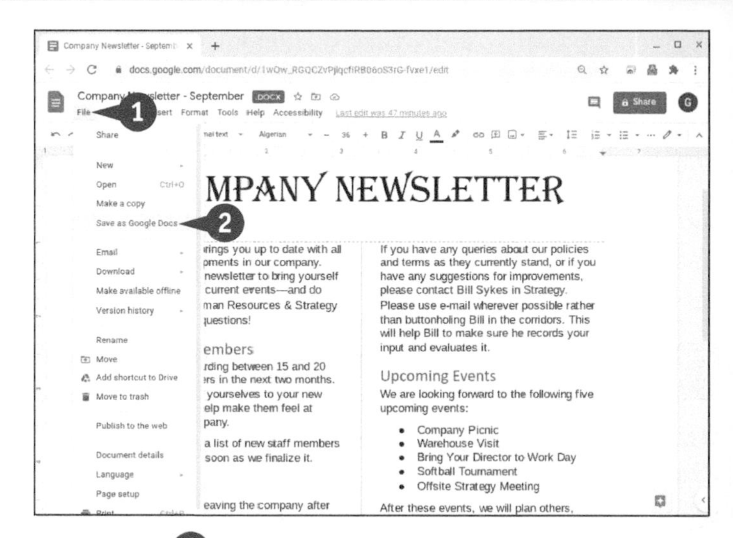

1. With a Microsoft Office document open in a Google Workspace app, click **File**.

   The File menu opens.

2. Click **Save as Google Docs**, **Save as Google Sheets**, or **Save as Google Slides**, depending on the app.

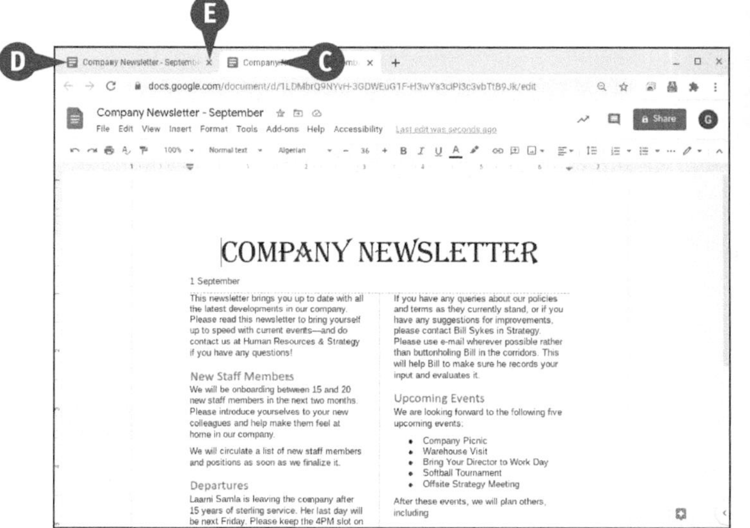

The app saves the document in the Google app's format in the same folder.

- C The new document appears in a new tab.
- D The original document is still open in its tab.
- E To avoid confusion, you may want to click **Close** (X) to close the original document at this point.

You can now work with the new document in its Google Workspace format.

TIP

Which Microsoft Office file types can the Google apps save?

The Google apps can save the most widely used Microsoft Office formats. For Microsoft Word, these are the Word Document format, which uses the .docx file extension, and the older Word 97–2003/2004 Document format, which uses the .doc file extension. For Microsoft Excel, these are the Excel Workbook format, which uses the .xlsx file extension, and the older Excel 97–2003/2004 Workbook format, which uses the .xls file extension. For Microsoft PowerPoint, these are the PowerPoint Presentation format, which uses the .pptx format, and the older PowerPoint 97–2003/2004 Presentation format, which uses the .ppt file extension. Google Drive automatically converts all other Word, Excel, and PowerPoint files to the equivalent Google Workspace apps formats.

continued ►

Keeping a Microsoft Office document in its original format can be helpful when you or colleagues need to work on the document in Microsoft Office. But if you will be using only Google Workspace apps to work on the document from now on, converting the document to the corresponding Google Workspace format is usually a good idea.

Google Workspace also enables you to upload and convert a Microsoft Office document in a single move. For example, you can upload an Excel workbook, converting it so that it arrives in Google Drive as a Google Sheets spreadsheet.

Work with Microsoft Office Documents (continued)

Upload and Convert a Microsoft Office Document

1. Open the Google Workspace app that can handle the format to which you want to convert the file. For example, in Google Drive, click **New** (+) to display the New pop-up menu, and then click **Google Sheets** (⊞) to open the Google Sheets app and create a new spreadsheet.

Following this example, the new spreadsheet opens in a new browser tab.

2. Click **File**.

The File menu opens.

3. Click **Open**.

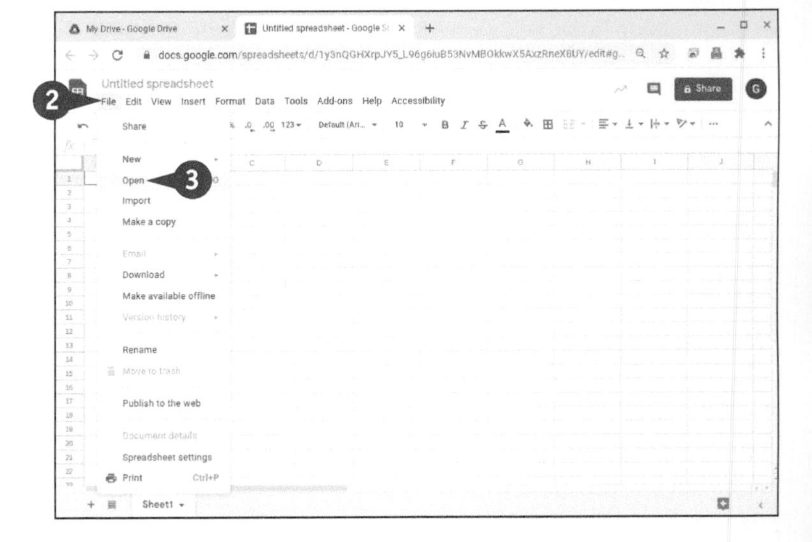

The Open a File dialog box opens.

4. Click **Upload**.

   The Upload tab appears.

5. Specify the file you want to upload:

   F. Either drag a file from a file-management window to the open area with the *Drag a file here* prompt.

   G. Or click **Select a file from your device**, use the Select a File to Open dialog box to select the file, and then click **Open**.

   The app uploads the file and converts it to the Google Workspace app's format.

   The Open a File dialog box closes.

   The file opens in the Google Workspace app you were using.

   You can now work with the file as normal.

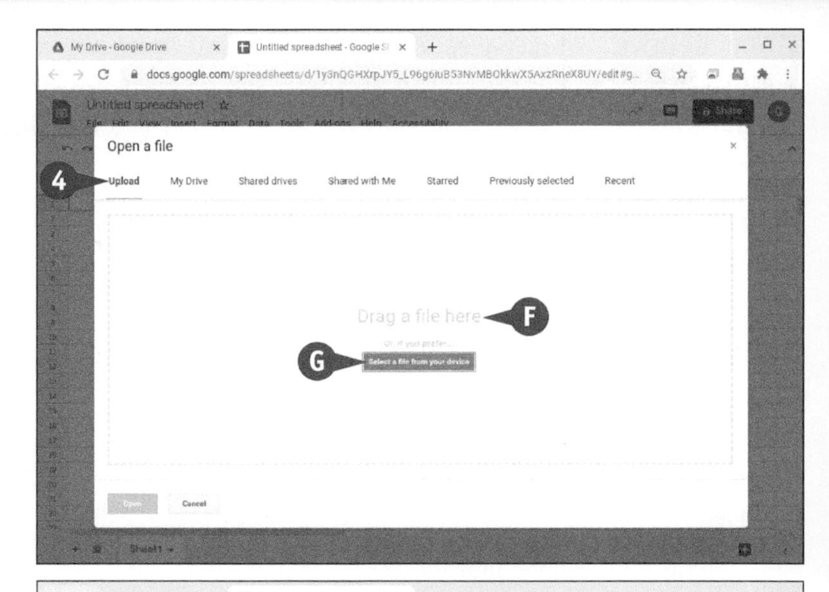

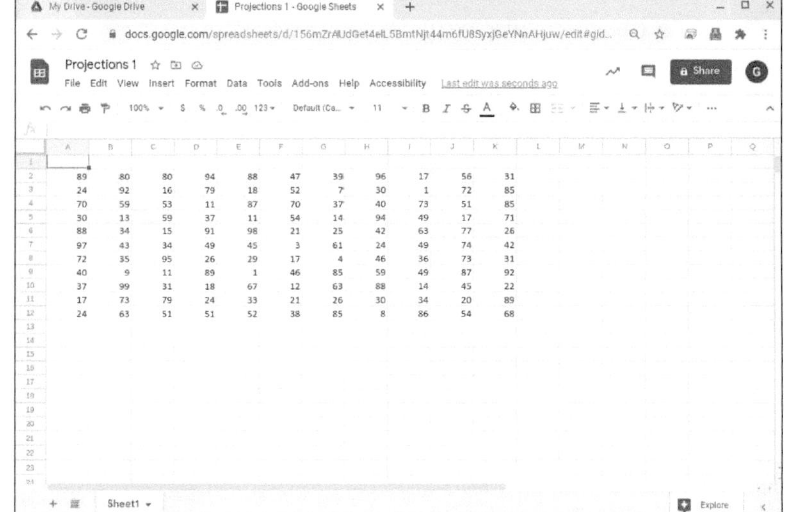

TIP

Can I create Microsoft Office documents from Google Workspace documents?

Yes — you can create Microsoft Word documents from Google Docs, Microsoft Excel workbooks from Google Sheets, and Microsoft PowerPoint presentations from Google Slides.

Open the Google Workspace document in its app — for example, open a Google Docs document in Google Docs. Click **File** to open the File menu, click or highlight **Download** to display the Download submenu, and then click **Microsoft Word (.docx)**. In Google Sheets, click **File**, click or highlight **Download**, and then click **Microsoft Excel (.xlsx)**. In Google Slides, click **File**, click or highlight **Download**, and then click **Microsoft PowerPoint (.pptx)**.

Streamline Your Work with Workspaces

Google Drive's Workspaces feature enables you to create groups of files called *workspaces*. Each workspace can contain up to 25 files, which can be located in any part of Google Drive to which you have access. After adding files to a workspace, you can display the screen for the workspace and quickly open or manage the files it contains.

You access your workspaces through the Priority category in Google Drive. From here, you can create new workspaces and manage existing workspaces.

Streamline Your Work with Workspaces

Create a Workspace and Add Files to It

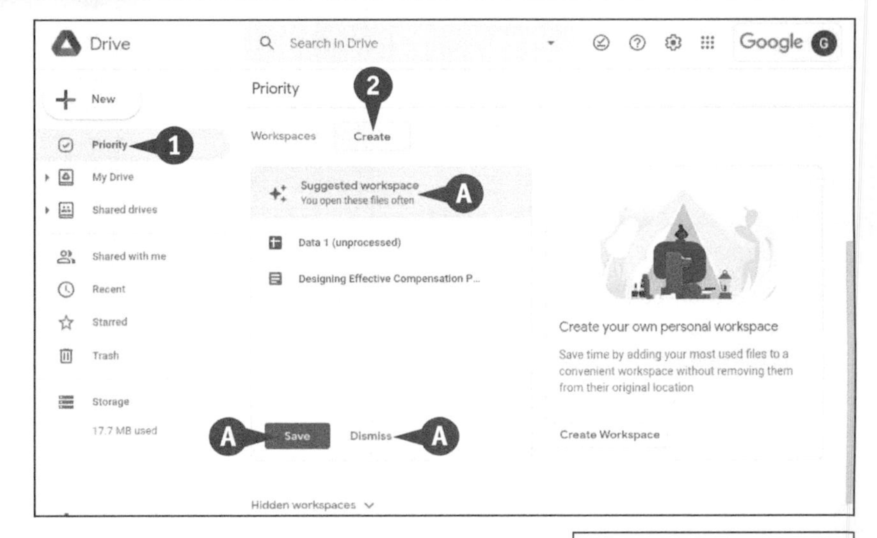

1. In Google Drive, click **Priority** (☑).

   The Priority category appears.

   A Google Drive may display Suggested Workspace (✦) based on files you open frequently. You can click **Save** to accept the suggestion and save the workspace or click **Dismiss** to dismiss the suggestion.

2. Click **Create.**

   The New Workspace dialog box opens.

3. Type the name for the new workspace.

4. Click **Create.**

   The New Workspace dialog box closes.

   The screen for the workspace appears.

   B A pop-up message saying *Workspace created* appears for a few seconds.

5. Click **Add files.**

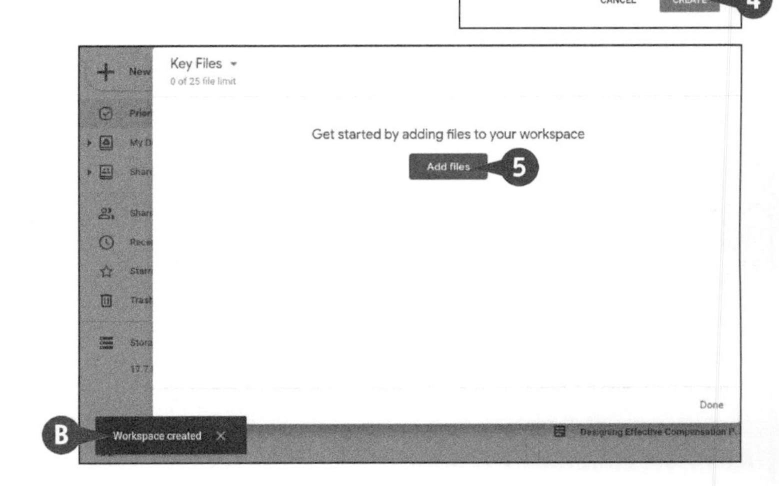

The screen for the workspace shrinks somewhat and moves to the left.

The Add to Workspace pane appears on the right.

6 On the tab bar at the top of the Add to Workspace pane, select the location that contains the files you want to add. In this example, you would click **RECENT**.

C You can click **Next** (›) to scroll along the bar. Click **Previous** (‹) to scroll back.

7 Click to select each file you want to add.

8 Click **INSERT**.

The Add to Workspace pane closes.

The files appear on the screen for the workspace.

D You can click **Add files** to add other files.

9 When you finish adding files to the workspace, click **Done**.

The workspace appears in the Workspaces section of the Priority category.

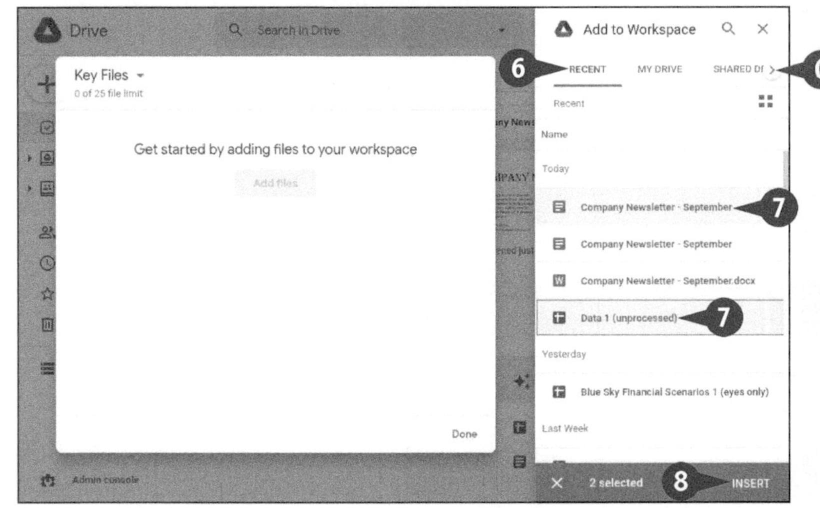

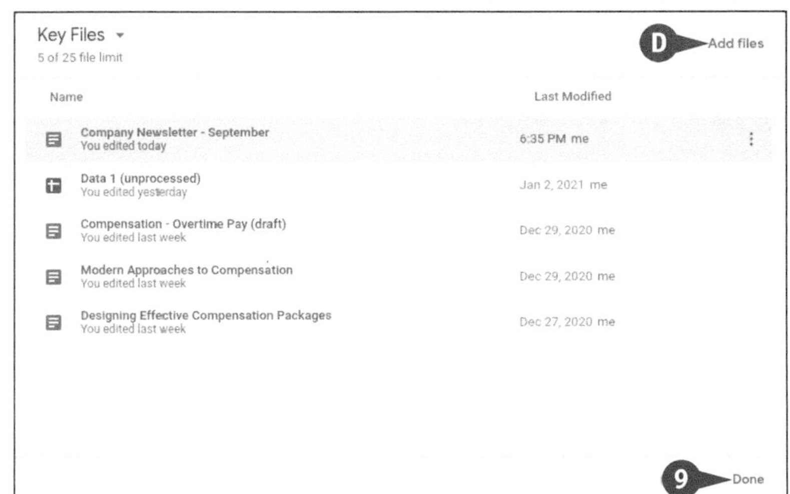

TIP

What other way can I start creating a workspace?

You can start creating a workspace by selecting one or more files you want to put in that workspace. Right-click in the selection, highlight or click **Add to workspace** (+), and then click **Create new workspace.** The New Workspace dialog box opens. Type the name for the workspace and click **Create.** Google Drive creates the workspace and adds the files to it.

continued ►

You can update a workspace by adding files to it — up to the maximum of 25 files — and removing files from it, as needed.

If you create many workspaces, you may have to scroll the Priority category in Google Drive to find the workspaces you need. To reduce clutter, you can hide any workspace, moving it out of sight until you need it again — at which point you can unhide it. When you no longer need a workspace, you can get rid of it by removing it.

Streamline Your Work with Workspaces (continued)

Work with a Workspace

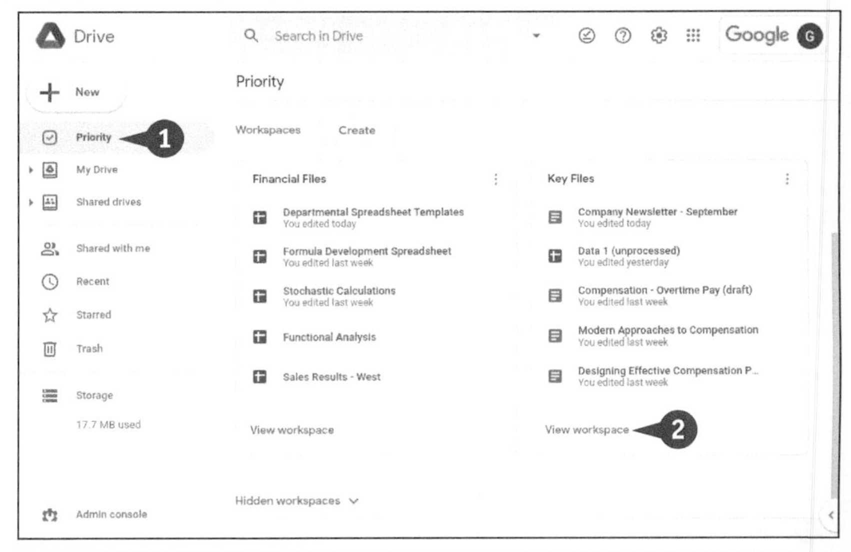

1. In Google Drive, click **Priority** (☑).

   The Priority category appears.

2. In the Workspaces section, click **View workspace** on the workspace you want to open.

Note: You can also click the workspace's name to open the workspace.

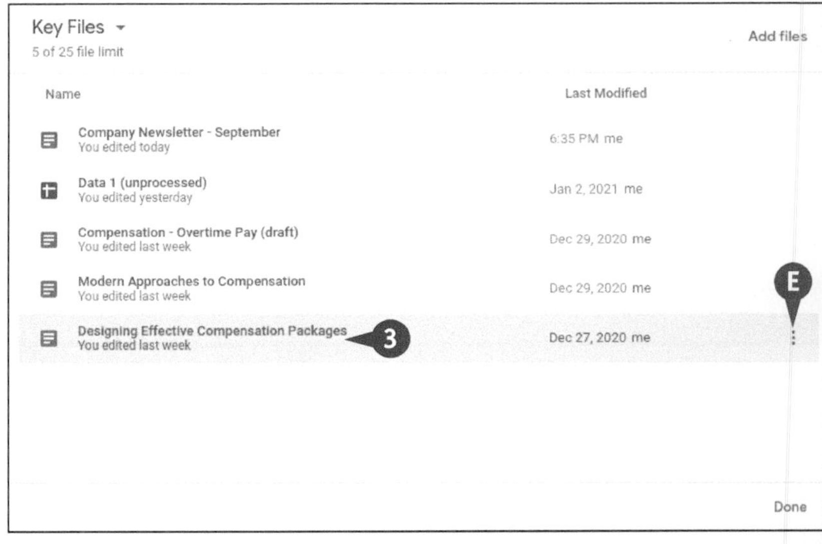

The screen for the workspace appears.

E You can take other actions with a file by clicking it, clicking **More actions** (⋮), and then clicking the appropriate menu item. For example, you can click **Show file location** (🗀) to display the file's location, or you can click **Remove from workspace** (⊖) to remove the file from the workspace.

3. Double-click the file you want to open.

The file opens in a new tab in the default Google Workspace app.

For example, a Google Docs document opens in the Google Docs app.

You can then work with the file as normal.

4 When you finish working with the file, click **Close** (✕).

The file's tab closes.

The tab containing the screen for the workspace appears again.

F You can open another file, if needed.

5 When you finish working with the workspace, click **Done**.

The screen for the workspace closes.

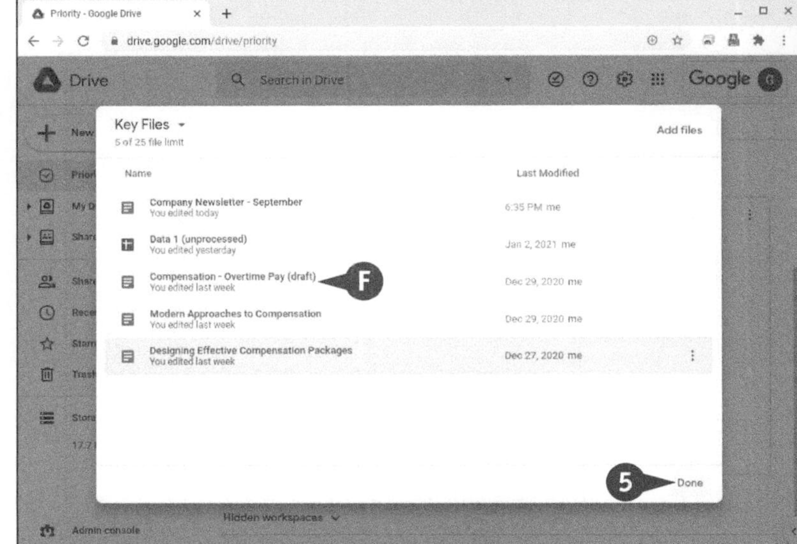

TIP

How — and why — do I hide a workspace?

If you create many workspaces, you may want to hide the ones you do not currently need so that you can focus on the other workspaces. To hide a workspace, go to the Priority category, click **More actions** (⋮) in the workspace's box, and then click **Hide workspace**. Google Drive moves the workspace to the Hidden Workspaces section of the Priority category. To show the workspace again, click **Hidden workspaces** (⌄ changes to ⌃), displaying the list of hidden workspaces. Click the workspace to display its screen, and then click **Unhide**.

CHAPTER 3

Performing Common Tasks in Google Docs, Google Sheets, and Google Slides

In this chapter, you learn to open apps, create and save documents, and perform other essential moves.

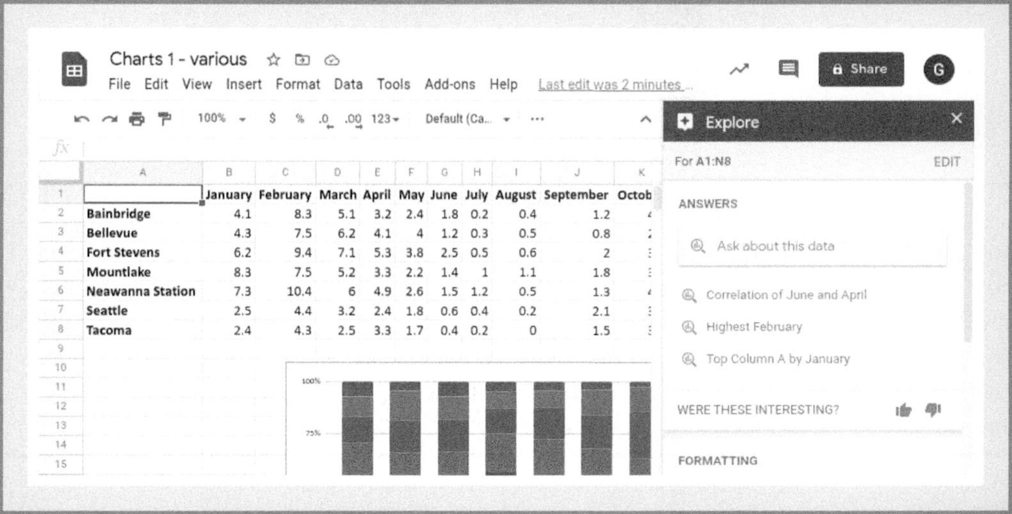

Open the App

To start creating a document, you first need to open the appropriate app — Google Docs, Google Sheets, or Google Slides. Generally, the easiest way to run the app is by opening the Google Apps pop-up panel, which appears in Google Drive, Gmail, and various other apps. But if you use Google's Chrome browser rather than another browser, you can also create a shortcut for the app so that you can launch it more easily from the Start menu in Windows, the Launchpad screen in macOS, or the Launcher screen on Chrome OS.

Open the App

Open the App from Google Drive

1 Open a browser window or tab to drive.google.com.

Note: If you want to create a shortcut, as explained in the next subsection, use Google's Chrome browser. If not, any widely used browser should work — for example, Microsoft Edge, Safari, or Firefox.

Note: If Google Drive does not sign you in automatically, follow the prompts to sign in manually.

2 Click **Google Apps** (such as ⋮⋮⋮).

The Google Apps pop-up panel opens.

3 Click the app you want to open. This example uses **Google Docs** (▤).

A The app opens in a new tab.

B You can now start to create a new document, as explained in the next section, "Create a New Document and Save It."

C Alternatively, you can open an existing document, as explained in the section after that, "Open and Close Documents."

With the app open, you can create a shortcut to run the app, as explained in the next subsection.

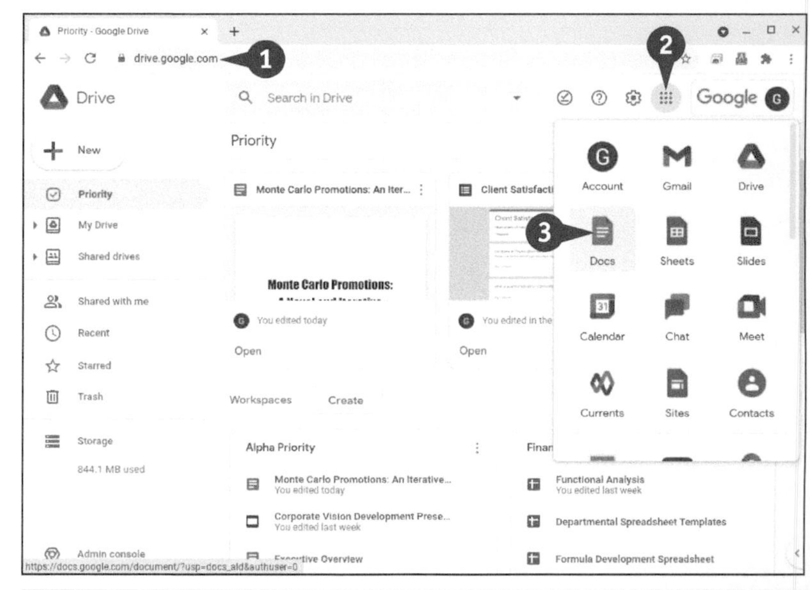

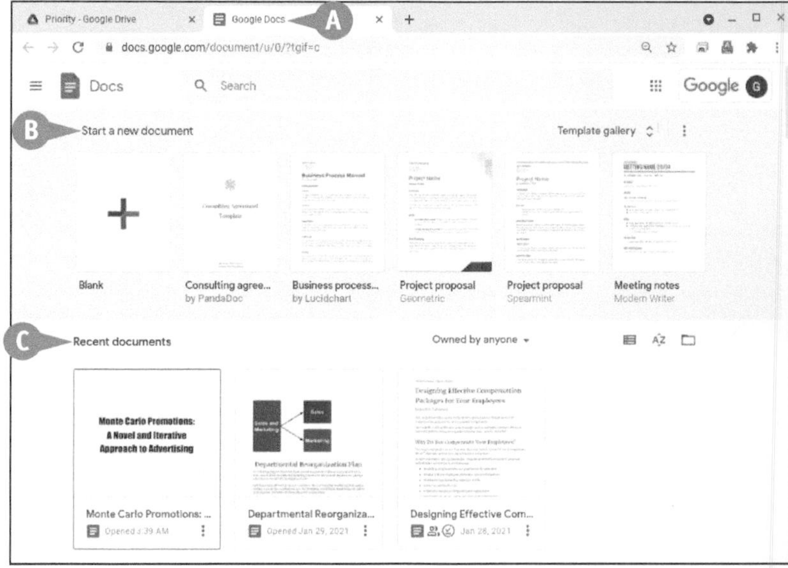

Create a Shortcut to Run the App

Note: To use this technique, you must use the Chrome browser rather than another browser.

1. In the Chrome tab showing the opening screen for the app you just launched, click **Menu** (⋮).

   The menu opens.

2. Click or highlight **More tools**.

   The More Tools submenu opens.

3. Click **Create shortcut**.

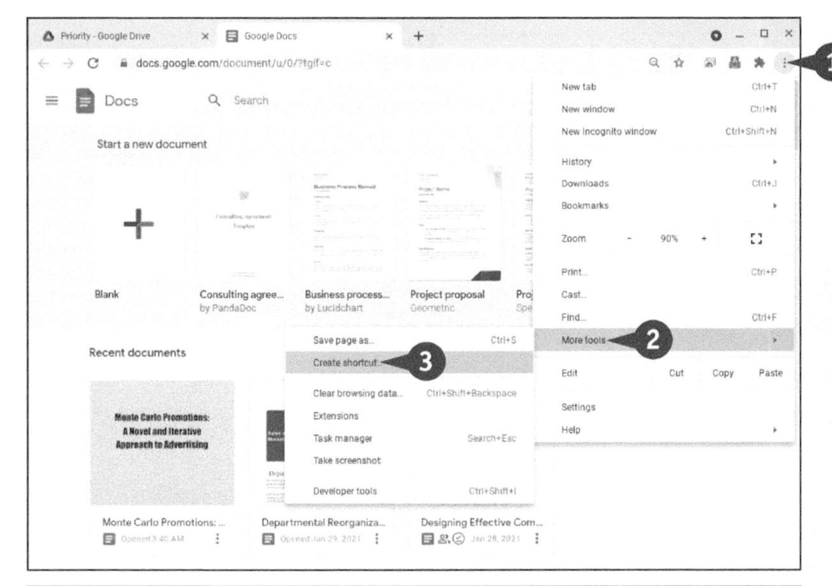

   The Create Shortcut? dialog box opens.

4. Optionally, edit the app's name.
5. Click **Open as window** (☐ changes to ☑).
6. Click **Create**.

   The Create Shortcut? dialog box closes.

   Chrome creates a Chrome web app for the app.

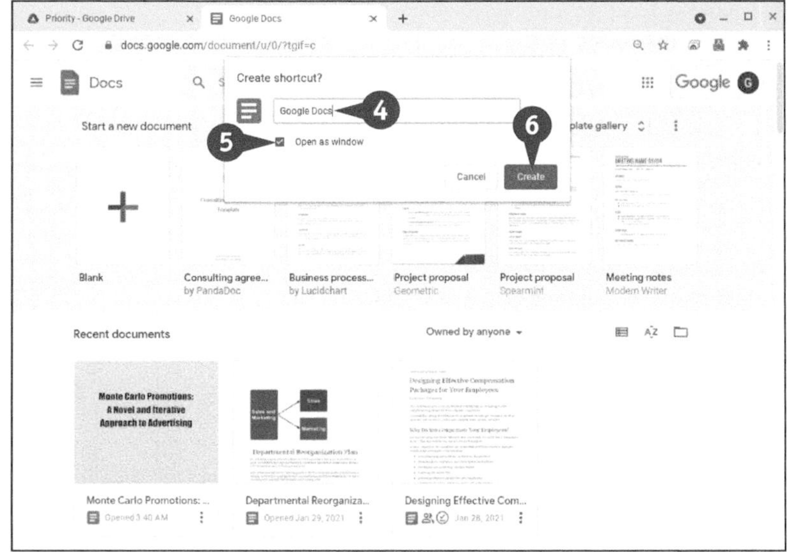

TIP

How do I run a Google Workspace app from a shortcut I created?

In Windows, click **Start** (⊞) to display the Start menu, and then click the app's icon. If you have trouble locating the app, start typing the app's name to search for it.

On macOS, click **Launchpad** (🚀), and then click the app's icon. To reduce the number of apps displayed, start typing the app's name.

On Chrome OS, press Shift+click **Launcher** (◉) to display the Launcher screen, and then click the app's icon. Here, too, you can start typing the app's name to locate it.

Create a New Document and Save It

You can create a new document in the Google Workspace apps either by giving a command from Google Drive or by opening the app and choosing the type of document. When working in an app, you can create a new blank document in another app. For example, when working in Google Slides, you can create a new blank spreadsheet document in Google Sheets.

When you start from Google Drive or from the app for the document type you want to create, you can create either a blank document or a document based on a template.

Create a New Document and Save It

Start a New Document from Google Drive

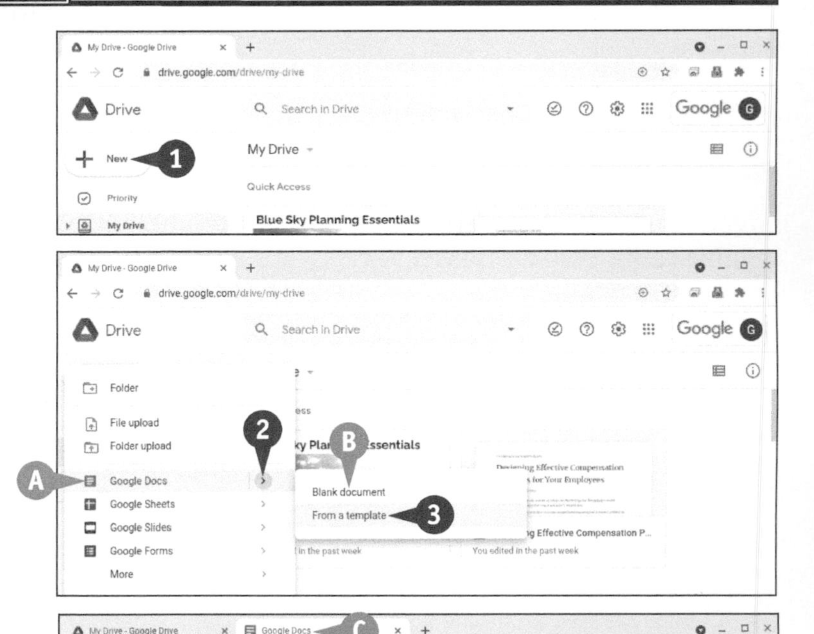

1 In Google Drive, click **New** (+).

The New menu opens.

A To create a new blank document, you can click the app's name. For example, click **Google Docs** (▤).

2 To create a document based on a template, click or highlight **More** (›).

The More submenu opens.

B You can click **Blank document** to create a new blank document. This has the same effect as clicking the app's name in step **A**.

3 Click **From a template**.

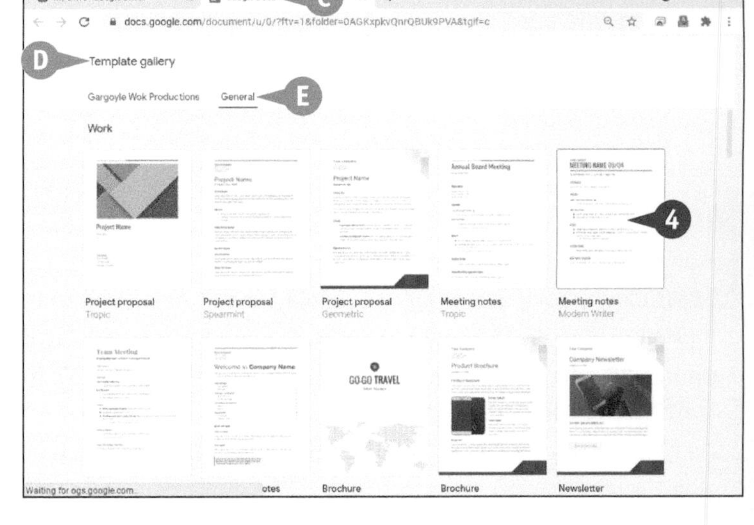

C The app you selected appears in a new Chrome tab.

D The app's Template Gallery screen appears.

E If necessary, click a different tab at the top of the Template Gallery.

Note: The General tab contains templates Google makes available through Google Workspace. The tab that bears your organization's name contains your organization's templates.

4 Click the template you want to use.

A new document based on that template opens.

F The app gives the document a default name based on the template. You can double-click the name and change it.

G The document contains sample text and placeholders that you can edit.

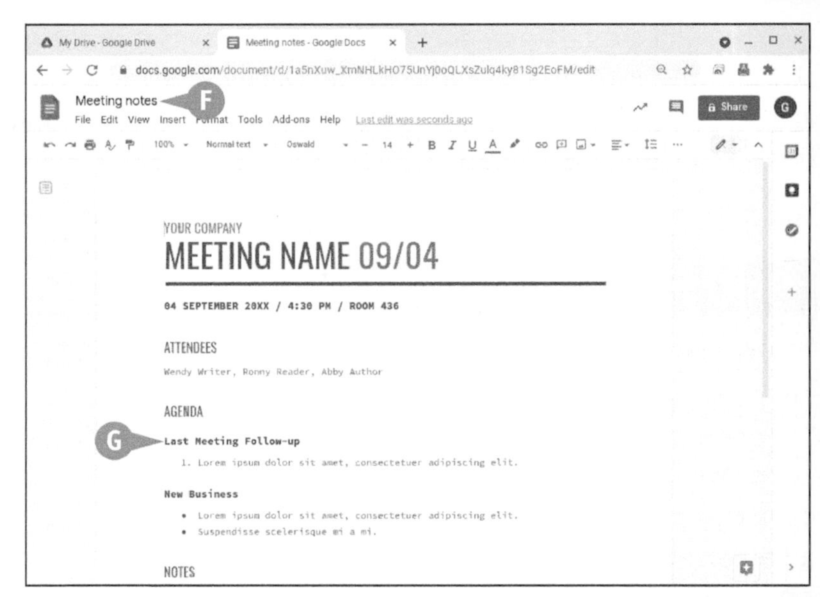

Start a New Document from Within an App

H In this example, the active app is Google Docs.

1 Click **File**.

The File menu opens.

2 Click or highlight **New**.

The New submenu opens.

I You can click **Document** (▤) to create a new blank document in Google Docs.

J You can click **From template** to display the Template Gallery in the active app — in this case, Google Docs.

K You can click **Presentation** (▭) to create a new blank presentation in Google Slides.

L You can click **Form** (▤) to create a new blank form in Google Forms.

M You can click **Drawing** (◩) to create a new drawing in Google Drawings.

3 For this example, click **Spreadsheet** (⊞).

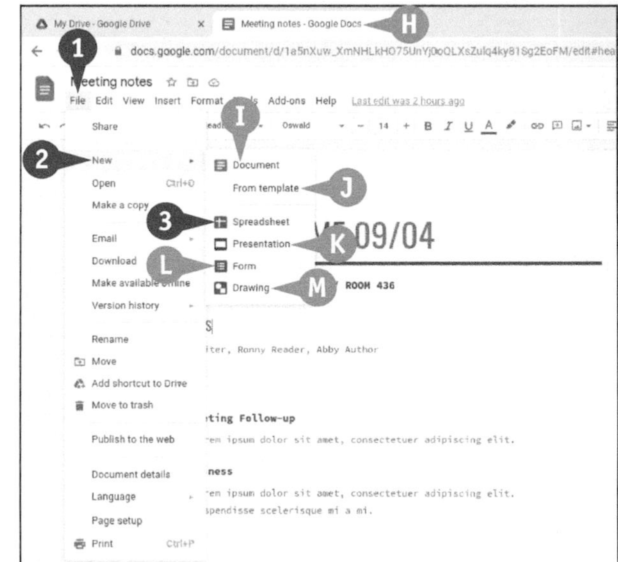

TIP

What is the purpose of the icon to the left of the File menu?

The icon to the left of the File menu and the document's name is the app's Home icon — Docs Home (▤), Sheets Home (⊞), Slides Home (▭), and so on. Click this icon to close the active document and display the app's Home screen, the screen from which you can create a new document or open an existing document.

continued ►

Create a New Document and Save It (continued)

When you create a new document, the app saves it in the root folder of your Google Drive. Once the document has been saved, you can move it to another folder by working directly from the app. For example, you may want to store the document in a folder that contains related documents rather than in the root folder.

You can also move the document to another folder later by working in Google Drive.

Create a New Document and Save It (continued)

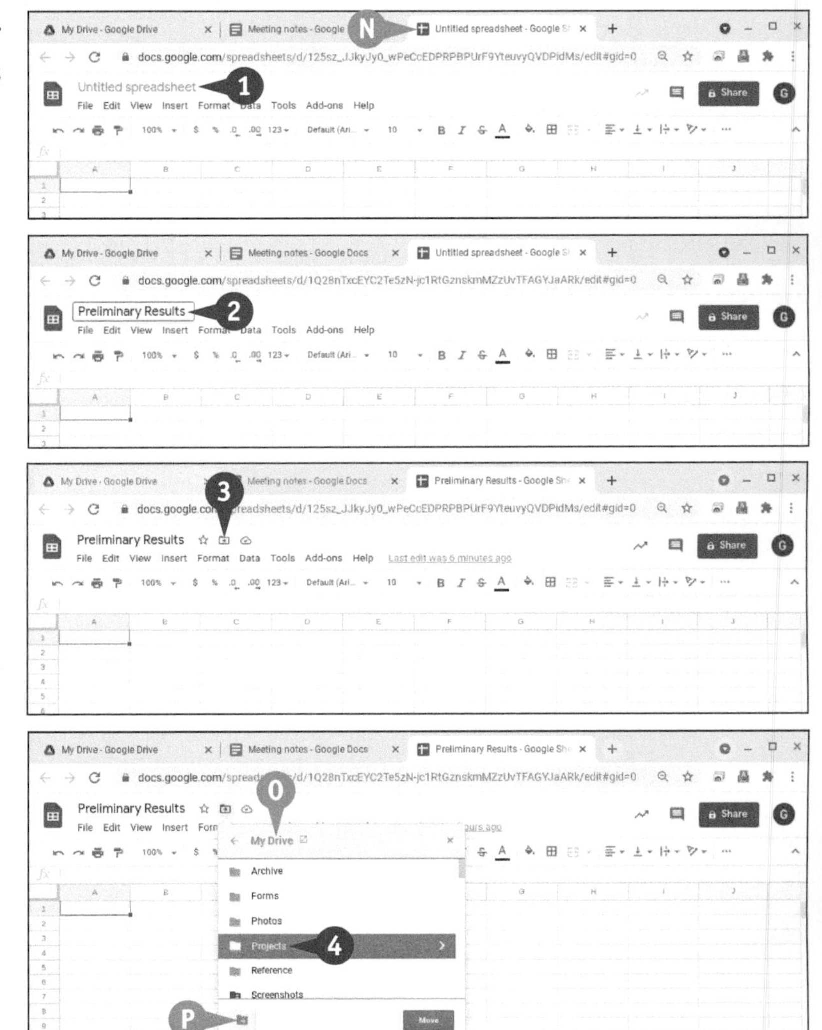

The new document opens in a new tab.

Ⓝ In this example, the new tab contains a Google Sheets spreadsheet with the default name, Untitled Spreadsheet.

Save the Document and Move It to a Folder of Your Choice

1. Double-click the document's name.

   The name becomes selected and highlighted.

2. Type the new name, and then press Enter or Return.

Note: You can also apply the new name by clicking outside the name.

The app saves the document under the new name, storing the document in your Google Drive's root folder.

Three icons — Star (☆), Move, and See Document Status — appear to the right of the name.

3. Click **Move**.

   A pop-up window opens.

Ⓞ The window's title bar shows the document's current folder — in this case, My Drive.

4. Double-click the folder you want to open.

Ⓟ You can click **New folder** to start creating a new folder in the current folder.

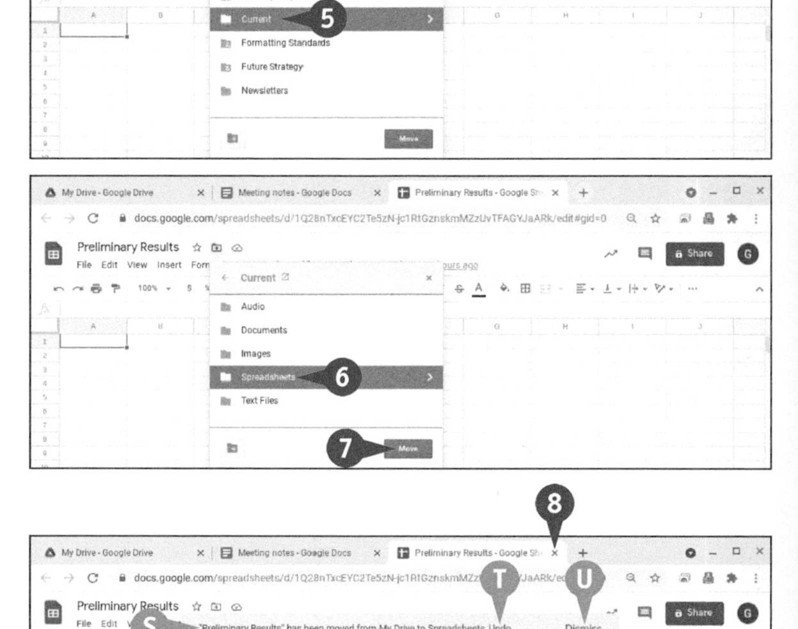

The pop-up window displays the contents of the folder you opened.

Ⓠ The window's title bar shows the current folder.

Ⓡ You can click **Back** (←) to return to the previous folder.

5 If you need to navigate further, double-click the folder you want to open. This example illustrates opening the Current folder.

6 When you reach the folder to which you want to move the document, click the folder.

7 Click **Move**.

The pop-up window closes.

The app moves the document to the folder you selected.

Ⓢ A pop-up message appears for a few seconds, confirming the Move operation.

Ⓣ You can click **Undo** to undo the Move operation.

Ⓤ You can click **Dismiss** to dismiss the pop-up message. Alternatively, wait a few seconds for it to disappear automatically.

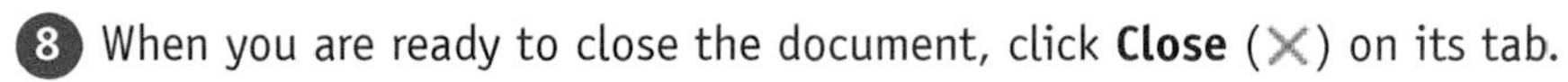

8 When you are ready to close the document, click **Close** (✕) on its tab.

The tab closes, closing the document with it.

TIP

How can I create a new document based on an existing document?

You can use the Make a Copy command from within the app. Open the existing document in its app, click **File** to open the File menu, and then click **Make a copy** to open the Copy Document dialog box. In the Name box, edit the default name — Copy of *filename* — as needed; if you will store the copy in the same folder as the original, the copy must have a different name. To store the copy in a different folder, click **Folder** (📁), use the Select a File pop-up window to navigate to the folder, and then click **Select**. Click **OK** to close the Copy Document dialog box and create the copy.

Open and Close Documents

To view or edit a document in Google Workspace, you open it in the appropriate app. For example, you open a spreadsheet file in Google Sheets or a presentation file in Google Slides. You can open a file either from the Google Drive app or from the File menu in the app.

As you make changes to the file, the app automatically saves changes, so you do not need to save them manually. When you finish working on the file, you close it by closing the browser tab that contains it.

Open and Close Documents

Open a File from Google Drive

1. In Google Drive, navigate to the location or folder that contains the file you want to open.
2. Double-click the file.

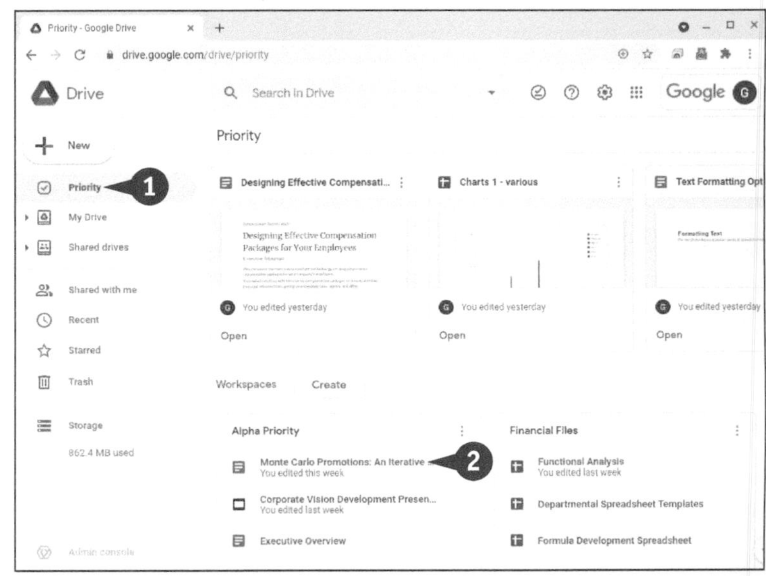

Google Drive automatically launches the right app for the file type — in this example, Google Docs.

A The app opens in a new browser tab.

B The file opens.

C The file's contents appear.

You can start working with the file. For example, you might add text.

3. When you finish working with the file, click **Close** (✕) on the browser tab.

The tab closes, closing the file with it.

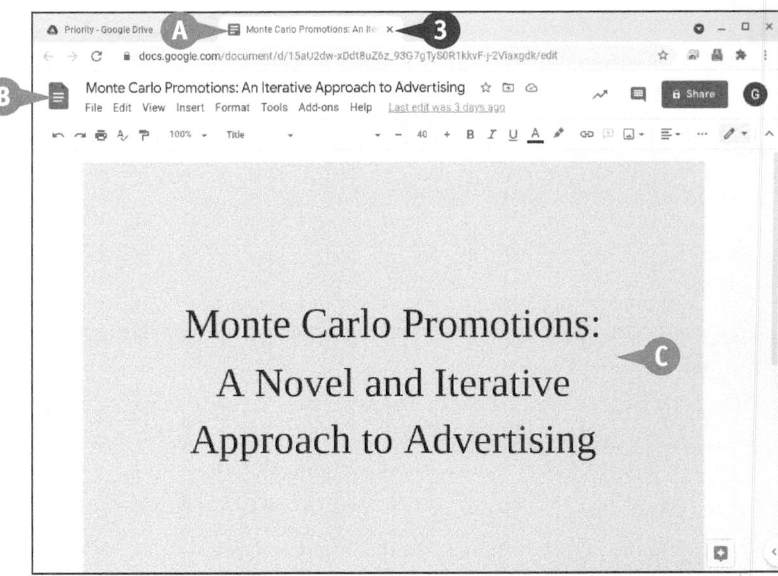

Open a File from Within an App

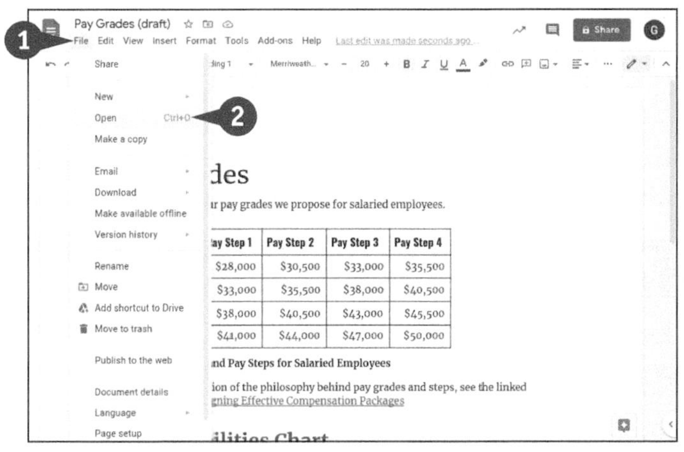

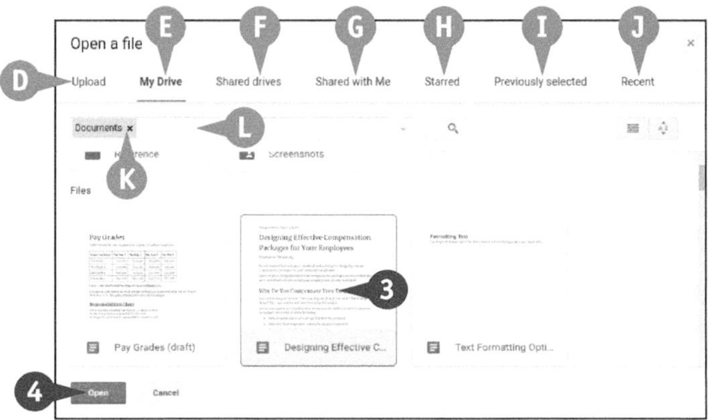

1. Click **File**.

   The File menu opens.

2. Click **Open**.

Note: From the keyboard, you can press Ctrl+O to display the Open a File dialog box. On the Mac, press ⌘+O.

The Open a File dialog box appears.

- D You can click **Upload** to upload a file from your computer.
- E You can click **My Drive** to display files on your Google Drive.
- F You can click **Shared drives** to display files on shared drives available to you.
- G You can click **Shared with Me** to display files shared with you.
- H You can click **Starred** to display files you have marked with a star.
- I You can click **Previously selected** to display files you have selected previously.
- J You can click **Recent** to display files you have used recently.
- K The app applies a search filter to find its own file type, such as Documents for Google Docs. You can click **Remove** (✕) to remove the filter.
- L You can click in the box, type a search term, and then click **Search** (🔍) to locate matches.

3. Click the file you want to open.
4. Click **Open**.

   The app opens the file.

TIP

In what other way can I open a document in a Google Workspace app?
When you are working in the app and you want to close the file you are currently using, click the app's Home button — **Docs Home** (▤), **Sheets Home** (▦), or **Slides Home** (▭) — to close the file and display the Home screen. Here, you can open a file from the Recent Documents list, or you can use the Search box to search for any file.

Zoom the View or Use Full-Screen Mode

To make the document you are working on easy to see, you can zoom in or out. Google Docs, Google Sheets, and Google Slides all offer fixed zoom percentages, such as 50%, 100%, and 200%, but you can also zoom to other percentages by using keyboard shortcuts.

To see as much as possible of a document within the app, you can use the Full Screen command, which hides the app's menu bar and toolbars to reclaim the space they normally occupy.

Zoom the View or Use Full-Screen Mode

Zoom the View

1. In the app, click **Zoom** (▾).

   The Zoom pop-up menu opens.

2. Click the zoom percentage you want. In this example, you would click **Fit** in Google Docs to make the document's width fit to the window.

Note: In Google Slides, click **Zoom** (🔍 ▾) on the toolbar to zoom.

Note: In Google Sheets, the Zoom command does not have a Fit option.

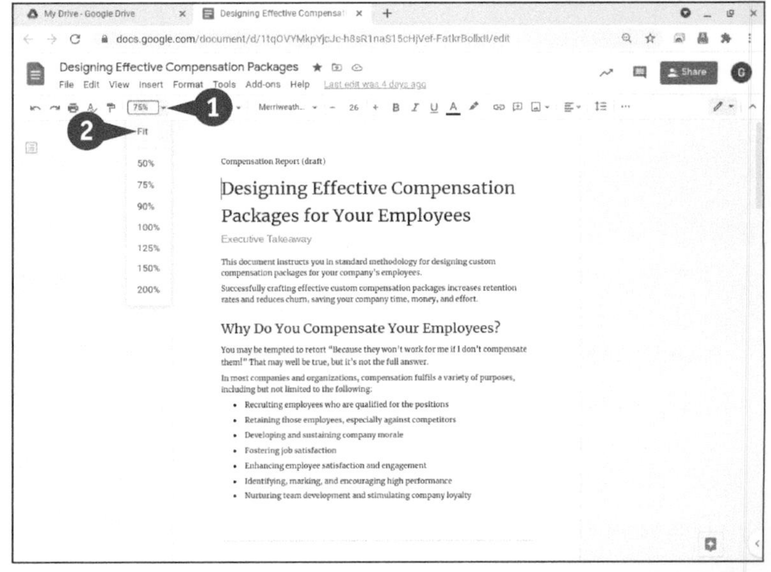

The app zooms the document to the degree you chose.

Note: From the keyboard, press Ctrl + + to zoom in. Press Ctrl + − to zoom out.

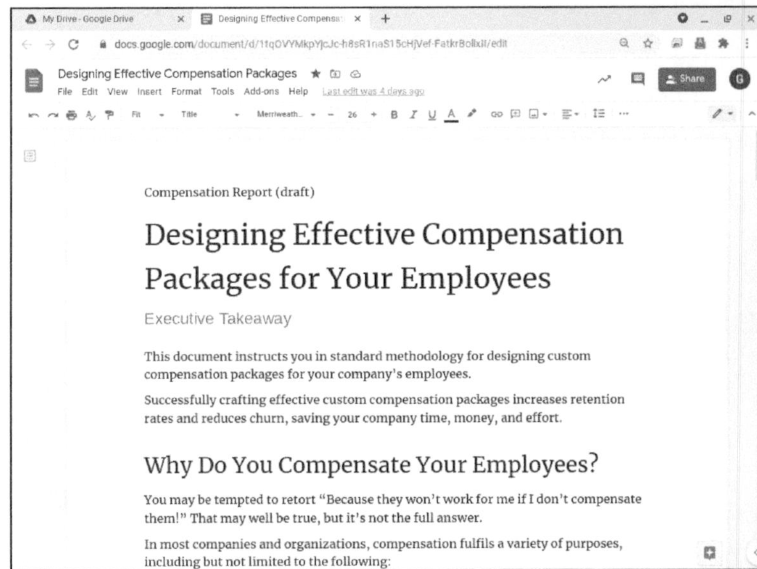

Using Full Screen Within the App

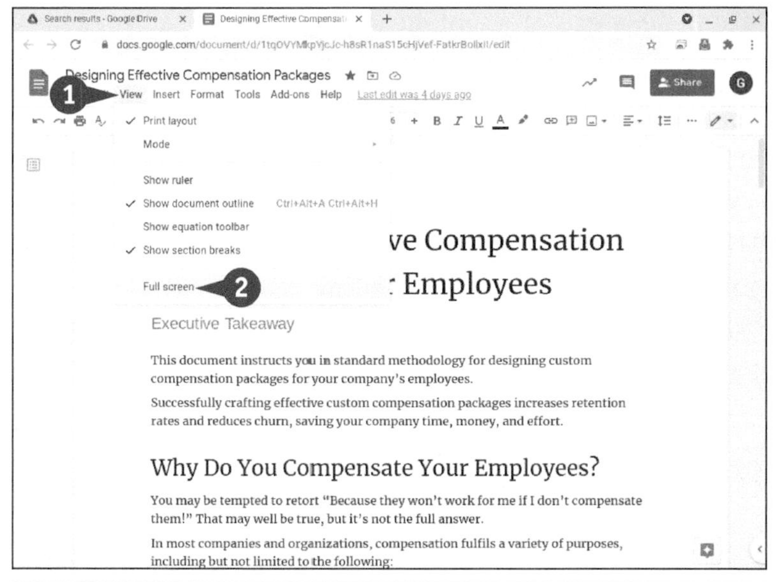

1 Click **View**.

The View menu opens.

2 Click **Full screen**.

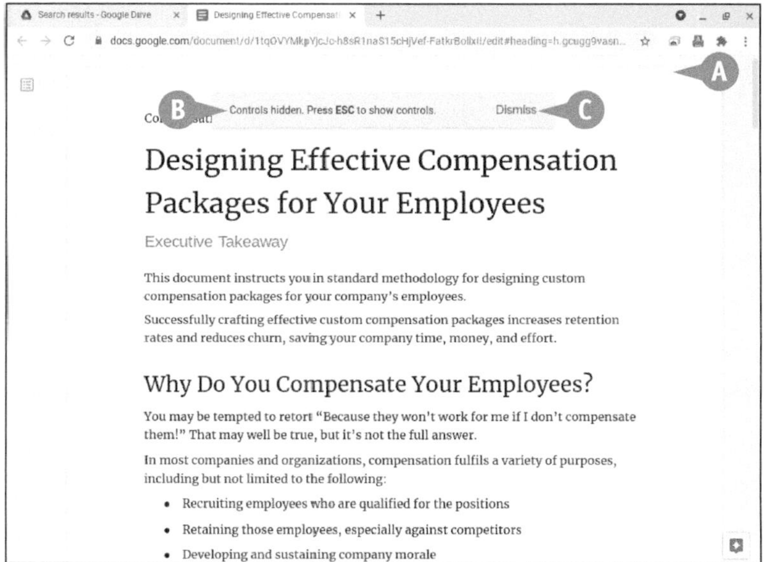

A The app hides the menu bar and toolbar.

B The *Controls hidden. Press ESC to show controls* message appears.

C Click **Dismiss** to dismiss the message.

When you want to display the menu bar and toolbar again, press Esc.

TIP

How can I display as much as possible of a document on the screen?

Try putting your browser into Full Screen Mode. In Chrome, click **Menu** (⋮) in the upper-right corner, and then click **Full screen** (⛶). In other browsers, such as Microsoft Edge or Firefox, look for a Full Screen button or a Full Screen command on the app's main menu.

On Windows, try pressing F11 to switch to Full Screen. On the Mac, try pressing ⌘+Ctrl+F. These commands work for most but not all apps.

Using Cut, Copy, and Paste

To include existing content in a Google Apps document, you can cut or copy that content and then paste it in. Cutting removes the content from the source document; copying does not.

You can paste many different kinds of material, from text and tables to images and videos. When you paste text, you can paste it either with or without its formatting. Some Google Apps have app-specific paste features. For example, Google Sheets has a Paste Special submenu that enables you to paste only part of the copied or cut data, such as only values or only conditional formatting.

Using Cut, Copy, and Paste

1. Select the material in the source document.
2. Right-click in the selection.

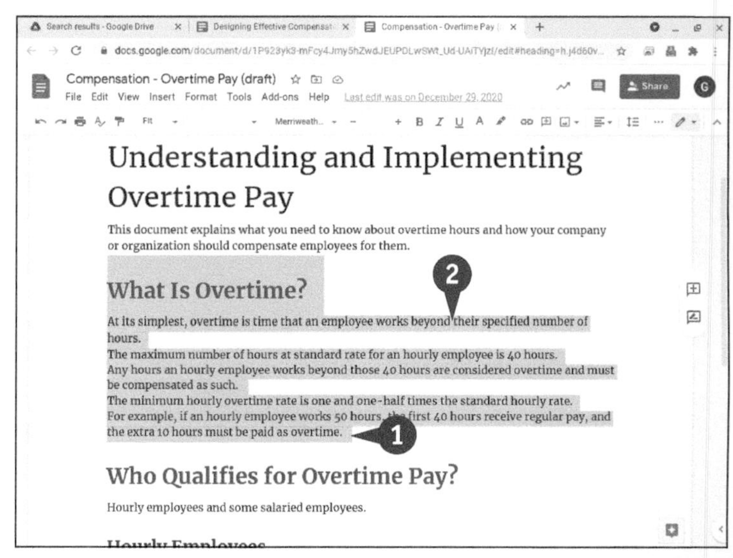

The contextual menu opens.

3. Click **Cut** (✂) or **Copy** (⧉), as appropriate. This example uses **Cut** (✂).

The app cuts or copies the material from the document and places it on the Clipboard, a dedicated temporary storage area maintained by the operating system.

If you gave the Cut command, the app removes the material from the document.

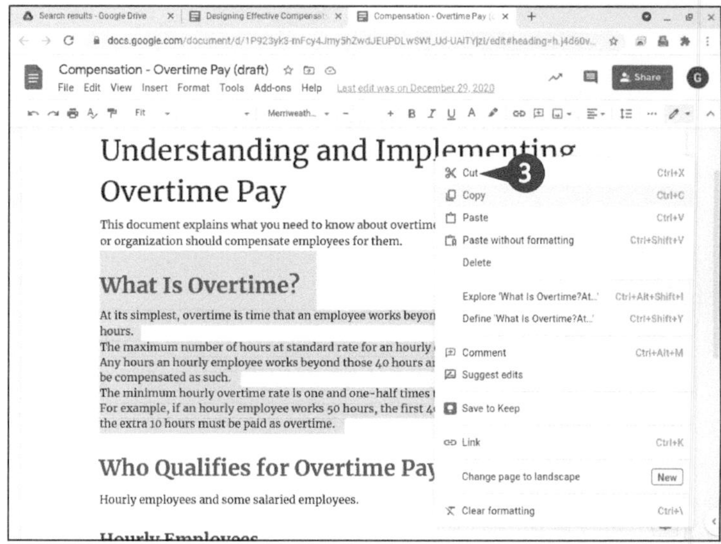

4 If you will paste the material into another document, activate that document. For example, click the document's tab.

5 In the destination document, right-click where you want to paste the material.

The contextual menu opens.

6 Click **Paste** (📋).

A If you want to retain only the text of the material you are pasting, click **Paste without formatting** (📋).

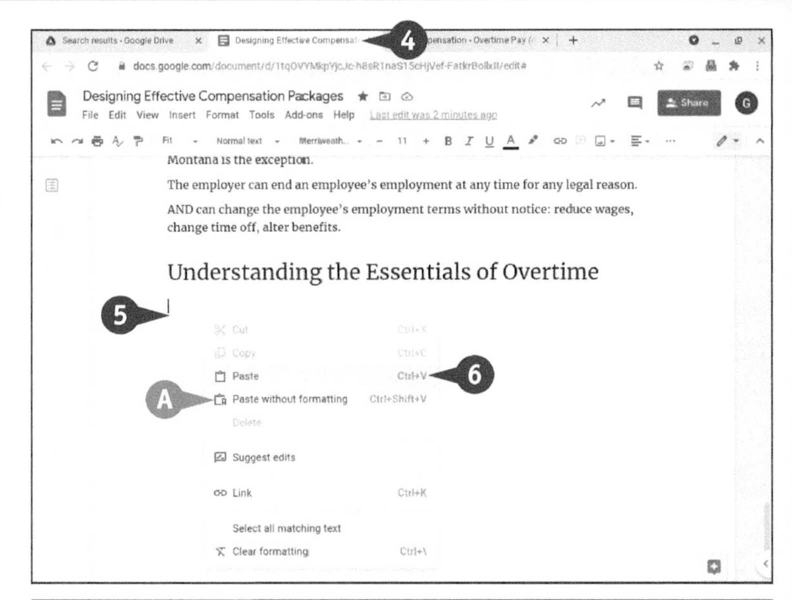

B The material appears in the document.

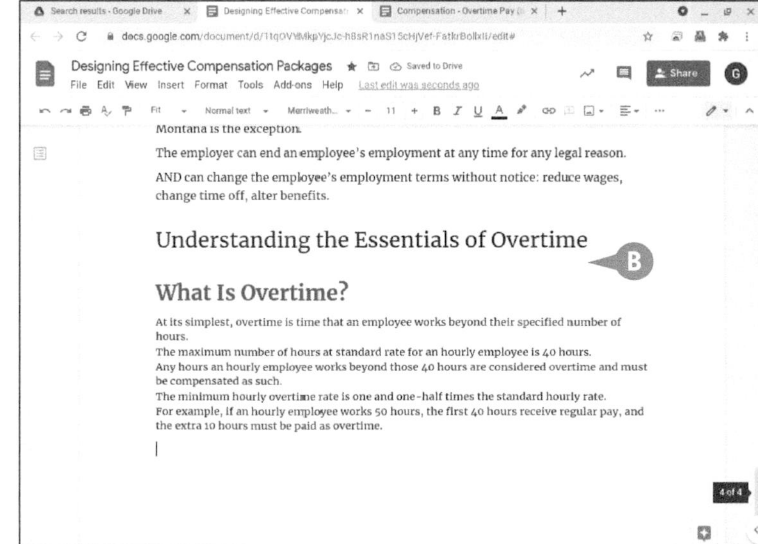

TIP

Can I use keyboard shortcuts for Cut, Copy, and Paste?

Yes. Press Ctrl+X to give the Cut command. Press Ctrl+C to give the Copy command. Press Ctrl+V to give the Paste command.

On the Mac, the modifier key is ⌘ rather than Ctrl, so the keyboard shortcuts are ⌘+X for Cut, ⌘+C for Copy, and ⌘+V for Paste.

To paste without formatting, press Ctrl+Shift+V; on the Mac, press ⌘+Shift+V.

Undo and Redo Actions

The Google Workspace apps provide an Undo feature and a Redo feature. Undo enables you to undo actions you have taken recently, starting with the latest action and proceeding backward from there. Undo can save you from disaster when you have taken an ill-advised or unintended action, but it is also a great time-saver for removing minor mistakes.

After using Undo to undo one or more actions, you can use Redo to reinstate the changes you have undone, starting with the last action undone and proceeding from there. Use Redo when you have undone more actions than necessary.

Undo and Redo Actions

Create Some Sample Text with Formatting

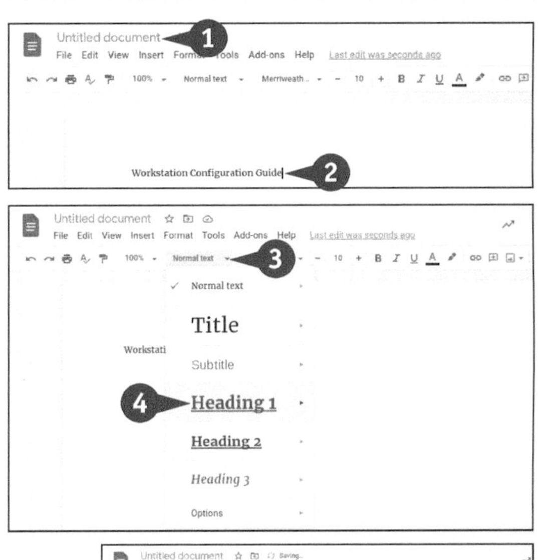

1. Create a new blank document in Google Docs. For example, in Google Drive click **New** (+) and then click **Google Docs** (▤) on the New pop-up menu.
2. Type the text for a first-level heading paragraph.
3. Click **Styles** (▾).

   The Styles pop-up menu opens.
4. Click **Heading 1**.

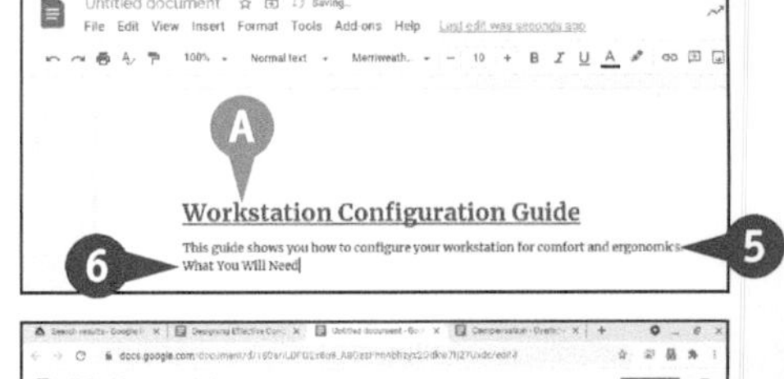

Ⓐ The paragraph takes on the Heading 1 style formatting.

5. Type the text for a body paragraph.
6. Type the text for another heading.
7. With the cursor still at the end of the second heading paragraph, click **Styles** (▾).

   The Styles pop-up menu opens again.
8. Click **Heading 2**.

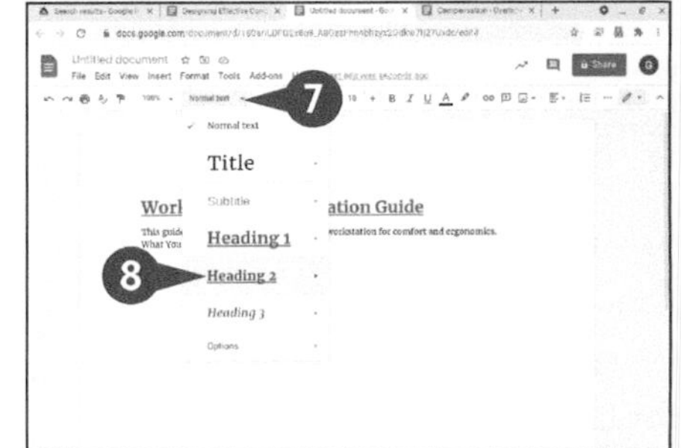

Ⓑ The second heading paragraph takes on the Heading 2 style formatting.

Undo and Redo Actions

1 Click **Undo** (↶).

Ⓒ Google Docs undoes the last action, which was applying the Heading 2 formatting to the second heading paragraph.

2 Click **Undo** (↶) again.

Google Docs undoes the second-to-last action, which was typing the second heading.

Note: Depending on how you typed the heading, Google Docs may have recorded it as multiple actions rather than a single action. If so, click **Undo** (↶) until the heading paragraph disappears.

3 Click **Undo** (↶) a third time.

Google Docs undoes the third-to-last action, which was typing the body paragraph.

4 Click **Redo** (↷).

Ⓓ Google Docs redoes the last undone action: It types the body paragraph again.

You can click **Redo** (↷) again if you need to redo other actions you have undone.

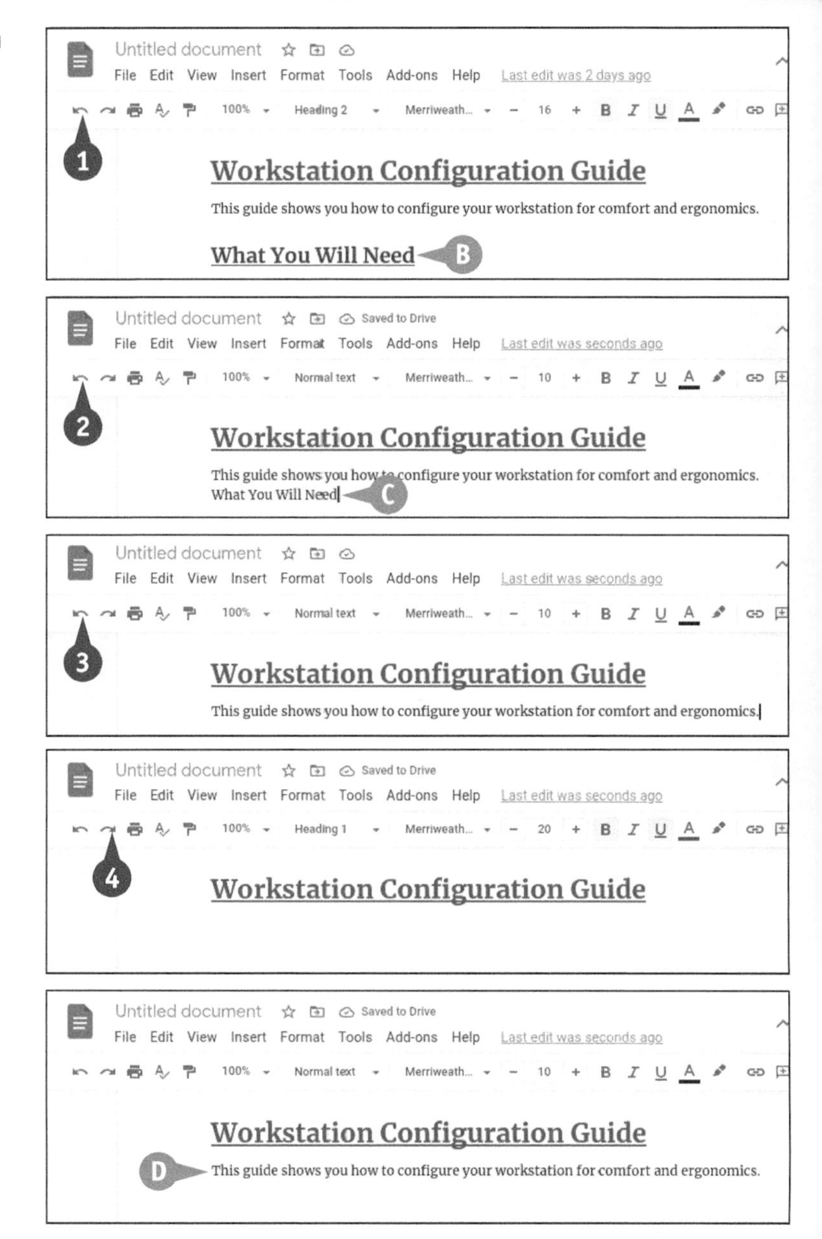

TIP

In what other ways can I give the Undo command and Redo command?

From the keyboard, press Ctrl+Z to issue the Undo command; press Ctrl+Y to issue the Redo command. On the Mac, press ⌘+Z for Undo and ⌘+Y for Redo.

You can also click **Edit** to open the Edit menu, and then click **Undo** (↶) or **Redo** (↷). There is no advantage to using the menu, unlike in some other apps, in which the commands include a brief description of the action — for example, "Undo style formatting" or "Redo typing."

Apply Basic Formatting to Text

Google Docs, Google Sheets, and Google Slides enable you to apply basic formatting from the toolbar to control how text appears. You can quickly change the font and font size; apply or remove boldface, italics, or underline; and change the text color. In Google Docs and Google Slides, you can change the highlight color; in Google Sheets, you can change the fill color for cells.

After using these commands to apply the formatting you want to some text, you can use the Paint Format tool to quickly apply the formatting to other text.

Apply Basic Formatting to Text

Apply Basic Formatting

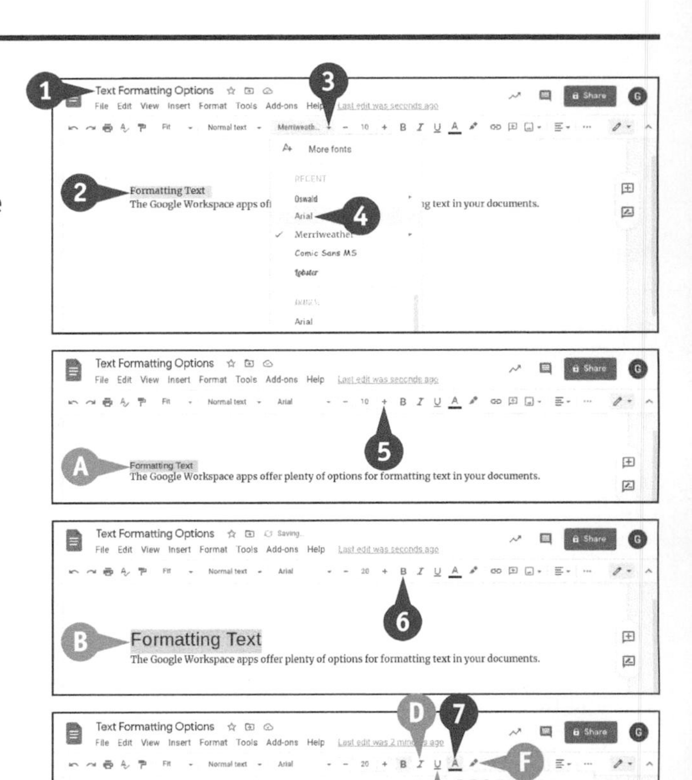

1. Open a document in Google Docs, Google Sheets, or Google Slides.

   This example uses an existing document in Google Docs.

2. Select the text you want to format.
3. Click **Font** (▾).

   The Font pop-up menu opens.

4. Click the font you want to apply.

Note: An arrow (▶) indicates that the font has a submenu of different font styles or weights, such as Extra Light or Semi Bold.

A. The text takes on the font formatting.

5. Click **Increase font size** (+) several times.

B. The text's font size increases.

6. Click **Bold** (**B**).

C. The text becomes boldface.

D. You can click **Italic** (*I*) to apply italics.

E. You can click **Underline** (U) to apply underline.

F. You can click **Highlight color** (🖉) to apply a highlight color.

7. To apply color, click **Text color** (A).

   The Text Color pop-up panel opens.

8. Click the color you want to apply.

   The text's color changes.

Copy Formatting with the Paint Format Feature

Note: This example uses an existing spreadsheet document in Google Sheets.

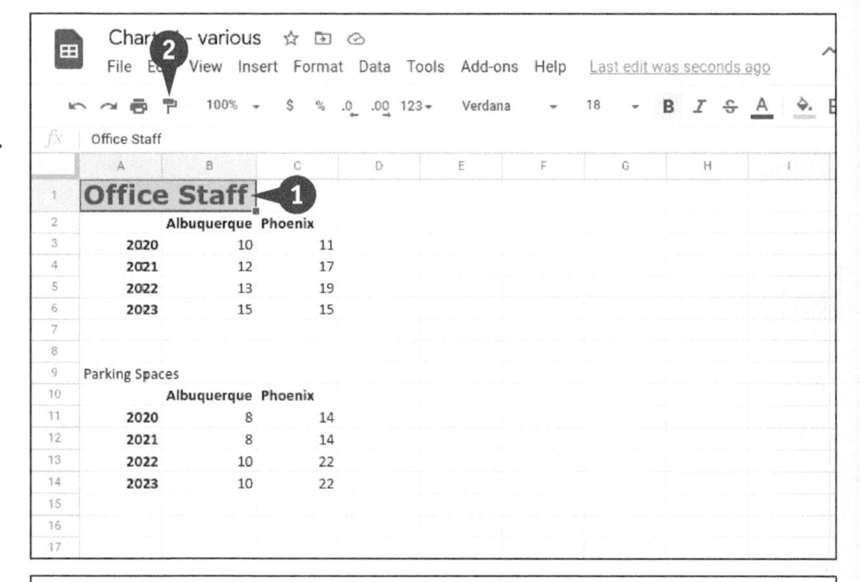

1. After applying formatting that you want to copy elsewhere, select the formatted text. For example, in Google Sheets, click the cell that contains the text.

2. Click **Paint format** (🖌).

   The app copies the formatting.

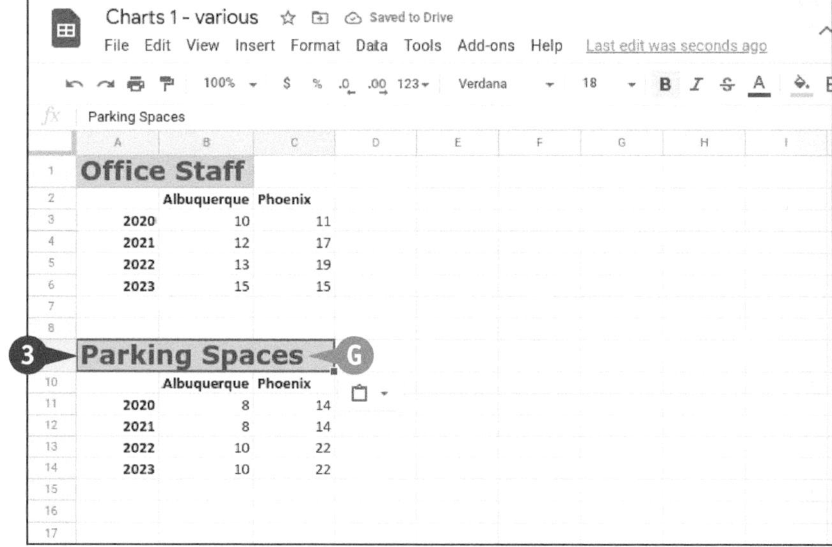

3. Select the text to which you want to apply the formatting. For example, in Google Sheets, click the cell that contains the text.

G The text takes on the pasted formatting.

TIP

Are there other ways of applying formatting quickly?

In Google Docs, you can use styles to apply formatting quickly. A *style* is a collection of formatting settings, including font formatting, indentation, and line spacing. See the section "Format a Document with Styles" in Chapter 5 for information on working with styles in Google Docs.

Using Find and Replace

Google Docs, Google Sheets, and Google Slides all provide tools for finding text in your documents and, optionally, replacing it with other text. When you need to find and review instances of particular text, you can use the Find in Document pop-up panel, which takes a minimal amount of space and so lets you see more of your document. When you need to replace the text or use other options, such as matching the capitalization you specify, you can open the Find and Replace dialog box, which is larger and obscures more of the document.

Using Find and Replace

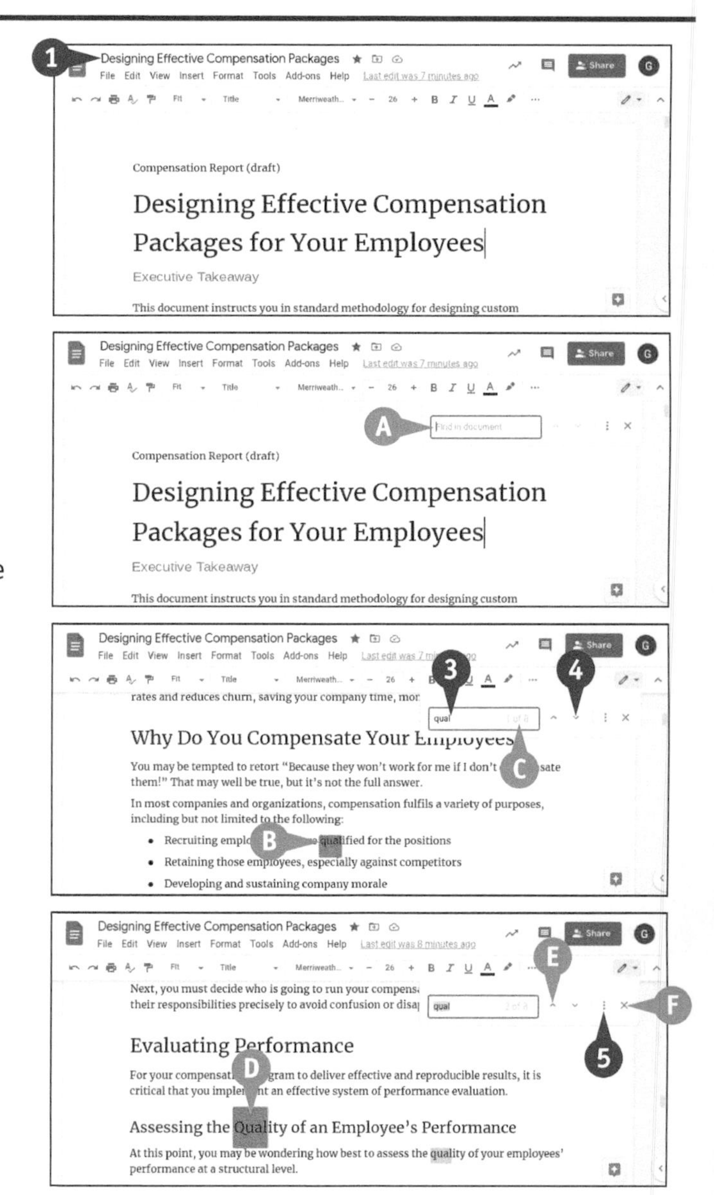

1. Open the document in which you want to use Find and Replace. This example uses a Google Docs document.
2. Press Ctrl + F.

Note: On the Mac, press ⌘ + F.

- A The Find in Document pop-up panel opens, with the cursor positioned inside its text field.

3. Start typing your search term.

- B If there are any matches, the app highlights them and scrolls as needed to display the first match.
- C The readout on the right side of the text field shows the number of the current match and the number of matches — for example, *1 of 8*.

4. Click **Next** (⌄).

- D The app displays the next instance, scrolling if necessary.
- E You can click **Previous** (^) to display the previous match.
- F You can click **Close** (✕) to close the Find in Document panel.

5. To replace, or to use other options, click **More options** (⋮).

The Find and Replace dialog box opens.

Note: At first, any search term from the Find in Document panel appears in the Find field of the Find and Replace dialog box.

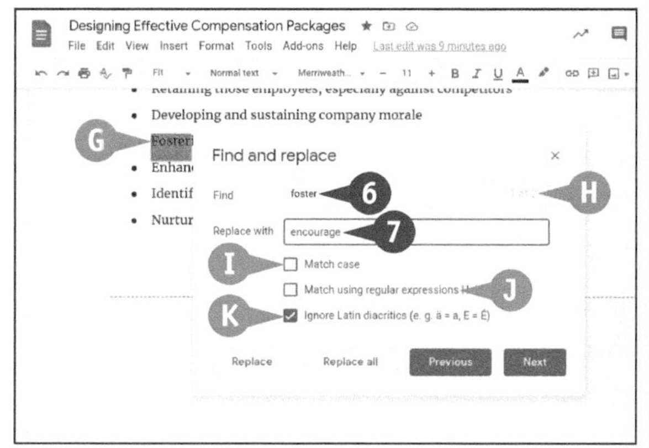

6 Click **Find** and type your search term.

G The app displays the next instance of the search term, scrolling if necessary.

H The readout shows the number of the current match and the number of matches.

7 Click **Replace with** and type the replacement term.

I You can select **Match case** (☑) if you want to find only matches that use the same capitalization.

J You can select **Match using regular expressions** (☑) to use regular expressions. See the next section, "Using Regular Expressions for Advanced Searching."

K You can select **Ignore Latin diacritics** (☑) if you want to ignore accented letters.

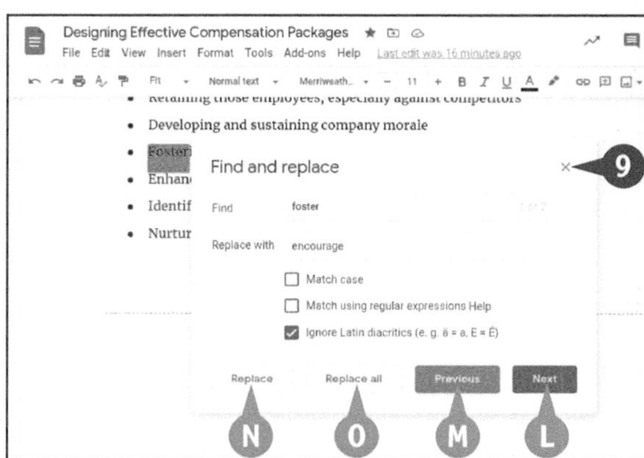

8 You can now take the following actions:

L Click **Next** to display the next instance of the term, leaving this instance unchanged.

M Click **Previous** to display the previous instance of the term, leaving this instance unchanged.

N Click **Replace** to replace this instance of the term and display the next instance.

O Click **Replace all** to replace all instances of the term.

9 When you finish working in the Find and Replace dialog box, click **Close** (✕).

The Find and Replace dialog box closes.

TIPS

How can I open the Find and Replace dialog box directly?
Click **Edit** to display the Edit menu, and then click **Find and Replace** to open the Find and Replace dialog box. Alternatively, press Ctrl+H; on the Mac, press ⌘+H.

What other Find and Replace options does Google Sheets provide?
You can limit the scope of the search by clicking **Search** (▾) and then clicking **This sheet**, **All sheets**, or **Specific range**; for Specific Range, specify the range on the active spreadsheet. You can select **Match entire cell contents** (☑) to restrict matches to entire cell contents. You can select **Also search within formulas** (☑) to search within formulas as well as results.

Using Regular Expressions for Advanced Searching

The Find and Replace dialog box makes straightforward searches easy, but in Google Docs and Google Sheets, this dialog box also provides more powerful searching using regular expressions, sequences of characters that express standard search patterns. For example, you can use a regular expression to search for one specified character or another specified character, or to search for two or more instances of a specified character.

This section shows you how to use regular expressions in Google Docs and Google Sheets and introduces you to some of the most useful regular expressions.

Enable the Use of Regular Expressions in Searches

To use regular expressions in your searches, open the Find and Replace dialog box by clicking **Edit** and then clicking **Find and Replace** on the Edit menu.

In Google Sheets, select **Search using regular expressions** (A, ☑) to enable the use of regular expressions. When you do this, Google Sheets automatically selects Match Case (B, ☑) as well.

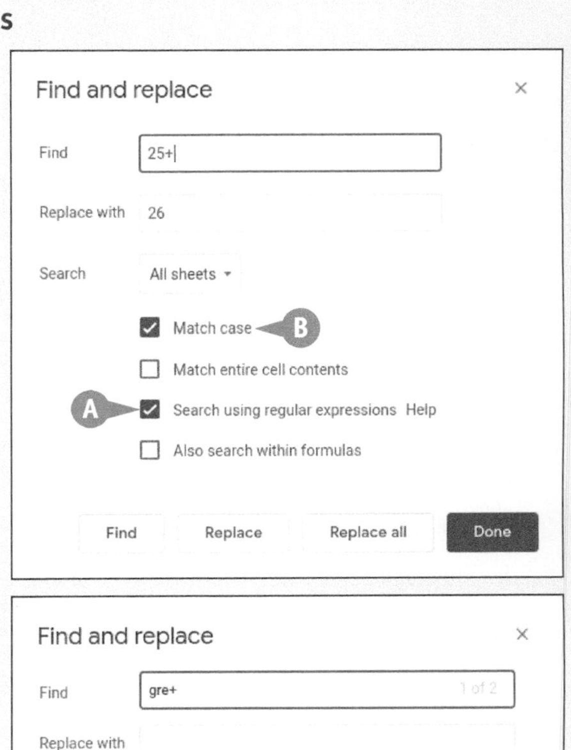

In Google Docs, select **Match using regular expressions** (☑, C). Google Docs does not automatically select Match Case, and you need not select it manually.

Meet the Most Useful Regular Expressions

The following table explains nine of the most widely useful regular expressions, giving examples of their usage and indicating matches and misses.

Regular Expression	Indicates	Example	Matches	Does Not Match
. (a period)	Any character	the.	they, them	the
*	The preceding character repeated 0 or more times	10*	10, 100, 1000, 11, 12	20, 21
+	The preceding character repeated 1 or more times	10+	10, 100, 1000	11, 12
?	The preceding character being optional	boa?rder	border, boarder	brder, barder
{*number1*,*number2*}	The preceding character repeated between *number1* and *number2* times	25(0{1,4})	250, 2500, 25000, 250000	25, 2500000, 25000000
[*character_list*]	One instance of any of the characters	b[aiu]t	bat, bit, but	bet, bot
[*character_range*]	One instance of any character in the range	h[a-n]t	hat, hit	hot, hut
[^*character_range*]	One instance of any character not in the range	s[^a-f]t	sit, sot	sat, set
\s	Any white-space character, such as a space or a tab	estimate\s:	estimate :, estimate :	estimate:, estimated:

Check Spelling in a Document

Google Docs, Google Sheets, and Google Slides share a powerful spell checker that helps you eliminate spelling errors in your documents. You can change either a single instance of an error or all the instances in the document, ignore either a single instance of an error or all the instances, and add words to your personal dictionary to prevent the spell checker from querying them in the future.

Google Docs and Google Slides also offer on-the-fly spell checking, which enables you to correct mistakes instantly via the contextual menu. Google Docs provides a pop-up panel for even quicker corrections.

Check Spelling in a Document

Check Spelling Using the Pop-Up Panel in Google Docs

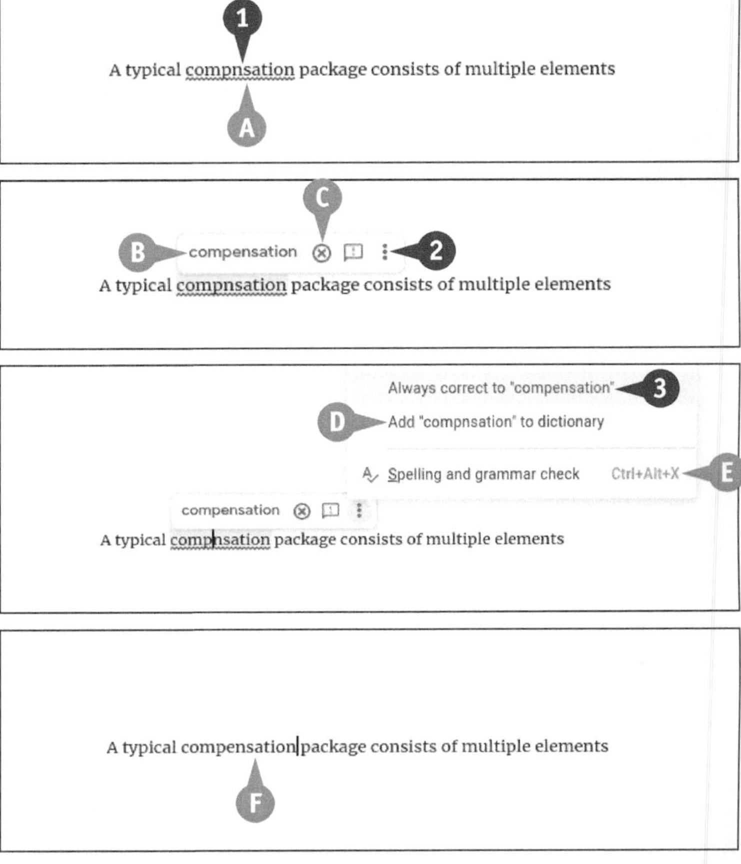

A When the spell checker identifies an apparent error, it displays a wavy red line beneath it.

1 Click the underlined word.

The pop-up panel opens.

B You can click the suggestion to replace the queried word with the suggested word.

C You can click **Ignore** (⊗) to make the spell checker ignore this instance of the apparent error.

2 For more options, and to follow this example, click **Menu** (⋮).

The pop-up menu opens.

D You can click **Add "*word*" to dictionary** to add this word to your personal dictionary, preventing the spell checker from querying it in the future.

E You can click **Spelling and grammar check** (A✓) to launch a full spelling and grammar check of the document.

3 Click **Always correct to "*suggestion*"** to create a text substitution that will automatically correct this error when you type it.

Note: Creating the substitution is usually the best choice if the apparent error is indeed an error.

F The corrected word appears in the document.

Check Spelling Using the Contextual Menu in Google Docs and Google Slides

- **G** When the spell checker identifies an apparent error, it displays a wavy red line beneath it.

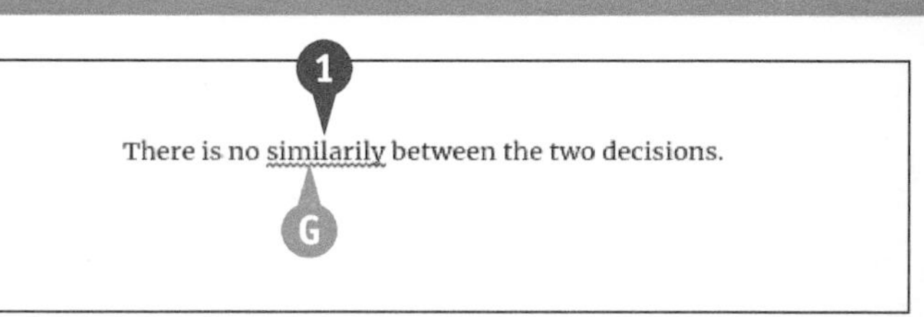

1. Right-click the underlined word.

   The contextual menu opens.

- **H** You can click the suggestion to replace the queried word with the suggested word.
- **I** You can provide feedback on the suggestion by clicking **Feedback on suggestion**, and then clicking **Suggestion is wrong**, **Suggestion is unclear**, or **Provide more details** on the Feedback on Suggestion submenu.

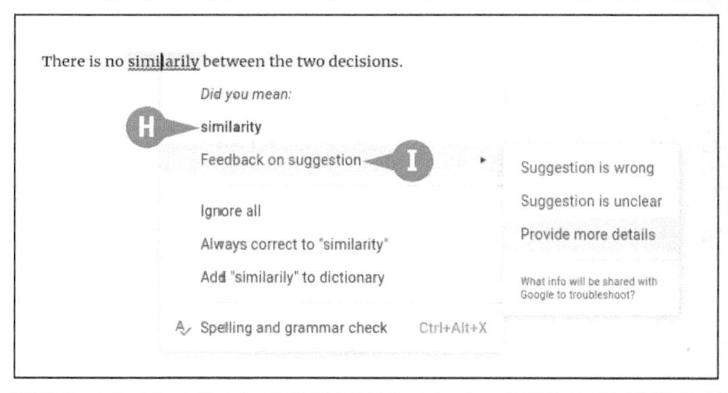

- **J** You can click **Ignore all** to make the spell checker ignore all instances of the apparent error in this document.
- **K** You can click **Add "*word*" to dictionary** to add this word to your personal dictionary, preventing the spell checker from querying it in the future.
- **L** You can click **Spelling and grammar check** (A✓) to launch a full spelling and grammar check of the document.

2. Click **Always correct to "*suggestion*"** to create a text substitution that will automatically correct this error when you type it.

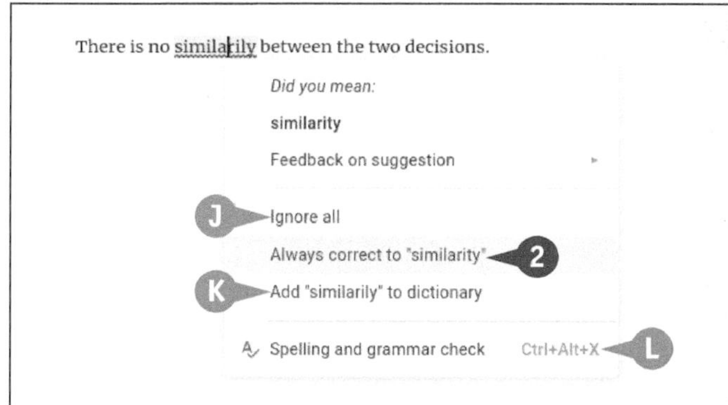

- **M** The corrected word appears in the document.

There is no similarity between the two decisions.

TIPS

Is there another way to launch the spell checker?

Yes. Only in Google Docs, you can click **Spelling & grammar check** (A✓) on the toolbar to launch the spell checker. You can also press Ctrl + Alt + X.

How do I use my personal dictionary on another computer or device?

Simply sign in to your Google Account on the other computer or device. The Google Workspace apps store your personal dictionary in your Google Account, making it available on any device to which you sign in.

continued ▶

Where possible, the spell checker attempts to analyze the context in which an apparent spelling error occurs, with the aim of making better suggestions for correcting the error. For example, if you write "HR approves all personel decisions," the spell checker suggests replacing "personel" with "personnel" — the correct word. But if you write "This is my personel decision," the spell checker suggests "personal" as the replacement word — again, correctly, unless perhaps you work in HR.

Check Spelling in a Document (continued)

Check Spelling Using the Spelling Dialog Box

1. Click **Tools**.

   The Tools menu opens.

2. Click or highlight **Spelling**.

   The Spelling submenu opens.

3. Click **Spell check**.

   The Spelling dialog box opens and displays suggestions for fixing the first error it identifies.

   N The spell checker highlights the error. For example, in Google Sheets, the spell checker selects the cell.

   O You can click **Change** to change this instance of the error.

   P You can click **Add to Dictionary** to add this word to your personal dictionary.

4. Click the Change pop-up menu button (▾), and then click **Change all** to change all instances of the error in this document.

Note: In Google Sheets, the Change All command and Ignore All command apply to the active sheet rather than the entire spreadsheet document.

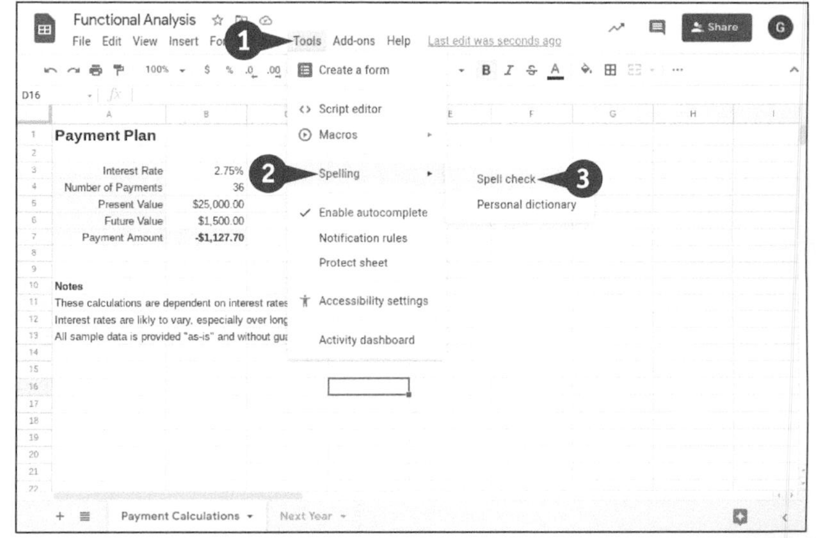

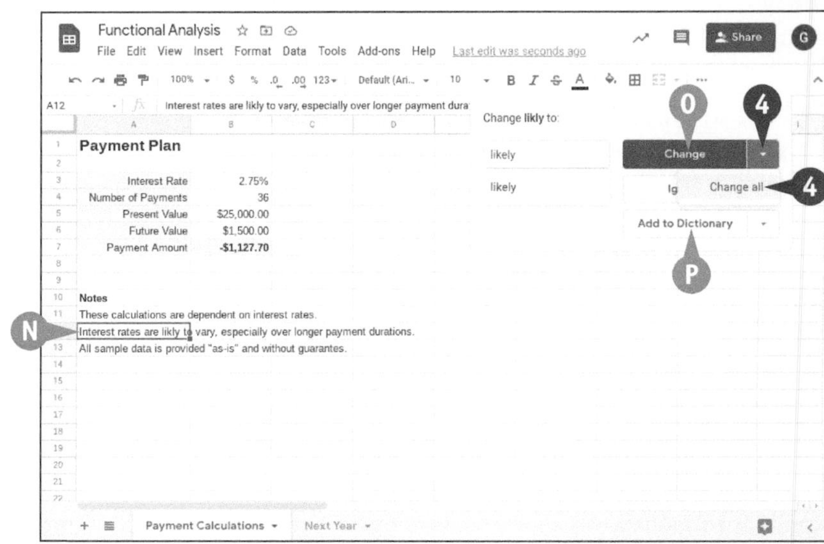

The spell checker makes the change, and then displays the next error, if there is one.

Ⓠ The spell checker highlights the error so that you can see it in context.

Ⓡ You can click **Ignore** to ignore this instance of the error.

Ⓢ You can click the Ignore pop-up menu button (▾), and then click **Ignore all** to ignore all instances of the error in this document.

5 To follow this example, click **Change**.

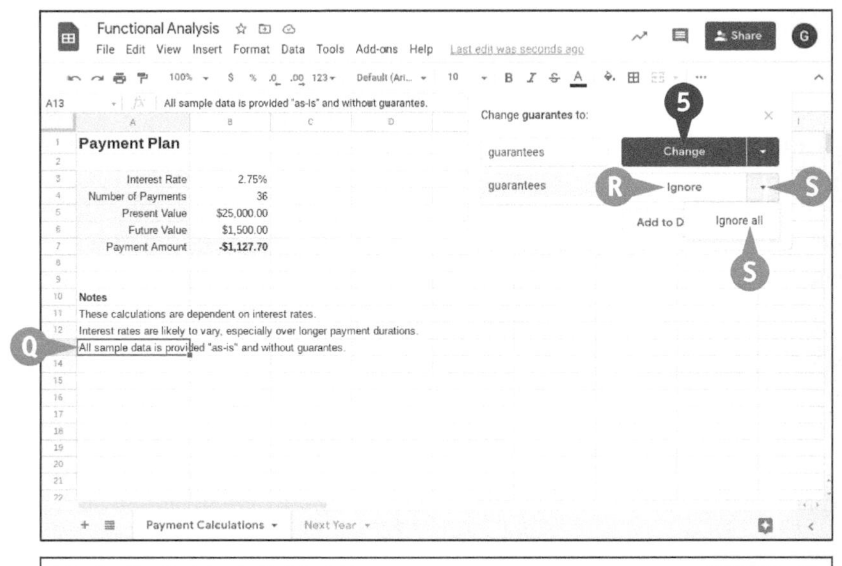

The spell checker replaces the queried word with the suggestion, and then continues the spell check.

When the spell checker finds no more errors, it displays a dialog box saying so, such as the No Spelling Suggestions dialog box in Google Sheets.

Ⓣ In Google Sheets, you can click **Search all sheets** to extend the search to the spreadsheet document's other sheets.

6 Click **Close** (✕).

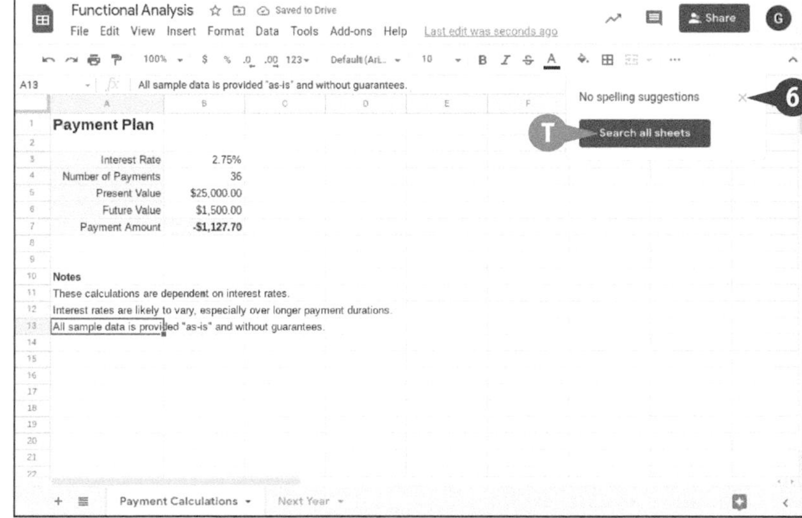

TIP

How do I remove a word I added to my personal dictionary?

Click **Tools** on the menu bar to open the Tools menu, click or highlight **Spelling and grammar** to open the Spelling and Grammar submenu, and then click **Personal dictionary.** The Personal Dictionary dialog box opens. Move the cursor over the word you want to remove, and then click **Remove** (🗑). While you have the Personal Dictionary dialog box open, you can add a new word by clicking **Add a new word**, typing the word, and then clicking **Add.** When you finish working on your personal dictionary, click **OK** to close the Personal Dictionary dialog box.

View History in Activity Dashboard

The Activity Dashboard feature in Google Docs, Google Sheets, and Google Slides enables you to review a document's sharing history and analyze how others have viewed the document and interacted with it. Activity Dashboard opens as a window containing five categories: Viewers, Viewer Trend, Comment Trend, Sharing History, and Privacy Settings.

The Viewers category lets you review the people who have viewed the document; you can also begin an email message to them. The Viewer Trend category shows you the number of unique viewers for the document and a histogram showing when the document has been viewed.

View History in Activity Dashboard

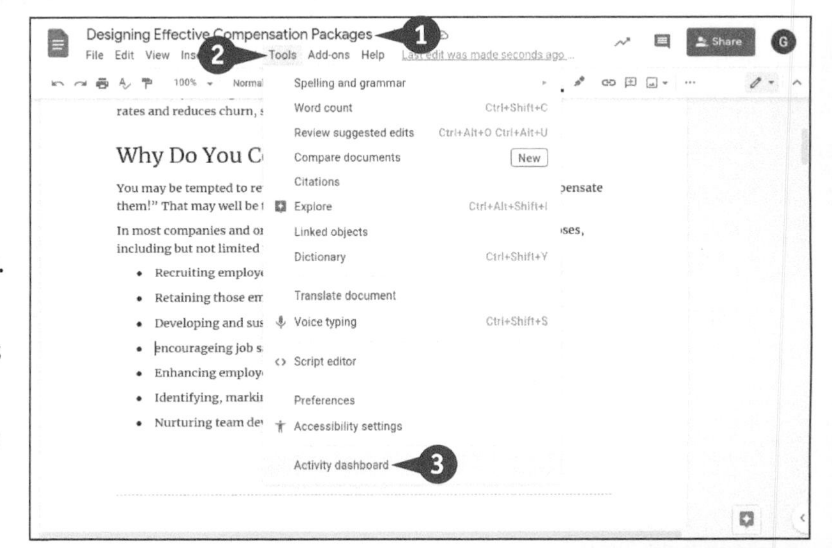

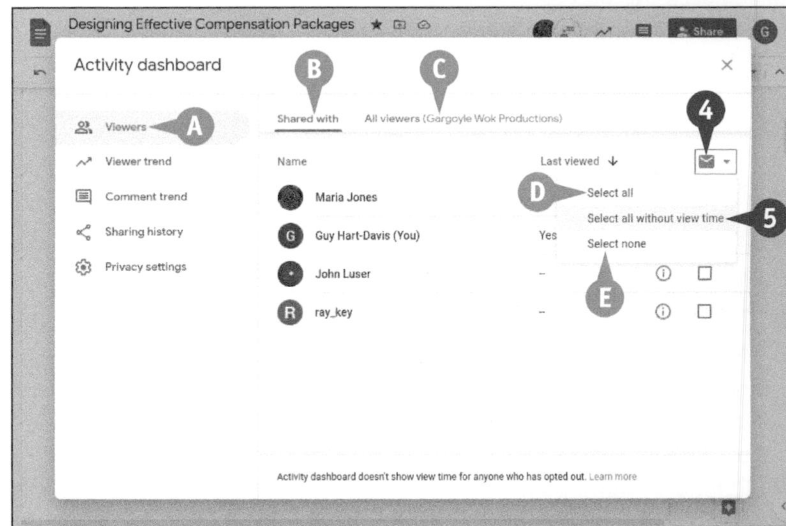

1. Open the document for which you want to view history.
2. Click **Tools**.

   The Tools menu opens.
3. Click **Activity dashboard**.

   The Activity Dashboard window opens.

   A. The Viewers category (👥) normally appears at first. If not, click **Viewers** (👥) to display it.

   B. The Shared With tab shows the people with whom the document is shared.

   C. You can click **All viewers** to display the list of viewers in your organization.
4. To contact some or all of the viewers, click **Send email** (✉ ▾).

   The Send Email pop-up menu opens.

   D. You can click **Select all** if you want to email all the viewers.
5. For this example, click **Select all without view time** if you want to email only those who have not viewed the document.

   E. You can click **Select none** to undo an existing selection.

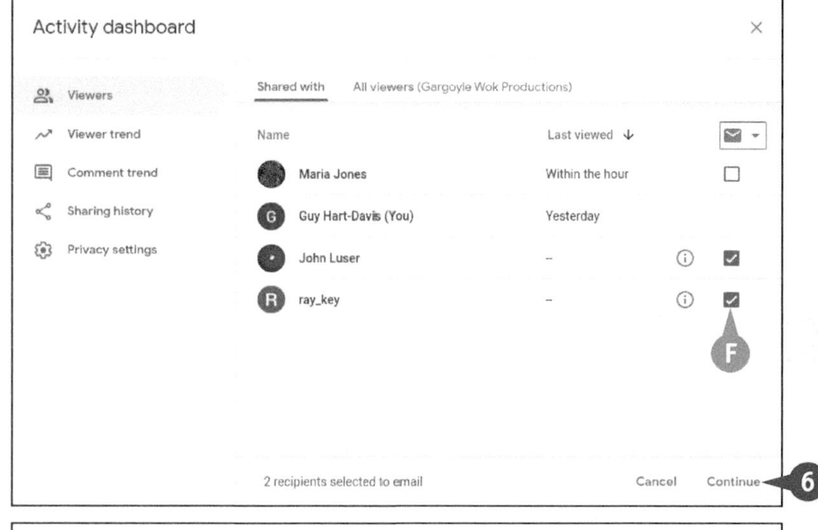

F The app selects the check box (☑) for each viewer specified.

6 Click **Continue**.

The Activity Dashboard window displays its Send Email screen, which contains the start of a message to the viewers you selected.

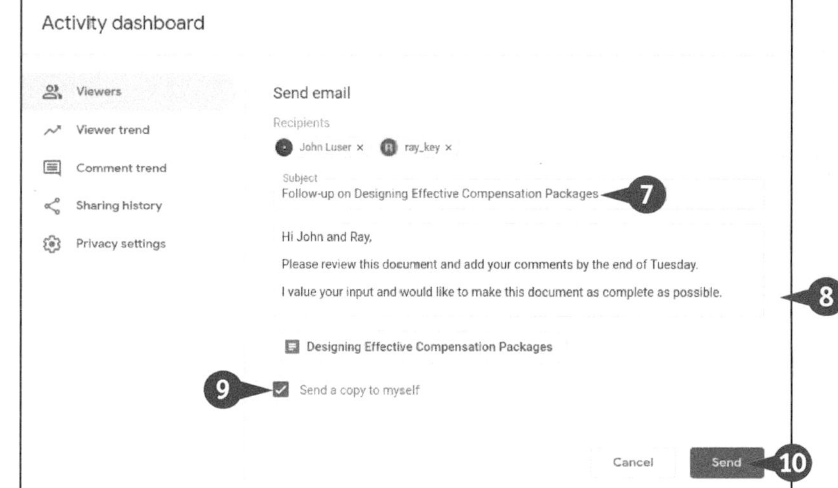

7 Edit the Subject line, as needed.

8 Type a message to the recipients.

9 Select **Send a copy to myself** (☑) if you want to send yourself a copy of the message — for example, for reference.

10 Click **Send**.

TIP

Are the Viewers and Viewer Trend statistics accurate?

The statistics in Activity Dashboard are usually accurate, but only up to a point. First, some users may hide their activity by using the settings in the Privacy Controls category; if so, the statistics omit these users, as you would expect. Second, an administrator can choose to hide all the views for a Google Workspace organization; this can seriously skew the viewer statistics. Third, if your document gets too many views or too many viewers, Activity Dashboard may simply fail to collect all the information.

continued ►

View History in Activity Dashboard (continued)

The Comment Trend category shows how many comments the document has received and when it received them. The Sharing History category lists the people the document is shared with and provides access to the sharing settings.

The Privacy Settings category lets you control your settings for the View History feature. You can set the Account Setting switch to enable or disable View History for your account as a whole. If you set the Account Setting switch to On, you can set the Document Setting switch to Off or On to enable or disable your View History for this document.

View History in Activity Dashboard (continued)

The app sends the email messages.

The Viewers category appears again.

11 Click **Viewer trend** (↗).

The Viewer Trend category appears.

G You can see the number of unique viewers.

H You can see the breakdown of viewers by dates.

I You can click **Time** (▾), and then click **Last 7 days**, **Last 14 days**, **Last 30 days**, or **All time** to change the time period displayed.

12 Click **Comment trend** (▤).

The Comment Trend category appears.

J You can see the total number of comments and replies the document has received.

K You can see the breakdown of comments by dates.

L The legend shows the colors for new comments, replies, and unresolved comments.

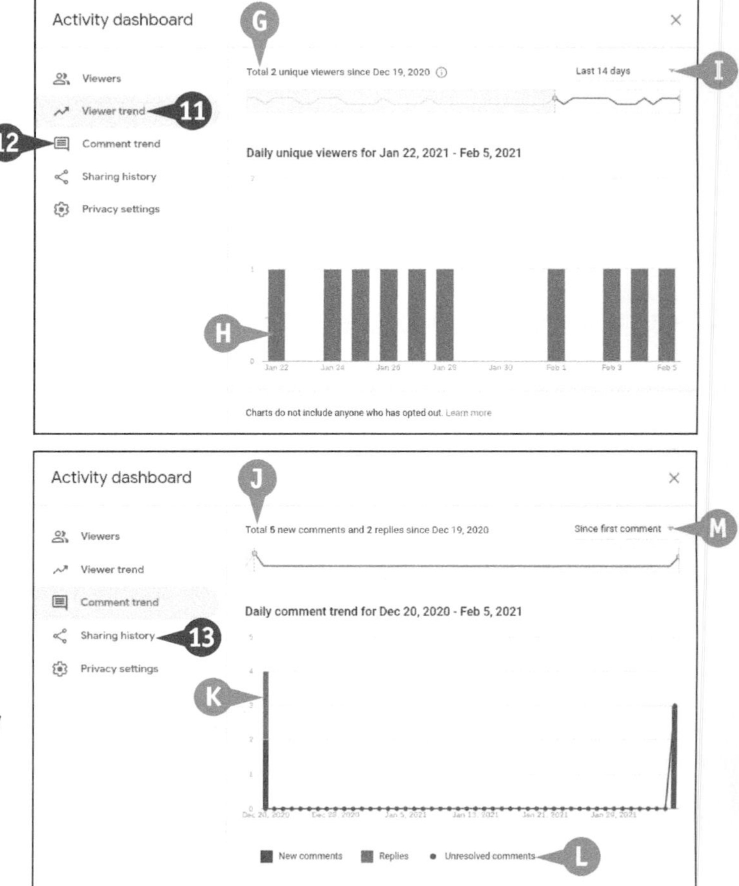

M You can click **Time** (▾), and then click **Last 7 days**, **Last 14 days**, **Last 30 days**, **Since first comment**, or **All time** to change the time period displayed.

13 Click **Sharing history** (<).

The Sharing History category appears.

N You can see the number of people with whom the document is shared.

O You can see sharing events for different time periods, such as Today and Last Week.

P You can see the sharing setting for each user, such as Can Edit.

Q You can click **Manage settings** to display the Share with People and Groups dialog box, in which you can adjust the sharing settings.

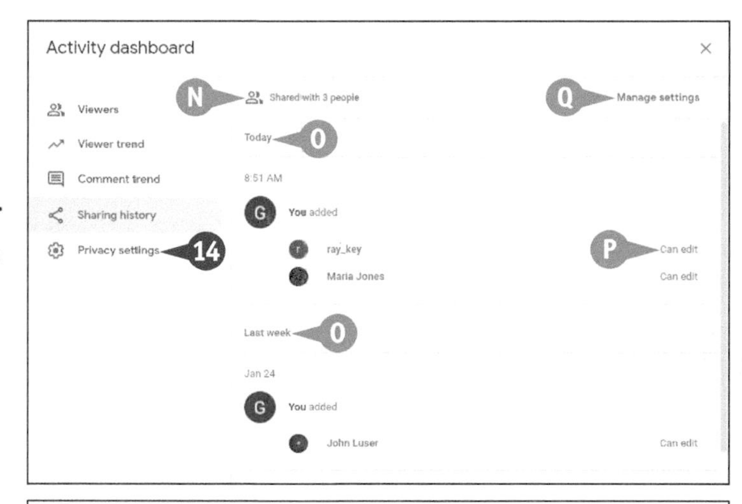

14 Click **Privacy settings** (⚙).

The Privacy Settings category appears.

15 Set the **Show my view history for all Docs, Sheets and Slides files** switch to On ( ) or Off ( ), as needed. See the tip for advice.

16 Assuming you set the upper switch to On ( ), set the **Show my view history for this document** switch to On ( ) or Off ( ), as needed.

17 Click **Save**.

Activity Dashboard saves your settings.

18 Click **Close** (✕).

The Activity Dashboard window closes.

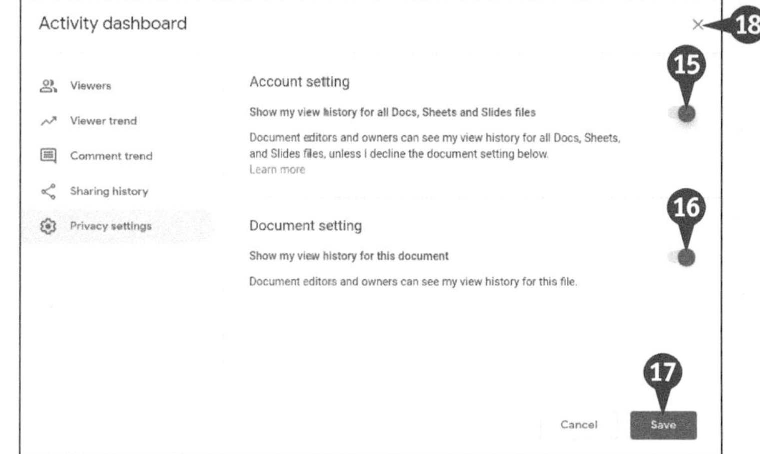

TIP

Should I enable or disable my View History?

Whether to enable or disable your View History can be a tricky decision — but you may be spared having to make it.

On the plus side, enabling your View History helps your colleagues to see what you do and may contribute to getting work done quickly and efficiently. On the minus side, the feeling of having your actions monitored may diminish your creativity, participation, and morale.

This decision may not be yours, as your organization's Google Workspace administrator may implement these settings via policy, preventing you from changing them.

Add Information with the Explore Feature

Google Docs, Google Sheets, and Google Slides include the Explore feature, which enables you to add information to your documents from your files on Google Drive or from web searches and recommendations. The Explore feature, which was previously known as the Research feature, uses machine learning to scan your documents and suggest links and material you might want to include in them.

In Google Sheets, the Explore feature also suggests ways of analyzing the data in the active spreadsheet. In Google Slides, the Explore feature suggests alternative designs for the current slide.

Activate the Explore Feature

In Google Docs or Google Slides, move the cursor over **Explore** (A, changes to Explore) in the lower-right corner of the window, and then click **Explore** (Explore) to open the Explore pane on the right side of the window.

Why Do You Compensate Your Employees?

You may be tempted to retort "Because they won't work for me if I don't compensate them!" That may well be true, but it's not the full answer.

In most companies and organizations, compensation fulfils a variety of purposes, including but not limited to the following:

- Recruiting employees who are qualified for the positions
- Retaining those employees, especially against competitors
- Developing and sustaining company morale

In Google Sheets, click **Open Explore** (Explore) in the lower-right corner of the window to open the Explore pane on the right side of the window. In Google Sheets, you can also press Alt + Shift + X to open the Explore pane. This keyboard shortcut does not work in Google Docs or Google Slides.

Using the Explore Feature in Google Docs

In Google Docs, the Quick Access section displays documents from Google Drive that Explore has determined are thematically linked to the content of the active document. In the screen, the active document covers designing compensation packages, and the Quick Access area shows three documents that discuss compensation, pay grades, and similar topics. You can click a document to open it (B), or move the cursor over it and then click **Add link** (C, +) to add a link to the document.

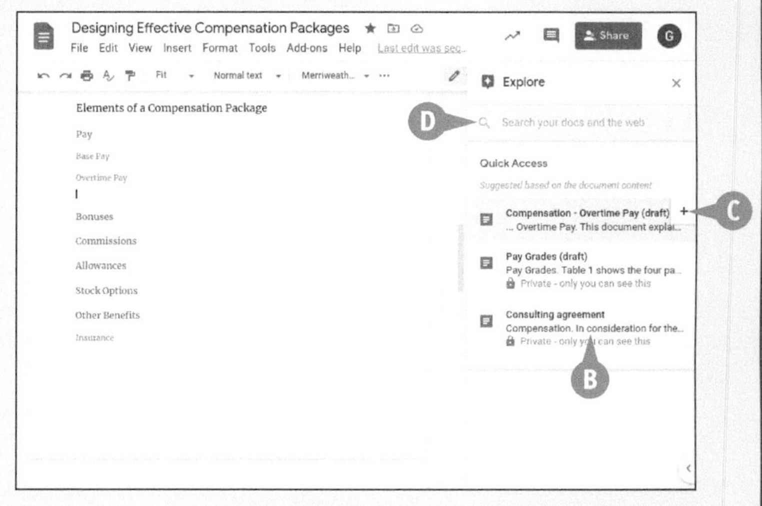

You can click **Search your docs and the web** (D,) and type keywords for which you want to search both in your documents and on the web.

Using the Explore Feature in Google Sheets

In Google Sheets, the Explore pane provides information, analysis, and actions for the active spreadsheet. In the example shown here, the Explore pane contains three sections — Answers, Formatting, and Analysis — for the data range shown at the top. You can click **EDIT** (E) to change the data range.

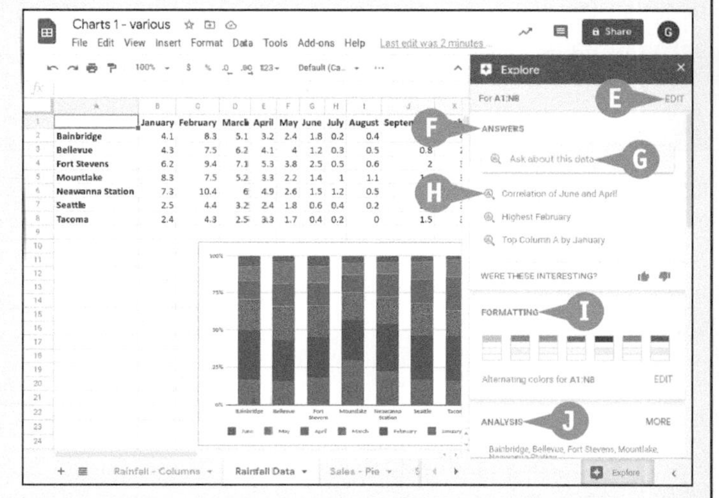

In the Answers section (F), you can click **Ask about this data** (🔍, G) to type keywords for analyzing the data, or you can click one of the suggested queries (🔍, H) to display its results.

In the Formatting section (I), you can click a formatting scheme to apply it to the data range.

In the Analysis section (J), you can click the analysis you want to view.

Using the Explore Feature in Google Slides

In Google Slides, the Explore pane enables you to access information resources and apply different layouts.

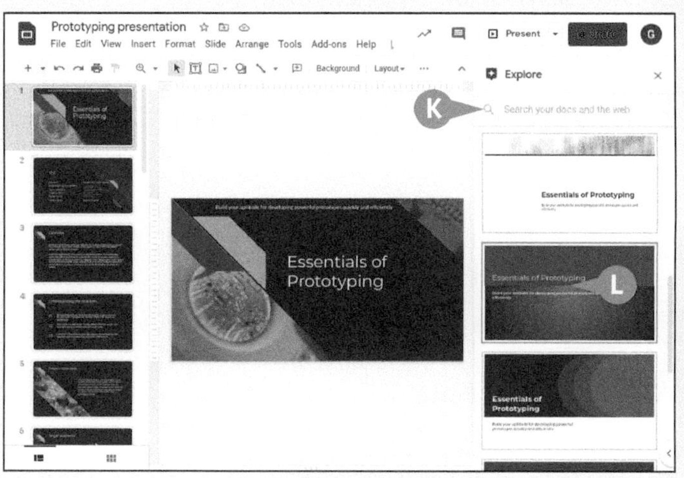

You can click **Search your docs and the web** (K, 🔍) and type terms for searching both in your Google Drive documents and on the web.

In the lower part of the Explore pane, you can browse the suggested alternative designs for the current slide. Click a design (L) to apply it.

Print a Document

If your computer has a printer available, you can print files from Google Docs, Google Sheets, and Google Slides. Printing works in the same way for each app, but there are minor differences between printing the different types of documents that the apps create — when you print documents in Google Docs, for example, you'll see different settings than when printing slides in Google Slides, as you would likely expect.

Printing generally works well, but you might find it helpful to know the capabilities of the printer, because the Print dialog box sometimes offers settings that require capabilities the printer does not actually have.

Print a Document

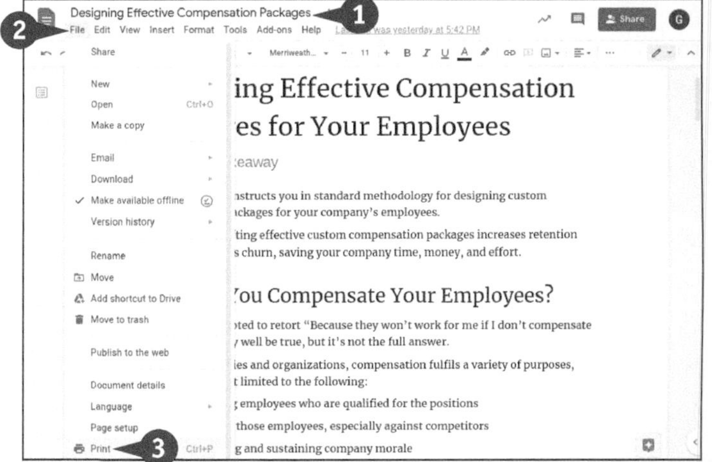

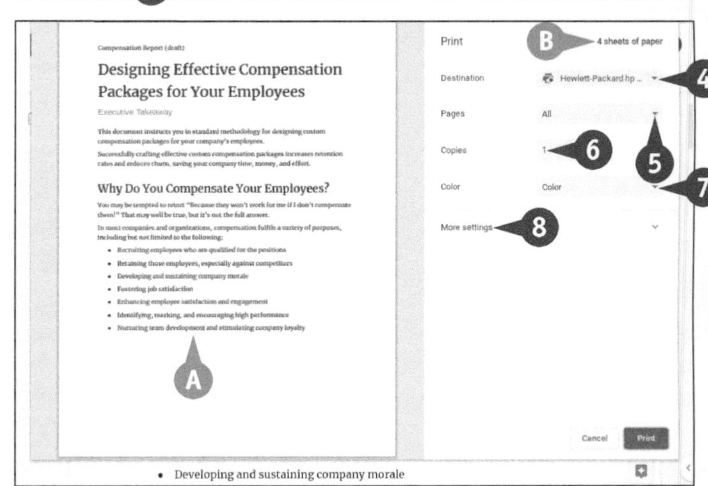

1. Open the file in the appropriate app.

   This example uses a document file in Google Docs.

2. Click **File**.

   The File menu opens.

3. Click **Print** (🖶).

   The Print dialog box opens.

   A The left pane shows a preview of how the printout will look. You can scroll up and down or press Page up and Page down.

   B The number of pages appears.

4. Click **Destination** (▾), and then click the appropriate printer on the pop-up menu.

5. Click **Pages** (▾), and then click **All** or **Custom**, as needed. If you click **Custom**, specify the pages in the box that appears. See the tip for details.

6. To print multiple copies, click **Copies** and enter the number.

7. To switch between color and black-and-white, click **Color** (▾), and then click **Color** or **Black and white**.

8. To choose further settings, click **More settings** (⌄ changes to ⌃).

The More Settings section expands, revealing its contents.

9. Choose other settings, as needed. For example, click **Paper size** (▼), and then click the paper size on which to print.

Note: The Print dialog box may offer settings beyond the printer's capabilities. For example, the example printer prints only in black and white and only on one side of the paper, but the Color pop-up menu offers Color as the default setting, and the Print on Both Sides check box is available.

10. Farther down the More Settings section, choose other settings, as needed.

C. You can click **Advanced settings** to display the Advanced Settings dialog box for the printer. These settings vary by printer model, but you can usually adjust the print quality between Draft — which saves ink or toner — and Normal, and add a cover sheet, such as Classified or Confidential, for each print job.

11. Click **Print**.

The Print dialog box closes.

The app sends the print job to the printer.

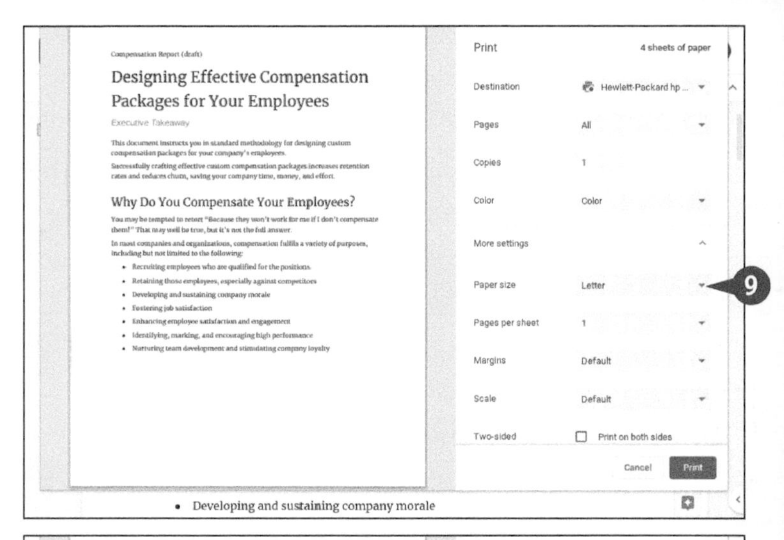

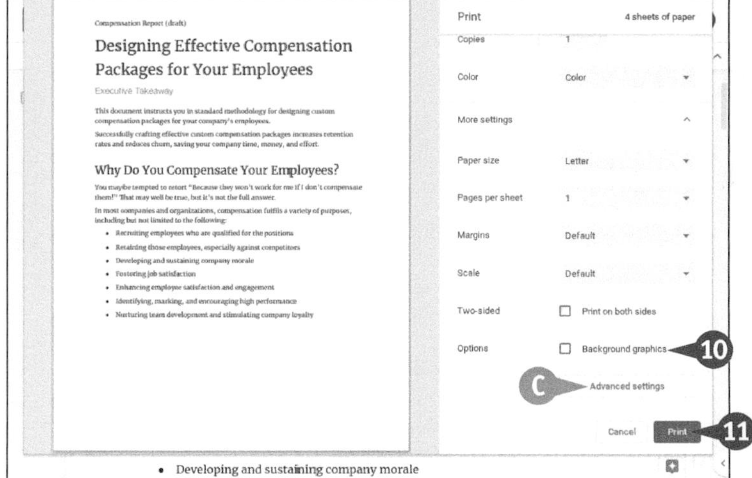

TIPS

How do I specify a custom page range?

Use a hyphen to designate a range, such as **3-6**. Use commas to separate pages and ranges, such as **1,3-6,10**.

How can I print when no printer is available?

You can "print" the document to a PDF file so that you can print it later. In the Print dialog box, click **Destination** (▼), and then click **Save as PDF**. The Save button replaces the Print button in the lower-right corner of the Print dialog box. Click **Save**, specify the filename and folder in the Save File As dialog box that opens, and then click **Save** again.

Send a File as an Email Attachment

Google Docs, Google Sheets, and Google Slides apps enable you to quickly send a file as an email attachment via your Gmail account. For example, you can open a presentation in Google Slides, work on it, and then send it from Google Slides without having to switch to the Gmail app.

When you send a file, you can include a message to the recipient or recipients, and you can choose the format in which to send the file. You can also choose to send yourself a copy of the file.

Send a File as an Email Attachment

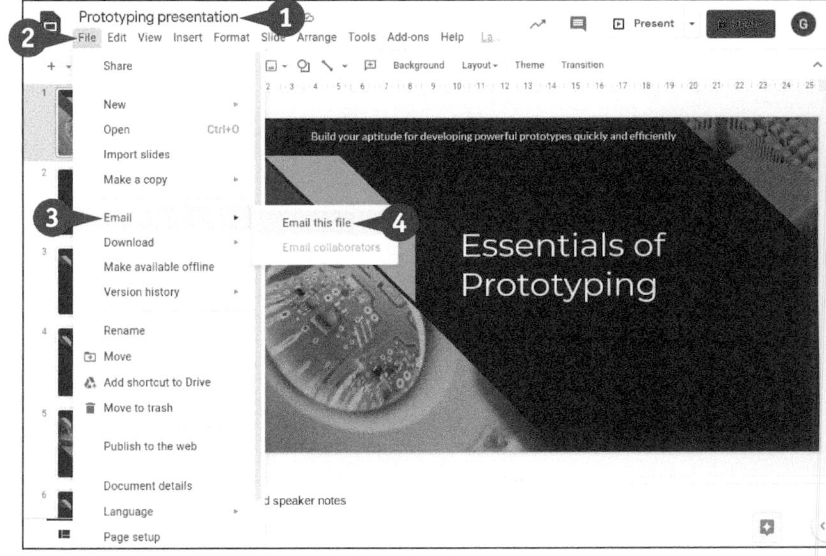

1. Open the file in the appropriate app.

   This example uses a presentation file in Google Slides.

2. Click **File**.

   The File menu opens.

3. Click or highlight **Email**.

   The Email submenu opens.

4. Click **Email this file**.

   The Email This File dialog box opens.

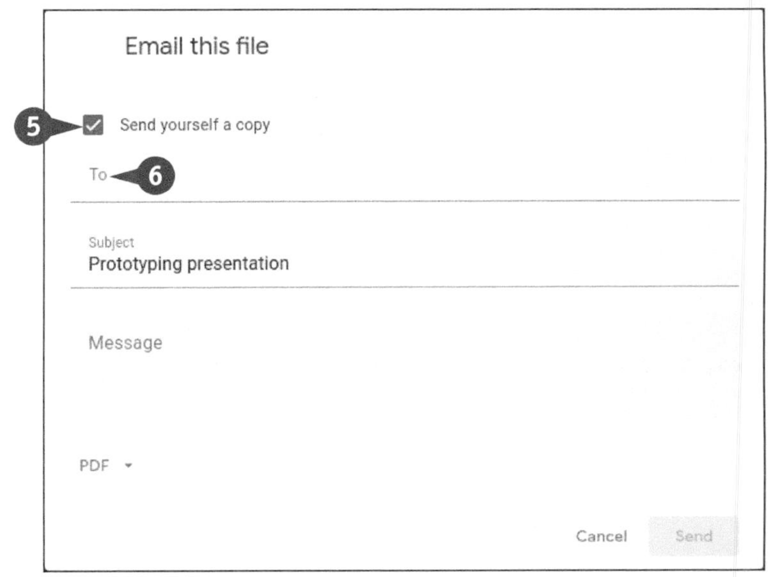

5. Click **Send yourself a copy** (☐ changes to ☑) if you want to email yourself a copy of the file.

Note: Sending yourself a copy of the file can be helpful for making sure it transfers satisfactorily.

6. Click **To**.

The To field becomes selected.

7 Start typing the first recipient's name or email address.

A list of matching results appears.

A You can hold the cursor over a result to display a pop-up window showing more detail.

8 Click the appropriate result.

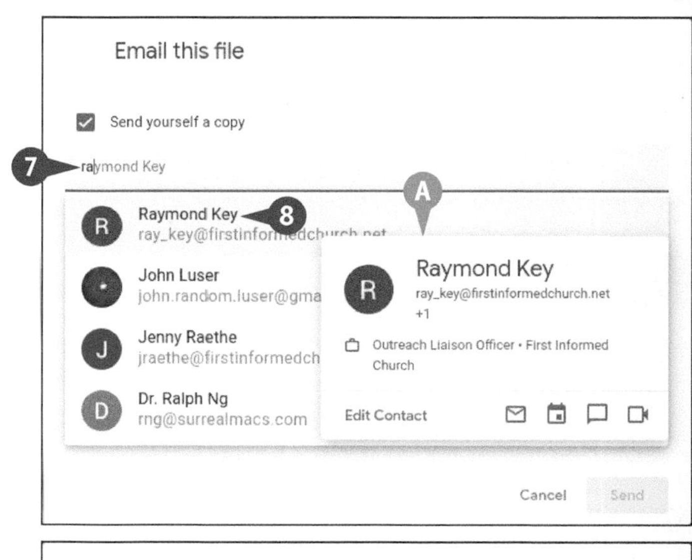

B The recipient's name appears as a button.

C You can click **Remove** (✕) to remove the recipient.

Note: You can add other recipients by repeating steps **6** to **8**.

9 If necessary, click **Subject** and edit the default subject, which is the filename.

10 Click **Message** and type any message needed for the recipient.

11 Click **Format** (▾), and then click the file type to send. See the tip for advice.

12 Click **Send**.

The app creates a file in the format you chose, and then sends it via email.

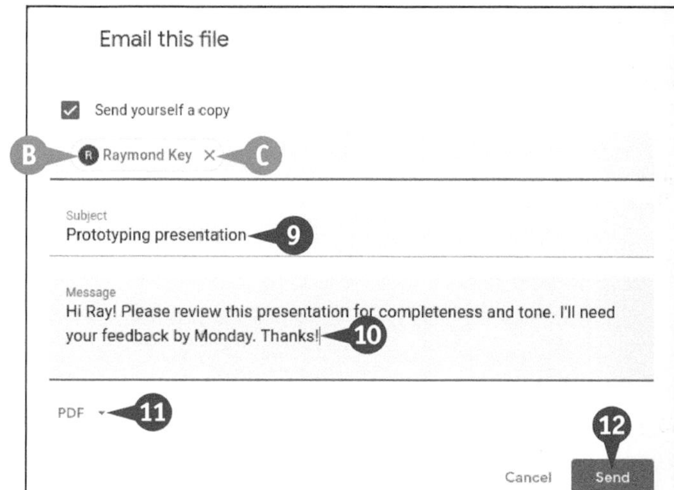

TIP

Which format should I use for sending files via email?

Your choices vary depending on the file type. For a Google Docs document, you can choose among PDF, Rich Text (RTF), Open Document, HTML, Microsoft Word, and Plain Text. For a Google Sheets spreadsheet, you can choose PDF, Open Office Spreadsheet, or Microsoft Excel. For a Google Slides presentation, your choices are PDF, Microsoft PowerPoint, and Plain Text.

Generally, you should choose PDF if the recipient needs to read the file but not edit it. If the recipient does need to edit the file, the Microsoft formats are the best bet, both because Microsoft Office is widely used and because other apps can open its files.

CHAPTER 4

Inserting Objects in Google Docs, Google Sheets, and Google Slides

In this chapter, you learn to insert objects in your work in Google Docs, Google Sheets, and Google Slides. In all three apps, you can insert images, charts, and links; you can work with comments; and you can resize, reposition, and format the objects you have inserted. In Google Docs and Google Slides, you can also insert special characters, such as symbols and emoji, tables, and drawings.

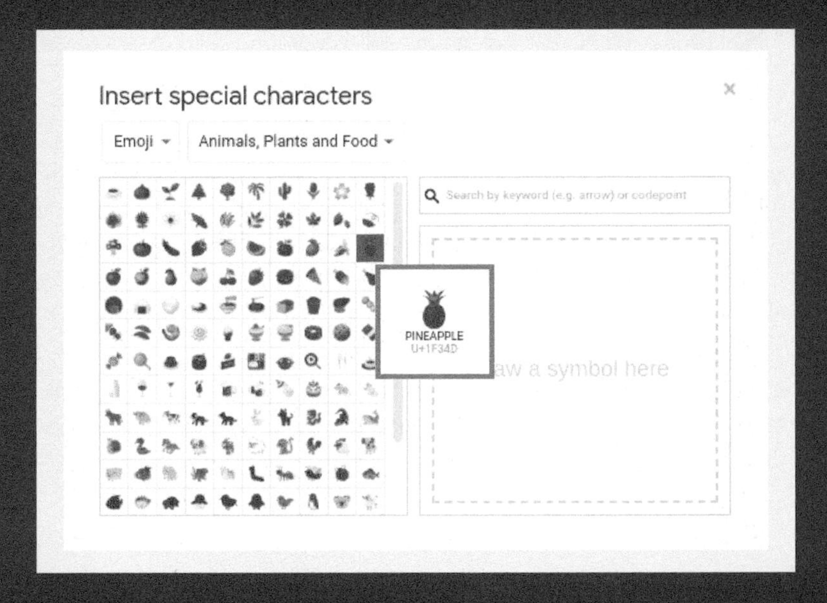

Insert Special Characters in Google Docs or Google Slides

In addition to regular text characters that you can type with your computer's keyboard, Google Docs and Google Slides enable you to insert special characters in your documents and slides. The apps provide a wide range of special characters, from symbols — such as arrows, currency icons, and keyboard characters — to emoticons, punctuation, and script characters.

You can search for symbols by name or description; by *codepoint*, the character number in the Unicode text-encoding system, such as for Á or for ç; or even by drawing an approximation of the symbol.

Insert Special Characters in Google Docs or Google Slides

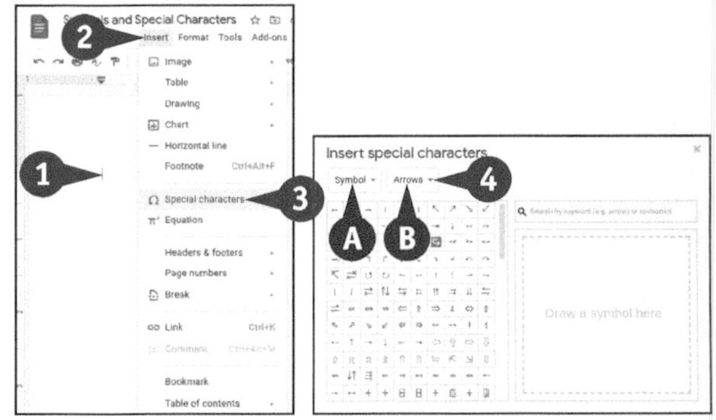

1. In the Google Docs document or Google Slides presentation, position the cursor where you want to insert the special character.
2. Click **Insert**.

   The Insert menu opens.
3. Click **Special Characters** (Ω).

   The Insert Special Characters dialog box opens.

   Ⓐ The left pop-up menu shows the current category, such as Symbol.

   Ⓑ The right pop-up menu shows the current subcategory within the category, such as the Arrows subcategory within the Symbol category.
4. Click the left pop-up menu button (▼).

   The pop-up menu opens.

   Ⓒ Click **Emoji** to enter emoji, also called "smileys."

   Ⓓ Click **Punctuation** to enter punctuation characters, such as ¶ or §.

   Ⓔ Click **Format & Whitespace** to enter formatting and whitespace characters, such as optional hyphens.

   Ⓕ Click **Modifier** to enter combining characters, such as ⃠.

   Ⓖ Click **Latin** to insert Roman alphabet–based characters, such as Æ and ð.

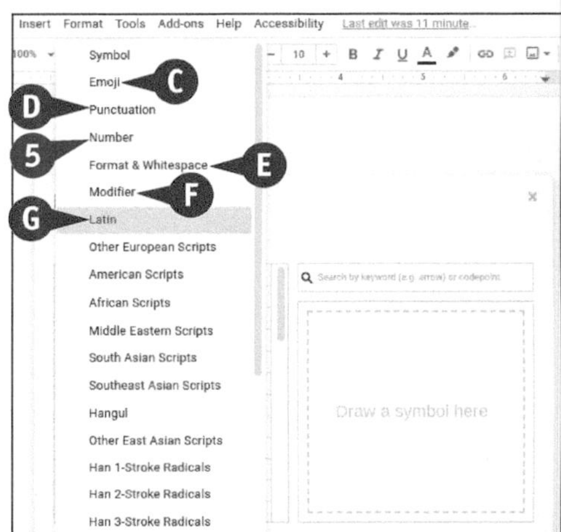

5. Click **Number** to enter fractions, superscript powers, or characters from other numbering systems, such as ௱ or ௲.

   This example uses **Number**.

Note: See the tip for information on the Scripts, Hangul, and Han Stroke Radicals options.

The options for the category you clicked appear.

6 Click the right pop-up menu button (▼), and then click the appropriate subcategory. For this example, click **Fractions/Related**.

The characters in the category appear.

H You can hold the cursor over a character to display a pop-up window showing the character, its name, and its Unicode codepoint.

7 Click the character you want to insert.

I The character appears in the document.

J Once you insert a character, a third pop-up menu appears to the left of the previous two. You can click this pop-up menu (▼) to switch among **Categories**, **Recent characters**, and — when you have searched — **Search results**.

K You can click **Search** (🔍) and type a search term, such as *accent* for characters or *grinning face* for emoji.

8 To search by drawing, click the box below the search field.

9 Draw the character you want.

L You can click **Erase** (↺) to erase what you have drawn.

M Matching characters appear.

10 Click the character you want to insert.

11 Click **Close** (✕).

The Insert Special Characters dialog box closes.

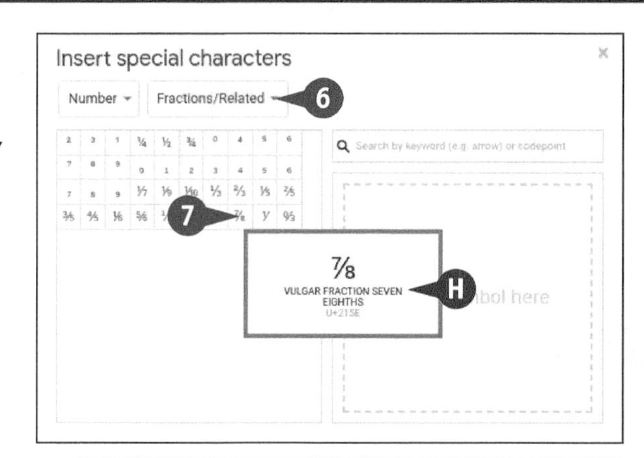

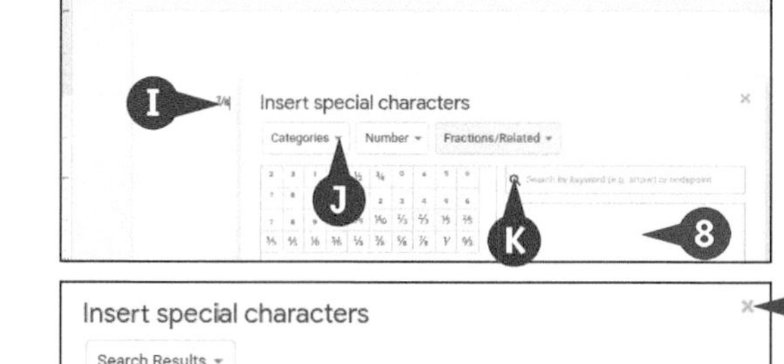

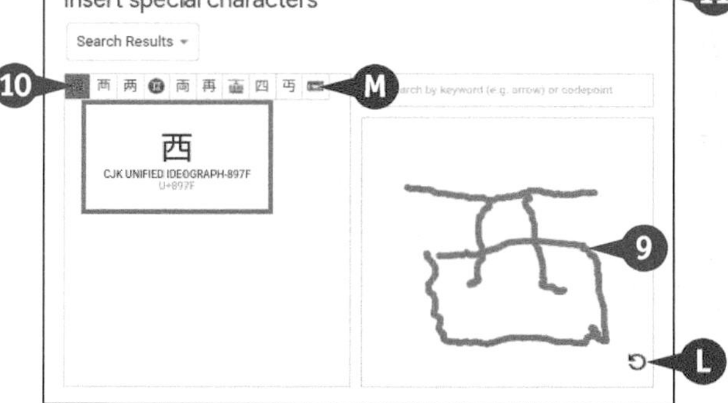

TIP

What are the other options on the left pop-up menu?

Click **Other European Scripts** to enter characters in scripts such as Cyrillic, Greek, and Armenian. Click **American Scripts** to enter characters in Canadian Aboriginal script, Cherokee script, or Historic Deseret script. Click **African Scripts** for scripts such as Ethiopic and Tifinagh. Click **South Asian Scripts** for scripts such as Bengali, Gujarati, and Tamil. Click **Southeast Asian Scripts** for scripts such as Balinese, Javanese, and Thai. Click **Hangul** for Korean script. Click **Other East Asian Scripts** for scripts including Japanese Hiragana and Katakana, Mongolian, and Old Turkic. For Han characters, click one of the Han *N*-Stroke Radicals items, such as **Han 5-Stroke Radicals**, or click **Han – Other**.

Insert an Image

Many documents benefit from the addition of images to illustrate key points graphically or simply to lighten dense text. The Google Workspace apps enable you to insert images easily from a variety of sources: from your computer; from your computer's camera, if it has one; from Google Drive; from Google Photos; from a URL you specify; or from the result of a web search you perform.

If you store your photos in Google Photos, you can quickly identify suitable photos and insert them in your documents, especially if you organize your photos into albums.

Insert an Image

Insert an Image from Google Photos

1. In Google Docs, place the cursor where you want the image to appear.
2. Click **Insert**.

   The Insert menu opens.
3. Click or highlight **Image** (🖼).

   The Image submenu opens.

Note: In Google Sheets, click **Insert**, click or highlight **Image** (🖼), and then click **Image in cell** or **Image over cells**, as needed. In the Insert Image dialog box that opens, click the appropriate tab — **UPLOAD**, **CAMERA**, **By URL**, **PHOTOS**, **GOOGLE DRIVE**, or **GOOGLE IMAGE SEARCH** — click the image, and then click **INSERT**.

4. Click **Photos** (✤).

   The Google Photos pane appears on the right side of the app.

   A. You can click **PHOTOS** to browse all the photos available to you in Google Photos.
5. Click **ALBUMS**.

   The Albums tab appears.
6. Double-click the album you want to open.

Note: If you have an iPhone, consider using the Google Photos app for iOS to upload your photos to the Google Photos service.

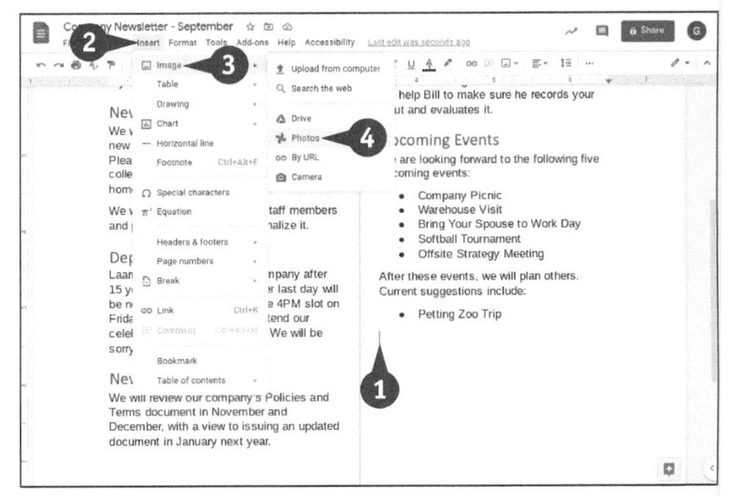

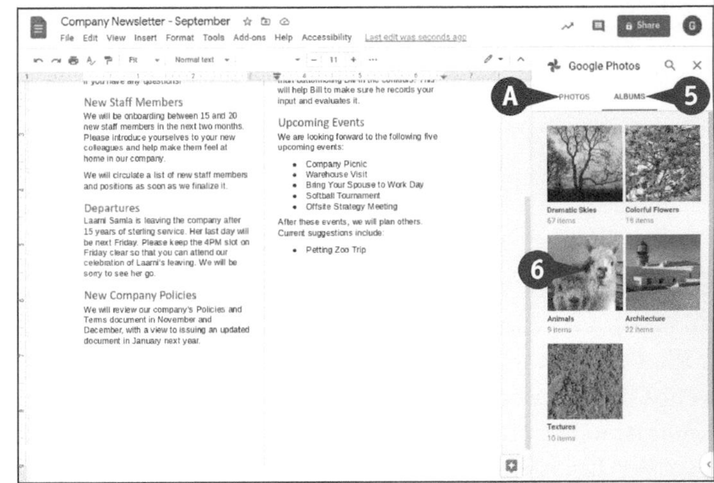

The photos in the album appear.

B You can click **Preview photo** (🔍) to display a preview of the photo — for example, to make sure it is the one you want. From the preview, you can click **INSERT** to insert the photo.

7 Click the photo you want to insert.

8 Click **INSERT**.

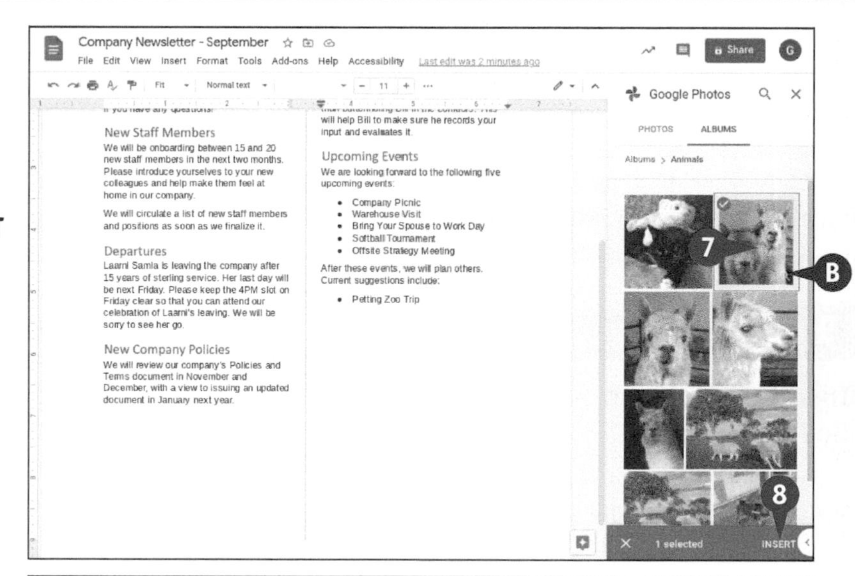

The image appears in the document.

C You can drag a handle to resize the image. See the section "Resize, Reposition, and Format an Object," later in this chapter, for more information.

D In Google Docs, you can click **In line** (▤) to position the image inline with the text, **Wrap text** (▤) to wrap the text around the image, or **Break text** (▤) to make the image interrupt the text.

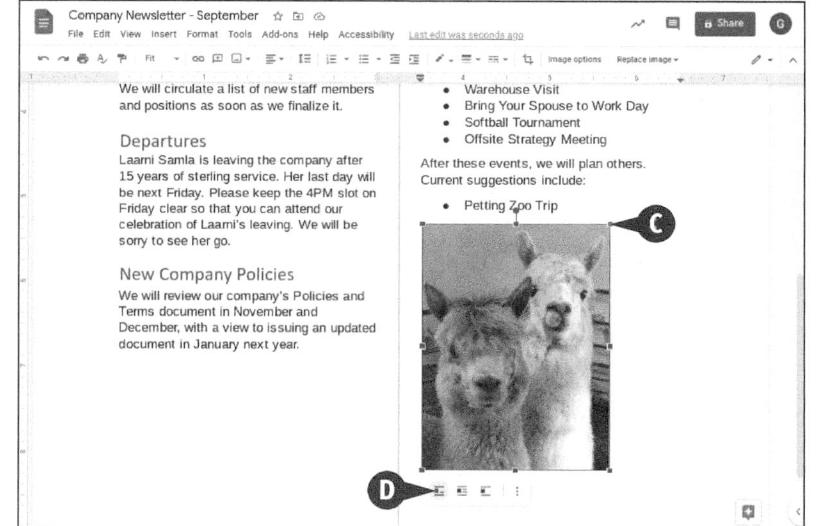

TIP

How can I use a photo from my computer's webcam?

Place the cursor where you want the photo to appear, click **Insert**, click or highlight **Image**, and then click **Camera** (📷). A Camera window opens, showing a preview of what the lens is seeing. Position your subject as needed, and then click **Take photo** (📷) to take one or more photos, as needed. Each photo appears as a thumbnail to the right of the Camera window. Click the photo you want to insert, and then click **INSERT**. The Camera window closes, and the photo appears in the document.

continued ▶

If you store images in Google Drive, you can insert them easily from there. Inserting images from Google Drive can be useful, especially if you or your company or organization use Google Drive to share image files.

You can also insert an image in a document by specifying the image's URL, its uniform resource locator — in other words, its web address. For example, you might insert a product photo from your company's website in a document.

Insert an Image (continued)

Insert an Image from Google Drive

1. In Google Slides, click the slide on which you want the image to appear.
2. Click **Insert**.

   The Insert menu opens.
3. Click or highlight **Image** (🖼).

   The Image submenu opens.
4. Click **Drive** (△).

   The Google Drive pane opens on the right side of the window.
5. On the tab bar at the top, click the tab you want to use to access the image. In this example, you would click **MY DRIVE**.

A. You can click **Next** (›) to display the next tabs, scrolling to the right. After scrolling right, you can click **Previous** (‹) to display previous tabs, scrolling to the left.

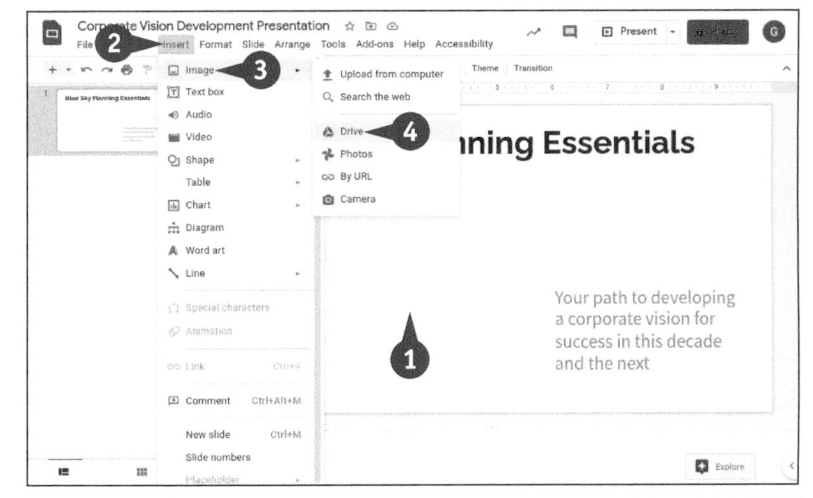

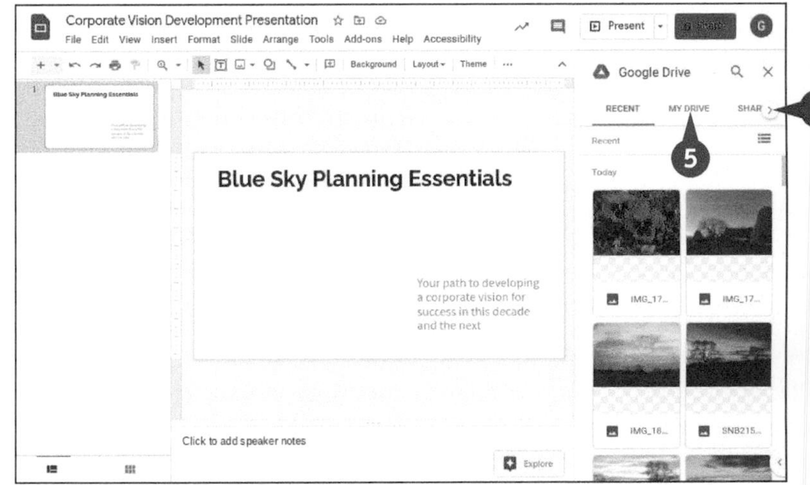

The contents of the tab appear.

In this example, the My Drive tab appears.

6 If necessary, navigate to the folder that contains the image. In this example, you would click **Photos** to display the contents of the Photos folder.

7 Click the image you want to insert.

8 Click **INSERT**.

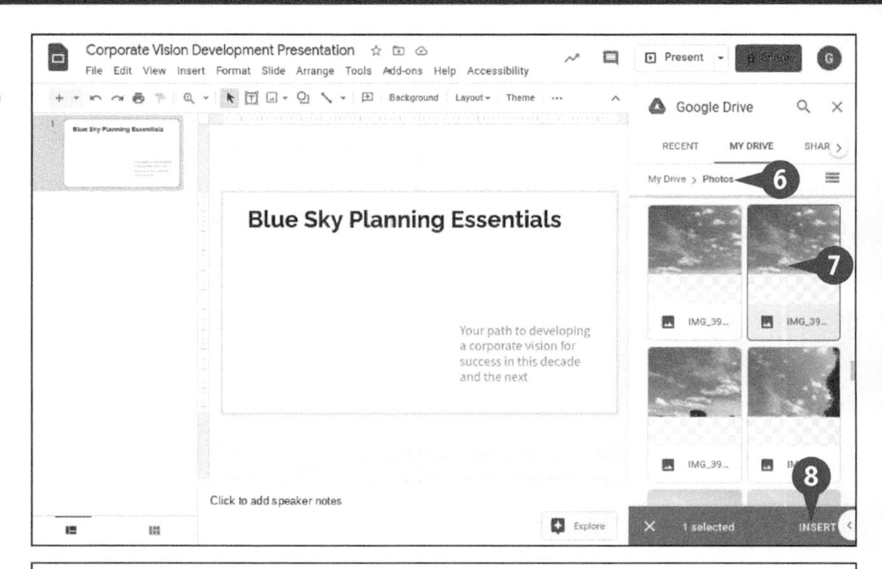

The Google Drive pane closes.

The image appears on the slide.

B You can drag a handle to resize the image. See the section "Resize, Reposition, and Format an Object," later in this chapter, for more information.

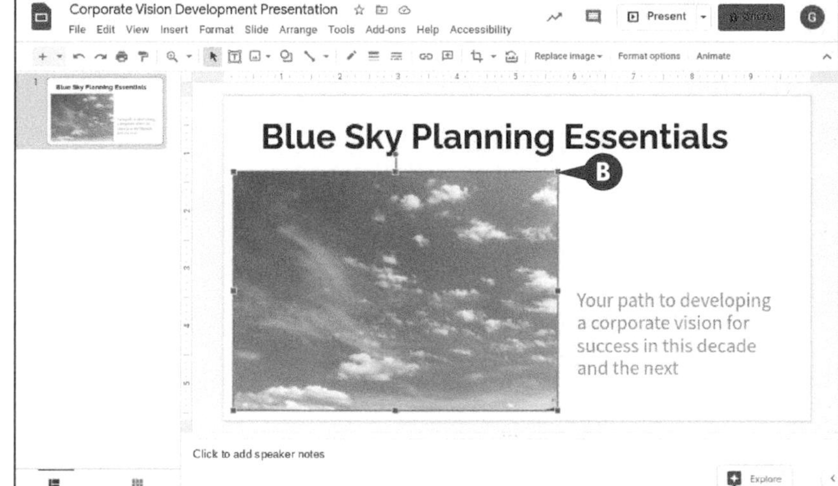

TIP

How do I insert an image from my company's website?

First, copy the image's URL, or web address. For example, open a browser tab, go to the web page that contains the image, right-click the image, and then click **Copy image address** on the contextual menu. Next, place the cursor where you want the photo to appear, click **Insert**, click or highlight **Image**, and then click **By URL** (⊖). In the Insert Image dialog box that opens, right-click **Paste URL of image**, and then click **Paste** on the contextual menu. Click **INSERT** to close the Insert Image dialog box. The app inserts the image in the document.

Insert a Table in Google Docs or Google Slides

Google Docs enables you to insert tables in your documents for laying out data in neat rows and columns. Similarly, Google Slides enables you to insert tables in slides to present data in a tabular format.

When inserting a table, you set the table's initial number of columns and rows. You can subsequently insert or delete rows or columns, as needed. You can also change column width; apply border formatting, such as changing the line weight and color; and format the table's contents.

Insert a Table in Google Docs or Google Slides

Insert a Table and Add Text

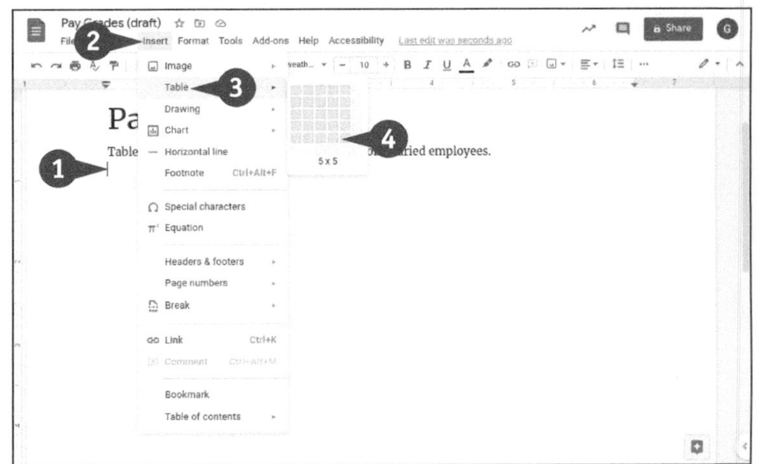

1. Position the cursor where you want the table to appear.

Note: This section uses Google Docs to illustrate inserting a table. The process is almost identical in Google Slides.

2. Click **Insert**.

   The Insert menu opens.

3. Click or highlight **Table**.

   The Table submenu panel opens.

4. Move the cursor over the grid until the readout shows the number of rows and columns you want, and then click.

   The table appears in the document.

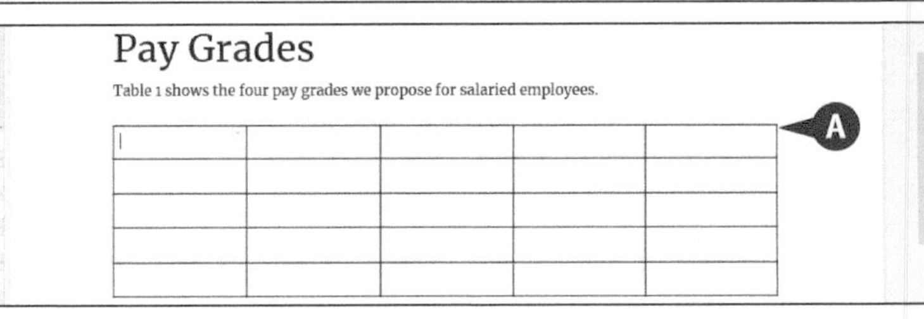

A. By default, the table has thin black borders applied. You can change them or remove them, as needed.

5. Type the contents of as many cells as you want to populate, pressing Tab to move the cursor from one cell to the next.

Note: Press Shift + Tab to move the cursor to the previous cell.

Note: Pressing Tab in the table's last cell creates a new row.

B. Text wraps automatically to new lines, as needed.

Pay Grades

Table 1 shows the four pay grades we propose for salaried employees.

Grades and Steps	Pay Step 1	Pay Step 2	Pay Step 3	Pay Step 4
Pay Grade 1	$28,000	$30,500	$33,000	$35,500
Pay Grade 2	$33,000	$35,500	$38,000	$40,500
Pay Grade 3	$38,000	$40,500	$43,000	$45,500
Pay Grade 4	$41,000	$44,000	$47,000	$50,000

Format the Table

1. Select the part of the table you want to format. For example, drag to select the top row.

2. Format the selected text as you wish. For example, you might apply boldface, as in this example; change the font; or change the font size.

3. Apply other formatting, as needed. For example, you might change the alignment of some cells.

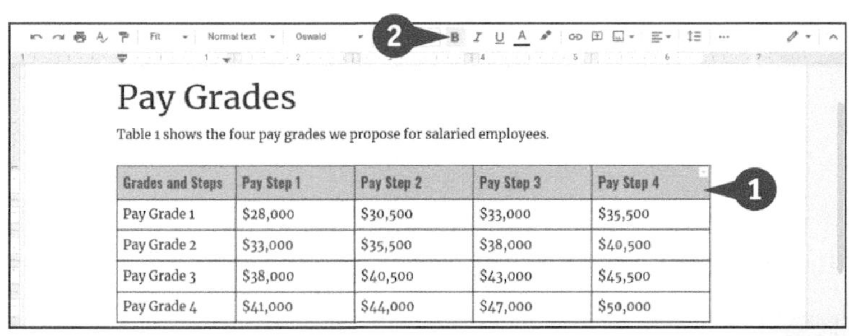

Pay Grades

Table 1 shows the four pay grades we propose for salaried employees.

Grades and Steps	Pay Step 1	Pay Step 2	Pay Step 3	Pay Step 4
Pay Grade 1	$28,000	$30,500	$33,000	$35,500
Pay Grade 2	$33,000	$35,500	$38,000	$40,500
Pay Grade 3	$38,000	$40,500	$43,000	$45,500
Pay Grade 4	$41,000	$44,000	$47,000	$50,000

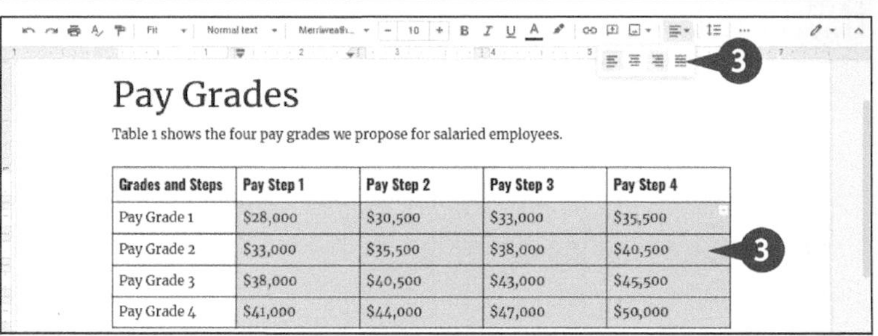

Pay Grades

Table 1 shows the four pay grades we propose for salaried employees.

Grades and Steps	Pay Step 1	Pay Step 2	Pay Step 3	Pay Step 4
Pay Grade 1	$28,000	$30,500	$33,000	$35,500
Pay Grade 2	$33,000	$35,500	$38,000	$40,500
Pay Grade 3	$38,000	$40,500	$43,000	$45,500
Pay Grade 4	$41,000	$44,000	$47,000	$50,000

4. To change the column widths, drag the right border of the column you want to affect.

C. The vertical blue line shows the border's new position.

Note: To format the table's borders, select the table or the cells you want to affect. Click **More** (···) if necessary to display the hidden section of the toolbar. You can then click **Border color** (✎) and click a color; click **Border width** (☰) and click a width; and click **Border dash** (☰) and click the line style — solid, dashed, or dotted.

Pay Grades

Table 1 shows the four pay grades we propose for salaried employees.

Grades and Steps	Pay Step 1	Pay Step 2	Pay Step 3	Pay Step 4	
Pay Grade 1	$28,000	$30,500	$33,000		$35,500
Pay Grade 2	$33,000	$35,500	$38,000		$40,500
Pay Grade 3	$38,000	$40,500	$43,000		$45,500
Pay Grade 4	$41,000	$44,000	$47,000		$50,000

Pay Grades

Table 1 shows the four pay grades we propose for salaried employees.

Grades and Steps	Pay Step 1	Pay Step 2	Pay Step 3	Pay Step 4
Pay Grade 1	$28,000	$30,500	$33,000	$35,500
Pay Grade 2	$33,000	$35,500	$38,000	$40,500
Pay Grade 3	$38,000	$40,500	$43,000	$45,500
Pay Grade 4	$41,000	$44,000	$47,000	$50,000

TIPS

How do I change the number of columns in a table?

Right-click anywhere in the column you want to remove or next to which you want to add a new column. On the contextual menu, click **Delete column** to delete the column; click **Insert column left** or **Insert column right** to insert a new column to the left or right of that column.

How can I make a larger cell in the table?

You can merge existing cells to create a larger cell. Select the cells, right-click in the selection, and then click **Merge cells** on the contextual menu. If you need to split the cells again, right-click the merged cell, and then click **Unmerge cells** on the contextual menu.

Insert a Drawing in Google Docs or Google Sheets

Google Docs and Google Sheets enable you to insert drawings in your documents and spreadsheets. Google Docs and Google Sheets handle drawings by inserting a blank drawing canvas that you populate with the objects your drawing needs. By contrast, Google Slides provides similar drawing tools, but the app lets you place objects directly on slides rather than inserting a drawing canvas.

If you already have a suitable drawing stored on Google Drive, you can quickly insert it in a document or spreadsheet. You can create drawings by using the Google Drawings app.

Insert a Drawing in Google Docs or Google Sheets

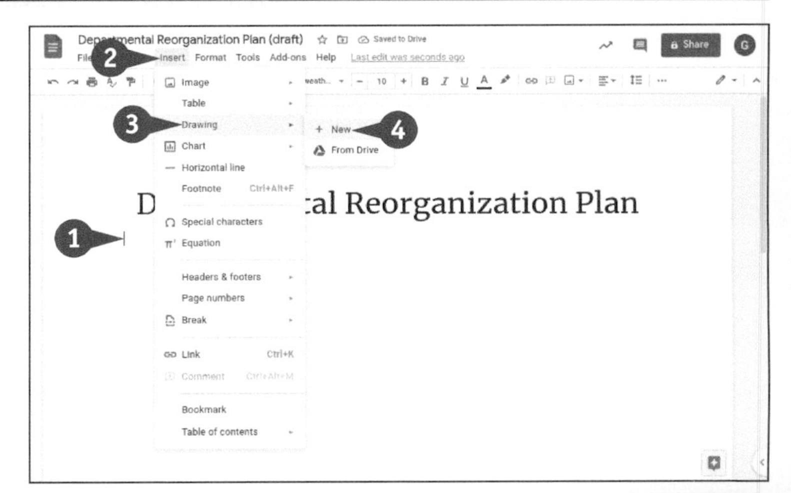

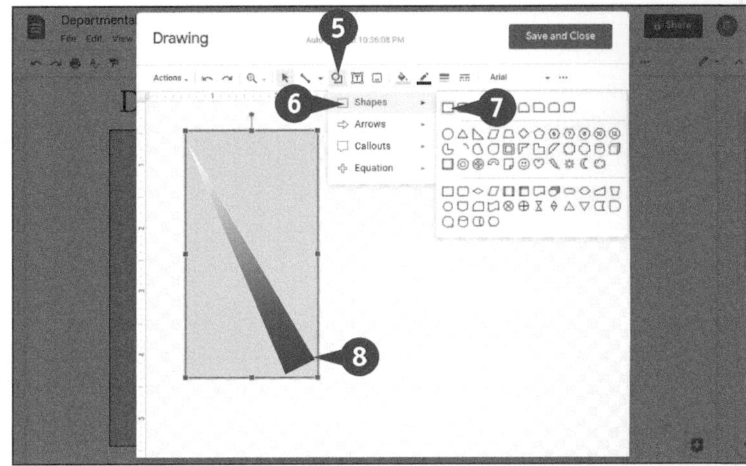

1. Position the cursor where you want the drawing to appear.
2. Click **Insert**.

   The Insert menu opens.
3. Click or highlight **Drawing**.

   The Drawing submenu opens.
4. Click **New** (+).

   The Drawing window opens in front of the app, showing an empty drawing canvas.

   You can now add components to the drawing, as needed. The following four steps add a rectangle as an example.
5. Click **Shape** (🔲).

   The Shape pop-up menu opens.
6. Click or highlight **Shapes** (□).

   The Shapes pop-up panel appears.
7. Click **Rectangle** (□).

   The Rectangle tool becomes active.
8. Drag on the canvas to set the size of the shape.

Note: To constrain a rectangle to a square, or to constrain an oval to a circle, hold down Shift while you drag on the canvas.

9. Make other changes to the drawing, as needed. Here are some examples:

A. To change a shape's fill color, click the shape, click **Fill color** (◈) on the toolbar, and then click the color on the pop-up panel.

B. To add text to a shape, double-click in it, and then type the text.

C. To add an arrow, click **Line** (↘), click **Arrow** (↘) on the Line pop-up menu, and then drag to place the arrow.

D. To change the color of selected text, click **More** (•••), click **Text color** (A), and then click the color on the pop-up panel.

10. Click **Save and Close**.

The Drawing window closes.

The Drawing canvas in the document updates to show your drawing.

E. You can drag a handle (■) to resize the drawing.

F. The Add Comment icon (⊞) and Suggest Edits icon (✎) appear when you select an object, such as a drawing. See the section "Work with Comments," later in this chapter, for details on using comments. See the section "Switch Among Editing, Suggesting, and Viewing Modes" in Chapter 5 for information on using Suggesting Mode.

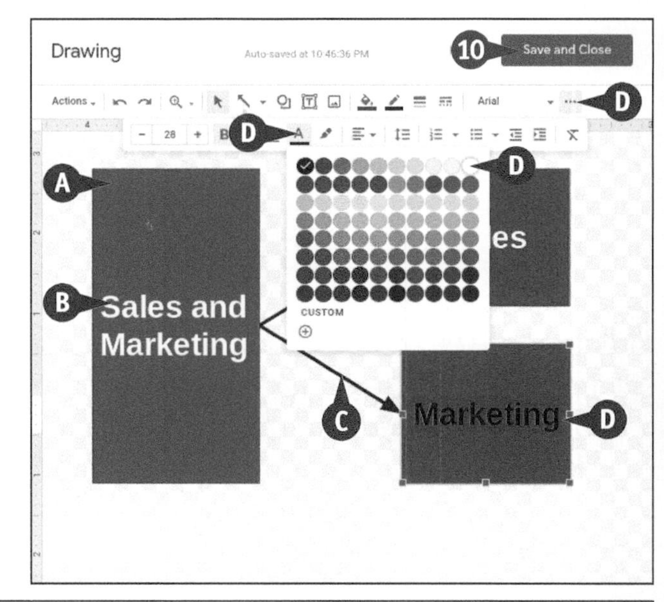

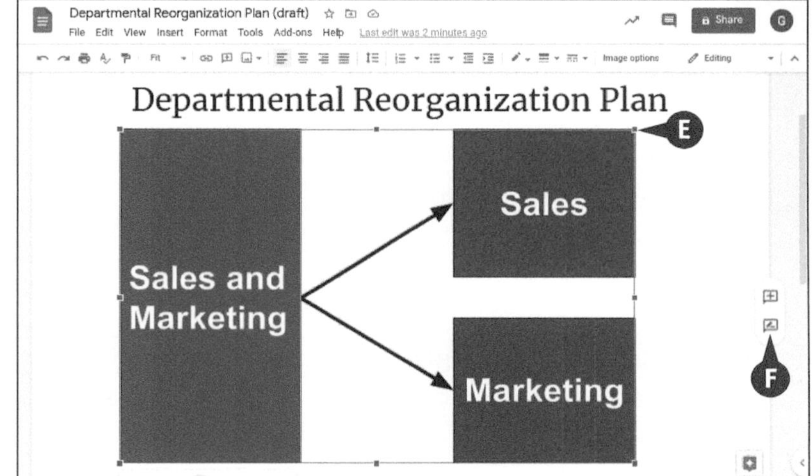

TIP

How do I add an existing drawing to a document?

If you have an existing drawing stored on Google Drive, position the cursor where you want to insert the drawing in the document. Click **Insert** to open the Insert menu, click or highlight **Drawing** to open the Drawing submenu, and then click **From Drive** (▲). In the Insert Drawing dialog box, click the drawing file, and then click **Select**. In the Insert Drawing dialog box that then opens, click **Link to source** (○ changes to ◉) or **Insert unlinked** (○ changes to ◉), as needed. Then click **Insert** to insert the drawing.

Insert a Chart

Google Docs and Google Slides enable you to insert a new chart quickly in a document or a presentation, respectively. You can insert four chart types this way: bar, column, line, or pie. The chart appears in the document or presentation using sample data, which you then edit as needed in Google Sheets. When the chart is ready, you update it in the document or presentation.

For greater flexibility, you can create a chart in Google Sheets, which offers far more chart types. You can then insert the chart in your document or presentation.

Insert a Chart

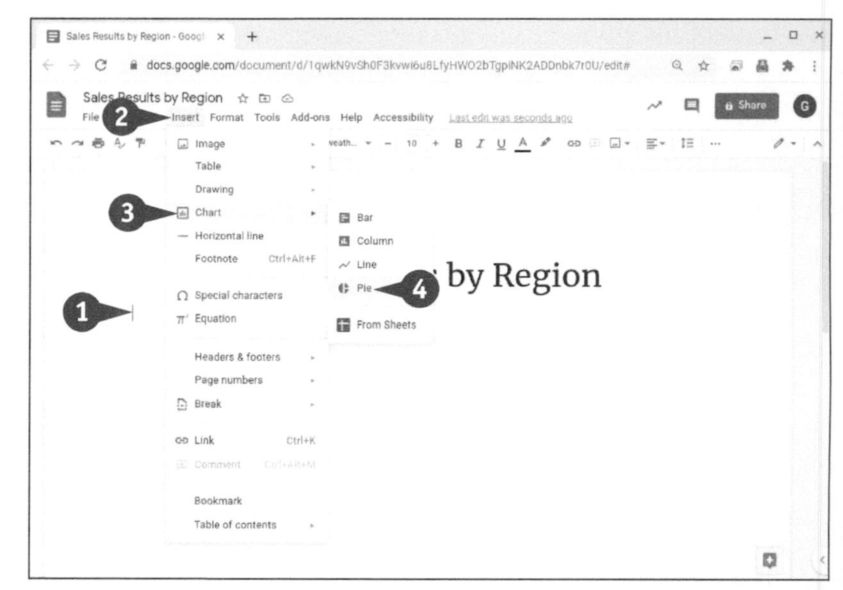

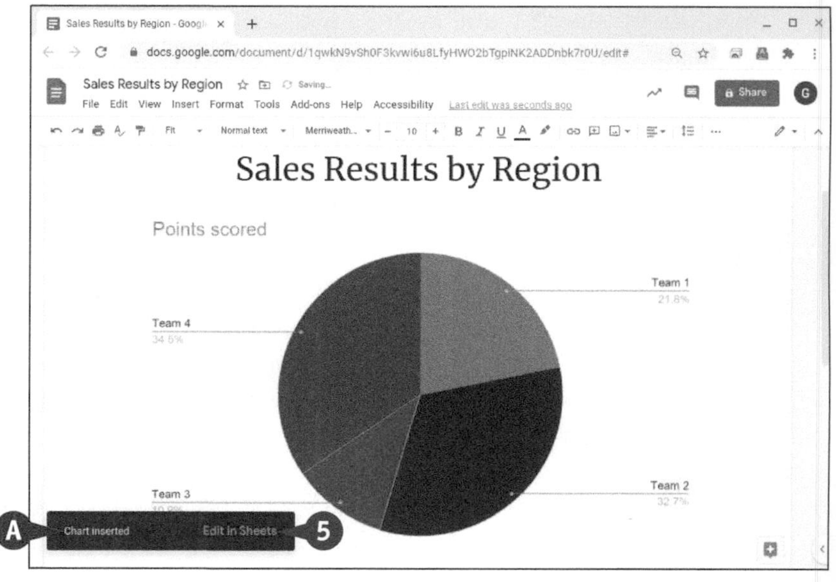

1. In Google Docs, position the cursor where you want the chart to appear.

Note: In Google Slides, select the slide on which you want to place the chart.

2. Click **Insert**.

   The Insert menu opens.

3. Click or highlight **Chart** ( ).

   The Chart submenu opens.

4. Click **Bar** ( ), **Column** ( ), **Line** ( ), or **Pie** ( ), as appropriate. This example uses **Pie** ( ).

   The app inserts a chart of that type containing sample data.

   A. The *Chart inserted* pop-up message appears briefly.

5. Click **Edit in Sheets**.

Note: If you miss the pop-up message, click the chart to select it, click **Linked chart options** ( ) in the upper-right corner, and then click **Open source** ( ) to open the chart in Google Sheets.

The chart opens in Google Sheets in a new browser tab.

6 Edit the chart data, as needed. For example, you would normally change the labels and the values.

B Google Sheet updates the chart automatically to show the changes.

7 Make any other changes needed. For example, you might change the colors: Double-click the color you want to change; then, on the Customize tab in the Chart Editor pane, click **Color** (▼), and then click the color you want.

8 Click **Close** (✕).

The Google Sheets tab closes, returning you to the document containing the chart.

9 Click **Update** (↻).

The chart in the document updates to match the version in Google Sheets.

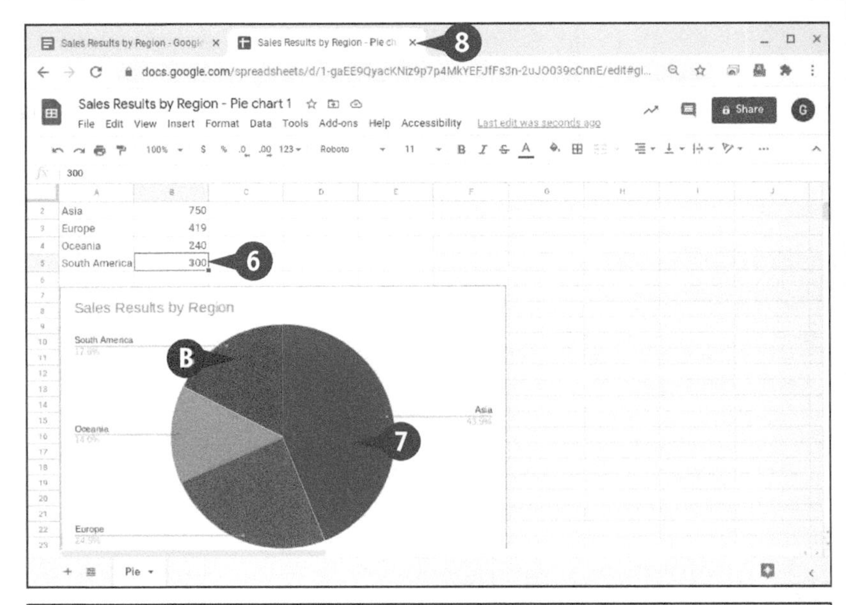

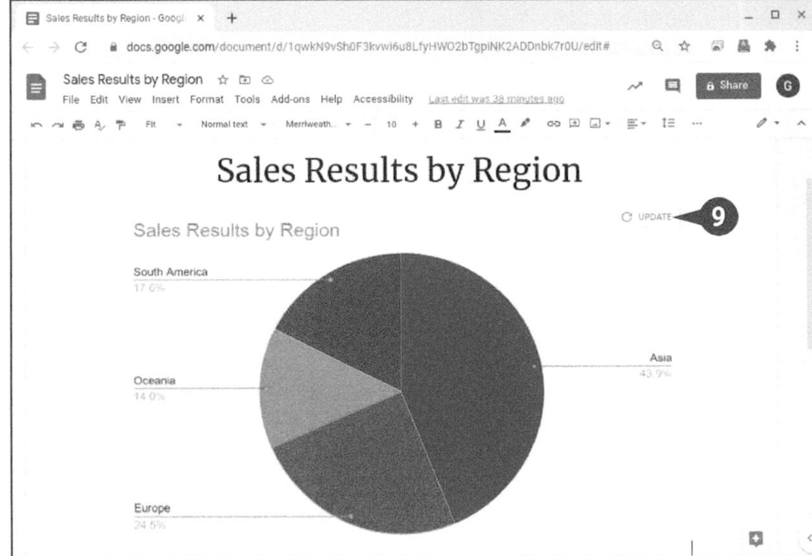

TIP

How do I insert a chart I created in Google Sheets in my Google Docs document?

Position the cursor where you want the chart to appear, click **Insert** to open the Insert menu, click or highlight **Chart** (📊) to open the Chart submenu, and then click **From Sheets** (⊞). In the Insert Chart dialog box that opens, click the spreadsheet, and then click **Select**. In the Import Chart dialog box that then opens, click the appropriate chart. Select **Link to spreadsheet** (☑) if you want to link the chart in the document back to the chart in the spreadsheet for updates. Then click **Import**. The Import Chart dialog box closes, and the chart appears in the document.

Insert a Link

The Google Workspace apps enable you to insert links in your documents, spreadsheets, and presentations. A link can go to any of various locations, such as another Google Workspace file, a file stored on Google Drive, or to a web page.

When you insert a link, you specify the text that the document should display for the link, such as a brief description of what the linked file contains. After inserting a link, you can use it, edit it, or remove it.

Insert a Link

1. In Google Docs, place the cursor where you want the link to appear in the document.

Note: In Google Slides, click in the text placeholder in which you want the link to appear.

Note: In Google Sheets, click the cell in which you want to place the link. Click **Insert** to open the Insert menu, and then click **Insert link** (🔗).

2. Click **Insert**.

   The Insert menu opens.

3. Click **Link** (🔗).

   The Link dialog box opens.

4. Specify the address for the link.

   A. You can click a suggested Google Workspace document to create a link to it quickly.

Note: The Link dialog box contains no Cancel button, but you can close the dialog box without inserting a link by simply clicking in the document outside the dialog box.

   B. You can paste a link into the Link box. For example, right-click, and then click **Paste** on the contextual menu.

Note: You can also type search terms to search for the web page or document you want.

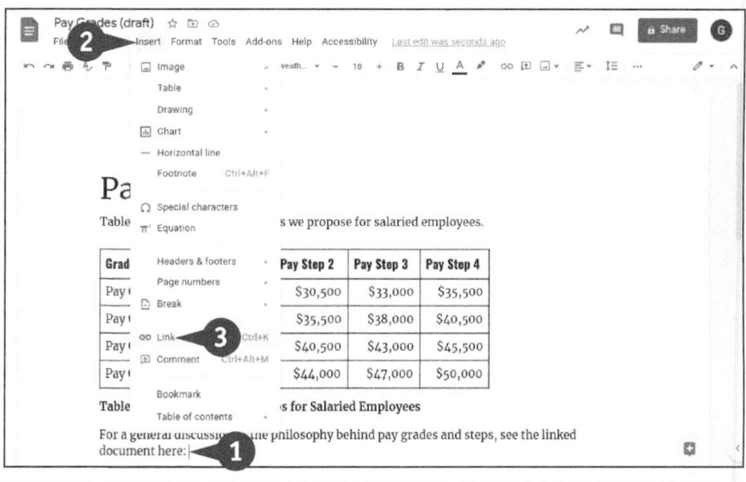

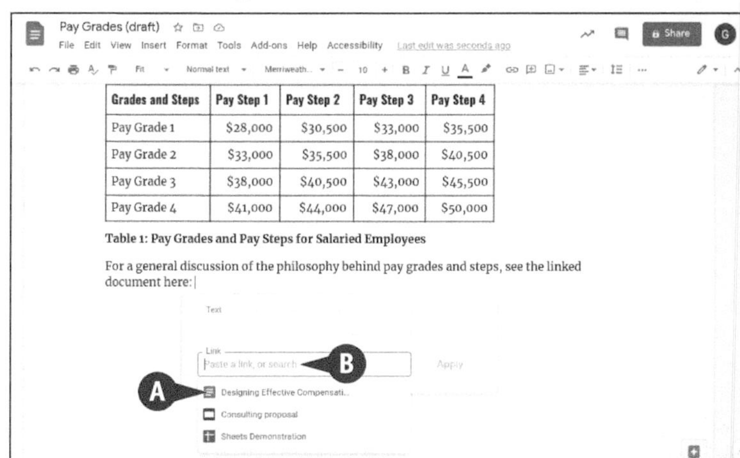

5 In the Text box, type the text you want the document to display for the link.

Note: If you click a suggested Google Workspace document, its name appears in the Text box automatically.

6 Click **Apply**.

Grades and Steps	Pay Step 1	Pay Step 2	Pay Step 3	Pay Step 4
Pay Grade 1	$28,000	$30,500	$33,000	$35,500
Pay Grade 2	$33,000	$35,500	$38,000	$40,500
Pay Grade 3	$38,000	$40,500	$43,000	$45,500
Pay Grade 4	$41,000	$44,000	$47,000	$50,000

Table 1: Pay Grades and Pay Steps for Salaried Employees

For a general discussion of the philosophy behind pay grades and steps, see the linked document here:

Text: Designing Effective Compensation Packages

Apply

The link appears in the document.

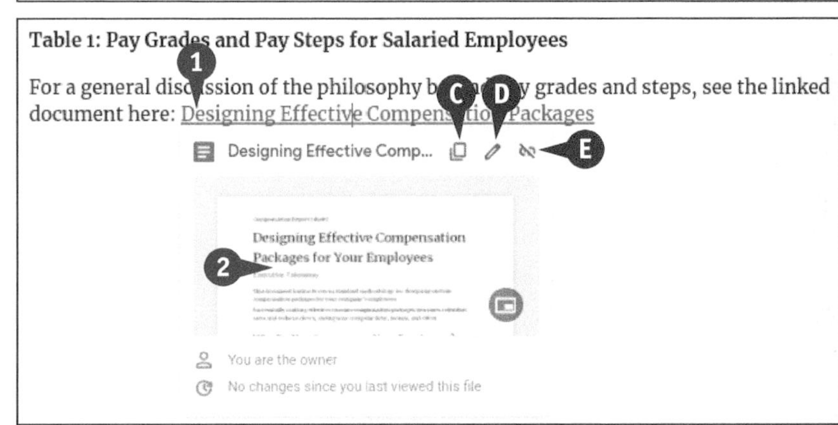

View, Edit, and Use a Link

1 Click the link.

A pop-up window displays a preview of the link.

C You can click **Copy link** (⧉) to copy the link's address.

D You can click **Edit link** (✎) to open the Link dialog box so that you can change the link address or the text.

E You can click **Remove link** (⛓) to remove the link from the document.

2 Click the preview.

The page opens in a new browser tab.

TIP

How do I create a link that starts an email message?

In the Link box in the Link dialog box, type **mailto:** followed by the email address, without a space — for example, **mailto:sales@gargoylewok.space**. To add a subject, type a question mark, **subject=**, and then the text of the subject, again without a space — for example, **mailto:sales@gargoylewok.space?subject=Customer query**. Click **Apply** to close the Link dialog box and enter the link.

Work with Comments

Google Docs, Google Sheets, and Google Slides enable you to add comments to your documents, spreadsheets, and presentations. Rather than appearing inline in the document, spreadsheet, or presentation, a comment appears as a separate entity, but it is attached to the text or object to which it refers.

In Google Docs, a comment is attached to a text selection — a word or multiple words; the text appears highlighted to indicate the comment's presence. In Google Sheets, a comment is attached to a cell and indicated by a triangular yellow marker (◥) in the upper-left corner of that cell.

Work with Comments

Work with Comments in Google Docs

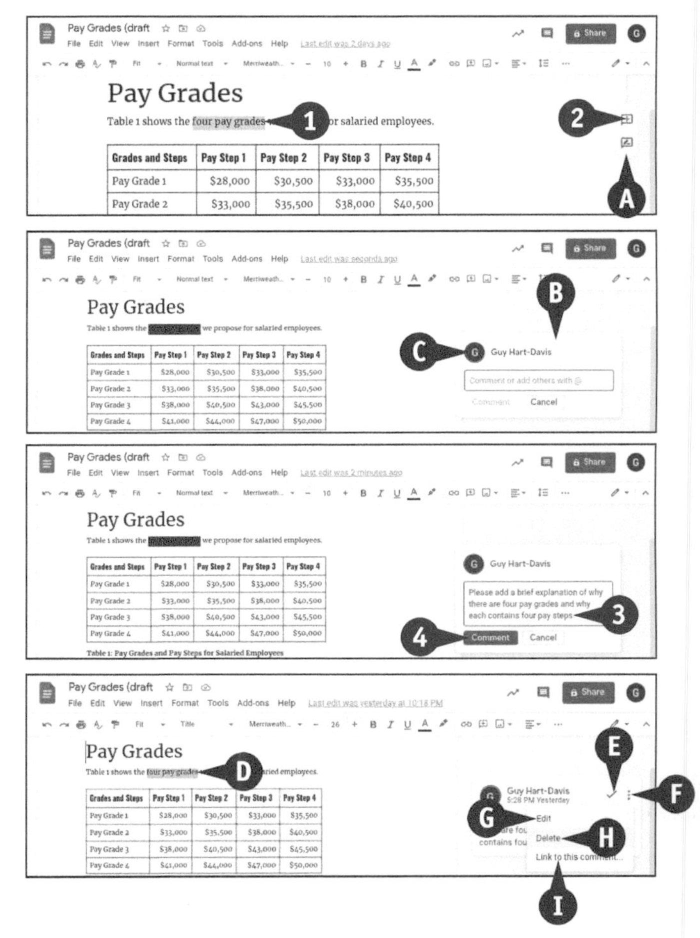

1 Select the text on which you want to comment.

A The Add Comment icon (⊞) and the Suggest Edits icon (✎) appear on the right side of the screen.

2 Click **Add comment** (⊞).

Google Docs shrinks the document to make space for the comment area on the right.

B A comment box opens.

C Your icon and name appear at the top of the comment box.

3 Type the text of your comment.

4 Click **Comment.**

The comment appears in the document.

D The highlight indicates that the text has a comment attached.

E You can click **Mark as resolved and hide discussion** (✓) to mark the comment as resolved and hide its contents.

F For further actions, click **Menu** (⋮).

The menu opens.

G You can click **Edit** to edit the comment.

H You can click **Delete** to delete the comment.

I You can click **Link to this comment** to create a link to the comment.

Insert a Comment in Google Sheets

1. Click the cell to which you want to attach the comment.

   The cell becomes selected.

2. Click **Insert**.

   The Insert menu opens.

3. Click **Comment** (⊞).

   J Google Sheets applies highlighting to the cell to indicate a comment is attached.

   A comment box opens.

4. Type the text of your comment.
5. Click **Comment**.

   The comment box closes.

   K A comment marker (◥) appears in the upper-right corner of the cell.

6. Move the cursor over the cell.

   The comment appears in a pop-up window.

   L You can click **Mark as resolved and hide discussion** (✓) to mark the comment as resolved and hide its contents.

7. To reply to the comment, click the comment.

   The cell becomes selected and highlighted.

8. Click the Reply box and type your reply.
9. Click **Reply**.

TIP

How do I direct a comment to one of my colleagues?

Open the comment window as usual; for example, click **Insert** to open the Insert menu, and then click **Comment** (⊞). Click in the text box, press + to display the pop-up list of your colleagues, and then click the appropriate person. Select **Assign to** (☑), which shows the colleague's name, if you want to assign responsibility for the comment to the colleague. Type the comment, and then click **Comment.** The app adds your colleague to the discussion and sends them an email telling them that the comment awaits their review.

continued ▶

In Google Slides, you can attach a comment to a text selection, which appears highlighted to indicate the comment; to an object, such as a shape or text box, which likewise appears highlighted; or to a slide, in which case no highlight appears. The Slides pane shows a comment marker (such as or) to the left of any slide that contains comments.

To help you deal with comments quickly and completely, each app provides the Comment History pane. Here, you can review each comment, edit it, reply to it, resolve it, link to it, or simply delete it.

Work with Comments (continued)

Insert a Comment in Google Slides

1. Select the text or object on which you want to comment.

Note: To comment on a slide as a whole, simply select that slide.

2. Click **Insert**.

   The Insert menu opens.

3. Click **Comment** ().

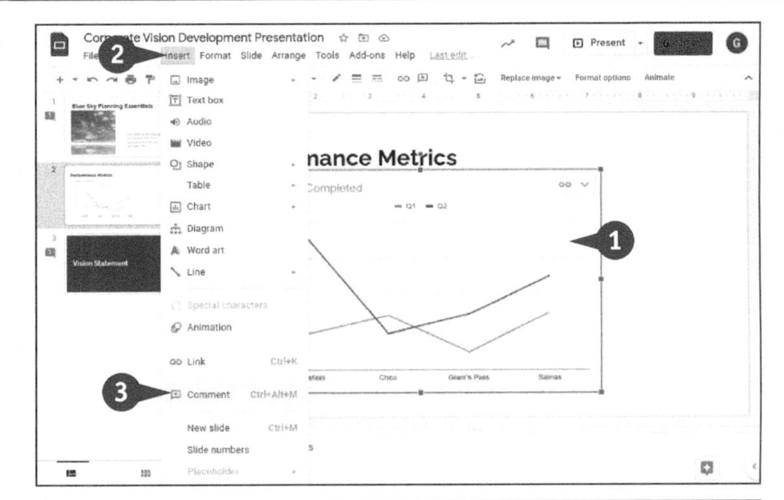

   A comment box opens.

Ⓜ A comment icon () appears to the left of the slide in the Slides pane.

4. Type the text of the comment.

5. Click **Comment.**

   The comment appears in the presentation.

Ⓝ You can click **Mark as resolved and hide discussion** (✓) to mark the comment as resolved and hide its contents.

Ⓞ You can click **Menu** (⋮) to edit the comment, delete it, or link to it.

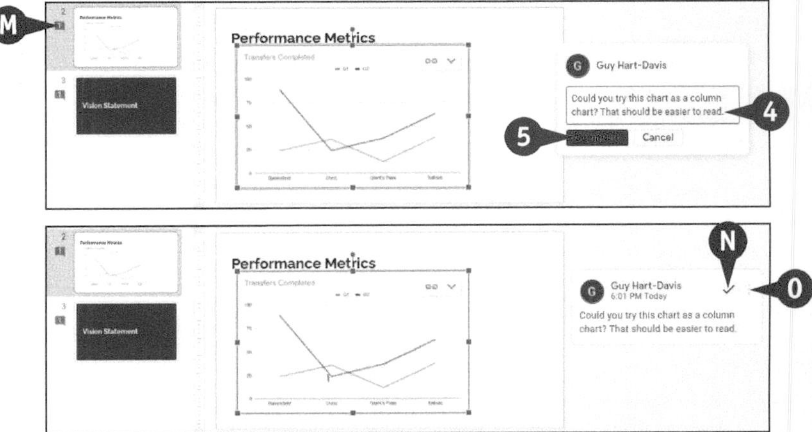

Open Comment History and Review Comments

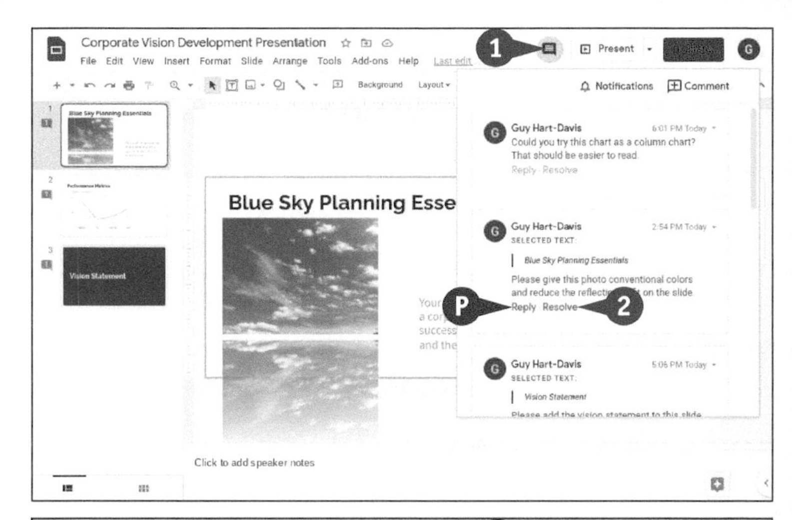

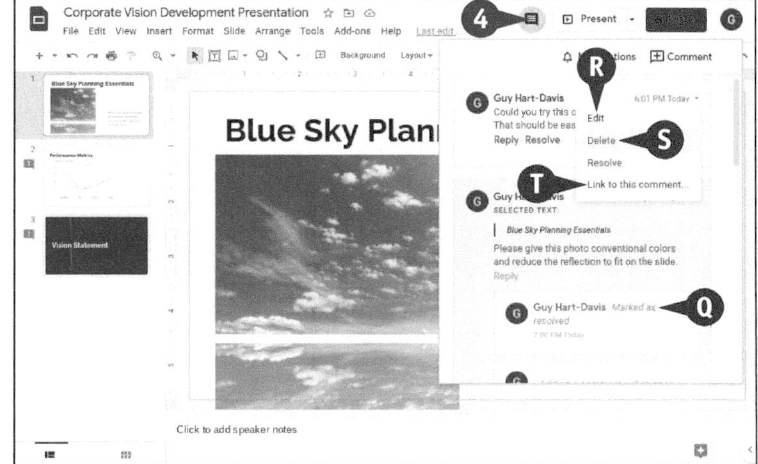

1. Click **Comment history** (💬).

Note: From the keyboard, you can press Ctrl + Alt + Shift + A to open the Comment History pane. On the Mac, press ⌘ + Option + Shift + A.

The Comment History pane opens.

P You can click **Reply** to begin replying to a comment.

2. To mark a comment as resolved, click **Resolve**.

Q The app marks the comment as resolved.

3. To take other actions, click **Menu** (⋮).

The menu opens.

R You can click **Edit** to edit the comment.

S You can click **Delete** to delete the comment.

T You can click **Link to this comment** to create a link to this comment.

4. When you finish working your way through the comments in the file, click **Comment History** (💬).

The Comment History pane closes.

TIP

What does the Notifications button at the top of the Comment History pane do?

The Notifications button at the top of the Comment History pane enables you to specify whose comments on this document should send email notifications. Click **Notifications** (🔔) to display the Notifications pop-up menu. Click **All** to have all users' comments send notifications, click **Only yours** to allow only your comments to send notifications, or click **None** to turn off email notifications for this document.

Resize, Reposition, and Format an Object

After inserting an object, such as a shape or a photo, in a Google Workspace document, you can resize the object, reposition it, and format it to look the way you want. You can choose between resizing or repositioning an object quickly using the mouse and using the Options pane to select precise settings for the size and position.

The formatting options available for an object depend on the object's type — for example, an image has settings that a shape or text box does not. This section concentrates on the core group of settings that most objects share.

Resize, Reposition, and Format an Object

Resize and Reposition an Object Using the Mouse

A In this example, the drawing object breaks the first body paragraph in a way that is widely considered poor placement.

1 Click the object to select it.

B A blue outline and sizing handles (■) appear around the object.

C The object formatting bar appears below the object.

2 Drag a handle to change the object's size.

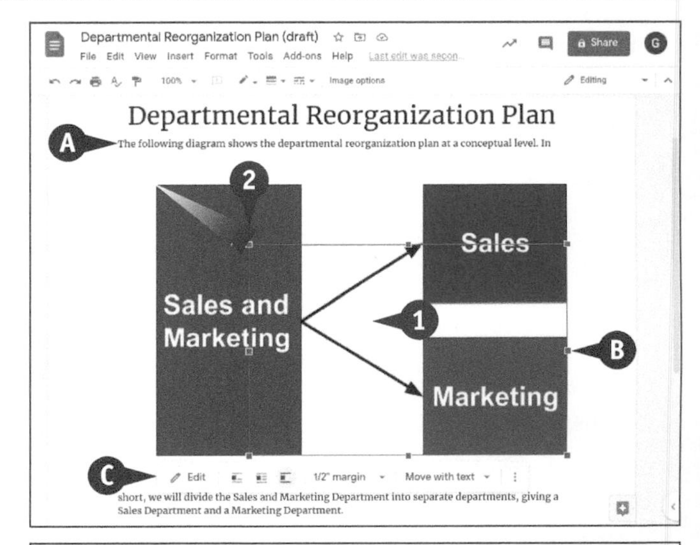

The object appears at its new size.

3 Drag the object to where you want it to appear.

D Red alignment guides appear when you drag the object near to an existing boundary to which the object will snap. In this case, the vertical red line indicates the text margin.

Note: You can hold down Alt to suppress the boundary checks and override snapping.

4 The object appears in its new position.

E For a drawing, you can adjust the margin around it by clicking **Drawing margin** (▾), and then clicking the appropriate value, such as **1/2"**.

Resize, Reposition, and Format an Object Using the Format Options Pane

1 Right-click the object.

The contextual menu opens.

2 Click the Options item. The item's name varies depending on the object and the app. In this example, you would click **Format options** (🖵).

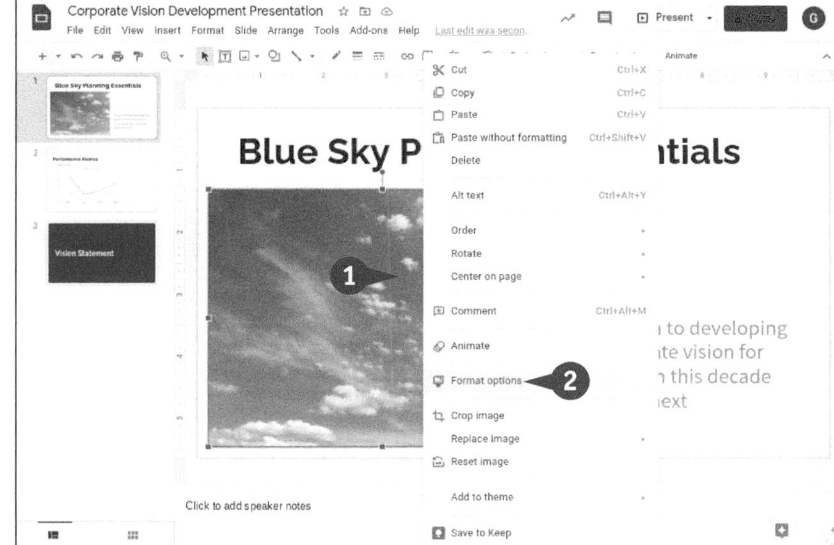

TIP

Why can I not move an object in a Google Docs document?

Most likely, the object is positioned "in line" with the text, which makes it act like a text character. Click the object to select it, verify that the In Line icon (▭) is selected, and then click **Wrap text** (▭) or **Break text** (▭) to move the object out of line. You can then drag the object to reposition it.

continued ►

Resize, Reposition, and Format an Object (continued)

The full name of the Options pane for formatting an object depends on the object type. For example, the pane for adjusting an image is the Format Options pane.

The Options pane contains multiple sections that you can expand and collapse. Most objects include the Size & Rotation section, the Position section, the Drop Shadow section, and the Reflection section. Other sections appear only for some objects. For example, the Recolor section and the Adjustments section appear for graphical objects but not for text boxes, whereas the Text Fitting section appears for text boxes but not for images.

Resize, Reposition, and Format an Object (continued)

The Options pane appears on the right side of the window. In this example, it is the Format Options pane.

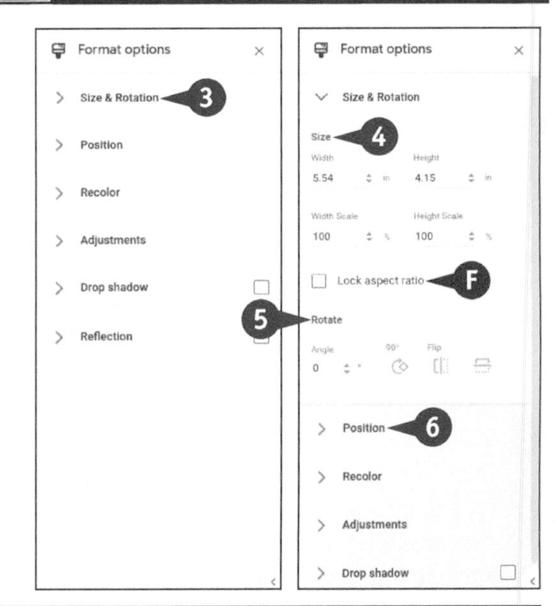

3 Click **Size & Rotation** (>).

Note: You can click either **Expand** (>) or the text of the section heading.

The Size & Rotation section expands.

4 Use the **Size** controls to adjust the object's size.

F You can select **Lock aspect ratio** (☑) to link the height and width adjustments proportionally.

5 Use the **Rotate** controls to rotate the object or flip it either horizontally or vertically.

6 Click **Position** (>).

The Position area expands.

7 Click **From** (▾), and then click **Top left** or **Center** to specify the starting position.

8 Click **X** and set the horizontal offset from the starting position.

9 Click **Y** and set the vertical offset from the starting position.

10 Click **Drop shadow** (>).

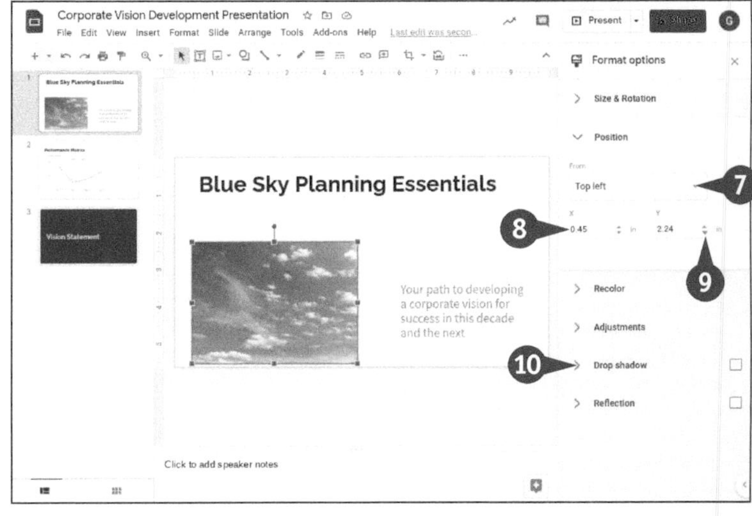

The Drop Shadow section expands.

The Drop Shadow check box becomes selected (☐ changes to ☑).

The Drop Shadow settings become active.

11 Click **Color** (▾), and then click the color for the drop shadow.

12 Drag the **Transparency** slider, **Angle** slider, **Distance** slider, and **Blur Radius** slider to create the drop-shadow effect you want.

Note: Click **Drop shadow** (☑ changes to ☐) to turn off the drop shadow effect temporarily.

13 Click **Reflection** (>).

The Reflection section expands.

The Reflection check box becomes selected (☐ changes to ☑).

The Reflection settings become active.

14 Drag the **Transparency** slider to adjust the reflection's transparency.

15 Drag the **Distance** slider to adjust the reflection's distance from the object.

16 Drag the **Size** slider to adjust the reflection's size.

17 Click **Close** (×).

The Options pane closes.

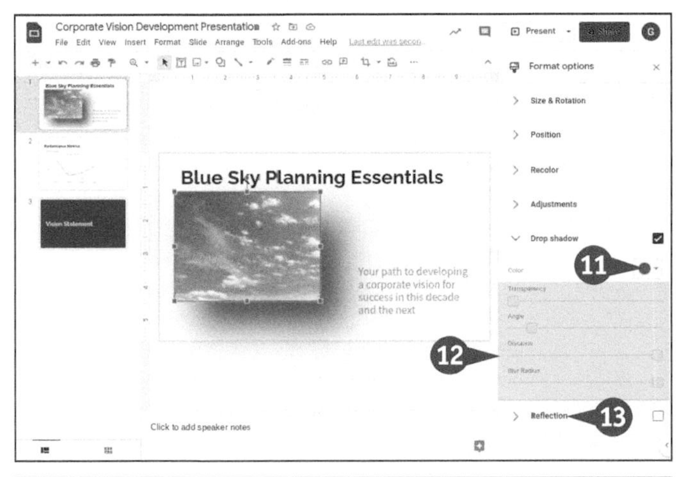

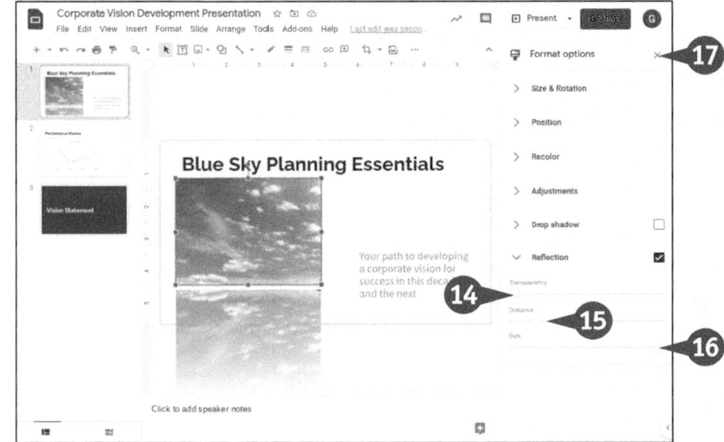

TIP

What do the Recolor and Adjustments controls do?

In the Recolor section of the Format Options pane, click **Recolor** (▾) to open the pop-up menu, and then click the recolor preset you want to apply. There are eight Light presets, Light 1 through Light 8; seven Dark presets, Dark 1 through Dark 7; and a single Sepia preset.

The Adjustments section of the Format Options pane contains three sliders and the Reset button. Drag the **Transparency** slider to adjust the transparency, from no transparency on the left to total transparency on the right. Drag the **Brightness** slider to increase or decrease the brightness. Drag the **Contrast** slider to adjust the contrast. Click **Reset** to restore the original settings.

CHAPTER 5

Working in Google Docs

In this chapter, you become productive in Google Docs, the word processing app in Google Workspace. You start by setting preferences and creating text substitutions; move on to setting page size and margins; and then learn how to enter text, make the most of formatting with styles, and navigate using the document outline. You also learn to insert page numbers; create either simple or complex headers and footers; and switch among Editing Mode, Suggesting Mode, and Viewing Mode.

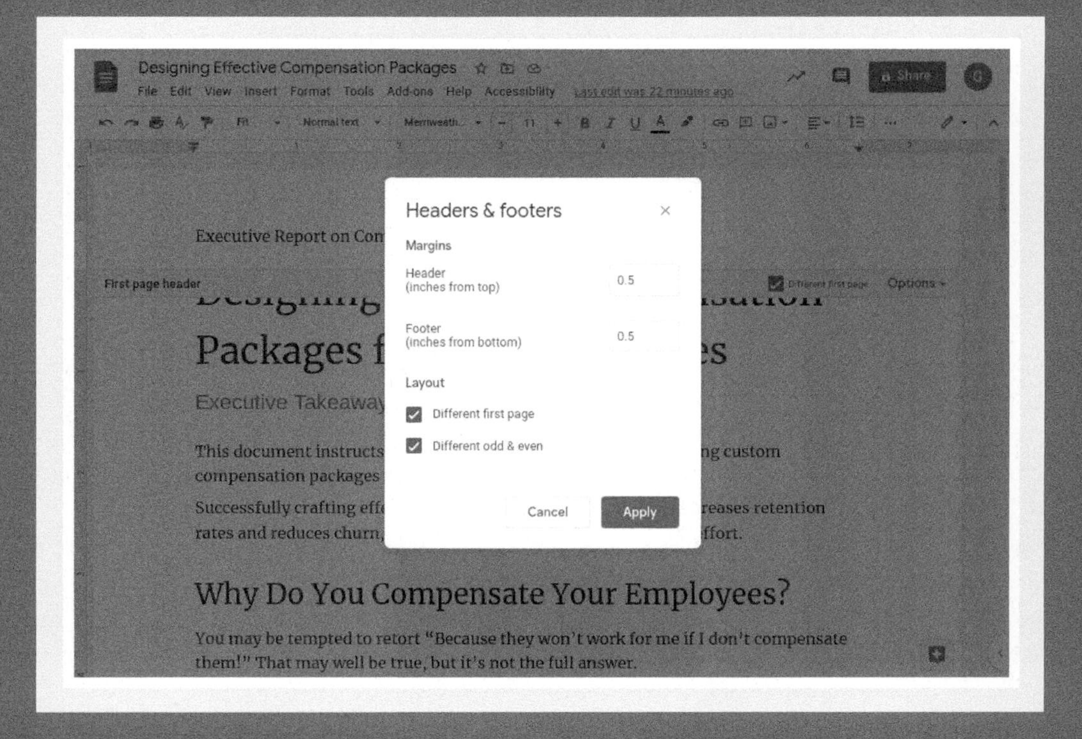

Set Preferences for Google Docs

Before you use Google Docs extensively, open the Preferences dialog box and set preferences on the General tab and the Suggestions tab.

On the General tab, you can enable or disable automatic features, such as automatic capitalization of the first letter in new sentences and paragraphs; use of smart quotes instead of straight quotes; and Smart Compose, which suggests the next word or phrase for you. On the Substitutions tab, you can customize the list of terms for which the app replaces a predefined shortcut or mistake, such as replacing *abbout* with *about*. Substitutions apply to all Google Workspace apps.

Set Preferences for Google Docs

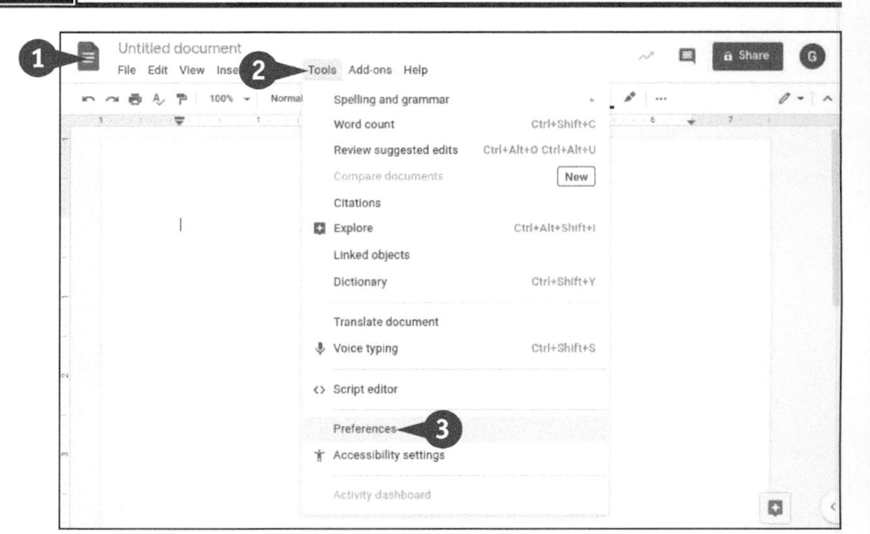

1. Open a Google Docs document.

   You can either open an existing document or create a new Google Docs document, as in the example screen.

2. Click **Tools**.

   The Tools menu opens.

3. Click **Preferences**.

   The Preferences dialog box opens, with the General tab selected.

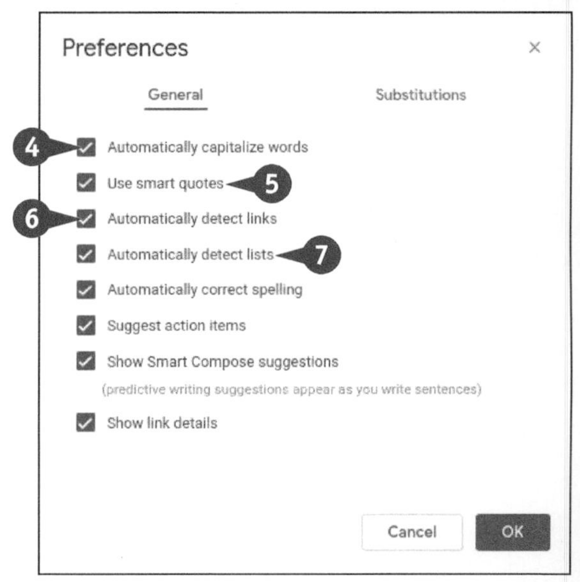

4. Select (☑) **Automatically capitalize words** if you want Google Docs to automatically capitalize the first letter of a new sentence, new line, new paragraph, or table cell.

5. Select **Use smart quotes** (☑) to have Google Docs automatically convert straight quotes to smart quotes.

6. Select **Automatically detect links** (☑) to have Google Docs identify links and apply link formatting.

7. Select **Automatically detect lists** (☑) to have Google Docs identify lists as you type.

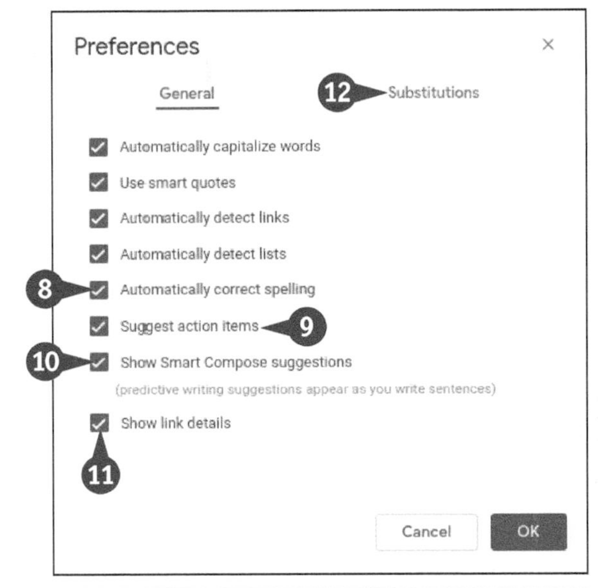

8 Select **Automatically correct spelling** (☑) to have Google Docs substitute correct spellings for apparently misspelled words.

9 Select **Suggest action items** (☑) to have Google Docs suggest action items from your input.

10 Select **Show Smart Compose suggestions** (☑) to have Google Docs suggest the next word or phrase for what you are typing. See the second tip.

11 Select **Show link details** (☑) to have Google Docs display a preview of the linked page when you click a link.

12 Click **Substitutions**.

The Substitutions tab appears.

13 Select **Automatic substitution** (☑) if you want Google Docs to replace predefined terms with their replacement text.

14 To deactivate a term, click it (☑ changes to ☐).

15 To delete a term, click **Delete** (✖).

16 To add a term, click the top box in the Replace column and type the text you want to replace.

17 Click the top box in the With column.

The Substitutions tab adds another row.

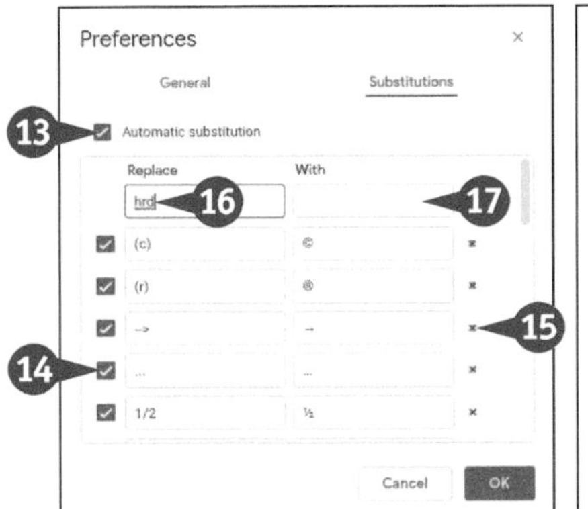

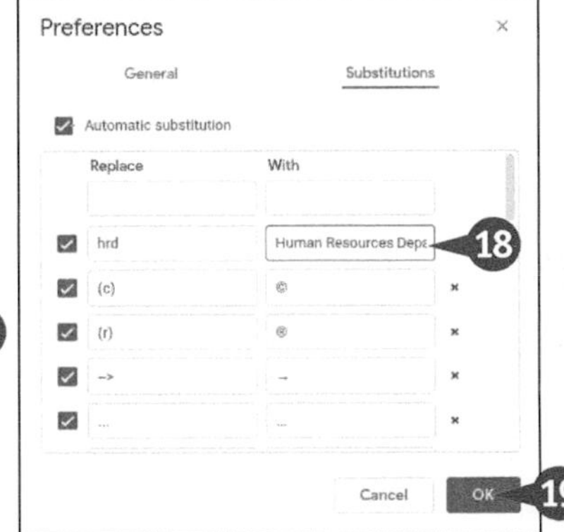

18 Type the replacement text.

19 When you finish choosing preferences, click **OK**.

The Preferences dialog box closes.

TIPS

How does Google Docs automatically detect lists?

Google Docs uses various algorithms to determine when you are starting a list. For example, if you type a number and a period followed by a space, Google Docs decides you are starting a numbered list. Similarly, if you type an asterisk followed by a tab or space, or a hyphen followed by a tab or space, Google Docs automatically creates a bulleted list for you.

What does Smart Compose do?

Smart Compose interprets what you type in real time and suggests words or phrases you might want to use next. For example, if you type *Your next ap*, Smart Compose may suggest *appointment*; press Tab to accept the suggestion.

Set Page Size and Margins

Google Docs enables you to use different page sizes for your documents, such as Letter size or Legal size. You can also choose the orientation of the page — either portrait, which is taller than it is wide, or landscape, which is wider than it is tall.

To make a document look the way you want, you can also change the settings for the top margin, bottom margin, left margin, and right margin.

Set Page Size and Margins

1. Open the document whose page size and margins you want to set.
2. Click **File**.

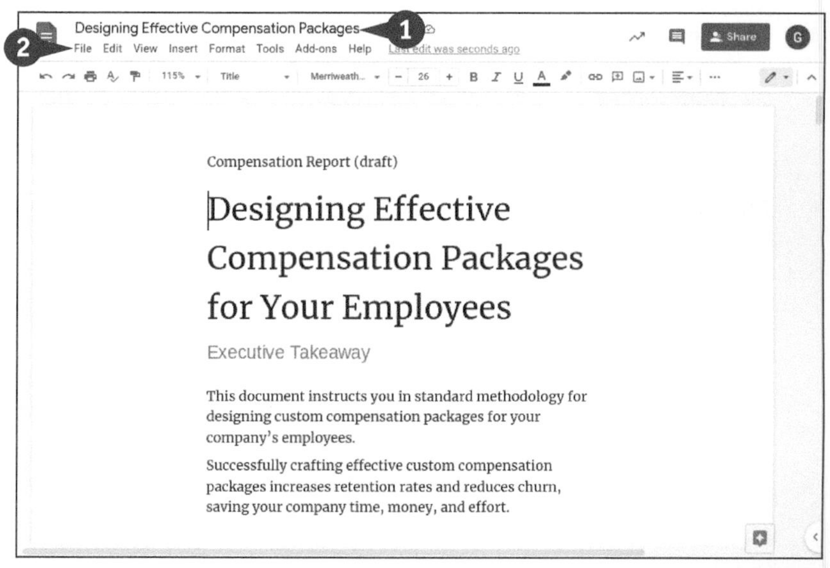

The File menu opens.

3. Click **Page setup**.

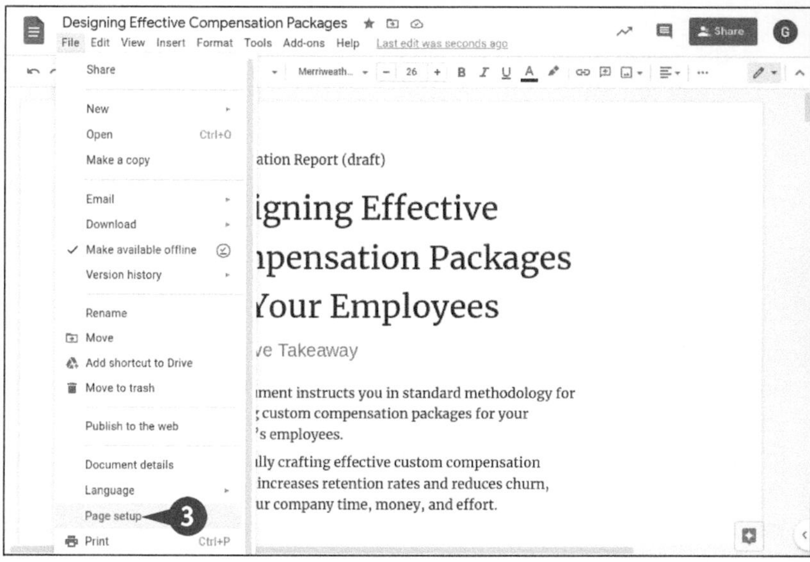

The Page Setup dialog box opens.

4. In the Orientation area, click **Portrait** (○ changes to ◉) or **Landscape** (○ changes to ◉) to set the orientation.

5. Click **Paper size** (▾), and then click the appropriate size, such as **Letter (8.5" x 11")** or **Legal (8.5" x 14")**.

6. Optionally, click **Page color** (▾), and then click the color.

7. In the Margins column, click **Top**, **Bottom**, **Left**, and **Right**, and type the appropriate margin measurements.

8. Click **OK**.

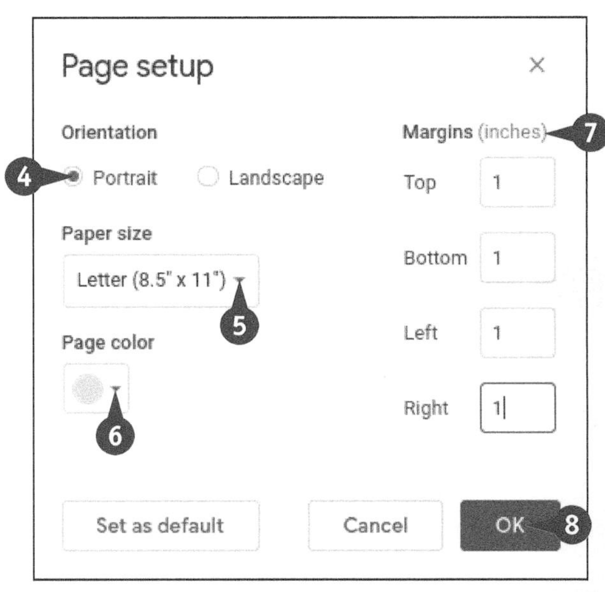

The Page Setup dialog box closes.

The changes appear in the document.

A The page color has been changed.

B The margins are narrower.

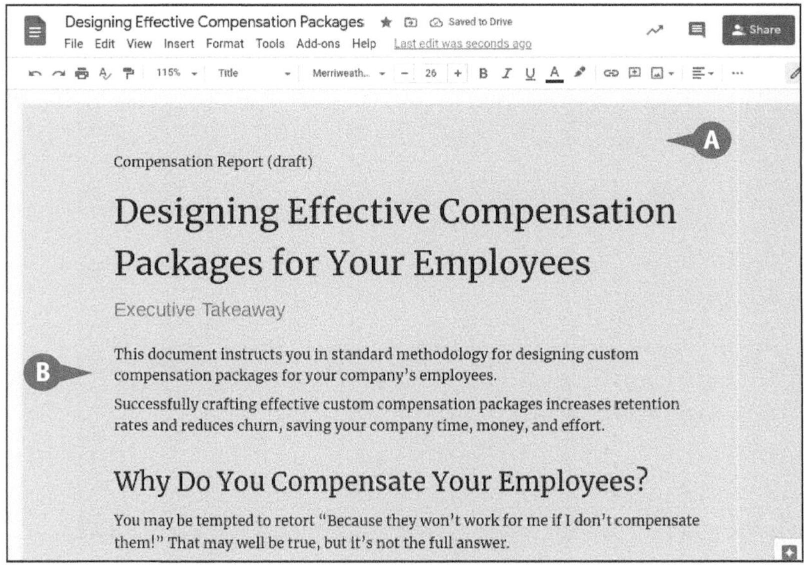

TIPS

How do I change the default page settings for my Google Docs documents?

In the Page Setup dialog box, click **Set as default** after setting the orientation, page size, page color, and margins you want for new documents you create that are not based on another template.

How can I get exactly the color I want for the page?

If none of the 80 preset colors on the Page Color pop-up menu meets your needs, click **Add custom color** (⊕) to display the Color Picker dialog box. Drag the **Hue** slider to select the hue you want, then drag the selection circle around the gradient rectangle to select the exact color. Click **OK**. The color then appears in the Custom list on the Page Color pop-up menu.

Enter Text in a Document

Google Docs enables you to insert text in your documents in three main ways. First, you can simply type text into a document. Second, you can dictate text using the Voice Typing feature, which can be impressively fast and accurate, especially if you use a high-quality microphone and speak clearly. Third, you can copy existing text from another file and paste it into a document. When you paste in text, you can choose between retaining any formatting on the text and inserting only the text's characters without formatting.

Enter Text in a Document

Type Text

1. Type the text that you want to appear in your document.

   A The text appears to the left of the cursor point as you type.

   B As the insertion point reaches the end of the line, Google Docs automatically starts a new one.

   Press Enter or Return only to start a new paragraph.

   C If the Smart Compose feature suggests a completion or a word or phrase, you can press Tab to accept it.

   In this example, typing *Nove* has caused Smart Compose to suggest *November*. The suggested *mber* appears in lighter font because it has not yet been accepted.

Note: To ignore a Smart Compose suggestion, simply keep typing.

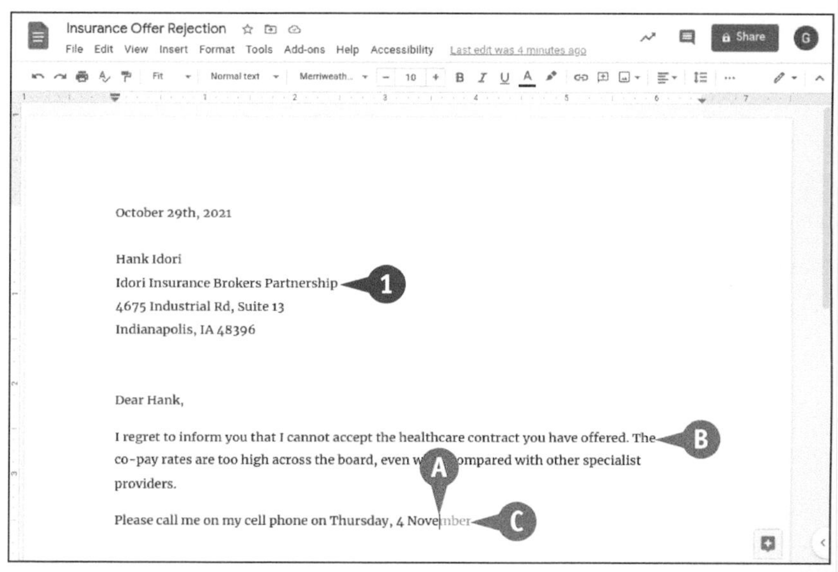

Dictate Text Using Voice Typing

1. Click **Tools**.

   The Tools menu opens.

2. Click **Voice typing** (🎙).

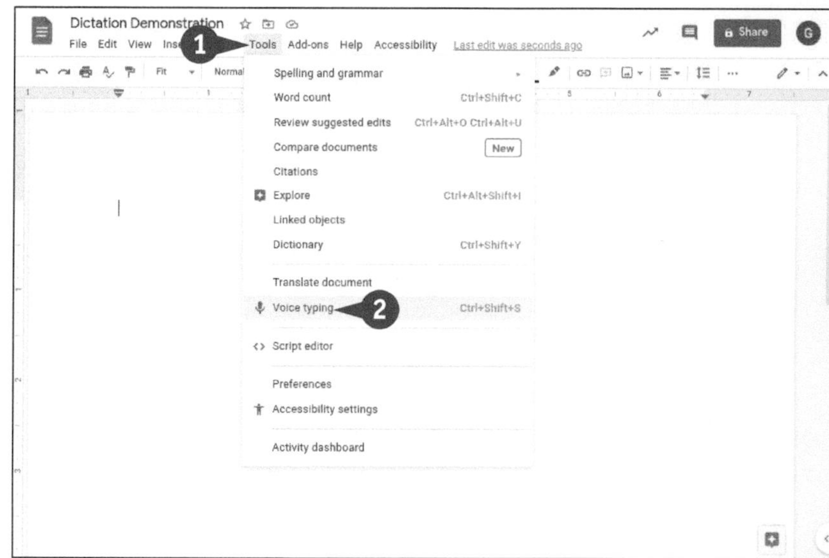

The Voice Typing icon appears.

3. Click **Voice Typing** (🎙).

   The Voice Typing feature becomes active and waits for input (🎙 changes to 🎙).

4. Start dictating text.

   D The Voice Typing feature starts processing input (🎙 changes to 🎙).

   Concentric circles appear around the Voice Typing icon to indicate activity.

   E Voice Typing enters the text in the document.

   F The Processing histogram indicates that Voice Typing is still interpreting input.

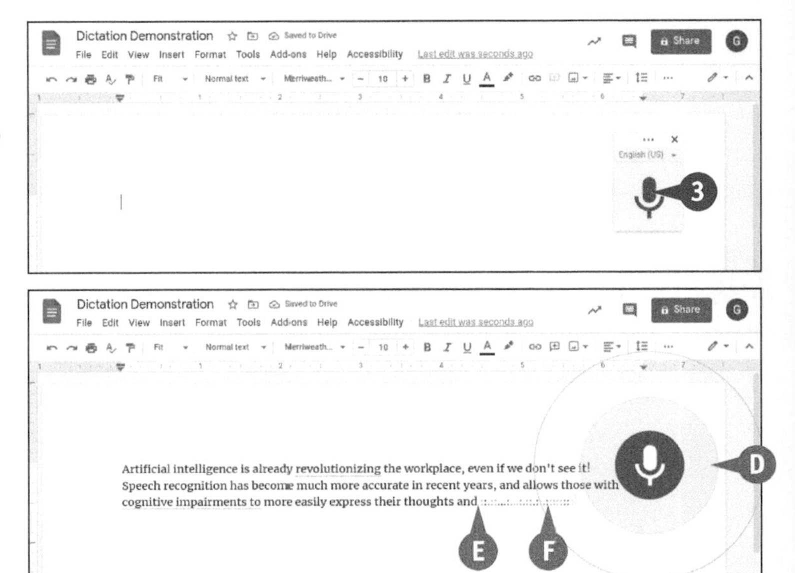

Paste Text with or Without Formatting

1. After copying text from another document, click **Edit**.

   The Edit menu opens.

   G You can click **Paste** (📋) to paste the text, including any formatting it has.

   H You can click **Paste without formatting** (📋) to paste only the text, removing any formatting.

   I This example shows text pasted with formatting.

   J This example shows the same text pasted without formatting.

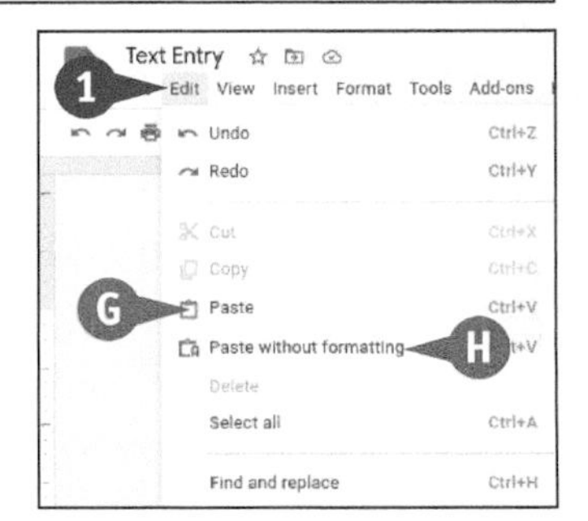

Understanding the Standard Elements of a Compensation Package

If asked, most employees would point to their salary as the key component of their compensation package. But while the salary is salient and essential, the less-considered components of a compensation package can be at least as important in the long run.

Understanding the Standard Elements of a Compensation Package

If asked, most employees would point to their salary as the key component of their compensation package. But while the salary is salient and essential, the less-considered components of a compensation package can be at least as important in the long run.

TIP

How can I get greater accuracy from Voice Typing?

First, use a dedicated microphone rather than one built into your computer. A headset microphone is usually the easiest choice, but you might prefer a lapel microphone or a microphone on a stand that you can position close to your mouth. Second, whichever type of microphone you choose, it is worth investing in a quality one rather than struggling with a basic model. Third, speak naturally — as you would to another person over the phone — but enunciate fully. Fourth, reduce extraneous noise as far as possible while dictating.

Switch Among Editing, Suggesting, and Viewing Modes

Google Docs provides three main modes for working with documents: Editing Mode, Suggesting Mode, and Viewing Mode. In Editing Mode, the document is open for you to make changes directly to the text, as usual. In Suggesting Mode, you can still make changes to the text, but they appear with change-tracking and change balloons. In Viewing Mode, you can only view the document or print it — unless you switch to Editing Mode or Suggesting Mode.

Switch Among Editing, Suggesting, and Viewing Modes

1. Open the document with which you want to work.

   Normally, the document opens in Editing Mode.

A. The toolbar appears.

B. The horizontal ruler and vertical ruler appear unless you have chosen to hide them.

C. The side panel appears.

D. The Explore button ( ) appears.

E. You can select text or objects in the document and manipulate them directly. For example, you can delete a word by selecting it and then pressing Del or Backspace.

2. Click **View**.

   The View menu opens.

3. Click or highlight **Mode**.

   The Mode submenu opens.

4. Click **Viewing** ( ).

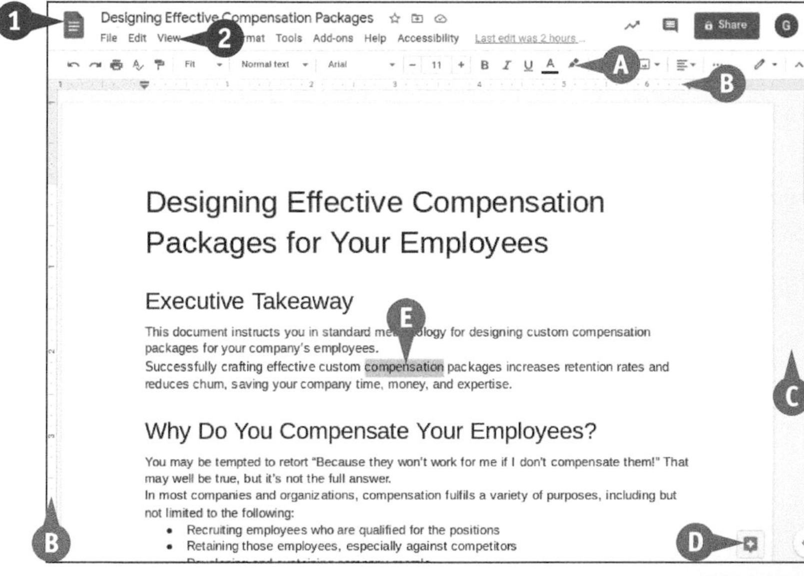

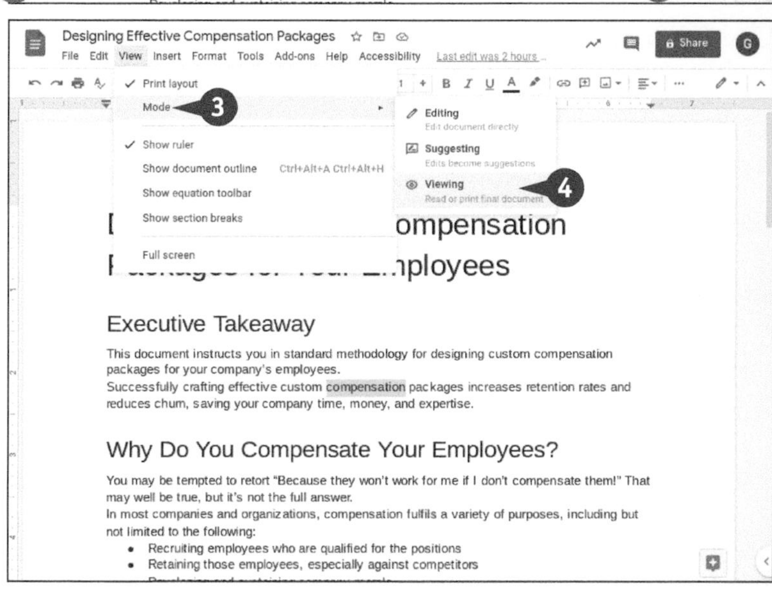

Google Docs switches the document to Viewing Mode.

F The *You're viewing* pop-up appears for a few seconds.

G A streamlined version of the menu bar appears.

The toolbar hides, as do the horizontal ruler and the vertical ruler.

H The side panel appears at a narrower width.

5 Click **Viewing mode** ( ).

The Viewing Mode pop-up menu opens.

6 Click **Suggesting** ( ).

Google Docs switches the document to Suggesting Mode.

I The *You're suggesting* pop-up appears for a few seconds.

J When you make a change, Google Docs applies change tracking to it.

K The change box shows the specifics of the change.

L You can click **Accept suggestion** ( ) to accept a suggestion or click **Reject suggestion** ( ) to reject it.

Note: To change back to Editing Mode, click **View**, click or highlight **Mode**, and then click **Editing**.

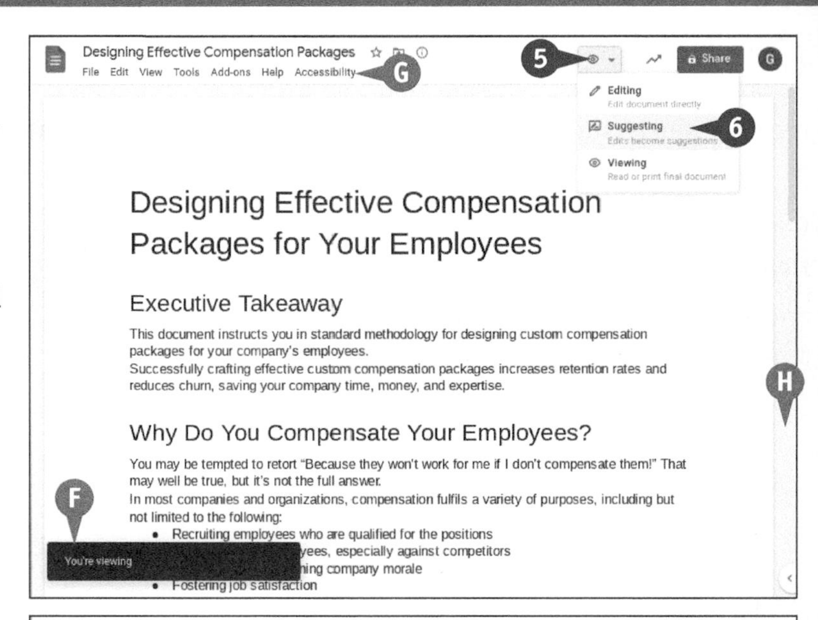

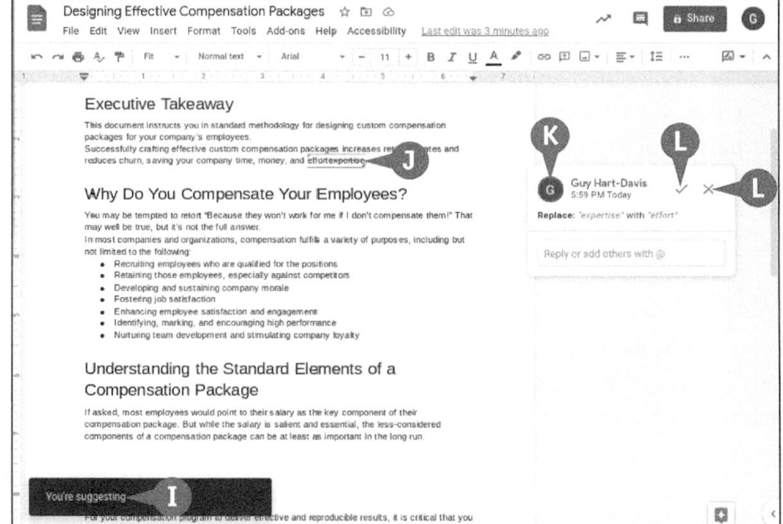

TIP

How do I set up a document so that other people can only suggest changes, not edit it directly?

To limit another person to suggesting changes, you share the document with them and specify the Commenter role. Open the document, and then click **Share** at the right end of the menu bar to open the Share with People and Groups dialog box. Click **Add people and groups**, start typing the person's Google address, and then click the appropriate match. In the upper-right corner of the dialog box, click , and then click **Commenter** in the pop-up menu; you can also click **Viewer** to restrict the person to viewing. Type any message needed in the Message box, and then click **Send**.

Format a Document with Styles

Google Docs provides built-in styles for formatting documents swiftly and consistently. A *style* is a collection of formatting that you can apply to a paragraph in a single click. The style includes the font name, such as Arial; font size, such as 12-point; font color, such as black; font weight, such as regular or bold; paragraph alignment, such as left; and line spacing, such as single.

Google Docs includes built-in styles for Title, Subtitle, Normal Text, and six levels of headings, from Heading 1 at the top level to Heading 6 at the bottom level.

Format a Document with Styles

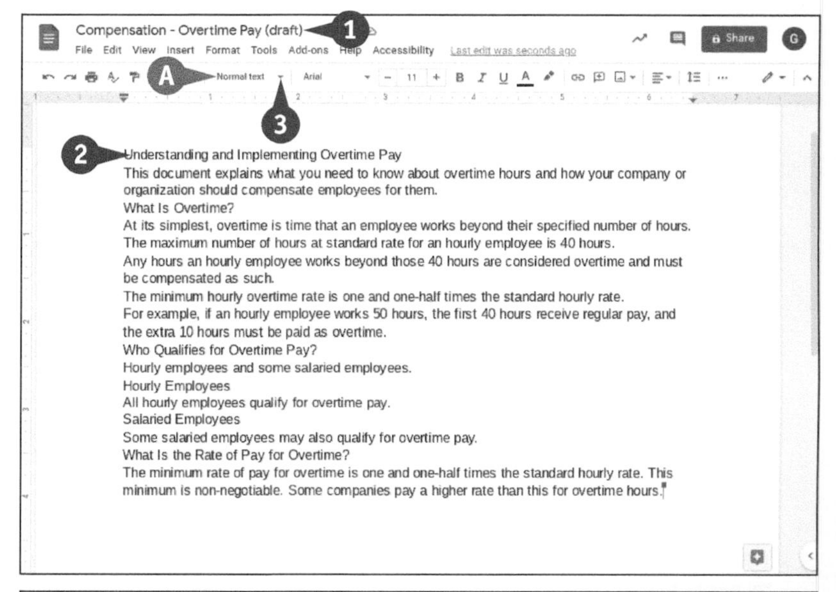

1. Open the document you want to format.
2. Click in the paragraph to which you want to apply a style.

   If you want to apply the same style to multiple contiguous paragraphs, select those paragraphs.

   A. The Styles pop-up menu shows the style currently applied to the paragraph.
3. Click **Styles** (▾).

   The Styles pop-up menu opens.
4. Click the style you want to apply.

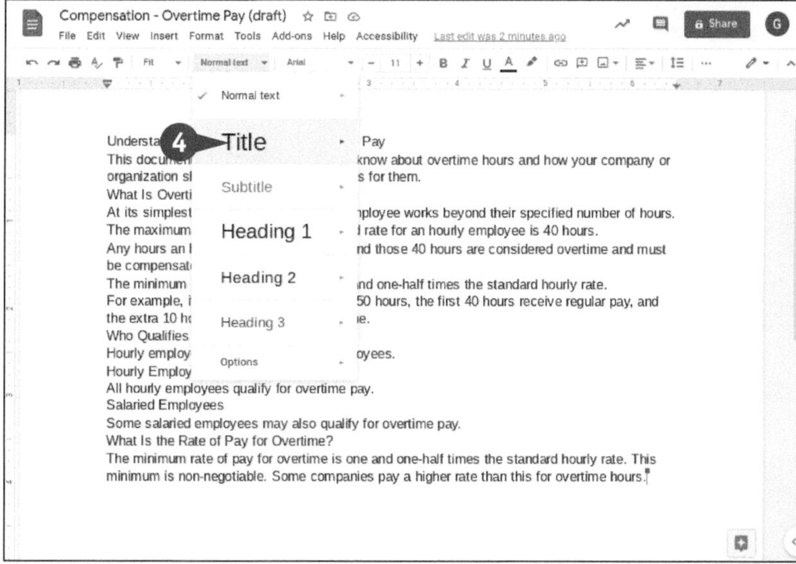

Note: The Styles pop-up menu includes only the first three heading styles, Heading 1 through Heading 3, at first. When you apply Heading 3, Heading 4 appears. Similarly, Heading 5 appears when you apply Heading 4, and Heading 6 appears when you apply Heading 5.

Note: You can quickly apply styles by using keyboard shortcuts. Press Ctrl+Alt+1 to apply Heading 1 style, Ctrl+Alt+2 to apply Heading 2 style, and so on up to Ctrl+Alt+6 for Heading 6 style. Press Ctrl+Alt+0 to apply Normal Text style. On the Mac, press ⌘+Option instead of Ctrl+Alt.

The Styles pop-up menu closes.

B The paragraph takes on the style's formatting.

5 Repeat steps **2** through **4** to format other paragraphs as needed.

Note: If the body text paragraphs of the document already have the Normal Text style applied, you do not need to reapply it.

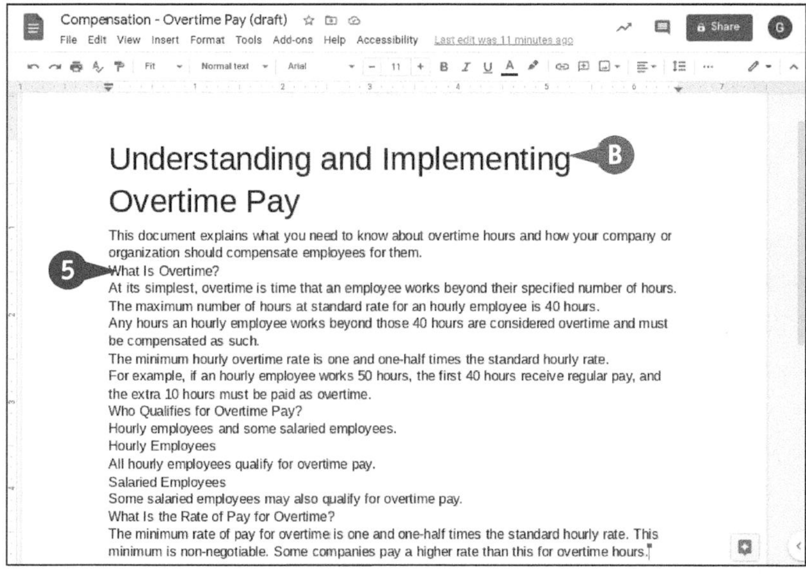

C Once you have applied styles, the document usually has more white space and is easier to read.

D In this example, the "What Is Overtime?" paragraph and the "Who Qualifies for Overtime Pay?" paragraph have Heading 1 style applied.

E The "Hourly Employees" paragraph has Heading 2 style applied.

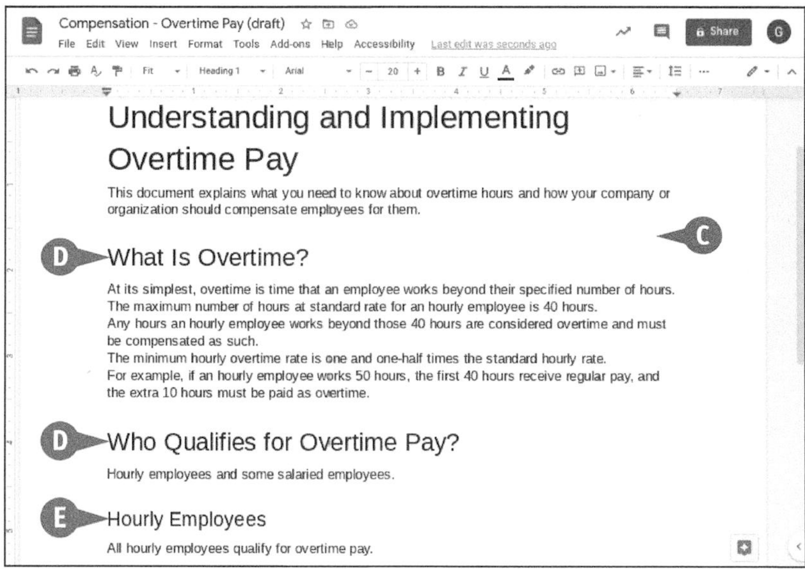

TIP

How can I quickly change all instances of one style to another style?

Right-click in a paragraph that uses the style you want to change. From the contextual menu that appears, click **Select all matching text**. Google Docs selects each paragraph that uses that style. You can then click **Styles** (▾) on the toolbar to open the Styles pop-up menu, and then click the replacement style.

The Select All Matching Text command also works for direct formatting, such as boldface or italics. For example, if a colleague has used 36-point boldface to indicate headings, you can use Select All Matching Text to select those paragraphs, and then apply a heading style to them.

Customize the Built-In Styles

As you saw in the previous section, you can use styles to format your documents quickly and consistently. Google Docs does not let you create your own styles, but you can customize the built-in styles so that they look exactly as you want.

To customize a style, you format a paragraph of text with the formatting you want the style to contain. You then update the style to match the formatting of that paragraph.

Customize the Built-In Styles

1. Open a document in Google Docs.

   If you have a document that contains the formatting you want for the styles, open that document. If not, open either a new document or an existing document in which you can make changes freely.

   This example shows a document that contains a paragraph for each built-in style, with a paragraph in Normal Text style separating each heading paragraph.

2. Select the paragraph you will use to adjust the style formatting.

3. Make any changes needed to the paragraph's formatting.

   (A) For instance, you might change the font or font size, or you might change the text color and apply boldface and underline. This is an example, not a recommendation.

4. Click **Styles** (▾).

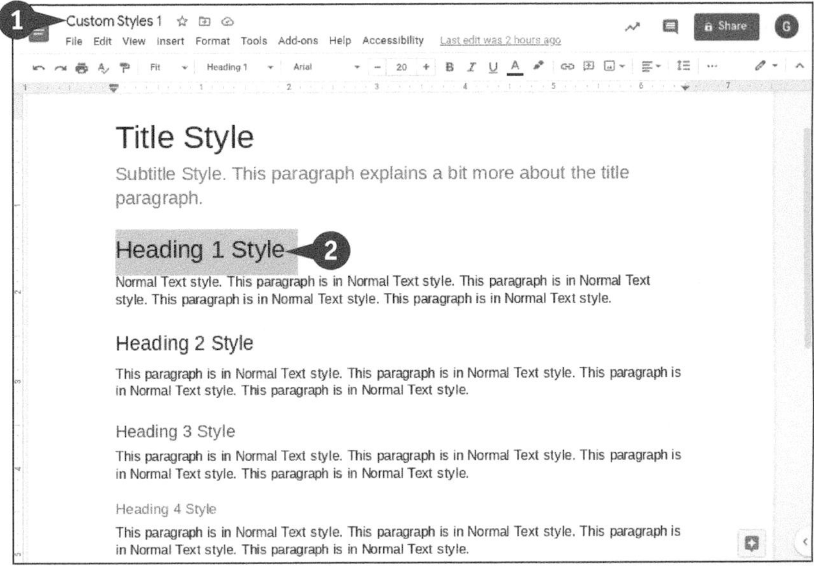

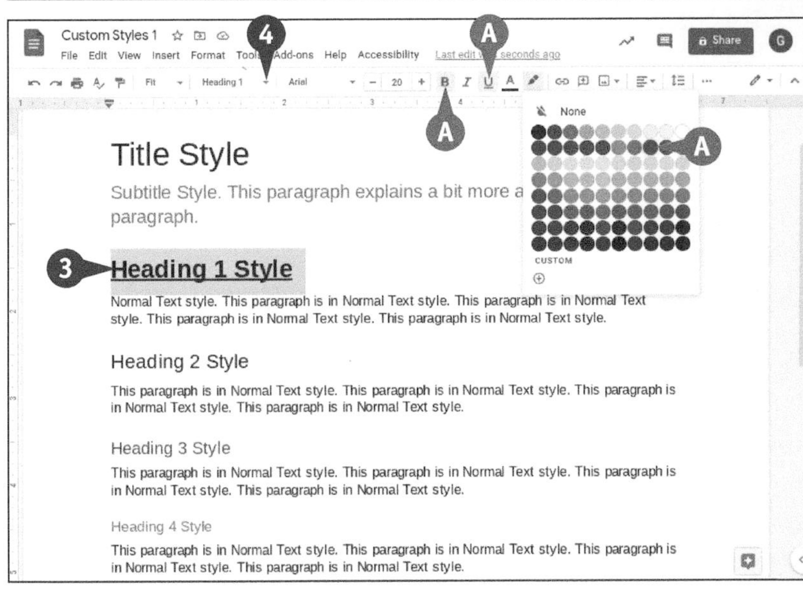

The Styles pop-up menu opens.

5. Without clicking, highlight the style you want to change.

   The style's submenu opens.

6. Click **Update *'Style'* to match**, where *Style* is the style's name.

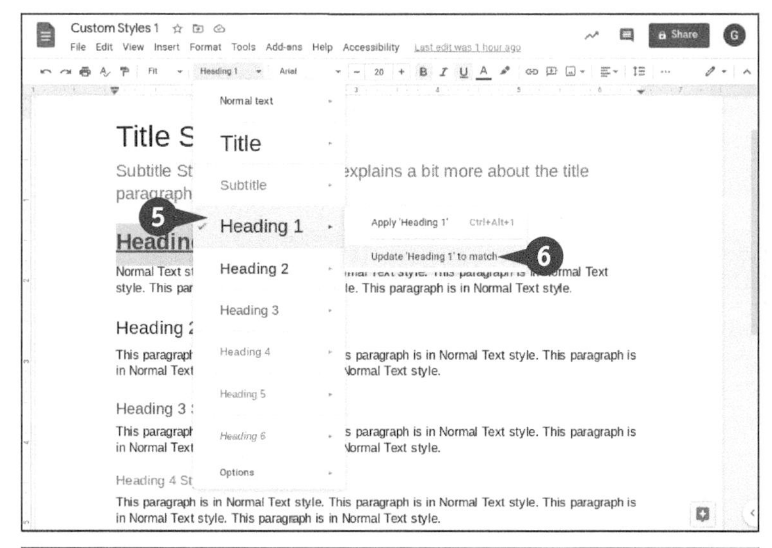

The Styles pop-up menu closes.

Google Docs updates the style but does not display any confirmation of having done so.

7. Repeat steps **2** through **6** to customize the other styles, as needed.

B. You can also update a style by right-clicking in it and then clicking **Update *'Style'* to match**, where *Style* is the style's name, on the contextual menu.

Note: To use your customized styles in other documents, save them as explained in the next section, "Save and Use Your Default Styles."

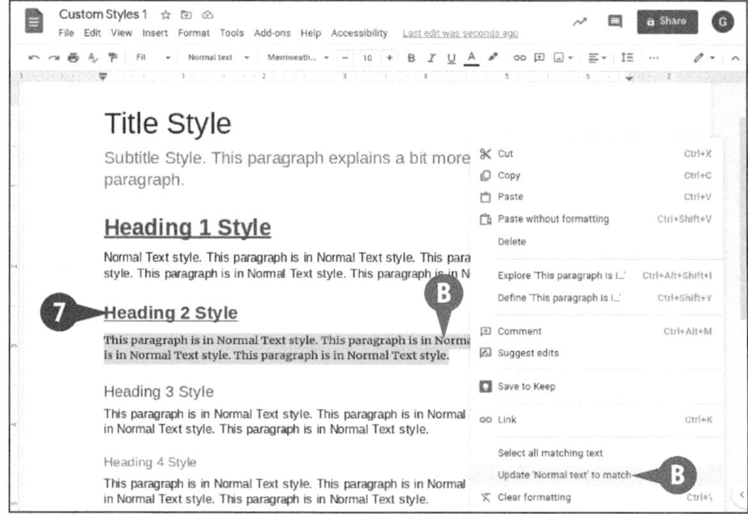

TIPS

How do I stop a sequence of Heading paragraphs from moving as a block from page to page?

Each Heading style has the Keep with Next setting enabled by default, so a sequence of Heading paragraphs without non-heading text between them will "walk" from page to page as a block. You can stop this "walking" by placing a Normal Text paragraph between each pair of Heading paragraphs. Alternatively, click a problem paragraph, click **Line spacing** (↕☰), and then click **Keep with next**, removing the check mark (✓).

Is there a way to create my own styles in Google Docs?

A third-party developer offers an add-on called Paragraph Styles+ that enables you to create styles, but Google currently blocks this add-on for safety.

Save and Use Your Default Styles

Once you have customized the Google Docs styles, as explained in the previous section, you should save those changes as your default styles so that you can use them in other documents. Once you have saved these default styles, each new document you create automatically uses the styles. Existing documents do not automatically pick up the new styles, but you can switch any existing document to use the new default styles in a couple of clicks.

Save and Use Your Default Styles

Save Your Default Styles

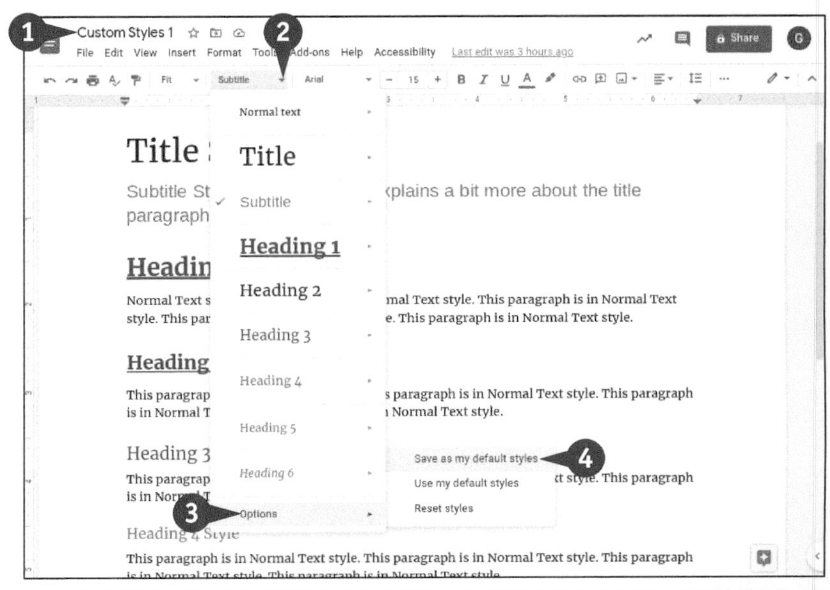

1. Open the document that contains your customized styles.

   If you have kept the document open from the previous section, "Customize the Built-In Styles," you are all set.

2. Click **Styles** (▾).

   The Styles pop-up menu opens.

3. Click or highlight **Options.**

   The Options submenu opens.

4. Click **Save as my default styles.**

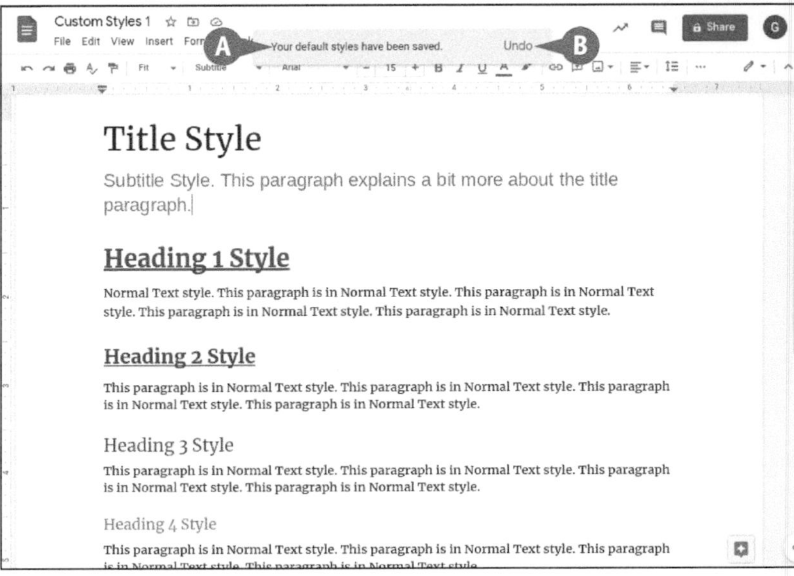

The Styles pop-up menu closes.

Ⓐ The *Your default styles have been saved* pop-up message appears for a few seconds and then disappears automatically.

Ⓑ You can click **Undo** to undo the change if necessary.

Apply Your Default Styles to a Document

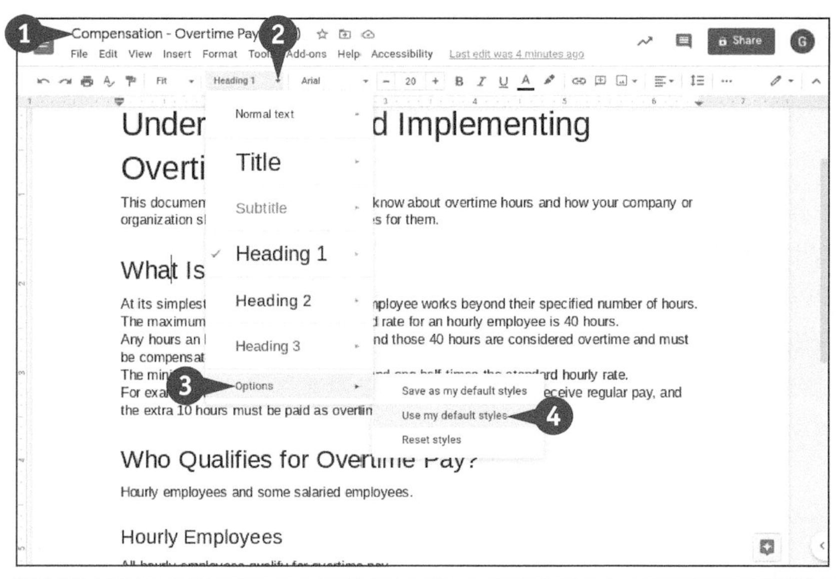

1. Open the document to which you want to apply your default styles.
2. Click **Styles** (▾).

   The Styles pop-up menu opens.
3. Click or highlight **Options.**

   The Options submenu opens.
4. Click **Use my default styles.**

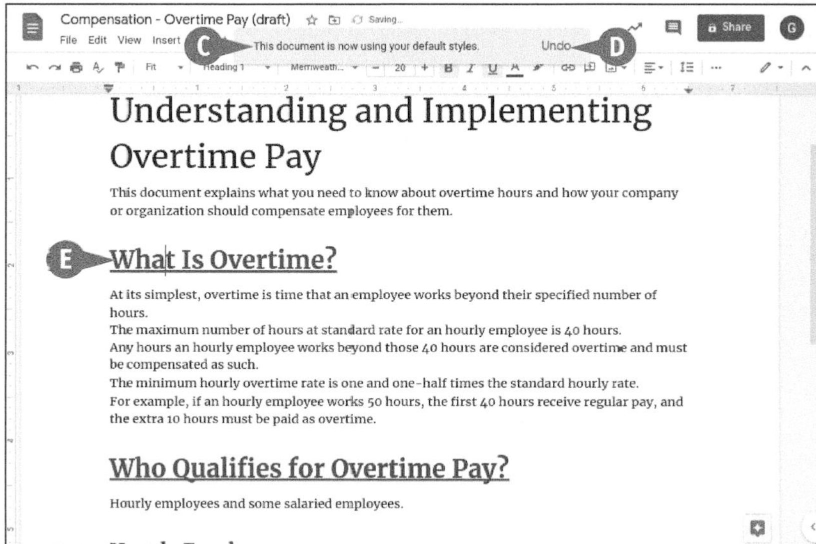

The Styles pop-up menu closes.

- C The *This document is now using your default styles* pop-up message appears for a few seconds, and then disappears automatically.
- D You can click **Undo** to undo the change if necessary.
- E The styles in the document change to your default styles.

Note: If the styles in the document do not change, click **Reload** (↻) to refresh the document.

TIP

Can I create multiple sets of default styles?

Yes, if you are prepared to keep swapping them around. For each style set, create a separate document and format the styles as you want them. When you need a style set, open the appropriate document and make its styles your defaults.

When creating new documents, you may find it easier to create a copy of the document that contains the styles. You can either create the copy in Google Drive, rename it there, and then open it in Google Docs; or you can open the original document in Google Docs, click **File**, click **Make a copy**, type the new name in the Copy Document dialog box, and then click **OK**.

Navigate with the Document Outline

The Google Docs Document Outline feature enables you to navigate quickly through longer documents. The document outline opens as a pane on the left side of the document window, displaying a hierarchical list of the headings in the document. You can click a heading in the document outline to display that part of the document in the main pane.

Using the Document Outline pane, you can also remove a heading from the document outline without removing its corresponding section from the document. After removing a headline from the document outline, you can put it back, if necessary.

Navigate with the Document Outline

1. Open the document through which you want to navigate.
2. Click **View**.

The View menu opens.

3. Click **Show document outline**.

Note: You can also display the Document Outline pane by holding down Ctrl + Alt and pressing A followed by H. On the Mac, hold down ⌘ + Ctrl and press A followed by H.

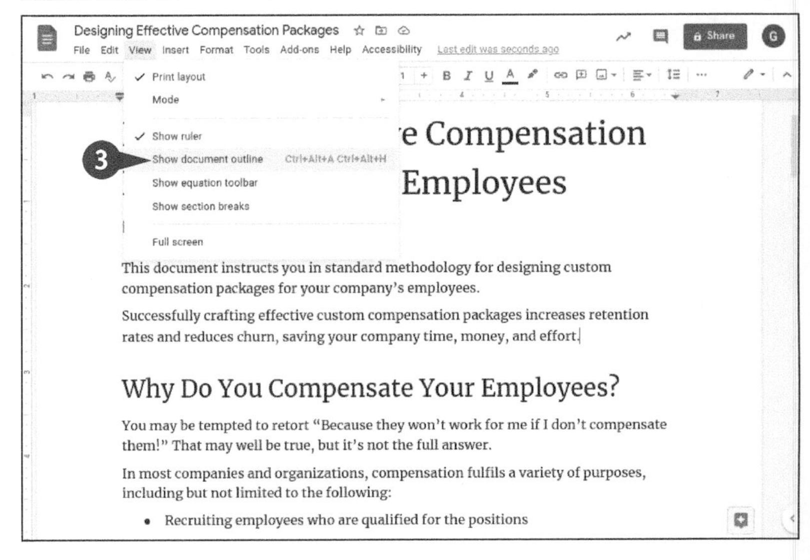

The Document Outline pane opens.

Ⓐ You can click **Close Document Outline** (←) to collapse the document outline. Click **Show document outline** (☰) to expand the document outline again.

Note: To get rid of the Document Outline pane altogether, click **View**, and then click **Show document outline**, removing the check mark (☰).

Ⓑ The heading levels appear at different sizes and with different indents to convey the outline's structure.

Ⓒ If a heading is truncated, you can hold the cursor over it to display a tooltip with the full text.

❹ Click the heading you want to display.

Ⓓ The heading appears at the top of the main pane.

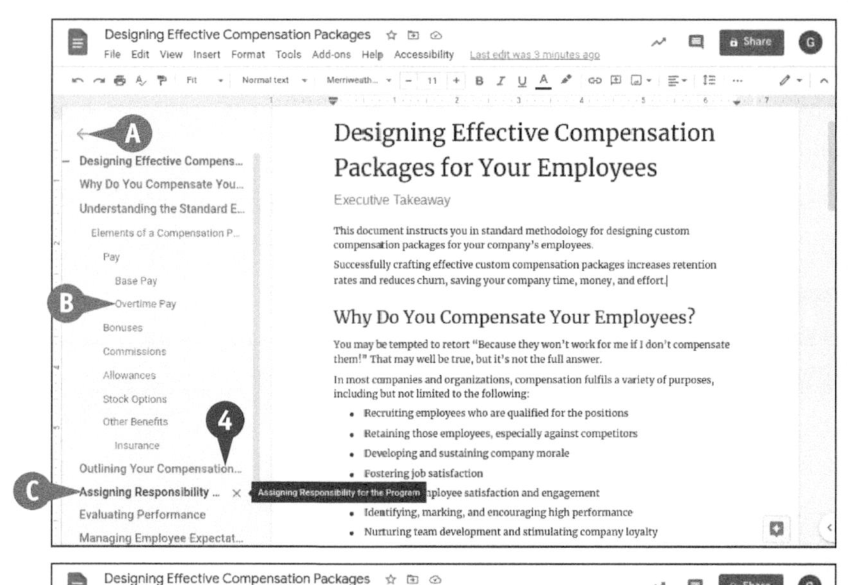

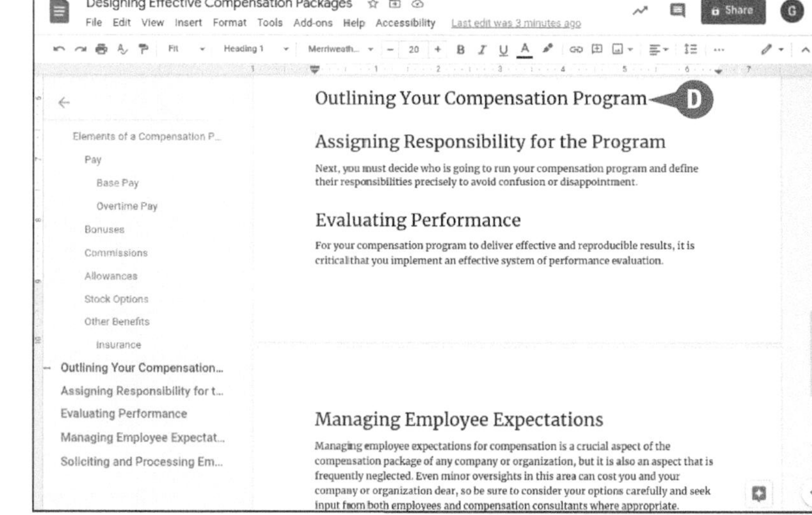

TIP

How do I remove a heading from the document outline?

To remove a heading, move the cursor over the heading in the document outline pane, and then click **Remove from outline** (✕). Google Docs removes the heading from the document outline but leaves the heading and any subparagraphs in the document itself.

If you need to restore the heading to the document outline, right-click the heading, and then click **Add to document outline** on the contextual menu.

Insert Page Numbers

If your documents need page numbers, you can use the Page Numbers feature to insert page numbers in either the header or the footer, where they repeat automatically on each page. You can choose to suppress page numbers on the first page of a document, and you can start page numbering at a value other than 1, if needed.

For some documents, you may want to use "Page X of Y" page numbering, letting the reader see the page count as well as the current page's number.

Insert Page Numbers

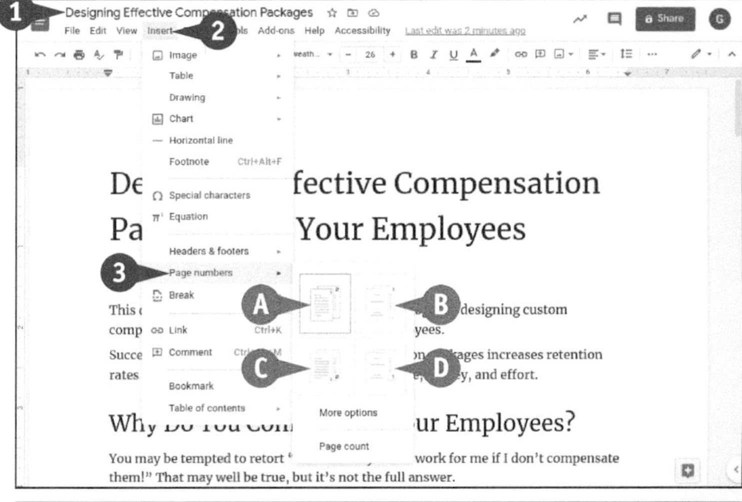

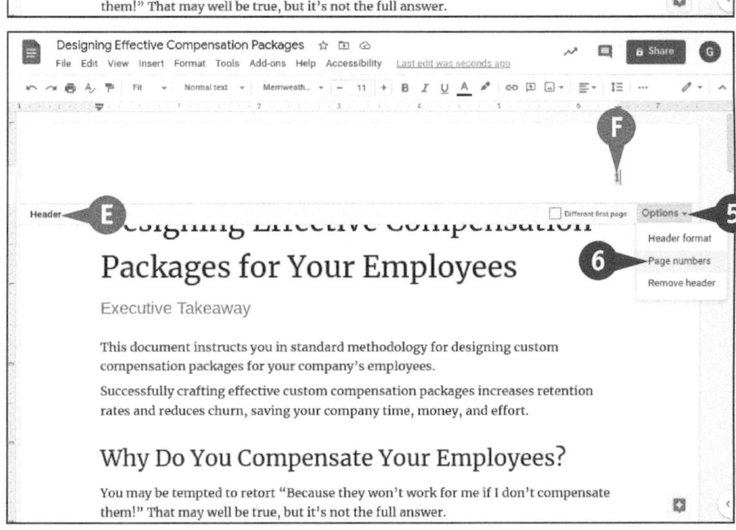

1. Open the document to which you want to add page numbers.
2. Click **Insert**.

   The Insert menu opens.
3. Click or highlight **Page numbers**.

   The Page Numbers submenu opens.
4. Click the appropriate icon:

   A. Click **Header** ( ) to put page numbers on each page in the header.

   B. Click **Header no first page** ( ) to put page numbers in the header, starting with the second page.

   C. Click **Footer** ( ) to put page numbers on each page in the footer.

   D. Click **Footer no first page** ( ) to put page numbers in the footer, starting with the second page.

   The header area or the footer area of the document opens, depending on your choice.

   E. This example uses the Header style, so the header area opens.

   F. The page number appears.
5. To customize the page numbering, click **Options** ( ).

   The Options pop-up menu opens.
6. Click **Page numbers**.

The Page Numbers dialog box opens.

7. In the Position area, click **Header** (◯ changes to ◉) or **Footer** (◯ changes to ◉), as needed.
8. Select **Show on first page** (☐ changes to ☑) if you want the page number to appear on the first page.
9. In the Numbering area, click **Start at** (◯ changes to ◉) or **Continue from previous section** (◯ changes to ◉), as needed.
10. If you select **Start at** (◉), adjust the number in the box, as needed. The number must be an integer between 0 and 999, inclusive; it cannot be negative.
11. Click **Apply**.

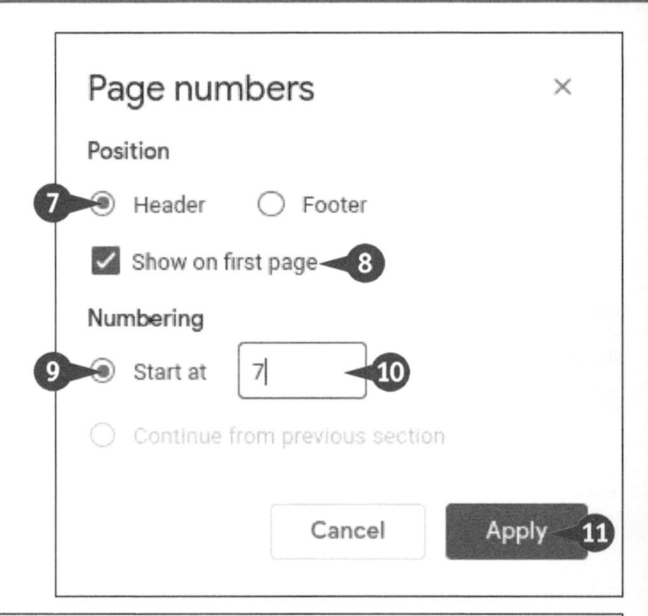

The Page Numbers dialog box closes.

The header area or footer area shows the updated numbering scheme.

12. Click in the main part of the document.

The header area or footer area closes.

G The page number appears in Print Layout view.

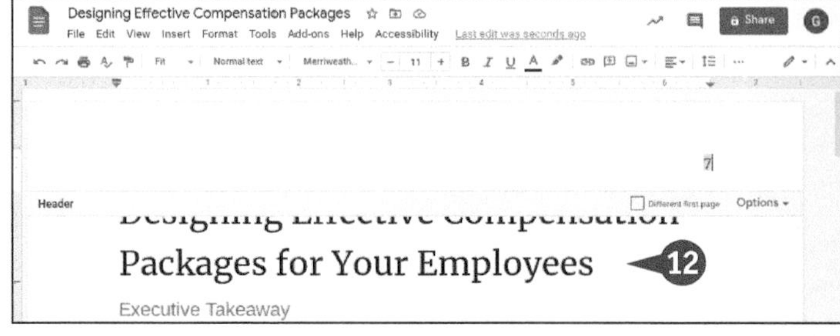

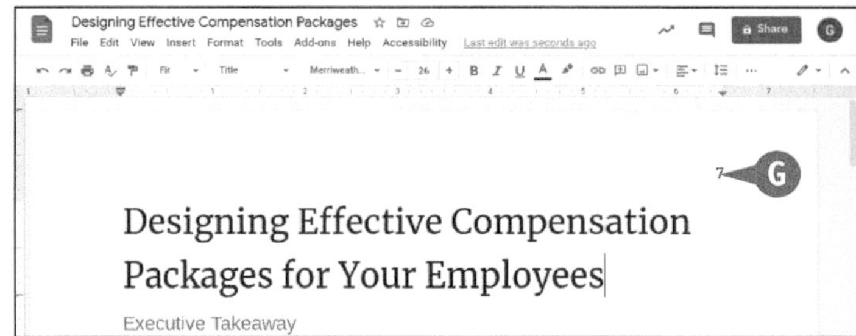

TIP

How can I create "Page 1 of 48" numbering?

Insert the page number as explained in the main text, and then type **Page** and a space before it. After it, press Spacebar, type **of**, and then press Spacebar again. Then click **Insert** to open to the Insert menu, click or highlight **Page numbers**, and then click **Page count**.

Be warned that the page count is the actual number of pages in the document, so if you specify a Start At number other than 1, you can create anomalies, such as Page 7 of 3.

Create Headers and Footers

Google Docs enables you to create headers and footers to make the pages of your documents easier to identify. The header area and footer area are separate from the main text of the document. The header or footer repeats automatically on each page of the document, but you can create different headers or footers for odd pages and even pages. You can also create a different header or footer for the first page of the document.

If you need to create different headers or footers for different parts of a document, see the next section, "Create Different Headers and Footers."

Create Headers and Footers

1. Open the document in which you want to create the headers or footers.
2. Click **Insert**.

   The Insert menu opens.
3. Click or highlight **Headers & footers**.

   The Headers & Footers submenu opens.
4. Click **Header** or **Footer**, as appropriate.

   This example uses **Header**.

Note: You can also display the Header pane by holding down Ctrl+Alt and pressing O followed by H; for the Footer pane, press O followed by F. On the Mac, hold down ⌘+Ctrl and press O followed by H for the header area or O followed by F for the footer area.

   The header area or footer area of the document opens.

   In this example, the header area opens.

A. The Header label shows the header type.

5. Type the text for the header.
6. If you want to use a different header on the first page, click **Different first page** (☐ changes to ☑).

B. The First Page Header label shows the header type.

7. Type the first page header.

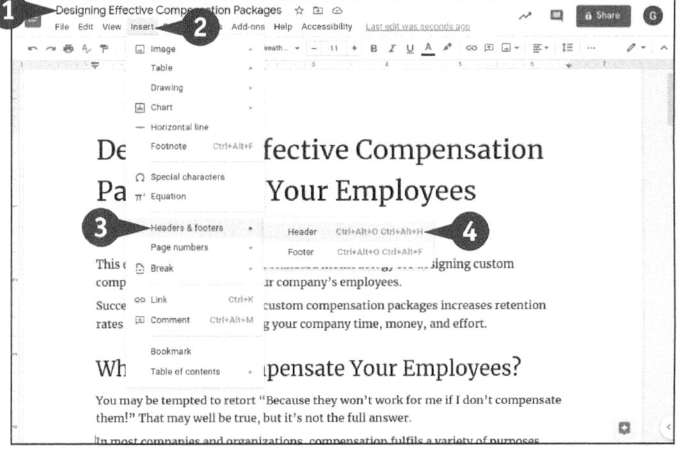

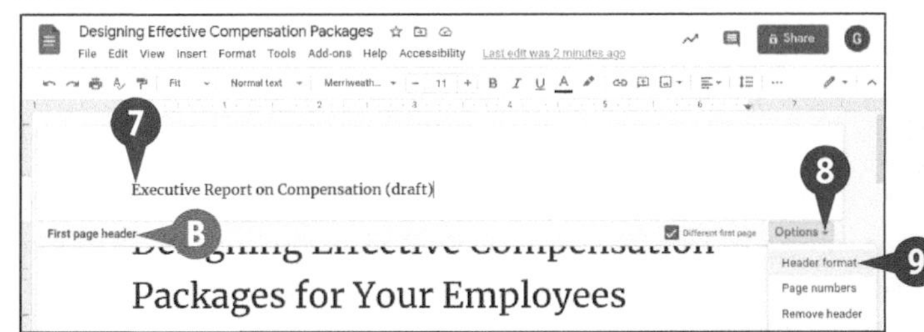

8. Click **Options** (▾).

   The Options pop-up menu opens.
9. Click **Header format**.

The Headers & Footers dialog box opens.

10 If necessary, click **Header** and adjust the distance from the top of the page.

11 If necessary, click **Footer** and adjust the distance from the bottom of the page.

12 If necessary, select (☑) or deselect (☐) **Different first page**. If you already chose the appropriate setting, you need not change it.

13 Select (☑) **Different odd & even** if you want the odd-numbered pages to have different headers or footers than the even-numbered pages.

Note: The existing header becomes the odd page header.

14 Click **Apply**.

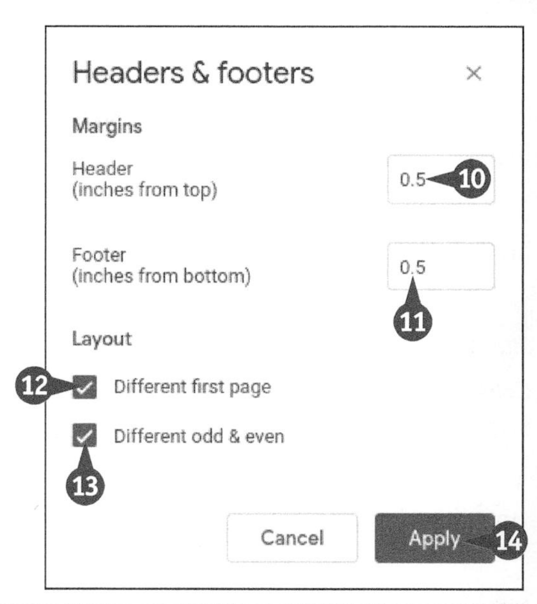

The Headers & Footers dialog box closes.

15 If you selected (☑) **Different odd & even**, navigate to an even-numbered page.

C The Even Page Header label indicates the header type.

16 Type the even page header.

17 When you finish working on your headers or footers, click in the main part of the document.

The header area or footer area closes.

D The header appears in Print Layout view.

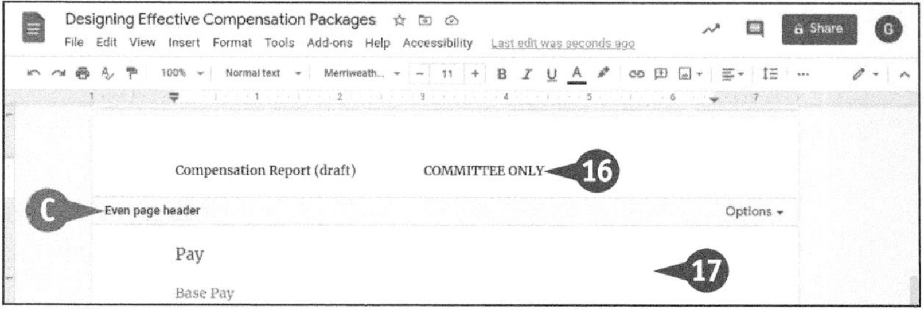

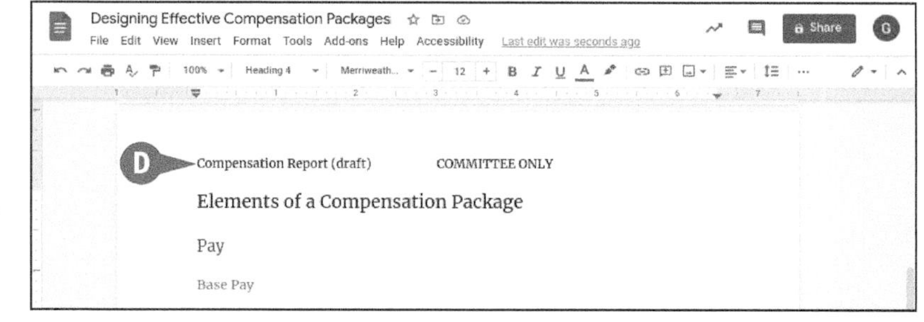

TIP

How do I delete a header or footer?

Open the header area or footer area either by double-clicking in it or by clicking **Insert**, clicking or highlighting **Headers & footers**, and then clicking **Header** or **Footer**, as appropriate. Click **Options** (▾) to display the Options pop-up menu, and then click **Remove header** or **Remove footer**. If you have created multiple headers or footers, such as a different first page header or different odd and even footers, you must go to each one and remove it separately.

Create Different Headers and Footers

As you saw in the previous section, "Create Headers and Footers," any header or footer you create normally repeats on each page of the document. When you need to create different headers or footers in different parts of a document, you must create a separate section for each part by inserting section breaks.

Google Docs provides two kinds of section breaks: continuous section breaks and next-page section breaks. You can set Google Docs to display section breaks, enabling you to see where they are.

Create Different Headers and Footers

Create Sections by Inserting Section Breaks

1. Open the document in which you want to create the headers or footers.
2. Click **View**.

   The View menu opens.
3. Click **Show section breaks**.

   The View menu closes.

   Any section breaks in the document appear. At this point, the example document contains no section breaks.
4. Position the cursor where you want a new section to start — for example, at the beginning of a paragraph.
5. Click **Insert**.

   The Insert menu opens.
6. Click or highlight **Break** (⎘).

   The Break submenu opens.
7. Click **Section break (next page)**.

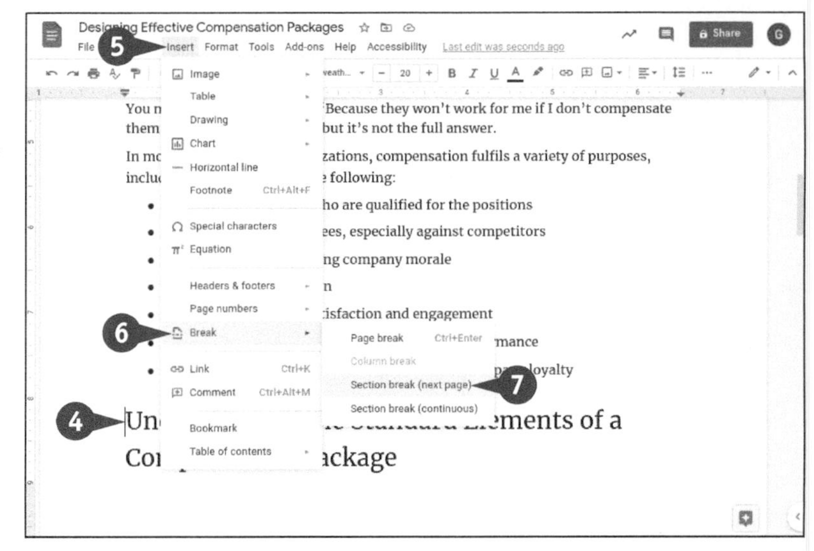

(A) The section break appears as a horizontal, light-blue dotted line.

(B) The paragraph before which you inserted the section break moves to the next page.

8 Repeat steps **4** through **7** to insert other section breaks, as needed.

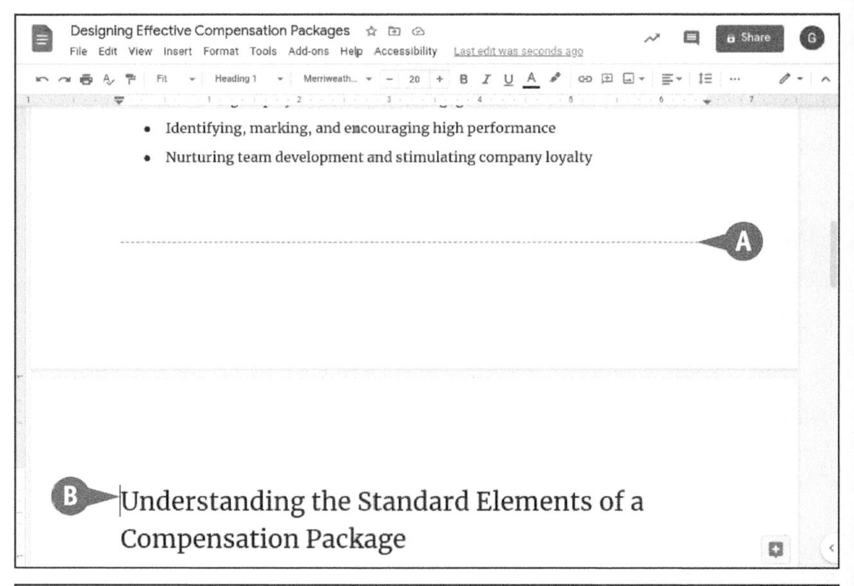

Insert Headers or Footers in the Document's Sections

1 Click in the first section of the document.

For example, you might scroll up to the top of the document.

2 Click **Insert**.

The Insert menu opens.

3 Click or highlight **Headers & footers**.

The Headers & Footers submenu opens.

4 Click **Header** or **Footer**, as appropriate.

This example uses **Header**.

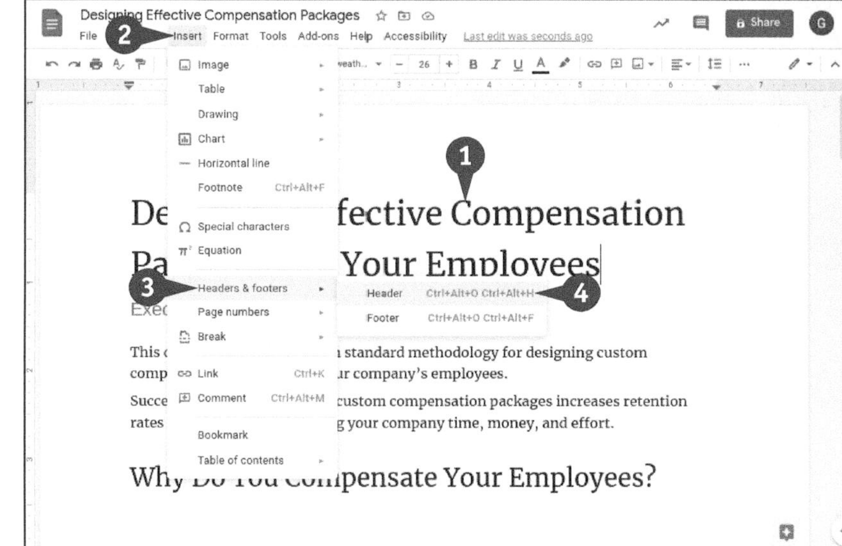

TIP

What other capabilities do sections offer?

Apart from enabling you to use different headers and footers for different parts of your documents, sections also allow you to use different margins on different pages. For example, Section 1 can have wide margins and Section 2 can have narrow margins.

continued ►

Once you have inserted section breaks to divide your document into as many sections as you need, you can go to each section and create the headers or footers it needs. By default, Google Docs automatically continues headers and footers from one section to the next by linking each header and footer to the header or footer in the previous section, but you can quickly break this link and create custom headers and footers in each section.

Create Different Headers and Footers (continued)

The header area or footer area opens.

C The *Header – Section 1* readout indicates the header type — a plain header, rather than a first page header or an even page header — and the section number.

5 Type the header for this section.

D You can click **Different first page** (☐ changes to ☑) if you want to create a different header on the first page of the section.

6 Click in the body of the document.

The header area closes.

7 Navigate to the next section, either by scrolling or by issuing the Next Section command — hold down Ctrl+Alt, and then press N followed by S.

Note: To navigate to the previous section, issue the Previous Section command — hold down Ctrl+Alt and then press P followed by S.

Note: On the Mac, hold down Ctrl+⌘ instead of Ctrl+Alt.

8 Double-click the header area.

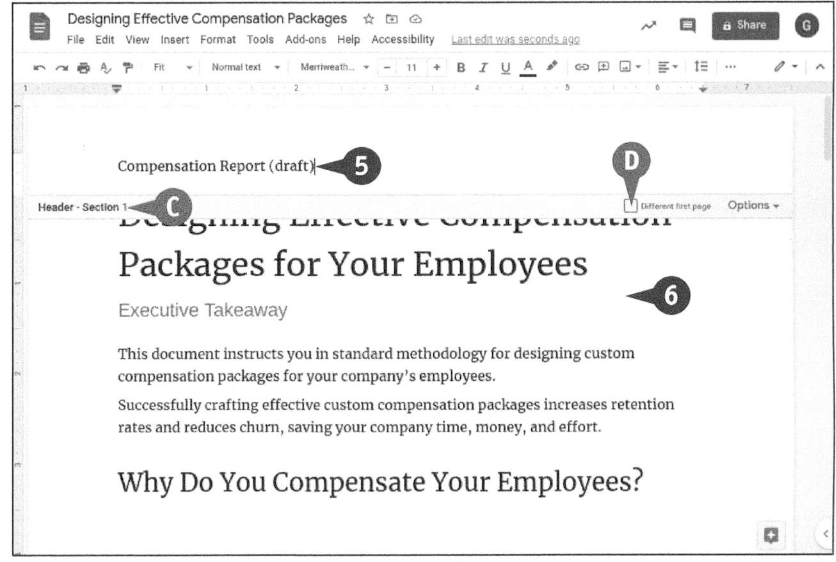

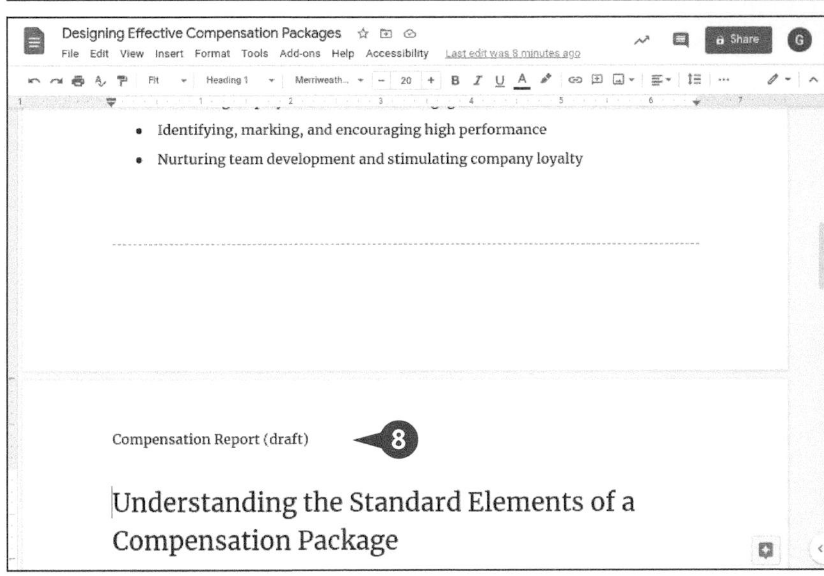

The header area opens.

Ⓔ The *Header – Section 2* readout indicates the header type — again, a plain header — and the section number.

Ⓕ The Link To Previous check box is selected (☑) by default.

Ⓖ The previous section's header appears because the Link To Previous check box is selected (☑).

9 Click **Link to previous** (☑ changes to ☐).

The previous section's header disappears.

10 Type the header for this section.

11 To configure other settings for headers and footers, click **Options** (▾).

The Options pop-up menu opens.

12 Click **Header format**.

The Headers & Footers dialog box opens.

13 To specify which section or sections of the document your changes will affect, click **Apply to** (▾).

The Apply To pop-up menu opens.

Ⓗ Click **Whole document** to affect all the sections.

Ⓘ Click **This section** to affect only the current section.

Ⓙ Click **This section forward** to affect the current section and all subsequent sections.

Ⓚ You can adjust the distance of the header from the top of the page.

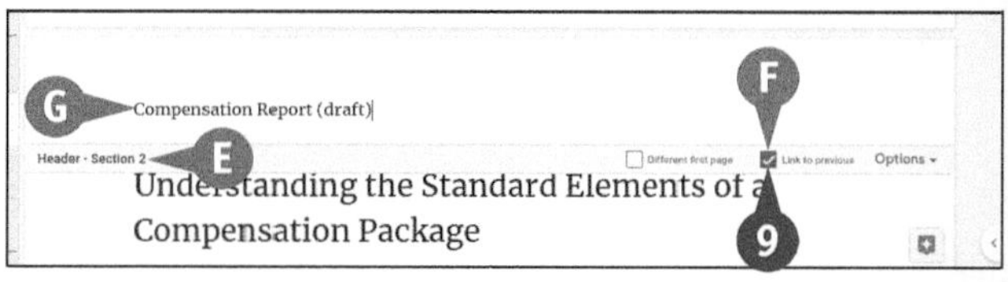

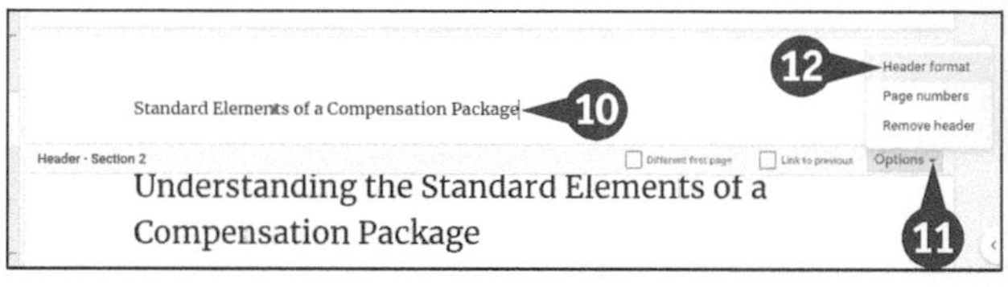

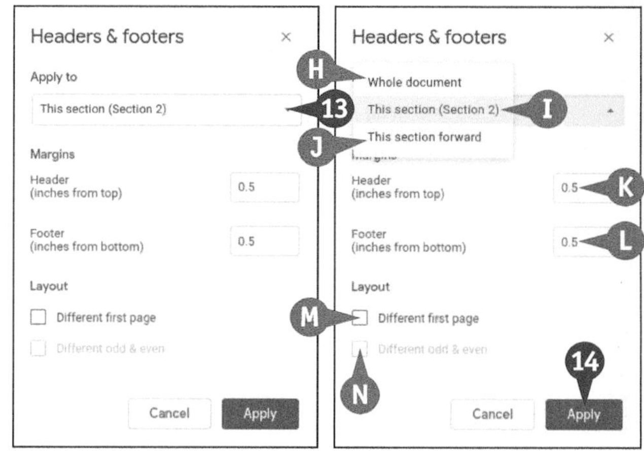

Ⓛ You can adjust the distance of the footer from the bottom of the page.

Ⓜ You can select **Different first page** (☑) to have a different first page header or footer.

Ⓝ You can select **Different odd & even** (☑) to have different headers or footers for odd and even pages.

14 Click **Apply**.

The Headers & Footers dialog box closes.

TIP

Should I use continuous section breaks or next-page section breaks?

If you are using sections to create different headers and footers, as explained in this section, next-page section breaks are usually the clear choice, because each page can show only the headers and footers from one section, not from two or more sections. But if you are using sections to effect other types of variations, such as having narrower margins for one paragraph than for other paragraphs on the same page, you will want to use continuous section breaks.

CHAPTER 6

Sharing and Collaborating on Files

In this chapter, you start by sharing a folder or a file with others, then move on to editing a document collaboratively in real time, optionally chatting with your co-editors as you work. Next, you learn to use collaborative tools such as comments, suggestions, and the Compare Documents feature in Google Docs. Finally, you learn how to revert to an earlier version of a document, how to change ownership of a file or folder, how to use Backup and Sync, and how to use Google Drive for Desktop.

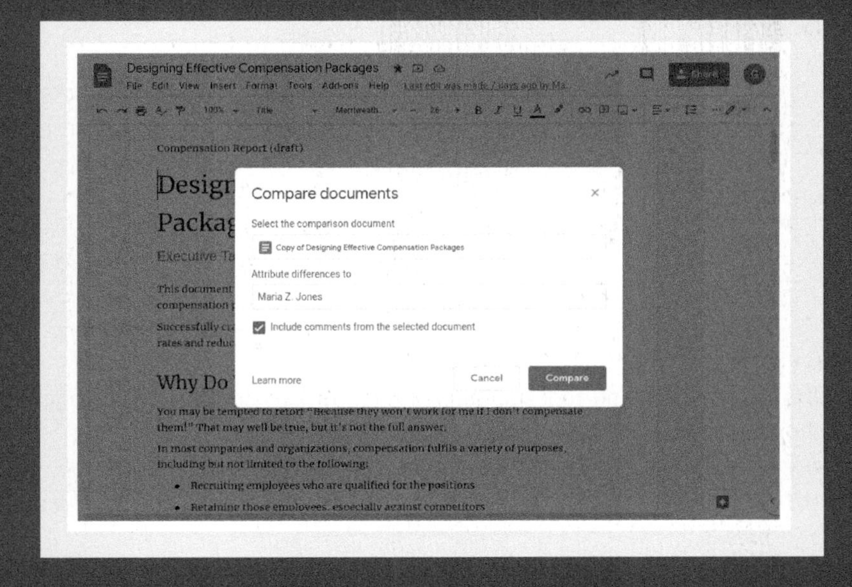

Understanding Your Options for Working with Others

Google Workspace gives you multiple ways of working with your colleagues in your organization and with people outside it. You can share documents or folders stored on Google Drive, specifying what level of permission to grant: Editor, Commenter, or Viewer. You can edit documents collaboratively in real time in Google Docs, Google Sheets, and Google Slides, optionally chatting with your collaborators as you work. You can review, reply to, and resolve the comments; revert to an earlier version of a document; and use Google Drive for Desktop to sync files to and from your computer.

Share a Document or Folder on Google Drive

The Google Workspace apps encourage you to store all your documents on your Google Drive, which gives you access to them anywhere you have a device with an Internet connection. Storing your documents on Google Drive also enables you to share them easily with your coworkers and with people outside your organization.

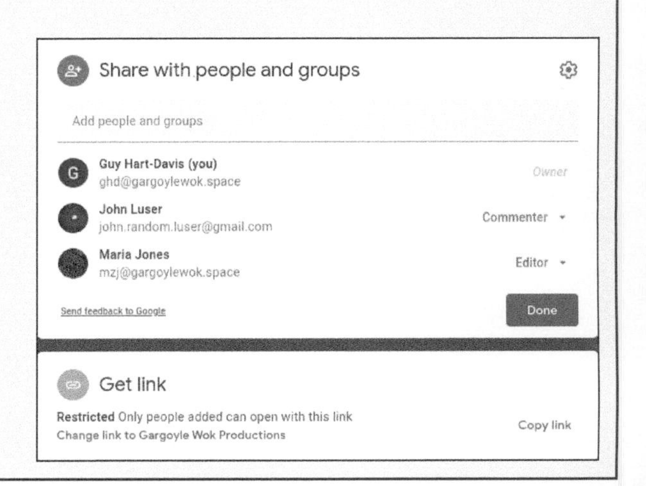

You can share either an individual document or an entire folder, including its contents. See the next section, "Share a Document on Google Drive," for instructions on sharing a document. See the section "Share a Folder on Google Drive," later in this chapter, for instructions on sharing a folder.

Collaborate on a Document in Real Time

Google Docs, Google Sheets, and Google Slides all enable you to collaborate on documents in real time with your colleagues. Real-time collaboration can be a great way to get a document created, edited, or finished — or all three — quickly. The apps let you see where each of your colleagues is working and update quickly with all changes made, making it easy to avoid interfering with one another's edits, especially if you use the apps' built-in Chat pane to communicate with your colleagues.

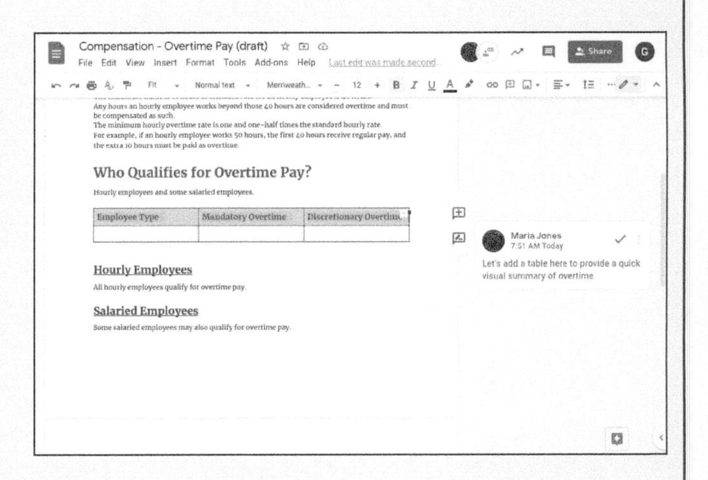

See the section "Collaborate in Real Time on a Document," later in this chapter, for details on real-time collaboration. See the section "Chat with Your Collaborators," also later in this chapter, for information on chatting while collaborating.

Collaborate via Comments

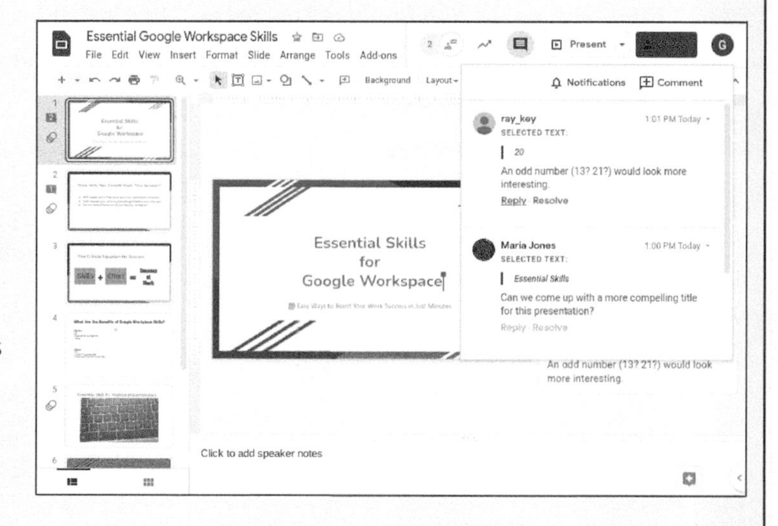

Google Docs, Google Sheets, and Google Slides enable you and your colleagues to collaborate on documents by using comments. A comment is not a direct edit to the document's content but rather a separate piece of text attached to part of the content. For example, you might attach a comment to a word in a Google Docs document, to a cell in a Google Sheets spreadsheet, or to a slide in a Google Slides presentation.

When you share a document with others, you can assign them the Commenter role, which allows them to insert comments but prevents them from making edits. You can then review the comments and incorporate their suggestions, as needed.

Revert to an Earlier Version of a Document

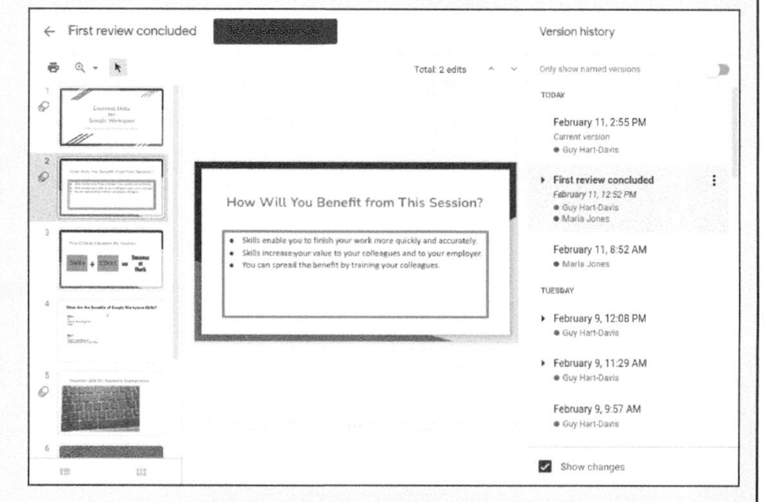

A *version* is a snapshot of a document that contains the state of the document at a particular point in time. Google Docs, Google Sheets, and Google Slides store information about different versions of your documents, enabling you to run through the edits made to the document at that point and allowing you to revert to an earlier version of a document when needed. Reverting to an earlier version lets you quickly recover from unsatisfactory changes or from accidental deletions.

The apps save the versions of each document automatically, marking each with the current date and time. You can also assign descriptive names manually to particular versions that you want to be able to identify easily.

Share a Document on Google Drive

Google Drive enables you to share a document with one or more other people, giving them access to the document so that they can open it and work with it.

For each person with whom you share a document, you specify a role to control the level of permission for viewing and changing the document. The Viewer role enables the person to open the document and view it; the Commenter role enables the person also to add comments to the document but not to edit it directly; and the Editor role enables the person to edit the document directly.

Share a Document on Google Drive

1. In Google Drive, right-click the document you want to share.

   The contextual menu opens.

2. Click **Share** (👤+).

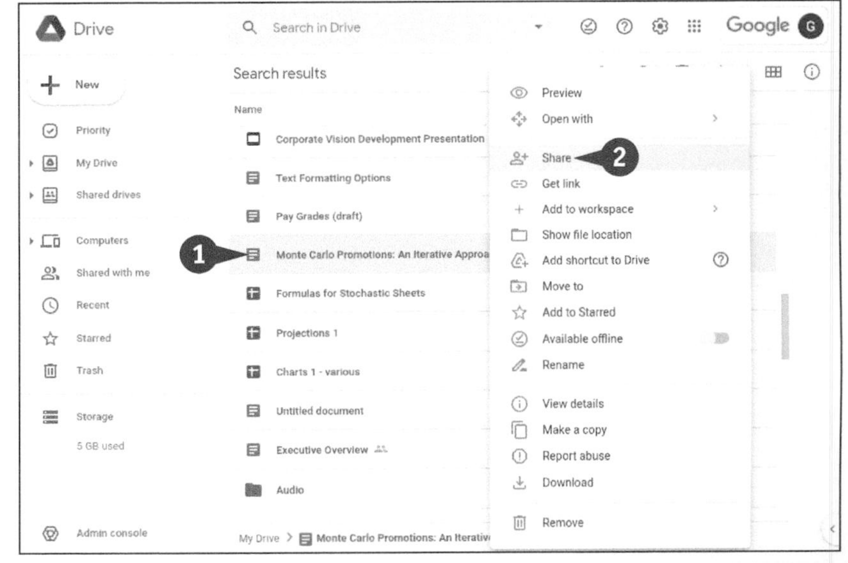

   The Share with People and Groups dialog box opens.

A. The folder's owner appears here.

3. Click **Settings** (⚙).

   The Share with People Settings dialog box opens.

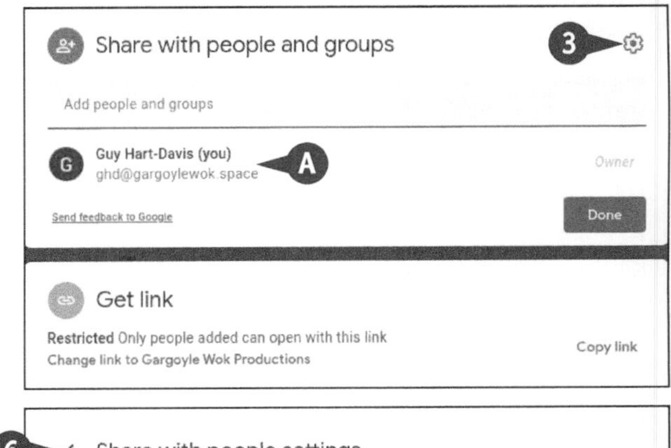

4. Select **Editors can change permissions and share** (☑) if you want people who have been assigned the Editor role to be able to change the document's permissions and share the document with others.

5. Select **Viewers and commenters can see the option to download, print, and copy** (☑) if you want viewers and commenters to be able to download the document, print it, and copy it.

6. Click **Back** (←).

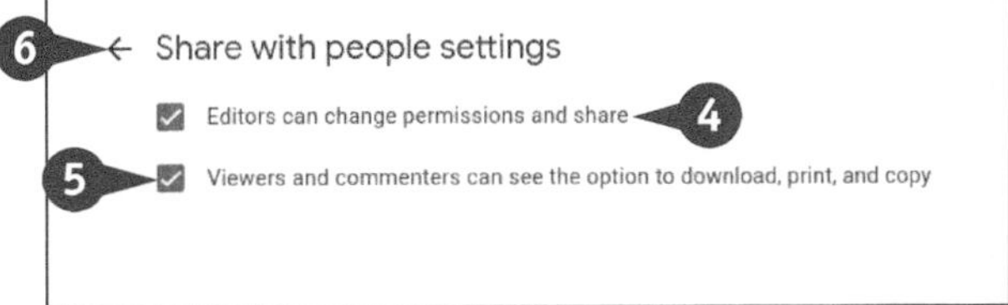

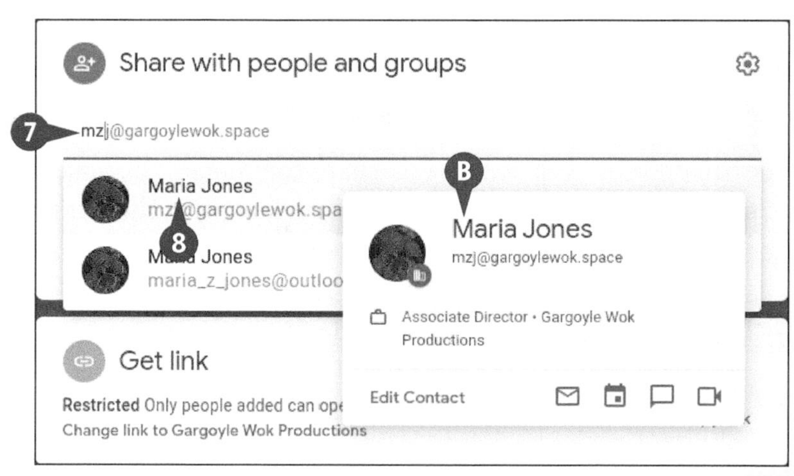

The Share with People and Groups dialog box reappears.

7 Start typing the name or email address of the person with whom you want to share the folder.

A list of matching results appears.

B You can hold the cursor over a result to display a pop-up window containing more contact information.

8 Click the appropriate result.

C The person's name appears as a button.

D You can click **Remove** (✕) to remove the person.

9 To change the person's role, click the pop-up menu (▾), and then click **Viewer**, **Commenter**, or **Editor**, as needed. See the tip for advice.

10 Select **Notify people** (☑) if you want to send the person a message telling them about the shared folder.

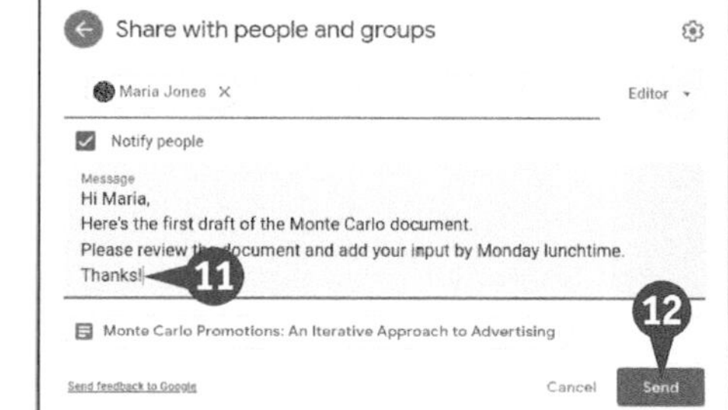

11 Type any custom message to include — for example, explaining what the folder contains.

12 Click **Send**.

Google Drive sends the message to the recipient or recipients and shares the folder.

A pop-up message appears briefly saying *Person added* or *People added* to confirm the change.

What role should I assign when sharing a document?

Assign the Viewer role by default. When you find that someone needs more extensive permissions, you can easily change them, as explained in the section "Manage Permissions on a Shared Document or Folder," later in this chapter.

If you know the person will need to provide input on the document, assign the Commenter role so that you will be able to see their input and integrate it or reject it, as appropriate. Assign the Editor role only to colleagues you trust to make extensive changes. Be even more selective with the Editors Can Change Permissions and Share permission. And when someone no longer needs elevated permissions, downgrade their permissions.

Share a Folder on Google Drive

Google Drive lets you share a folder with one or more other people. Sharing a folder can be an easy means of collaborating with others, enabling each person to access the folder's contents and work on them.

For each person with whom you share the folder, you can select one of three roles — Viewer, Commenter, or Editor — to specify which actions the person can take on the folder and its contents. See the tip for details of the three roles.

Share a Folder on Google Drive

1. In Google Drive, navigate to the location or folder that contains the folder you want to share.
2. Click the folder.
3. Click **Share** (👤+).

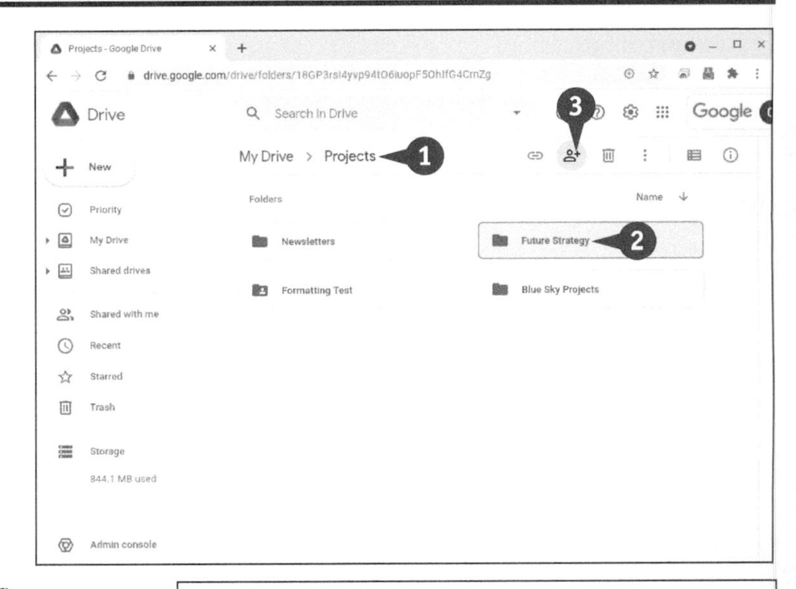

The Share with People and Groups dialog box opens.

Ⓐ The folder's owner appears here.

4. Click **Settings** (⚙).

The Share with People Settings dialog box opens.

5. Select **Editors can change permissions and share** (☑) if you want people who have been assigned the Editor role to be able to change permissions on the folder and share it with others.
6. Click **Back** (←).

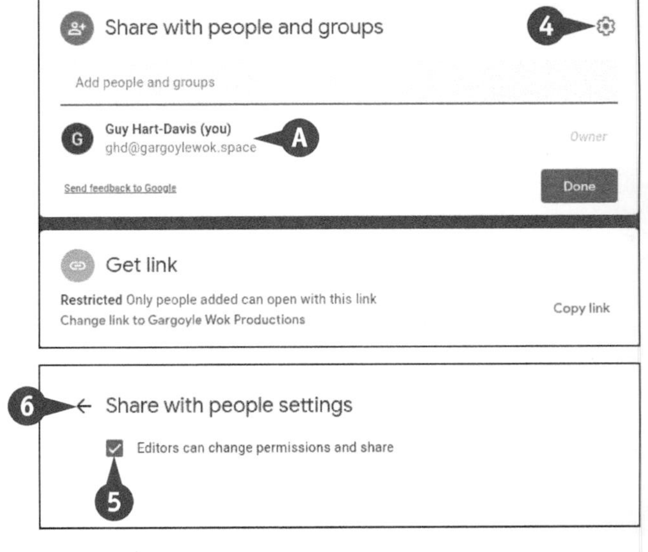

The Share with People and Groups dialog box reappears.

7 Start typing the name or email address of the person with whom you want to share the folder.

A list of matching results appears.

8 Click the appropriate result.

B The person's name appears as a button.

C You can click **Remove** (✕) to remove the person.

9 To change the person's role, click the pop-up menu (▾), and then click **Viewer**, **Commenter**, or **Editor**, as needed. See the tip for advice.

10 Select **Notify people** (☑) if you want to send the person a message telling them about the shared folder.

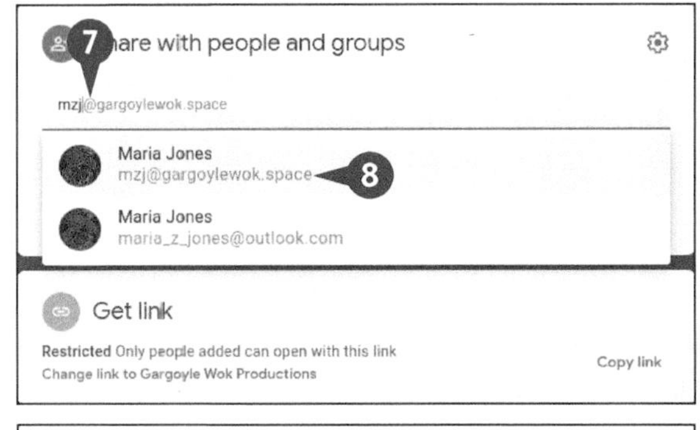

11 Type any custom message to include — for example, explaining what the folder contains.

12 Click **Send**.

Google Drive sends the message to the recipient or recipients and shares the folder.

A pop-up message appears briefly saying *Person added* or *People added* to confirm the change.

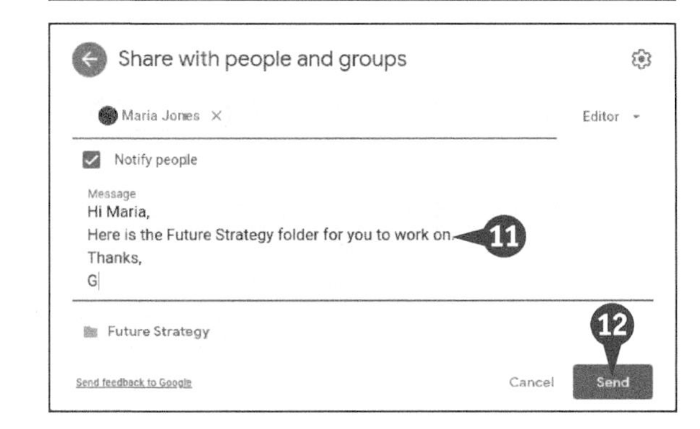

TIP

What are the differences between the Viewer, Commenter, and Editor roles for folders?

A Viewer can open the folder's files for viewing but cannot change them. However, they can make copies of the files, and then change those copies.

A Commenter can open the folder's files for viewing and can make comments and suggestions on them but not edit them directly. An Editor subsequently reviews the comments and suggestions and decides which to implement, if any.

An Editor can open the folder's files and edit them directly, and can create and delete files in the folder. If you selected Editors Can Change Permissions and Share (☑) for the Editor, the Editor can change permissions on the files and share them with other users.

Manage Permissions on a Shared Document or Folder

After sharing a document or a folder with other people, you can manage the permissions on it. You may simply need to view the list of people with whom the document or folder is shared. Other times, you may need to change the details of the sharing, either by adding or removing people, or by changing the roles assigned to them.

You can also change the ownership of a shared document or shared folder. See the section "Change Ownership of a File or Folder," later in this chapter, for details.

Manage Permissions on a Shared Document or Folder

Open the Share with People and Groups Dialog Box and Adjust Settings

A The Shared Folder icon () indicates a shared folder.

B The Shared icon () indicates a shared file.

1 In Google Drive, click the shared folder or shared document for which you want to adjust sharing.

2 Click **Share** ().

The Share with People and Groups dialog box opens.

C You can see who the owner of the document or folder is.

D You can see each person or group with whom the document or folder is shared.

E You can see the role assigned to each person or group.

3 Click **Settings** ().

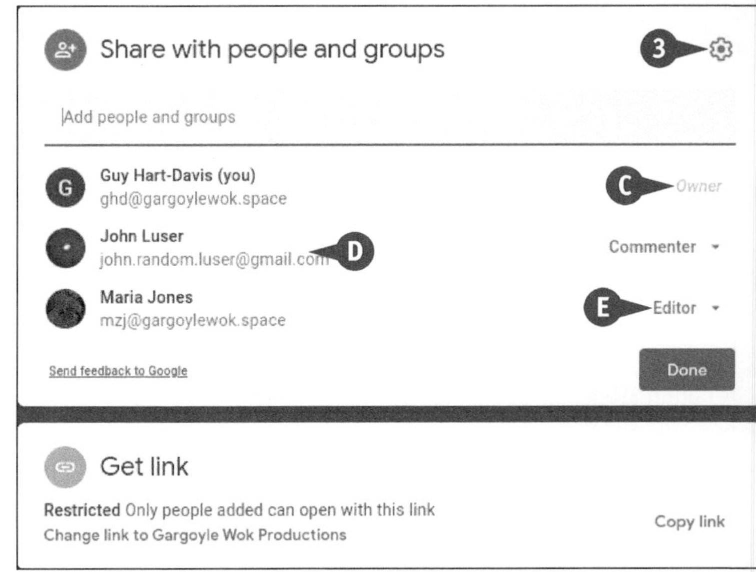

The Share with People Settings dialog box opens.

4 Select **Editors can change permissions and share** (☑) if you want people who have been assigned the Editor role to be able to change permissions on the folder and share it with others.

Note: For a shared document, the Share with People Settings dialog box contains a second check box. Select **Viewers and commenters can see the option to download, print, and copy** (☑) if you want viewers and commenters to be able to download the document, print it, and copy it.

5 Click **Back** (←).

The Share with People and Groups dialog box appears again.

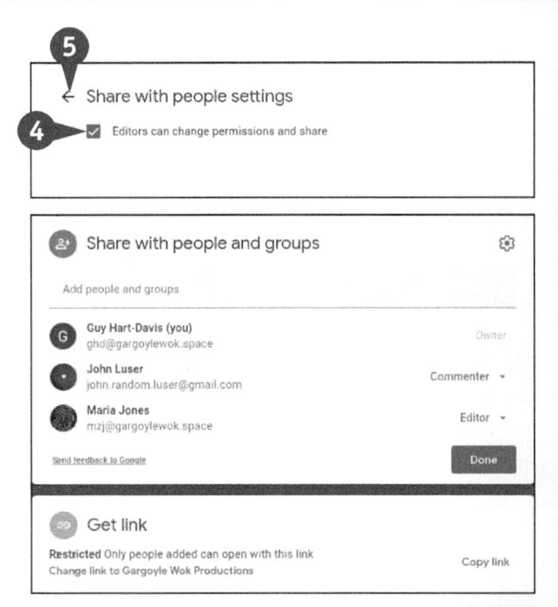

Add People or Groups to a Shared Document or Folder

1 To add a person or group, click **Add people or groups**.

2 Start typing the name or email address of the person with whom you want to share the folder. For a group, start typing the group name.

A list of matching results appears.

F You can hold the cursor over a result to display a pop-up window containing more contact information.

3 Click the appropriate result.

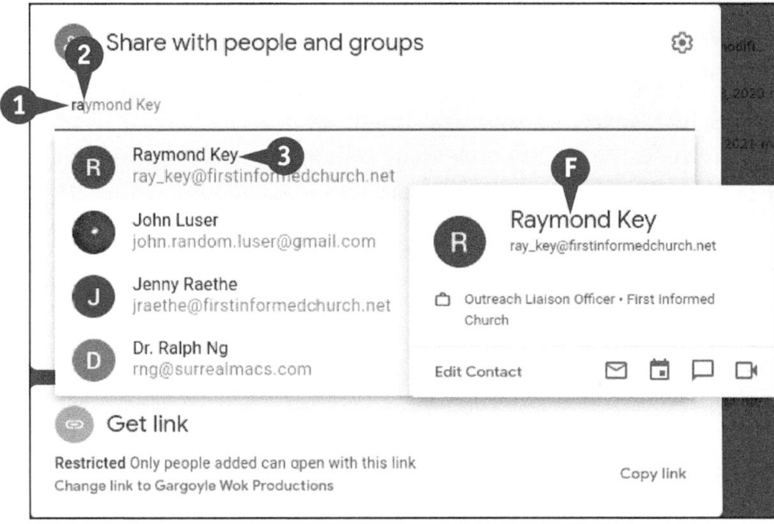

TIP

What happens if I change a person's permission while they have the shared document open?
If the person makes changes to the document before the app implements the permission change, those changes will likely be lost. On the person's computer, the app displays the Your Access Has Expired dialog box, telling the person that they need to reload the document to regain access to it. The person can click **Reload without your unsaved changes** to reload the document.

continued ►

Manage Permissions on a Shared Document or Folder (continued)

When you add a person to a shared document or folder, you can choose to notify them via email. Sending this notification message is usually helpful, especially if you include an explanation of why you are sharing the document or folder with them.

To keep close control of folders and documents, you may frequently need to change the roles assigned to the people with whom you share files and folders. For example, you may need to upgrade a person with Viewer permissions to Commenter permissions so that they can provide input on document contents.

Manage Permissions on a Shared Document or Folder (continued)

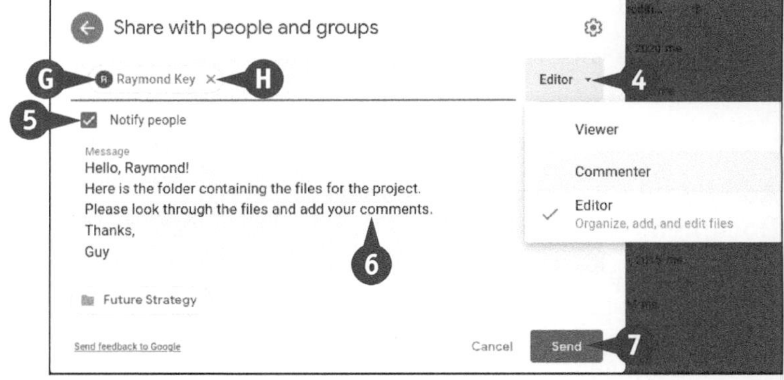

G The person's name appears as a button.

H You can click **Remove** (✕) to remove the person.

4 To specify the person's role, click the pop-up menu (▾), and then click **Viewer**, **Commenter**, or **Editor**, as needed.

5 Select **Notify people** (☑) if you want to send the person a message telling them about the shared folder.

6 Type any custom message to include — for example, explaining what the folder contains.

7 Click **Send**.

Google Drive sends the message to the recipient or recipients and shares the folder.

A pop-up message appears briefly saying *Person added* or *People added* to confirm the change.

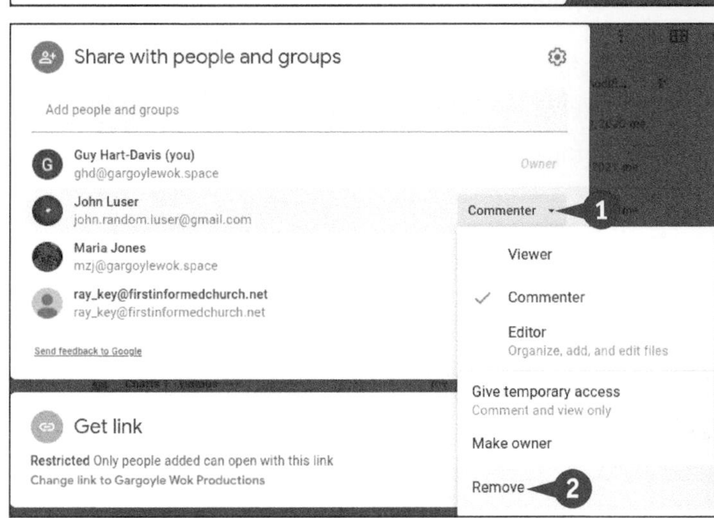

Remove People or Groups or Change Roles

1 In the Share with People and Groups dialog box, click **Role** (▾) on the right of the row for the person or group you want to remove.

The Role pop-up menu opens.

2 Click **Remove**.

The entry for the person or group disappears from the list.

I The *Pending changes* readout appears as a reminder that there are unsaved changes.

3 Make any other changes needed. For example, click **Role** (▾) to the right of the row for a person or group, and then click a different role, such as **Viewer**. The example shows changing a person from the Commenter role to the Viewer role.

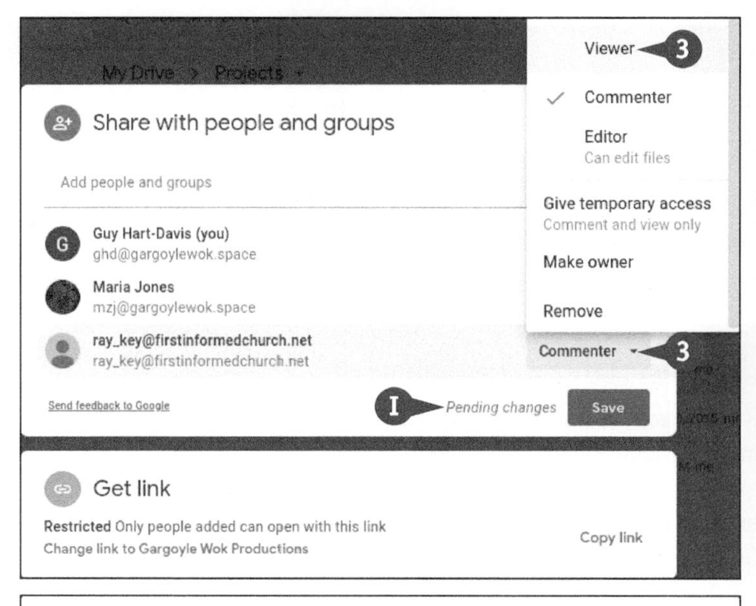

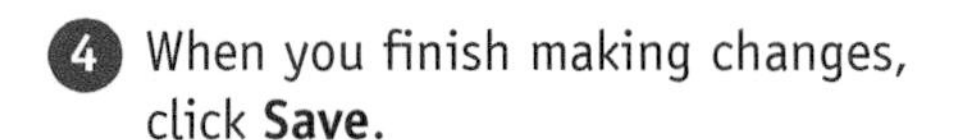

4 When you finish making changes, click **Save**.

The Share with People and Groups dialog box closes.

A pop-up message appears briefly in the lower-left corner of the screen with a readout summarizing the changes, such as *Person removed* or *Permissions updated*.

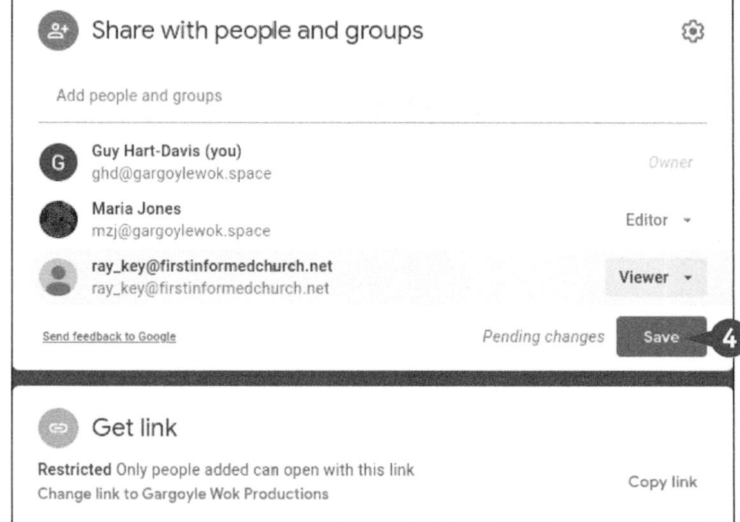

TIP

What should I do when the Share Outside of Organization dialog box opens?

The Share Outside of Organization dialog box opens when you are sharing a document or folder outside your Google Workspace organization. If you are sure you want to proceed, click **Share anyway** to share the item. Otherwise, click **Cancel** and check with your Google Workspace administrator or with a supervisor whether you should share the document or folder with outside people.

Google Docs, Google Sheets, and Google Slides let you collaborate in real time on documents with your colleagues. Real-time collaborative editing can be a great way to create or edit a document quickly, especially when a deadline is imminent. It can also be useful when each person working on the document is focusing on a separate section.

When working collaboratively on a document in real time, you may want to communicate with your colleagues via chat so that you can assign responsibilities and resolve minor queries orally. See the next section, "Chat with Your Collaborators," for information.

Collaborate in Real Time on a Document

Note: Each document on which you collaborate must be shared with each collaborator. For example, if you own the document, share it as explained in the section "Share a Document on Google Drive," earlier in this chapter.

1. Open the document. For example, in Google Drive, right-click the document, click or highlight **Open with** (✥), and then click the appropriate app, such as **Google Docs** (▤).

Ⓐ The Shared icon (👥) indicates that the document is shared.

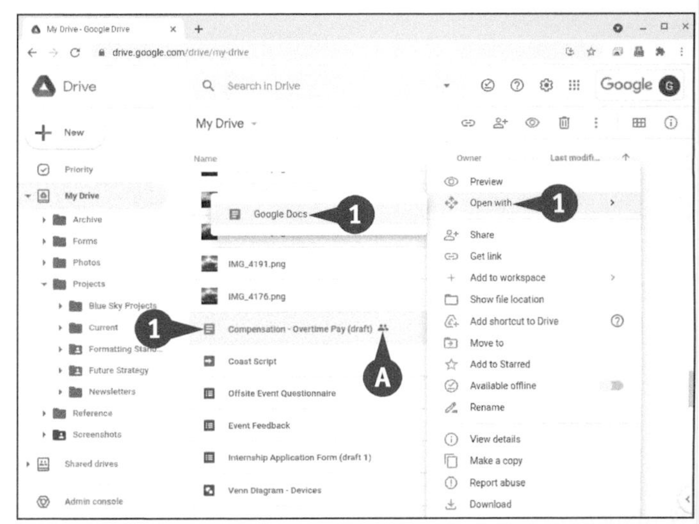

Ⓑ A new browser tab opens.

The document opens in the app.

In this example, the document opens in Google Docs.

2. Move the cursor over **Share** (👥).

Ⓒ The pop-up message shows the number of people with whom the document is shared.

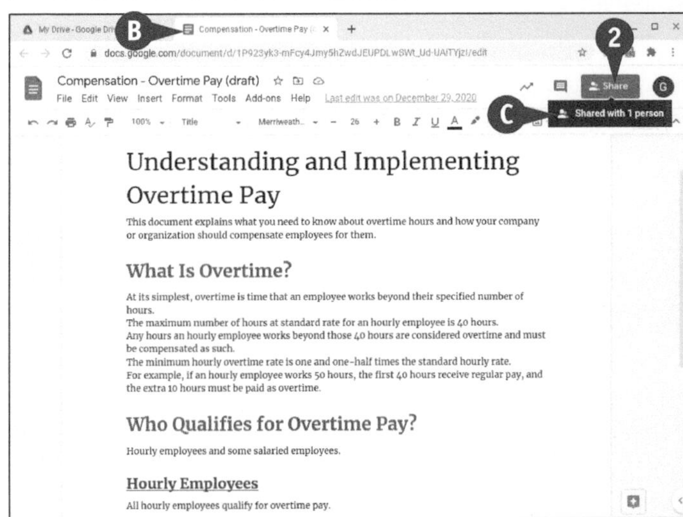

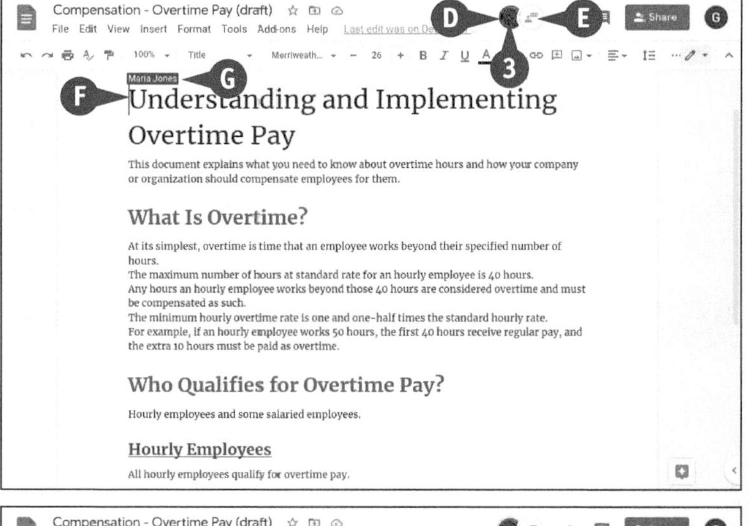

D When a collaborator opens the document, the collaborator's icon (such as M or ●) appears.

E The Show Chat icon (💬) also appears.

F A colored cursor (such as |) indicates the position of the collaborator's cursor.

G A tooltip showing the collaborator's name appears for a few seconds. You can display it again by moving your cursor over the collaborator's cursor.

3 To view a collaborator's information, move the cursor over their icon.

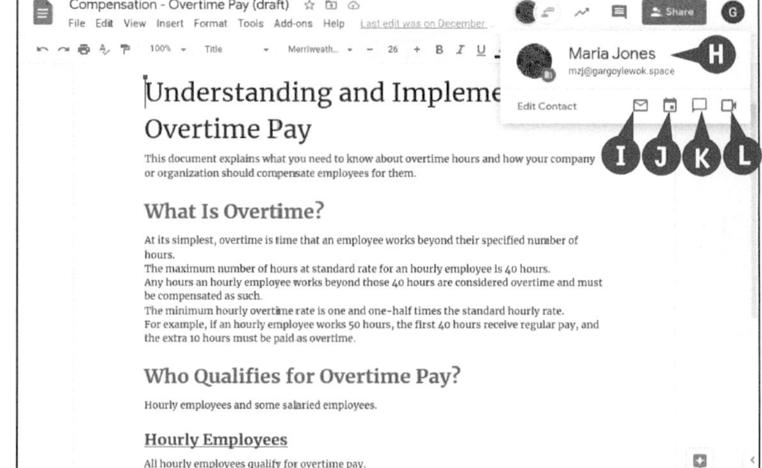

H A pop-up panel opens, showing the collaborator's name and email address, plus control buttons.

I You can click **Send email** (✉) to start an email message to the collaborator.

J You can click **Schedule event** (📅) to start scheduling an event, such as a meeting.

K You can click **Send message** (💬) to send an instant message.

L You can click **Start video call** (📹) to start a video call to the collaborator.

TIPS

What happens if a collaborator loses their network connection?

If the collaborator has set up Google Drive's Offline Mode, as explained in the section "Enable and Use Google Drive's Offline Mode" in Chapter 2, the collaborator can continue working on the document. When their computer reconnects, the app synchronizes the changes. Generally speaking, however, it is better to stop making changes once offline, because the chance of creating conflicting changes rises steeply.

Are there limitations on collaborative editing?

The main limitation to be aware of is that the documents must be stored on Google Drive rather than in other locations. Google Drive provides the necessary tracking of editors and commenters and management of different versions.

continued ▶

Collaborate in Real Time on a Document (continued)

Real-time collaborative editing has long appeared to be the ultimate in collaboration tools, which has created a widespread perception that whenever collaborative editing is available, people should use it so as to avoid missing out on its benefits. But in fact, though collaborative editing does offer real benefits, they are worthwhile for only some documents and situations — so do not allow yourself to be pressured to use collaborative editing if you find it does not suit particular documents; particular activities, such as outline development or fact checking; or even your work style, your concentration, or your mood.

Collaborate in Real Time on a Document (continued)

When a collaborator is editing the document, the app updates the document on your screen as quickly as possible. There may be a slight lag.

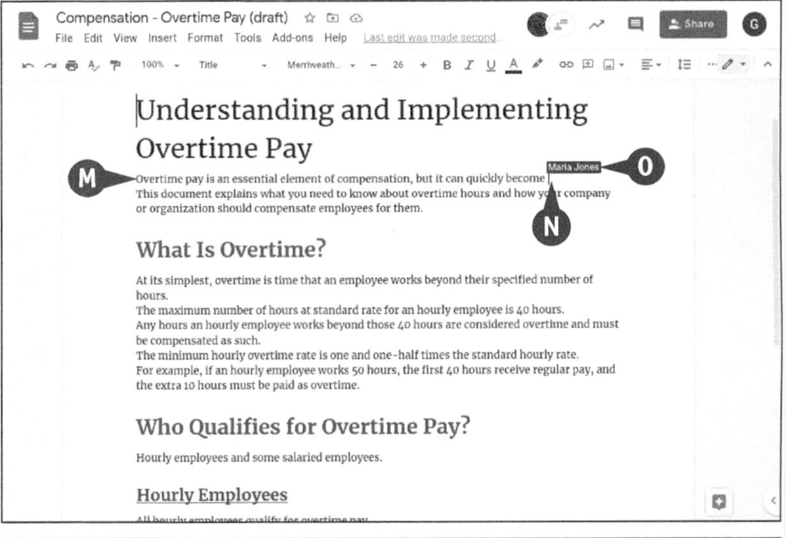

M When the collaborator makes edits, the edits appear without revision marks. In this example, the collaborator is adding a new first body paragraph under the heading.

N The colored cursor shows where the collaborator is working.

O The name pop-up button appears briefly when the collaborator is making a change.

P When the collaborator inserts a comment, the comment appears in the markup pane, as usual.

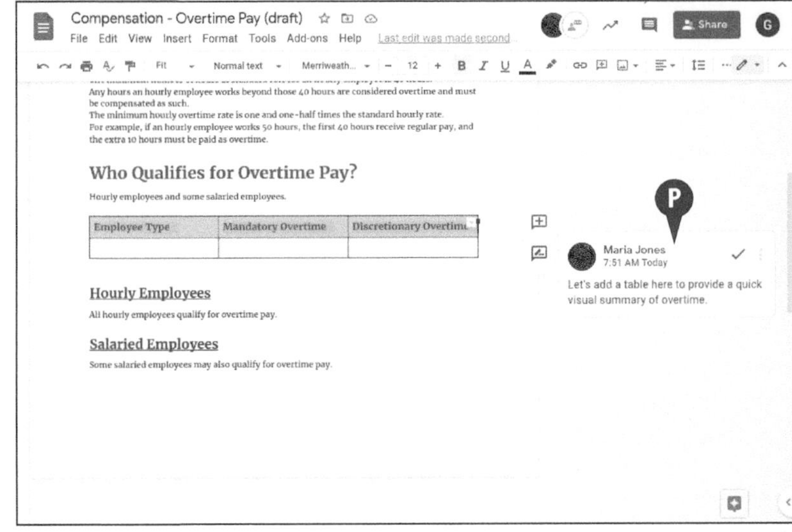

Q When the collaborator makes a suggestion, the document shows inserted text in color and deleted text with a color strikethrough.

R The summary of the suggestion appears in the markup pane.

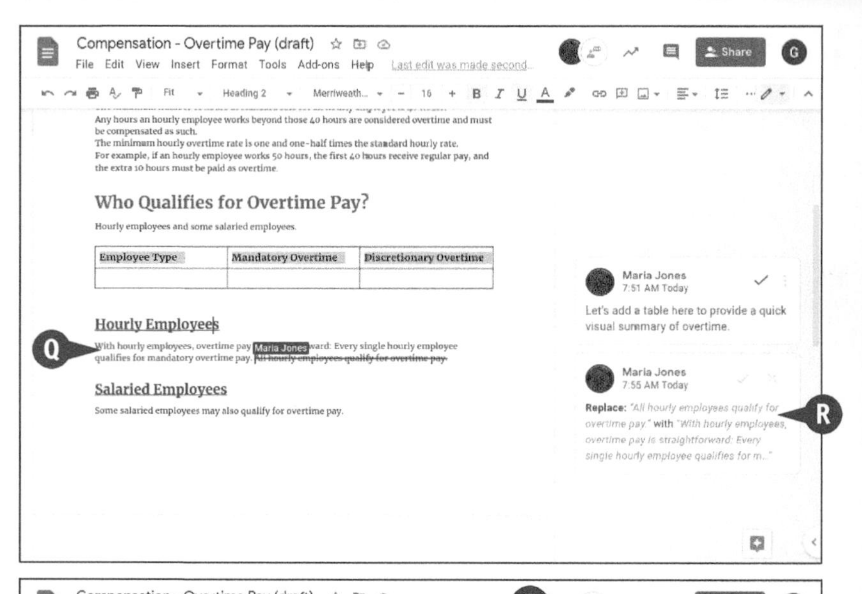

S When the collaborator closes the document, their icon disappears but the Show Chat icon ( ) remains.

There is no other notification that the collaborator has closed the document.

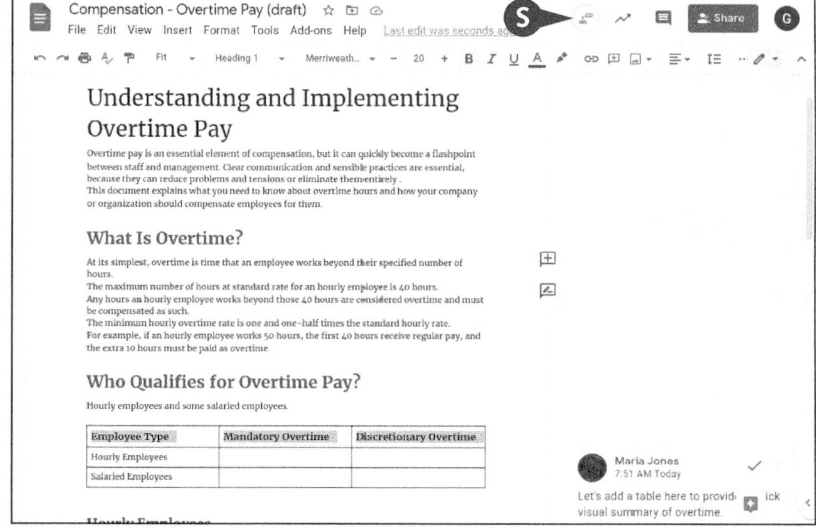

TIP

Can two editors work on the same part of the document at once?

This depends on the app and what the part of the document consists of, but generally speaking, the apps permit multiple editors to work on nearby parts of the document. For example, in Google Docs two editors can usually make edits in the same paragraph without the app blocking either of them from making changes.

Chat with Your Collaborators

When you collaborate in real time on a document, you may find it helpful to chat with your collaborators. For example, you may need to agree who will write, develop, or edit each section of a document, or you may want to discuss the best resolution for suggestions and comments.

Google Docs, Google Sheets, and Google Slides include a built-in Chat feature that enables you to start a chat from within the app. You can toggle the display of the Chat pane on and off, as needed.

Chat with Your Collaborators

Ⓐ When a collaborator has opened the document, the collaborator's icon (such as Ⓜ or ●) appears.

1 Click **Show chat** ( ).

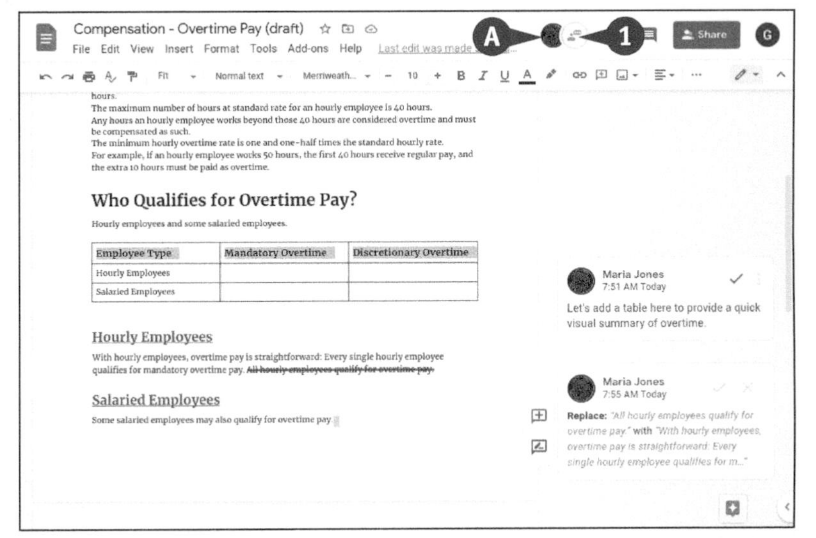

Ⓑ The Chat pane opens on the right of the window.

Ⓒ The readout at the top of the pane shows the number of editors and their names.

2 Click the **Type here to chat** prompt, type your message, and then press Enter or Return.

The app sends the message.

3 If you need to reclaim the space the Chat pane occupies, click **Close** (✕).

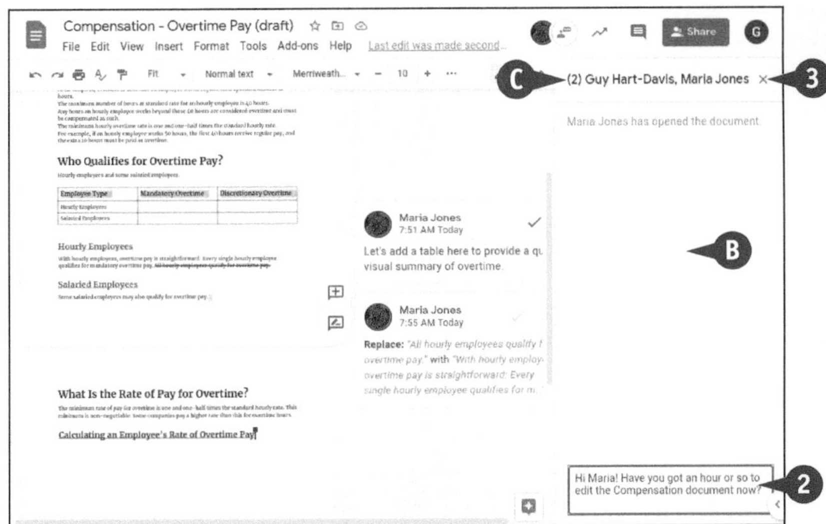

Note: If your computer's monitor permits a wide enough window to keep the Chat pane visible without shrinking the document's contents awkwardly, you may prefer to simply keep the Chat pane open.

The Chat pane closes.

D The Show Chat button displays a red badge ( ) to indicate when you have unread messages.

4 Click **Show chat** ( ).

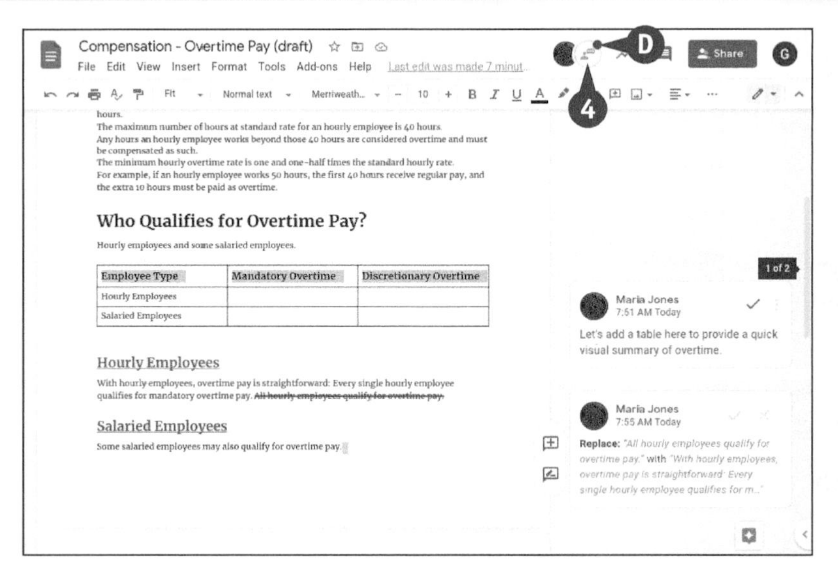

The Chat pane opens again.

E Any replies or new messages from your collaborators appear.

F To reply, click the **Type here to chat** prompt, type your message, and then press Enter or Return.

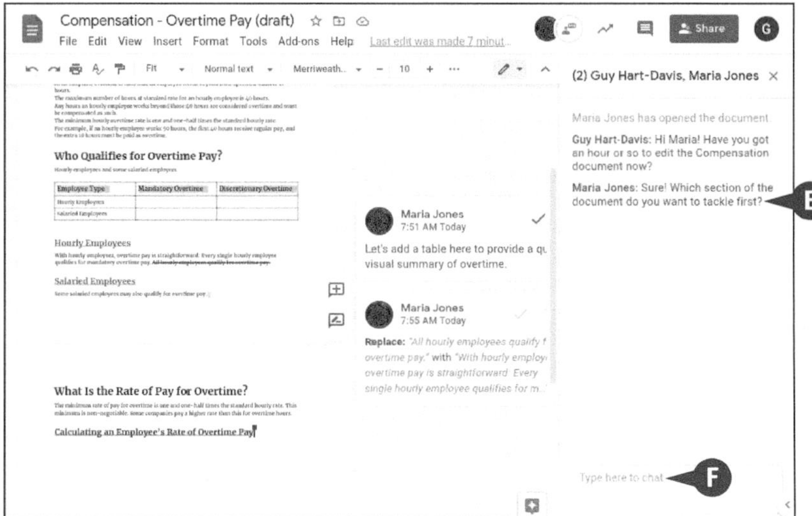

TIP

Can I chat with collaborators outside my organization?

Yes, you can, but each outside collaborator must be using a Google Account for the sharing. If you share a document with an outside collaborator who uses a different account type, you cannot chat with that collaborator. Instead, send an email message. Move the cursor over the collaborator's account icon (such as M) to display the pop-up panel for the collaborator, and then click **Send email** ( ) to start an email message.

Compare Two Documents in Google Docs

The Compare Documents feature in Google Docs enables you to compare two versions of the same document and automatically mark the differences between them. Compare Documents is great for reconciling separate copies of the document that contain different edits made directly in the file rather than using suggestions or comments.

The terminology for comparing documents is somewhat awkward. The document you use as the basis for the comparison is typically termed the "original document." The document you compare with it is the "comparison document." The new document that shows the changes between the two is the "comparison results document."

Compare Two Documents in Google Docs

1. Open the document you want to use as the basis for the comparison — for example, the original document.
2. Click **Tools**.

   The Tools menu opens.
3. Click **Compare documents.**

   The Compare Documents dialog box opens.
4. In the Select the Comparison Document box, click the current location, such as **My Drive** (📁).

   The Open a File dialog box appears.
5. Navigate to the location that contains the comparison document. For example, click **Recent** to display the Recent tab.
6. Click the comparison document.
7. Click **Open**.

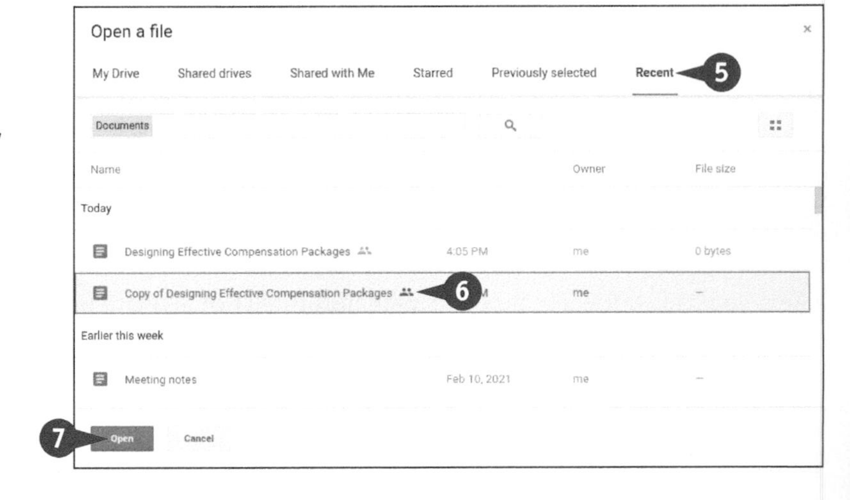

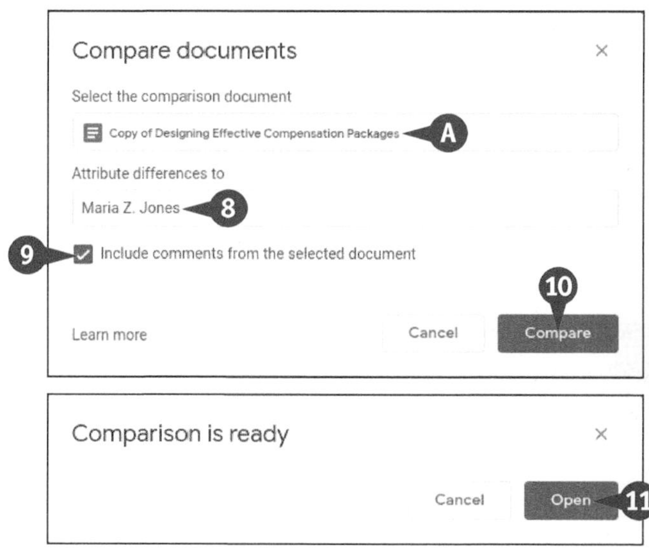

The Compare Documents dialog box appears again.

A The comparison document's name appears.

8 In the **Attribute differences to** box, enter the name with which to mark the changes from the comparison document.

9 Select **Include comments from the selected document** (☑) if you want to include comments.

10 Click **Compare**.

The Compare Documents dialog box closes.

The Comparison Is Ready dialog box opens.

11 Click **Open**.

The comparison results document, named *Comparison of* and the document names, opens in a new browser tab.

B The changes appear with tracking.

You can now review the changes, accepting or rejecting them, as needed.

Note: See the next section, "Review Comments," for coverage of reviewing comments and suggestions.

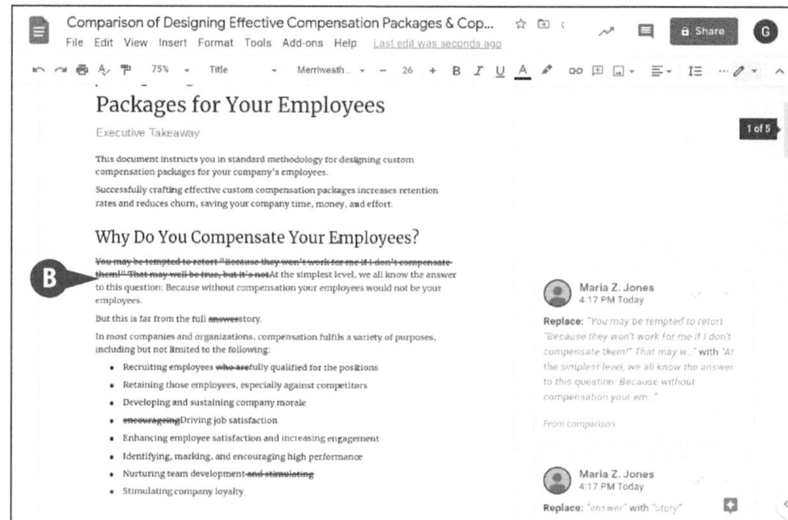

TIP

How can I compare three documents?

You can run the Compare Documents command twice — but you need to do so the right way.

First, run Compare Documents on the original document and the comparison document, as discussed in the main text. Review the comparison results document, removing all the tracked changes by either accepting them or rejecting them; you need to do this because otherwise the next Compare Documents operation will accept all the changes. If you want to leave a question open, insert a comment containing the question.

Once you have removed all tracked changes, run Compare Document from the comparison results document, and select the third document as the comparison document.

Review Comments

Google Docs, Google Sheets, and Google Slides let you insert comments attached to items in the document. For example, in Google Docs, you might comment on a particular sentence or paragraph; in Google Sheets, you might comment on a cell or a chart; and in Google Slides, you might comment on a slide or an image.

When you share a document, you can assign the Commenter role to enable a colleague to insert comments but not make edits. You can review the comments, replying to them, resolving them, or deleting them, as needed.

Review Comments

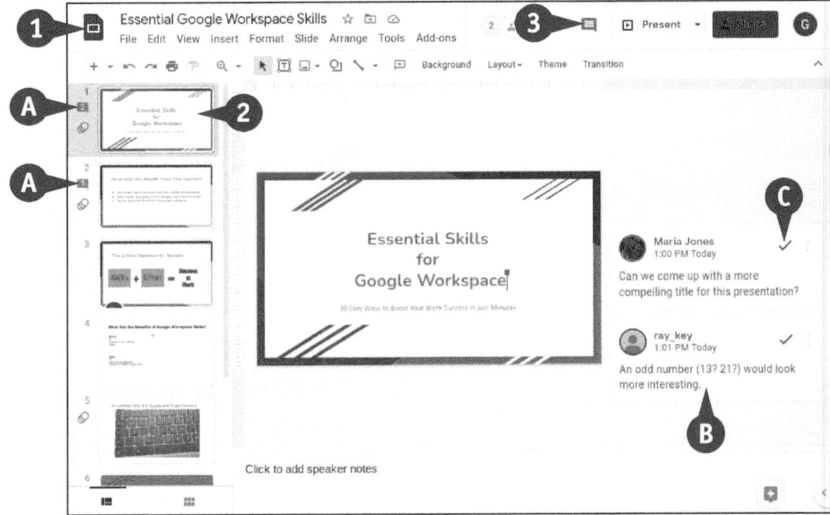

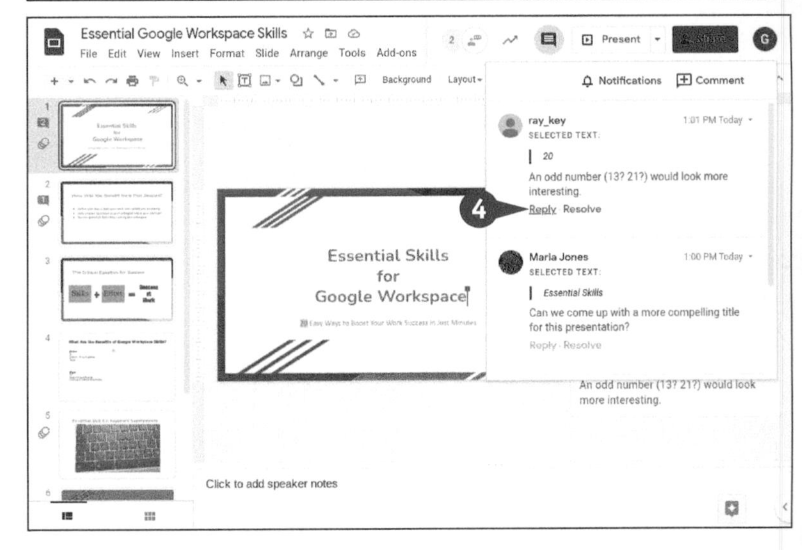

1. Open the document in which you want to review comments.

   This example shows a presentation document in Google Slides.

   A. A Comment indicator (such as 1 or 2) indicates that a slide contains comments.

2. Click the slide you want to view.

   The slide appears.

   B. The comments automatically appear.

   C. You can click **Mark as resolved and hide discussion** (✓) to mark the comment as resolved and hide it.

3. For more options than marking the comment as resolved, click **Comment history** (▤).

   The Comment History pane opens, showing the comments for the current slide.

4. Click **Reply**.

The comment expands to show the Reply field.

5. Click in the box and type the text of your reply.
6. Click **Reply**.

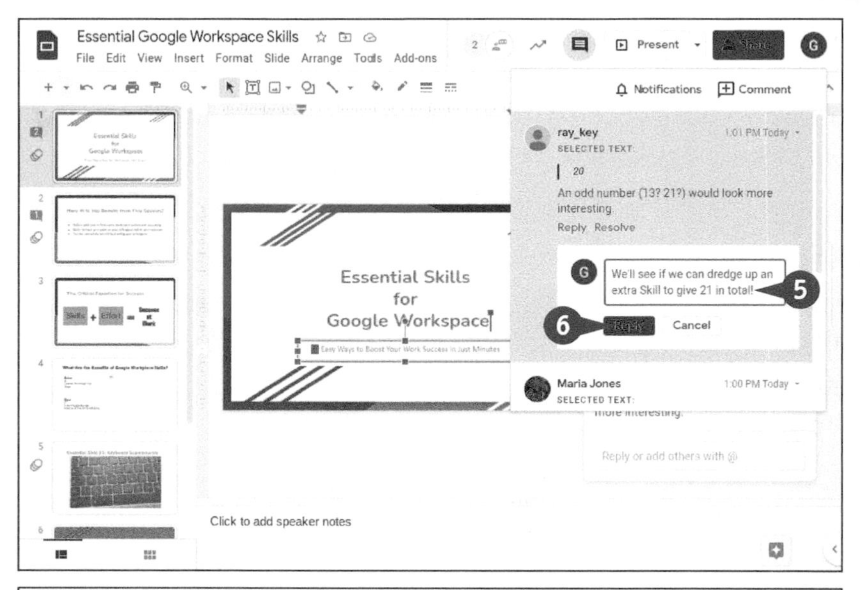

- D Your reply appears in the Comment History pane.
- E You can click **Edit** to edit your reply.
- F You can click **Delete** to delete your reply.

A second Reply box appears in case you need to add more text or direct a reply to someone by entering @ followed by their name or email address.

7. When you finish reviewing comments, click **Comment history** (▤).

The Comment History pane closes.

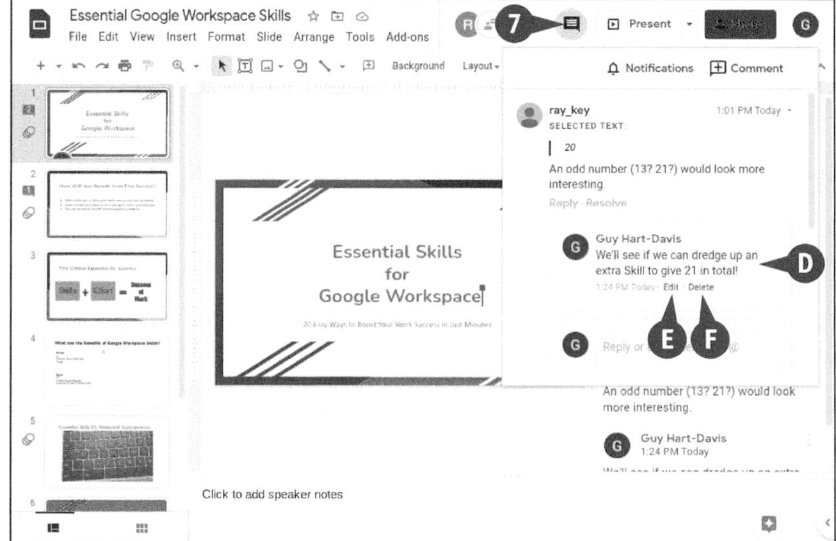

TIP

What does the Menu icon (⋮) on a comment let me do?

It lets you create a link to the comment. Click **Menu** (⋮) to open the menu, and then click **Link to this comment** to display the Link to This Comment dialog box, in which the text box contains the link. Click **Copy Link** to copy the link to your computer's Clipboard, from which you can paste it into a message or a document.

Revert to an Earlier Version of a Document

Google Docs, Google Sheets, and Google Slides store information about different versions of your documents, where a *version* contains the state of a document at a particular point in time. The apps enable you to revert to an earlier version of a document when needed. Reverting can be a great way to recover from ill-advised changes or from accidental deletions that go unnoticed until later.

To help you identify key versions of a document, the apps let you assign a descriptive name to the current version and to browse all extant versions or all versions that you have named.

Revert to an Earlier Version of a Document

Assign a Name to the Current Version

1. With the document open, click **File**.

   The File menu opens.

2. Click or highlight **Version history**.

   The Version History submenu opens.

3. Click **Name current version**.

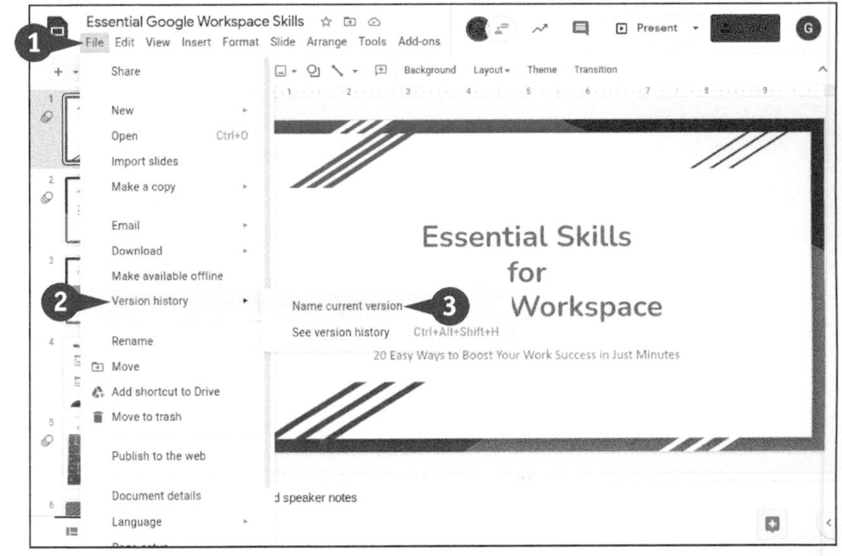

The Name Current Version dialog box opens.

4. Type the name for the version.
5. Click **Save**.

   The Name Current Version dialog box closes.

A. A pop-up message saying *Named in version history* appears for a few seconds.

B. You can click **View** to open the Version History pane and display the version.

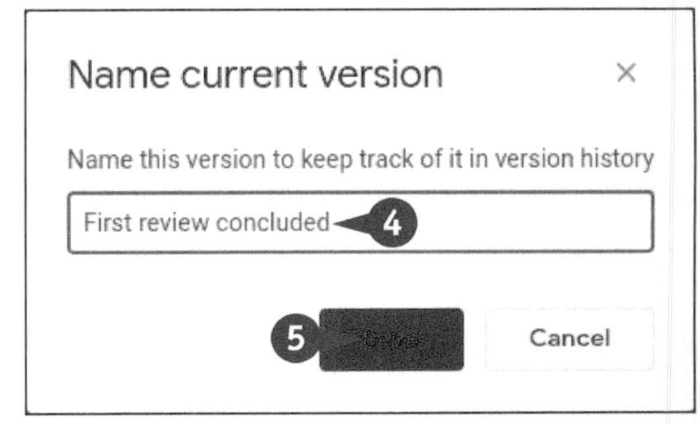

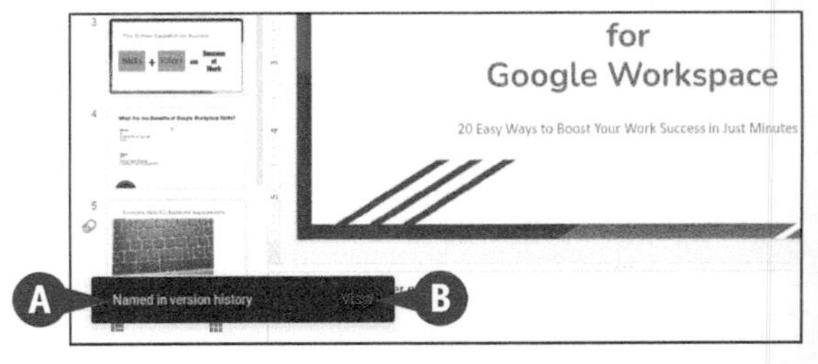

Revert to an Earlier Version of the Document

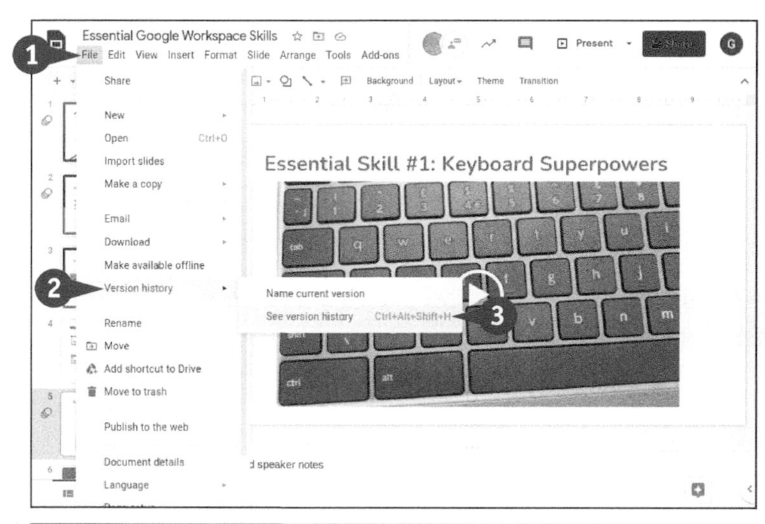

1. With the document open, click **File**.

   The File menu opens.

2. Click or highlight **Version history**.

   The Version History submenu opens.

3. Click **See version history**.

   The Version History pane appears.

C You can set the **Only show named versions** switch to On (changes to) to display only versions you and your colleagues have named.

4. Click the version you want to review.

5. Select **Show changes** (☑).

D Details of the version's edits appear. You can click **Previous** (^) and **Next** (v) to move through the edits to make sure this is the version you want.

6. When you identify the version you want to restore, click **Restore this version**.

E If you decide not to restore a version, click **Back** (←) to return to the document.

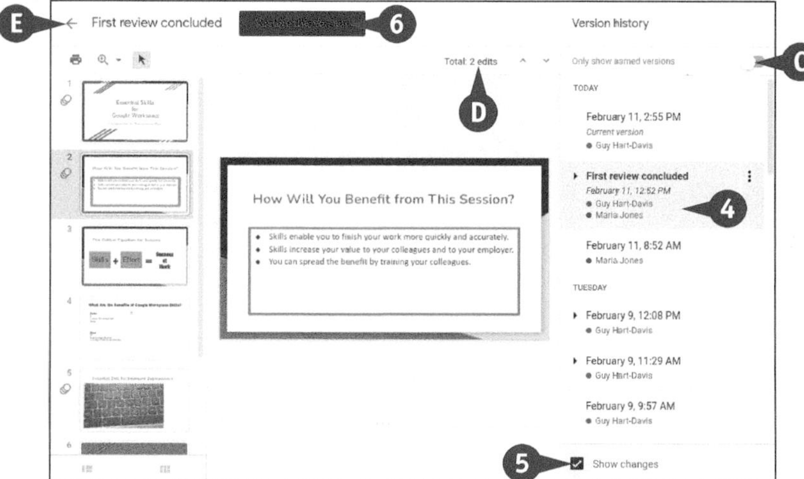

TIPS

What other actions can I take in the Version History pane?

You can rename a version, remove the name from a named version, or make a copy of a version. Click the version you want to affect; click **Menu** (⋮) in the upper-right corner of the version to open the pop-up menu; and then click **Rename**, **Remove name**, or **Make a copy**, as needed.

Can I restore a version while other people are working on the document?

Yes, but warn your collaborators before you do. Otherwise, they see the document refresh, and then the restored version appears without explanation, often apparently losing their current work. Worse, a collaborator can then restore the latest version, or another version, exacerbating the confusion.

Change Ownership of a File or Folder

When you create a new file or folder on Google Drive, or when you upload a file or folder to Google Drive, you become the owner of that file or folder. The *owner* is the person who has ultimate control of a file or folder. The owner can give others permission to view and change the file or folder. The owner can also delete the folder.

Each file or folder can have only one owner at any given time. Normally, you would retain ownership of your files and folders, but you may sometimes need to transfer ownership to someone else.

Change Ownership of a File or Folder

Note: Before you can change ownership of a file or folder, you must share the file or folder with the person to whom you want to transfer ownership.

1. In Google Drive, navigate to the location or folder that contains the file or folder whose ownership you want to transfer.

Note: You can also transfer ownership of a file by opening it in Google Docs, Google Sheets, or Google Slides, and then clicking **Share**.

2. Right-click the file or folder.

   The contextual menu opens.

3. Click **Share** (👤+).

   The Share with People and Groups dialog box opens.

   A. Your Google Account, identified by "(you)," is the owner.

4. Click **Role** (▾) on the row for the person to whom you want to transfer ownership.

   The Role pop-up menu opens.

5. Click **Make owner**.

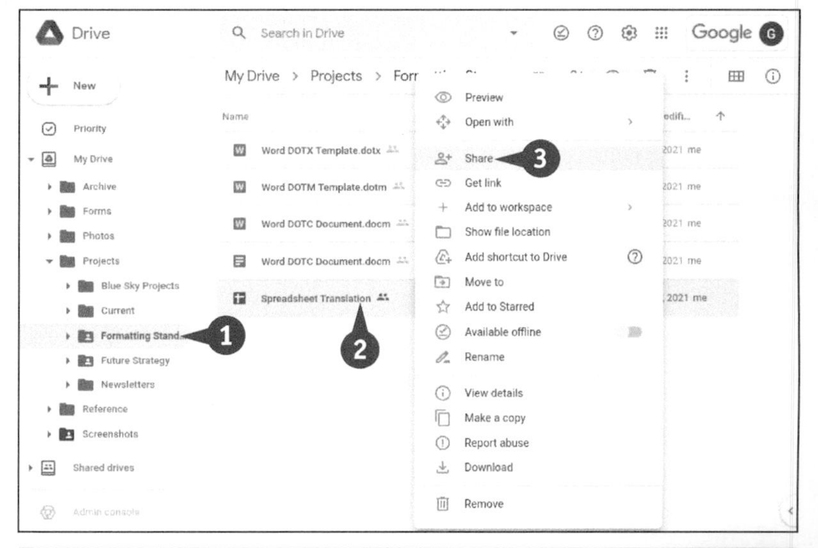

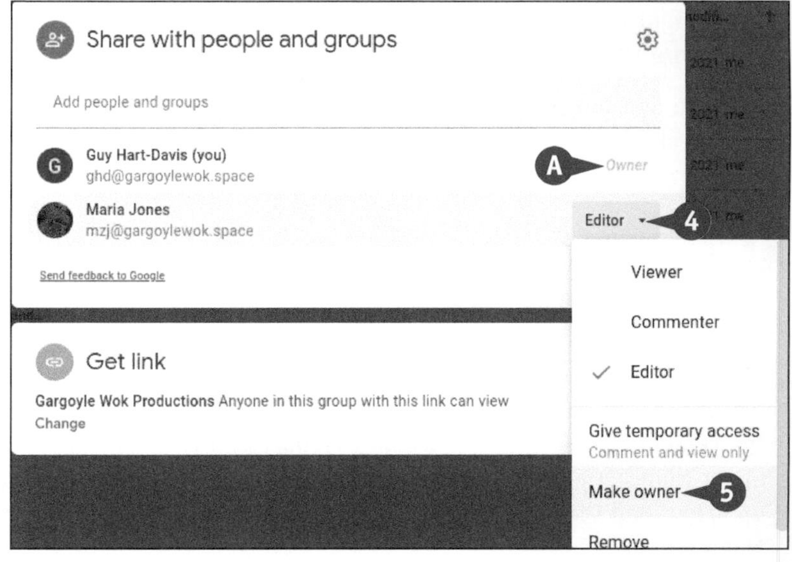

The Make This Person the Owner? dialog box opens.

6 Read the warning about how the new owner might remove you from the file or folder.

7 Click **Yes** if you want to proceed.

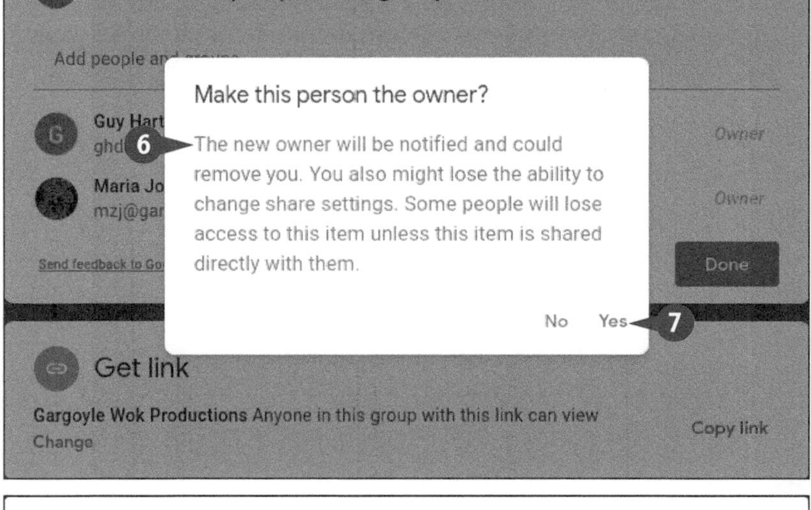

The Make This Person the Owner? dialog box closes.

The Share with People and Groups dialog box appears again.

B The *Owner* readout appears for the new owner.

C Your role changes to Editor, because Editor has the next highest level of permissions.

8 Click **Done**.

The Share with People and Groups dialog box closes.

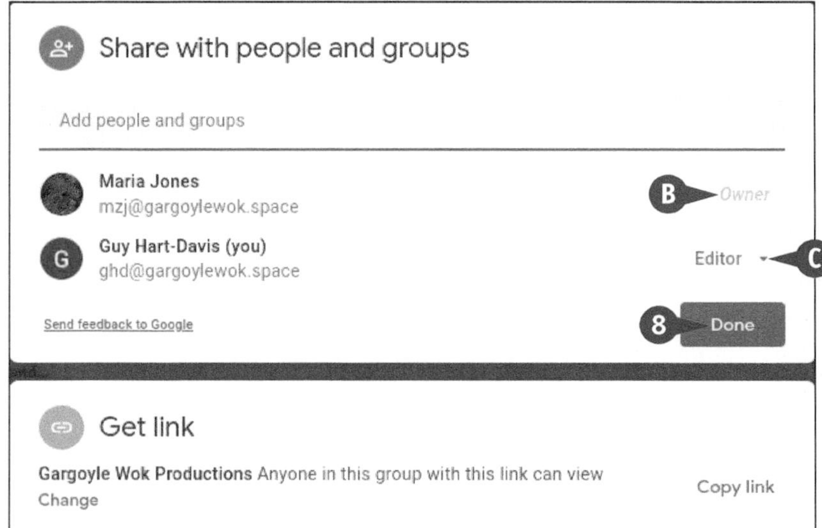

TIPS

When I transfer ownership of a folder, what happens to the files it contains?
When you transfer ownership of a folder, the new owner owns the folder, but you retain ownership of the files and subfolders inside the folder. If you want to transfer ownership of the files and subfolders as well, you must do so explicitly.

Can I transfer ownership of any type of file?
No. You can transfer ownership of folders and of the following file types: Google Docs, Google Sheets, Google Slides, Google Drawings, and Google My Maps. You cannot transfer ownership of other file types, such as image files, audio files, or Microsoft Office documents.

Understanding Backup Tools for Windows and Mac

Over the years, Google has provided several different tools for backing up and synchronizing files from your Windows PC or your Mac to Google Drive. These tools enable you to keep local copies of the files you store in your Google Drive and to work on those local copies with the apps installed on your computer.

For consumers, Google has offered the Backup and Sync app for Windows and macOS. For G Suite and Google Workspace, Google has provided Google Drive File Stream. Google is now replacing both Backup and Sync and Google Drive File Stream with Google Drive for Desktop.

Understanding Backup and Sync

Backup and Sync is an app targeted at consumers but also usually available to Google Workspace users, depending on how the organization's administrator configures Google Workspace.

Backup and Sync enables you to choose which folders to sync from your PC or Mac to your Google Drive and which folders to sync from your Google Drive to your PC or Mac.

On the My PC screen or the My Mac screen, select **Desktop** (☑, A), **Documents** (☑, B), and **Pictures** (☑, C), as needed. You can add other folders by clicking **CHOOSE FOLDER** (D) and following the prompts. In the Photo and Video Upload Size area, click **High quality** (◉, E) or **Original quality** (◉, F), as needed. In the Google Photos area, select **Upload photos and videos to Google Photos** (☑, G) to upload photos. Click **Next** (H) to continue.

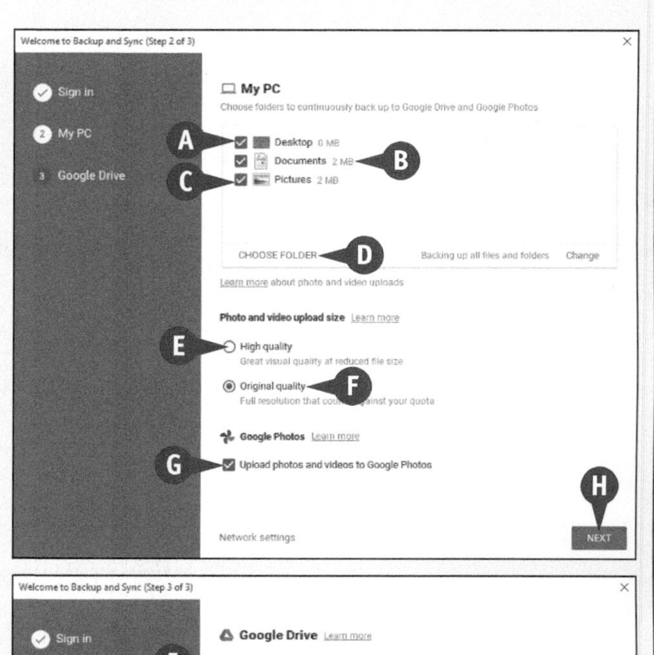

On the Google Drive screen, select **Sync My Drive to this computer** (☑, I). Then either select **Sync everything in My Drive** (◉, J) to sync all the files from your Google Drive, or select **Sync only these folders** (◉, K), and then select the individual folders to sync. Click **START** (L) to start syncing.

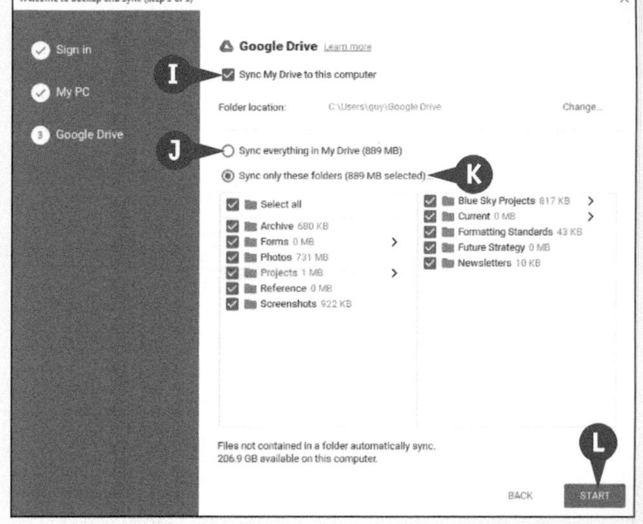

Understanding Google Drive File Stream

Unlike Backup and Sync, Google Drive File Stream is only available for business, enterprise, and education users through Google Workspace and G Suite. Whereas Backup and Sync provides consumer-focused features, such as syncing your photos to Google Photos, Google Drive File Stream is intended only for directly working with files on Google Drive.

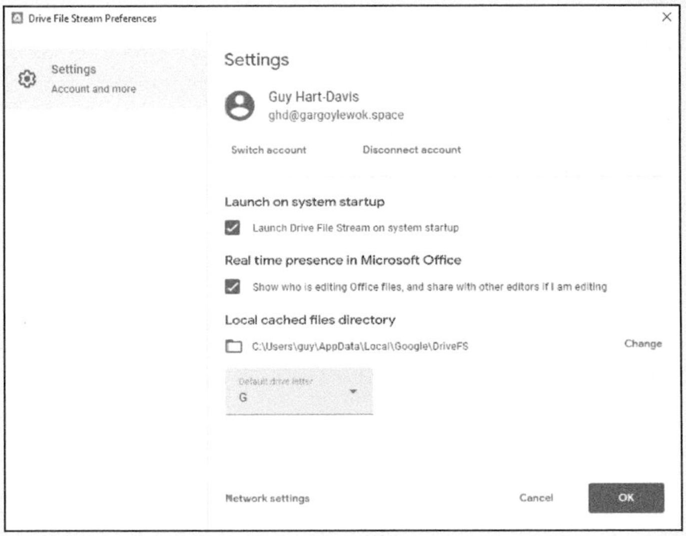

Google Drive File Stream is not intended to sync your computer's data to Google Drive, or vice versa — instead, it enables your computer to use Google Drive as if it were a local drive, either by streaming files across the Internet or by maintaining local copies of files or folders you explicitly choose.

Google Drive File Stream is a great tool for power users, because it allows them to quickly and reliably upload, download, and manipulate files by streaming them across the Internet in real time.

The streaming element in Google Drive File Stream allows your PC or Mac request to download particular segments of a file rather than the entire file, which can vastly speed up the process of working with files up to 5 terabytes — 5TB — in size.

As of this writing, Google is replacing Google Drive File Stream with Google Drive for Desktop. See the next section, "Using Google Drive for Desktop," for details.

Using Google Drive for Desktop

Google Drive for Desktop is Google's latest tool for both backing up and syncing files to and from Google Drive and for streaming them from there. As of this writing, Google is gradually replacing both the consumer-focused Backup and Sync tool and the business-oriented Google Drive File Stream tool with Google Drive for Desktop.

If you are still using either Backup and Sync or Google Drive File Stream, you will likely need to move to Google Drive for Desktop in the near future.

Install Google Drive for Desktop on Windows

To start installing Google Drive for Desktop on Windows, open a browser window and go to the Google Drive Download page, www.google.com/drive/download. Locate the link for downloading the installer file, and then click it to start the download.

When the download is complete, run the installer file. In the User Account Control dialog box that opens, confirm that the Verified Publisher is Google LLC (A), and then click **Yes** (B).

In the Install Google Drive? dialog box, select **Add an application shortcut to your Desktop** (☑, C) if you want to create a Google Drive shortcut on your Desktop; if you prefer to run the app automatically on startup, you may not need a shortcut. Select **Add desktop shortcuts to Google Docs, Sheets, and Slides** (☑, D) if you want shortcuts for the three apps. Then click **Install** (E).

When the Google Drive Successfully Installed dialog box opens, click **Close** (F). You can then run the app by clicking **Google Drive** (△) on your Desktop, if you chose to create the shortcut, or on the Start menu.

The first time you run Google Drive for Desktop, you must sign in to your Google Account, providing your credentials and usually satisfying the 2-Step Verification requirement. Once authenticated, you see the Welcome to Google Drive dialog box, which gives you a short introduction to the app and its capabilities.

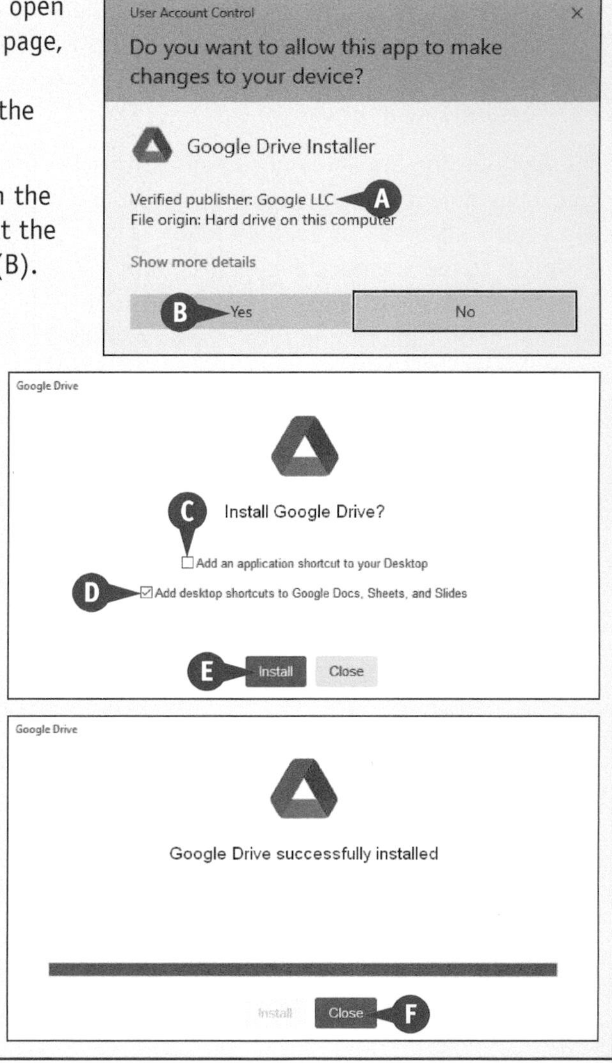

Use and Configure Google Drive for Desktop on Windows

When you dismiss the Welcome to Google Drive dialog box, a File Explorer window opens, showing your Google Drive folder. Here, you can click **My Drive** (, G) to display the contents of your Google Drive, or click **Shared drives** (, H) to display the content of shared drives available to you.

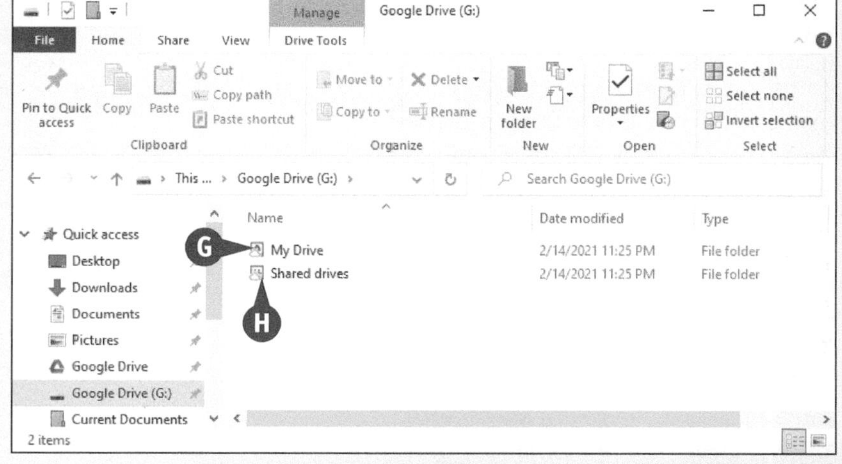

When you are not actively using the app, Google Drive for Desktop runs in the background, syncing your files automatically. To view current activity or notifications, click **Google Drive** (, I) in the system tray, and then look at the Activity tab or the Notifications tab.

To configure preferences, click **Settings** (, J), and then click **Preferences** (K) on the pop-up menu.

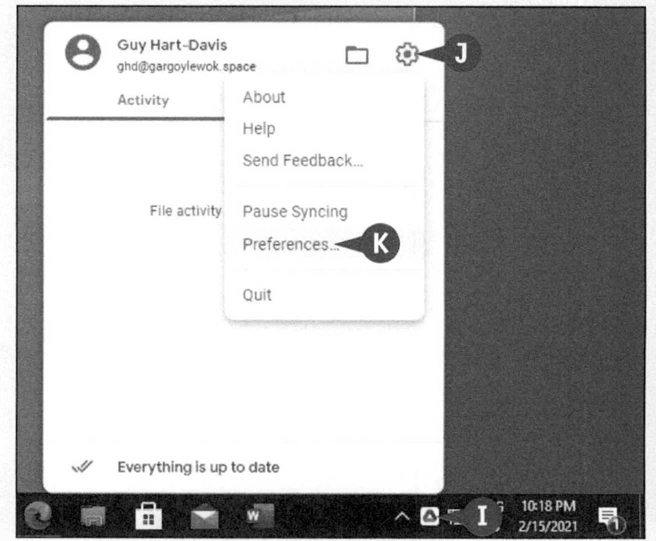

continued ▶

Google Drive for Desktop requires Windows 7 or a later desktop version, or Windows Server 2012 or a later version. On the Mac, Google Drive for Desktop requires macOS 10.11, El Capitan, or a later version: macOS 10.12, Sierra; macOS 10.13, High Sierra; macOS 10.14, Mojave; macOS 10.15, Catalina; or macOS 11, Big Sur.

As of this writing, Google Drive for Desktop does not yet support Apple's M1 processors, but Google may well have added support by the time you read this.

Use and Configure Google Drive for Desktop on Windows (continued)

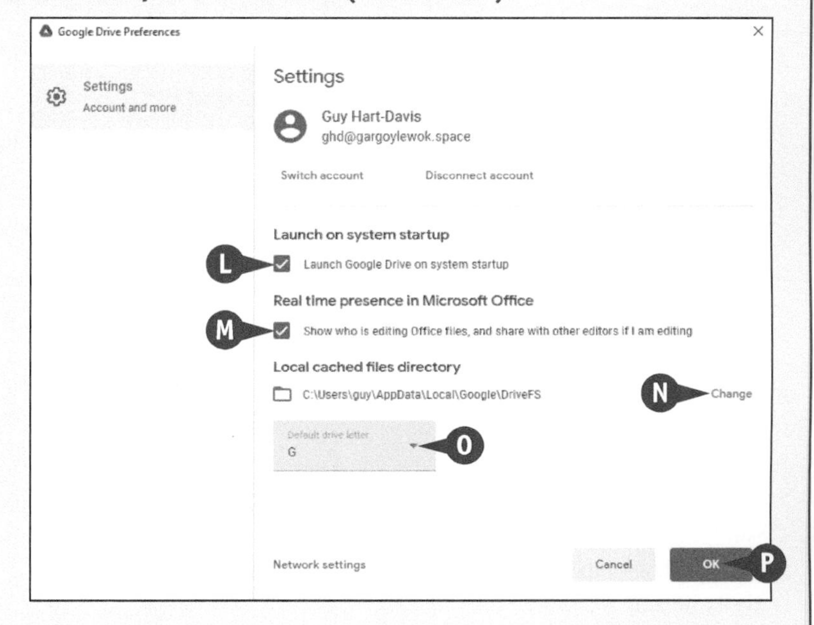

The Google Drive Preferences dialog box opens.

In the Launch on System Startup section, select **Launch Google Drive on system startup** (☑, L) if you want Windows to run Google Drive for Desktop on startup. This is usually more convenient than running it manually.

In the Real Time Presence in Microsoft Office section, select **Show who is editing Office files, and share with other editors if I am editing** (☑, M) if you want to share information about editing Microsoft Office files. This setting applies only to Office documents stored on Google Drive, not to Office documents stored elsewhere. When you open a shared document on Google Drive, its real-time status appears in the lower-right corner of the window: Safe to Edit, which means you can safely open it; Wait to Edit, which means what it says, but you can click **Notify me when it's safe to edit** to get a notification; or New Version Created, in which case you can click **Get latest** to get that version.

In the Local Cached Files Directory section, you can click **Change** (N) if you need to move your cache folder. You would not normally need to do this. You can click **Default drive letter** (▾, O) and change the default drive letter assigned to Google Drive. You might want to change the default drive letter if your computer sometimes starts with removable drives connected that change the drive letter assignments.

When you finish configuring preferences, click **OK** (P) to close the Google Drive Preferences dialog box.

Install Google Drive for Desktop on the Mac

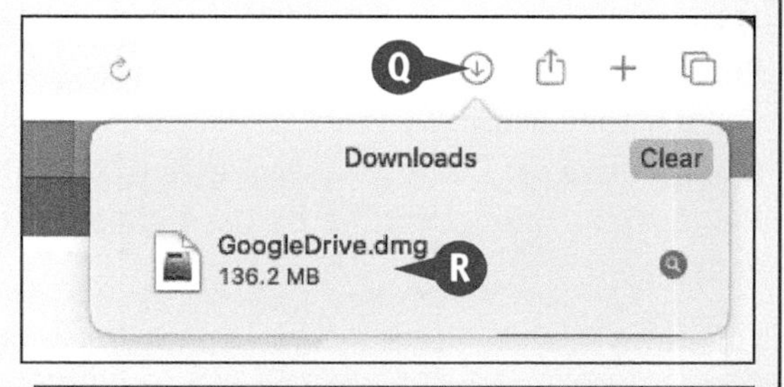

To start installing Google Drive for Desktop on macOS, open a browser window and go to the Google Drive Download page, www.google.com/drive/download. Locate the link for downloading the installer disk image file, and then click it to start the download. If the Do You Want to Allow Downloads on "support.google.com"? dialog box opens, click **Allow** to permit the download.

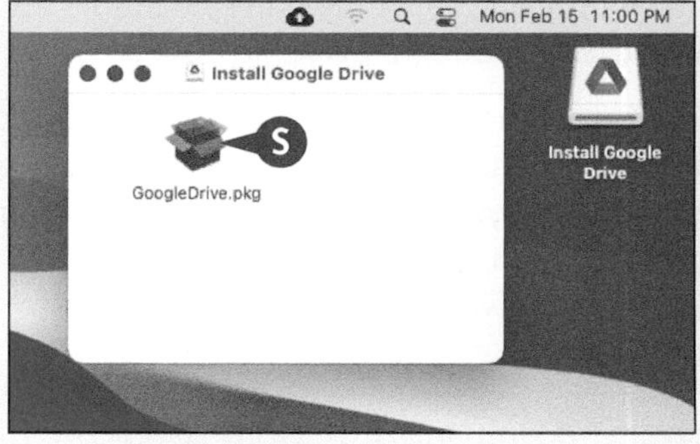

Once the download is complete, click **Downloads** (⊕, Q), and then double-click the installer disk image file (R) on the Downloads pop-up panel.

macOS expands the disk image, mounts it in the file system, displays an icon for it on the Desktop, and displays a window showing its contents. Double-click the package file (S) to run the installer.

Click **Continue** (T) on the Welcome to the Google Drive Installer screen, and then follow through the remaining screens.

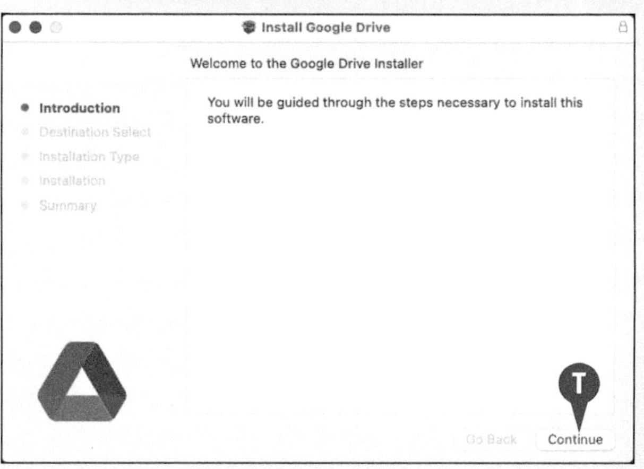

continued ►

Using Google Drive for Desktop (continued)

When installing Google Drive for Desktop on the Mac, you may find that the Gatekeeper security feature in macOS blocks the running of a system extension file that Google Drive for Desktop requires. If this happens, you will need to allow the system extension file in the Privacy & Security category of System Preferences. You may also need to restart your Mac to get macOS to run the system extension file.

Install Google Drive for Desktop on the Mac (continued)

If the System Extension Blocked dialog box opens, click **Open Security Preferences** (U) to open the System Preferences app and display the General pane in the Security & Privacy category, and then click **Allow** (V) to allow the Google Drive for Desktop system extension. If the A Restart Is Required Before New System Extensions Can Be Used dialog box opens, click **Restart** to restart your Mac.

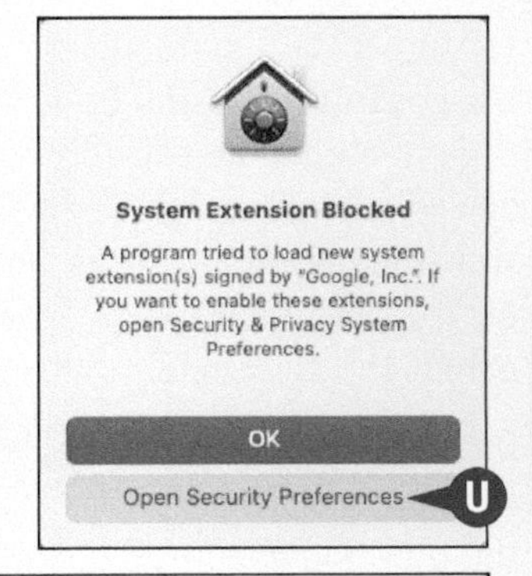

When the installation finishes, and after any necessary restart, you can run the app by clicking **Launchpad** (on macOS Big Sur, on earlier versions) and then clicking **Google Drive** ().

The first time you run Google Drive for Desktop, you must sign in to your Google Account, providing your credentials and usually satisfying the 2-Step Verification requirement. Once authenticated, you see the Welcome to Google Drive dialog box, which gives you a short introduction to the app and its capabilities.

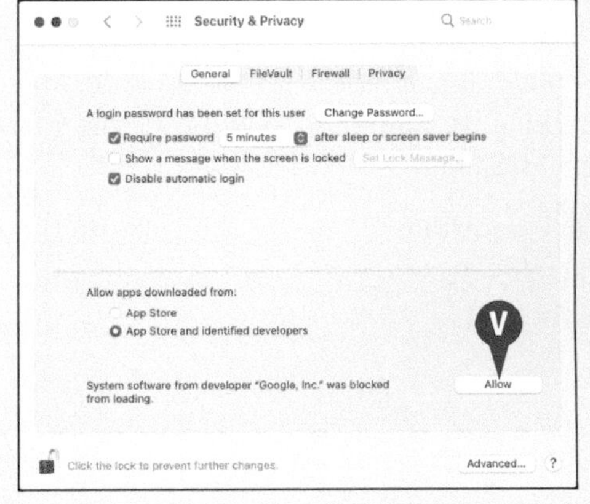

Use and Configure Google Drive for Desktop on macOS

When you dismiss the Welcome to Google Drive dialog box, a Finder window opens, showing your Google Drive mounted in the Locations list (W), and with the contents of the My Drive folder displayed. You can click **Shared drives** (X) to display the content of shared drives available to you.

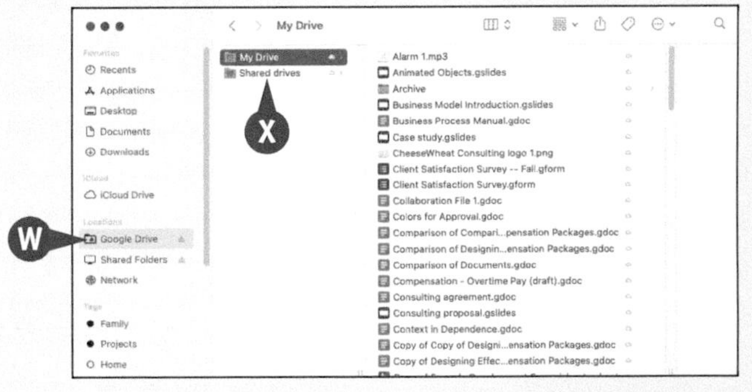

When you are not actively using the app, Google Drive for Desktop runs in the background, syncing your files automatically. To view current activity or notifications, click **Google Drive** (, Y) on the menu bar, and then look at the Activity tab or the Notifications tab in the pop-up panel.

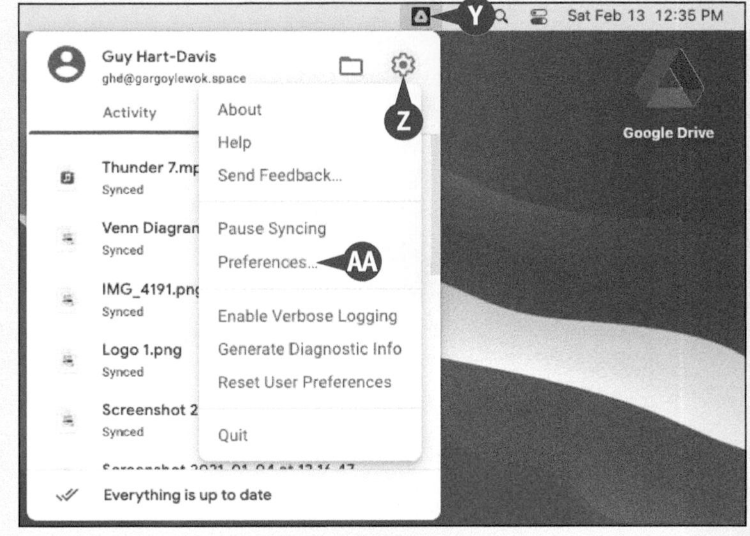

To configure preferences, click **Settings** (, Z), and then click **Preferences** (AA) on the pop-up menu. The Google Drive Preferences dialog box opens.

In the Launch on System Startup section, select **Launch Google Drive on system startup** (, AB) if you want macOS to run Google Drive for Desktop automatically on startup. This is usually more convenient than running it manually.

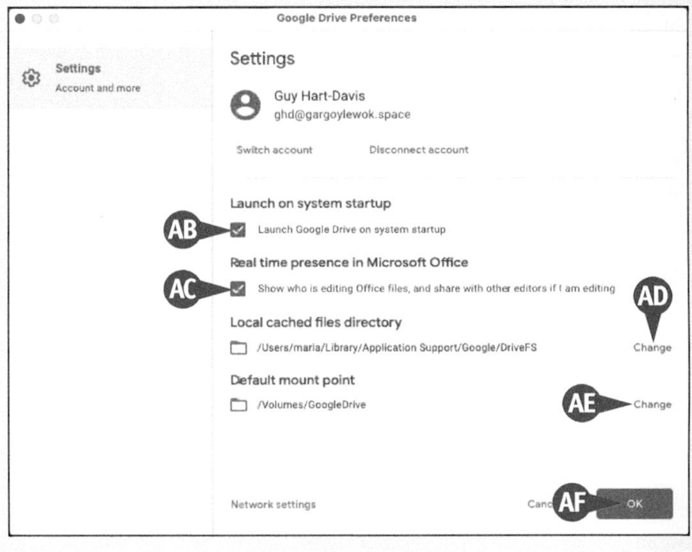

In the Real Time Presence in Microsoft Office section, select **Show who is editing Office files, and share with other editors if I am editing** (, AC) if you want to share information about editing Microsoft Office files.

In the Local Cached Files Directory section, you can click **Change** (AD) if you need to move your cache folder. You would not normally need to move this folder.

In the Default Mount Point section, you can click **Change** (AE) if you want to change the default mount point. You would not normally need to change this mount point.

When you finish configuring preferences, click **OK** (AF) to close the Google Drive Preferences dialog box.

CHAPTER 7

Working in Google Sheets

In this chapter you learn the essentials of working in Google Sheets. You start by selecting cells and ranges and entering data either manually or by importing existing data. You then develop the skills of rearranging your worksheets, inserting functions, and applying the most widely useful formatting. You also learn to insert notes and choose spreadsheet settings.

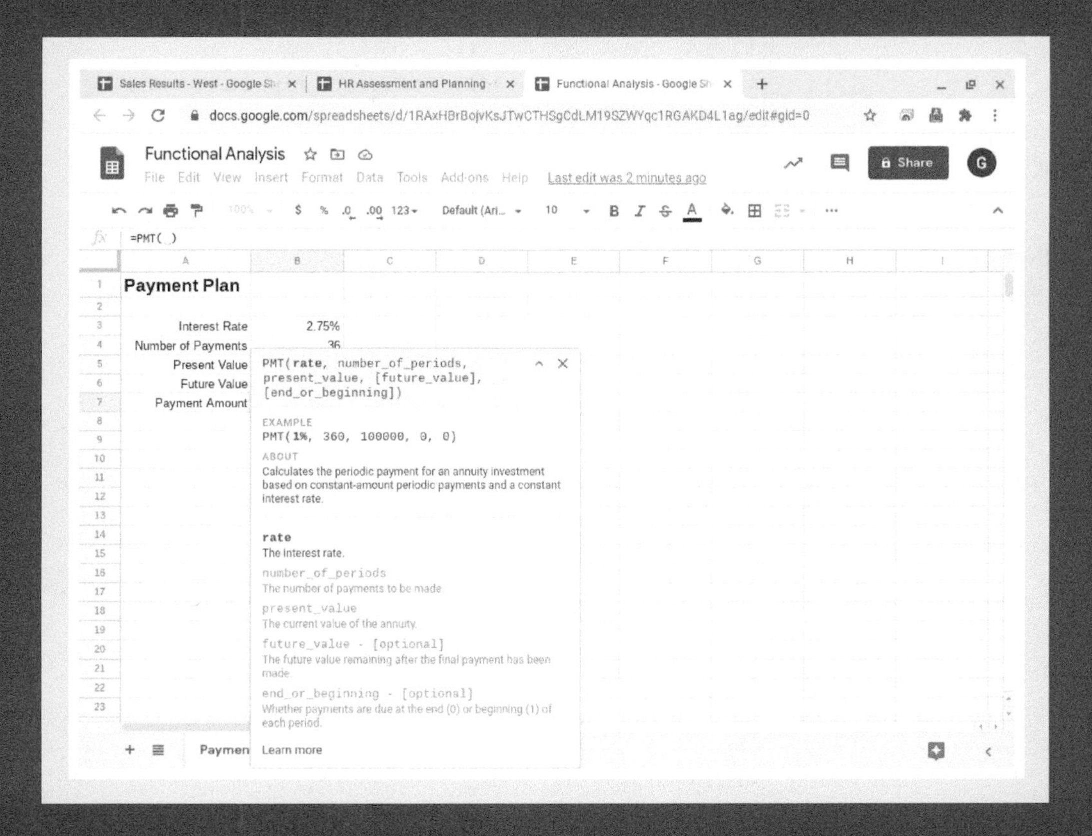

Select Cells and Ranges

To take actions in Google Sheets, you frequently need to select cells or ranges. For example, to enter data in a cell, you select the cell, and to apply formatting to a group of cells, you select that range of cells. You can select cells and ranges using the cursor, using the keyboard, or using both together.

A *range* is either a single cell or multiple cells. In a multiple-cell range, the cells can be in a single block; they can be separated from each other; or they can be a mix of adjacent cells and separate cells.

Select Cells and Ranges

Select a Cell

1. In a spreadsheet in Google Sheets, click the cell.

   The cell becomes active.

   Ⓐ A blue outline appears around the active cell.

Note: The active cell is the cell that receives keyboard input when you type.

Note: Press ← or → to move the active cell left or right by one column. Press ↑ or ↓ to move the active cell up or down by one row.

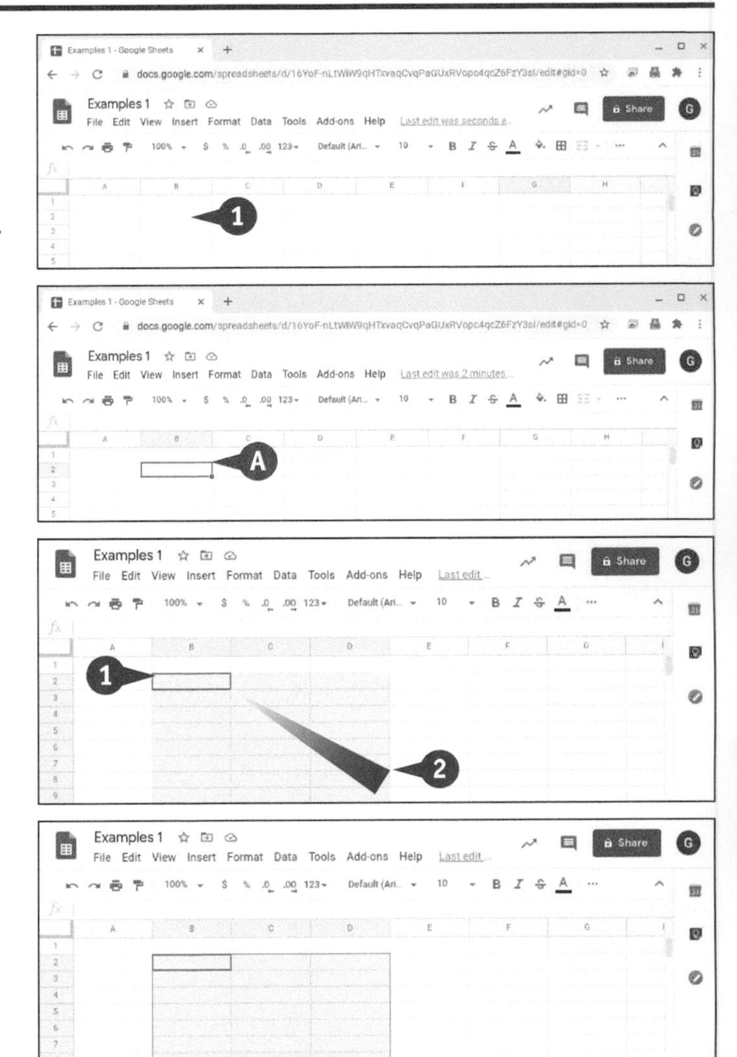

Select a Range of Contiguous Cells

1. Click a cell at one corner of the range, and keep holding down the mouse button.

Note: You can start selecting from any corner of the range. Often, starting from the upper-left corner is easiest.

2. Drag to the opposite corner of the range.

   For example, if you started at the upper-left corner, drag to the lower-right corner.

3. Release the mouse button.

   The range becomes selected.

Select a Range of Noncontiguous Cells

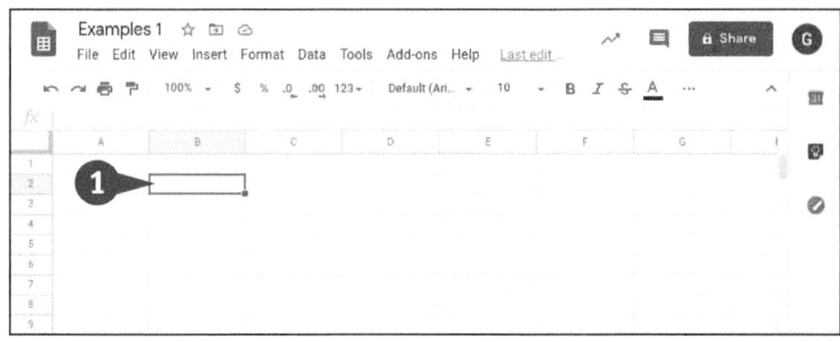

1 Click the first cell you want to include in the range.

Alternatively, press ←, →, ↑, or ↓ to select the cell.

The cell becomes active.

2 Press Ctrl+click each cell you want to add to the range.

Note: On the Mac, press ⌘ rather than Ctrl.

Each cell you click becomes part of the range and displays blue shading.

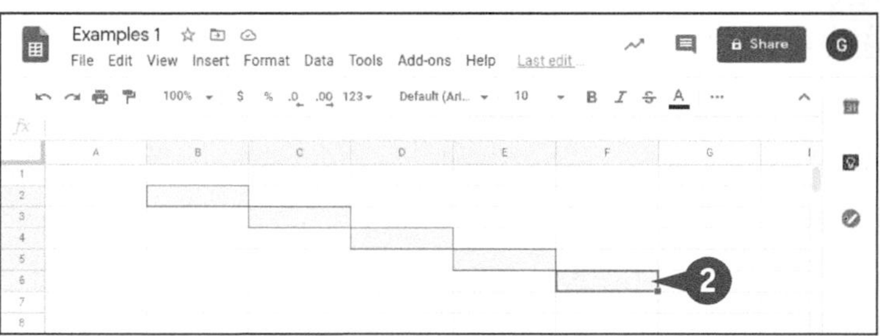

Select a Mixed Range

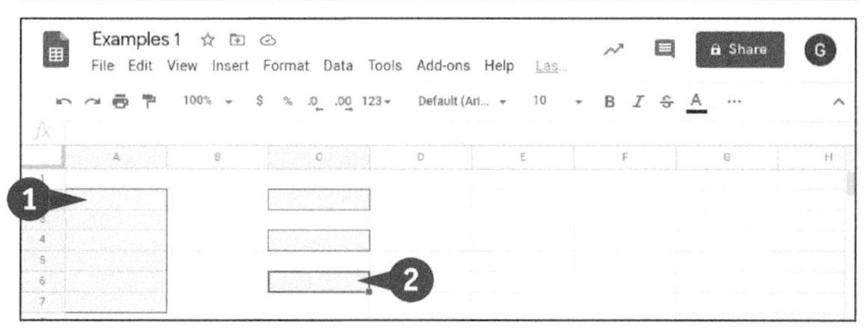

1 Select the first cell or contiguous group of cells you want to include in the range.

2 Press Ctrl+click each individual cell you want to add to the range.

Note: On the Mac, press ⌘ rather than Ctrl.

3 Press Ctrl+drag through each contiguous group of cells you want to add.

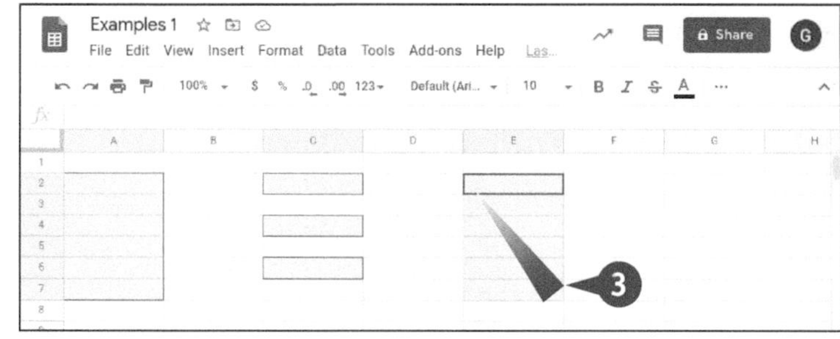

TIP

How do I select a range using the cursor and the keyboard together?
Start by clicking the cell at one corner of the range. Which corner does not matter, but the upper-left corner is usually easiest. Then press Shift+click the cell in the opposite corner of the range — for example, the lower-right corner of the range. Google Sheets selects all the cells in between.

Enter Content in Cells

You can enter content in a spreadsheet cell by typing it in or by pasting in content you have copied or cut from elsewhere. You can also enter the same content into multiple cells quickly by entering it in the first cell and making Google Sheets repeat it.

The Autofill feature can automatically enter a series of data starting from one or more values you supply. For example, Autofill can enter the days of the week starting from a cell containing *Monday* or infer a mathematical sequence starting from two cells, one containing *5* and the other containing *10*.

Enter Content in Cells

Type Content into a Cell

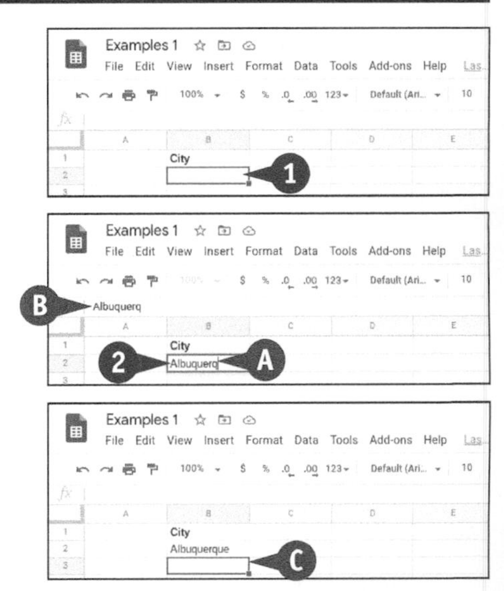

1. Click the cell.

   The cell becomes active.

2. Start typing the content.

   Google Sheets opens the cell for editing.

   A The content appears in the cell with a cursor.

   B The content also appears in the Formula bar. You can click in the Formula bar and edit there instead of in the cell.

3. When you finish typing the content, press Enter or Return.

   Google Sheets closes the cell.

   C The next cell becomes active.

Enter Content in Multiple Cells Using Repeat

1. Select the cells in which you want to enter the content.
2. Type the content in the first cell.
3. Press Enter or Return.

   Google Sheets enters the content in the first cell.

   D The second cell becomes active.

4. Press Ctrl + Enter.

Note: On the Mac, press ⌘ + Return.

Google Sheets enters the content in the remaining selected cells.

fx Southwest

	A	B	C	D	E
1		City	Region		
2		Albuquerque	Southwest		
3		El Paso			
4		Phoenix			
5		Tucson			

	A	B	C	D	E
1		City	Region		
2		Albuquerque	Southwest		
3		El Paso			
4		Phoenix			
5		Tucson			

fx Southwest

	A	B	C	D	E
1		City	Region		
2		Albuquerque	Southwest		
3		El Paso	Southwest		
4		Phoenix	Southwest		
5		Tucson	Southwest		

Enter a Common Sequence of Data with Autofill

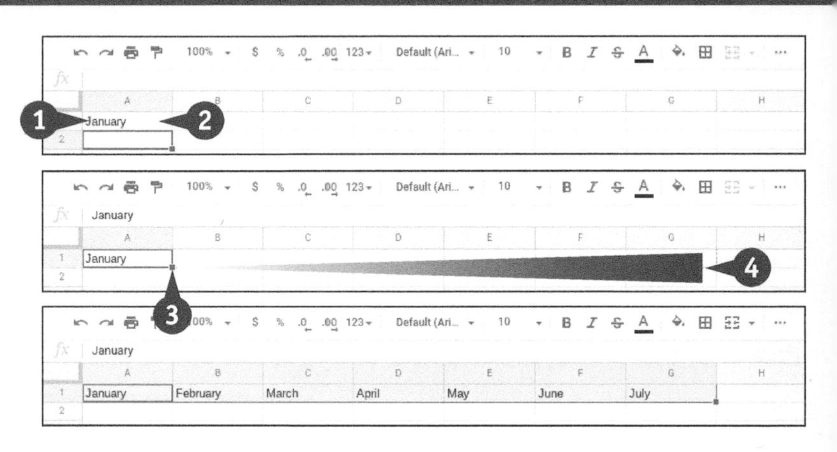

1. Click the first cell, type the starting value for the sequence, and then press Enter or Return.

   The next cell becomes active.

2. Click the first cell.

   The cell becomes active.

3. Click **Autofill** (■).

4. Drag to select the cells you want to fill, and then release the mouse button.

   Autofill enters the values in the cells.

Enter a Custom Sequence of Data with Autofill

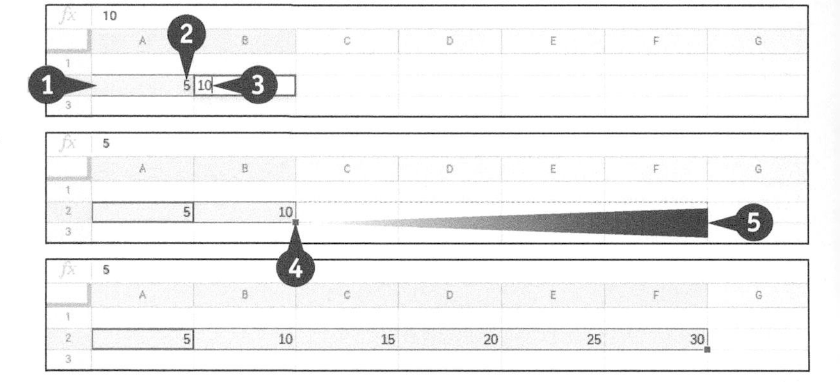

1. Select the first two cells of the range.

2. Type the starting value in the first cell, and then press Enter or Return.

   The second cell becomes active.

3. Type the second value, and then press Enter or Return.

   The cells remain selected.

4. Click **Autofill** (■).

5. Drag to select the cells you want to fill, and then release the mouse button.

   Autofill infers the sequence and enters the values in the cells.

TIP

What types of data series can I enter using Autofill?
You can enter text series, date and time series, and math series using Autofill. A text series needs to be a common one, such as the days of the week or the months of the year. A date series or time series requires one date or time for default date or time increments or two dates or times in the same format for custom increments. For example, if you autofill from the date 5/21/2021, you get one-day increments — 5/22/2021, 5/23/2021, and so on; if you autofill from the values 5/21/2021 and 5/25/2021, you get four-day increments. A math series needs two values from which Autofill can determine the series.

Import Data into Google Sheets

If you have data stored in an existing spreadsheet you have created in another app, you can import it into Google Sheets. You can choose among various options for placing the imported data, such as appending it to the current spreadsheet, inserting a new sheet, or creating a new spreadsheet file.

You can import data in various formats, including Microsoft Excel workbook formats and the OpenOffice.org/LibreOffice Calc format. For even wider compatibility, you can import data in comma-separated values format, CSV; in tab-separated values format, TSV; or even in a plain-text format.

Import Data into Google Sheets

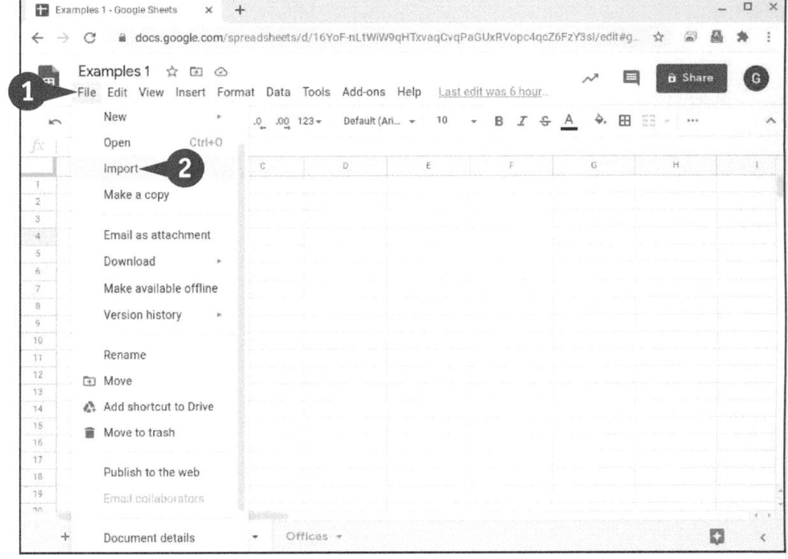

Note: If you are going to import the data into an existing spreadsheet file, open that spreadsheet file. If you are going to replace a sheet, or place data on the sheet, make that sheet active by clicking it in the tab bar at the bottom of the window.

1. In Google Sheets, click **File**.

   The File menu opens.

2. Click **Import**.

   The first Import File dialog box opens.

   A. The My Drive tab is displayed by default.

   B. You can click **Shared with me** to display the list of files that people have shared with you.

   C. You can click **Recent** to display the list of files you have used recently.

   D. You can click **Upload** to upload a file from your computer to Google Drive.

3. Click the file you want to import.
4. Click **Select**.

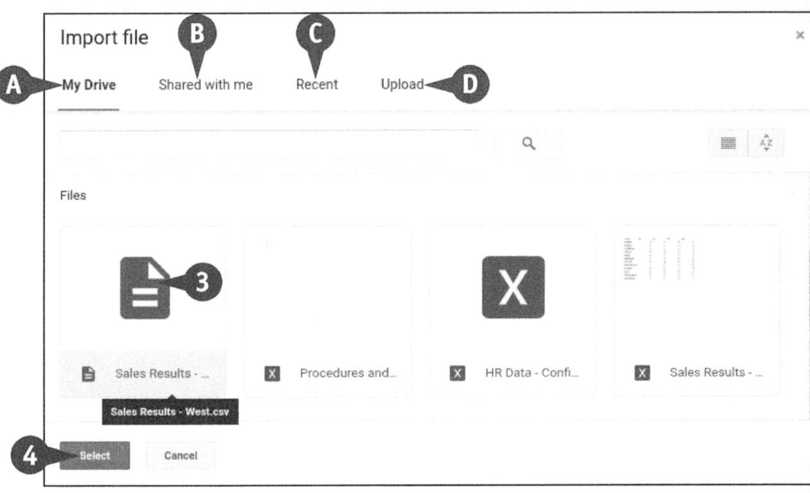

The second Import File dialog box opens.

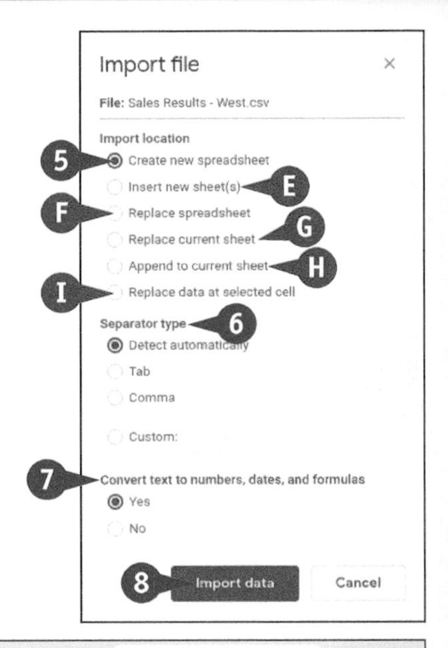

5 Select **Create new spreadsheet** (◉) to create a new spreadsheet file to contain the imported data. This is often the best choice.

E You can select **Insert new sheet(s)** (◉) to insert the data on new sheets in the existing spreadsheet.

F You can select **Replace spreadsheet** (◉) to replace the existing spreadsheet with the incoming data.

G You can select **Replace current sheet** (◉) to replace the current sheet with the incoming sheet.

H You can select **Append to current sheet** (◉) to add the incoming data after the existing data on the current sheet.

I You can select **Replace data at selected cell** (◉) to replace data starting at the selected cell.

6 For a CSV or TSV file, click **Detect automatically** (◉), **Tab** (◉), **Comma** (◉), or **Custom** (◉) in the Separator Type area.

7 For a CSV or TSV file, select **Yes** (◉) or **No** (◉) in the Convert Text to Numbers, Dates, and Formulas area, as needed.

8 Click **Import data.**

Note: If you chose to create a new spreadsheet, the second Import File dialog box stays open but displays the message *File imported successfully*. Click **Open now** to open the new file, or click **Cancel** to close the dialog box.

The second Import File dialog box closes.

The imported data appears in the location you specified.

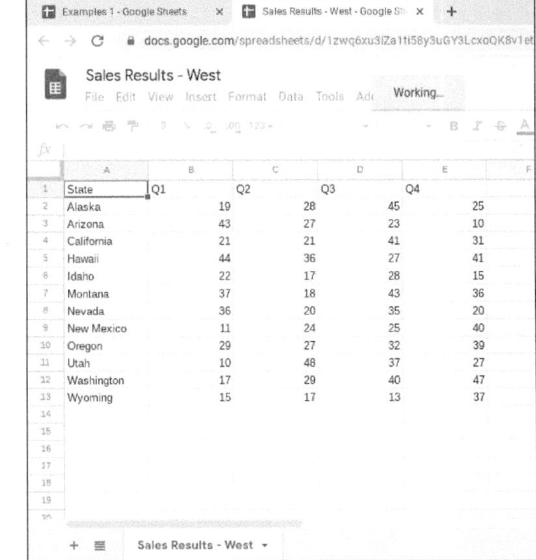

TIP

Can I just copy data from an Excel workbook and paste it into Google Sheets?

Yes. You can open an Excel workbook, either in Excel or in Google Sheets, copy the data you want, and then paste it into a spreadsheet in Google Sheets.

Copy and paste is quick and effective, especially for small amounts of text-based data. Where you need to get a whole spreadsheet's worth of data, importing it is usually easier. Copy and paste tends to work less well for complex objects. For example, if you paste a chart into Google Sheets, you may get only a picture of the chart, not its underlying data.

Laying out the data in a spreadsheet often involves trial and error. For example, you may need to add columns of data to your initial design or delete rows that have proved superfluous. Google Sheets enables you to insert and delete cells, rows, and columns in your spreadsheets easily.

Inserting or deleting cells, rows, or columns helps you avoid having to move large blocks of data when rearranging your spreadsheets. But you can use whichever layout technique you find easiest.

Insert and Delete Cells, Rows, and Columns

Insert or Delete a Row or Column

1. Right-click a cell in the row above which or the column before which you want to insert the new row or column.

   The contextual menu opens.

2. Click **Insert row**.

- A You can click **Insert column** to insert a column.
- B You can click **Delete row** to delete the row that contains the cell.
- C You can click **Delete column** to delete the column that contains the cell.

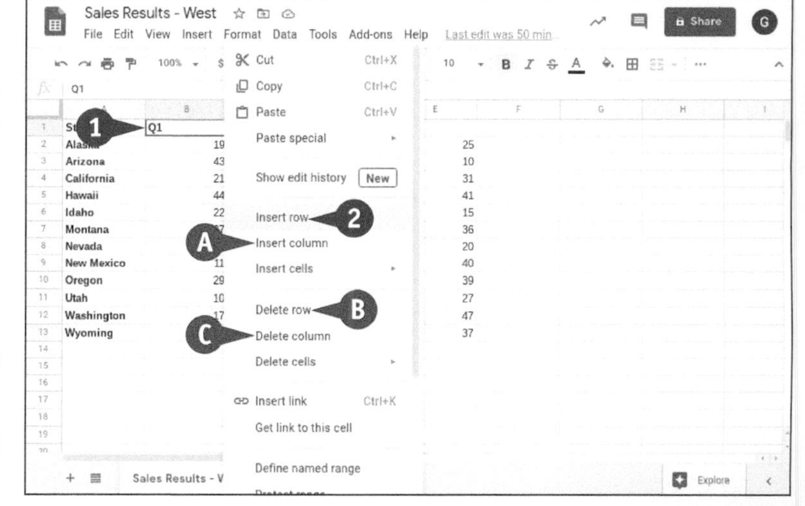

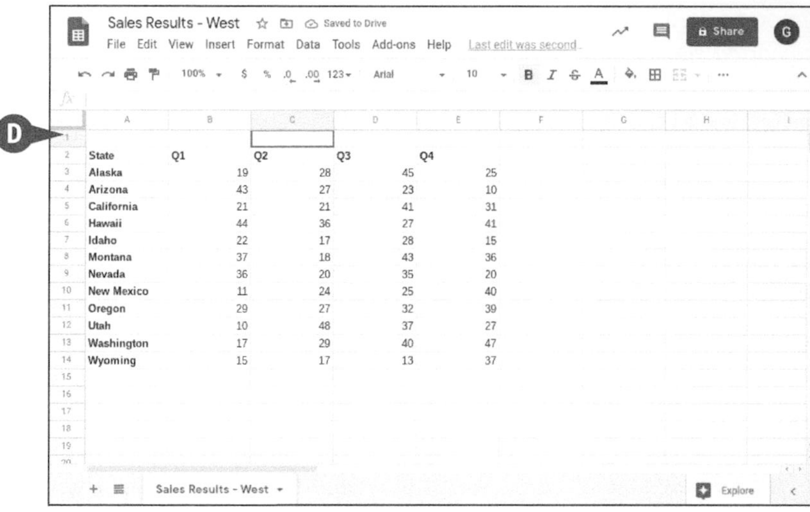

- D The new row appears in the spreadsheet.

Note: You can also insert a row by right-clicking a row heading and then clicking **Insert 1 above** or **Insert 1 below** on the contextual menu. Similarly, you can right-click a column heading, and then click **Insert 1 left** or **Insert 1 right**.

Delete a Block of Cells

1. Select the block of cells you want to delete.
2. Right-click anywhere in the selection.

   The contextual menu opens.
3. Click or highlight **Delete cells**.

   The submenu opens.
4. Click **Shift left** or **Shift up**, as needed.

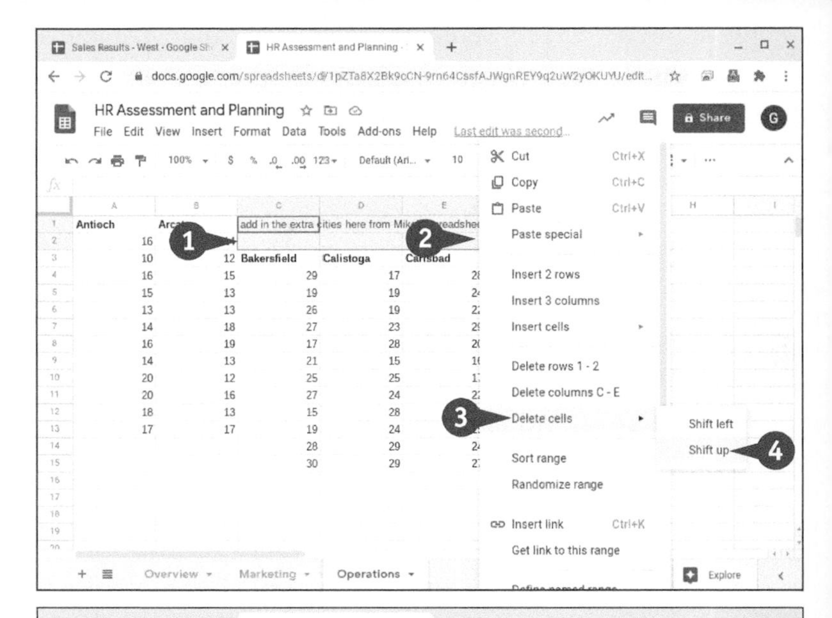

Google Sheets deletes the cells and moves the remaining cells as you specified.

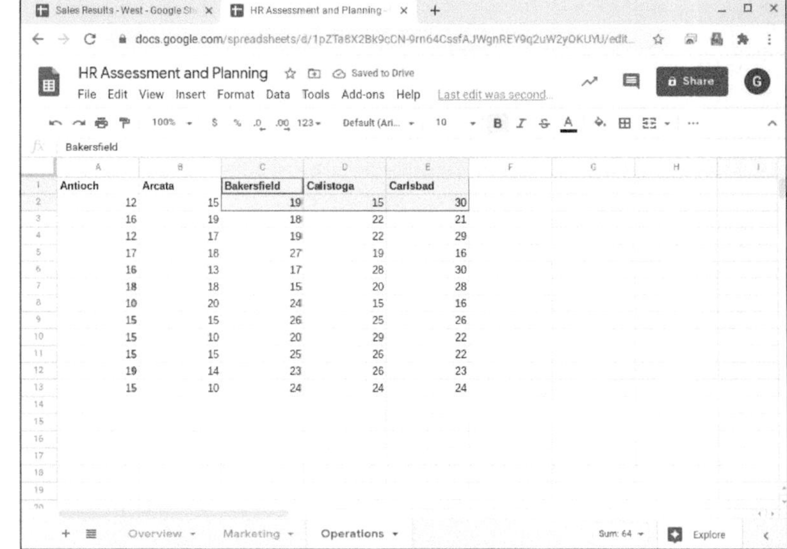

> **TIP**
>
> **How do I insert a block of cells?**
>
> Select the block of cells that currently occupy the range you want the new block of cells to occupy. Right-click anywhere in the selection to display the contextual menu, click or highlight **Insert cells** to display the Insert Cells submenu, and then click **Shift right** or **Shift down** to tell Google Sheets which direction to move the current cells.

Insert, Delete, and Manage Sheets

A blank Google Sheets spreadsheet contains only a single sheet by default, whereas template files may contain multiple sheets. You can add further sheets as needed to store and manipulate data. Each sheet you add receives a default name, such as Sheet2 or Sheet3, but you can rename each sheet to make them easier to identify. You can also change the color of a sheet's tab for visual reference.

You can arrange a spreadsheet file's sheets into your preferred order, and you can delete any sheet that you no longer need.

Insert, Delete, and Manage Sheets

Insert a Sheet and Rename It

1. In a Google Sheets spreadsheet, click **Add Sheet** (+).

   Google Sheets adds a new sheet to the spreadsheet, giving it a default name, such as Sheet2.

2. Click ▾.

   The pop-up menu opens.

3. Click **Rename**.

Note: You can also double-click the sheet's existing name on the tab to select it for renaming.

   Google Sheets selects the current name, displaying a blue border around it.

4. Type the new name.

Note: A sheet name can be up to 100 characters long. If you exceed this limit, the blue border changes to red.

5. Click anywhere in the sheet.

Note: You can also press Enter or Return to apply the name.

   The sheet becomes active again.

   The tab shows the sheet's new name.

A. You can change the tab's color by clicking ▾, clicking or highlighting **Change color**, and then clicking the color.

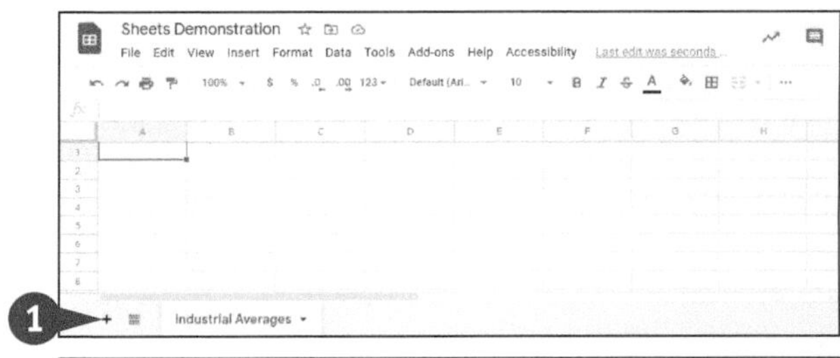

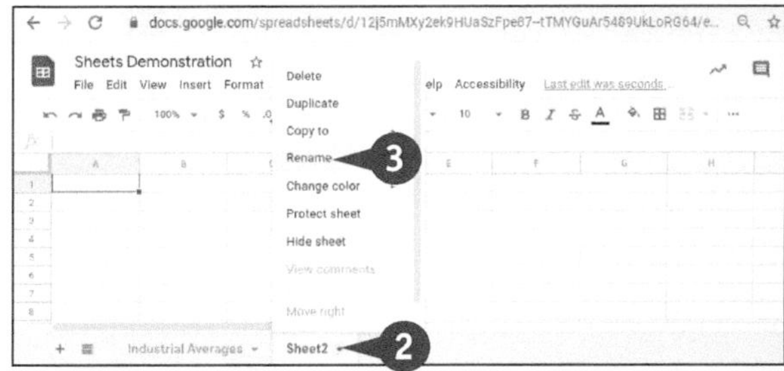

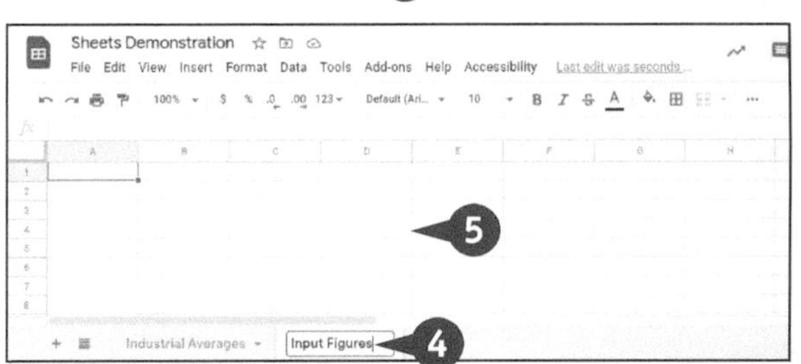

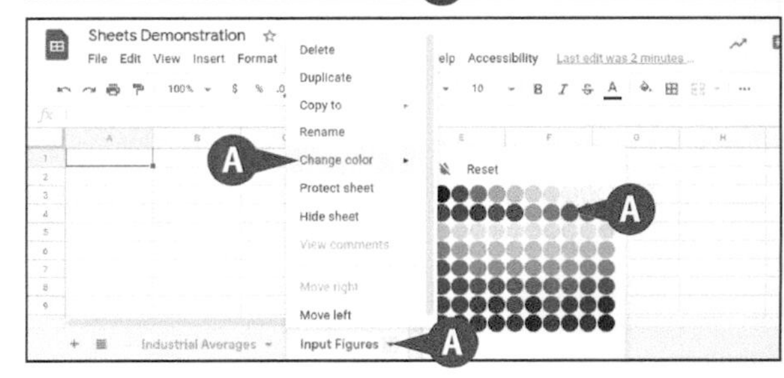

Rearrange Sheets

1. Drag the tab for the sheet left or right along the tab bar.

Note: When you want to switch the position of two adjacent sheets, click ▼ on one of the sheets, and then click **Move right** or **Move left** on the pop-up menu, as needed.

2. When the tab is where you want it, release the mouse button.

   The tab appears in its new location.

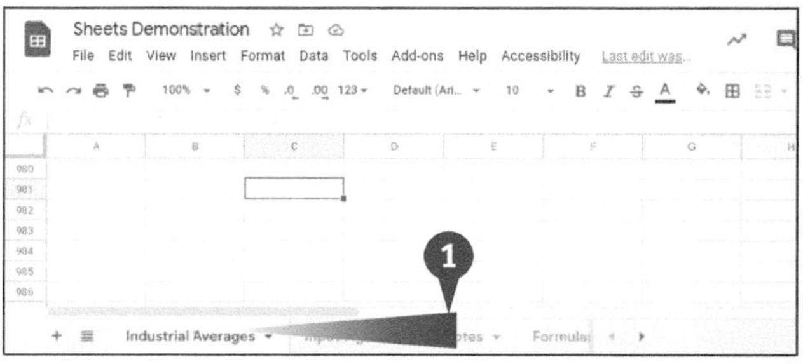

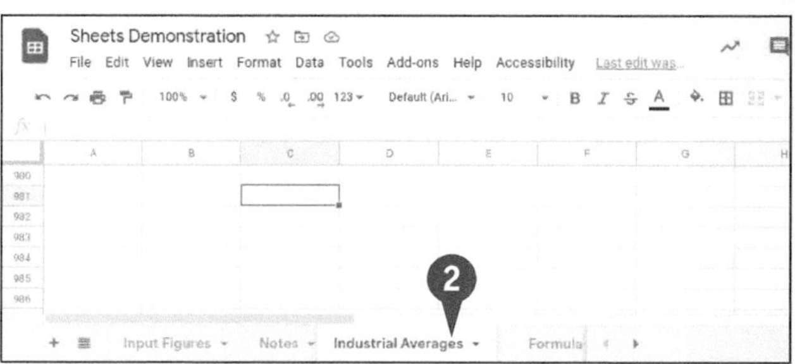

Delete a Sheet

1. Click ▼ on the sheet you want to delete.

   The pop-up menu opens.

2. Click **Delete**.

   The Heads Up! dialog box opens, making sure you want to delete the sheet.

3. Click **OK**.

   The Heads Up! dialog box closes.

   Google Sheet deletes the sheet.

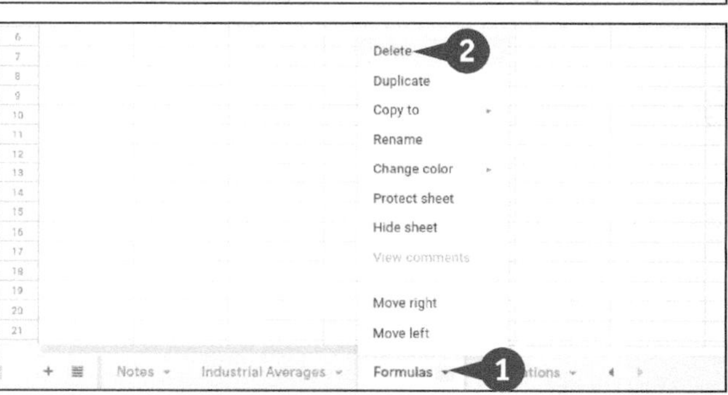

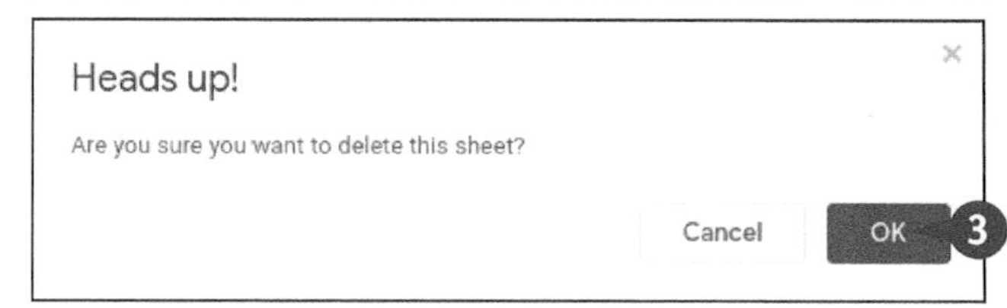

TIPS

What is the horizontal-lines button to the left of the leftmost sheet tab?

This is the All Sheets button, which enables you to navigate easily between sheets. Click **All Sheets** (≡) to display a pop-up menu listing all the sheets, and then click the sheet you want to display. This pop-up menu is especially convenient when a spreadsheet contains more sheets than the tab bar can display at once.

What is the maximum number of sheets a Google Sheets spreadsheet can contain?

There is no hard-and-fast maximum number of sheets, but the maximum number of cells is 5 million. Using the default number of cells per sheet, this gives a practical maximum of about 192 sheets.

Insert a Function

Google Sheets includes hundreds of functions, prebuilt formulas that you can use to perform calculations in your spreadsheet. For example, when you need to add the values of cells, you can use the `SUM()` function instead of creating a formula from scratch.

Google Sheets breaks down its functions into various categories, such as Date functions, Financial functions, Logical functions, and Math functions. You can browse these categories to locate the functions you need. If you prefer to navigate by name, you can display a list of all the functions.

Insert a Function

1. Enter any data the function will need.

   This example uses the `PMT()` function, which calculates periodic payments for an investment item.

2. Click the cell in which you want to enter the function.

3. Click **Insert**.

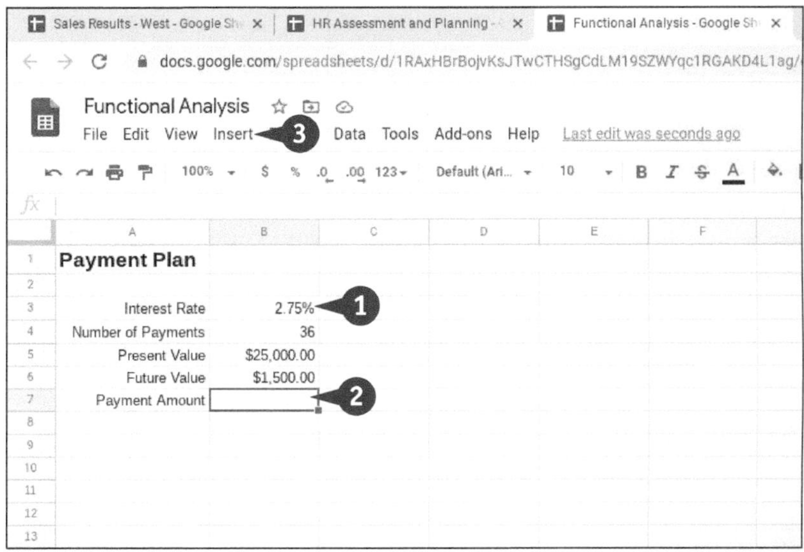

The Insert menu appears.

4. Click or highlight **Function** (Σ).

   The Function submenu appears.

   A. You can click one of the five widely used functions — `SUM()`, `AVERAGE()`, `COUNT()`, `MAX()`, and `MIN()` — at the top of the Function submenu.

   B. You can click **All** to display the list of all functions.

5. Click the category of function you want to use.

   To follow this example, you would click **Financial**.

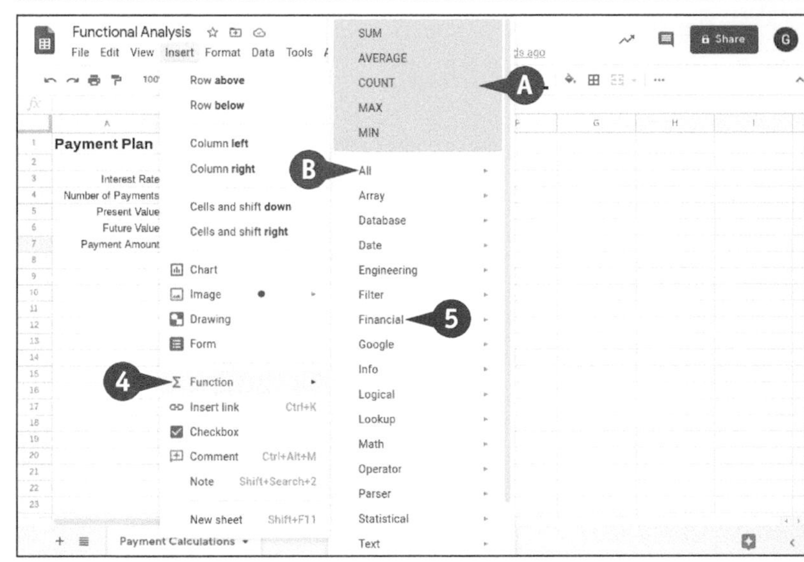

The category's submenu appears, showing the functions in the category.

C You can hold the cursor over a function to display its description, which can be helpful in distinguishing between functions with similar names.

6 Click the function you want to insert.

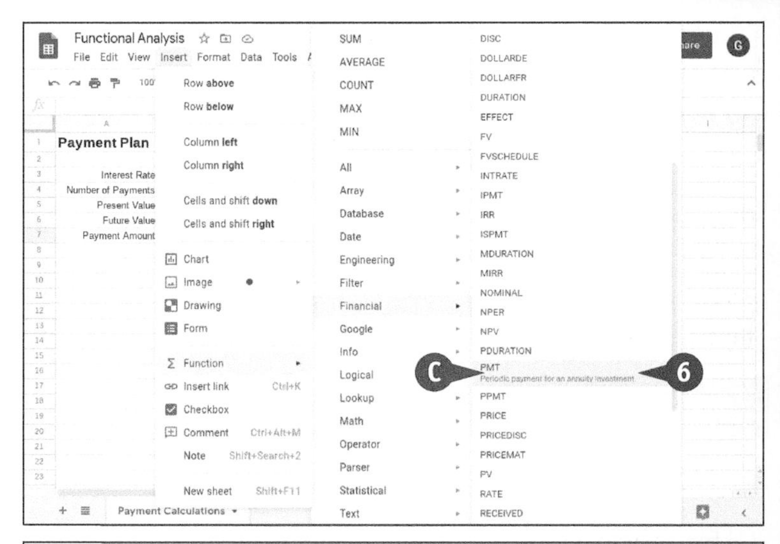

Google Sheets inserts the function and displays its information panel.

D The function's syntax appears at the top of the panel.

E The Example section shows a brief example.

F The About section describes what the function does.

G The lower part of the panel shows information about the *arguments*, the pieces of information the function uses.

7 Click **Minimize** (^).

Note: If the information panel does not obscure anything you want to see, you need not minimize it.

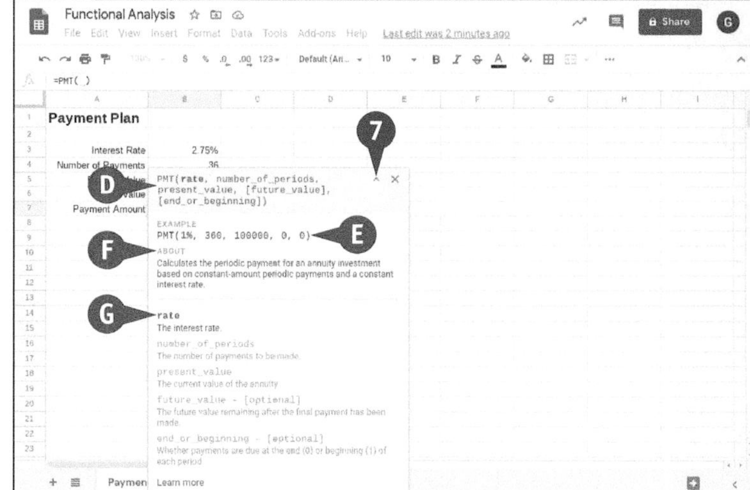

TIPS

How can I see all the functions in a spreadsheet?

Click **View** on the menu bar to open the View menu, and then click **Show formulas** to display all the formulas and functions in the spreadsheet.

Does Google Sheets have all the same functions as Microsoft Excel?

Not quite. Google Sheets has most of the same functions as Microsoft Excel, so if you convert an Excel workbook to a Google Sheets spreadsheet, most of the formulas will still work in the same way. However, Excel does have some functions — mostly specialized ones — that Google Sheets does not have.

continued ▶

Each function has a unique name, which is followed by a pair of parentheses that encloses the list of arguments the function uses. Most functions take one or more arguments, although a few functions take no arguments. Some arguments are required, but others are optional. Optional arguments appear in brackets in the function syntax.

For example, the syntax for the PMT function is `PMT(rate, number_of_periods, present_value, [future_value], [end_or_beginning])`. The first three arguments — `rate`, `number_of_periods`, and `present_value` — are required, and you supply them in that order. The last two arguments — `future_value` and `end_or_beginning` — are optional.

Insert a Function (continued)

The information panel becomes smaller, showing only the function's syntax.

H The first part of the function appears in the cell.

I The current argument appears in green boldface in the syntax.

8 Click the cell that contains the value for the first argument.

The information panel hides.

J Google Sheets highlights the cell.

K The cell reference appears in the formula in the matching color.

9 Type a comma to indicate the first argument is complete.

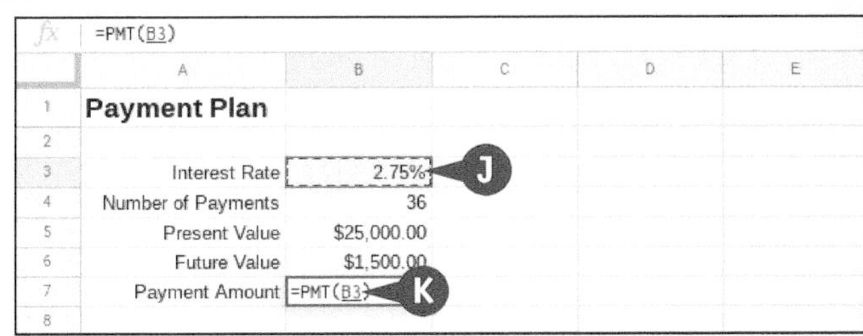

The information panel appears again.

L The next argument appears in green.

10 Click the cell that contains the value for the second argument.

The information panel hides.

Ⓜ Google Sheets highlights the cell in a different color.

Ⓝ The cell reference appears in the formula in a matching color.

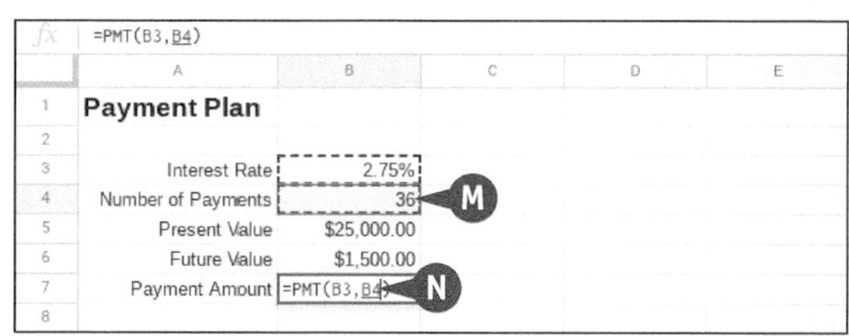

11 Type a comma to indicate the first argument is complete.

The information panel appears again.

Ⓞ The next argument appears in green.

12 Continue to provide the information for the remaining required arguments and any optional arguments you will use.

In this example, you would click the cell that contains the value for the third argument.

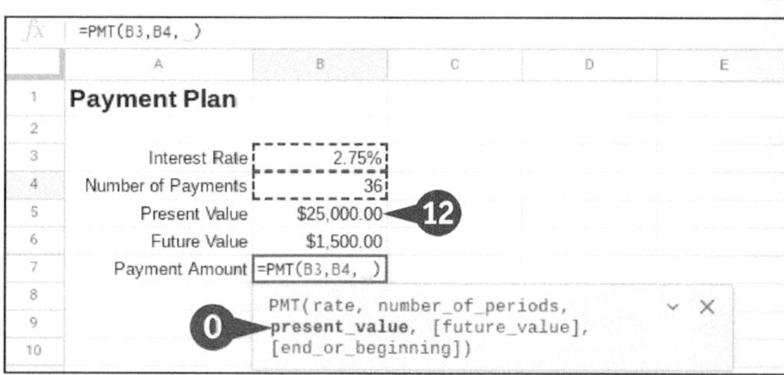

Ⓟ Google Sheets uses a different color for each argument, helping you to see which cell supplies which value.

Note: The example formula uses the first optional argument, `future_value`, but not the second optional argument, `end_or_beginning`.

13 When you finish entering the arguments, press Enter or Return.

Ⓠ The formula result appears in the cell.

TIP

Can I enter values for arguments directly instead of putting them in cells?

Yes, you can enter values directly in functions. You can also use functions to provide values for arguments. For example, the function `HOUR()` returns the hour for the time provided, and the function `NOW()` returns the current date and time. You can use `=HOUR(NOW())` to return the current hour.

Format Spreadsheets, Cells, and Ranges

Google Sheets enables you to apply a wide range of formatting to cells and ranges in your spreadsheets. The easiest place to start is with the theme, the overall formatting scheme applied to the spreadsheet. You can switch to a different theme, and you can customize the current theme, as needed.

You can also apply formatting to cells and ranges to emphasize key data. For example, you can apply boldface to headings to make them stand out, or apply a different fill color to cells that need input.

Format Spreadsheets, Cells, and Ranges

Change the Spreadsheet's Theme

1. Click **Format**.

   The Format menu opens.

2. Click **Theme**.

   The Themes pane appears on the right side of the window.

   A. A default spreadsheet uses the Standard theme unless you change it.

3. Click the theme you want to apply.
4. To customize the theme, click **Customize**.

   The controls for customizing the theme appear.

5. Click **Font** (▾) and then click the font.
6. In the Colors section, click each pop-up button (▾), and then click the color you want.

   B. For example, click **Text**.

   The pop-up color picker appears.

   C. Click the color you want.

7. When you finish choosing colors, click **Done**.
8. Click **Close** (✕).

   The Themes panel closes, and the changes appear in the spreadsheet.

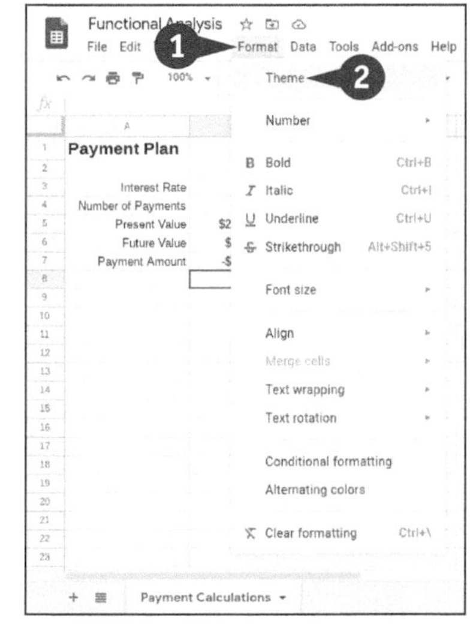

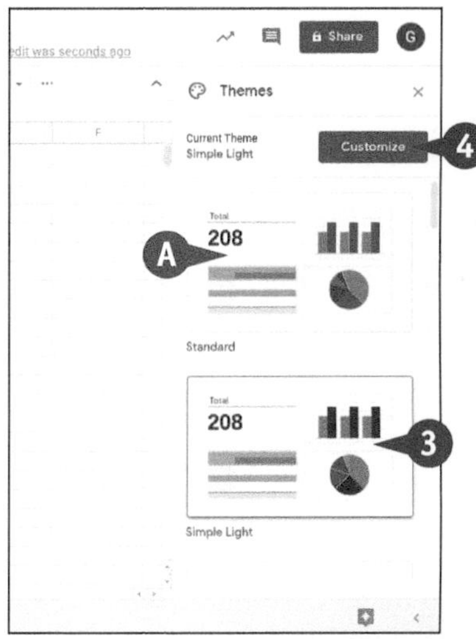

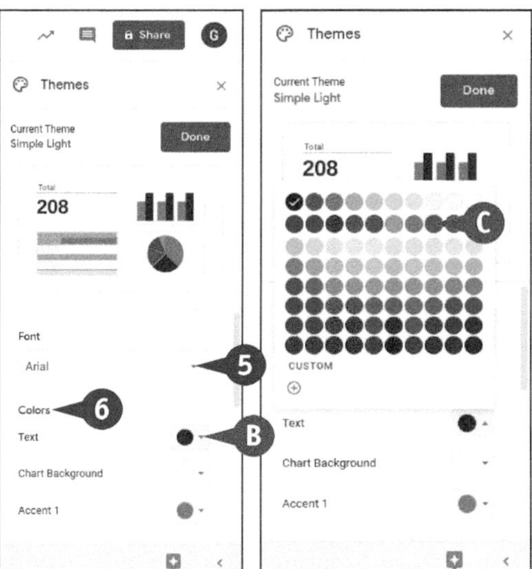

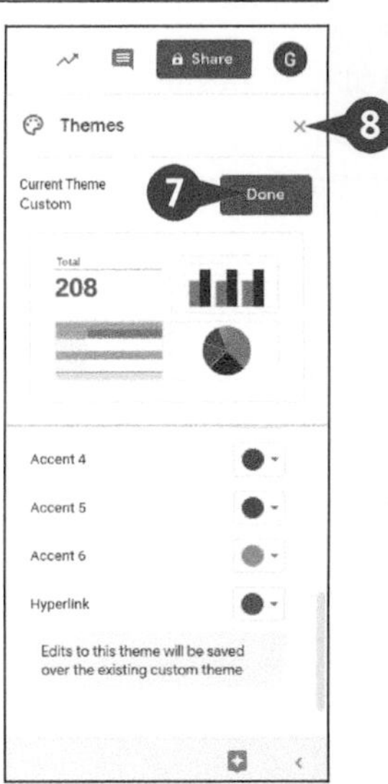

Format Cells and Ranges

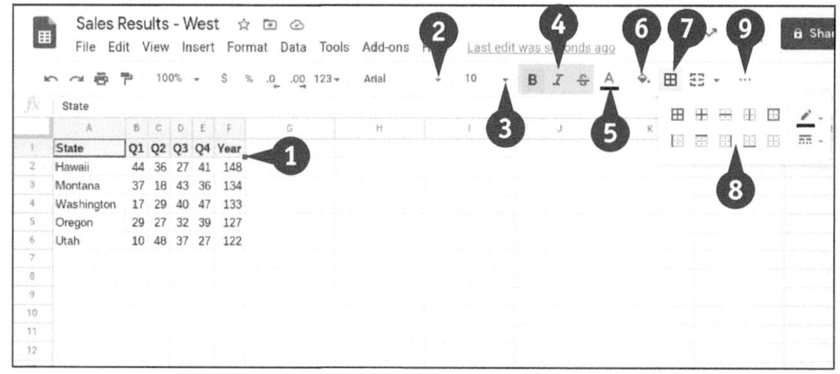

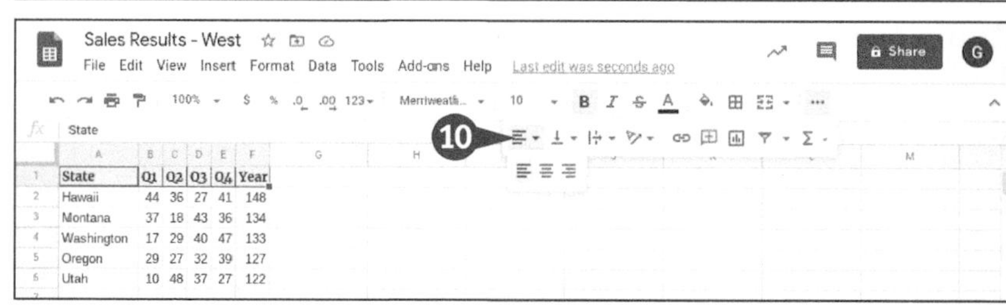

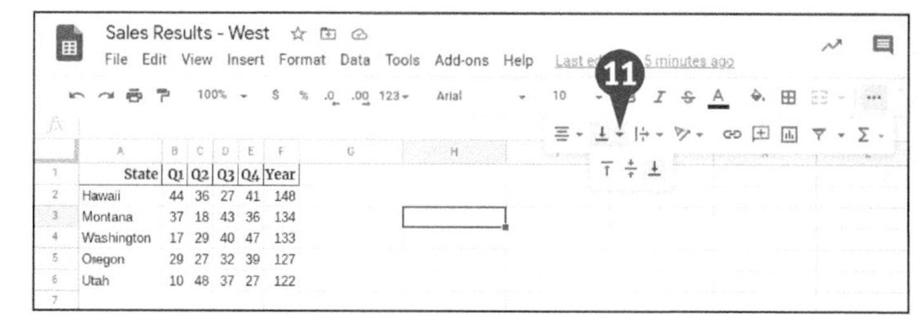

1. Select the cell or range.
2. Click **Font** (▾), and then click the font.
3. Click **Size** (▾), and then click the size.
4. Click **Bold** (B), **Italic** (I), or **Strikethrough** (S), to toggle that property on or off.
5. Click **Text color** (A), and then click the color.
6. Click **Fill color** (◈), and then click the color.
7. Click **Borders** (⊞).

   The Borders pop-up panel opens.
8. Click the border style.
9. Click **More** (•••).

Note: The More button (•••) does not appear when the Google Sheets window is wide enough to accommodate the entire toolbar.

   The remaining section of the toolbar appears.

10. Click **Horizontal align** (≡ ▾), and then click **Left** (≡), **Center** (≡), or **Right** (≡), as needed.
11. Click **Vertical align** (⊥ ▾), and then click **Top** (⊤), **Middle** (÷), or **Bottom** (⊥), as needed.

   The cell or range takes on the formatting you applied.

TIPS

How do I remove formatting?
Select the cell or range, click **Edit** to open the Edit menu, and then click **Clear formatting**.

What keyboard shortcuts can I use to apply formatting?
Google Sheets supports three standard shortcuts for formatting: Press Ctrl+B to toggle bold, press Ctrl+I to toggle italics, and press Ctrl+U to toggle underline. On the Mac, use ⌘+B, ⌘+I, and ⌘+U instead.

Press Alt+Shift+5 to toggle strikethrough formatting. When you need to remove formatting, press Ctrl+\ to give the Clear Formatting command.

Apply Number Formatting

Numbers are vital to most spreadsheets, and Google Sheets provides easy ways to format numbers to look the way you need them to. Beyond the Automatic format used by default and the Plain Text format for text, the quickly accessible formats include three widely used number formats — Number, Percent, and Scientific; four monetary formats — Accounting, Financial, Currency, and Currency (Rounded); and four date and time formats — Date, Time, Date Time, and Duration. You can also use other currency formats and other date and time formats; you can even create custom number formats, if needed.

Apply Number Formatting

Apply the Currency Format and the Percentage Format

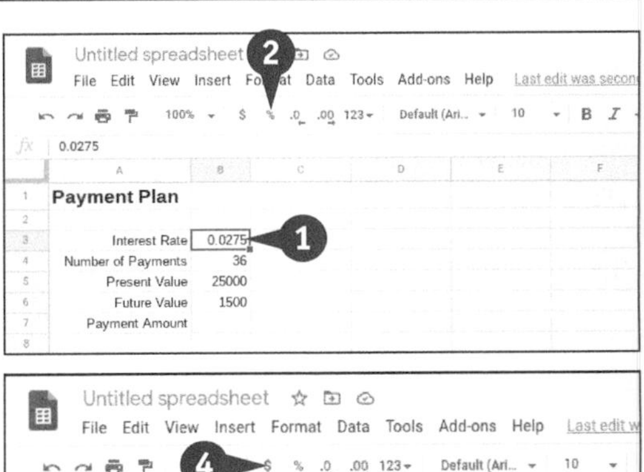

1. Select the cell or range you want to format.
2. Click **Format as percent** (%).

Ⓐ The cell takes on the Percent format.

3. Select the next cell or range.
4. Click **Format as currency** ($).

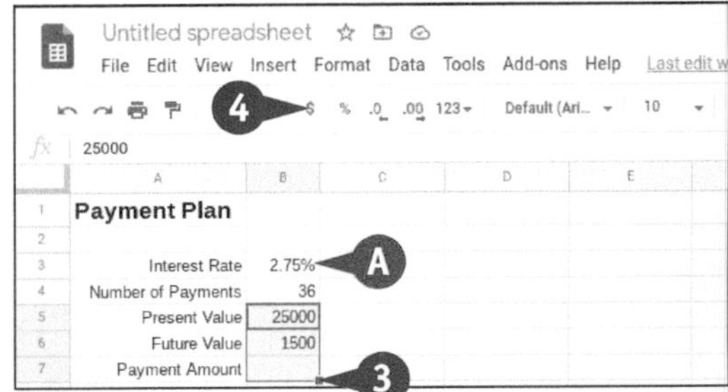

Ⓑ The cell or range takes on the Currency format, which uses two decimal places by default.

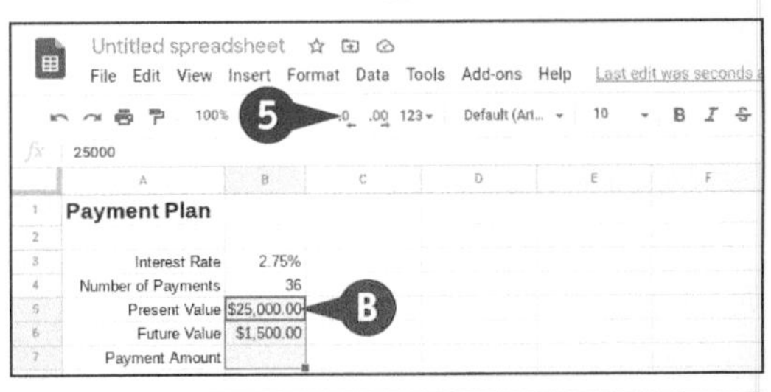

5. Click **Decrease decimal places** (.0) twice.

Note: You can click **Increase decimal places** (.00) to increase the number of decimal places displayed.

Ⓒ The cell or range shows two decimal places fewer.

Note: Changing the number of decimal places affects only the displayed number, not the underlying number.

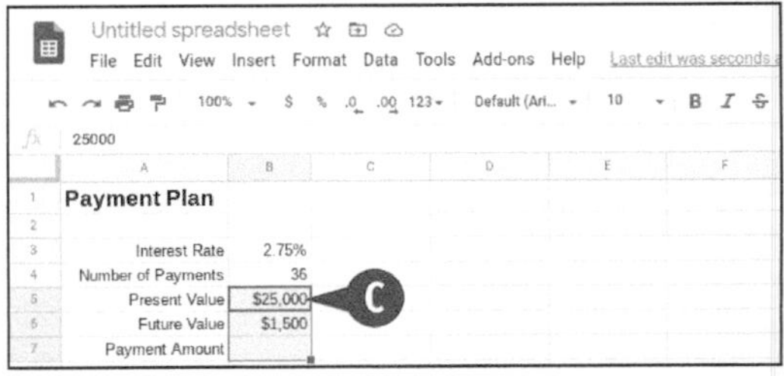

Apply Other Number Formats

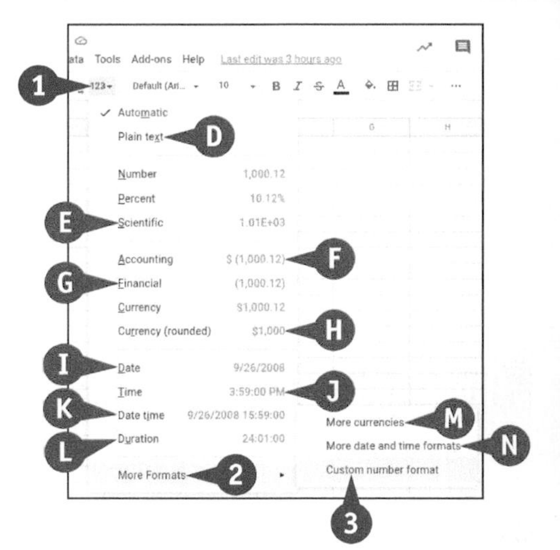

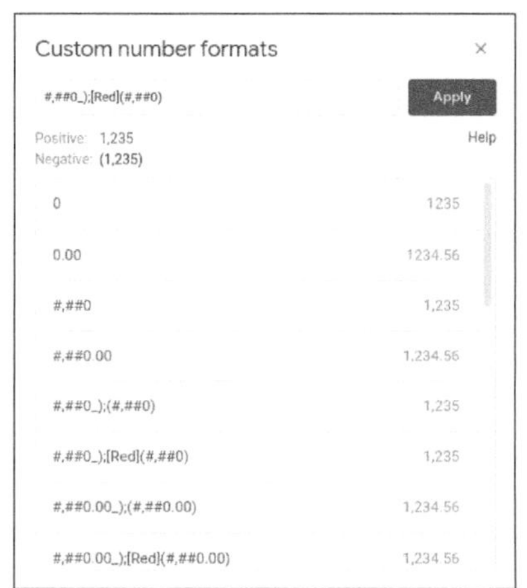

1 After selecting the cell or range, click **More formats** (123▾).

The More Formats menu opens.

D Click **Plain text** to make Google Sheets treat a number as text.

E Click **Scientific** to apply exponential notation.

F Click **Accounting** to display the currency symbol and negative numbers in parentheses.

G Click **Financial** to display negative numbers in parentheses.

H Click **Currency (rounded)** to show numbers rounded to the major unit, such as the dollar.

I Click **Date** to display a date format.

J Click **Time** to display a standard time format.

K Click **Date time** to display a date and time format.

L Click **Duration** to display the elapsed time.

2 If no format is suitable, click or highlight **More Formats.**

The More Formats submenu opens.

M Click **More currencies** to display the Custom Currencies dialog box, in which you can create a currency format.

N Click **More date and time formats** to display the Custom Date and Time Formats dialog box, in which you can create a custom date and time format.

3 Click **Custom number format.**

The Custom Number Formats dialog box opens.

You can then apply one of the formats provided or create a custom number format. See the tip for information on creating a custom number format.

TIP

How do I create a custom number format?

Select the appropriate cell or range. Open the Custom Number Formats dialog box by clicking **More formats** (123▾), clicking or highlighting **More Formats**, and then clicking **Custom number format.** In the list of formats, click the format closest to what you want. The format appears in the box at the top, and you can edit it as needed. In the codes, # represents a digit, and ; represents the division between the formatting for positive numbers and the formatting for negative numbers. Other characters — (and), , and . — appear literally. Watch the sample readout below the box to see the effect of your changes. Click **Apply** when the format is correct.

Highlight Data Using Conditional Formatting

As well as regular formatting, which appears all the time once you have applied it, Google Sheets provides *conditional formatting*, formatting that appears only when the conditions you specify are met.

Conditional formatting enables you to identify out-of-band values in your spreadsheets. For example, you might use conditional formatting to highlight any values that fell outside of a normal range so that you can pick out those values at a glance. It also enables you to apply a color scale to values, making it easy to determine how they compare to each other.

Highlight Data Using Conditional Formatting

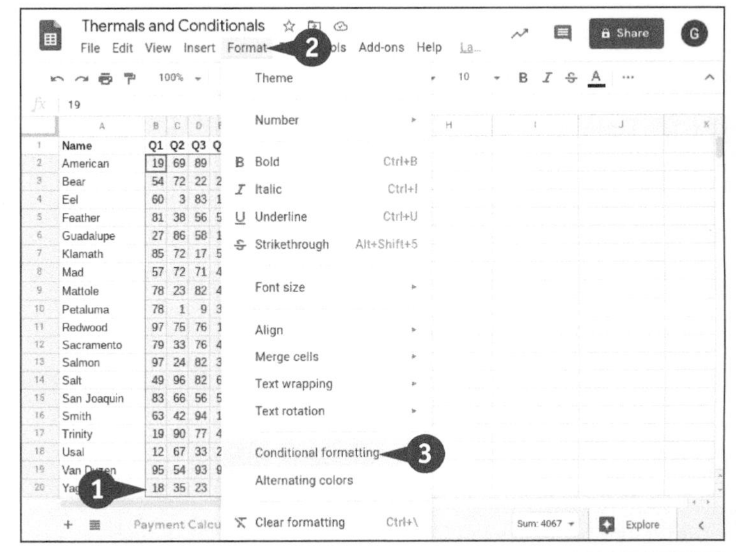

1. Select the cell or range that you will format.

   Usually, you will format a range rather than a single cell.

2. Click **Format**.

   The Format menu opens.

3. Click **Conditional formatting**.

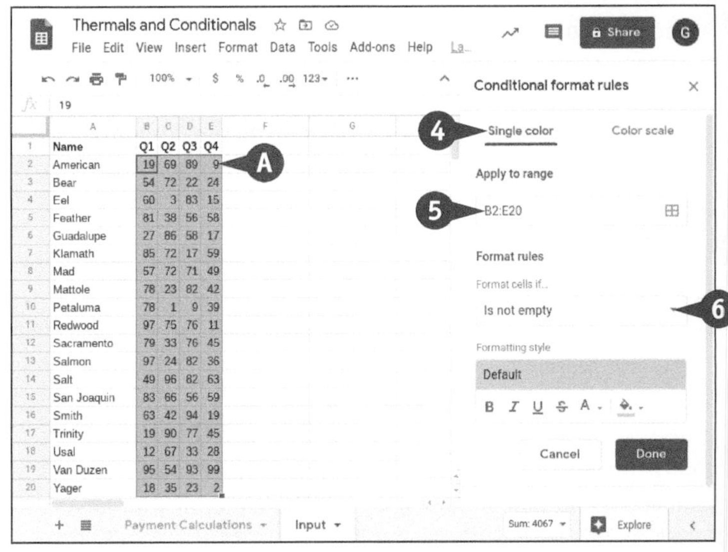

The Conditional Format Rules pane opens.

A. The cell or range may take on the default conditional formatting, as in this example, where the default setting is to format cells if they are not empty, applying the default formatting style.

4. Click **Single color**.

5. Verify that the Apply to Range box shows the correct range. If not, click **Select data range** (⊞) to open the Select a Data Range dialog box, select the range, and then click **OK**.

6. Click **Format cells if** (▾).

The Format Cells If pop-up menu opens.

7. Click the appropriate comparison.

   In this example, you would click **Is not between.**

   The area below the Format Cells If box displays controls for you to enter the data required for the comparison.

   For example, the Is Not Between comparison needs a lower value or formula and an upper value or formula.

8. Click **Value or formula** and enter a suitable lower value, such as **10**, or formula.

9. Click **Value or formula** and enter a suitable upper value, such as **90**, or formula.

10. Click **Default.**

    The Default pop-up panel opens.

11. Click the default format you want to apply.

    B The selected cell or range shows the formatting.

12. Click **Done.**

13. Click **Close** (×).

    The Conditional Format Rules pane closes.

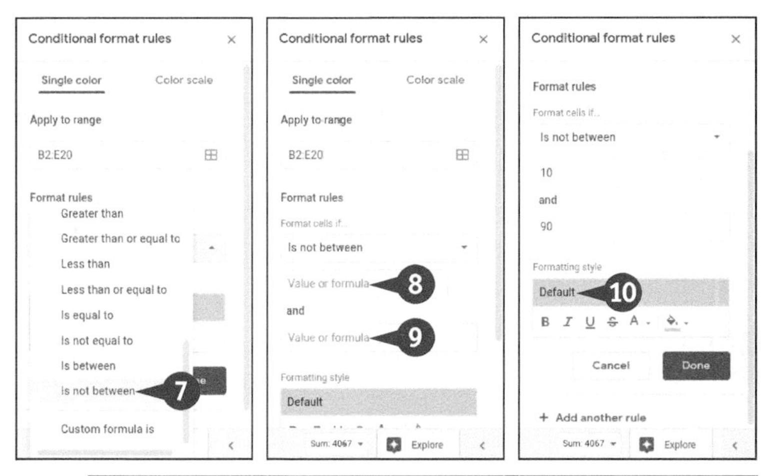

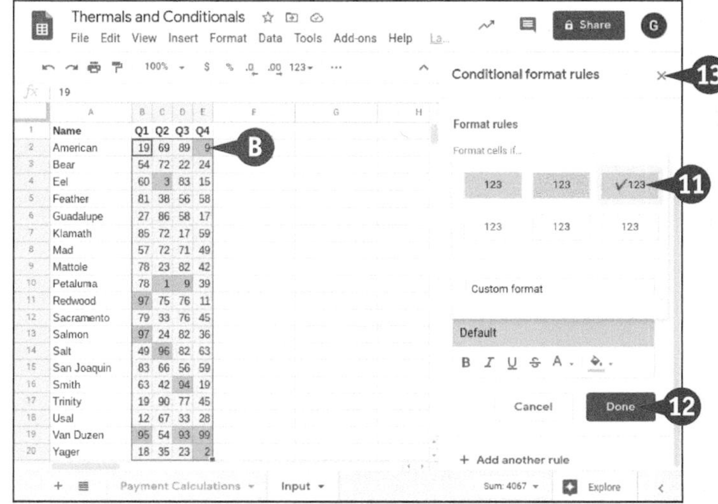

TIP

How do I change a default format for conditional formatting?

Click **Default** in the Formatting Style section of the Conditional Format Rules pane, and then click the default format you want to change. Then use the row of buttons below the Default button to customize the format. Click **Bold** (B) to toggle boldface. Click **Italic** (*I*) to toggle italic. Click **Underline** (U) to toggle underline. Click **Strikethrough** (S) to toggle strikethrough. Click **Text color** (A) to open the Text Color panel, and then click the text color. Click **Fill color** (◆) to open the Fill Color panel, and then click the fill color.

Apply Alternating Colors

To help make your spreadsheets more readable, Google Sheets enables you to apply alternating colors to rows. Having rows appear in alternating colors makes it easier for your eye to follow along a row of data without straying to another row. This is especially helpful when the spreadsheet is packed with data. The Alternating Colors feature can also apply different formatting to the header row or footer row in a range.

Google Sheets provides various default styles for alternating colors. You can also create custom styles using your own colors.

Apply Alternating Colors

1. Select the range of cells you want to affect.
2. Click **Format.**

   The Format menu opens.
3. Click **Alternating colors.**

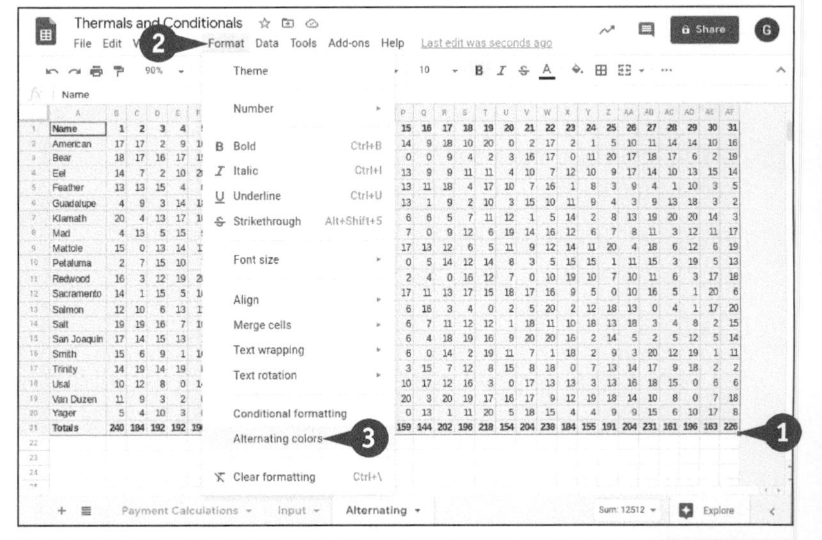

The Alternating Colors pane opens on the right side of the window.

4. Verify that the Apply to Range box contains the correct range. If not, click **Select data range** (⊞) to display the Select a Data Range dialog box, drag through the range in the spreadsheet to enter it in the box, and then click **OK.**
5. In the Styles area, select **Header** (☑) if you want to format the header row.

Note: If the top row of the selected range has different formatting from the following rows, Google Sheets may select Header (☑) automatically.

6. Select **Footer** (☑) if you want to format the footer row.

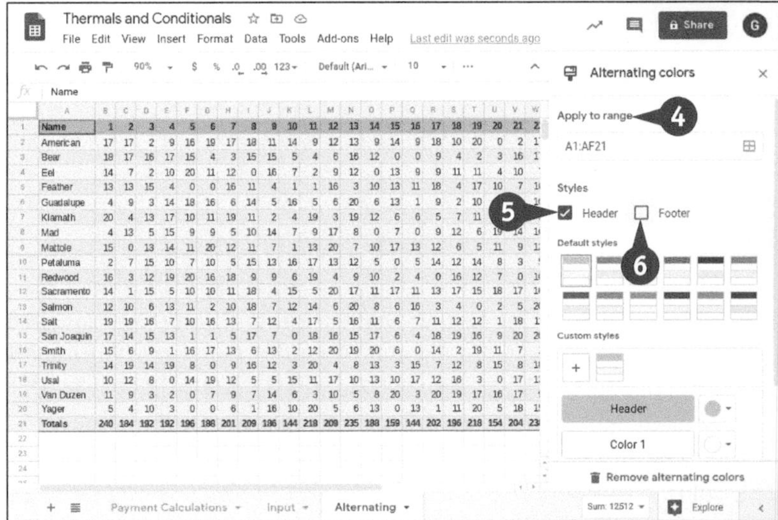

7. In the Default Styles box, click the default style you want to apply.

8. To change the header color, click **Header** (▾), and then click the color on the pop-up panel.

9. To change Color 1, click **Color 1** (▾), and then click the color on the pop-up panel.

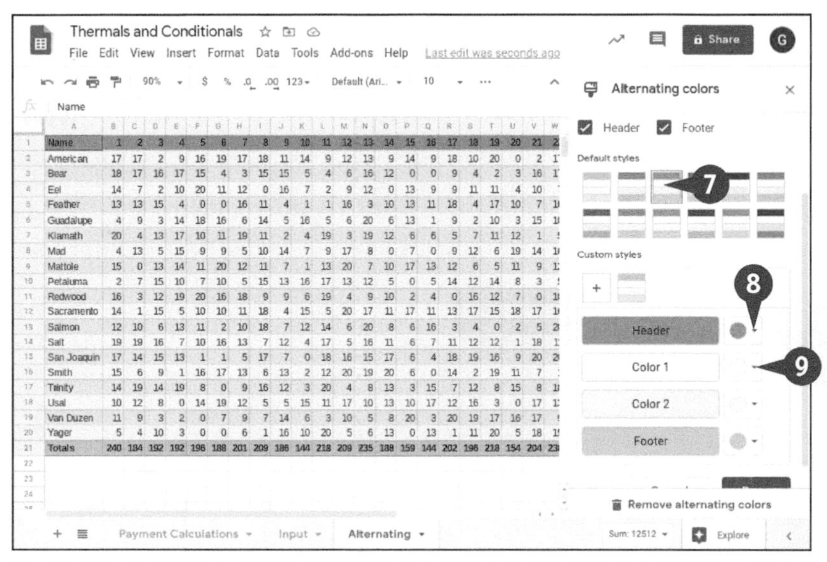

10. To change Color 2, click **Color 2** (▾), and then click the color on the pop-up panel.

11. To change the footer color 1, click **Footer** (▾), and then click the color on the pop-up panel.

12. Click **Done**.

The Alternating Colors pane closes.

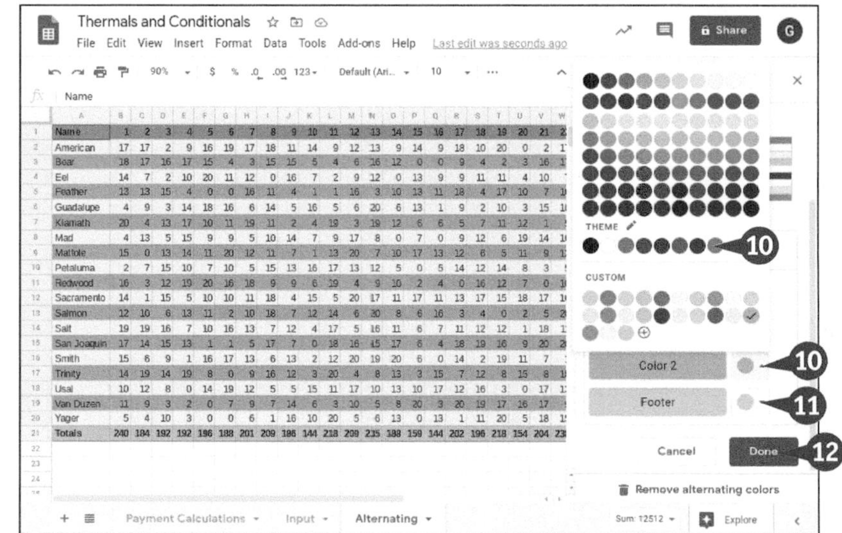

TIP

How do I remove alternating colors from a spreadsheet?

Click anywhere in the range that has the alternating colors applied. Click **Format** to open the Format menu, and then click **Alternating colors** to display the Alternating Colors pane. At the bottom of the pane, click **Remove alternating colors** (🗑).

Insert and View Notes

When you need to add some explanation or clarification to a cell, you can insert a note. For example, you might want to explain what type of data a user should enter in a particular cell or display other information you did not want to include in a cell.

Notes consist of text with no formatting. Google Sheets displays a black triangle in the upper-right corner of a cell to indicate the cell has a note inserted. Notes are different from comments, which are explained in the section "Work with Comments" in Chapter 4.

Insert and View Notes

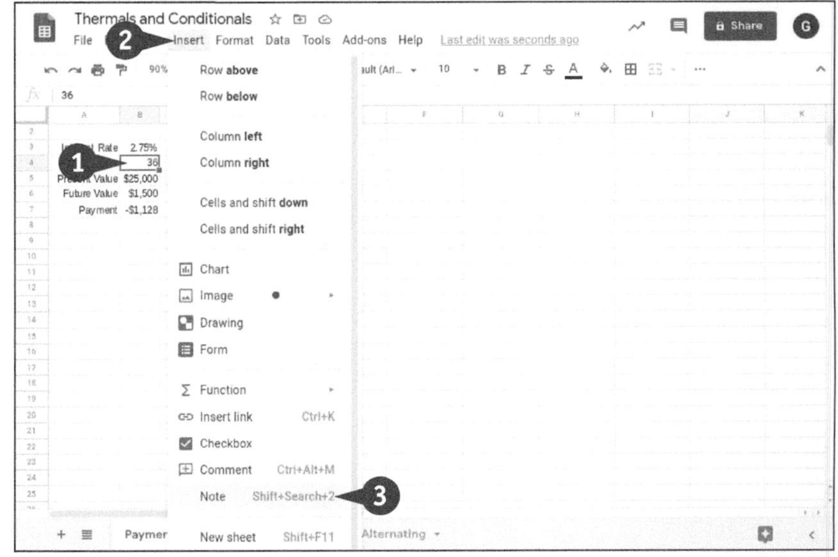

1. Click the cell in which you will insert the note.
2. Click **Insert**.

   The Insert menu opens.
3. Click **Note**.

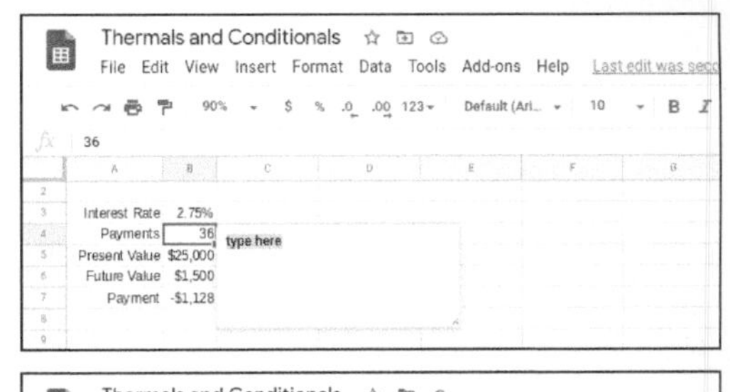

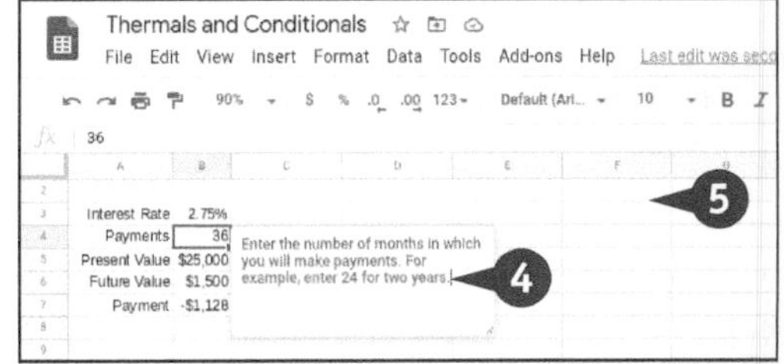

Google Sheets displays a note box with the prompt *type here* selected so that you can type over it.

4. Type the text of the note.
5. Click in any other cell.

Google Sheets hides the note.

Ⓐ The note marker (◥) appears in the upper-right corner of the cell.

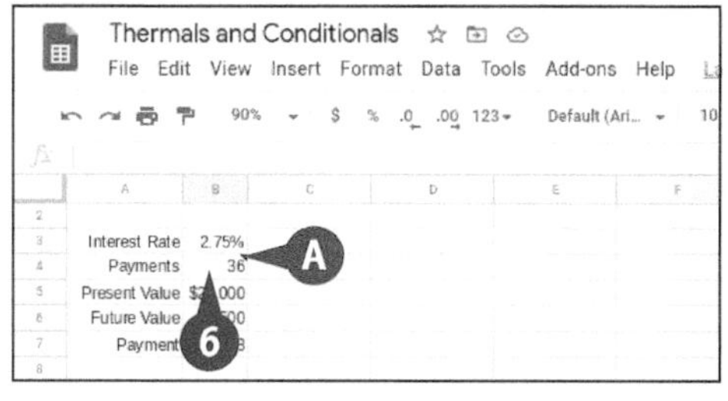

6 Move the cursor over the cell.

Note: You can also click the cell to display its note.

The note appears.

7 If you want to edit the note, click it.

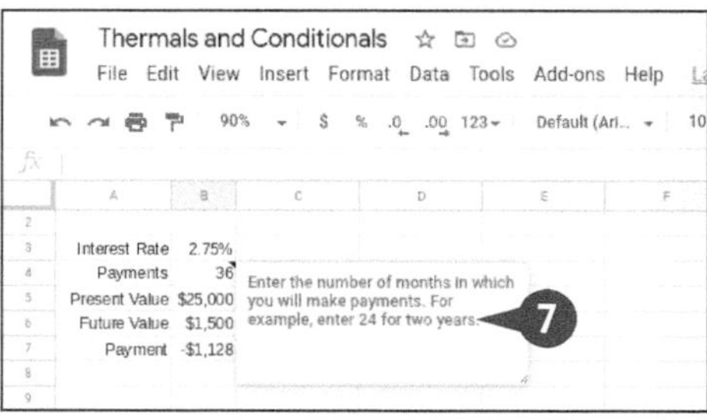

Ⓑ The insertion point appears in the note.

8 Edit the note, as needed.

Note: You can resize the note window by dragging the handle at its lower-right corner.

9 Click outside the note.

The note window closes.

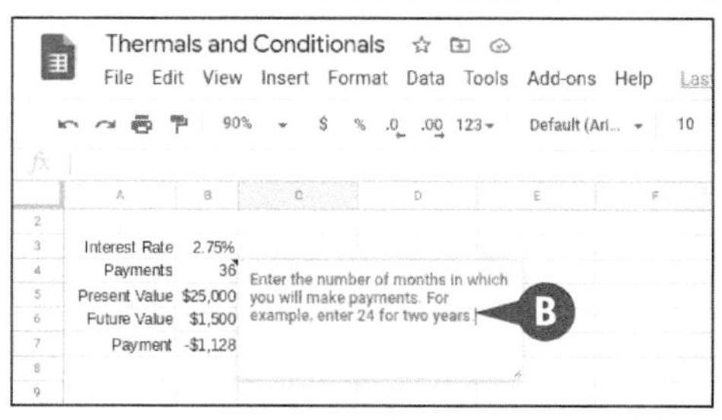

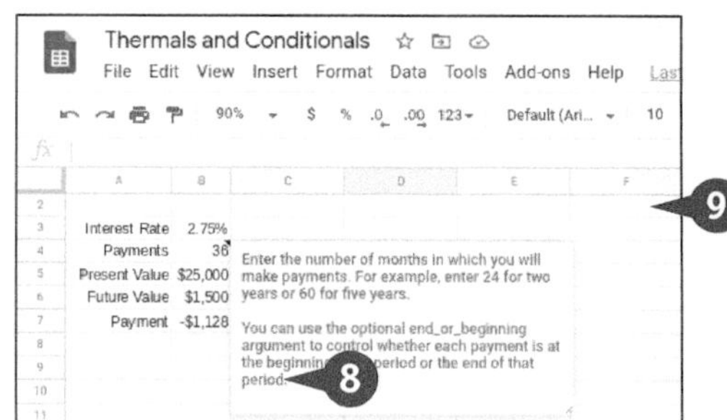

TIP

How do I delete a note?

Select the cell that contains the note, click **Edit** on the menu bar to open the Edit menu, and then click **Clear notes**.

To delete multiple notes at once, first select a range encompassing the cells that contain the notes. To delete all the notes from the spreadsheet, first click **Select all** ( ) at the intersection of the row headings and the column headings to select the whole spreadsheet. Then click **Edit** on the menu bar, and click **Clear** on the Edit menu.

Choose Spreadsheet Settings

Google Sheets enables you to configure various settings for a spreadsheet file as a whole by working in the Settings for This Spreadsheet dialog box. On the General tab of this dialog box, you can set the spreadsheet's locale, such as the United States, and the time zone, such as Eastern. On the Calculation tab, you can control when the spreadsheet recalculates four specific functions: `NOW()`, `TODAY()`, `RAND()`, and `RANDBETWEEN()`.You can also enable or disable *iterative calculation*, calculation that occurs when a formula contains a circular reference — a reference that includes the formula's cell.

Choose Spreadsheet Settings

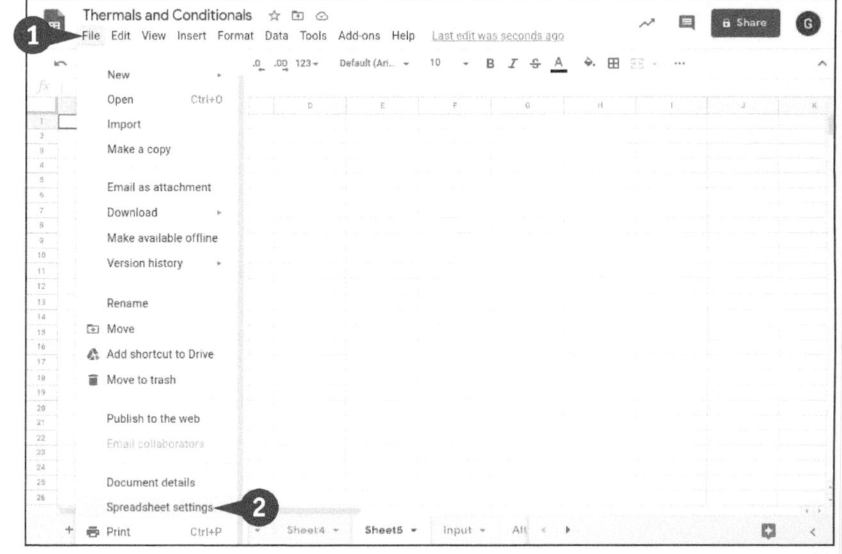

1. Click **File**.

   The File menu opens.

2. Click **Spreadsheet settings**.

   The Settings for This Spreadsheet dialog box opens.

   The General tab is displayed at first.

3. Verify that Locale shows the correct locale. If not, click **Locale** (▼), and then click the appropriate locale.

4. Verify that Time Zone shows the correct time zone. If not, click **Time zone** (▼), and then click the appropriate time zone.

5. Click **Calculation**.

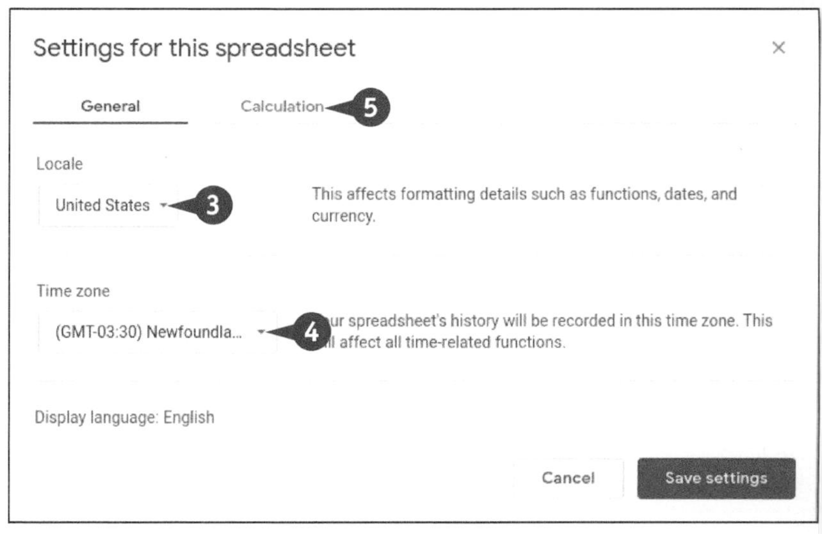

The Calculation tab appears.

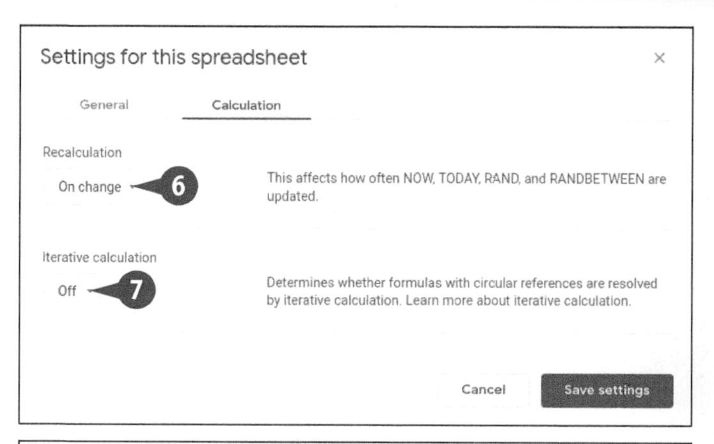

6 Click **Recalculation** (▾), and then click **On change**, **On change and every minute**, or **On change and every hour**, as needed.

7 Click **Iterative calculation** (▾), and then click **On** or **Off**, as needed. If you click **Off**, go to step **10**.

If you click **On**, the Max Number of Iterations box and the Threshold box appear.

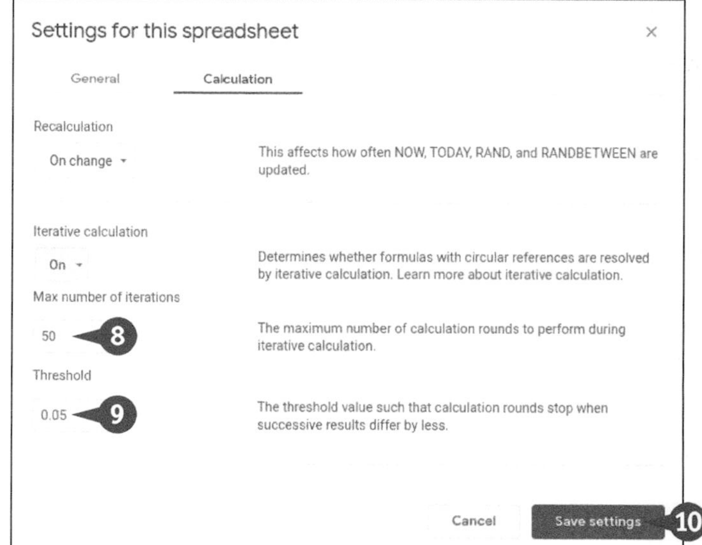

8 Click **Max number of iterations**, and then type the maximum number of iterations you want to allow.

9 Click **Threshold**, and then type the threshold value for continuing iterative calculation.

Note: Iterative calculation stops when successive calculation results differ by less than the threshold value.

10 Click **Save settings.**

The Settings for This Spreadsheet dialog box closes.

TIP

What do the `NOW()`, `TODAY()`, `RAND()`, and `RANDBETWEEN()` functions do?

`NOW()` returns the current date and time. `TODAY()` returns the computer system's current date. `RAND()` returns a random number between 0 and 1, including the value 0 but excluding the value 1. `RANDBETWEEN()` returns a random number between the two numbers provided — for example, `RANDBETWEEN(20,50)` returns a random number between 20 and 50, including the values 20 and 50.

Technically, `RAND()` and `RANDBETWEEN()` return pseudo-random numbers rather than genuinely random numbers. For most spreadsheet purposes, this is an academic distinction, because the pseudo-random numbers are random enough to perform effective randomization.

Merge Cells

Google Sheets enables you to merge the contents of two or more cells together into a single cell. You can merge cells horizontally, vertically, or as a block. Merging cells can be helpful for creating display elements in your spreadsheets, such as headings that span multiple columns.

When you merge cells that contain data, Google Sheets retains only the data from the upper-left cell in the range. Given this, you should either leave the other merge cells empty for the merge operation or copy their data elsewhere so that you can enter it in the merged cell.

Merge Cells

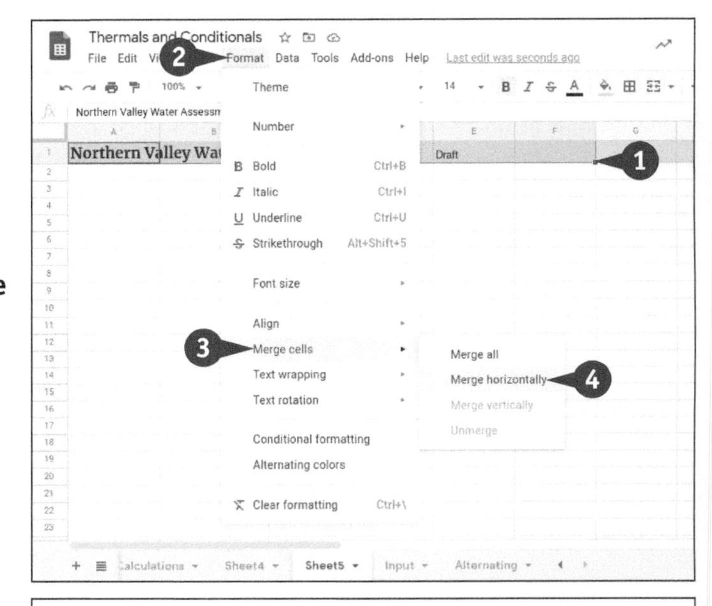

1. Select the cells you want to merge.
2. Click **Format**.

   The Format menu opens.
3. Click or highlight **Merge cells**.

   The Merge Cells submenu opens.
4. Click **Merge all**, **Merge horizontally**, or **Merge vertically**, as appropriate.

Note: If your selected cells occupy multiple rows and columns, click **Merge all** to create a single cell from all the selected cells. Click **Merge horizontally** to merge each row's cells separately. Click **Merge vertically** to merge each column's cells separately.

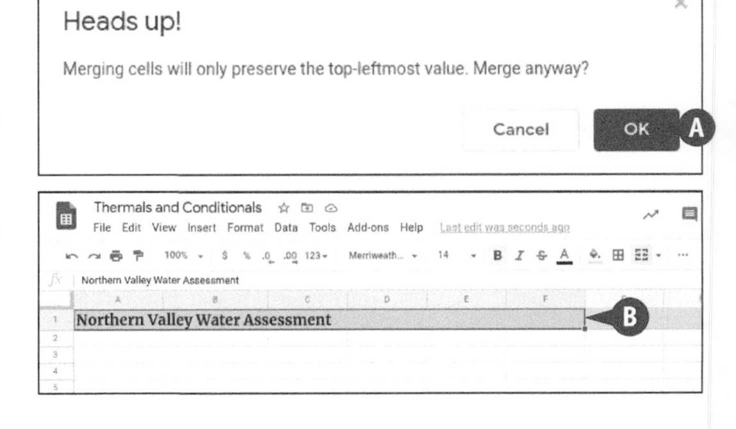

A. If the merge will delete data, the Heads Up! dialog box opens. Click **OK** if you want to proceed.

B. Google Sheet merges the selected cells into a single cell.

Note: To separate cells you have merged, select the merged cell, click **Format** to open the Format menu, click or highlight **Merge cells**, and then click **Unmerge** on the submenu.

Wrap and Rotate Cell Contents

When a cell contains more text than can be displayed at its current width, Google Sheets can handle the extra text in three ways. With the default setting, Overflow, the extra text appears in the next cell to the right, provided that cell is empty; if not, the extra text is hidden. With the Wrap setting, the text wraps to two or more lines within the cell. With the Clip setting, the text stops at the cell's right border even if the next cell is empty.

Google Sheets also enables you to rotate the contents of a cell for visual effect.

Wrap and Rotate Cell Contents

Wrap Cell Contents

1. Click the cell whose contents you want to wrap.
2. Click **More** (•••).

   The extra section of the toolbar appears.
3. Click **Text wrapping** (|⇾| -).

   The Text Wrapping pop-up menu opens.
4. Click **Wrap** (|⇾|).

A. Google Sheets wraps the text in the cell and automatically adjusts the row height.

Note: Click **Overflow** (|÷) to apply Overflow formatting, or click **Clip** (|⊣) to apply Clip formatting.

Rotate Cell Contents

1. Click the cell whose contents you want to rotate.
2. Click **More** (•••).

   The extra section of the toolbar appears.
3. Click **Text rotation** (⊳ -).

   The Text Rotation pop-up menu opens.
4. Click **Tilt up** (⊳), **Tilt down** (⊲), **Stack vertically** (|A), **Rotate up** (◁|), **Rotate down** (|▷), as needed.

B. You can click **Custom angle** (▾), and then specify a custom angle.

C. You can click **None** (A) to remove rotation.

D. Google Sheets applies the rotation.

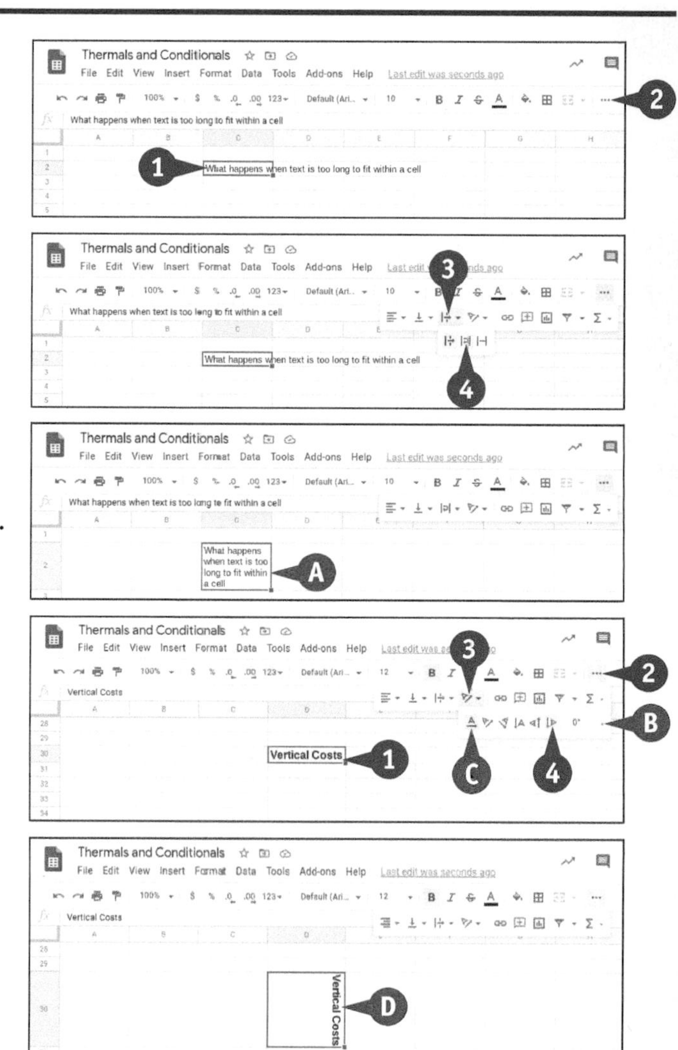

CHAPTER 8

Learning Advanced Google Sheets Features

In this chapter, you learn how to use advanced features in Google Sheets. You start by using the Paste Special command, and then move on to sorting data, filtering data, and applying data validation. After that, you apply protection to ranges and sheets, and learn to automate procedures by creating and running macros.

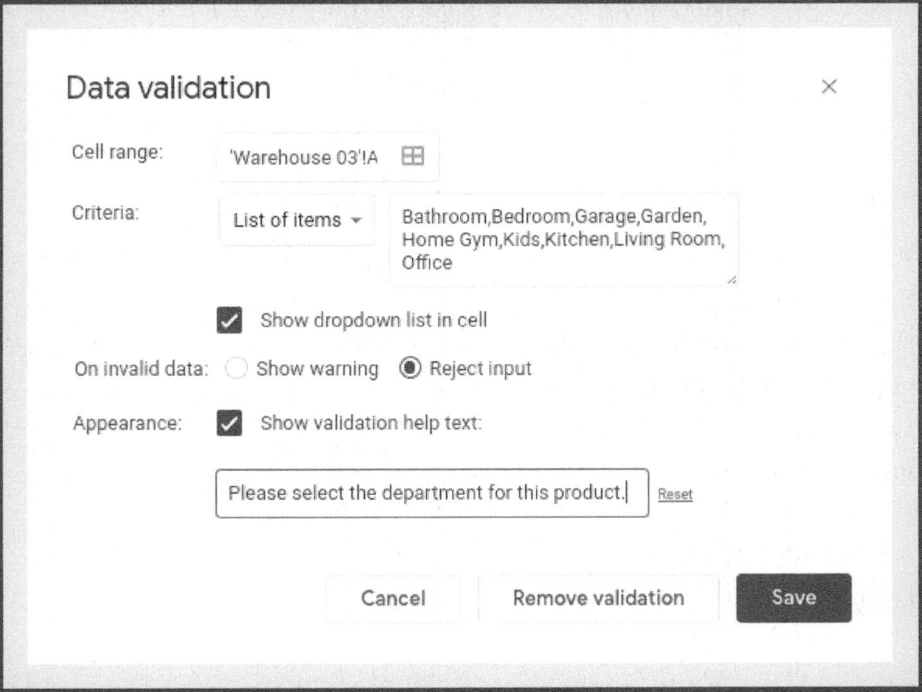

Using Paste Special and Transposing Data

Beyond regular pasting, Google Sheets offers eight Paste Special commands that enable you to paste only certain aspects of what you have cut or copied. You can paste only values with no formulas or formatting, paste only formatting, paste everything except borders, or paste only the column widths. You can also paste only formulas, paste only data validation, or paste only conditional formatting.

You can also paste data with the rows and columns transposed. Paste transposed can be an easy way to fix a spreadsheet that you have laid out the wrong way.

Using Paste Special and Transposing Data

Using Paste Special

1. In a spreadsheet in Google Sheets, select the data you want to copy.
2. Right-click anywhere in the selection.

   The contextual menu opens.
3. Click **Copy** (⧉).

   Google Sheets copies the selected data to the Clipboard.
4. Click **New Sheet** (+).

   Ⓐ Google Sheets adds a new worksheet and makes it active.
5. Right-click the upper-left cell in which you want to paste the data.

   The contextual menu opens.
6. Click or highlight **Paste Special**.

   The Paste Special submenu opens.
7. Click **Paste values only**.

   The pasted data appears in the worksheet.

Note: This example shows the pasted data after resizing the columns to fit the data.

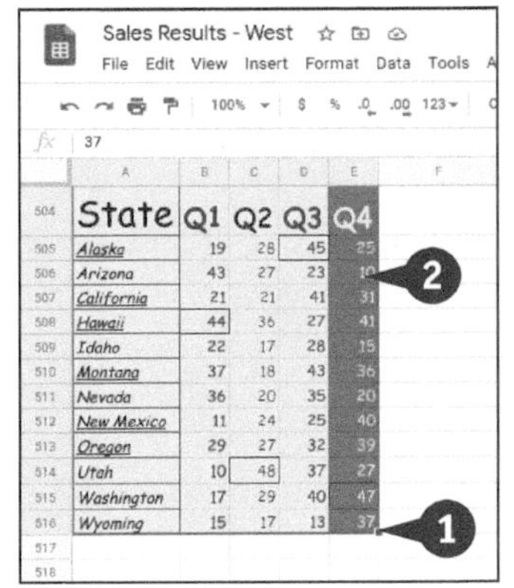

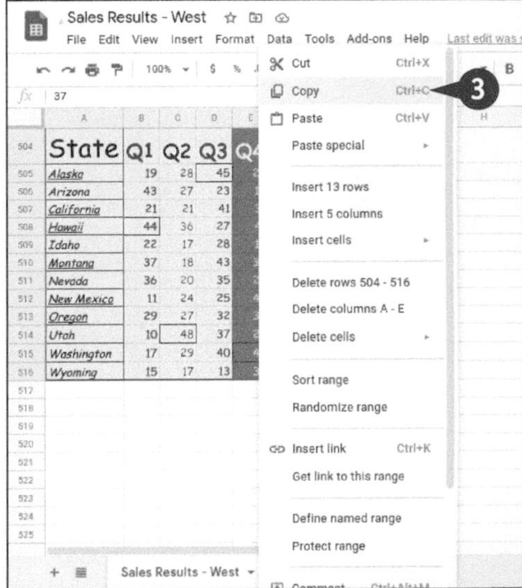

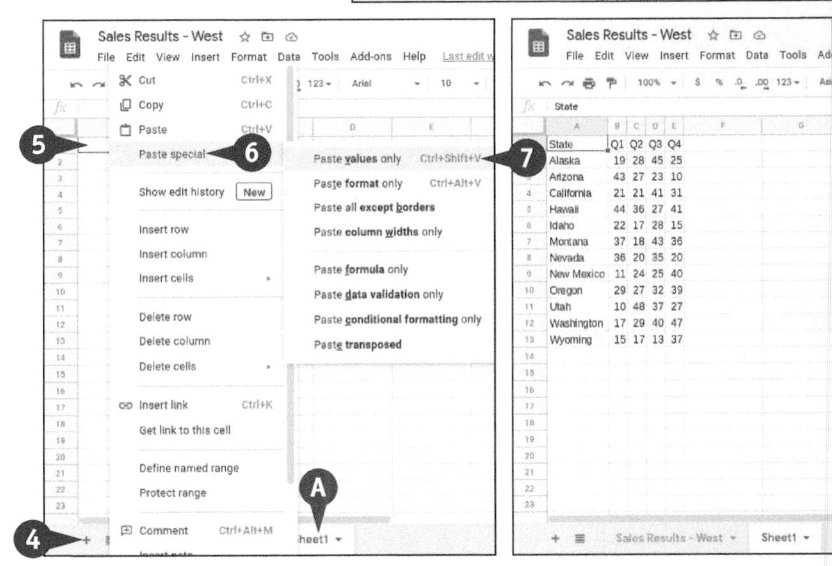

Transpose Data

1. Select the data you want to transpose.
2. Right-click anywhere in the selection.

   The contextual menu opens.
3. Click **Copy** (⧉).

   Google Sheets copies the selected data to the Clipboard.
4. Click **New Sheet** (+).

   Google Sheets adds a new worksheet and makes it active.
5. Right-click the upper-left cell in which you want to paste the transposed data.

   The contextual menu opens.
6. Click or highlight **Paste special**.

   The Paste Special submenu opens.
7. Click **Paste transposed**.

   The transposed data appears in the worksheet.

Note: After transposing data, you may need to resize the columns, as in this example.

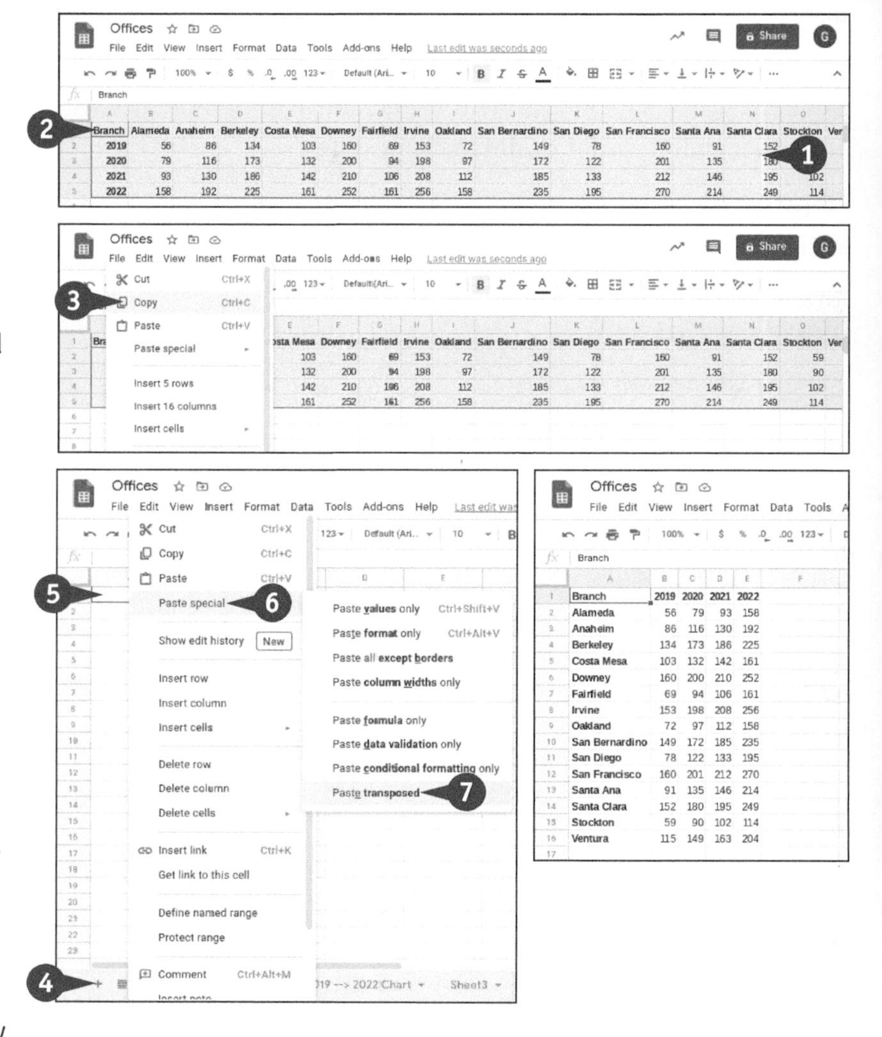

TIP

What is the point of pasting only the column widths?

Pasting the column widths enables you to quickly format new worksheets or imported worksheets for easy viewing on-screen. This is especially helpful when you work with multiple worksheets that share a layout. Once you have set the column widths on one worksheet, you can use Paste Special to apply the width to other worksheets that use that layout.

Sort Your Data

To locate the data you want or to display it in your preferred order, you will often need to sort it. Google Sheets makes sorting easy, enabling you to sort either a range or an entire sheet. You can sort either by a single field or by multiple fields in the order you specify, sorting each field into either ascending order or descending order.

To reduce the amount of data displayed, you can also apply filters. See the following section, "Filter Data in a Sheet," for details.

Sort Your Data

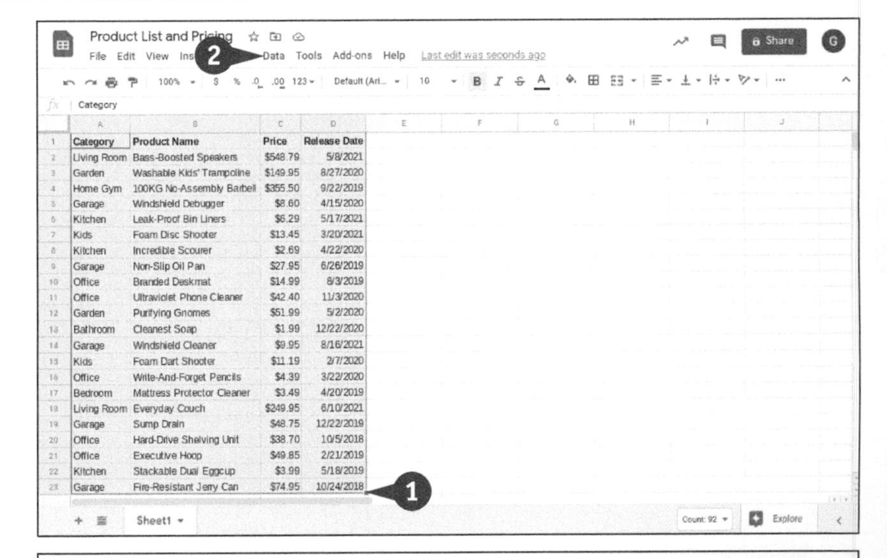

1. In a spreadsheet in Google Sheets, select the data you want to sort.

2. Click **Data**.

Note: Google Sheets can sort data in either ascending order or descending order. *Ascending order* means from A to Z, from smaller numbers to larger numbers, and from earlier dates and times to later ones. *Descending order* is the opposite: from Z to A, from larger numbers to smaller numbers, and from later dates and times to earlier ones.

The Data menu opens.

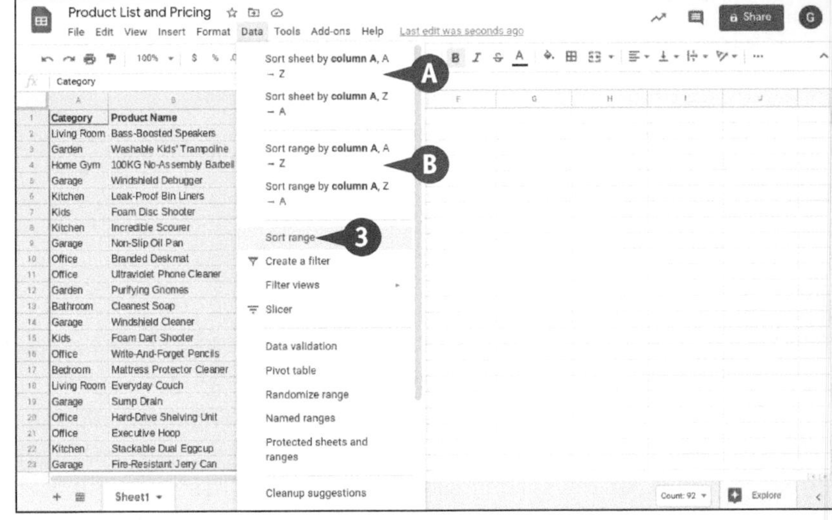

Ⓐ You can quickly sort the entire sheet by the column that contains the active cell.

Ⓑ You can quickly sort the selected range by the column that contains the active cell.

3. Click **Sort range**.

The Sort Range dialog box opens.

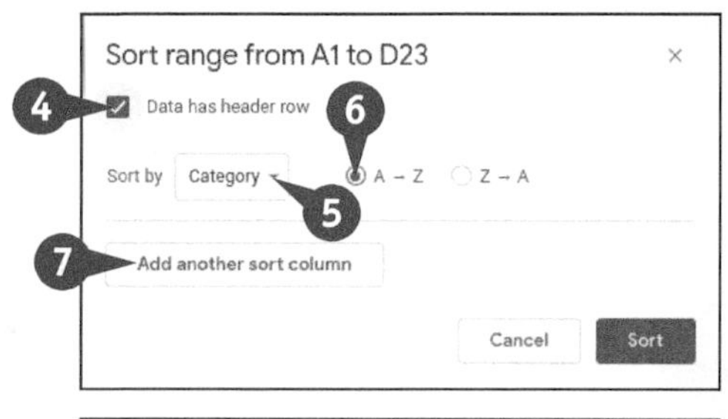

4. Click **Data has header row** (☐ changes to ☑) if your selection has a header row.

5. Click **Sort by** (▾), and then click the appropriate column.

Note: If you have selected **Data has header row** (☑), the Sort By list shows the header text. Otherwise, the Sort By list shows the column lettering, such as Column A or Column ZX.

6. Click **A–Z** (○ changes to ◉) for an ascending sort or **Z–A** (○ changes to ◉) for a descending sort.

7. To add another sort column, click **Add another sort column**.

   Another sort column appears.

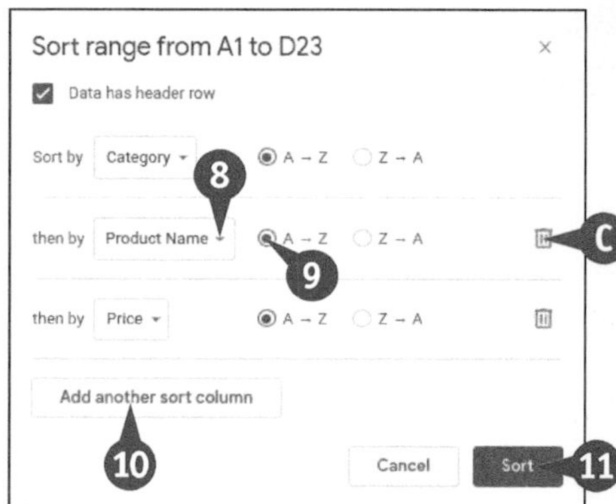

8. Click **Sort by** (▾), and then click the appropriate column.

9. Click **A–Z** (○ changes to ◉) for an ascending sort or **Z–A** (○ changes to ◉) for a descending sort.

C. You can click **Delete** (🗑) to delete a sort column.

10. If necessary, repeat steps **7** to **9** to add further sort columns.

11. Click **Sort**.

    The Sort Range dialog box closes.

    Your data appears sorted in the order you specified.

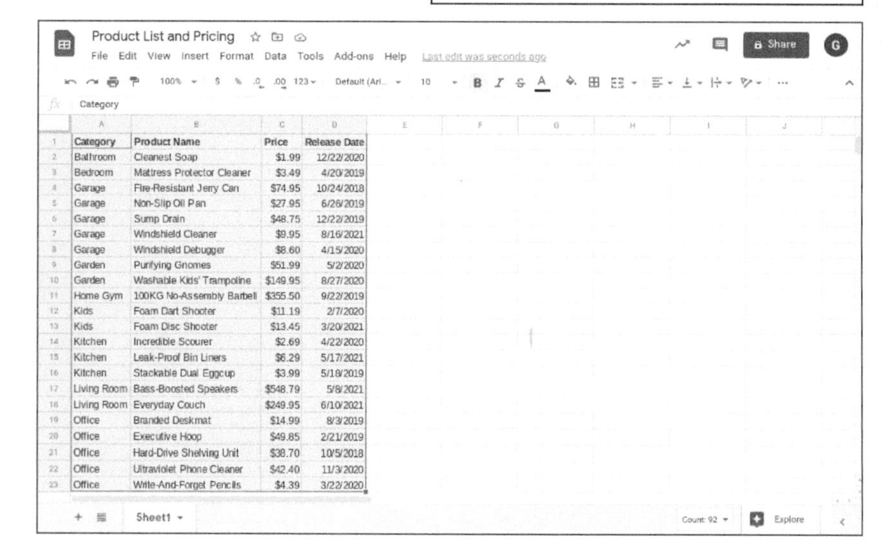

Category	Product Name	Price	Release Date
Bathroom	Cleanest Soap	$1.99	12/22/2020
Bedroom	Mattress Protector Cleaner	$3.49	4/20/2019
Garage	Fire-Resistant Jerry Can	$74.95	10/24/2018
Garage	Non-Slip Oil Pan	$27.95	6/26/2019
Garage	Sump Drain	$48.75	12/22/2019
Garage	Windshield Cleaner	$9.95	8/16/2021
Garage	Windshield Debugger	$8.60	4/15/2020
Garden	Purifying Gnomes	$51.99	5/2/2020
Garden	Washable Kids' Trampoline	$149.95	8/27/2020
Home Gym	100KG No-Assembly Barbell	$355.50	9/22/2019
Kids	Foam Dart Shooter	$11.19	2/7/2020
Kids	Foam Disc Shooter	$13.45	3/20/2021
Kitchen	Incredible Scourer	$2.69	4/22/2020
Kitchen	Leak-Proof Bin Liners	$6.29	5/17/2021
Kitchen	Stackable Dual Eggcup	$3.99	5/18/2019
Living Room	Bass-Boosted Speakers	$548.79	5/8/2021
Living Room	Everyday Couch	$249.95	6/10/2021
Office	Branded Deskmat	$14.99	8/3/2019
Office	Executive Hoop	$49.85	2/21/2019
Office	Hard-Drive Shelving Unit	$38.70	10/5/2018
Office	Ultraviolet Phone Cleaner	$42.40	11/3/2020
Office	Write-And-Forget Pencils	$4.39	3/22/2020

TIP

How can I easily revert to the original order of my data?

If you need to be able to return your data to its original order, add a column containing sequential numbers before you sort the data. You can use Autofill to enter sequential numbers quickly in the column.

When you want to restore the original order, sort the data again and specify an ascending sort by the column containing the sequential numbers.

Filter Data in a Sheet

The Filter feature in Google Sheets enables you to reduce the amount of data displayed in a worksheet to only what you need to see. For example, you can filter an address database to display only customers in specific states or in specific cities in those states.

Google Sheets lets you filter by the values in a column in the dataset; filter by a condition, such as whether a cell includes specified text or a value in a specified range; or by text color or fill color.

Filter Data in a Sheet

1. Click a cell in the dataset you want to filter.

   The cell becomes active.

2. Click **Data**.

   The Data menu opens.

3. Click **Create a filter** (⧩).

   - **A** Google Sheets applies green shading to the row headers and column headers of the data range to be filtered.
   - **B** A Filter icon (⩸) appears in the top row of each column.

4. Click **Filter** (⩸) in the column by which you want to filter.

   The Sort and Filter panel opens, with the Filter by Values section expanded by default.

   - **C** The list shows an item for each unique value in the filter column.
   - **D** At first, each item is selected (✓).

5. Click **Clear**.

   Google Sheets removes the check marks from all the items.

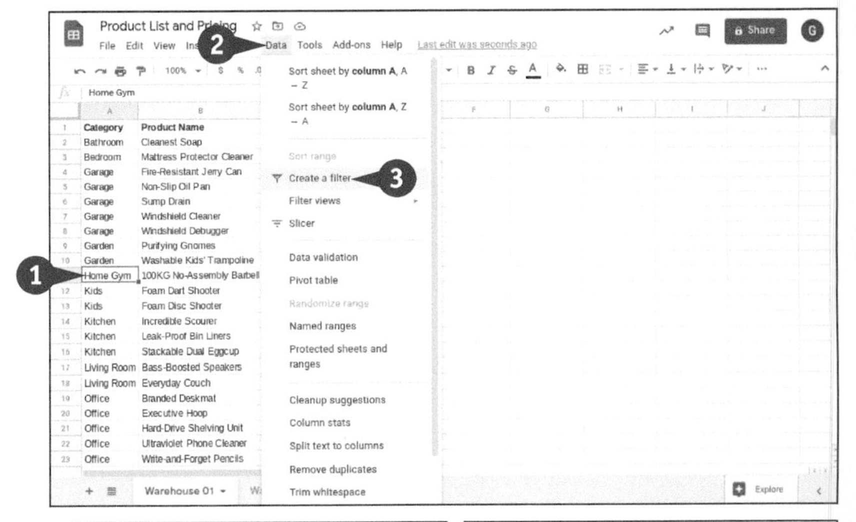

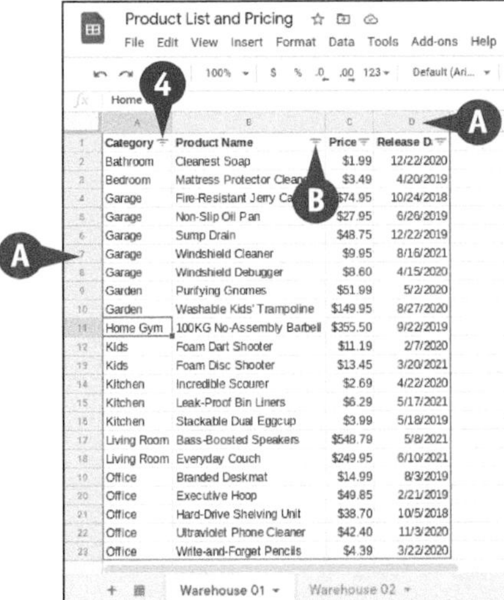

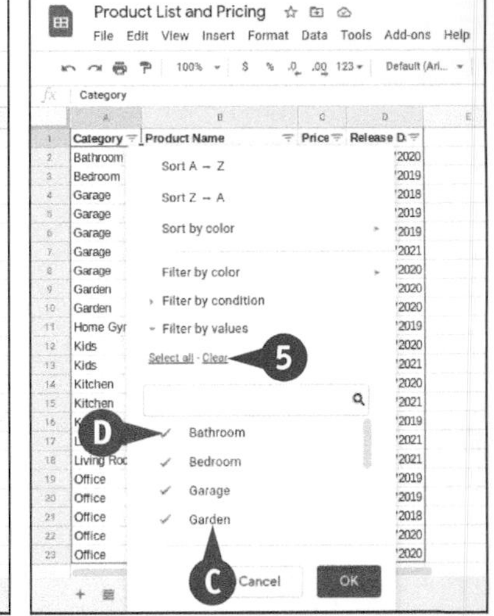

6. Click each item (✓ appears) by which you want to filter.

7. Click **OK**.

   The Sort and Filter panel closes.

   The filtered dataset appears. In this example, only the Kitchen category and the Office category appear.

E. The Filter Applied icon (▼) indicates a filter applied to that column.

8. Click **Filter** (≡) in the next column by which you want to filter.

   The Sort and Filter panel opens.

9. Click **Filter by condition** (▸).

   The Filter by Condition section expands.

10. Click **Condition** (⬍) and then click the condition, such as **Greater than or equal to**. See the tip for more information.

11. Enter the data for the comparison.

12. Click **OK**.

    The Sort and Filter panel closes.

    The filtered dataset appears.

Note: To remove the filters, click **Data**, and then click **Turn off filter** (▼).

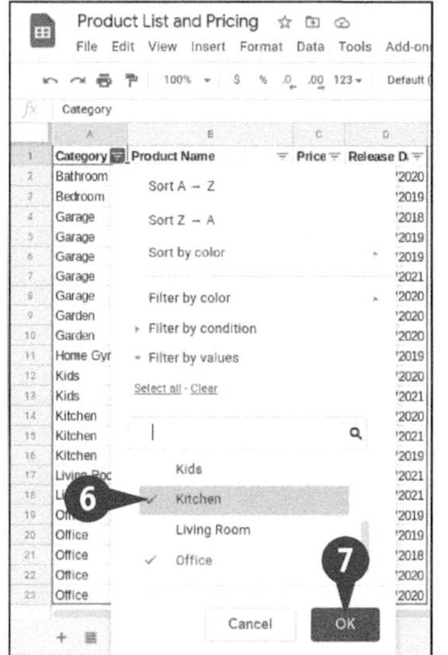

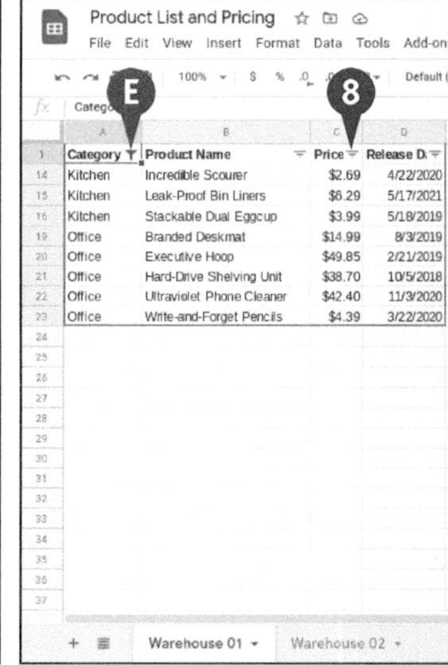

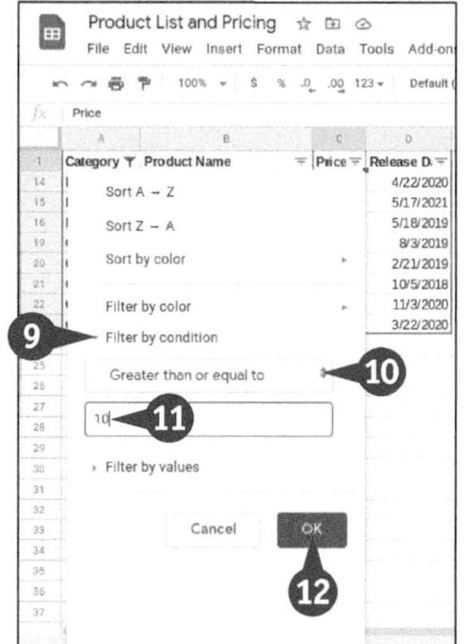

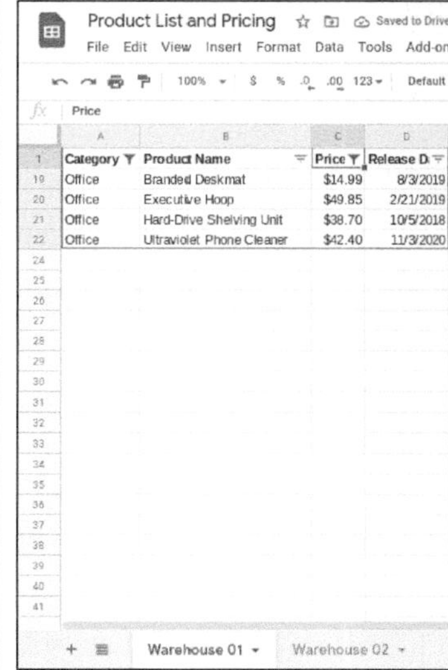

TIP

What types of conditions can I filter by?

You can filter by emptiness, by text contents, by date contents, by mathematical value, or by using a custom formula.

To filter by emptiness, choose Is Empty or Is Not Empty, as needed. To filter by text, choose Text Contains, Text Does Not Contain, Text Starts With, Text Ends With, or Text Is Exactly, and enter the comparison text.

To filter by date, choose Date Is, Date Is Before, or Date Is After, and enter the value.

To filter by value, choose the comparison, such as Greater Than or Equal To, and provide the value.

To filter by custom formula, choose Custom Formula Is, and then enter a value or a custom formula.

Apply Data Validation to Your Sheets

The data validation feature in Google Sheets can help you make sure that you and your colleagues enter suitable types of data in your sheets. For example, you can set up a range of cells to accept only numbers rather than text, dates, or other data types; and you can specify constraints for those numbers, such as that they must be between a lower limit and an upper limit.

You can add help text to ensure users know what data type is needed. You can also set Google Sheets to warn users about noncompliant data or simply to reject noncompliant data.

Apply Data Validation to Your Sheets

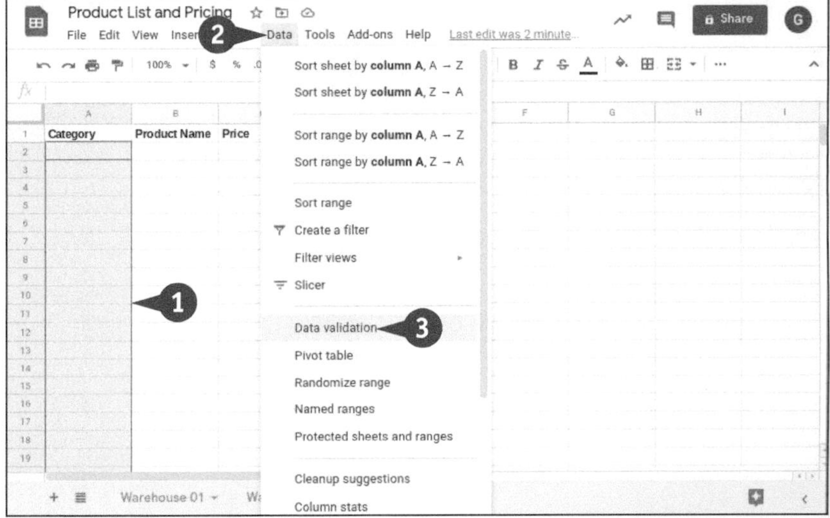

1. Select the range to which you want to apply data validation.
2. Click **Data**.

   The Data menu opens.
3. Click **Data validation**.

   The Data Validation dialog box opens.
4. Click **Criteria** (▼).

   The Criteria pop-up menu opens.
5. Click the validation criterion you want to use. This example uses **List of items**.
6. Use the controls to complete the validation criterion. In this example, you would click the text box that appears, and then enter the items, separated by commas.
7. For the List from a Range criterion or the List of Items criterion, select **Show dropdown list in cell** (☑) to display the items as a drop-down list from which the user can select.
8. On the On Invalid Data line, click **Show warning** (○ changes to ◉) or **Reject input** (○ changes to ◉), as needed.
9. To display text to help the reader surmount the validation, select **Show validation help text** (☑).

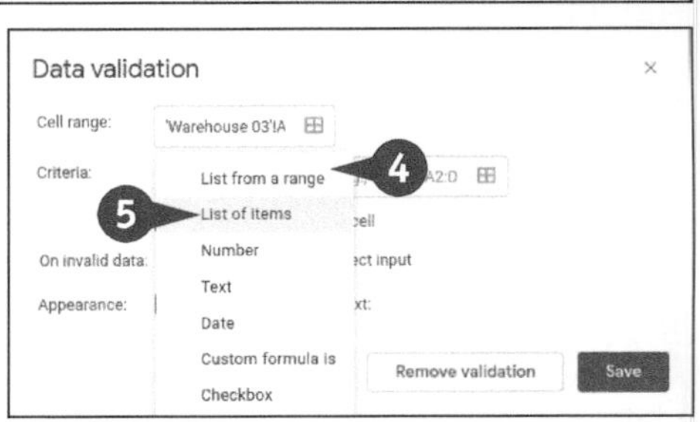

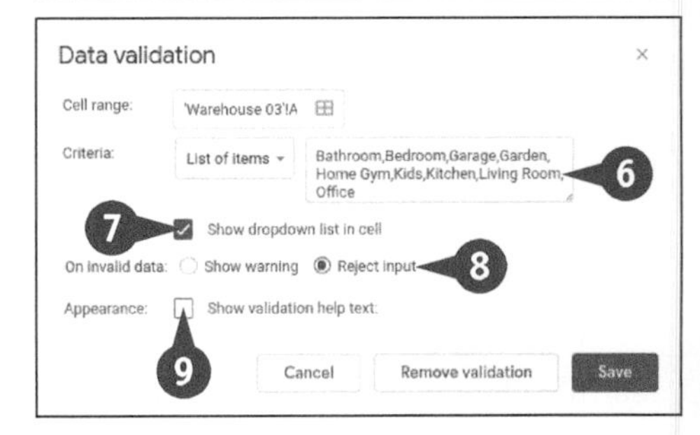

A text box appears below the Show Validation Help Text check box.

Ⓐ You can click **Reset** to delete the contents of the text box.

⑩ Enter the help text in the box.

⑪ Click **Save**.

The Data Validation dialog box closes.

Google Sheets applies the validation to the range.

Each cell in the range displays a pop-up menu button (▾).

⑫ Click ▾ in a cell.

The pop-up menu opens.

Ⓑ The Validation panel appears with the help text.

⑬ Click the item you want to enter.

Ⓒ The item appears in the cell.

⑭ In the next cell, start typing the item you want.

Ⓓ The pop-up menu displays matching items.

If you enter an invalid item, the There Was a Problem dialog box opens.

⑮ Click **OK**.

The There Was a Problem dialog box closes.

The same cell remains active, so you can type a valid value.

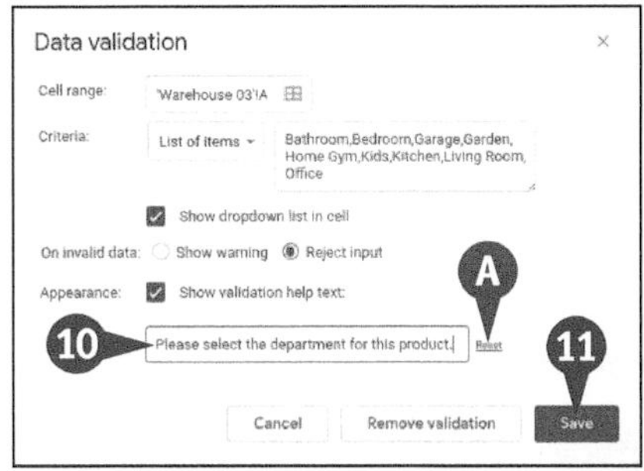

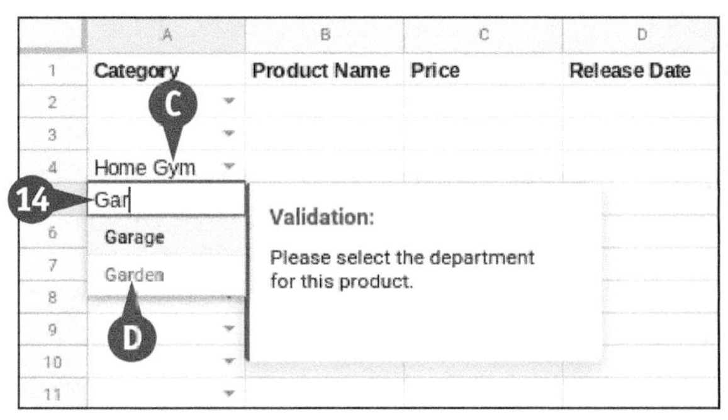

TIP

How do I use validation to get a suitable numeric value?

Click **Data** to display the Data menu, and then click **Data Validation** to open the Data Validation dialog box. Click **Criteria** (▾), and then click **Number**. Click the pop-up menu (▾) to the right of Number, and then choose the appropriate comparison — **between**, **not between**, **less than**, **less than or equal to**, **greater than**, **greater than or equal to**, **equal to**, or **not equal to**. In the box or boxes that appear, enter suitable values to make the condition — for example, *between 100 and 500*. The "between" values are inclusive, whereas the "not between" values are exclusive.

Protect Ranges in a Sheet

Google Sheets enables you to protect ranges in your sheets to reduce the risk of unwanted changes or data loss. You can protect either a single range or multiple ranges, as needed.

You can apply two types of protection. First, you can set Google Sheets to warn users that they are editing part of a sheet that should not be changed accidentally. This protection is largely useless. Second, you can restrict editing to only yourself or to yourself and other people you specify. This protection is effective and is a better choice.

Protect Ranges in a Sheet

1. Select the first range you want to protect.
2. Click **Data**.

   The Data menu opens.
3. Click **Protected sheets and ranges**.

   The Protected Sheets & Ranges pane appears, with the Range tab displayed.

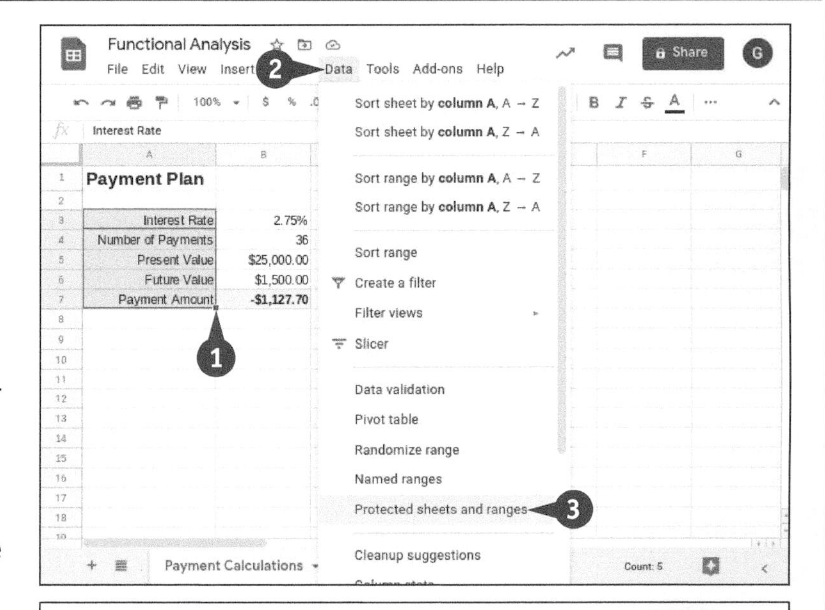

4. Click here and type a description for the range you are protecting.

Note: The description is to help you identify the protected range. The more ranges you protect, the more helpful the descriptions tend to be.

- **A** This box shows the sheet name and the range. You can adjust these manually if necessary.
- **B** You can click **Select data range** (⊞) to select the data range in the sheet.

5. Click **Set permissions**.

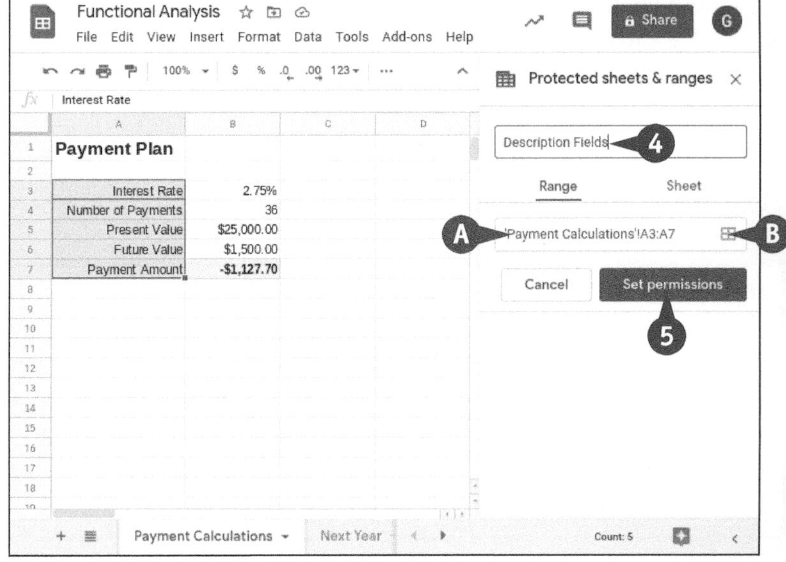

The Range Editing Permissions dialog box opens.

6 Make sure **Restrict who can edit this range** is selected (◉).

C The default permission is Only You.

D To allow others to edit the range, click ▾, click **Custom**, and then type the names or email addresses in the Add Editors box.

7 Click **Done**.

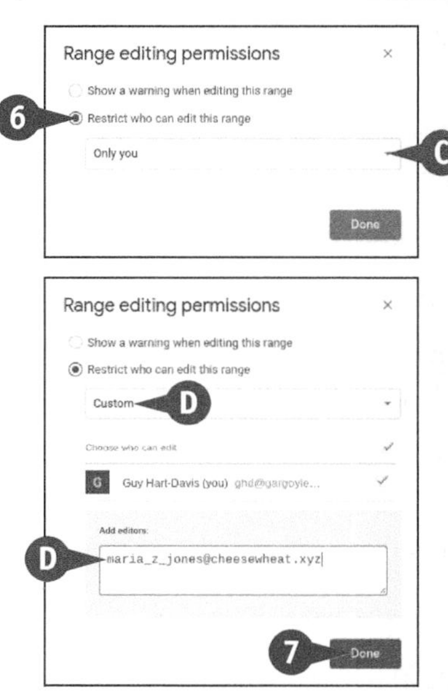

The Range Editing Permissions dialog box closes.

E The *Permissions* readout shows the permission status for the range.

F You can click **Change permissions** to open the Range Editing Permissions dialog box again and change the permissions.

8 Click **Done**.

9 Click **Close** (✕).

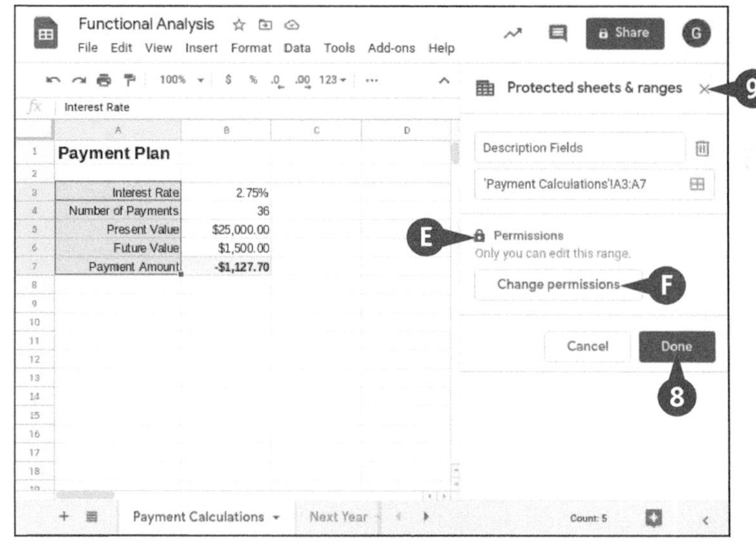

TIPS

What does the Show a Warning When Editing the Range setting do?

This setting causes the Heads Up! dialog box to open when you or someone else attempt to make changes to the protected cells. You can click **Don't show this again for 5 minutes** (☐ changes to ☑) to suppress the warning temporarily. Click **OK** to make the changes despite the warning, or click **Cancel** to undo the change.

Is there a way to duplicate permissions?

In the Range Editing Permissions dialog box, click ▾, and then click **Copy permissions from another range**; click the existing range whose permissions you want to duplicate; make any changes needed; and then click **Done**.

Protect a Sheet

As well as protecting one or more ranges on a sheet, Google Sheets enables you to protect an entire sheet. As with ranges, you can apply effective protection by restricting editing to only yourself or to yourself and other people you specify, or you can apply token protection by configuring Google Sheets to warn users that they are editing a sheet that should not be changed accidentally.

When protecting a sheet, you can exclude certain cells from the protection.

Protect a Sheet

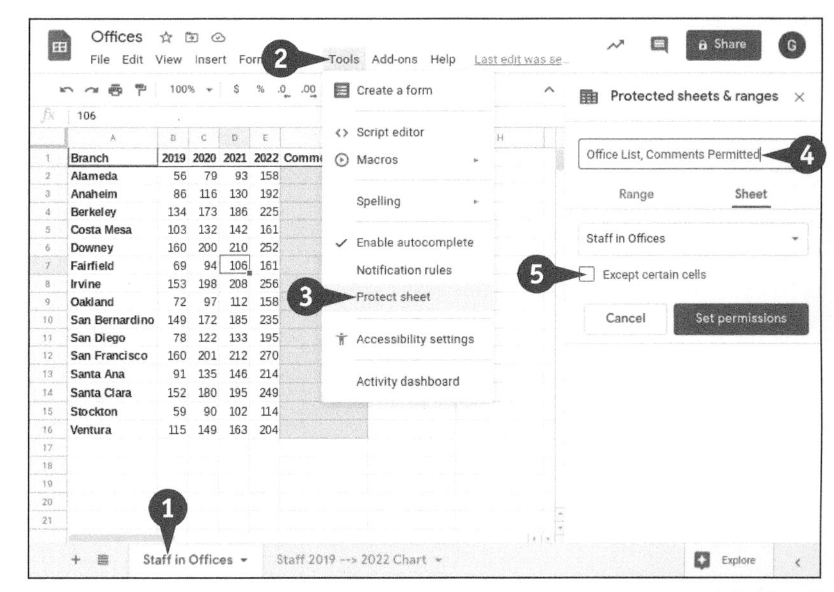

1. Activate the sheet you want to protect.
2. Click **Tools**.

   The Tools menu opens.
3. Click **Protect sheet.**

   The Protected Sheets & Ranges pane opens, with the Sheet tab displayed.
4. Type a description in this field.
5. To exclude some cells from the protection, click **Except certain cells** (☐ changes to ☑).

   Further controls appear.
6. Click **Select data range** (⊞).
7. Drag to select the cells you want to exclude from the protection.

Ⓐ You can click **Add another range** to exclude another range from the protection.

8. Click **OK**.

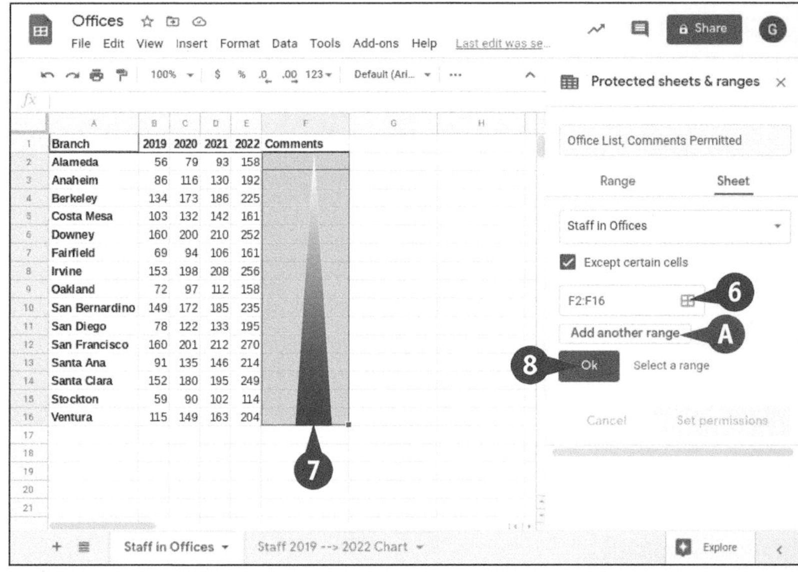

The Set Permissions button becomes available.

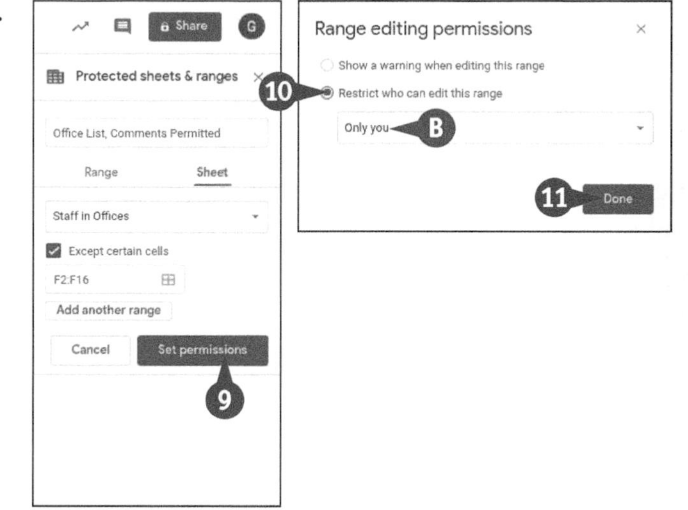

9 Click **Set permissions.**

The Range Editing Permissions dialog box opens.

10 Make sure **Restrict who can edit this range** is selected (◉).

B The default permission is Only You. To allow others to edit the range, click ▾, click **Custom**, and then type the names or email addresses in the Add Editors box.

11 Click **Done**.

Note: You can duplicate protection permissions from other sheets in the same document. See the second tip in the previous section for details.

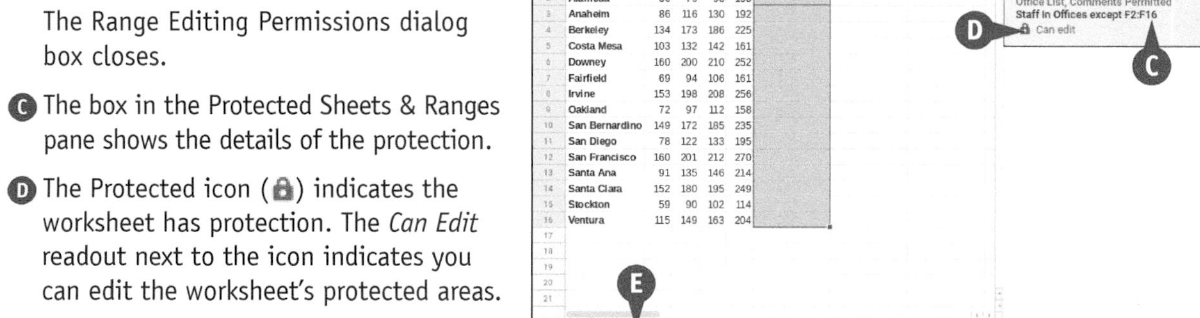

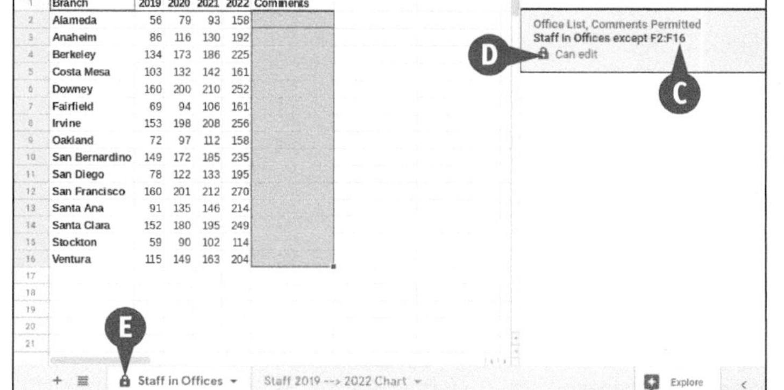

The Range Editing Permissions dialog box closes.

C The box in the Protected Sheets & Ranges pane shows the details of the protection.

D The Protected icon (🔒) indicates the worksheet has protection. The *Can Edit* readout next to the icon indicates you can edit the worksheet's protected areas.

E The Protected icon (🔒 for the active sheet, 🔒 otherwise) indicates that the sheet is protected.

12 Click **Close** (✕).

The Protected Sheets & Ranges pane closes.

TIP

How do I remove protection from a sheet?

First, make the sheet active. Next, click **Data** to open the Data menu, and then click **Protected sheets and ranges** to open the Protected Sheets & Ranges pane. Click the entry for the sheet to display the settings for the protection, and then click **Delete range or sheet protection** (🗑). In the Are You Sure You Want to Remove This Protected Range? dialog box, click **Remove**. You can then click **Close** (✕) to close the Protected Sheets & Ranges pane.

Create a Macro

Google Sheets enables you to create macros to automate repetitive tasks. A *macro* is a sequence of commands. You typically create a macro by switching on the macro recorder and then performing the actions you want the macro to take. After you stop the macro recorder, you can run the macro, making Google Sheets play back the actions you took.

For example, you might record a macro to enter specific data and apply complex formatting to it. You could then run the macro to enter that data and formatting in other sheets or spreadsheet documents.

Create a Macro

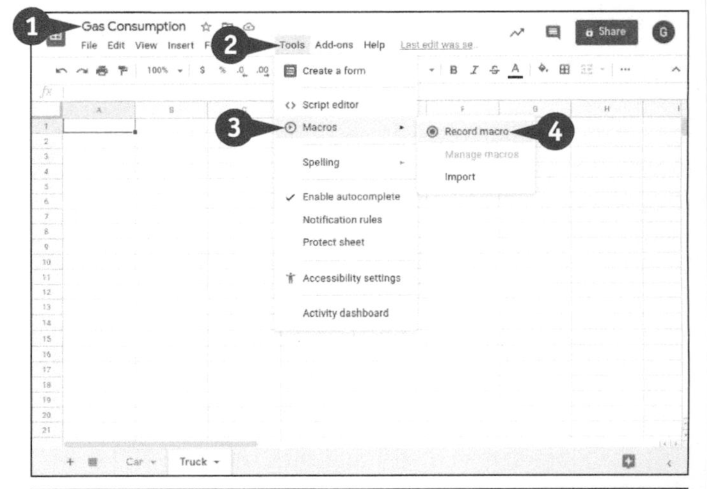

1 Open the spreadsheet document you will use for creating the macro.

Note: At this point, you should also perform any preparation needed to create suitable conditions for the macro. For example, you might position the active cell or add values that the macro will manipulate.

2 Click **Tools**.

The Tools menu opens.

3 Click or highlight **Macros** (⦿).

The Macros submenu opens.

4 Click **Record macro** (◉).

The Recording New Macro panel opens.

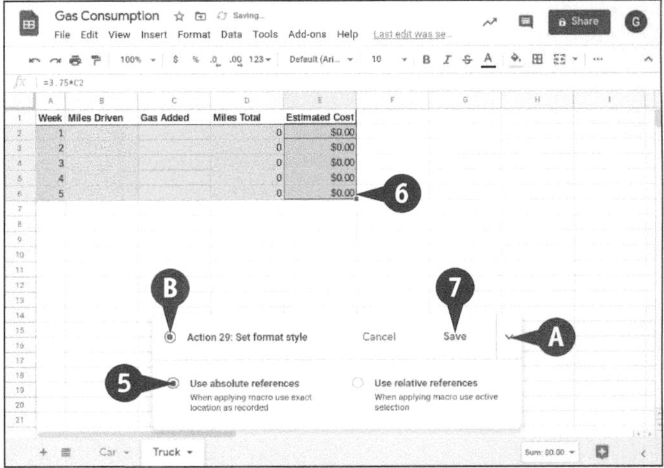

5 Before you start taking actions, click **Use absolute references** (○ changes to ◉) or **Use relative references** (○ changes to ◉), as needed. See the tip for advice.

A You can click **Collapse** (⌄) to hide the References section of the Recording New Macro panel.

6 Perform the actions you want the macro to take. In this example, you would enter headings and formulas in the range A1:E6 and apply formatting.

B After each action, the Recording New Macro panel briefly displays a readout of the action recorded, such as *Action 29: Set format style*, before again displaying *Recording new macro* (◉).

7 Click **Save**.

Google Sheets stops recording.

The Save New Macro dialog box opens.

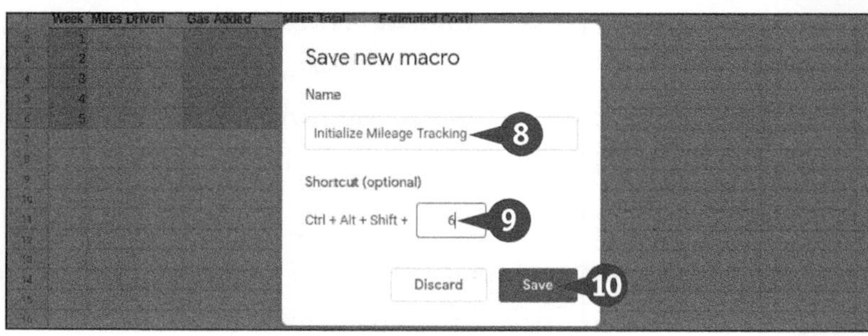

8 Type a descriptive name for the macro.

9 Optionally, click the **Shortcut (optional)** box and type the number you will use with Ctrl + Alt + Shift to invoke the macro.

Note: You can create shortcuts for only 10 macros, using the numbers 0 through 9, so you will likely want to save the numbers for macros you will run frequently.

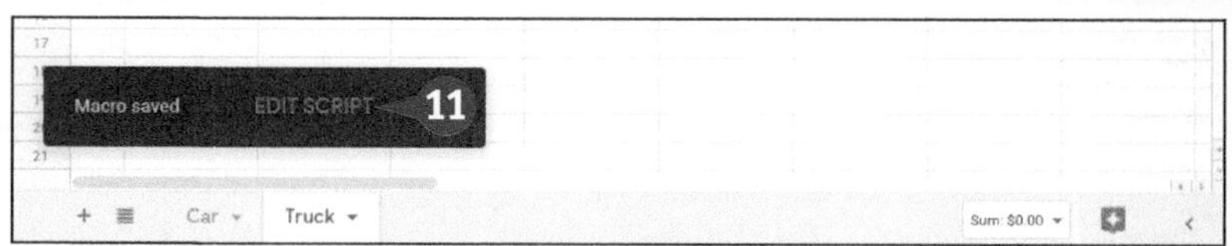

10 Click **Save**.

The Save New Macro dialog box closes.

The Macro Saved pop-up message appears for a few seconds.

11 Optionally, click **EDIT SCRIPT**.

The macro opens in a new tab.

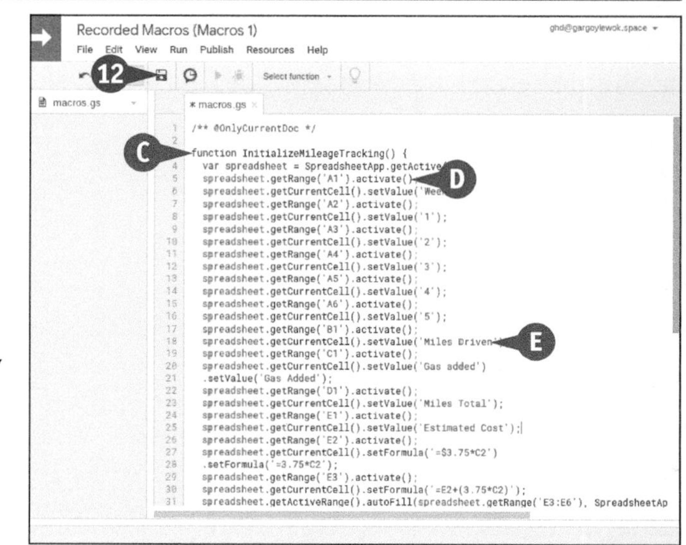

C The function statement begins the macro.

D Even if you do not know the Apps Script language, you can see which commands represent the actions you took. For example, `spreadsheet.getRange('A1').activate()` is the command for selecting cell A1.

E You can change values or text if you made a mistake.

12 After making changes, click **Save** (💾). You can then click **Close** (✕) to close the tab.

TIP

Should I choose Use Absolute References or Use Relative References for my macro?

Click **Use absolute references** (○ changes to ◉) if you want the macro to run on the same cells in each spreadsheet. For example, if you record a macro that enters data in the range A1:C4 with absolute references, the macro will use that range each time you run it.

Click **Use relative references** (○ changes to ◉) if you want to be able to run the macro on different ranges. For example, if you record a macro that enters data in the range A1:C4 with relative references, the macro will use a range three columns wide by four rows high wherever you run it.

Run a Macro

After recording a macro, as explained in the previous section, you can run it any time you need to. Running the macro plays back the recorded actions, such as entering text in cells and applying formatting. Before running a macro, you will want to make the appropriate sheet active and undertake any other preparation needed, such as positioning the active cell in a suitable place or making the type of selection the macro uses.

If you assigned a keyboard shortcut to the macro, you can run it by pressing that shortcut. Otherwise, you can run the macro from the Macros submenu on the Tools menu.

Run a Macro

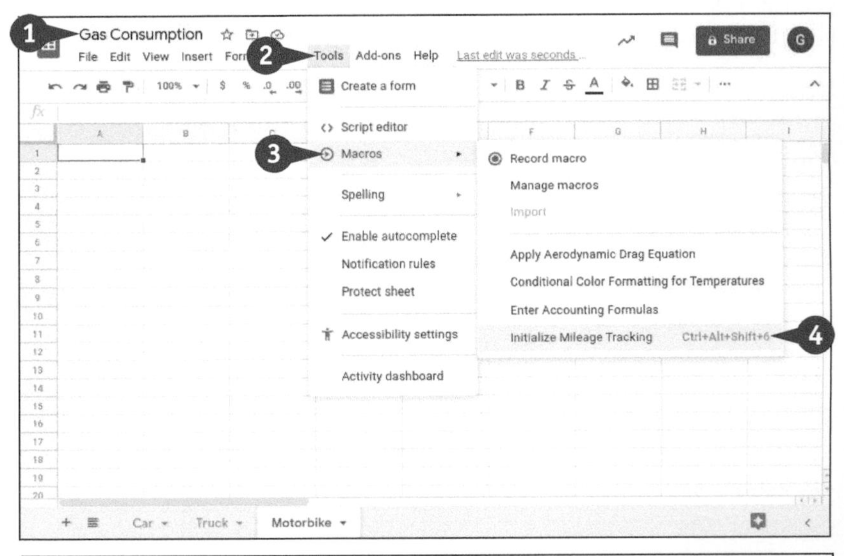

1. Open the spreadsheet document on which you will run the macro.

Note: Add a new sheet to the spreadsheet document if necessary.

Note: If needed, make the appropriate cell, or select a range.

2. Click **Tools**.

   The Tools menu opens.

3. Click or highlight **Macros** (⊙).

   The Macros submenu opens.

4. Click the macro's name.

   Google Sheets starts running the macro.

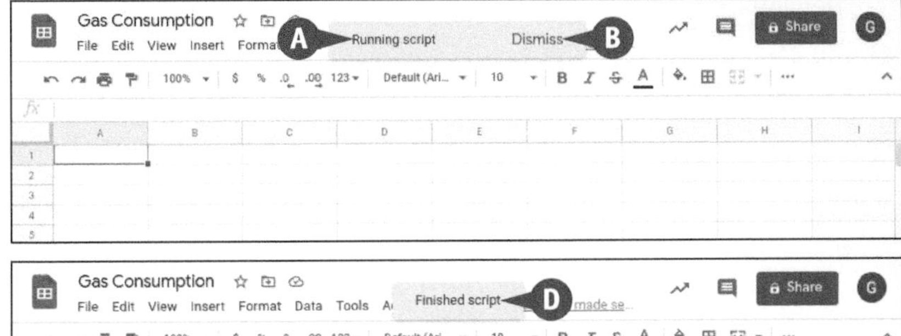

Ⓐ The *Running script* pop-up appears briefly.

Ⓑ You can click **Dismiss** to dismiss the pop-up.

Ⓒ The macro performs its actions. In this example, the macro creates the table in the range A1:E6.

Ⓓ The *Finished script* pop-up appears, letting you know that the script has finished running.

Gas Consumption — Finished script (D)

=3.75*C2

Week	Miles Driven	Gas Added	Miles Total	Estimated Cost
1			0	$0.00
2			0	$0.00
3			0	$0.00
4			0	$0.00
5			0	$0.00

Manage Your Macros

CHAPTER 8

Google Sheets gives you straightforward tools for managing the macros you record. You can rename a macro — for example, to give it a name that is more descriptive or easier to understand. You can assign a keyboard shortcut to a macro that does not have one, or remove the existing keyboard shortcut from a macro. And if you find that a macro has outlived its usefulness, you can remove it.

Manage Your Macros

1. In a spreadsheet document, click **Tools**.

   The Tools menu opens.

2. Click or highlight **Macros** (⊙).

   The Macros submenu opens.

3. Click **Manage macros.**

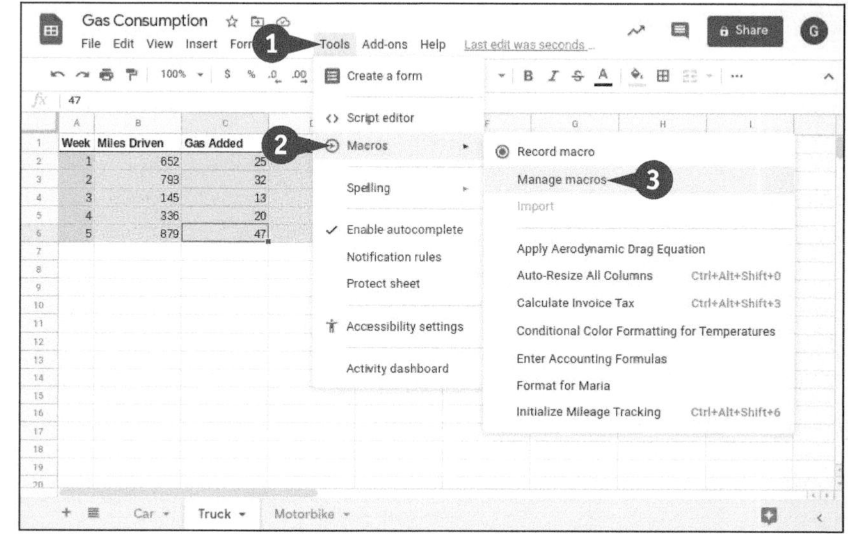

The Manage Macros dialog box opens.

Ⓐ To change a macro's name, edit it in the Name box.

Ⓑ To change the keyboard shortcut for a macro, type the number or delete the existing number.

Ⓒ To delete a macro, click **More** (⋮), and then click **Remove** on the pop-up menu.

4. When you finish making changes, click **Update**.

   The Manage Macros dialog box closes.

   Google Sheets saves your changes.

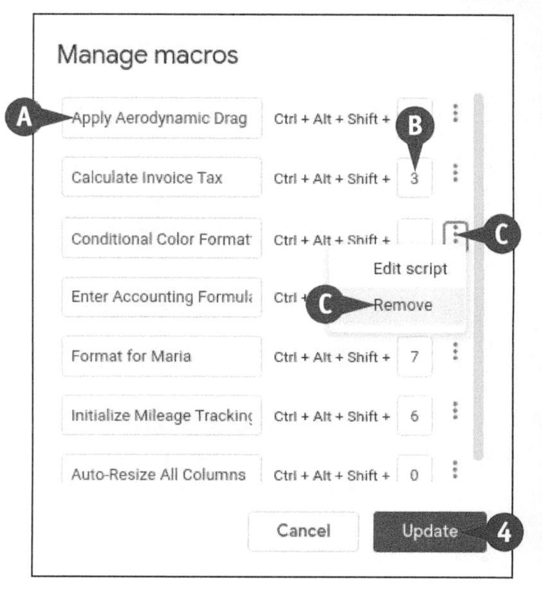

CHAPTER 9

Working in Google Slides

In this chapter, you first set preferences for Google Slides, including Autofit behavior. You then learn to add new slides to a presentation and import existing slides, use different views, and add audio, video, and other content to slides. You add transitions and animations, insert slide numbers, edit the slide master templates, and organize the slides into the appropriate order. Finally, you learn how to preview and print a presentation, how to create handouts for a presentation, and how to deliver a presentation.

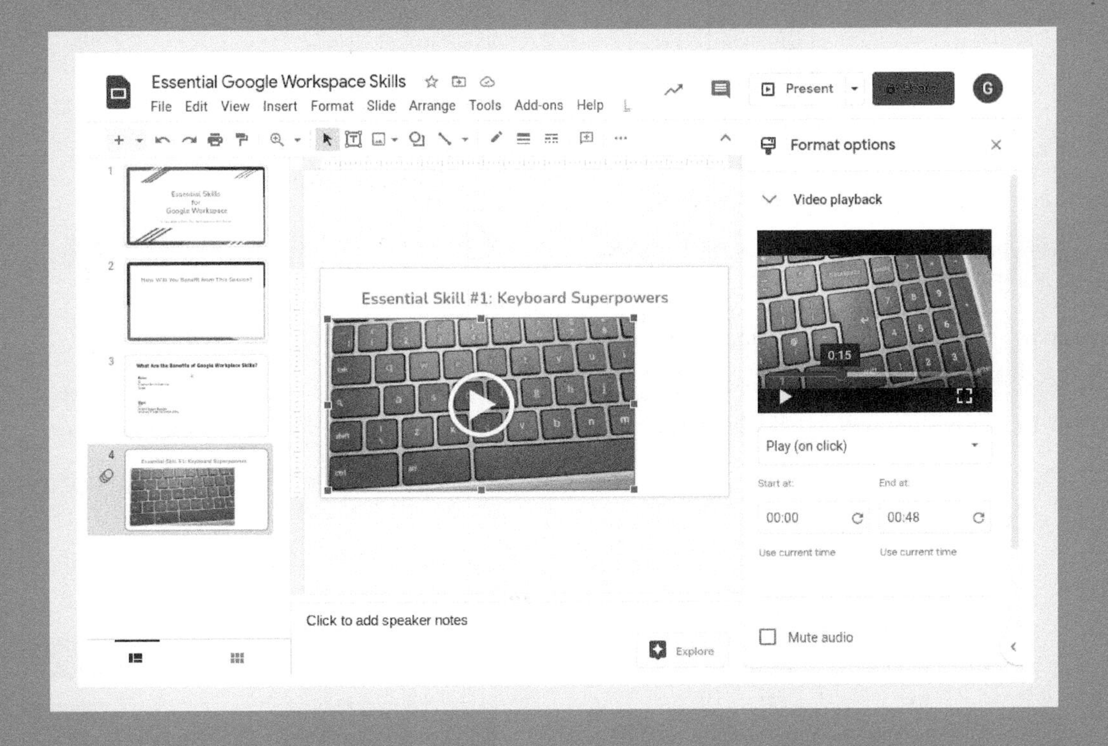

Set Preferences for Google Slides

Before you start working with Google Slides, take a minute to visit the app's Preferences dialog box and choose settings that will suit the way you work. Some of the settings on the General tab of the Preferences dialog box are similar to those in Google Docs — for example, settings for automatically capitalizing words, using smart quotes, and automatically detecting lists as you type. But the Use Custom AutoFit Preferences settings are only in Google Slides, and you will likely benefit from configuring them.

Set Preferences for Google Slides

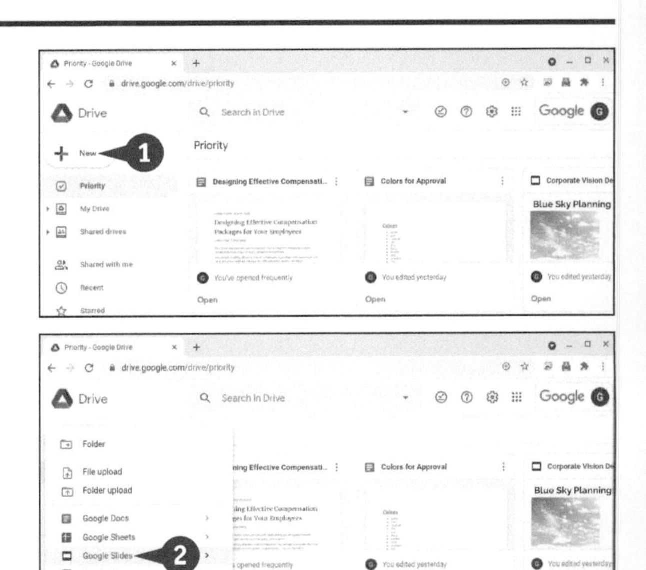

1. In Google Drive, click **New** (+).

   The New pop-up menu opens.

2. Click **Google Slides** (▭).

   Google Slides opens in a new browser tab, creating a new presentation that appears as Untitled Presentation.

3. Click **Tools**.

   The Tools menu opens.

4. Click **Preferences**.

   The Preferences dialog box opens.

   The General tab appears at the front at first.

Note: If you want to configure text substitutions, click **Substitutions** and work on the Substitutions tab. See the section "Set Preferences for Google Docs" in Chapter 5 for advice.

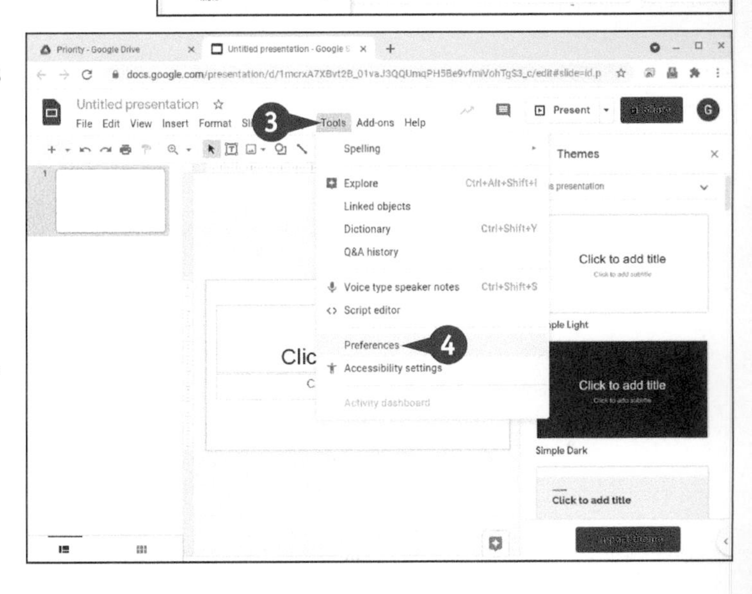

5 Select (☑) **Automatically capitalize words** if you want the app to automatically capitalize the first letter of a new sentence, new line, new paragraph, or table cells.

6 Select **Use smart quotes** (☑) to have the app automatically convert straight quotes to smart quotes.

7 Select **Automatically detect links** (☑) to have the app identify links and apply link formatting.

8 Select **Automatically detect lists** (☑) to have the app identify lists as you type.

9 Select **Show link details** (☑) to have the app display a preview of the linked page when you click a link.

10 Select **Use custom autofit preferences** (☑) to display the Theme Text Placeholders pop-up menu and New Text Boxes pop-up menu.

11 Click **Theme text placeholders** (▾).

12 Click **Do not autofit**, **Shrink text on overflow**, or **Resize shape to fit text**, as needed. See the tip for advice.

13 Click **New text boxes** (▾).

14 Click **Do not autofit**, **Shrink text on overflow**, or **Resize shape to fit text**, as needed. Again, see the tip for advice.

15 When you finish working in the Preferences dialog box, click **OK**.

The Preferences dialog box closes.

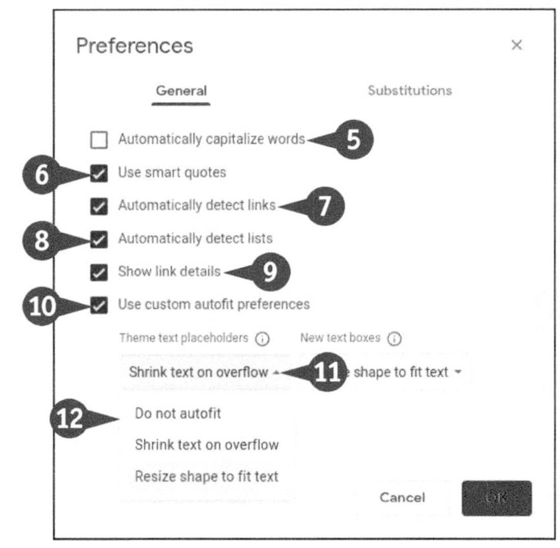

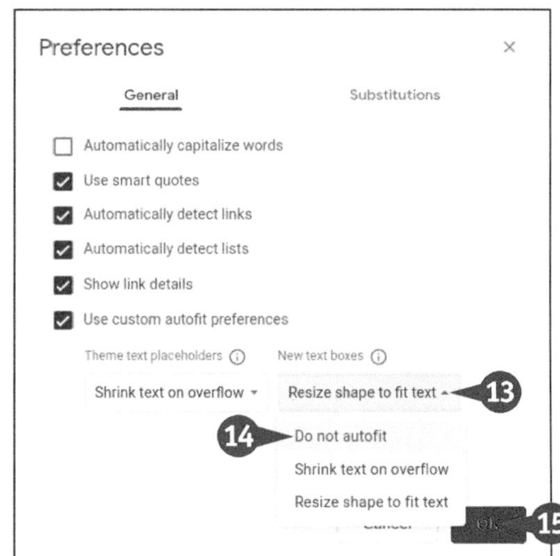

TIP

Which autofit preference should I choose for Theme Text Placeholders and New Text Boxes?

Click **Shrink text on overflow** if you want Google Slides to automatically reduce the text size when the text becomes too long to fit in the placeholder or the text box. This behavior is helpful when you are working fast and need to make sure all the text remains visible. Click **Resize shape to fit text** if you prefer to keep the text size the same but change the placeholder or the text box to accommodate the text. Click **Do not autofit** if you prefer to make any changes in font size or shape size manually. This setting gives you greater control but may take more time.

Add a Slide to a Presentation

A new, blank presentation in Google Slides contains only a single slide, so you will almost always need to create new slides in the presentation. By contrast, a new presentation based on a template typically contains enough slides for a complete presentation, but unless you rigidly follow the template's format, you will likely need to add slides to it, too.

You can add either a blank slide or a slide containing a standard layout, such as the Title and Body layout. After adding the slide, you can enter text and other content on it, as needed.

Add a Slide to a Presentation

Note: This section assumes you have created a presentation in Google Slides. See the section "Create a New Document and Save It" in Chapter 3 for coverage of creating a new document based on a template.

1. In the Filmstrip pane on the left, click the thumbnail of the slide after which you want to add the new slide.

Note: You can also click below the existing slide's thumbnail so that a horizontal yellow line appears for the cursor.

A. You can click **New slide** (+) to add a blank slide.

2. Click **New slide with layout** (+ ▾).

   The New Slide with Layout pop-up panel opens.

B. You can click **Blank** to add a blank slide if none of the slide layouts seems suitable and you decide to start from scratch.

3. Click the slide layout you want. This example uses **Title and body**.

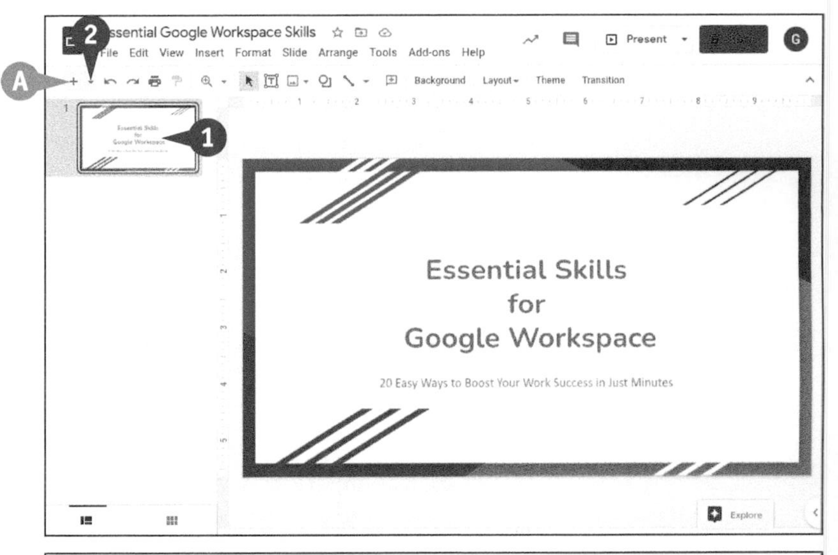

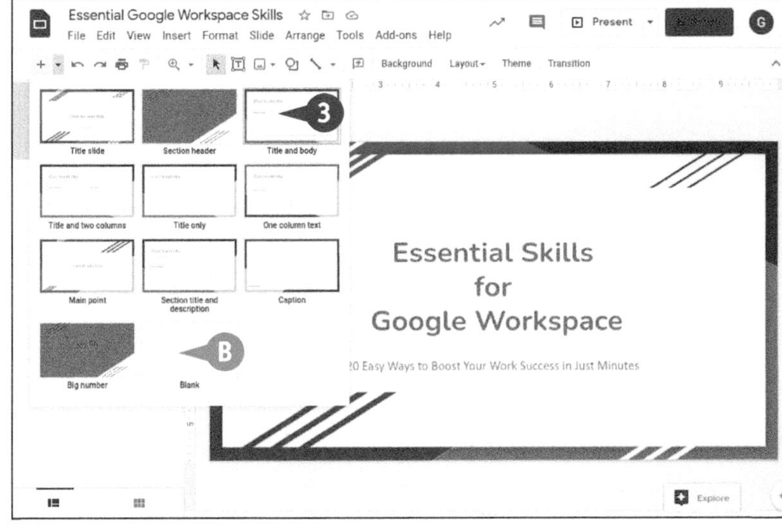

The New Slide with Layout pop-up panel closes.

- C The slide's thumbnail appears in the Filmstrip pane.
- D The slide appears in the Slide pane.

4 Click a placeholder on the slide. This example uses **Click to add title**.

- E A blue outline and resizing handles appear around the placeholder.
- F The Autofit Behavior button appears. See the tip for details.

The cursor appears in the placeholder.

5 Type the text for the placeholder.

- G The text appears on the slide's thumbnail.

6 Click the next placeholder, and continue adding text or other content to the slide.

- H You can click the **Click to add speaker notes** prompt and type notes for the speaker — for example, telling the speaker how to present the slide's content.

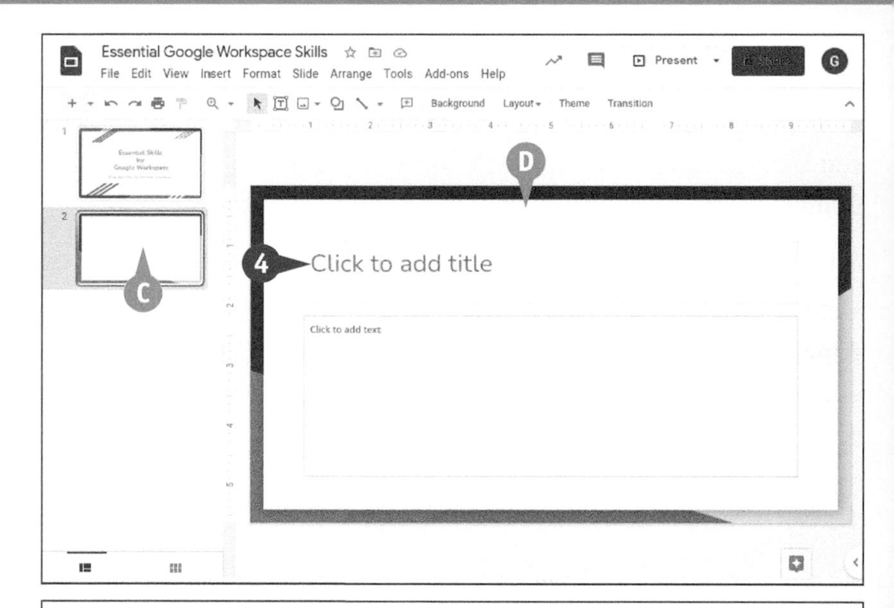

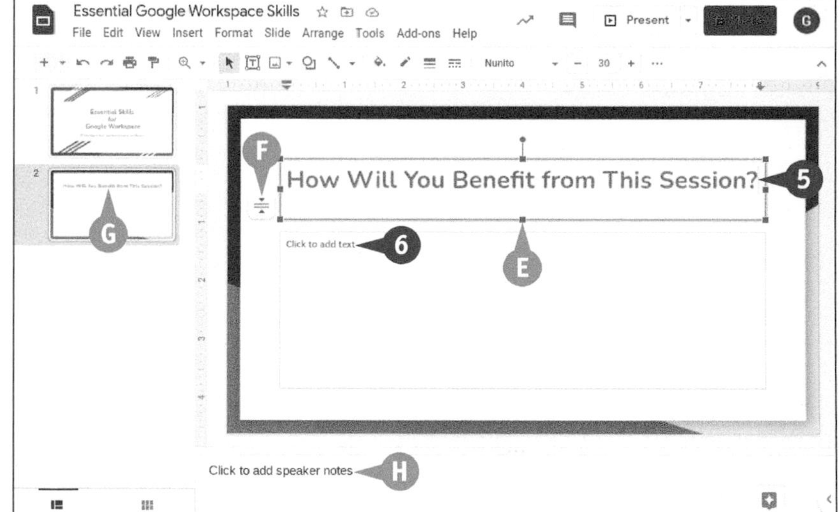

TIP

What does the Autofit Behavior button do?

Click **Autofit behavior** (, , or , depending on the current setting) to display the Autofit Behavior pop-up menu. You can then click **Do not autofit** () to turn off autofitting for this shape, click **Shrink text on overflow** () to have Google Slides automatically reduce the font size to make text that is too long for the shape fit within the shape, or click **Resize shape to fit text** () to have Google Slides enlarge the shape to accommodate the overlong text.

Import Slides from an Existing Presentation

Google Slides enables you to import slides from an existing presentation into the presentation on which you are working. Importing existing slides can be a great way to develop or complete a presentation quickly without having to recreate content. The presentation that contains the slides can be one stored on Google Drive or one that you upload from your computer. It can be in either Google Slides format or Microsoft PowerPoint format.

After importing the slides, you can edit them as needed. For example, you may want to change the slides' theme to match the theme of the current presentation.

Import Slides from an Existing Presentation

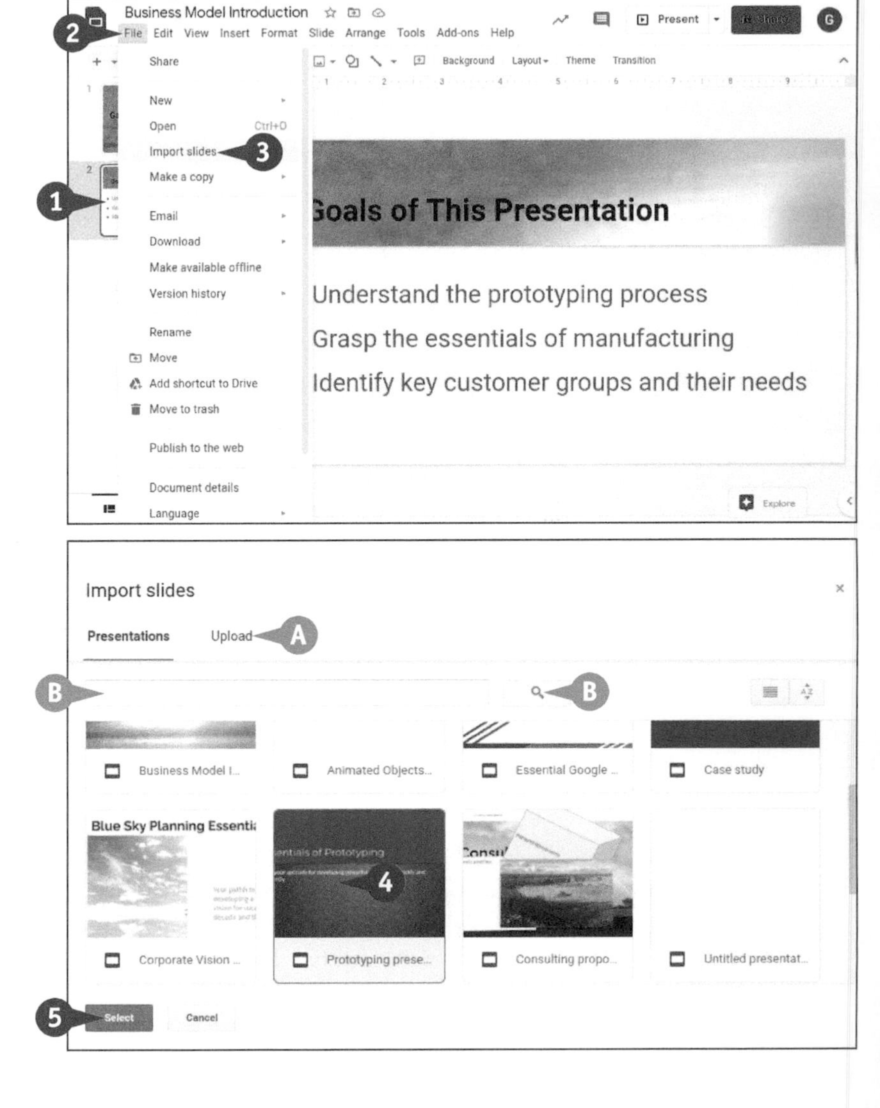

1. In the Filmstrip pane on the left, click the slide after which you want to place the imported slides.
2. Click **File**.

   The File menu opens.
3. Click **Import slides**.

   The Import Slides dialog box opens.

   A. You can upload a presentation from your computer by clicking **Upload** and working on the Upload tab. See the tip for details.

   B. You can search by clicking in the Search box, typing one or more search terms, and then clicking **Search** (🔍).
4. Click the presentation that contains the slides you want to import.
5. Click **Select**.

The Import Slides dialog box shows the slides in the presentation.

6 Click each slide you want to import.

A blue outline appears around the slide, and the slide number background turns blue.

C You can click **All** to select all the slides.

D You can click **None** to deselect any selected slides.

Note: You can select a range of slides by clicking the first slide in the range and then pressing Shift+clicking the last slide in the range.

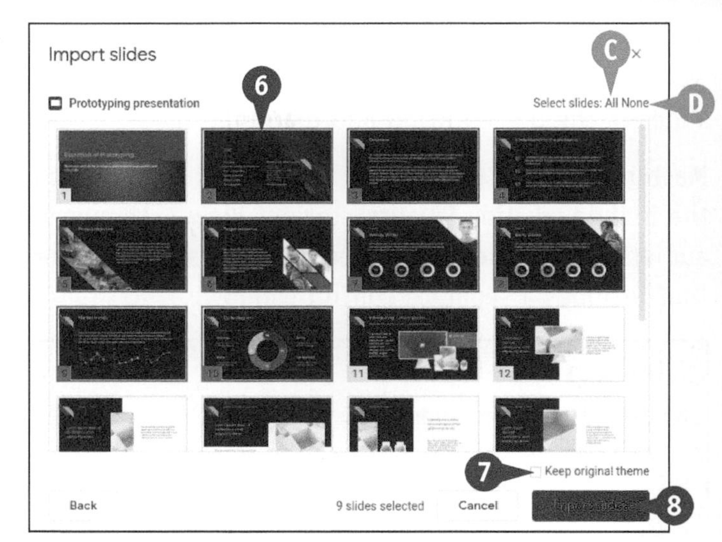

7 Select **Keep original theme** (☑) if you want the slides to retain the source presentation's theme. Deselect **Keep original theme** (☐) if you want the slides to pick up the destination presentation's theme.

8 Click **Import slides**.

The Import Slides dialog box closes.

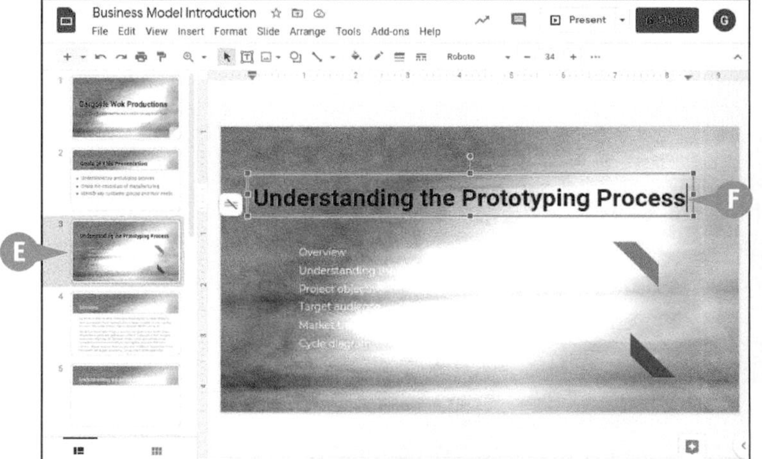

E The slides appear in your presentation.

In this example, the slides take on the destination presentation's theme.

F You can edit the slides, as needed, to make them fit thematically and visually in the presentation.

TIP

How do I upload a presentation and import slides from it?

In the Import Slides dialog box, click the Upload tab to display its contents. Identify the presentation file in one of these two ways: Either click **Select a file on your device** to open the Select a File to Open dialog box, click the presentation, and then click **Open**, or open a file-management window, such as a File Explorer window on Windows or a Finder window on macOS, and then drag the presentation file to the Drag a File Here prompt on the Upload tab. The Import Slides dialog box then shows the slides, and you can select the ones you want, as explained in the main text.

Understanding and Using Views

Google Slides provides five main views for working with presentations. Filmstrip View is the default view for creating and editing slides, whereas Grid View enables you to get an overview of the slides in the presentation and rearrange them as needed.

Master View is a special view that allows you to edit the slide masters, the templates used to create the individual slide layouts. Present View is the view in which you present a presentation to its audience, with the slides appearing full screen. Presenter View is an enhanced form of Present View that includes a separate control window.

Filmstrip View

By default, a presentation opens in Filmstrip View, which is the view shown in the screens so far in this chapter. On the left of the view is the Filmstrip pane (A), which shows a thumbnail image of each slide in the presentation; you may need to scroll the Filmstrip pane up and down to see all the slides. The slide currently selected in the Filmstrip pane appears in the Slide pane (B), the main part of the window, where you can edit it. Below the Slide area, the Speaker Notes pane (C) may appear; you can display it or hide it by clicking **View** and then clicking **Show speaker notes** on the View menu, either adding or removing the check mark (✓). At the top of the view, the menu bar and toolbar appear, as usual.

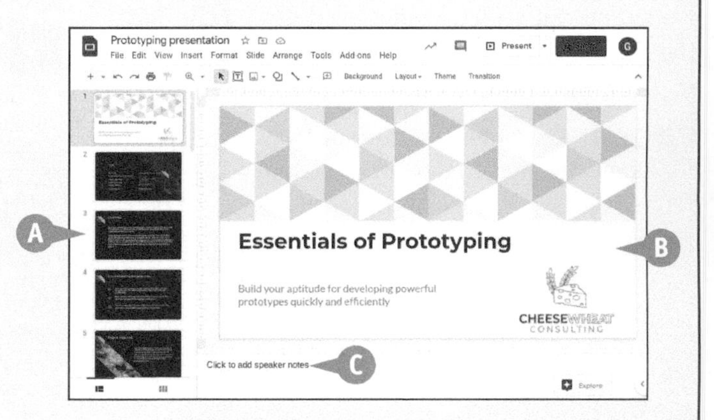

Grid View

Grid View displays thumbnail images of the presentation's slides in a grid arrangement. Grid View enables you to get a more extensive overview of the presentation's slides than Filmstrip View provides and to drag them into a different order.

To switch to Grid View, either click **Grid View** (⊞, D) on the status bar at the bottom of the screen or click **View** on the menu bar and then click **Grid view** on the View menu. To switch back to Filmstrip View, either click **Filmstrip View** (☰, E) on the status bar or click **View** on the menu bar and then click **Grid view** again, this time removing the check mark (✓). You can also press Ctrl + Alt + 1 to toggle between Filmstrip View and Grid View; on the Mac, press ⌘ + Option + 1.

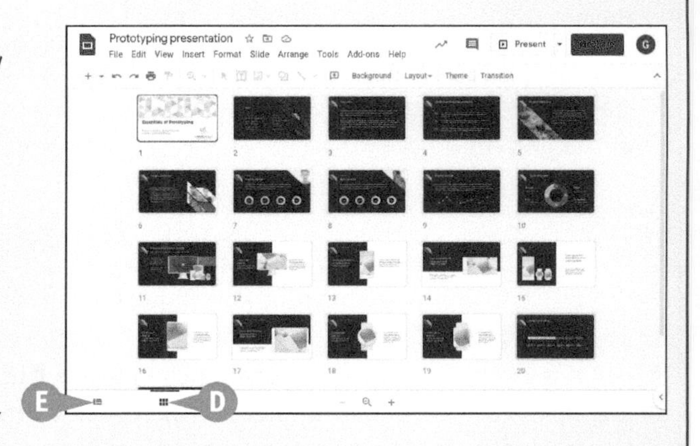

See the section "Organize the Slides in a Presentation," later in this chapter, for full coverage of Grid View.

Master View

Each slide layout is based on a template called the *slide master*, often referred to as simply as the *master*. You can edit a slide master to make changes to its layout. When you edit a master, you can reapply the master to all the slides in the presentation based on the master, extending your changes to the slides in a single, easy move.

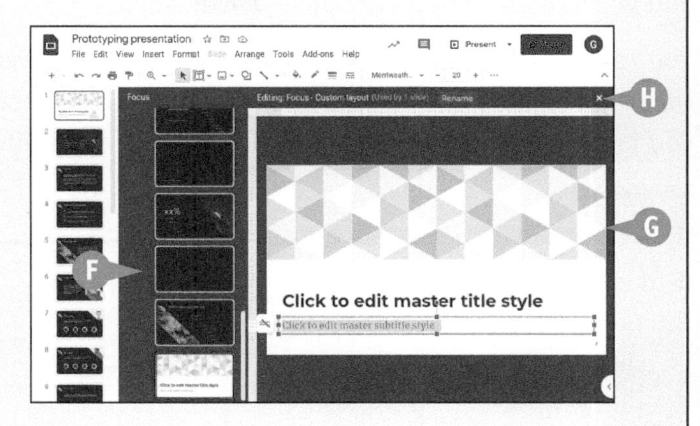

In Filmstrip View, Google Slides hides the slide masters from you, letting you change the layout of individual slides without inadvertently affecting their masters. To edit a slide master, you switch to Master View by clicking **View** on the menu bar, and then clicking **Master** on the View menu.

In Master View's Filmstrip pane (F), click the master you want to edit, and then work in the Master pane (G). When you finish, you can click **Close** (✕, H) to close Master View; alternatively, click **View** on the menu bar, and then click **Master** again, removing the check mark (✓).

See the section "Edit a Slide Master," later in this chapter, for more information on Master View.

Present View and Presenter View

Present View is the view you use for delivering a presentation on a single screen. This view displays one slide at a time, as large as the screen will allow, plus a pop-up control bar (I) that provides tools for navigating the slides and managing the presentation.

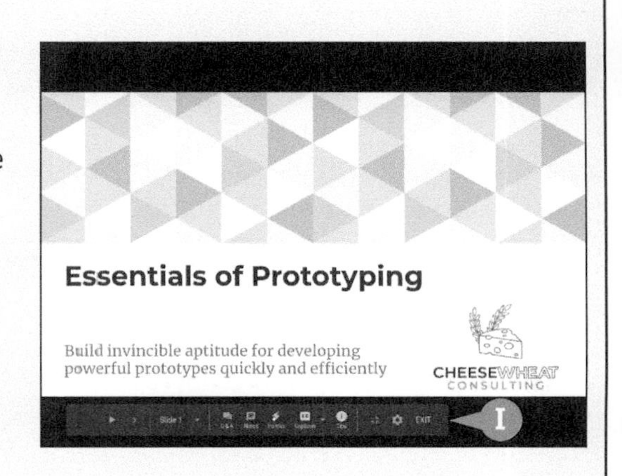

Presenter View is an enhanced version of Present View that opens a separate browser window containing tools for helping you deliver the presentation. These tools include a timer, previews of the previous slide and next slide, any speaker notes for the slides, and a feature for holding a question-and-answer session with the audience.

To switch to Present View, click **View** on the menu bar, and then click **Present** on the View menu. Alternatively, click **Present** (▶) in the upper-right corner of the screen. To switch to Presenter View, click the Present pop-up menu (▾), and then click **Presenter view** (💬).

See the section "Deliver a Presentation," later in this chapter, for more information on both Present View and Presenter View.

Work with Text Boxes

Many slides need at least some text to convey their meanings fully, and so most slide masters contain one or more text boxes for you to populate. You can delete any superfluous text boxes, and you can add other text boxes, as needed.

You can configure the Autofit feature either to automatically reduce the font size of overlong text to fit inside its text box or to enlarge the text box to accommodate the text at its current font size. If you prefer, you can turn off Autofit and resize the font, the text box, or both manually.

Work with Text Boxes

Add a Text Box

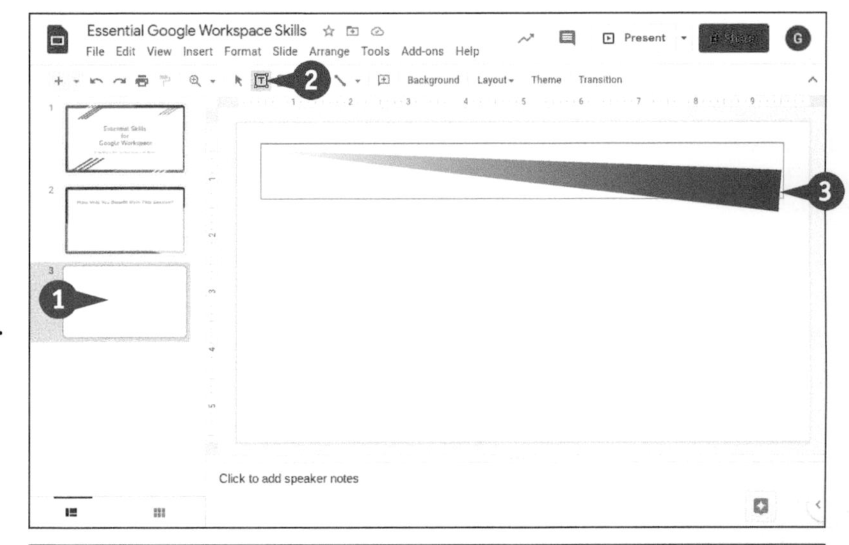

1. In the Filmstrip pane, click the slide to which you want to add the text box.

   The slide appears in the Slide pane.

2. Click **Text box** (T).

   The Text Box tool becomes active.

3. Click where you want to place one corner of the text box, and then drag to the opposite corner.

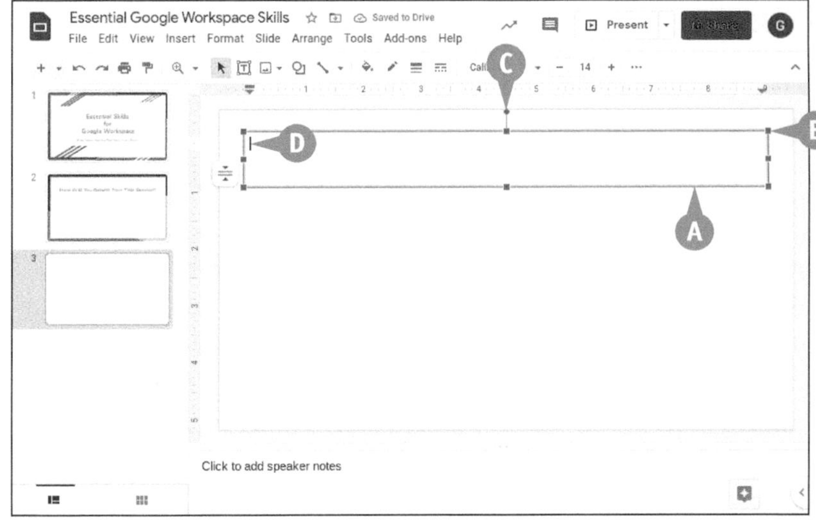

- A The text box appears with a blue outline.
- B A sizing handle (■) appears at each corner and in the middle of each side.
- C The rotation handle (●) appears at the top, connected to a side handle.
- D The cursor appears in the text box, ready for text entry.

Enter Text and Apply Formatting

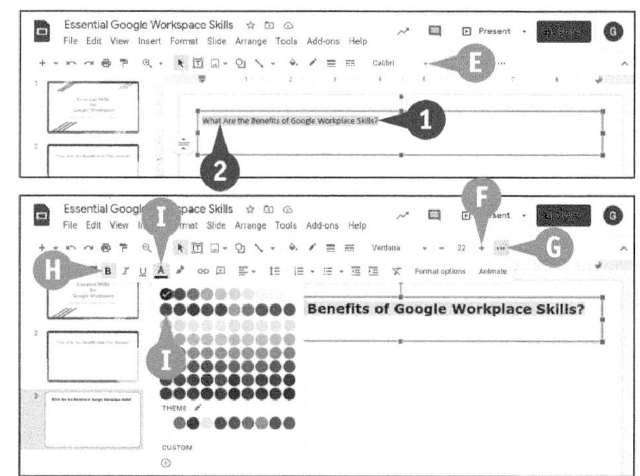

1. Type the text for the text box.
2. Select the text. For example, press Shift + ↑, or drag with the mouse.
3. Apply formatting to the text, as needed. For example:

- E Click **Font** (▾), and then click the font you want to apply.
- F Click **Increase font size** (+) to increase the font size.
- G Click **More** (···) to display the extra section of the toolbar.
- H Click **Bold** (B) to apply boldface.
- I Click **Text color** (A) to open the Text Color pop-up panel, and then click the color you want to apply.

Control Autofit Behavior for a Text Box

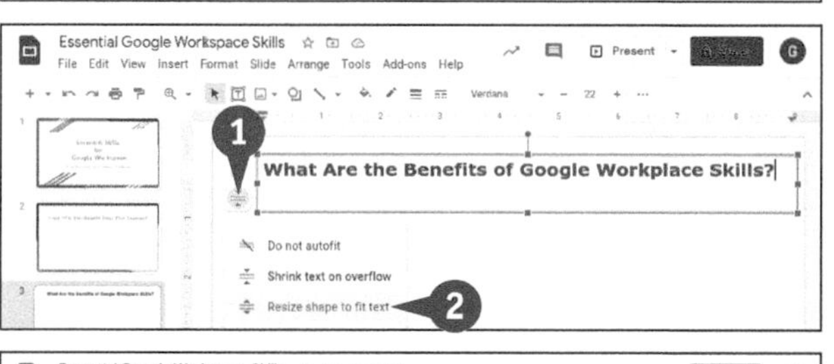

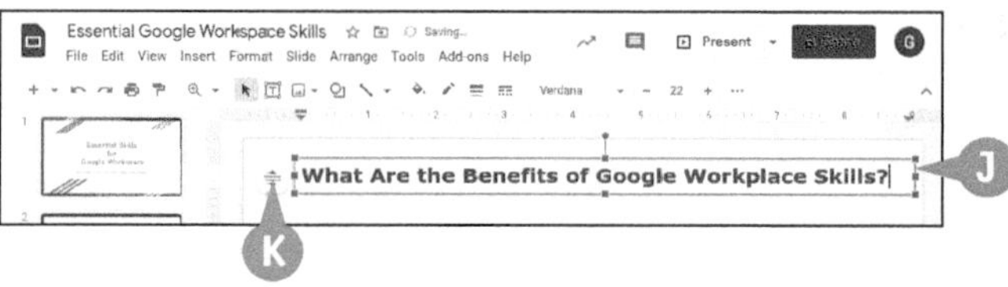

1. Click **Autofit behavior** (≑, ⍀, or ≑).

   The Autofit Behavior pop-up menu opens.

2. Click **Do not autofit** (⍀), **Shrink text on overflow** (≑), or **Resize shape to fit text** (≑). This example uses **Resize shape to fit text** (≑).

- J Google Slides resizes the text box to fit the text.
- K The Autofit Behavior button displays the button for the behavior you chose.

TIP

How do I add other formatting to a text box?

Right-click the text box, and then click **Format options** (⌨) on the contextual menu. The Format Options pane opens. Click the appropriate heading — **Size & Rotation**, **Position**, **Text fitting**, **Drop shadow**, or **Reflection** — to display the controls it contains, and then use the controls to adjust the formatting. For example, click **Text fitting** to expand the Text Fitting section, which contains three sections: Indentation, Autofit, and Padding. The Indentation controls enable you to adjust left and right indentation and apply a first-line indent or a hanging indent. Autofit is explained in the main text. The Padding controls enable you to adjust the amount of space between text and the text-box borders.

continued ▶

You can resize a text box in a single dimension by dragging one of its side handles, or resize it in two dimensions at once by dragging one of its corner handles. You can reposition a text box freely by dragging it to where you want it to appear.

You can also rotate a text box, which enables you to display text at any angle you choose, including upside down. You can adjust the rotation either freely or in 15-degree steps.

Work with Text Boxes (continued)

Resize, Reposition, or Rotate a Text Box

1. Click the text box.

   A blue outline and sizing handles appear around the text box.

   L If the Autofit Behavior button is set to Resize Shape to Fit Text (≑), click **Resize shape to fit text** (≑), and then click **Do not autofit** (⋠).

2. Drag a sizing handle to resize the text box, as needed.

   The text box appears at the new size.

3. Move the cursor over the text box.

   M The cursor changes to a four-headed arrow (✥).

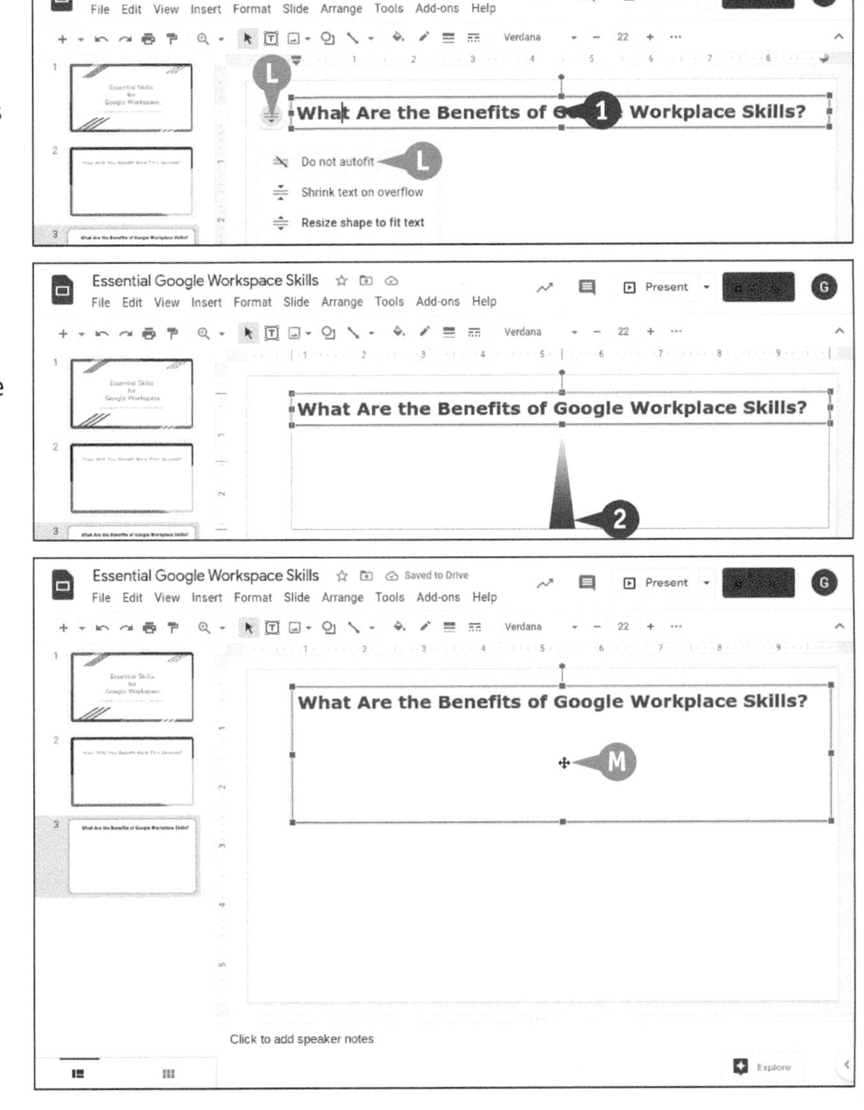

4 Drag the text box to where you want it to appear.

N The outline shows where the text box will land when you drop it.

O A red alignment guide appears when the text box is in alignment with its previous position. In this instance, the horizontal alignment guide indicates that the upper border is aligned with the previous position.

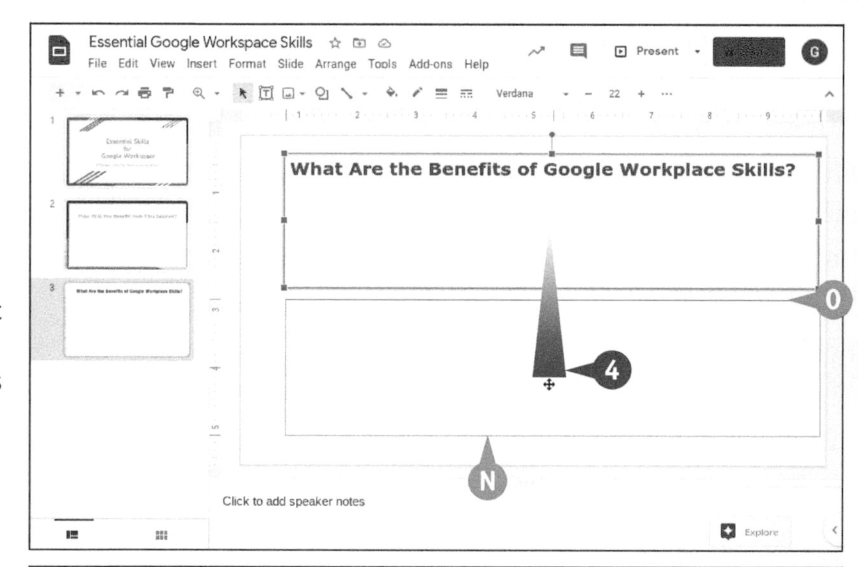

The text box appears in its new position.

5 To rotate the text box, move the cursor over the blue rotation handle (●), and then drag left or right.

P The outline shows how the text box will end up when you stop dragging.

Q The readout indicates the current angle.

Note: Hold down Shift while you drag to constrain the movement to 15-degree increments.

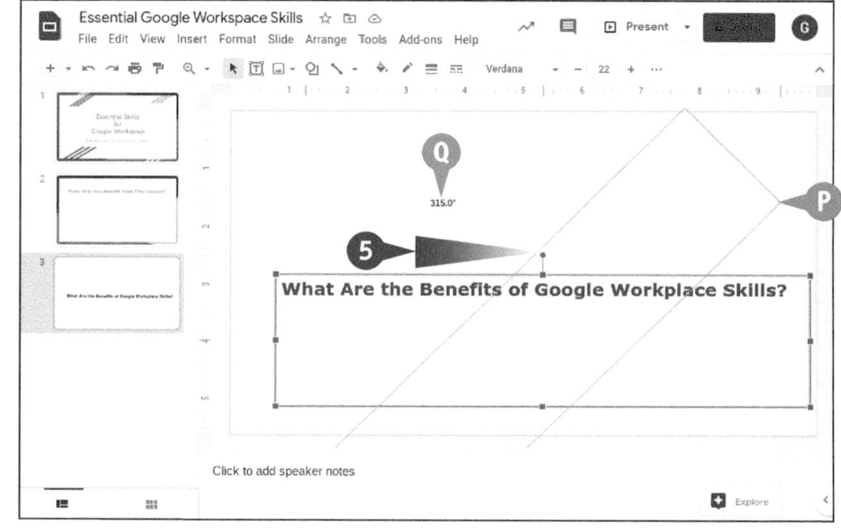

TIP

How do I tell Google Slides to always resize a text box proportionally?

If you want to ensure that a text box or other object always resizes proportionally so that adjusting the width or height always adjusts the other dimension correspondingly, you need to lock the aspect ratio. Right-click the text box to display the contextual menu, and then click **Format options** to display the Format Options pane. Click **Size & Rotation** to expand the Size & Rotation heading, and then select **Lock aspect ratio** (☑).

Add Audio to a Slide

Google Slides enables you to add audio files to a slide. This capability is useful both for playing back sounds to the audience and for adding narration to a presentation. The audio can be in either of two widely used formats, MP3 or WAV.

After adding an audio file to a slide, you can configure it to play the way you want. You can start it playing either automatically, when the slide is displayed, or when the presenter clicks it. You can set the playback volume, choose whether the audio plays a single time or repeats, and control whether the audio stops when a different slide is displayed.

Add Audio to a Slide

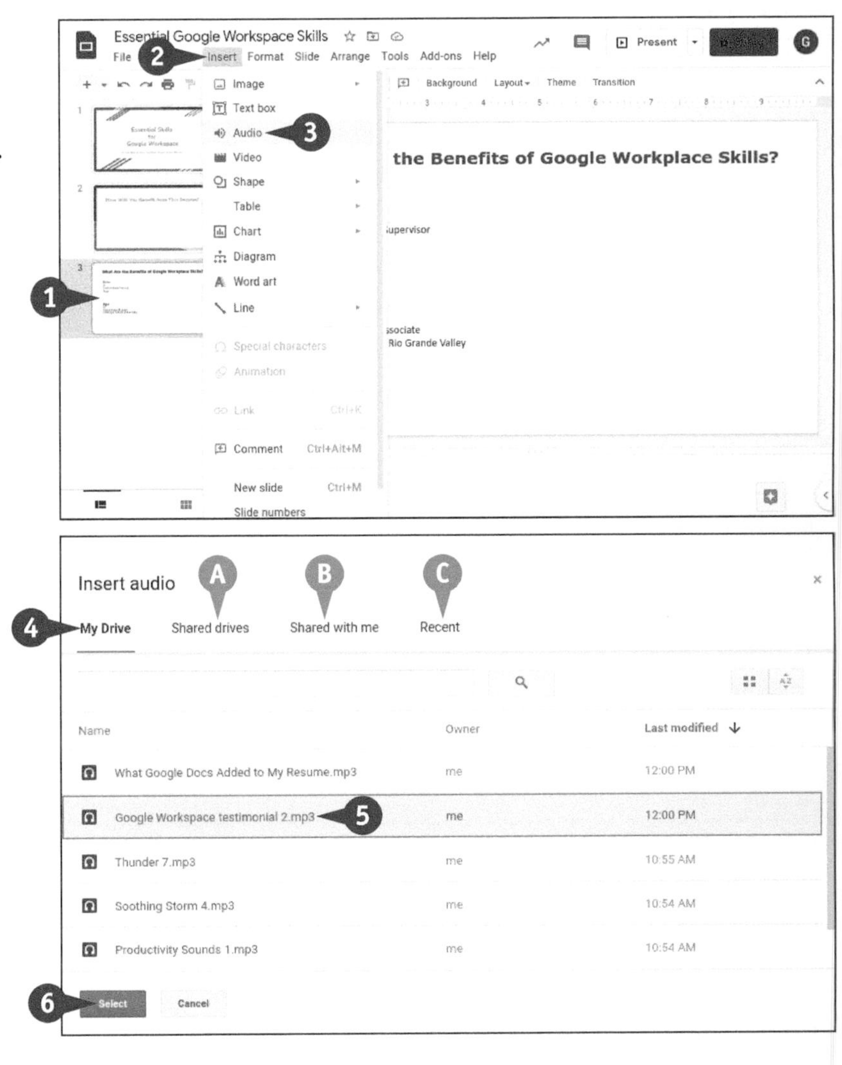

1. In the Filmstrip pane, click the slide to which you want to add the audio.

   The slide appears in the Slide pane.

2. Click **Insert**.

   The Insert menu opens.

3. Click **Audio** (🔊).

   The Insert Audio dialog box opens.

4. Navigate to the location or folder that contains the audio file you want to insert. For example, click **My Drive**.

   A. You can click **Shared drives** to display shared drives available to you.

   B. You can click **Shared with me** to display files that others have shared with you.

   C. You can click **Recent** to display files you have used recently.

5. Click the audio file.

6. Click **Select**.

The Insert Audio dialog box closes.

Google Slides inserts the audio file in the slide.

D The audio icon (🔊) appears, with sizing handles around it.

E The Format Options pane appears automatically, with the Audio Playback section expanded.

7 In the Start Playing area, select **On click** (○ changes to ◉) or **Automatically** (○ changes to ◉), as needed.

8 In the Options area, drag the **Volume while presenting** slider to set the playback volume.

9 Select **Loop audio** (☑) if you want the audio to play back repeatedly until the presenter stops it.

10 Select **Stop on slide change** (☑) if you want the audio to stop when a different slide is displayed.

11 Click **Close** (✕).

The Format Options pane closes.

12 Click the audio icon (🔊).

The playback controls appear.

13 Click **Play** (▶).

The audio plays, and you can verify that the volume is suitable.

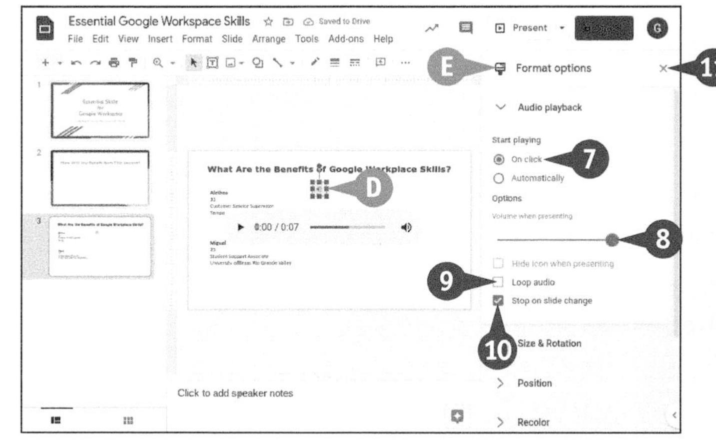

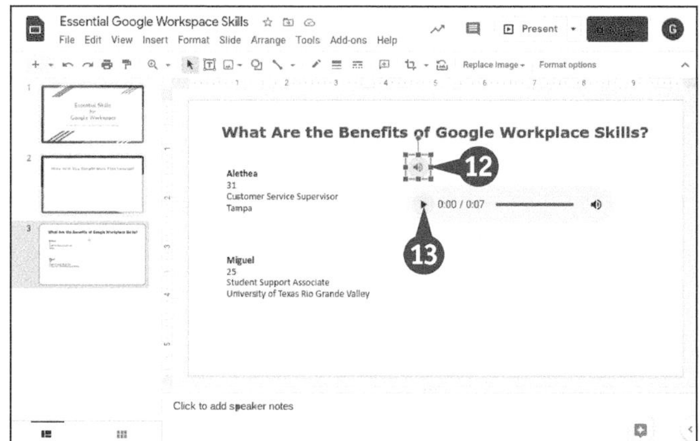

TIP

How do I hide the icon for an audio file on a slide?

If you want to hide the icon for an audio file, you must set the file to play automatically rather than when clicked, as the latter requires the icon. Right-click the icon, and then click **Format options** on the contextual menu to open the Format Options pane with the Audio Playback section expanded. In the Start Playing area, select **Automatically** (○ changes to ◉). Then, in the Options area, select **Hide icon when presenting** (☑). Click **Close** (✕) to close the Format Options pane.

Add a Video to a Slide

A video can be a great way to enliven a monotonous presentation. Google Slides enables you to insert a video on a slide and control how it plays back. You can set the video to play back automatically, manually, or when clicked, and you can choose which part of the video to play.

You can insert either a video to which you have access on Google Drive or a video on YouTube. For example, if your organization creates training videos, you can upload them to Google Drive and then insert them in your presentations.

Add a Video to a Slide

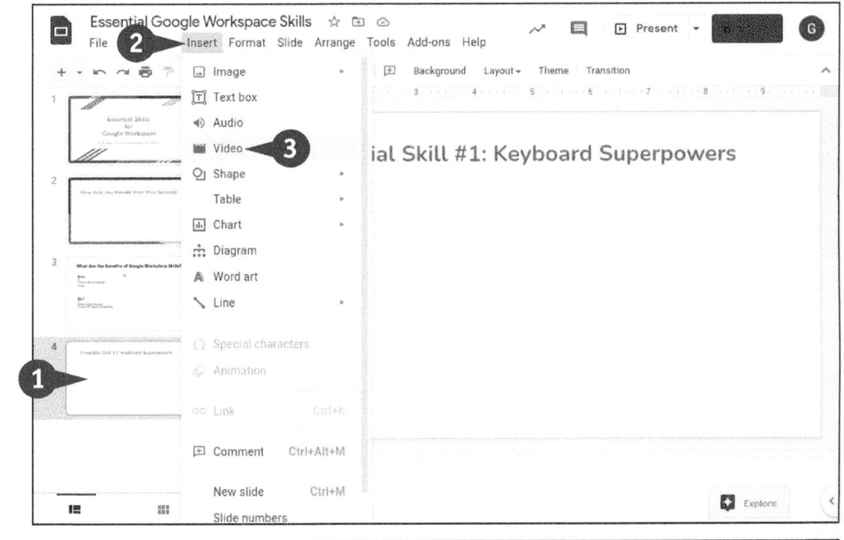

1 In the Filmstrip pane, click the slide to which you want to add the video.

The slide appears in the Slide pane.

2 Click **Insert**.

The Insert menu opens.

3 Click **Video** (🎬).

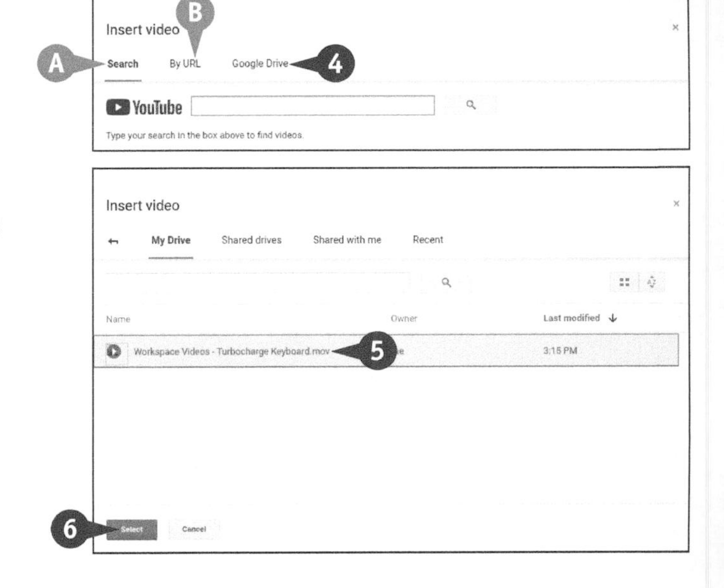

The Insert Video dialog box opens.

A The Search tab enables you to search YouTube by keyword.

B The By URL tab enables you to enter the YouTube URL for the video.

4 Navigate to the location or folder that contains the video file you want to insert. To follow this example, you would click **My Drive**.

5 Click the video you want to insert.

6 Click **Select**.

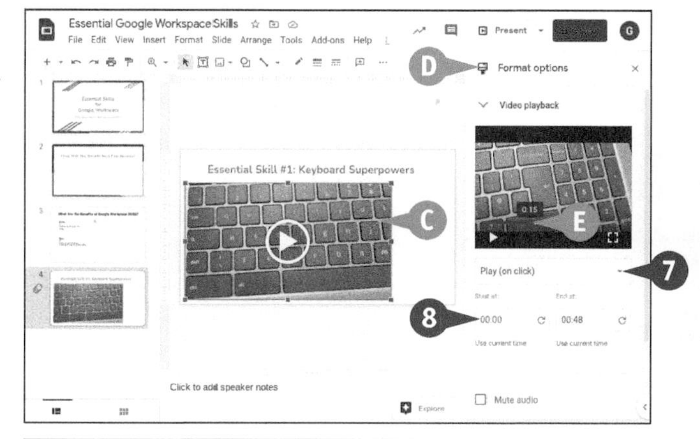

The Insert Video dialog box closes.

Google Slides inserts the video file in the slide.

C The video file's poster frame appears, with sizing handles around it.

You can resize and reposition the video frame, as needed.

D The Format Options pane appears automatically, with the Video Playback section expanded.

E You can play the video, or drag the playhead (■), to locate the frame at which you want to start or end playback.

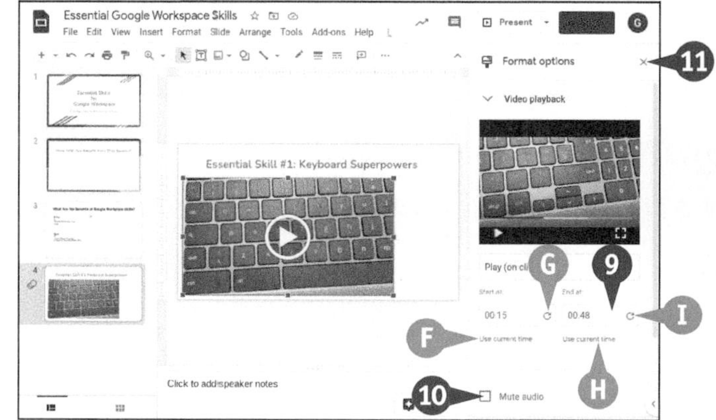

7 Click **Play** (▾), and then click **Play (on click)**, **Play (automatically)**, or **Play (manual)**, as appropriate. See the tip for more information.

8 Optionally, click **Start at** and enter the start time, such as 00:20.

F You can click **Use current time** to use the preview's current time as the start time.

G You can click **Reset to start** (↻) to reset the time to the start.

9 Optionally, click **End at** and enter the end time.

H You can click **Use current time** to use the preview's current time as the end time.

I You can click **Reset to end** (↻) to reset the time to the end.

10 Select **Mute audio** (☑) if you want to mute the video's audio.

11 Click **Close** (✕).

The Format Options pane closes.

TIP

What is the difference between "Play (on Click)" and "Play (Manual)" for a video?

The terminology is awkward, but the difference is straightforward. Choose **Play (on click)** to make the video play when this slide is displayed, whether via a literal click or a keystroke from the presenter or via automatic advancing. Choose **Play (manual)** to make the video play only when the presenter actually clicks it.

Insert Shapes

Google Slides enables you to insert a wide variety of shapes in your slides: standard shapes, such as rectangles, ovals, and cubes; arrows, from straight arrows and curved arrows to quad arrows; callouts, such as explosions, stars, and scrolls; and equation symbols, such as + and =. You can place these shapes directly on your slides, format them to look the way you prefer, and even add text to them.

Insert Shapes

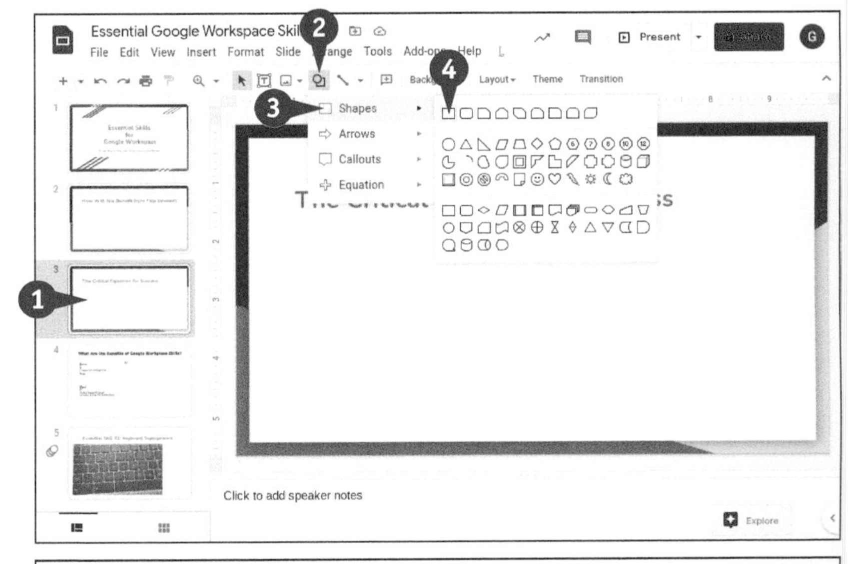

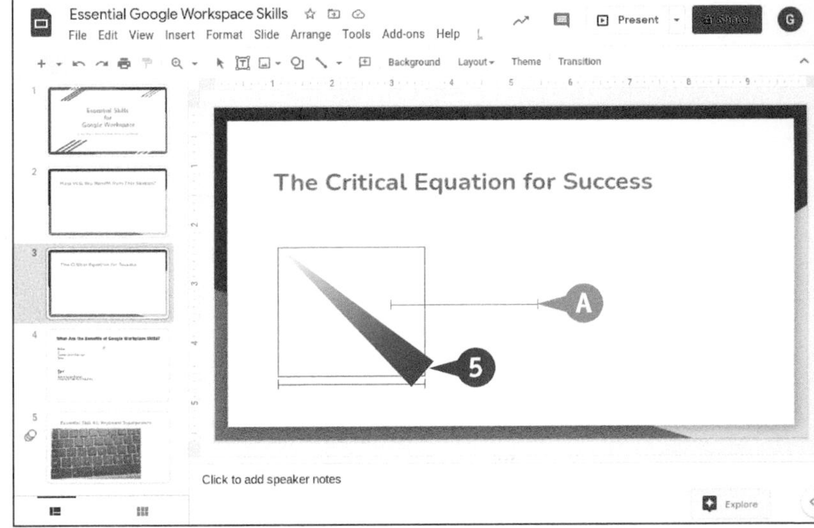

1. In the Filmstrip pane, click the slide on which you want to insert one or more shapes.

   The slide appears in the Slide pane.

2. Click **Shape** (⬚).

   The Shape pop-up menu opens.

3. Click or highlight **Shapes** (□), **Arrows** (⇨), **Callouts** (🗨), or **Equation** (✚), as needed.

   This example uses **Shapes** (□).

4. Click the shape you want to insert. This example uses **Rectangle** (□).

5. Click and drag to insert the shape.

A. Google Slides may display sizing and alignment guides as you drag.

The shape appears, with an outline and sizing handles around it.

6. Apply any formatting needed. For example:

B. Click **Fill color** (), and then click the fill color.

C. Click **Border color** (), and then click the border color.

7. Double-click in the shape.

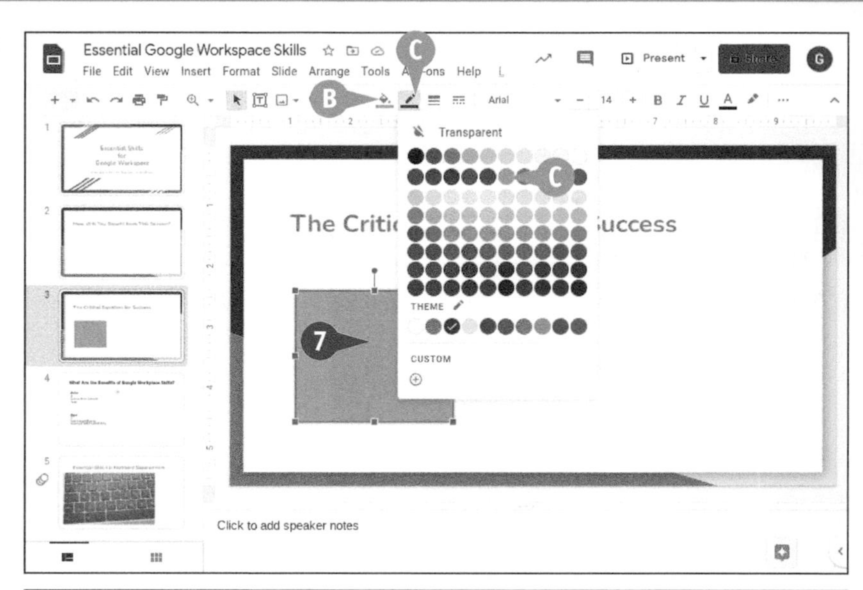

The cursor appears in the shape.

8. Type the text for the shape.

9. Select the text, and then apply any formatting needed.

10. Click outside the shape.

The shape becomes deselected, and you can better judge whether it needs further formatting.

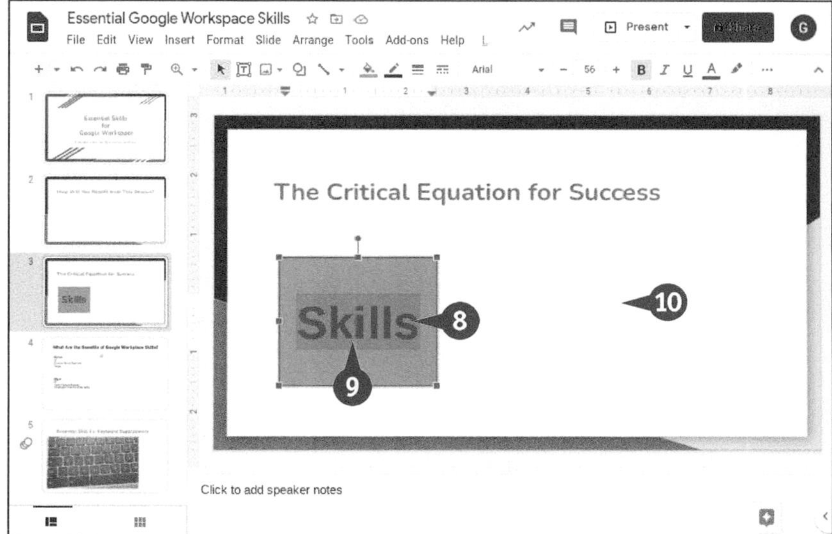

TIP

How can I connect the shapes I add to slides?

You can add lines to connect the shapes. Click **Line** () on the toolbar to display the pop-up menu of seven different line tools. Click **Line** () on the pop-up menu to draw a straight line. Click **Arrow** () to draw a straight arrow. Click **Elbow connector** () to create a three-segment line with two 90-degree bends. Click **Curved connector** () to a two-segment line with smooth curves. Click **Curve** () to draw a complex curved line. Click **Polyline** () to create a complex shape from straight lines. Lastly, click **Scribble** () when you need to draw freely on the screen — for example, to illustrate a point.

Insert Word Art

The Word Art feature in Google Slides enables you to make graphical elements consisting of text. Word Art gives you greater flexibility than text in text boxes, because it lets you format the text with both a fill color and an outline color, change the outline thickness, and stretch or compress the text horizontally or vertically.

Insert Word Art

1. In the Filmstrip pane, click the slide on which you want to insert one or more shapes.

   The slide appears in the Slide pane.

2. Click **Insert**.

   The Insert menu opens.

3. Click **Word art** (A).

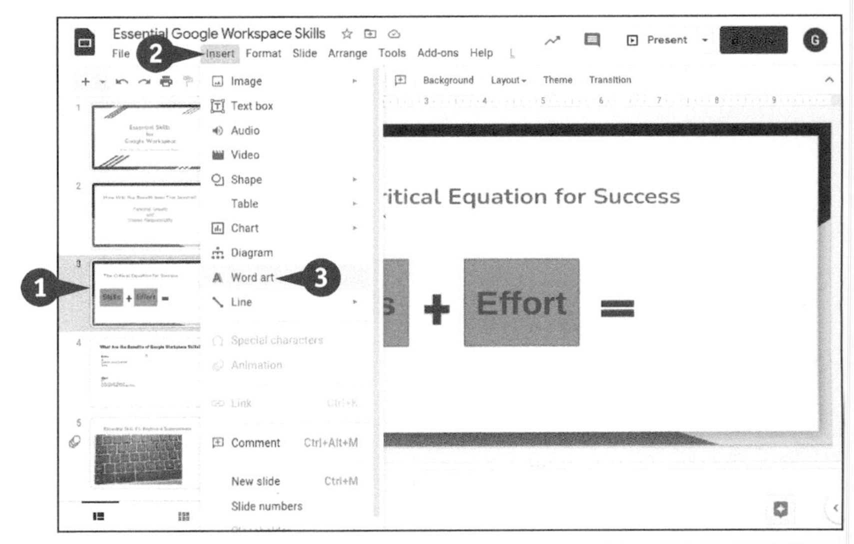

   The Word Art text entry box opens.

4. Type the text you want to use in the Word Art.

Note: Press Shift + Enter if you need to start a new line. On the Mac, press Shift + Return.

5. Press Enter or Return to enter the text.

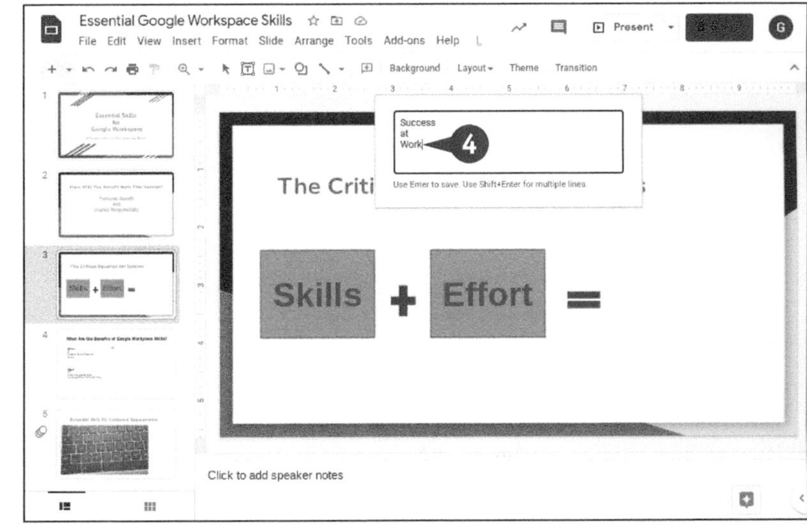

The Word Art text entry box closes.

The Word Art item appears in the middle of the slide.

6 Drag the Word Art item to where you want it.

A Google Slides may display alignment guides or spacing guides to help you position the item.

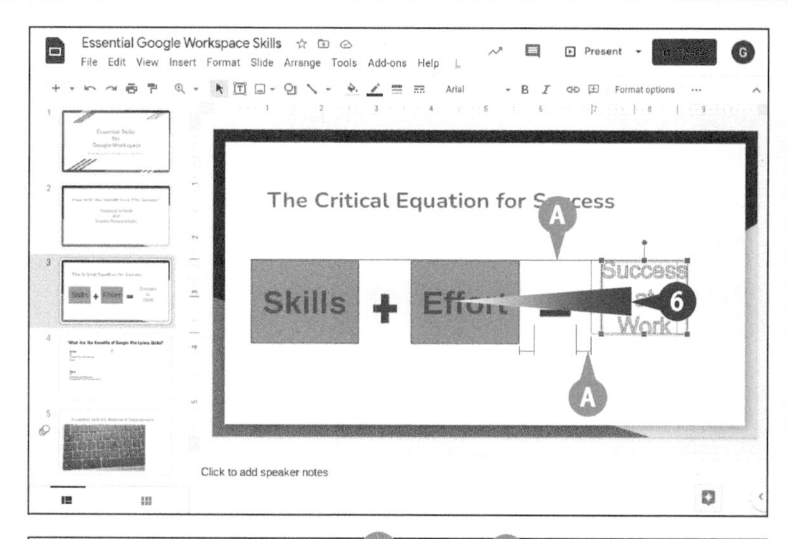

7 With the Word Art item still selected, apply any formatting needed. For example:

B Click **Fill color** (), and then click the fill color.

C Click **Border color** (), and then click the border color.

D Click **Font** (), and then click the font you want to use.

8 Click outside the Word Art item.

The Word Art item becomes deselected, letting you better judge whether it needs other formatting.

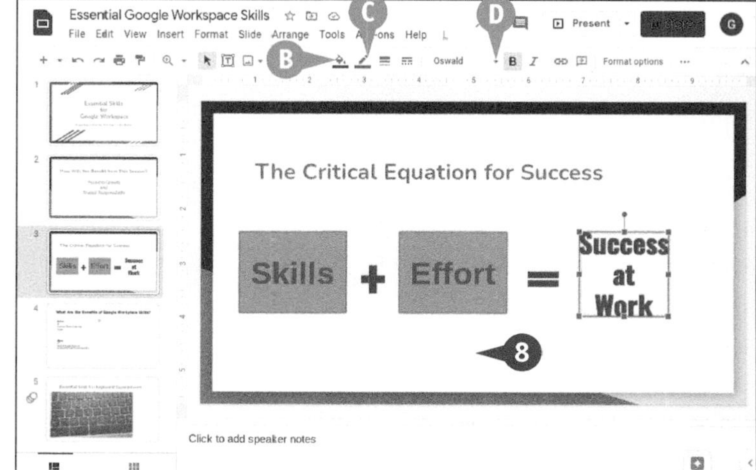

TIP

How else can I make a Word Art item look different?

Try applying a drop shadow. Click the Word Art item, and then click **Format options** on the toolbar to open the Format Options pane. Select the check box () to the right of the Drop Shadow heading, and then click **Drop shadow** to display the individual controls. Click **Color** (), and then click the color for the drop shadow. Then drag the **Transparency** slider to adjust the transparency and opacity of the drop shadow, drag the **Angle** slider to adjust the shadow's angle, drag the **Distance** slider to adjust the shadow's distance from the text, and drag the **Blur Radius** slider to adjust the blurring. Click **Close** (×) to close the Format Options pane.

Add a Transition and Animations

To help bring your slides to life, you can add animations and transitions to them. An *animation* is an effect that you apply to a particular object; for example, you could animate a text box so that its paragraphs fly in one at a time from the top of the screen. A *transition* is an effect that plays as one slide replaces another. For example, you can apply the Dissolve transition to have the current slide appear to gradually dissolve and be replaced by the next slide. The Motion pane enables you to configure both animations and transitions.

Add a Transition and Animations

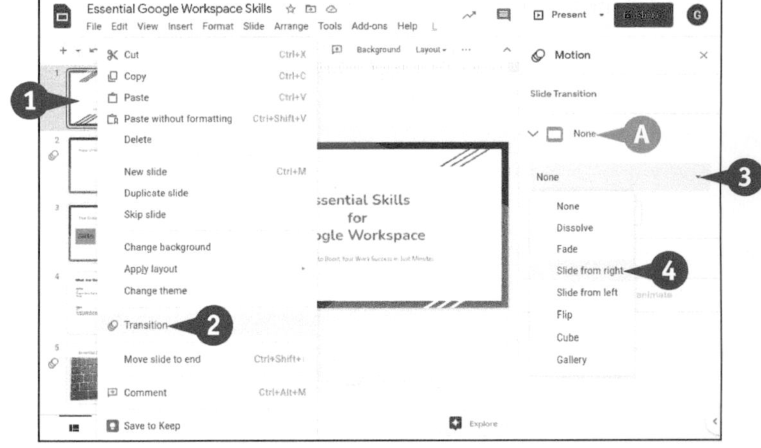

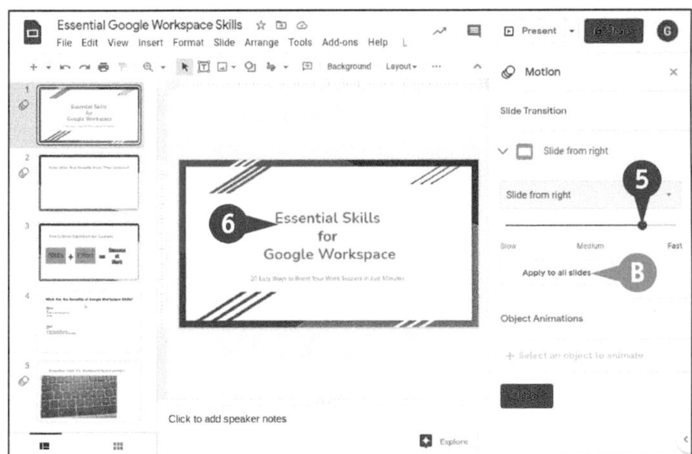

1 In the Filmstrip pane, right-click the slide to which you want to apply an animation or a transition.

The slide appears in the Slide pane.

The contextual menu opens.

2 Click **Transition** (◎).

The Motion pane opens.

Note: If the Slide Transition section is collapsed so that the Transition pop-up menu is not visible, click **Expand** (>) to expand the section.

A The section heading shows the name of the current transition or None if there is no current transition.

3 Click **Transition** (▾).

The Transition pop-up menu opens.

4 Click the transition you want to apply, such as **Slide from right**.

The Speed slider appears.

5 Drag the slider (●) to set the speed of the transition.

B You can click **Apply to all slides** if you want to apply the same transition to each slide. If not, select each slide in turn, and then apply a transition, as needed.

6 In the Slide pane, click the first object on the slide that you want to animate.

The object becomes selected.

Google Slides collapses the Slide Transition section of the Motion pane.

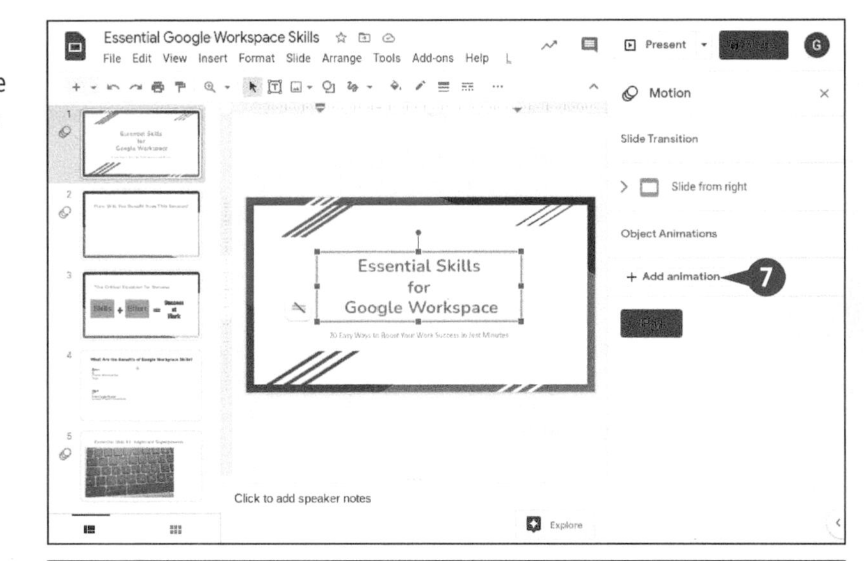

7 In the Object Animations section of the Motion pane, click **Add animation** (+).

Further controls appear in the Object Animations section.

8 Click **Animation type** (▾), and then click the appropriate animation, such as **Fly in from bottom**.

9 Click **Start condition** (▾), and then click **On click**, **After previous**, or **With previous**, as appropriate.

C For a text object, you can select **By paragraph** (☑) to animate each paragraph separately.

10 Drag the slider (●) to set the speed of the animation.

11 Click **Play**.

The animation plays in the Slide pane, and you can judge whether it requires further adjustment.

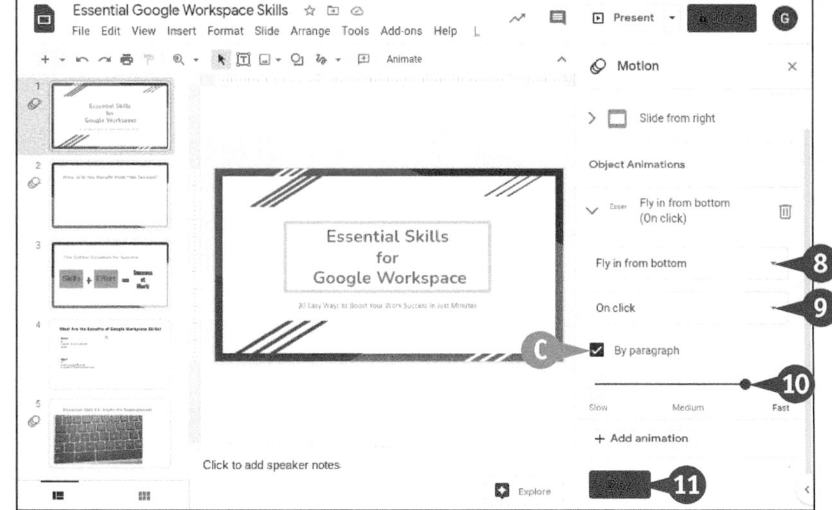

You can now add further animations as necessary by repeating steps **6** to **11**.

TIP

How do I change the order of animations?

Right-click the slide in the Filmstrip pane, and then click **Transition** (◎) on the contextual menu to open the Motion pane. In the Object Animations section, click **Collapse** (⌄) to collapse the controls for the animation you want to move. You can then drag the handle (⋮⋮) to move the animation up or down in the Object Animations section to its new position.

Edit a Slide Master

Each slide layout is based on a template called the *slide master*. You can edit a slide master to make changes to its layout. For example, you may want to change the font used for the master title style, change the font size for a single level of heading text, or add your organization's logo to the master to make it appear on all the slides.

When you edit a master, you can reapply the master to all the slides in the presentation based on the master.

Edit a Slide Master

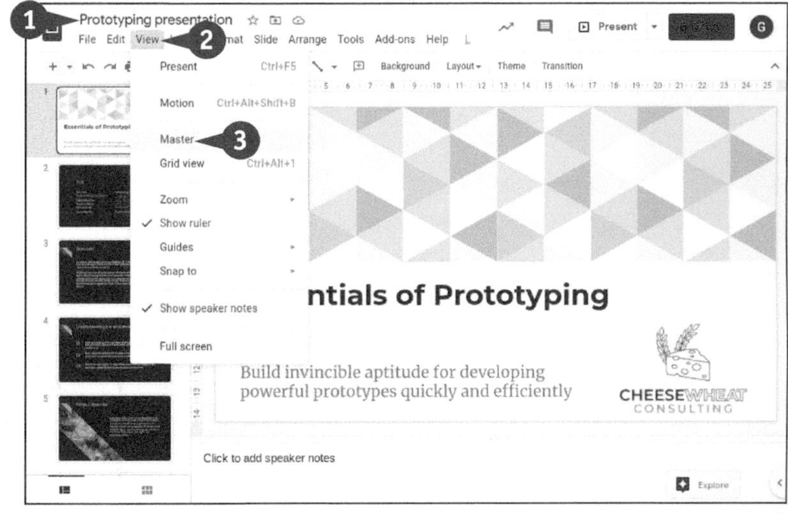

1. Open the presentation whose slide master you want to change.
2. Click **View**.

   The View menu opens.
3. Click **Master**.

   Google Slides switches to Master View.

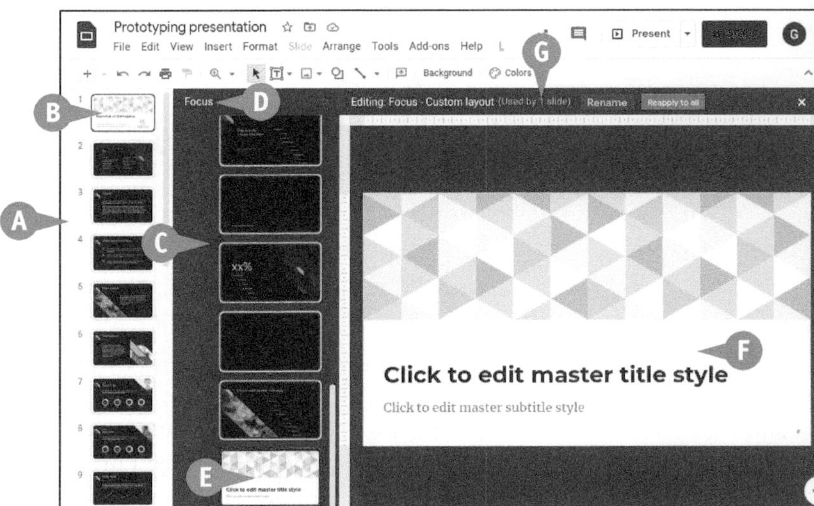

- **A** The Filmstrip pane displays the slides in the presentation, as usual.
- **B** The active slide appears with a yellow outline.
- **C** The second pane, the Slide Masters pane, shows the slide masters in the presentation.
- **D** The presentation template's name appears in the upper-left corner.
- **E** The yellow outline indicates the slide master used for the slide selected in the Filmstrip pane.
- **F** The Master pane shows the slide master.
- **G** The readout shows the number of slides using this slide master.

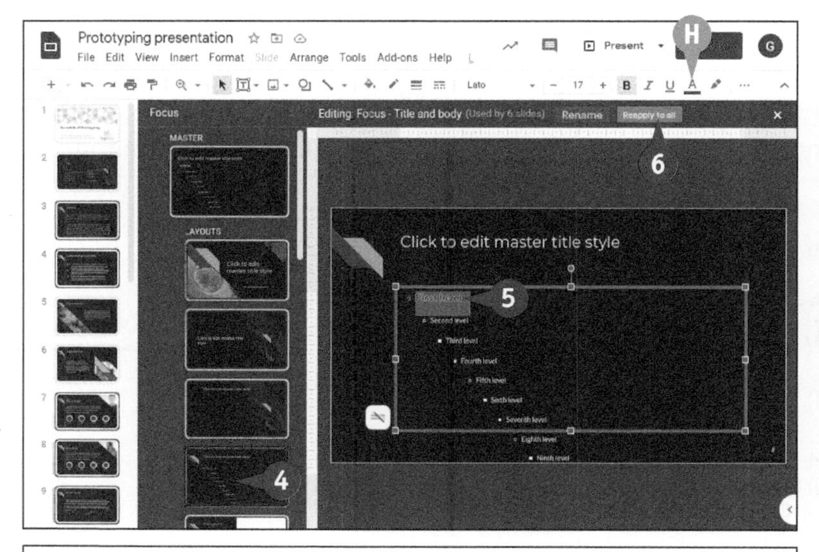

4. In the Slide Masters pane, click the slide master you want to edit.

   The slide appears in the Master pane.

5. Select the first element you want to change, and then make the changes needed.

   H. For example, you can click **Text color** (A) and then click the text color you want.

6. When you finish making changes to the slide master, click **Reapply to all** to reapply the master to the slides.

   Google Slides reapplies the slide master.

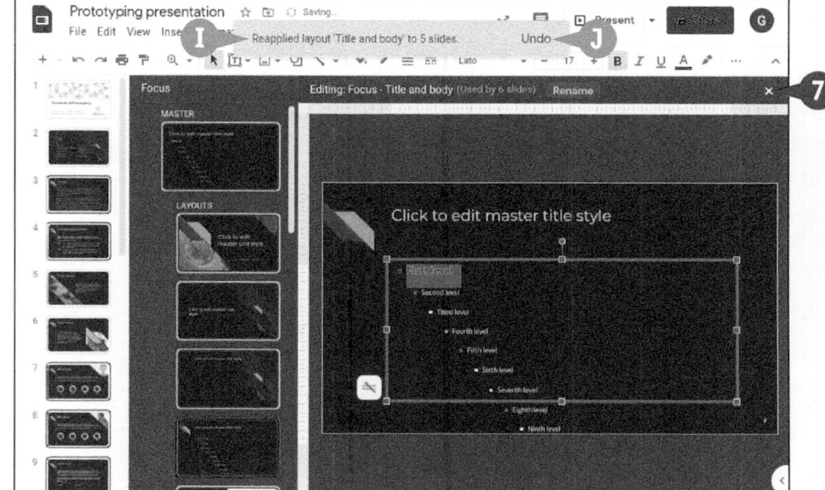

   I. A pop-up message summarizes the change made.

   J. You can click **Undo** to undo the change.

7. When you finish editing the slide masters, click **Close** (☒).

   Google Slides closes Master View.

   Filmstrip View appears again.

TIP

How can I make changes to all the slide masters at once?

Click **View** on the menu bar, and then click **Master** to switch to Master View. In the Slide Masters pane, click **MASTER** at the top. This is the root master, which is used by all slides. Changes you make on this master will carry through to the slide master layouts.

Organize the Slides in a Presentation

Sometimes, you may create all the slides in a presentation in exactly the right order, but more often, you will need to organize a presentation's slides into a different order. You can perform minor reorganizing in Filmstrip View by working in the Filmstrip pane, but unless your presentation is very short or your monitor permits a very tall window, your movements are likely to be constrained.

For serious reorganizing, you can switch to Grid View, which enables you to reorganize slides swiftly and efficiently.

Organize the Slides in a Presentation

1. Click **View**.

   The View menu opens.

2. Click **Grid view**.

   Ⓐ You can also click **Grid view** (▦) to switch to Grid View from Filmstrip View.

Note: You can press Ctrl + Alt + 1 to toggle between Filmstrip View and Grid View. On the Mac, press ⌘ + Option + 1.

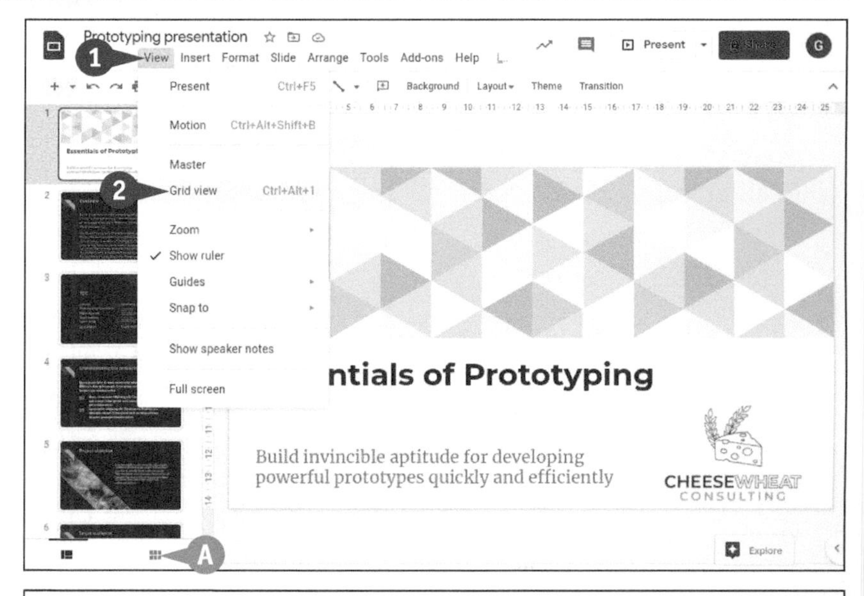

The presentation appears in Grid View.

3. If you want to change the number of slides displayed, click **Decrease thumbnail size** (—) or **Increase thumbnail size** (+), as needed.

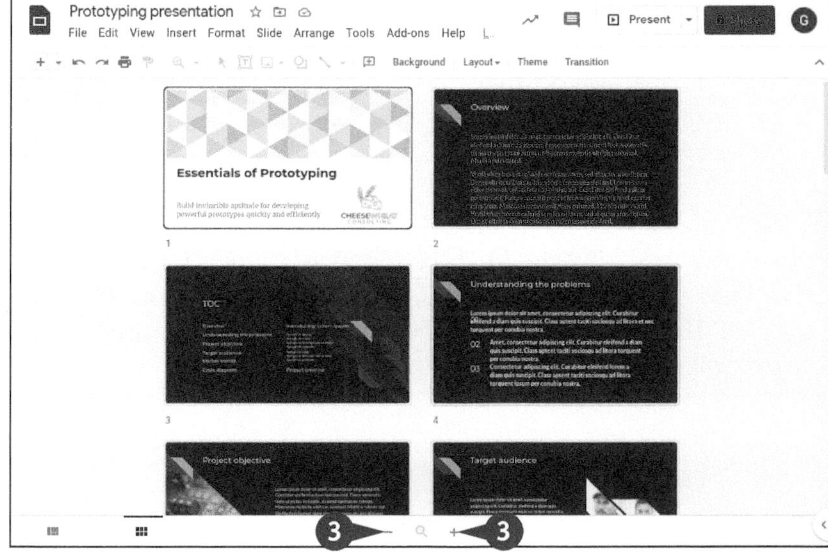

B You can click **Reset thumbnail size** (🔍) to reset the thumbnails to their default size.

4 Select the slides you want to move.

Note: To select a contiguous range of slides, click the first slide in the range, and then press Shift+click the last slide in the range. To select noncontiguous slides, click the first slide, and then press Ctrl+click each other slide; on the Mac, press ⌘+click.

5 Drag the slides to where you want them to appear.

C The vertical yellow line shows the new position.

D The slides appear in their new position.

6 When you finish working in Grid View, click **Filmstrip view** (▮☰).

The presentation appears in Filmstrip View again.

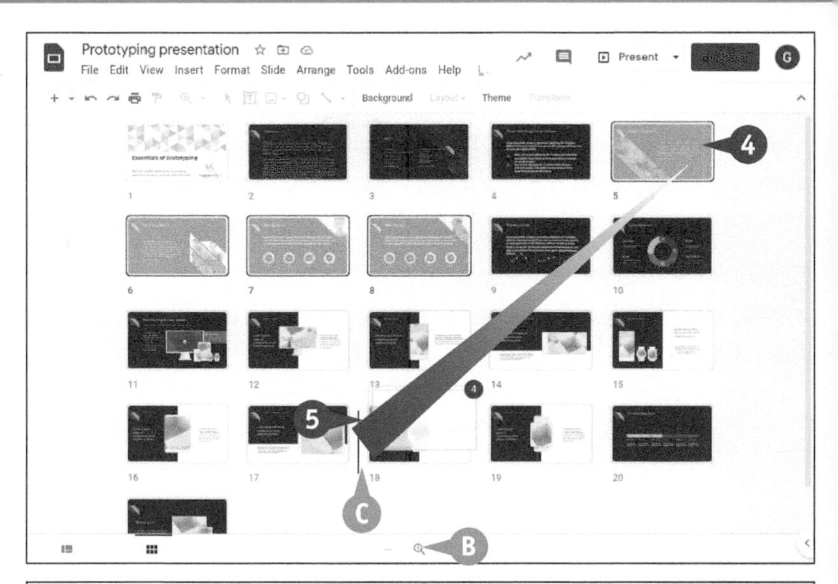

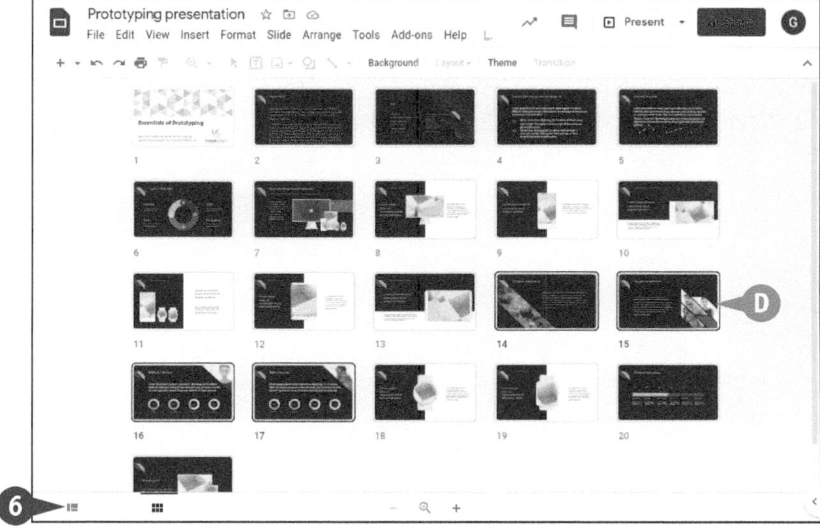

TIP

How do I reorganize slides in the Filmstrip pane?

In two ways. First, you can simply drag a slide up or down the Filmstrip pane; when the horizontal yellow bar appears where you want to position the slide, drop it. You can also select multiple slides in the Filmstrip pane and then drag them up or down. Select the slides by clicking the first slide, and then pressing Ctrl+clicking each other slide you want to select; on the Mac, press ⌘+click.

Second, you can quickly move a slide to the beginning or end of the presentation. Right-click the slide, and then click **Move slide to beginning** or **Move slide to end** on the contextual menu.

Insert Slide Numbers

Slide numbers are useful when you need to be able to refer to particular slides clearly — for example, you may want to ask your audience to read particular slides in a handout.

Google Slides enables you to insert slide numbers in either Filmstrip View or Grid View. You can simply assign a number to each slide, or you can select only certain slides and assign slide numbers to them, leaving the other slides unnumbered. For numbering only some slides, Grid View is usually easier.

Insert Slide Numbers

1. Click **View**.

   The View menu opens.

2. Click **Grid view**.

   A You can also click **Grid view** (▦) to switch to Grid View from Filmstrip View.

Note: You can press Ctrl + Alt + 1 to toggle between Filmstrip View and Grid View. On the Mac, press ⌘ + Option + 1.

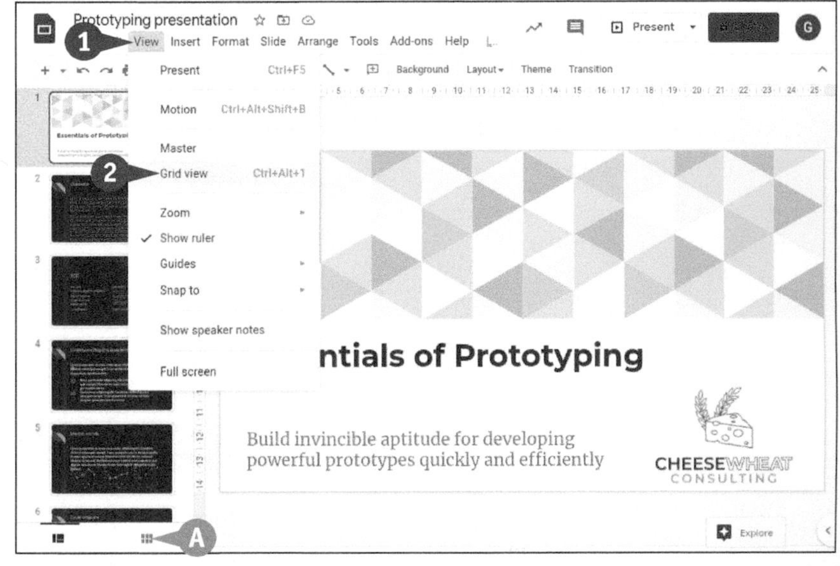

3. If you want to apply slide numbers to only some slides, select those slides.

   If you want to apply slide numbers to all slides, you do not need to select any.

Note: To select a contiguous range of slides, click the first slide in the range, and then press Shift + click the last slide in the range. To select noncontiguous slides, click the first slide, and then press Ctrl + click each other slide; on the Mac, press ⌘ + click.

4. Click **Insert**.

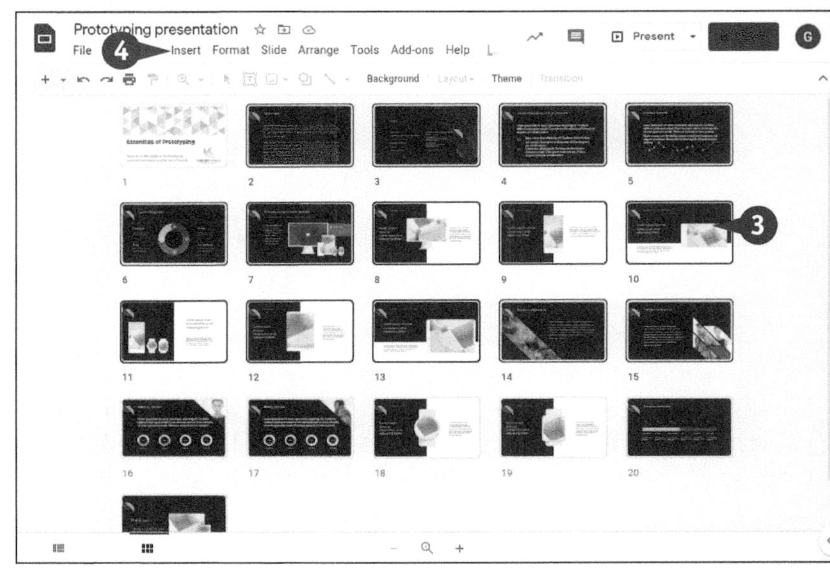

The Insert menu opens.

5. Click **Slide numbers**.

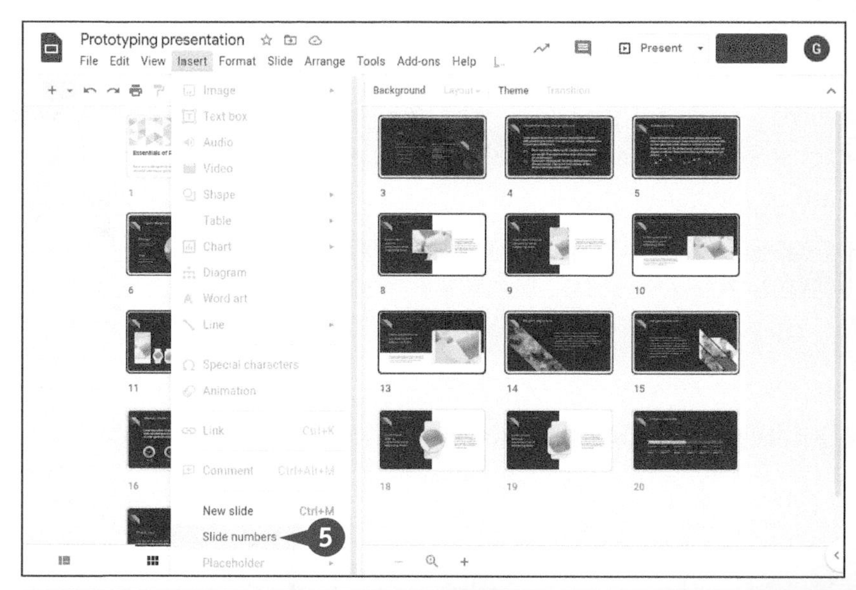

The Slide Numbers dialog box opens.

6. Select **On** (◉).
7. Select **Skip title slides** (☑) if you want the numbering to omit title slides.
8. If you selected some slides, click **Apply to selected**. Otherwise, click **Apply**.

The Slide Numbers dialog box closes.

Google Slides applies slide numbers to the slides you specified.

9. Click **Filmstrip view** (▤).

The presentation appears in Filmstrip View again.

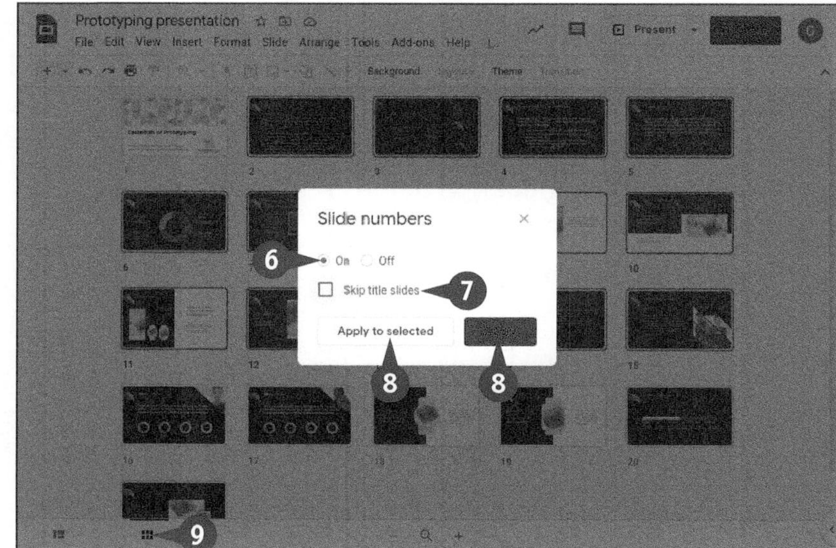

TIP

How do I remove slide numbers I have applied?

Click **Insert** to open the Insert menu, and then click **Slide numbers** to open the Slide Numbers dialog box. Select **Off** (◉), and then click **Apply**.

Preview and Print a Presentation

When your presentation is ready to meet its audience, you can print it, either on paper or as a PDF file. But before you print the presentation, you should preview it to make sure that it looks the way you want it to look. You can preview the slides either with notes or without notes. You can choose to hide the background — for example, because the background will make the printed slides hard to read. You can also choose whether to include or omit skipped slides in the printout.

Preview and Print a Presentation

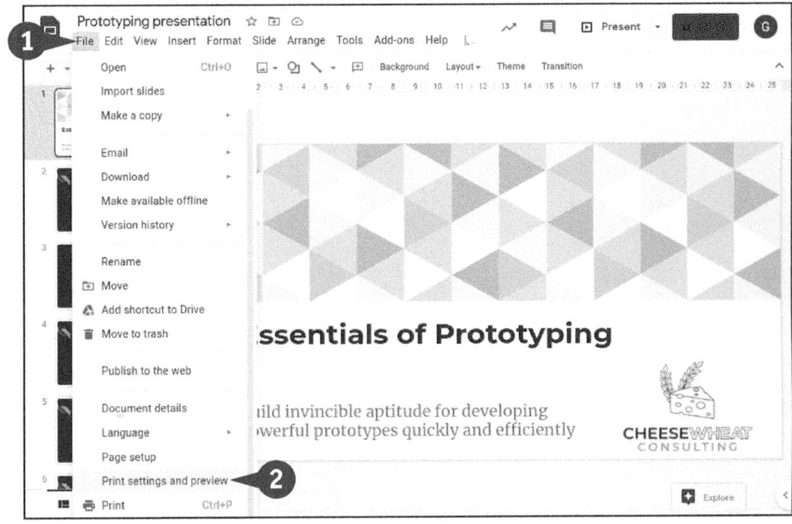

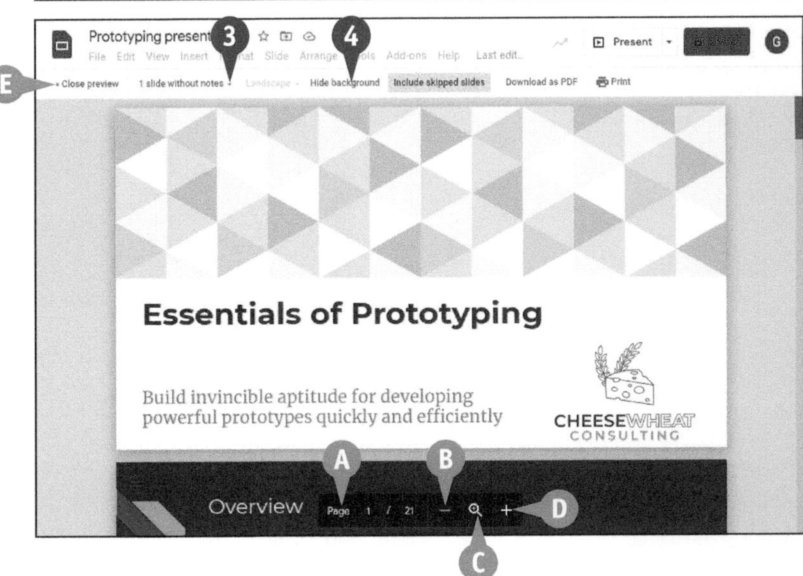

1. Click **File**.

   The File menu opens.

2. Click **Print settings and preview**.

   The preview appears.

   A The pop-up bar shows the page number and the total number of pages.

   B You can click **Zoom out** (−) to zoom the preview out.

   C You can click **Fit to width** (🔍) to fit the preview to the window's width.

   D You can click **Zoom in** (+) to zoom the preview in.

   E You can click **Close preview** if you want to close the preview.

3. Click **Printout type** (▾), and then click the printout type you want, such as **1 slide without notes** or **1 slide with notes**.

4. If you want to hide the background to make the text and other objects more visible, click **Hide background**. When this setting is On, the button has a light-orange highlight.

The slides appear without their backgrounds.

5 If you want to include skipped slides in the printout, click **Include skipped slides**. When this setting is On, the button has a light-orange highlight.

6 When you have previewed the presentation to your satisfaction and want to print, click **Print** (🖶).

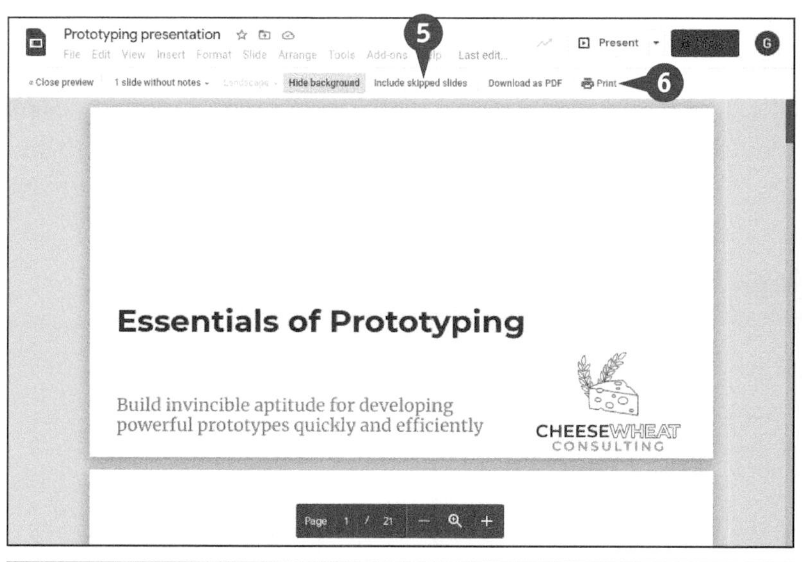

The Print dialog box opens, showing a preview on the left and settings on the right.

F The Print readout shows how many sheets of paper the printout will occupy.

7 Click **Destination** (▾), and then click the printer you want to use.

8 Choose other settings, as needed. For example, you can click **Pages** (▾), click **Custom**, and then specify which pages to print.

9 Click **Print**.

The Print dialog box closes.

The app prints your presentation on the selected printer.

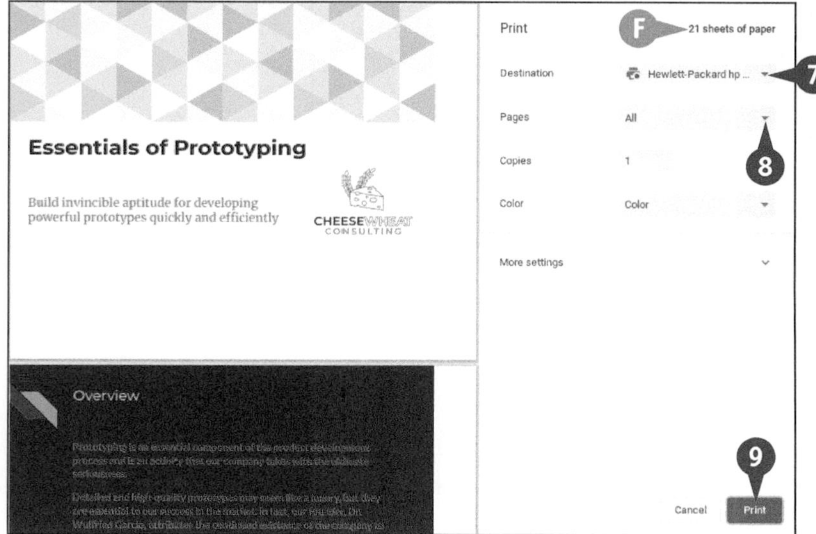

TIP

How do I print a presentation to a PDF file?

Follow the instructions in the main text to preview the presentation and open the Print dialog box. Click **Destination** (▾) to open the Destination pop-up menu, and then click **Save as PDF**. Select **Print as image** (☑) if you want to print the presentation file as an image rather than as a file containing text that is editable in some PDF editor apps. Click **Save**. In the Save File As dialog box that opens, select the folder in which to save the file, specify the file name, and then click **Save** again.

Create Handouts for a Presentation

A handout can be a great tool both for increasing your audience's interaction with a presentation and its presenter and for cementing the presentation's key points in the audience's memory. Google Slides makes it easy to create handouts from your presentations. You can either print a handout on paper or "print" it to a PDF file that you can distribute online. You can choose how many slides to display per page, choose between portrait and landscape orientations, and decide whether to include skipped slides or to omit them.

Create Handouts for a Presentation

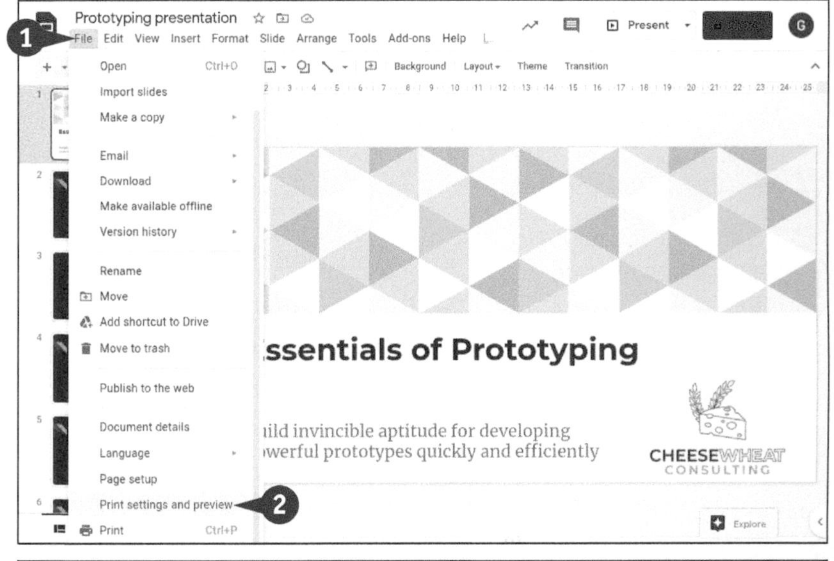

1 Click **File**.

The File menu opens.

2 Click **Print settings and preview**.

The preview appears.

A The pop-up bar shows the page number and the total number of pages at the current number of slides per page.

B If you want to hide the background to make the text and other objects more visible, click **Hide background**. When this setting is On, the button has a light-orange highlight.

C If you want to include skipped slides in the handout, click **Include skipped slides**. When this setting is On, the button has a light-orange highlight.

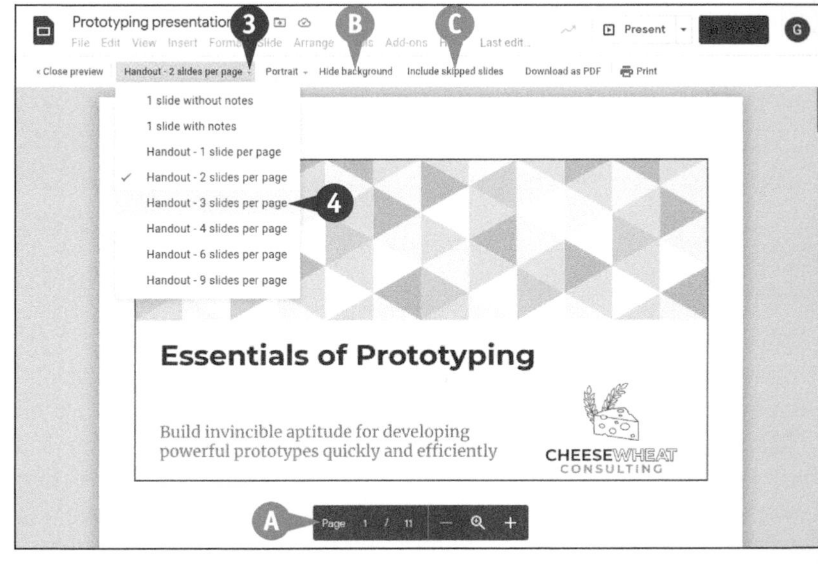

3 Click **Printout type** (▼).

The Printout Type pop-up menu opens.

4 Click the handout type you want, such as **Handout – 3 slides per page**.

Google Slides switches the preview to the format you chose.

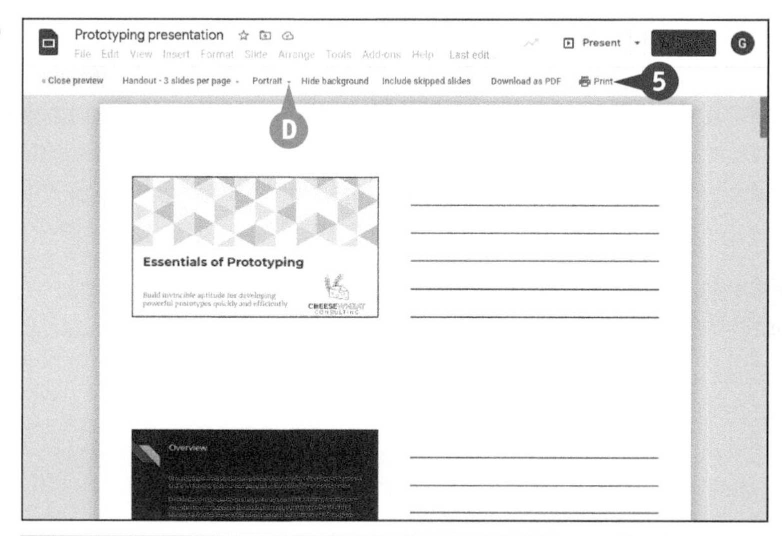

D You can click **Orientation** (▾), and then click **Portrait** or **Landscape**, as needed.

5 When you are satisfied with the layout, click **Print** (🖶).

The Print dialog box opens, showing a preview on the left and settings on the right.

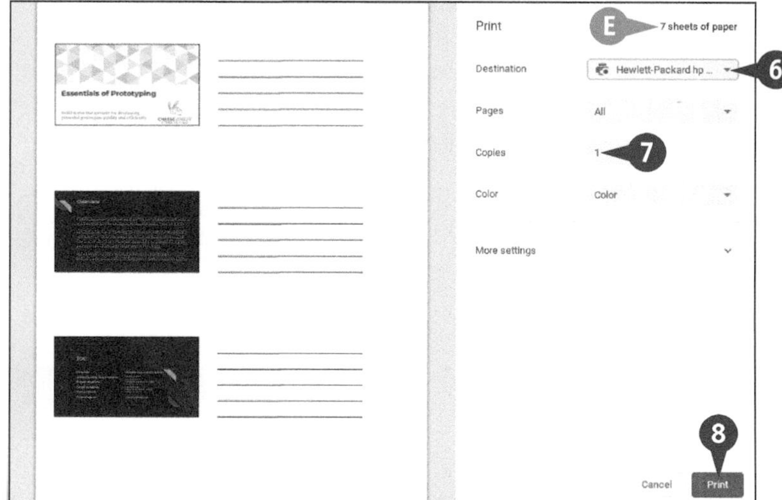

E The Print readout shows how many sheets of paper the printout requires.

6 Click **Destination** (▾), and then click the printer you want to use.

7 Choose other settings, as needed. For example, you can click **Copies** and then type the number of copies you want to print.

8 Click **Print.**

The Print dialog box closes.

The app prints your handout on the selected printer.

TIP

Which handout layout is the best choice?

There is no single answer, as the best layout depends on your presentation and your audience, but here are three suggestions:

- If you need the handout to show only the slides, and to show them as large as possible, choose **Handout – 1 slide per page** and set the orientation to **Landscape**.
- If the audience will need to take handwritten notes, choose **Handout – 3 slides per page** and set the orientation to **Portrait.** This layout displays lines for handwritten text alongside each slide.
- If you need a compact format, choose **Handout – 6 slides per page** and set the orientation to **Portrait**.

Deliver a Presentation

When the time comes to deliver a presentation, you can choose between two views: Present View and Presenter View. Present View is the more straightforward of the two views and is widely useful for giving presentations, since it requires only a single screen. Present View puts most of its controls on a pop-up control bar that you can display when you need it — for example, when you want to navigate to a particular slide. You can also control the presentation from the keyboard; see the tip for details.

Deliver a Presentation

Deliver a Presentation in Present View

1. In the Filmstrip pane, click the slide you want to display at first.

Note: For many presentations, you will want to display the first slide initially. But for other presentations, you may find it helpful to start partway through the presentation.

The slide appears in the Slide pane.

2. Click **Present** (▶).

The slide appears full screen in Present View.

A. Depending on the screen resolution, the slide may be letterboxed with black bands at the top and bottom.

B. The pop-up control bar appears for a few seconds, and then disappears if you do not use it.

3. Click the slide.

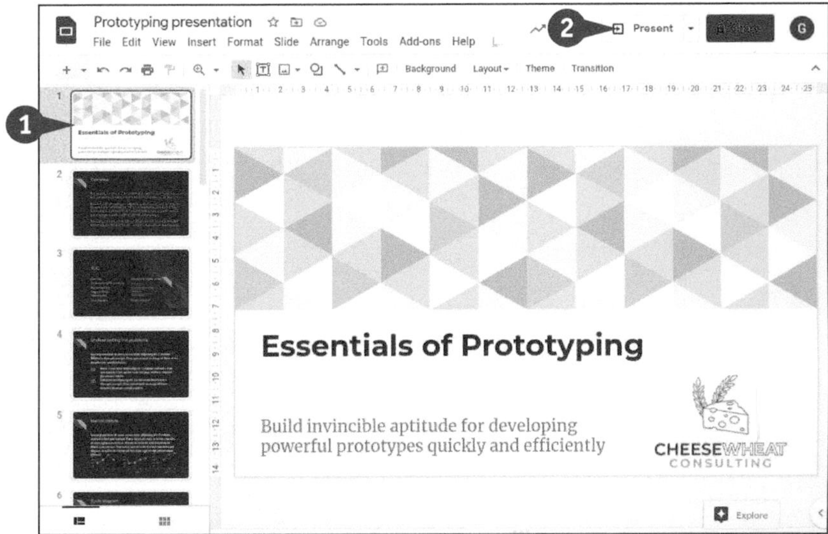

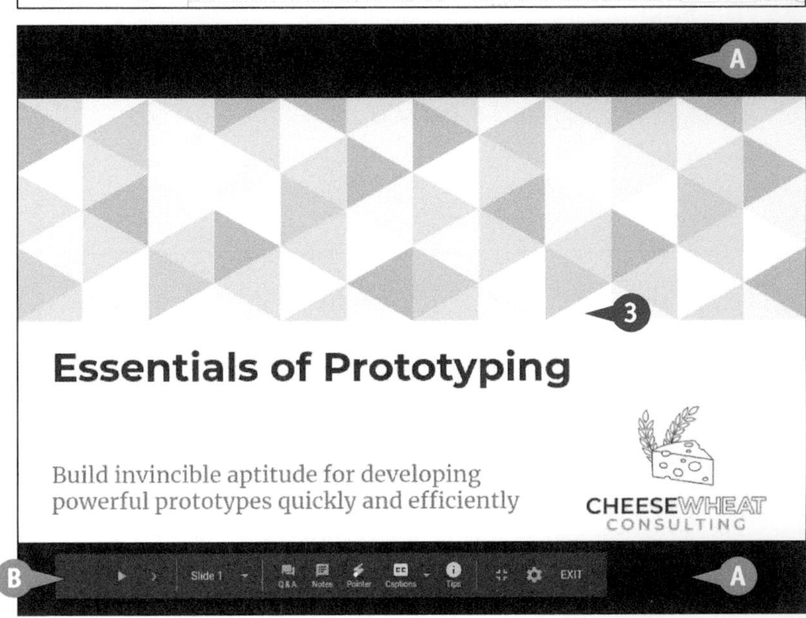

The next slide appears.

4. Move the pointer over the bottom of the screen.

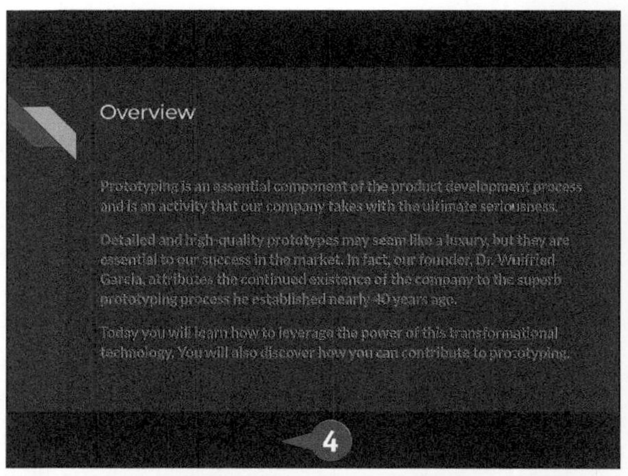

The pop-up control bar appears.

Ⓒ You can click **Back** (◀) to go back to the previous slide.

Ⓓ You can go to a slide by name or number by clicking **Go to slide** (▾) and then clicking the slide on the pop-up menu.

Ⓔ You can click **EXIT** to end the presentation.

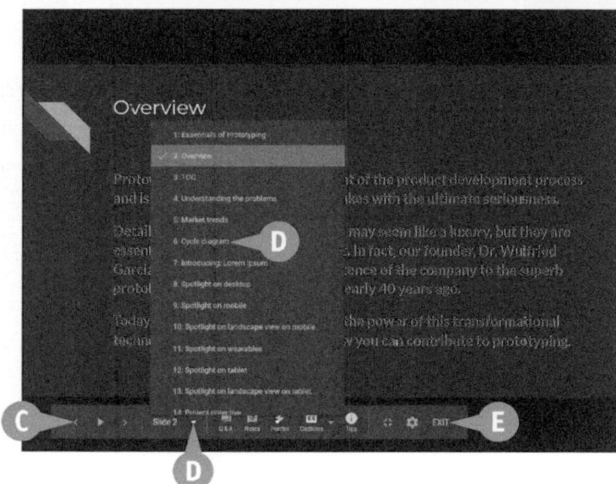

TIP

How can I control a presentation using the keyboard?

Use the keystrokes in the following list. There are various alternatives, but these are usually the easiest to remember.

- Press → or N to display the next slide.
- Press ← or P to display the previous slide.
- Press Home to display the first slide or End to display the last slide.
- Press B to display a blank black slide. Press W to display a blank white slide. Press any key to return to the slide.
- Press L to toggle the red laser pointer.
- Press Esc to stop the presentation.

continued ▶

As well as Present View, Google Slides provides Presenter View, an enhanced presentation view that gives you extra tools for practicing and delivering your presentations. These tools appear in a separate window, so when using Presenter View, you will normally want to have two monitors, one for the presentation as the audience will see it and the other for the presenter tools.

The Presenter View window includes a clock showing the time elapsed since the start of the presentation, speaker notes for the current slide, and thumbnails of the next slide and previous slide for reference.

Deliver a Presentation (continued)

5. When you reach the final slide and are ready to end the presentation, press Esc.

   Google Slides displays the presentation in Filmstrip View again.

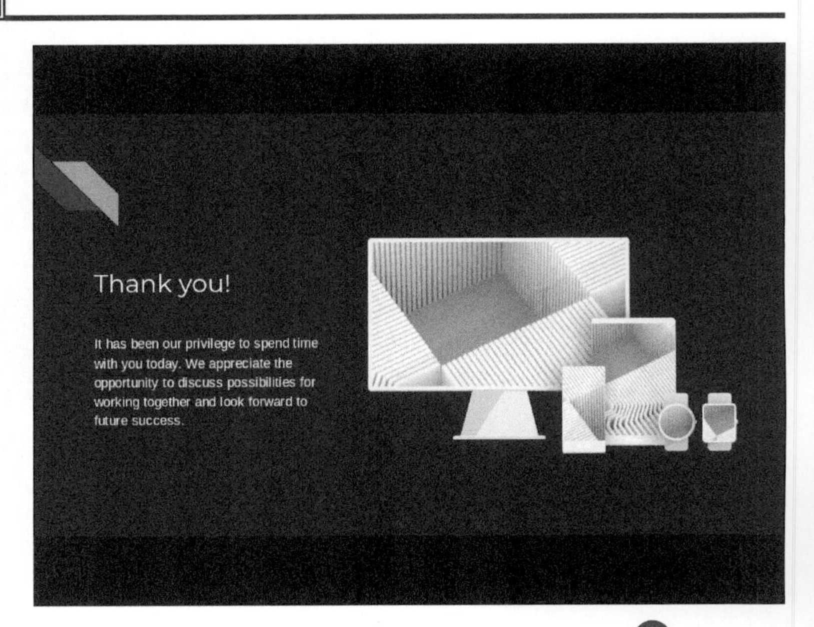

Practice or Present Using Presenter View

1. In the Filmstrip pane, click the slide you want to display at first.

   The slide appears in the Slide pane.

2. Click the **Start presentation** pop-up button (▼).

   The Start Presentation pop-up menu opens.

3. Click **Presenter view** (▆).

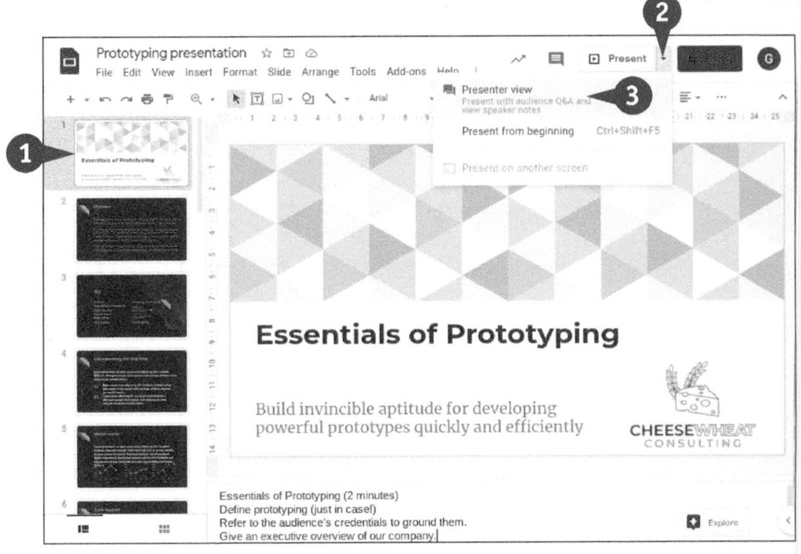

Google Slides switches the presentation to Presenter View.

F The slide appears in presentation mode, but within the original browser window rather than full screen.

G The pop-up control bar appears for a few seconds, but then disappears if you do not use it.

H The Presenter View window appears in front of the presentation window.

I The clock readout shows elapsed time since you started the presentation.

J The main image shows the current slide for your reference.

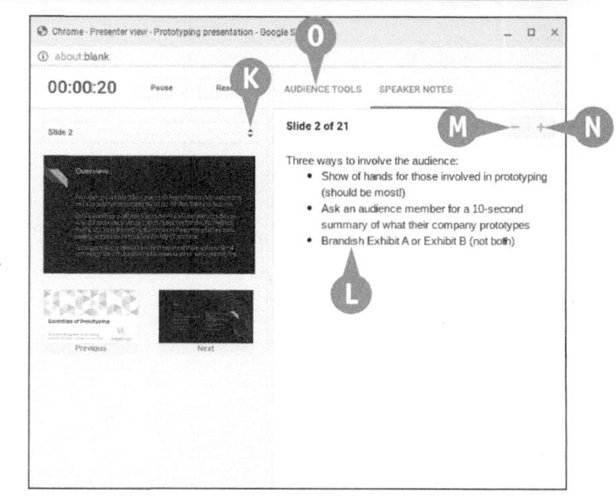

4 Click **Next** — either the text or the thumbnail.

The next slide appears.

K You can click **Go to slide** (⇕) to display the list of slides, and then click the slide you want to show.

L The speaker notes for the slide appear.

M You can click **Zoom out** (—) to make the speaker notes smaller.

N You can click **Zoom in** (+) to make the speaker notes larger.

O You can click **AUDIENCE TOOLS** to display the Audience Tools tab, which enables you to start an audience question-and-answer session.

5 When you are ready to stop practicing or presenting, press Esc.

The Presenter View window closes.

The original window switches back to Filmstrip View.

TIP

Why is the Present on Another Screen command not available when my computer has two monitors?
The Present on Another Screen command is designed for use with Google's Chromecast devices. To make this command available, connect your computer to a video-capable Chromecast device.

CHAPTER 10

Sending and Receiving Email

Google's Gmail service makes it easy to send and receive email messages. The Gmail app connects to your Google email account automatically, but you can use other email accounts as well.

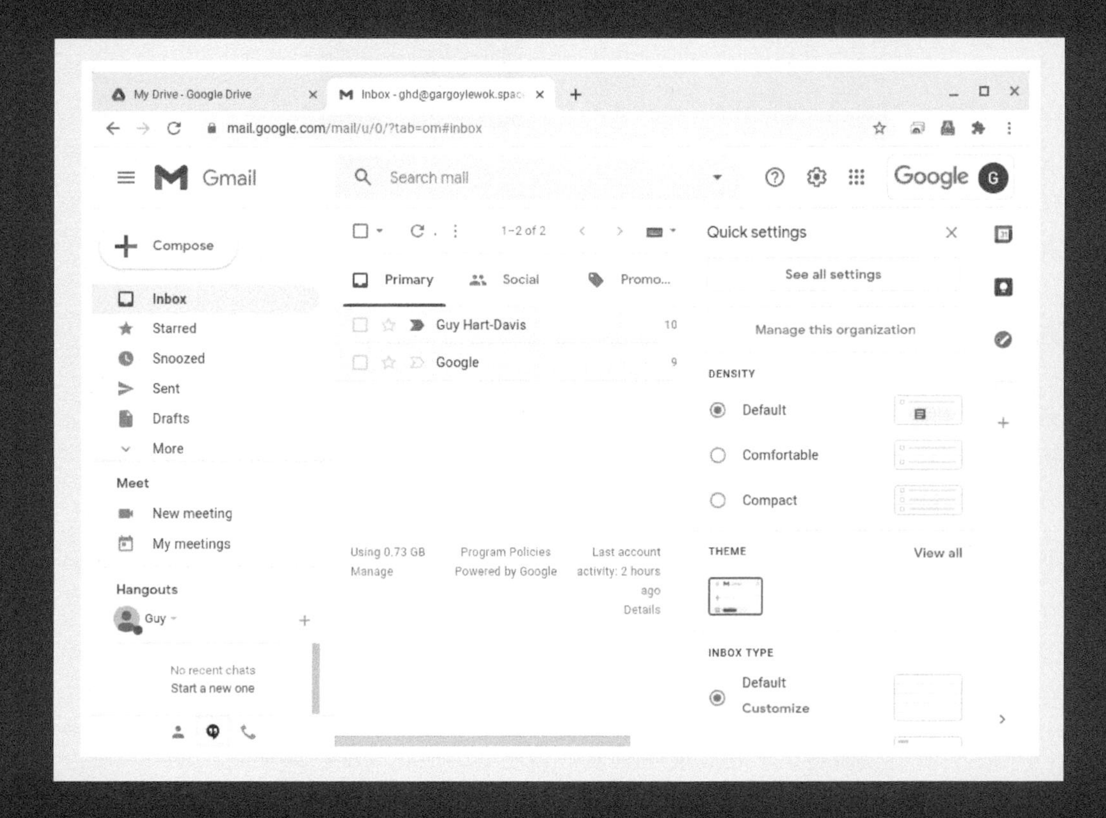

Add External Email Accounts to Gmail

After you sign in to your Google Account, the Gmail web app automatically connects to the email account for that Google Account, enabling you to send and receive email messages on that account.

If you want, and your organization's policies permit, you can use the Gmail web app to check other email accounts. Doing so can help simplify your email management by removing the need to use multiple email apps or services. To check your other accounts via Gmail, you must add each account to your Gmail setup.

Add External Email Accounts to Gmail

1. Open the Gmail app in your browser. For example, in Google Drive, click **Google apps** (⋮⋮⋮) to open the Google Apps panel, and then click **Gmail** (M).

Note: You can also open Gmail quickly from the Google home page by simply clicking the **Gmail** link.

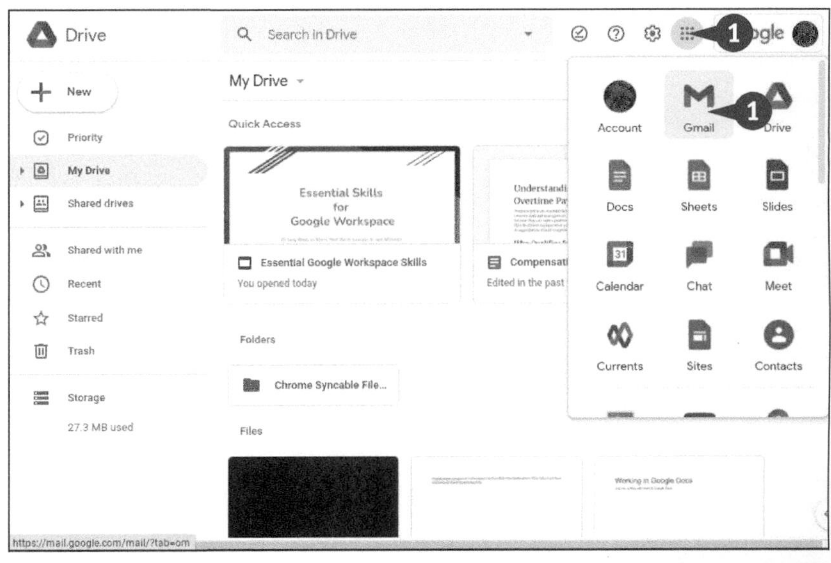

The Gmail web app opens in a new tab.

2. Click **Settings** (⚙).

The Quick Settings pane opens.

3. Click **See all settings**.

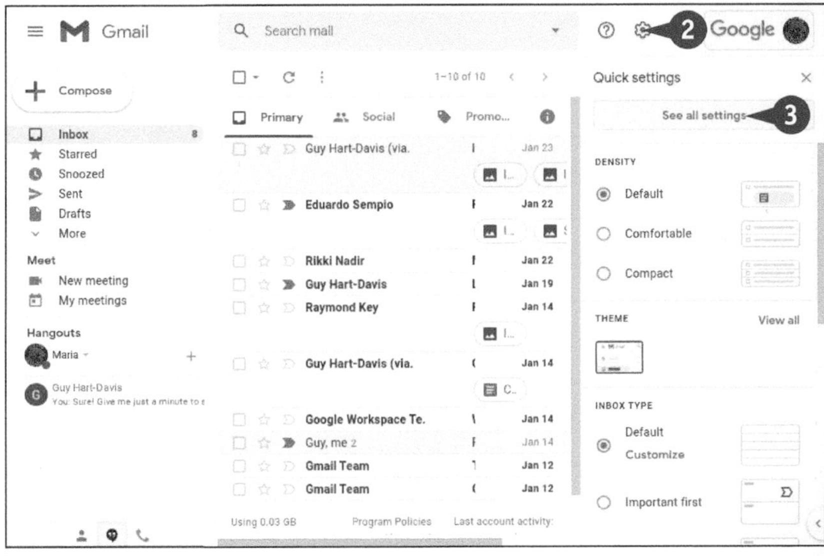

The Settings screen appears.

4 Click **Accounts**.

The Accounts tab appears.

5 On the Check Mail from Other Accounts row, click **Add a mail account**.

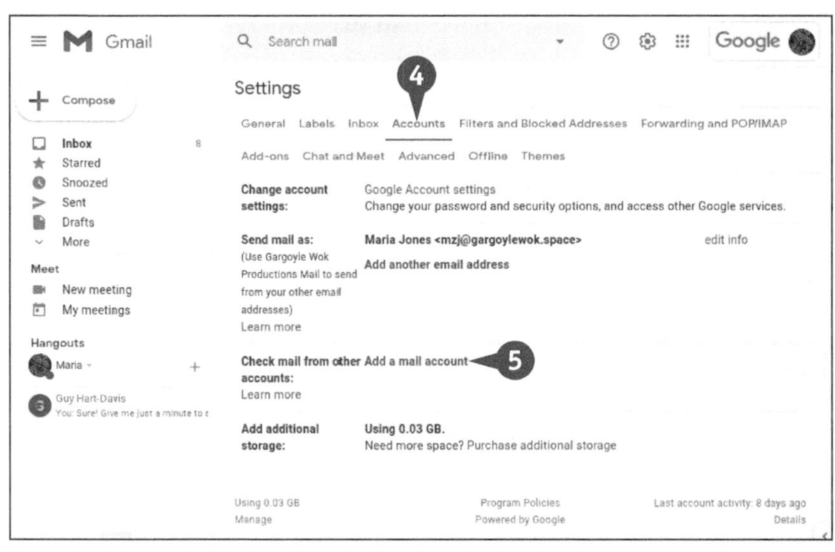

A new window opens, showing the Add a Mail Account screen.

6 In the Email Address box, type the email address for the account you want to add.

7 Click **Next**.

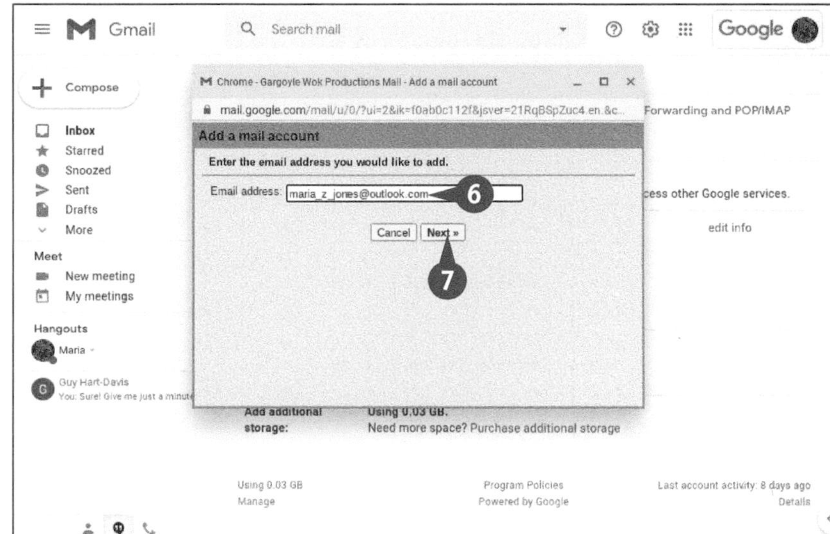

TIP

Should I add my external email accounts to Gmail?

Adding your external email accounts — or some of them — to Gmail can save you time and effort by enabling you to manage other accounts from Gmail. However, bear in mind that adding external accounts makes your Google email account a more tempting and disruptive target for hackers — by taking control of your Google email account, a hacker can also take control of your connected accounts. If this is a concern, consider setting your other email accounts to automatically forward messages to your Gmail account, without linking the email accounts.

continued ►

Add External Email Accounts to Gmail (continued)

Gmail can synchronize some email account types by using a connector feature. As of this writing, the connector works for Yahoo! accounts, AOL accounts, Hotmail accounts, Outlook accounts, and a few other types.

For email account types that the connector cannot synchronize, Gmail can import messages from the email account, enabling you to read the messages in Gmail. But it cannot synchronize the messages, so you will still need to use another email app or service to manage the messages — for example, to file, archive, or delete them.

Add External Email Accounts to Gmail (continued)

The Add a Mail Account screen appears.

Note: The controls on the Add a Mail Account screen vary depending on the provider of the email account you are adding.

8. Click **Password** and type the password for the account.
9. If necessary, click **POP Server** (⌄), and then click the appropriate mail server.
10. Select **Leave a copy of retrieved message on the server** (☑) if you want Gmail to leave a copy of each message it retrieves on the mail server.
11. Select **Always use a secure connection (SSL) when retrieving mail** (☑) to use a secure connection.
12. If you want Gmail to apply a label to messages it retrieves from this account, select **Label incoming messages** (☑), click the pop-up menu (⌄), and then click the label to apply.
13. If you want Gmail to archive incoming messages rather than putting them in the Inbox, select **Archive incoming messages (Skip the Inbox)** (☑).
14. Click **Add Account.**

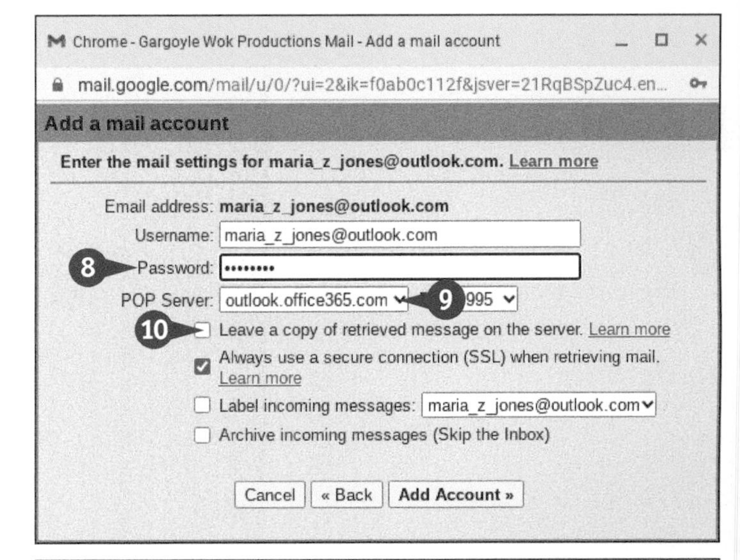

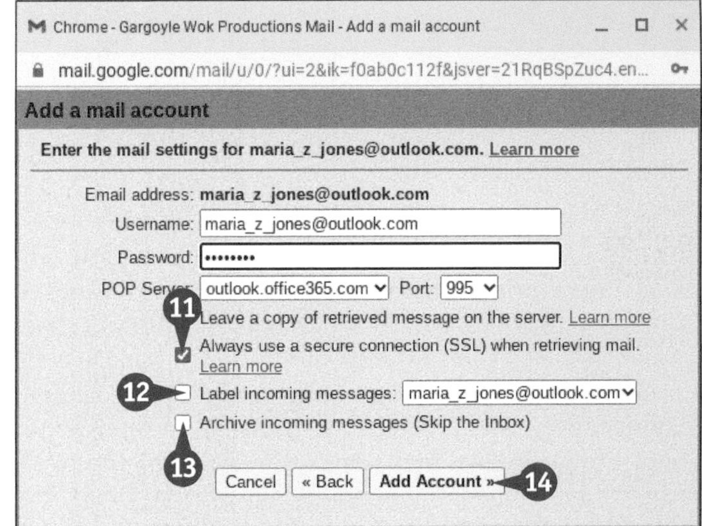

The Your Mail Account Has Been Added screen appears.

15 If you want Gmail to be able to send email from this account, click **Yes, I want to be able to send mail as** (○ changes to ◉). Otherwise, click **No** (○ changes to ◉).

16 Click **Next.**

If you chose to have Gmail send mail, follow the prompts to provide the information needed.

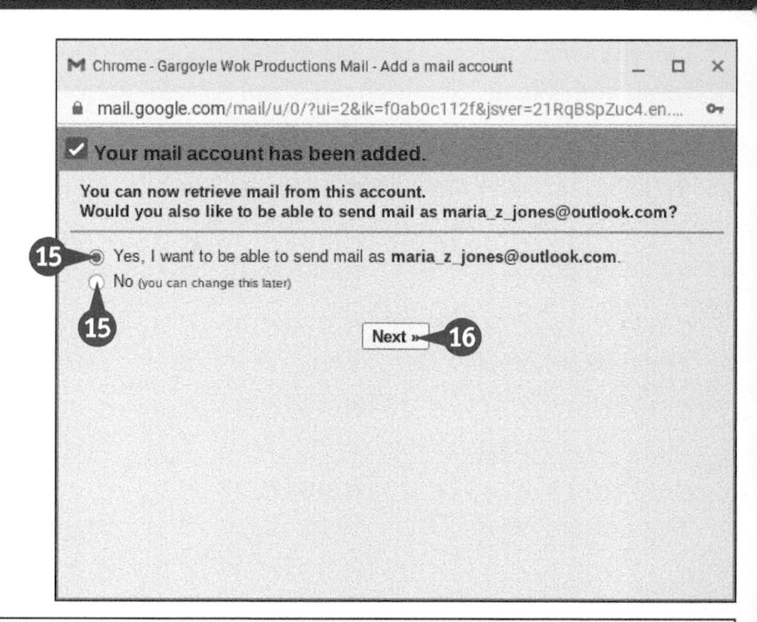

When you finish, the Accounts tab of the Settings screen appears.

A The account you added appears in the Check Mail from Other Accounts section.

17 Click **Inbox** (☐ changes to ☐).

Your Inbox appears, showing your messages from your Google email account and each account you have added.

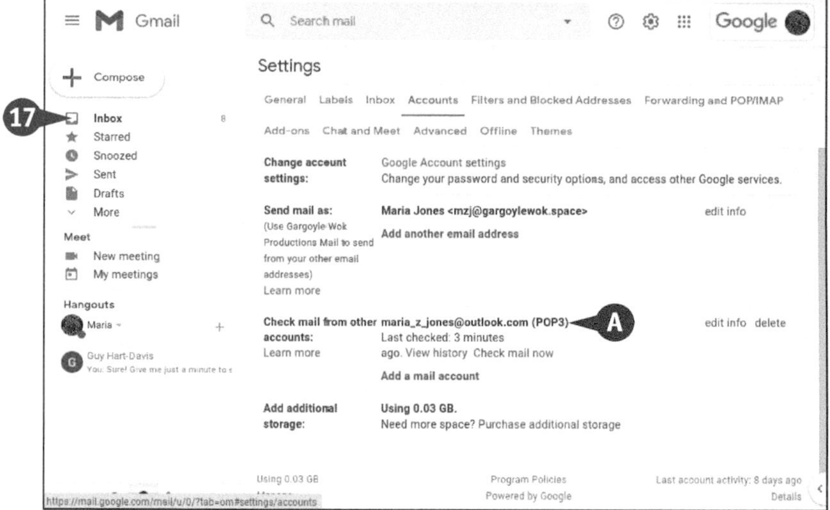

TIP

How do I remove an external email account?

Click **Settings** (⚙) to open the Quick Settings pane, and then click **See all settings** to display the Settings screen. Click **Accounts and Import** to display the Accounts and Import tab. Go to the Check Mail from Other Accounts row, and then click **unlink** to the right of the appropriate account. In the Unlink Account dialog box, click **Keep a copy of the imported messages in Gmail** (○ changes to ◉) or **Delete the copied emails** (○ changes to ◉), as needed; and then click **Unlink.**

Navigate the Gmail Interface

The Gmail web app packs a lot of functionality into a single screen. As well as giving you access to all your email, Gmail enables you to take actions such as starting meetings in Google Meet; communicating via Google Hangouts; and managing your calendar, tasks, and notes.

By default, Gmail filters out spam — junk mail — and divides the remaining incoming messages into four categories in your Inbox: Primary, for significant messages; Social, for messages relating to social media; Promotions, for advertising and marketing messages; and Updates, for service notifications, bills, and receipts.

Navigate the Gmail Interface

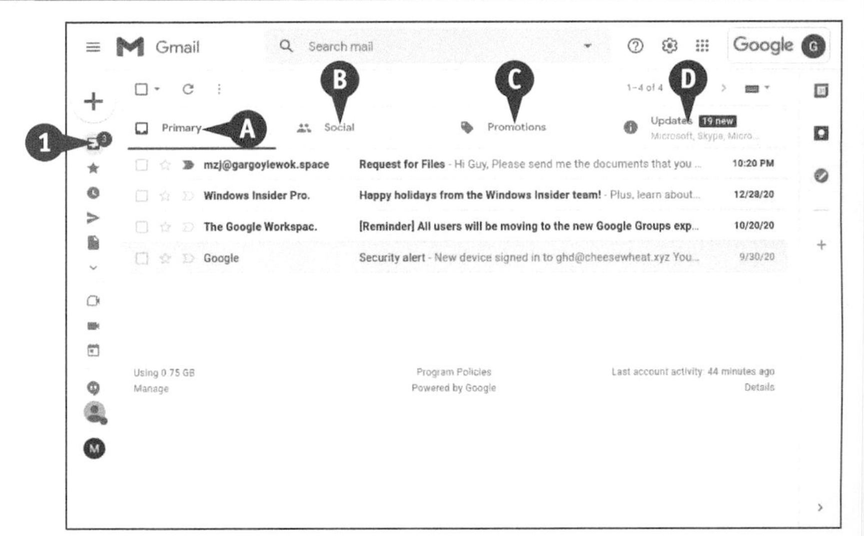

1. In Gmail, click **Inbox** (changes to).

   The Inbox appears.

A. Gmail normally displays the Primary tab of the Inbox at first.

B. You can click **Social** (changes to) to display the Social tab.

C. You can click **Promotions** (changes to) to display the Promotions tab.

D. You can click **Updates** (changes to) to display the Updates tab.

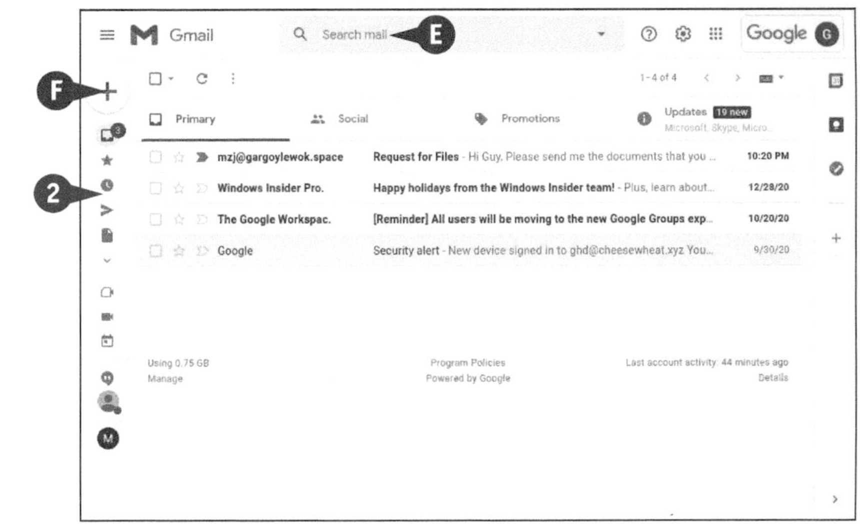

E. You can click **Search mail** () and type the keywords by which you want to search.

F. You can click **Compose** (+) to start a new message.

2. Move the cursor over the navigation bar, the column of icons on the left.

The navigation bar expands.

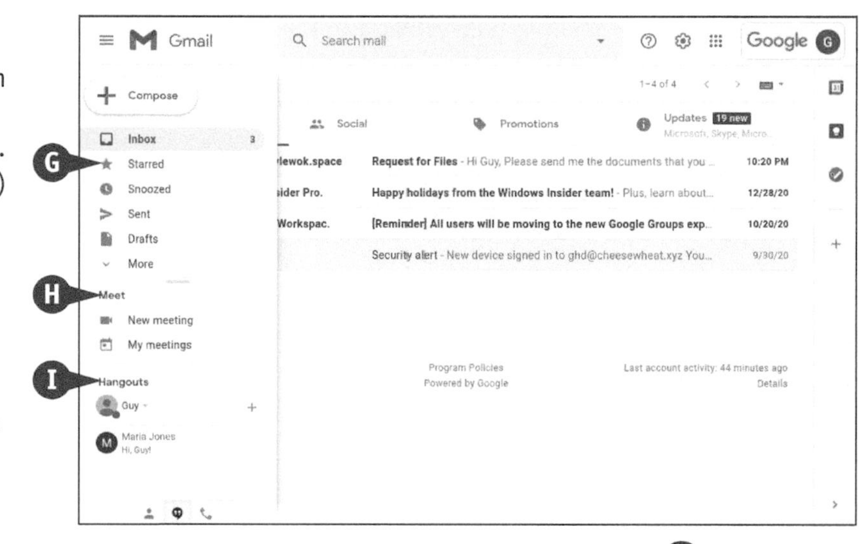

G In the upper section, you can click a label to display messages assigned that label. For example, click **Starred** (★) to display all messages assigned the Starred label.

H In the Meet section, you can start or join a meeting in Google Meet.

I In the Hangouts section, you can interact with a Google Hangouts contact. For example, you can start a video chat or send an email message.

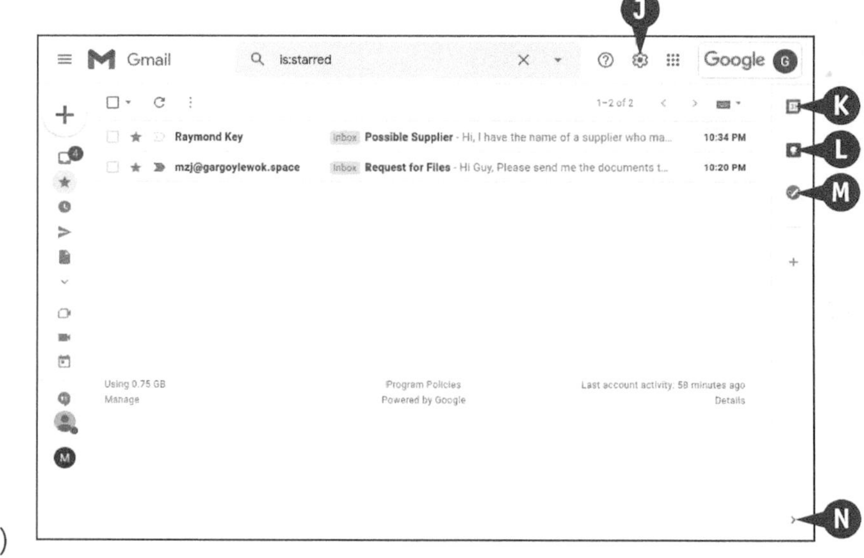

J You can click **Settings** (⚙) to display the Quick Settings pane.

K You can click **Calendar** (📅) to expand the side panel to show a Calendar pane.

L You can click **Keep** (💡) to expand the side panel, showing your notes in Google Keep.

M You can click **Tasks** (✔) to expand the side panel, showing your tasks in Google Tasks.

N You can click **Hide side panel** (›) to hide the side panel.

TIP

How do I change the tabs displayed at the top of the default Inbox?

Click **Settings** (⚙) to open the Quick Settings pane, go to the Inbox Type section, and then click **Customize** under the Default item. In the Select Tabs to Enable dialog box, select (☑) the check box for each tab you want to show, and deselect (☐) all the other check boxes. Select (☑) **Include starred in Primary** if you want to include starred messages in the Primary Inbox. Click **Save** to close the Select Tabs to Enable dialog box.

Receive and Read Your Email Messages

Gmail enables you to receive your incoming messages easily and read them in whatever order you prefer. A message sent to you goes to Google's email servers. To receive the message, you cause the Gmail web app to connect to the email servers so that it can display the message.

Google's division of the Inbox into four categories — Primary, Social, Promotions, and Updates — helps you to focus on particular types of messages. For example, you might choose to deal with all messages in the Primary category before going on to the Social category.

Receive and Read Your Email Messages

1. In Gmail, click **Inbox** (☐ changes to ☐).

   The Inbox appears.

   A. Gmail normally displays the Primary tab of the Inbox at first.

   B. You can click another category, if necessary. For example, click **Social** (👥 changes to 👥) to display the Social category.

   C. Boldface on the sender and the subject indicates an unread message.

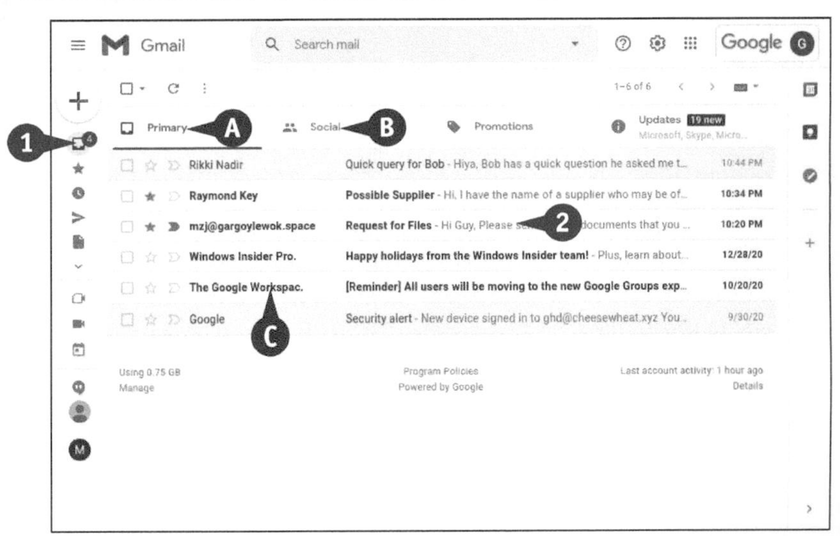

2. Click a message you want to open.

   The contents of the message appear.

   D. You can click **Archive** (📥) to archive the message, removing it from your Inbox.

   E. You can click **Report spam** (❗) to report the message as spam.

   F. You can click **Delete** (🗑) to delete the message.

   G. You can click **Mark as unread** (✉) to mark the message as not having been read, so it still appears to be new.

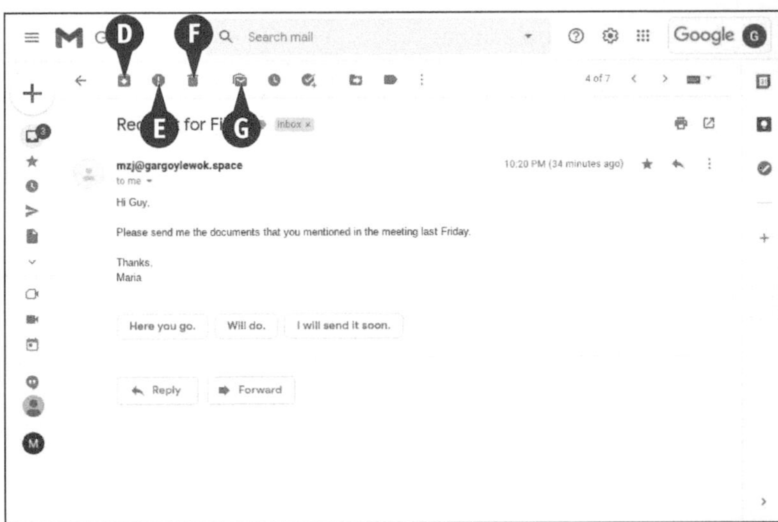

H You can click **Snooze** (🕓) to open the Snooze pop-up menu, and then click the date and time until which you want to snooze the message.

I You can click **Pick date & time** (📅) to choose exactly the date and time you want for the snooze to end.

J You can click **Newer** (<) to display the next newer message.

3 Click **Older** (>).

The next older message appears.

K Gmail displays the Be Careful with This Message dialog box if the sender's email address is new to you.

L You can click **Report phishing** to report the message as phishing, which is an attempt to scam you.

M Once you establish the sender's address is genuine, click **Looks safe** to close the Be Careful with This Message dialog box.

4 Click **Back** (←).

Your Inbox appears again.

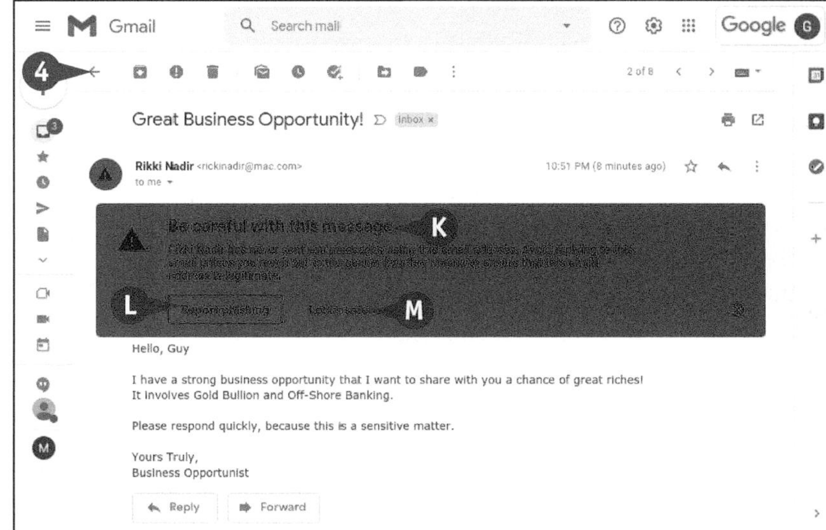

TIP

When I have read a message, why would I mark it as unread?

You might want to mark a read message as unread to indicate to yourself that you need to read it more closely or devote more time to it. Doing so is especially helpful if you tend to "triage" your incoming messages to determine which you must deal with first.

Many productivity methods recommend looking at each incoming item only once and dealing with the item at that point. For example, following the 4 Ds approach, you would Do, Defer, Delegate, or Delete each message you open, where "Do" might encompass actions such as replying, creating a task, or archiving the message.

Send an Email Message

The Gmail web app enables you to send an email message to anybody whose email address you know. After starting a new message, you can specify the recipient's address either by typing the whole address in the To field or by accepting a suggestion that Gmail displays as you start typing the address.

You can send an email message to a single recipient or to multiple recipients. You can send copies to Cc, or carbon-copy, recipients or send hidden copies to Bcc, or blind carbon-copy, recipients.

Send an Email Message

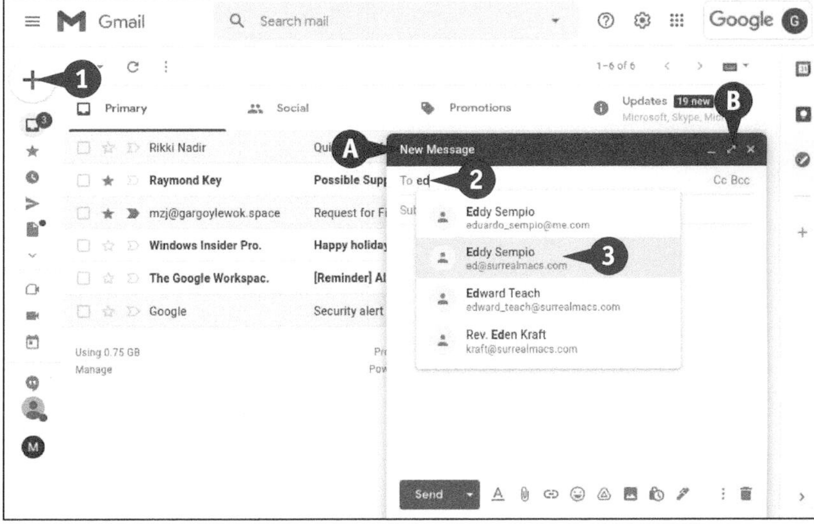

1. In Gmail, click **Compose** (+).

   A A New Message window opens as a pop-up window within the Gmail window.

   B You can click **Full screen** (⤢) to expand the New Message window; if necessary, click **Exit full screen** (⤡) to reduce it again.

Note: If you have configured Gmail with more than one email account, the From pop-up menu appears at the top of the New Message window. You can click **From** (▾) and then click the email address from which to send the message.

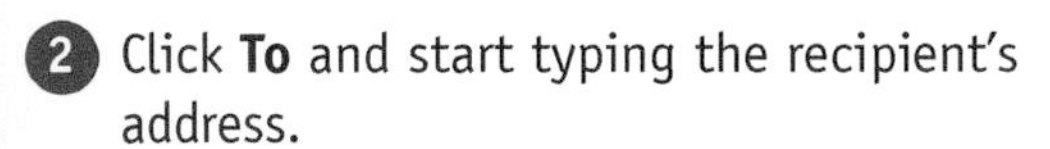

2. Click **To** and start typing the recipient's address.

   A list of matches from your contacts appears.

3. To see more information, move the cursor over a contact.

   A pop-up panel displays more information about the contact.

4. Click the appropriate contact and email address.

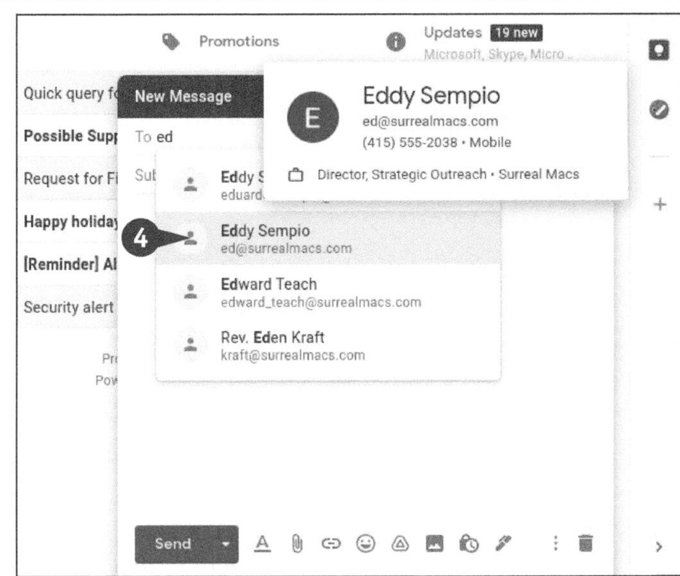

The contact's name appears in the To field as a button.

C You can click **Remove** (×) to remove the recipient.

You can now add another recipient to the To field by following steps **2** to **4**.

D To add a Cc recipient, click **Cc**.

E To add a Bcc recipient, click **Bcc**.

5 Click **Subject**.

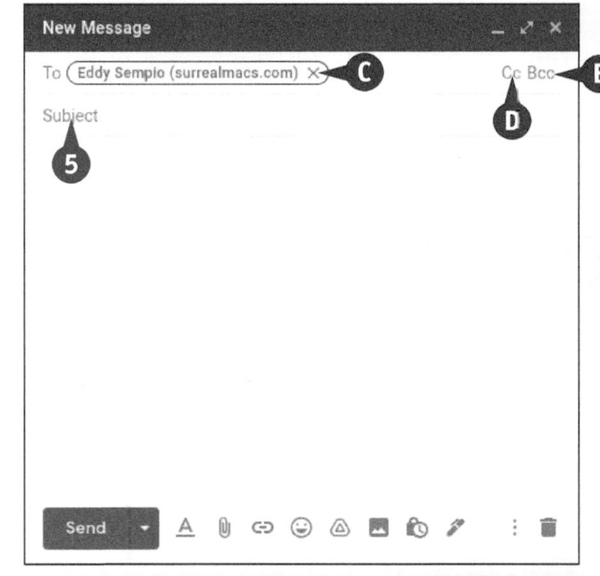

6 Type the subject.

7 Click the body area. Alternatively, press Tab.

F The title bar shows the subject.

8 Type the body of the message.

Note: As you type your message, the Smart Compose feature may suggest completions for the current word or phrase. Press Tab to accept a suggestion; keep typing to reject a suggestion.

9 Click **Send**.

Gmail sends the message.

Note: When you send a message, a *Message sent* pop-up appears for a few seconds. You can click **Undo** on this pop-up to undo the sending. You can adjust the time delay by clicking **Settings** (⚙), clicking **See all settings**, clicking **Send cancellation** (∨) in the Undo Send section of the General tab, and then clicking the time.

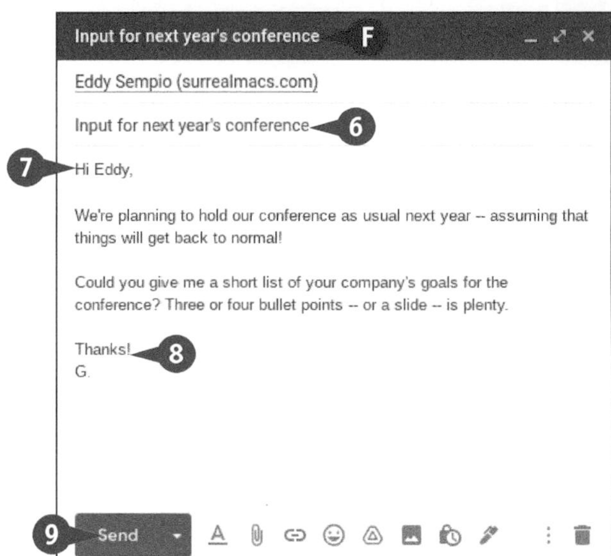

TIP

Can I write a message in a separate window from the main Gmail window?

Yes. Press Shift+click **Full screen** (⤢) or press Shift+click **Exit full screen** (⤡) to switch the pop-up New Message window to a separate window titled Compose Mail. Doing so gives you more flexibility in positioning the window so that you can see other windows and apps, which can be useful for reference.

After switching the message to a separate window, you can click **Pop-in** (↘) to switch the message back to a pop-up window in the main window.

Reply to a Message

Gmail makes it easy to reply to any message you receive. When you reply, you can include either the whole of the original message or just parts of it.

If the message had multiple recipients, you can choose between replying only to the sender and replying to both the sender and all the other recipients other than Bcc recipients. You can also customize the list of recipients manually, removing existing recipients and adding other recipients, as needed.

Reply to a Message

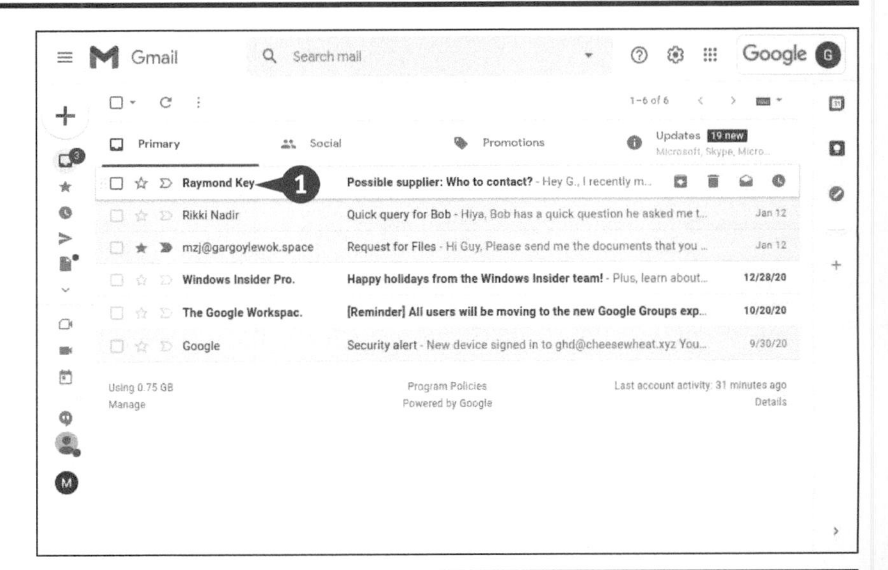

1. In Gmail, click the message to which you want to reply.

   The message can be in your Inbox or in another mailbox.

The message opens.

A The Reply All button appears if the message had multiple recipients, either To recipients or Cc recipients.

The To readout shows the recipients.

B You can click **to** (▾) to display a pop-up panel containing more information, including the names and email addresses of the recipients.

2. Click **Reply** (↩) or **Reply All** (↩↩), as appropriate.

The Reply panel opens.

C You can click **more** to expand the address area so that you can see the recipients.

3 Type your reply to the message.

Note: As you type your reply, the Smart Compose feature may suggest completions for the current word or phrase. If the suggestion is what you want, press Tab to accept it; if not, continue typing.

D You can click **Pop-out reply** (↗) to move the Reply panel to a pop-up window.

4 Click **Send**.

Gmail sends the reply.

E The *Message Sent* pop-up appears for a few seconds, confirming that the message was sent.

F The Undo button appears for the Send Cancellation period you set in Gmail settings. Until it disappears, you can click **Undo** to undo the sending of the message.

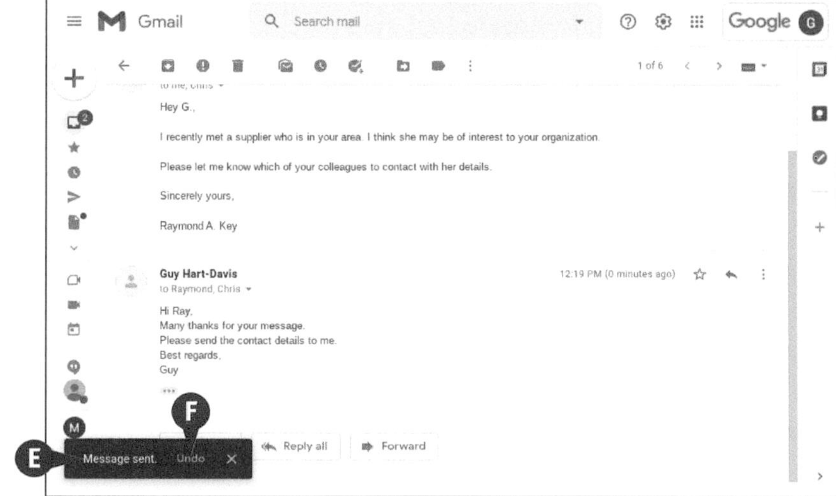

TIPS

How do I change the subject line when I reply to a message?

Click **Type of response** (such as ↩ ▾) to display the Type of Response pop-up menu, and then click **Edit subject**. The reply message opens in a pop-up window with the subject line selected. You can then edit the existing subject line or type a new subject line.

How do I include only part of the original message in my reply?

Start your reply, and then click **Show trimmed content** (···). Gmail shows the original content in an editable format, and you can delete the parts you do not want to include. You can also reply inline — for example, putting an answer straight after a question in the original message.

Forward a Message

Rather than replying to the sender of a message, you may want to forward the message to other people. Gmail enables you to forward either an entire message or only those parts you choose.

When you forward a message, you can add your own comments to the message. For example, you might want to tell the recipient something about the person or organization that sent you the original message, why you are forwarding it, and what action — if any — you expect the recipient to take.

Forward a Message

1. In Gmail, right-click the message you want to forward.

   The contextual menu opens.

2. Click **Forward** (➡).

Note: You can also click the message to open it and then click **Forward** (➡) to start the forwarding process.

Gmail displays the message to be forwarded in a pop-up window.

A. The title bar and subject show *Fwd:* and the previous subject to indicate that this is a forwarded message.

3. To get a larger window to work in, click **Full screen** (⤢).

Note: You can press Shift+click **Full screen** (⤢) to open the message in a separate window.

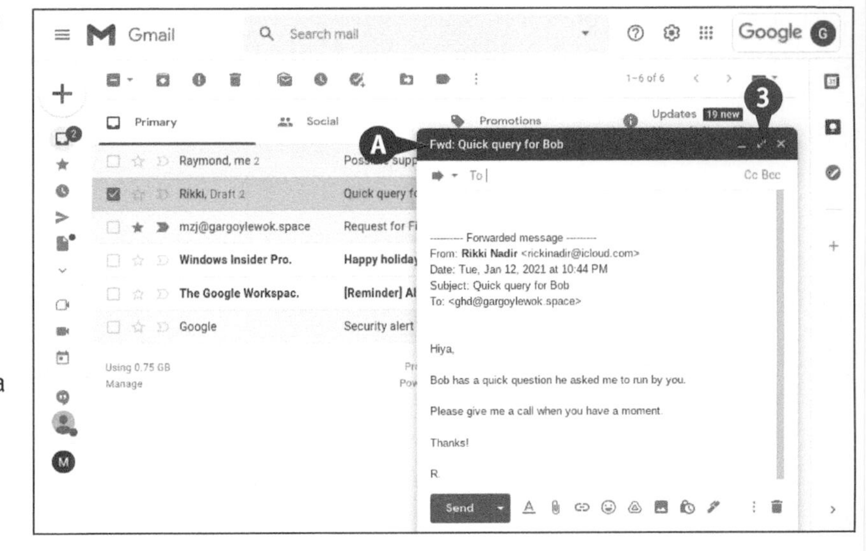

Gmail switches the pop-out window to what it terms full screen — what would normally be considered a larger window — and darkens the Gmail window to indicate it is not active.

4 Click **To** and start typing the recipient's email address.

The list of matches appears.

5 Click the appropriate match.

Note: At this point, you can add further recipients, including Cc or Bcc recipients.

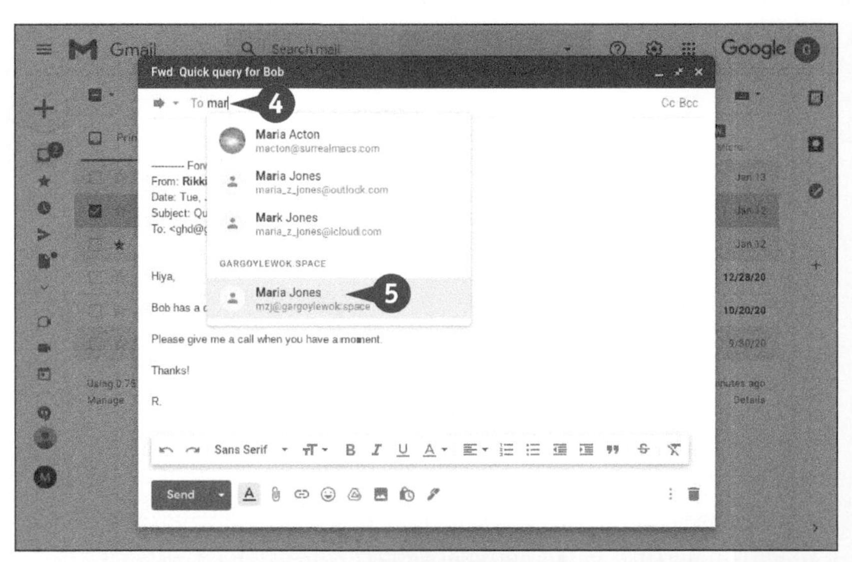

6 Click the body area or press Tab.

The body area becomes active.

7 Type any message needed to the recipient.

For example, you might explain why you are forwarding the message.

8 Click **Send**.

Gmail forwards the message to the recipient.

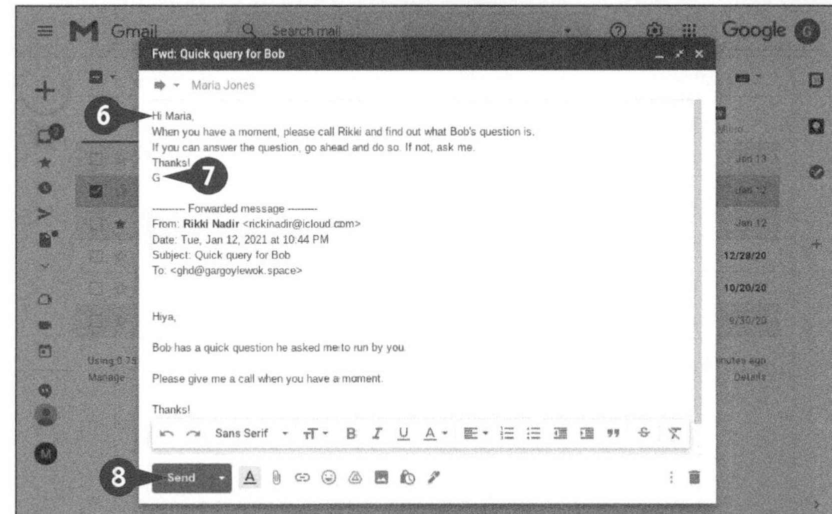

TIP

What does the Forward as Attachment command on the contextual menu do?

Click **Forward as attachment** (📎) to send a copy of the message as an attachment to a message instead of in the message itself. This command is useful when you want to forward a formatted message in a plain-text message.

Include Formatting, Emojis, and Pictures in Messages

You can communicate effectively via email by using nothing more than unformatted text in your outgoing messages. But Gmail enables you to include a wide variety of formatting, should you need it. You can also add emoji icons to help convey your meaning. When you need to convey a graphical concept without using a thousand words, you can insert a picture — or indeed several pictures — in a message.

Start by opening Gmail and clicking **Compose** (+) to create a new message.

Add Formatting to a Message

Click **Full screen** (⤢) to switch the new message window to full screen; when you do this, Gmail automatically displays the Formatting Options bar. If you prefer to work in the smaller window, click **Formatting options** (A) to display the Formatting Options bar.

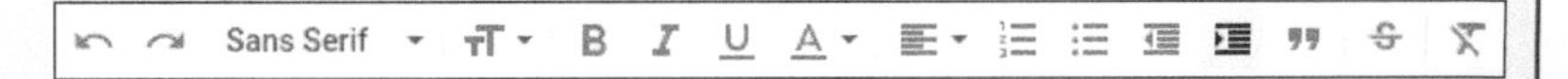

You can then use the controls on the Formatting Options bar to apply formatting:

Font (Sans Serif ▾). Select the font or font family, such as **Sans Serif** or **Tahoma**.

Size (TT ▾). Select the font size: **Small**, **Normal**, **Large**, or **Huge**.

Bold (B). Click to toggle boldface on or off.

Italic (I). Click to toggle italics on or off.

Underline (U). Click to toggle underlining on or off.

Text color (A ▾). Click to display the Text Color panel, and then click the background color or text color you want to apply.

Align (≡ ▾). Click to display the Align toolbar, and then click **Align left** (≡), **Align center** (≡), or **Align right** (≡), as needed.

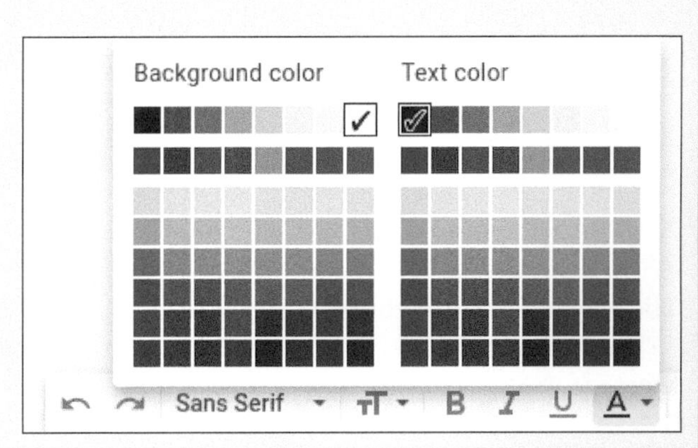

Numbered list (☰). Click to toggle list numbering on or off.

Bulleted list (☰). Click to toggle list bulleting on or off.

Indent less (☰). Click to reduce the indent.

Indent more (☰). Click to increase the indent.

Add Formatting to a Message (continued)

Quote (❞). Click to indent the paragraph both left and right.

Strikethrough (S̶). Click to toggle strikethrough on or off.

Remove formatting (T̸). Click to remove formatting from the selection.

Click **Undo** (↶) to undo a change. Click **Redo** (↷) to redo a change.

Insert Emojis in a Message

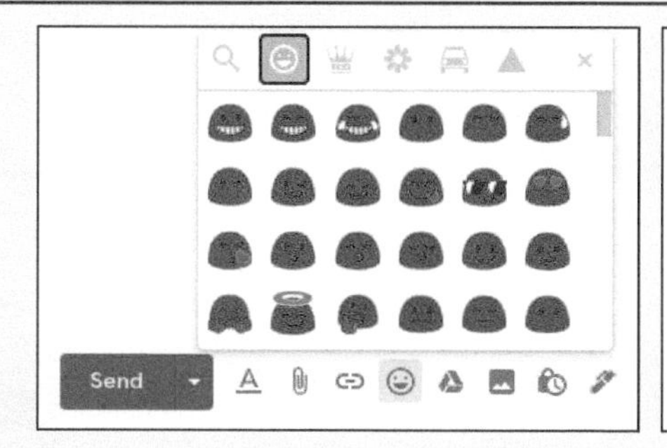

When you want to insert an emoji at the cursor position, click **Insert emoji** (☺) to display the Emoji pane. Display the emoji category you want by clicking **Show face emoticons** (☺), **Show object emoticons** (♕), **Show nature emoticons** (✿), **Show transportation emoticons** (🚗), or **Show symbol emoticons** (▲). You can then browse to locate the emoji you want and click the emoji to insert it.

Alternatively, click **Search** (🔍) to display the Search pane, and then type a keyword describing what you want to find.

Insert Pictures in a Message

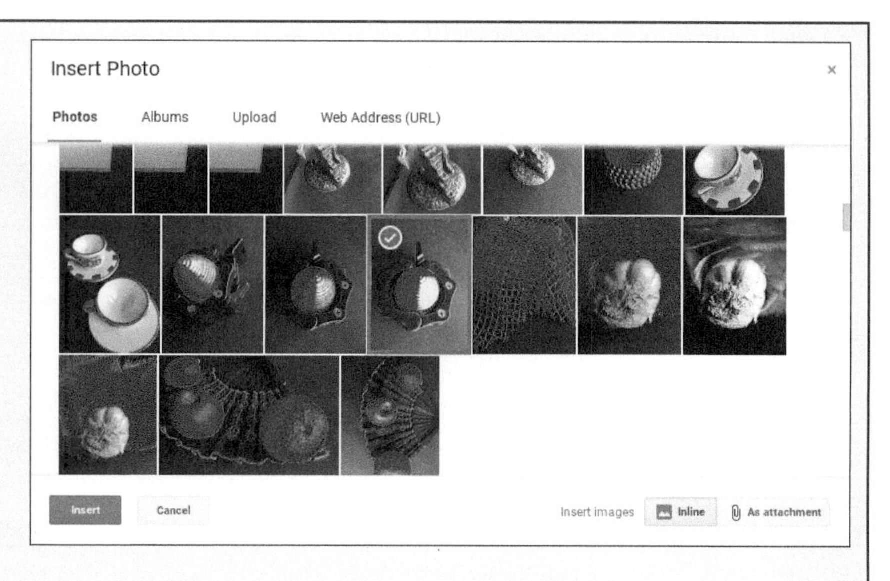

To insert a picture in a message at the cursor position, click **Insert photo** (▣). In the Insert Photo dialog box that opens, click the appropriate category — **Photos**, **Albums**, **Upload**, or **Web Address (URL)** — on the tab bar. Within the category, click the photo you want to insert. In the Insert Images area, click **Inline** (▣) if you want to insert the photo as a display element in the message; click **As attachment** (📎) if you want to attach the photo as a file. Then click **Insert**.

Send an Email Message Using Confidential Mode

When including sensitive information in an email message, you may want to enable Gmail's Confidential Mode for that message. Confidential Mode prevents the recipient from forwarding, copying, printing, or downloading the message. You can also specify an expiry date for the message and choose whether the recipient must use an SMS passcode.

Before using Confidential Mode, be aware that the protections it offers are largely "security theater" rather than effective protection; they do not meet serious information-security requirements, such as those of HIPAA. For example, the recipient can take screenshots or photographs of the content, transcribe it, or memorize it.

Send an Email Message Using Confidential Mode

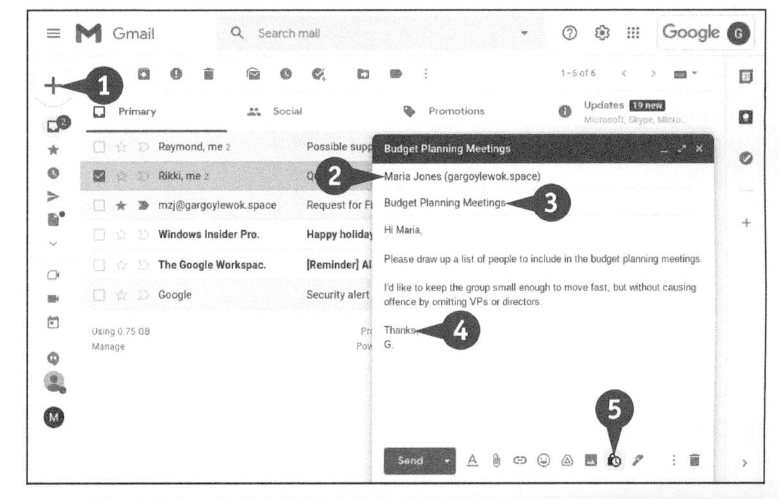

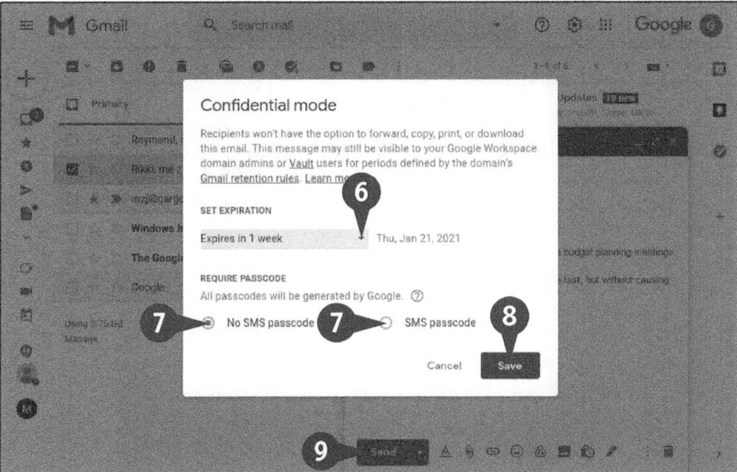

1. In Gmail, click **Compose** (+).

   A new message window opens.

2. Address the message.
3. Enter the subject.
4. Enter the body of the message.
5. Click **Confidential Mode** ( ).

   The Confidential Mode dialog box opens.

6. Click **SET EXPIRATION** ( ), and then click **Expires in 1 day**, **Expires in 1 week**, **Expires in 1 month**, **Expires in 3 months**, or **Expires in 5 years**, as appropriate.
7. In the REQUIRE PASSCODE area, select **No SMS passcode** (changes to) or **SMS passcode** (changes to), as needed.
8. Click **Save**.

   The Confidential Mode dialog box closes.

9. Click **Send**.

Note: If you chose to use an SMS passcode, type the recipient's phone number in the Confirm Phone Numbers dialog box, and then click **Send**.

Gmail sends the message.

Schedule a Message for Sending Later

Normally, Gmail sends each outgoing message when you click Send — or, more precisely, Gmail sends each message after a 5-second delay that gives you the chance to not only recognize you have made a dreadful mistake but also recover from it.

Sometimes, however, you may want to write a message and have Gmail send it later. Gmail makes scheduled sending easy.

Schedule a Message for Sending Later

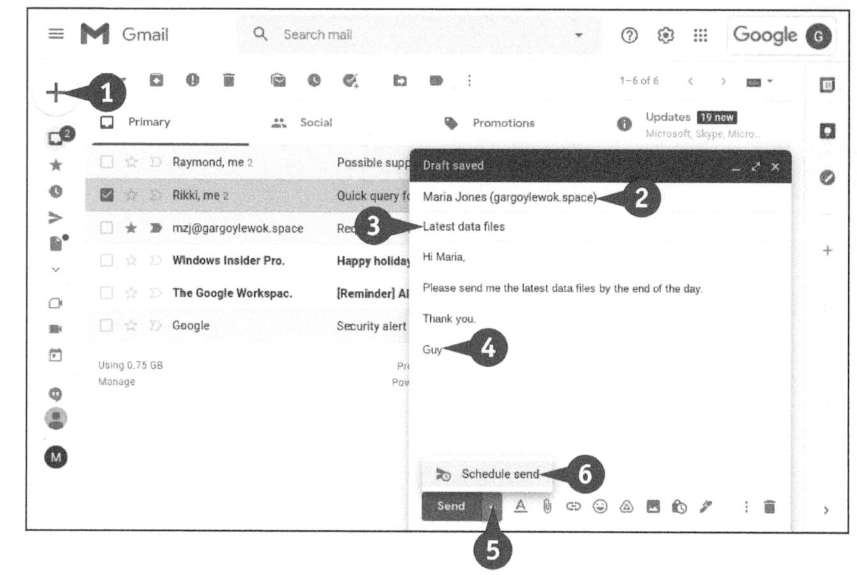

1. In Gmail, click **Compose** (+).

   A new message window opens.

2. Address the message.
3. Enter the subject.
4. Enter the body of the message.
5. Click the **Send** pop-up button.

   The Send pop-up menu opens (changes).

6. Click **Schedule send**.

   The Schedule Send dialog box opens.

7. If the appropriate time appears in the list, click it. Otherwise, click **Pick date & time**.

   The Pick Date & Time dialog box opens.

8. Click the date.
9. Click the time readout, and then adjust it as needed.
10. Click **Schedule send**.

    The Pick Date & Time dialog box closes.

    The message pop-up window closes.

    Gmail schedules the message for sending at the time and date you specified.

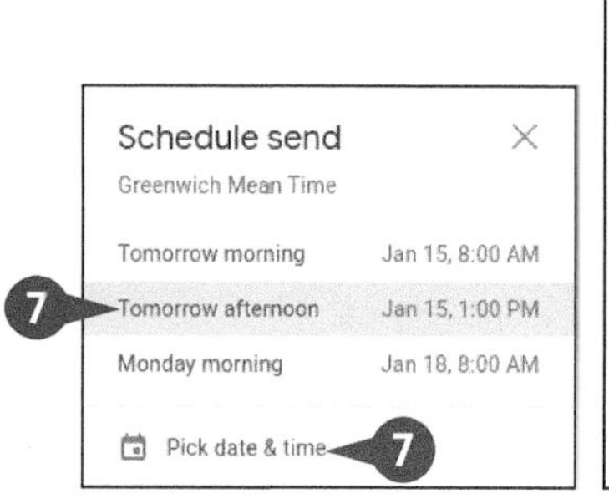

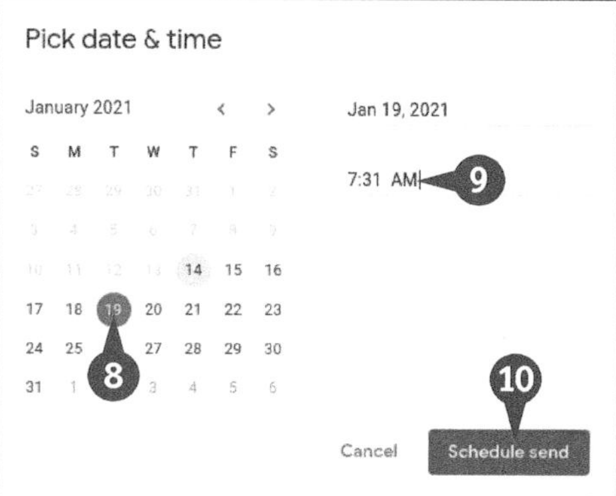

Send a File or a Link via Email

Gmail provides an easy way to transfer files to other people. You can attach one or more files to an email message so that the files travel as part of the message. The recipient can then save the files on their computer, open the files, and work with them.

Files you send can be stored on Google Drive, on your computer's local storage, or on a network drive. Gmail enables you to send up to 25MB from Google Drive; for larger files, Gmail automatically creates a link for you to send instead.

Send a File or a Link via Email

Send Files via Email

1. In Gmail, click **Compose** (+).
2. Address the message.
3. Enter the subject.
4. Enter the body of the message.
5. Click **Attach files** (📎).

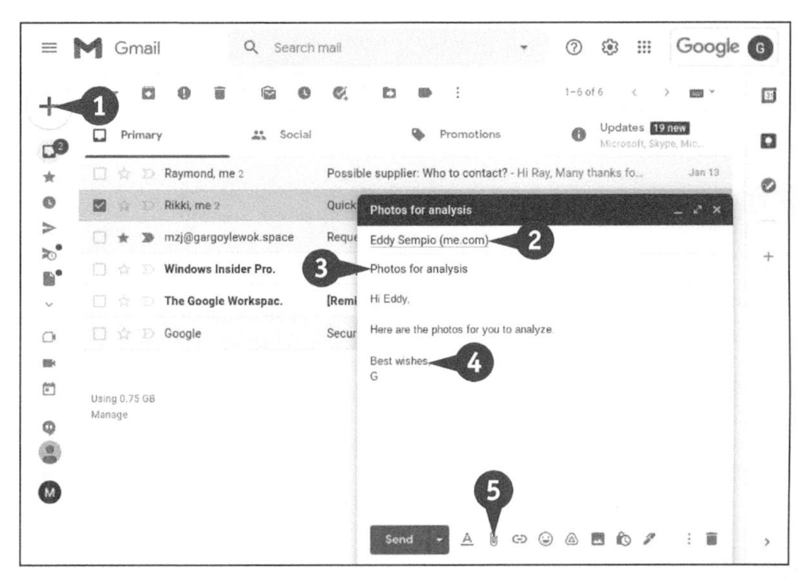

The Select One or More Files dialog box opens.

6. Navigate to the folder that contains the file or files you want to attach.
7. Select the file or files.
8. Click **Open**.

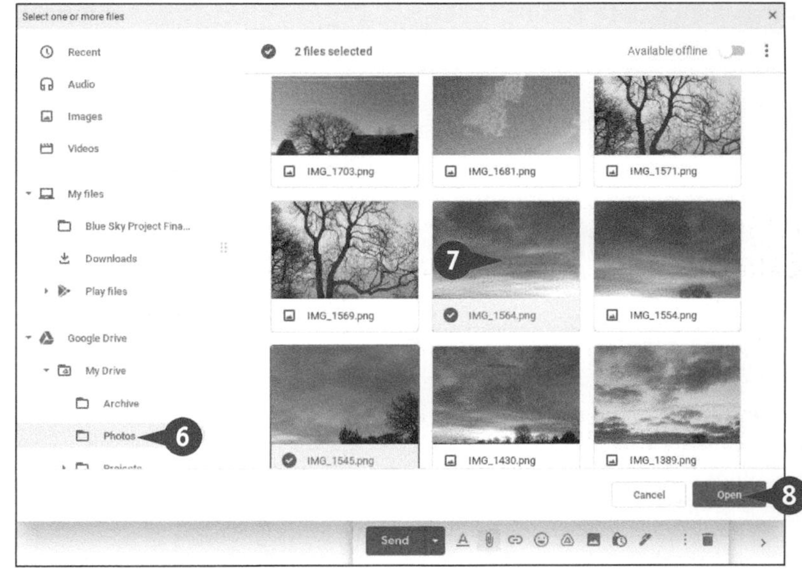

The Select One or More Files dialog box closes.

Note: If the files' total size is more than 25MB, Gmail tells you it will send links instead. See the following subsection.

Ⓐ Gmail adds each file to the message.

Ⓑ You can click **Remove attachment** (✕) to remove an attachment.

9 Click **Send**.

Gmail sends the message, including the files.

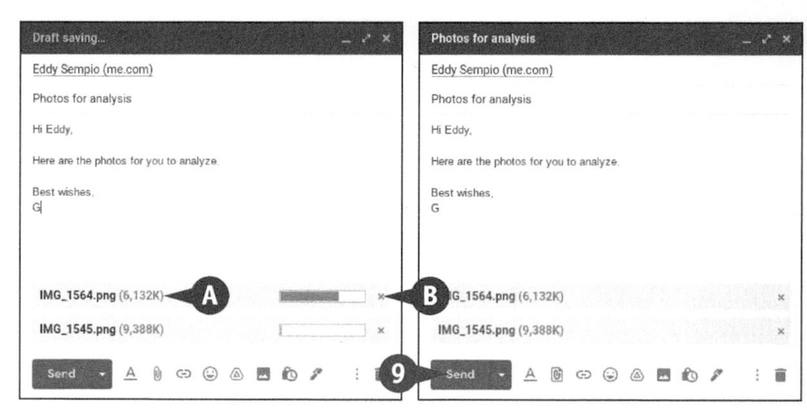

Send Links for Large Files via Email

If the files' total size is more than 25MB, the Attaching Files dialog box opens.

Ⓒ Gmail copies each file to storage that the message's recipients will be able to access via links included in the message.

When copying finishes, the Attaching Files dialog box closes.

The message window becomes active again.

Ⓓ The message includes a link for each file.

1 Click **Send**.

Gmail sends the message.

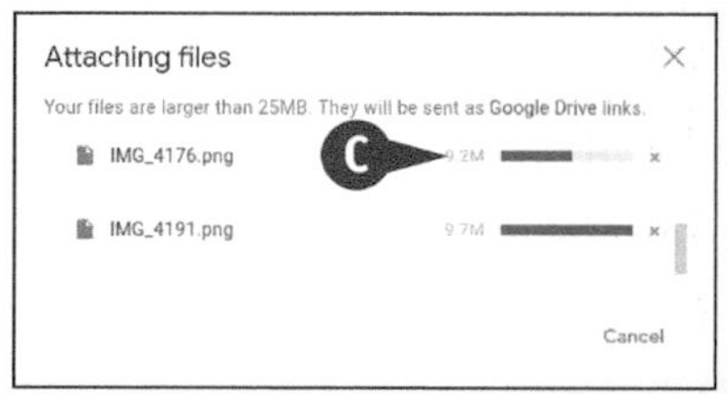

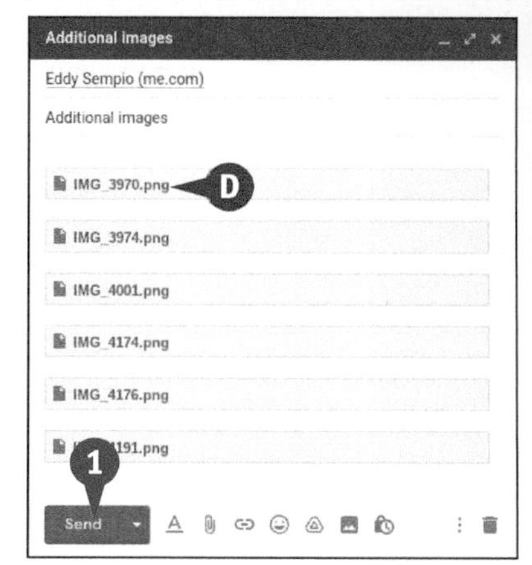

TIP

Why does Google limit the size of messages with attachments to 25MB?

Although email is an easy and convenient way to share files, it is not very efficient, especially when one person sends files to multiple recipients. Huge email messages clog up email servers and email inboxes, and many email servers are configured to reject messages over a certain size. This size varies but is often less than 25MB.

Sending a link to a file, enabling each recipient to download the file at a suitable time and — preferably — over a fast connection is much more efficient.

Receive a File or a Link via Email

When you receive a file via email, it appears as an attachment to a message in your Inbox. Similarly, when you receive a link via email, it appears as a button in an email message. Gmail makes it easy to view the attached files and the links you receive. You can preview an attached file or open a linked file directly from your Inbox, without having to open the message.

Receive a File or a Link via Email

Open Gmail and View a File from the Inbox

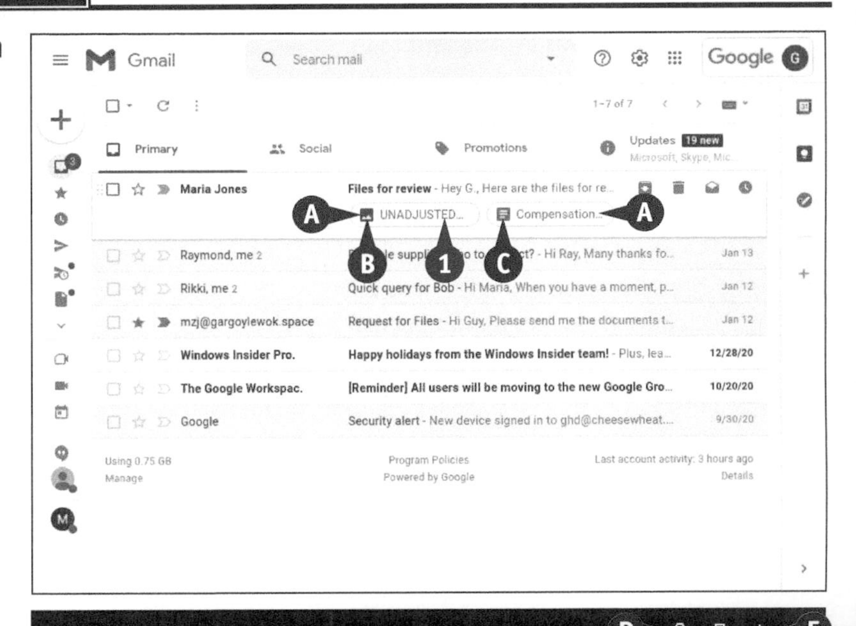

A In the Gmail Inbox, any attachments or links appear as buttons.

The icon indicates the file's type.

B The Image icon ( ) indicates an image file, such as a photo.

C The Docs icon ( ) indicates a Google Docs document.

1 To see an attached file, such as an image, without opening the message, click the file's button.

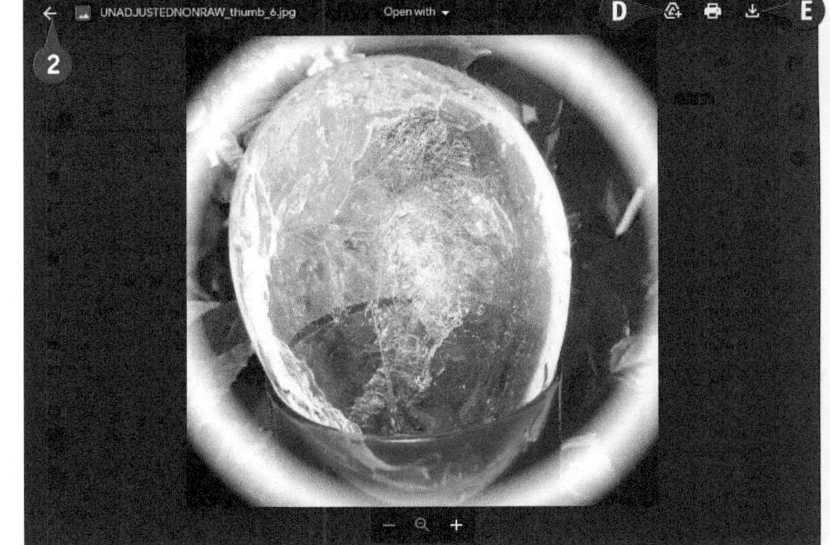

The image opens in the file viewer.

D You can click **Add to My Drive** ( ) to add the image to your Google Drive.

E You can click **Download** ( ) to download the file to your browser's Downloads folder.

2 Click **Close** ( ).

Your Inbox appears again.

3. Click a link included in a message in the Inbox.

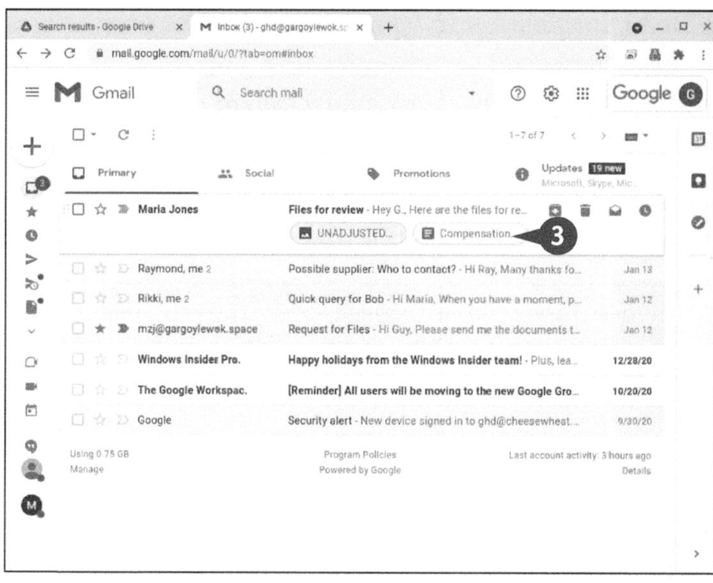

The file opens in the associated app in a new tab in the browser.

In this example, the Docs document opens in Google Docs.

You can now work with the document as usual.

4. When you finish working with the document, click **Close** (✕).

The tab containing the document closes.

Your Inbox appears again.

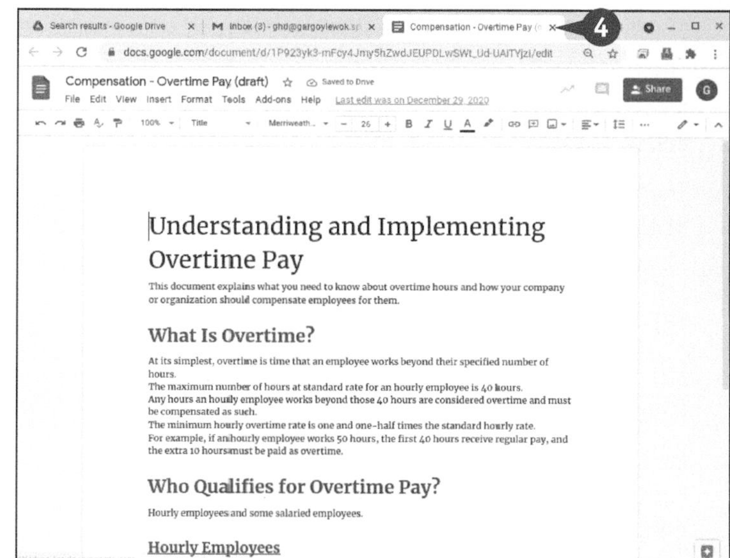

TIP

Pictures in incoming messages sometimes appear as blank boxes. How do I fix this?

You need to turn on the display of external images. Click **Settings** (⚙) to open the Quick Settings pane, and then click **See all settings** to display the Settings screen. On the General tab, which appears by default, go to the Images section, and then click **Always display external images** (☐ changes to ☑).

View Email Messages by Conversations

Gmail enables you to view an exchange of email messages as a conversation instead of viewing each message as a separate item. Conversations, also called *threads*, let you browse and sort messages on the same subject more easily by separating them from other messages in your mailboxes.

Conversation View is enabled by default in Gmail. But if you prefer not to use Conversation View, you can disable it easily; see the tip for instructions.

View Email Messages by Conversations

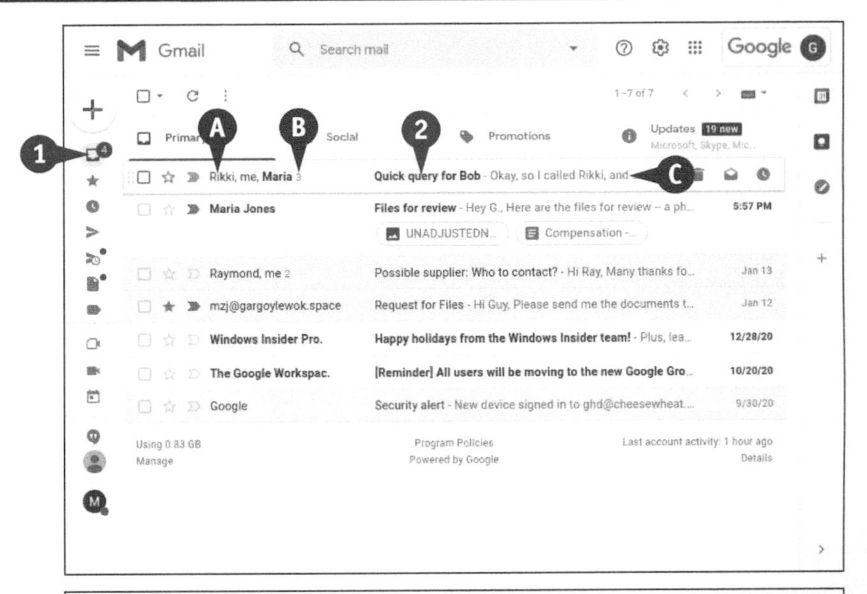

1. In Gmail, open the appropriate mailbox. For example, click **Inbox** (☐ changes to ☐) to display the Inbox.

   A. The readout summarizes the people involved in the conversation, in sequence.

   B. The number shows how many messages the conversation contains.

   C. The preview shows the beginning of the most recent message.

2. Click the conversation.

   The conversation appears.

   D. The latest message in the conversation appears in full.

   E. Each earlier message in the conversation appears reduced to its minimal length.

   F. If Gmail's Smart Compose feature is on, buttons for suggested quick replies appear.

   G. The Show Trimmed Content button (...) indicates that content has been trimmed. Normally, this is the part of the message that consists of replies.

3. To view the full text sent for a particular message, click it.

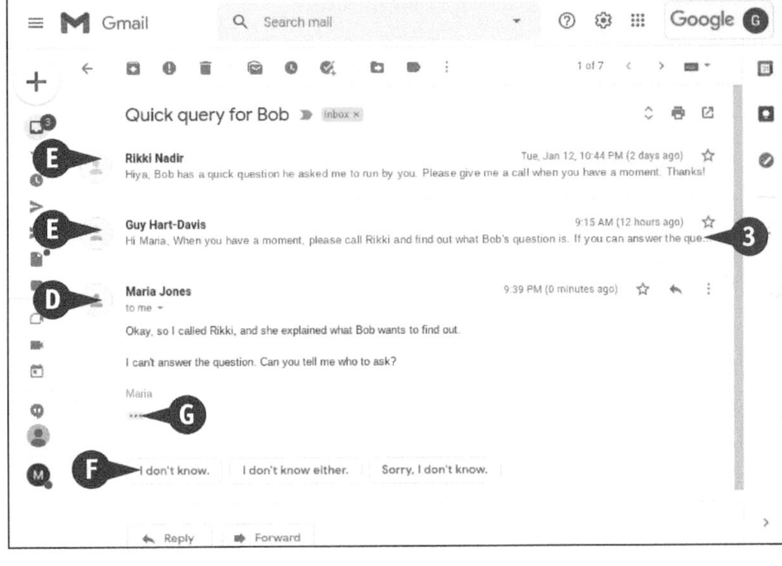

H The full text of the message appears.

Any parts of the message that were replies do not appear.

I You can click the sender bar to reduce the message to its summary again.

4 To view the trimmed content, click **Show trimmed content** (…).

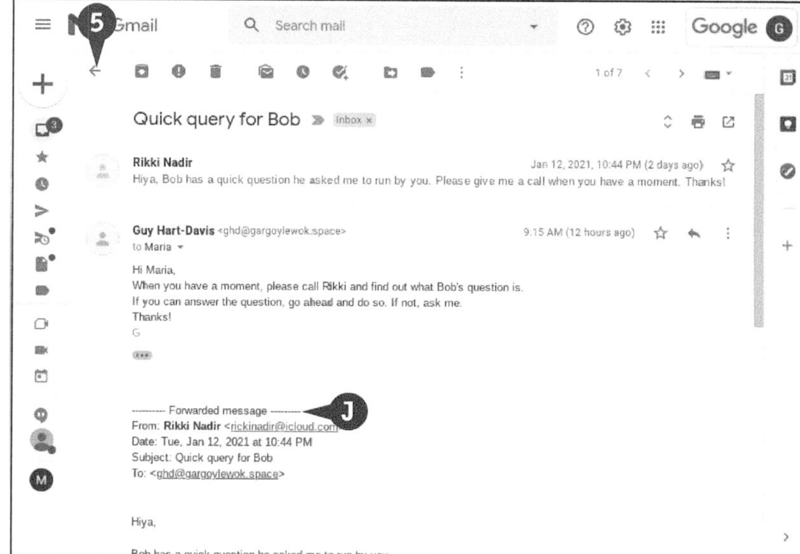

J The trimmed content appears, enabling you to see the full details of the message, including the sender, the date, the subject, and the recipients.

5 When you finish working with the conversation, click **Back** (←).

Your Inbox appears again.

TIP

How do I enable or disable Conversation View?

Click **Settings** in the upper-right corner of the Gmail screen to display the Quick Settings pane, and then scroll all the way to the bottom. In the Email Threading section, select (✓) or deselect **Conversation view**, as needed. A message box opens, telling you that Gmail needs to reload to turn Conversation View on or off. Click **Reload**, and then wait while Gmail reloads.

Block and Unblock Senders

If you receive unwanted messages in Gmail, you can block the message's sender. After you implement the blocking, Gmail directs any incoming messages from that sender to your Spam folder, so they do not appear in your Inbox. You can then review the messages in your Spam folder at your leisure to make sure the folder has not caught any useful messages.

If you decide that you do want to receive messages from a blocked sender after all, you can unblock the sender easily.

Block and Unblock Senders

1. In Gmail, click a message from the sender you want to block.

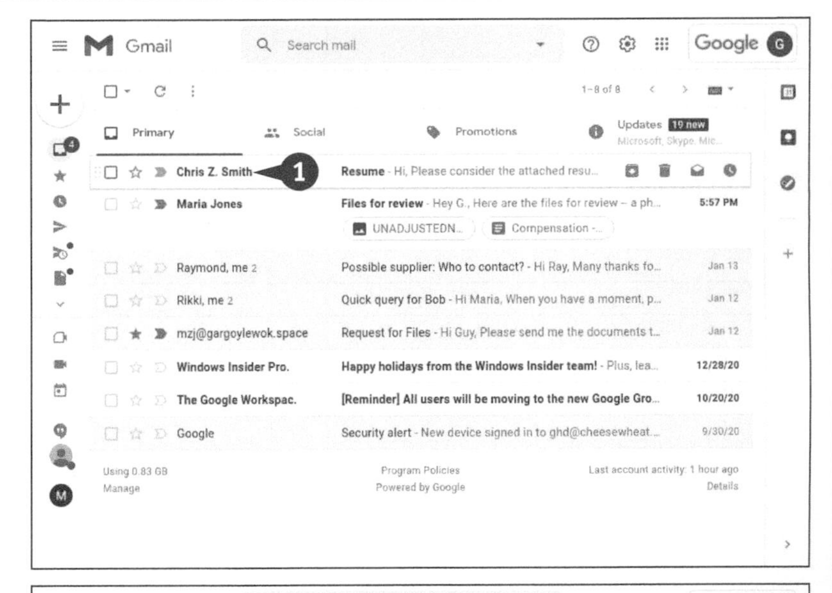

The message opens.

2. Click **Menu** (⋮).

The menu opens.

3. Click **Block "[sender]"**.

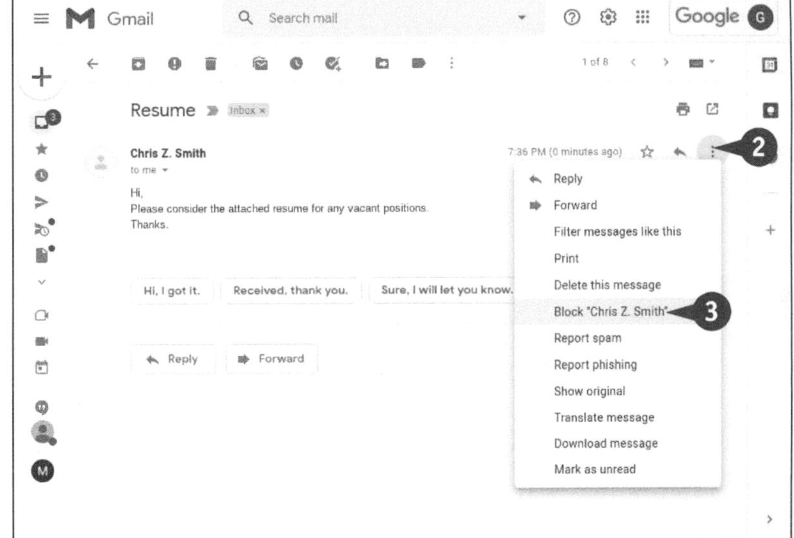

The Block This Email Address dialog box opens.

4 Click **Block**.

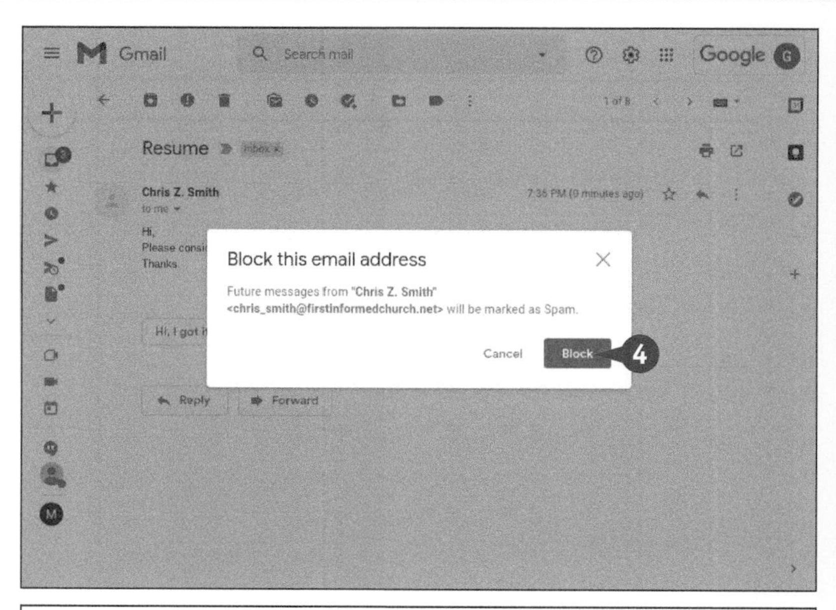

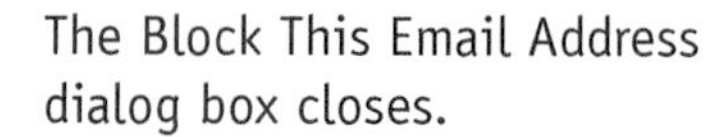

The Block This Email Address dialog box closes.

The You Have Blocked [Sender] dialog box opens, telling you that new messages from this sender will go to the Spam folder.

A You can click **Unblock sender** if you blocked the sender by mistake.

5 Click **Move to spam** to move the current message to the Spam folder as well.

B The *Email address blocked* readout appears briefly in the lower-left corner of the Gmail screen, confirming the blocking.

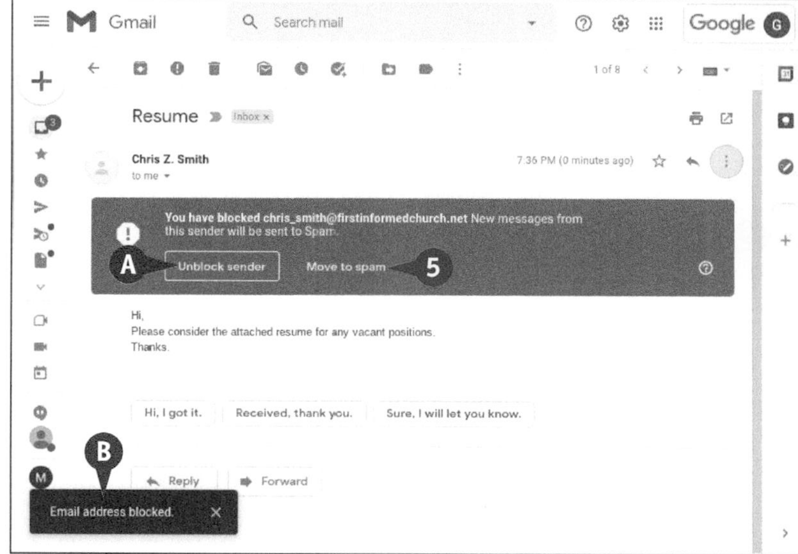

TIP

How do I unblock a sender I have blocked?

In Gmail, click **Settings** (⚙) to open the Quick Settings pane, and then click **See all settings** to display the Settings screen. On the tab bar at the top, click **Filters and Blocked Addresses** to display the Filters and Blocked Addresses tab. Go to the "The Following Email Addresses Are Blocked" section, and then click **unblock** on the right side of the row for the sender you want to unblock.

Create Email Filters

An *email filter* is a rule for automatically processing email messages. Gmail uses a wide range of filters automatically — for example, to weed out as much spam as possible and to sort your remaining incoming messages into the Primary, Social, Promotions, and Updates categories.

Gmail also enables you to create custom filters of your own. For example, you might create a filter to apply a particular label to high-priority messages or to forward such messages to a colleague — or to do both.

Create Email Filters

Display the Filters and Blocked Addresses Tab in Gmail Settings

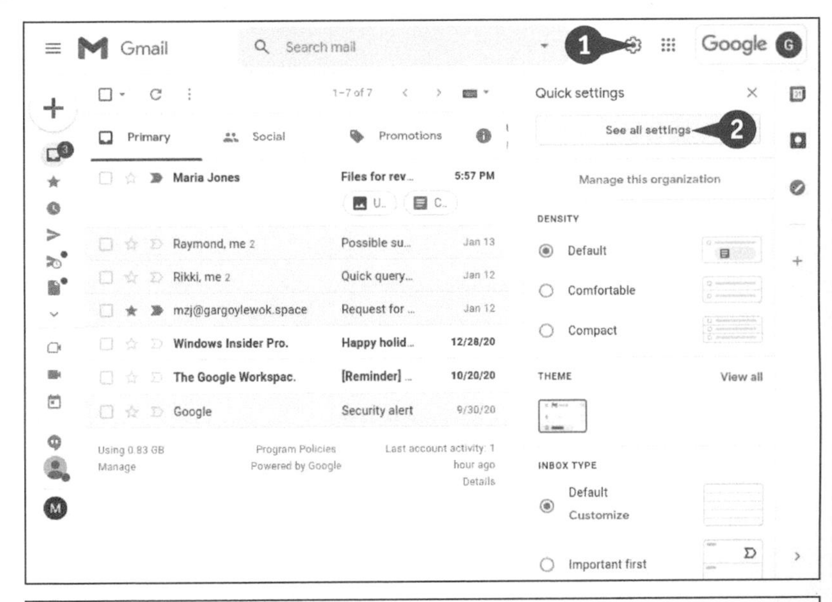

1. In Gmail, click **Settings** (⚙).

   The Quick Settings pane opens.

2. Click **See all settings**.

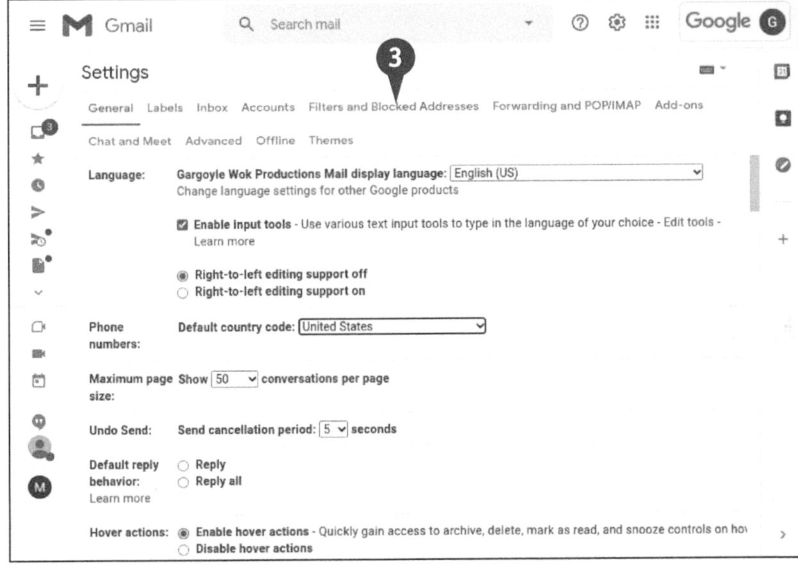

The Settings screen appears.

The General tab normally appears at first.

3. Click **Filters and Blocked Addresses**.

The Filters and Blocked Addresses tab appears.

A The "The Following Filters Are Applied to All Incoming Mail" list shows your existing filters. If you are just getting started with filters, this list may be empty.

B You can click **Create a new filter** to start creating a new filter.

C The "The Following Email Addresses Are Blocked" list shows email addresses you have blocked.

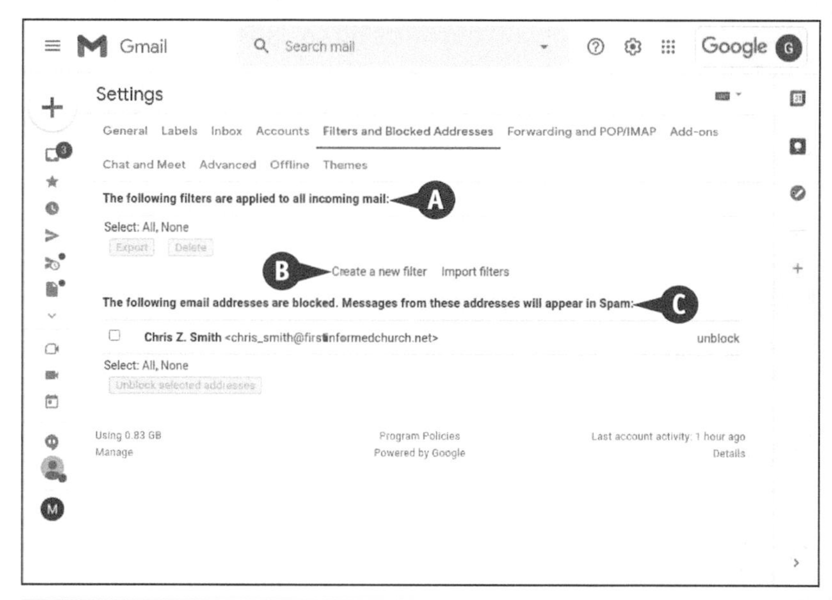

Create a New Filter

1. On the Filters and Blocked Addresses tab, click **Create a new filter**.

   The Create Filter dialog box opens.

2. Click the first field you want to use in the filter.

   For this example, you would click **From**.

3. Enter the data required to specify your first criterion.

   For this example, you would type or paste the appropriate email address.

Note: If Gmail suggests the appropriate item when you start typing, click the item to enter it.

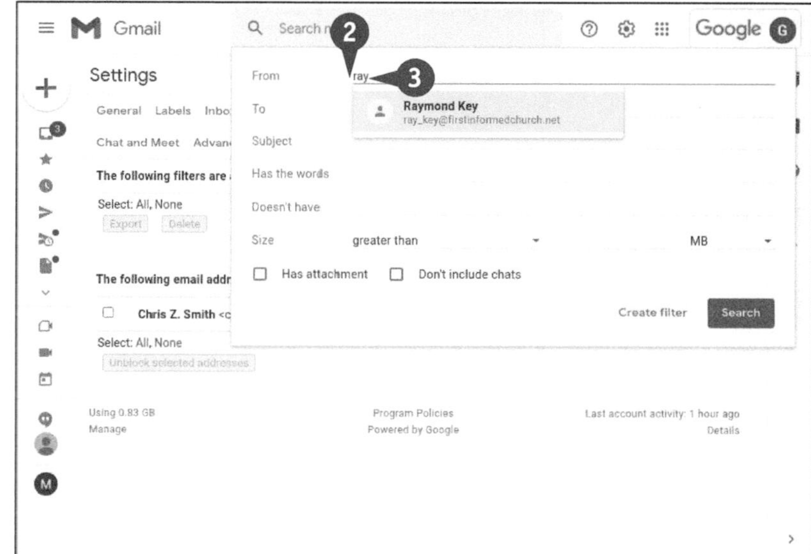

TIP

How else can I start creating a filter?

You can start creating a filter in various other ways. For example, open a message from a sender whose email address you want to use in a filter, click **Menu** (⋮) to open the menu, and then click **Filter messages like this** to open the Filter dialog box with the sender's email address entered in the From field.

continued ▶

Your home base for working with filters is the Filters and Blocked Addresses tab on the Settings screen for Gmail. From this tab, not only can you start creating a new filter of your choosing, but you can also manage, edit, and delete the filters you create. For example, after creating a number of filters, you may choose to apply only some of them to incoming mail rather than apply all of them.

Create Email Filters (continued)

The criterion appears.

4. Specify other criteria, as needed.

   For example, you might click **Subject** and specify a keyword.

   D. You can use the controls on the Size row to specify a minimum size or a maximum size for messages.

   E. You can select **Has attachment** (☑) to include only messages that have attachments.

   F. You can select **Don't include chats** (☑) to exclude Hangouts chats from the filter.

5. When you finish specifying your criteria, click **Create filter**.

   A screen for specifying the filter actions appears.

6. Use the controls in the When a Message Is an Exact Match for Your Search Criteria list to specify what to do with the message.

   For example, select **Apply the label** (☑), click ▾, and then click the label you want to apply.

7. Click **Create filter**.

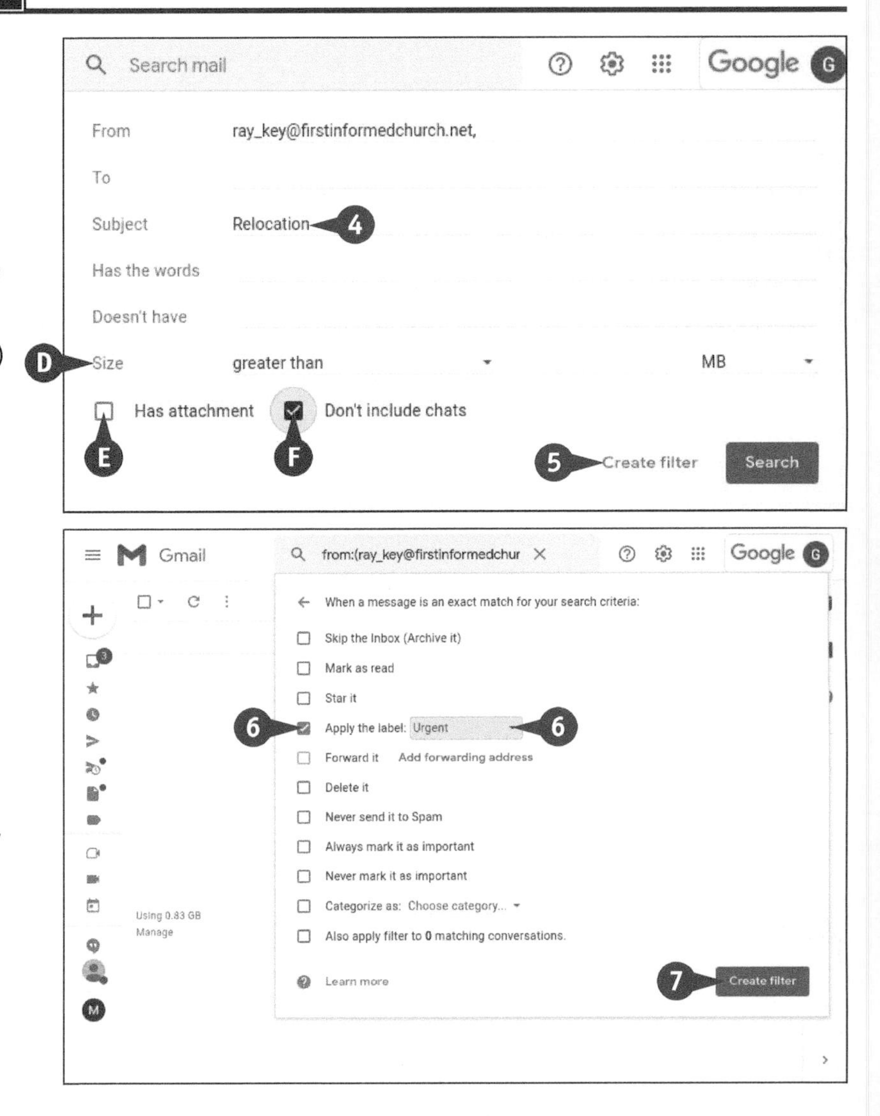

The filter appears in the "The Following Filters Are Applied to All Incoming Mail" list.

8. Select the check box (☑) for the filter.

The filter becomes active.

G You can click **edit** to edit a filter you have created.

H You can click **delete** to delete a filter you have created.

I You can click **Create a new filter** to start creating another filter.

9. When you finish creating filters, click **Inbox** (☐ changes to ☐).

Your Inbox appears.

The filter or filters that you created and applied are now in effect.

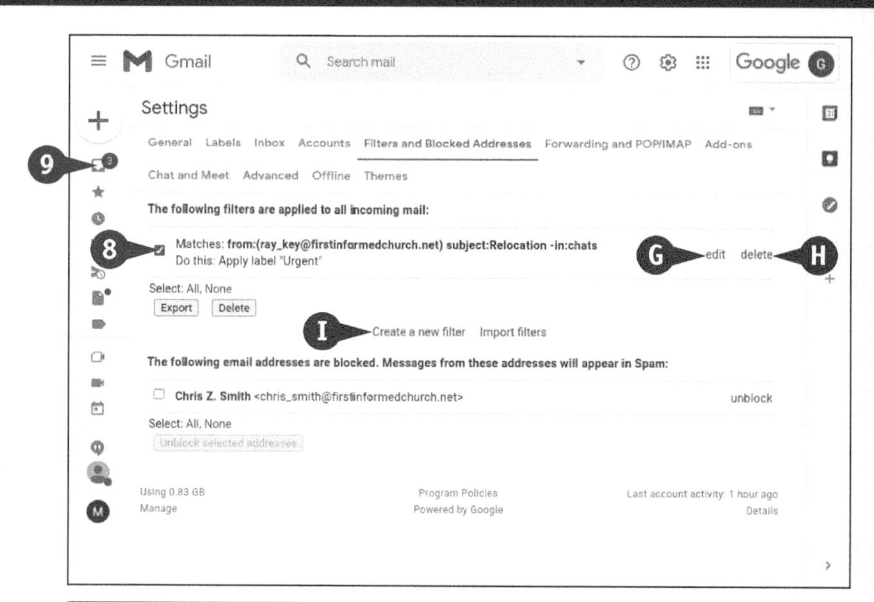

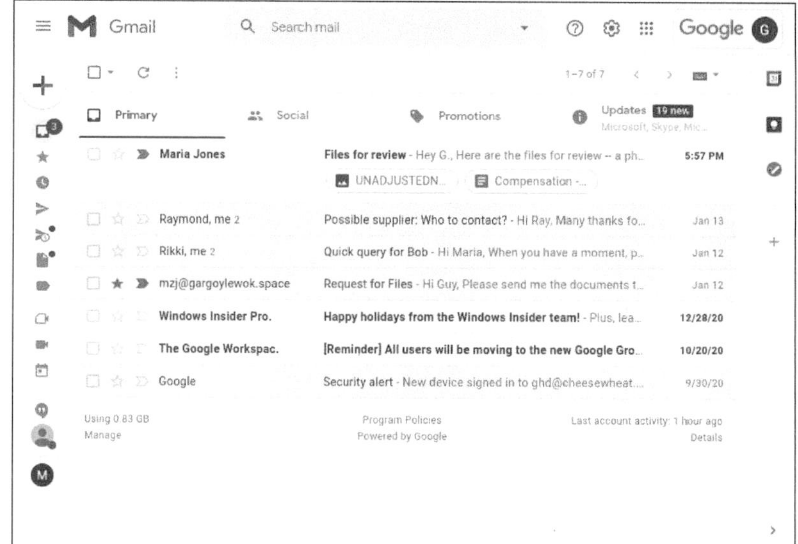

TIP

How can I quickly implement a standard set of filters?

Usually, the quickest way to implement a standard set of filters is to import the filters. For example, if your company or organization has created filters and saved them to a file, you can import them by clicking **Import filters** on the Filters and Blocked Addresses tab of the Settings screen, clicking **Choose file** to display the Select a File to Open dialog box, selecting the file, and then clicking **Open**.

CHAPTER 11

Organizing Your Life

In this chapter, you learn to use some of the key tools that Google Workspace provides for organizing your life. First, you learn about Google's assorted chat apps: Google Meet, Google Hangouts, and Google Chat. Next, you explore the options Google offers for managing and configuring your Google Account. After that, you organize your schedule with Google Calendar and your contact data with Google Contacts. Lastly, you take control of your notes with Google Keep and your tasks with Google Tasks.

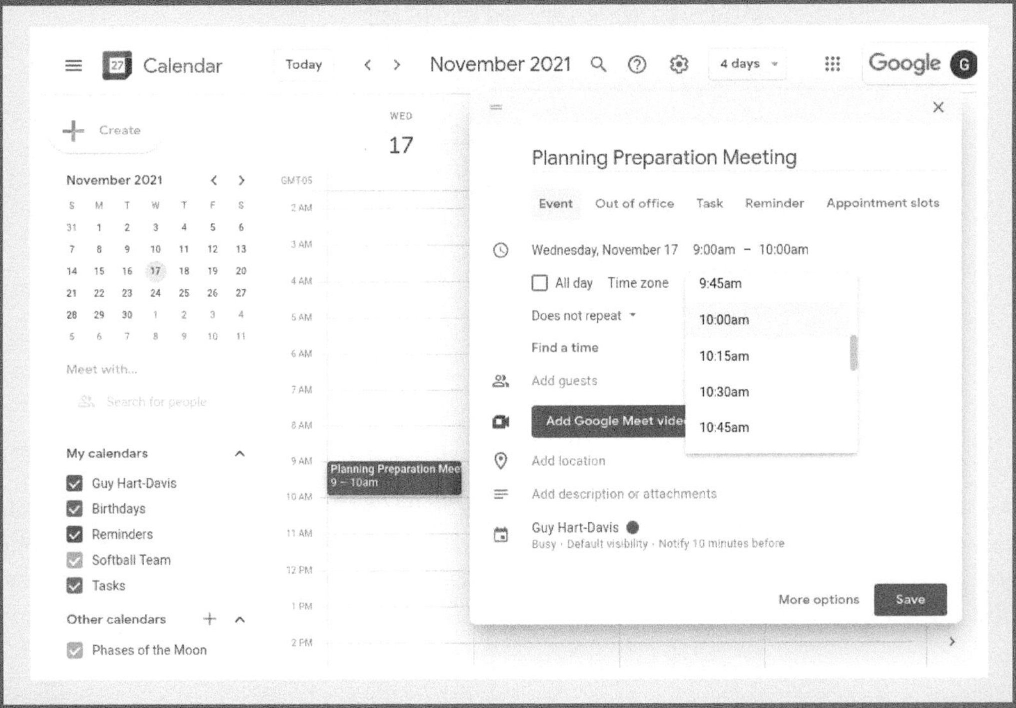

Understanding Google Meet, Google Hangouts, and Google Chat

Google Workspace provides you with three chat and conferencing apps whose capabilities overlap: Google Meet, Google Hangouts, and Google Chat. This section introduces you to these apps, explaining their functionality and their key differences.

Google has integrated both Google Meet and Google Hangouts into Gmail, enabling you to start a chat or a meeting directly from the browser tab containing your email. You may find this capability helpful for using text chat to resolve queries that arise while you are working on email. You can also run each app independently from the Google Apps pop-up panel.

Understanding Google Meet

Google Meet is a business-grade videoconferencing app that enables you to pack up to 250 users into a single meeting. Google Meet is available only to Google Workspace users, whereas both Google Hangouts and Google Chat are freely available to anyone who has a Google Account. Google Meet also includes features that Google Hangouts does not, such as recording your videoconferences and taking polls of attendees.

The standard way to launch Google Meet is to click **Google Apps** (⋮⋮⋮) and then click **Meet** (▣), but you can launch Google Meet from the Meet section of the left panel in Gmail. Click **New meeting** (■, A) to open the Share Your New Meeting dialog box, and then click **Send Invite** (<, B).

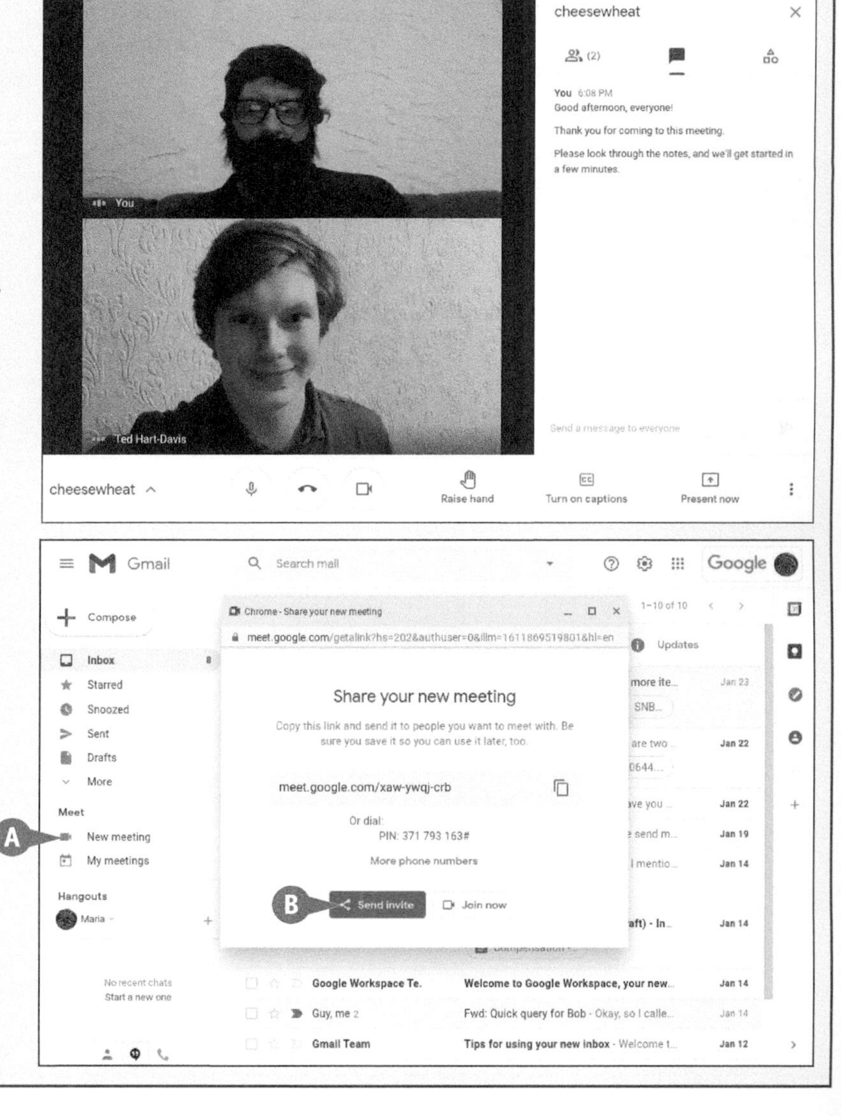

Understanding Google Hangouts

Google Hangouts is Google's all-in-one app for chat, audio calls, and video calls. Google Hangouts is available to anyone with a Google Account.

To launch Google Hangouts, click **Google Apps** (⋮⋮⋮), and then click **Hangouts** (💬). Alternatively, starting from the Gmail web app, you can quickly start a chat with another Google Account holder through the Google Hangouts service. The chat is primarily text based, but you can also send emoji and photos. You can turn a private chat into a group chat by adding more members to it.

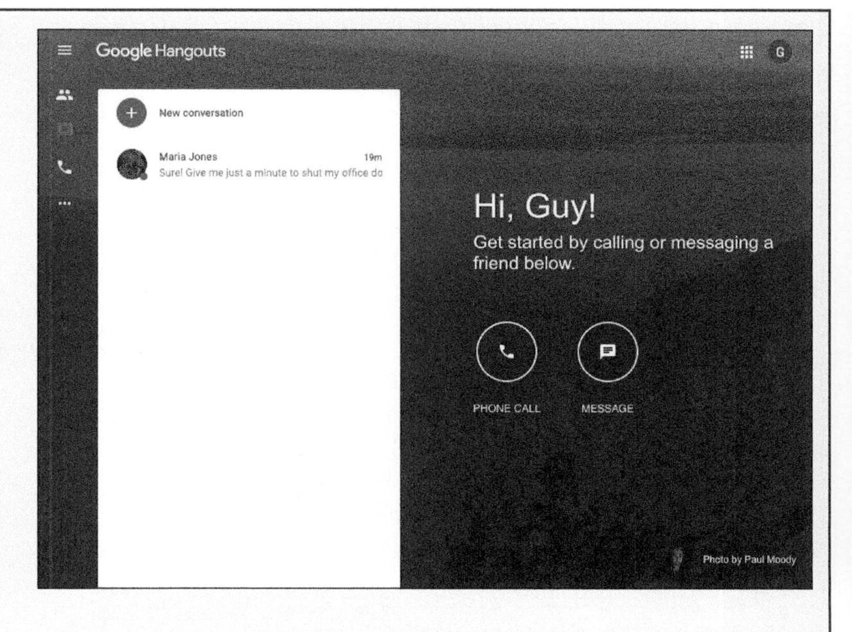

Understanding Google Chat

Google Chat, which you can launch by clicking **Google Apps** (⋮⋮⋮) and then clicking **Chat** (💬), is a chat app that focuses on text-based communication. You can create chat rooms to corral separate groups of people, and you can use bots to assign tasks and schedule meetings.

Google Chat enables you to share files from Google Drive and to launch video meetings in Google Meet.

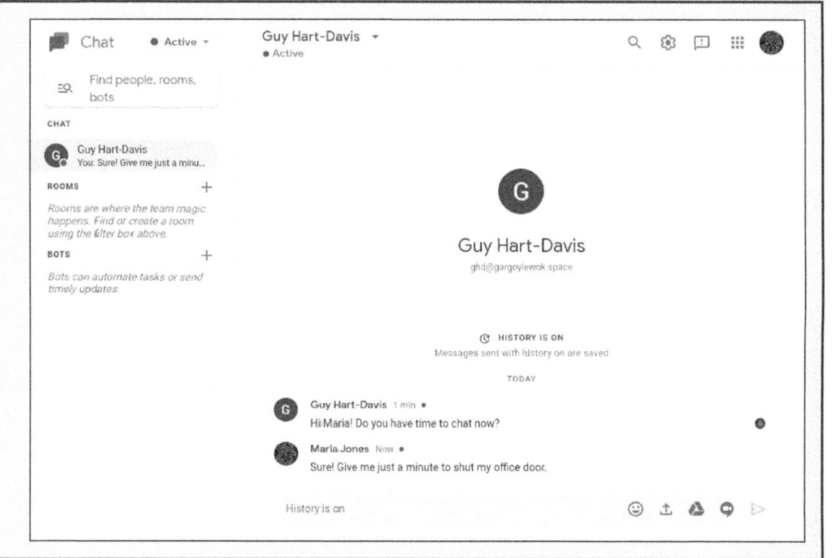

Manage Your Google Account

Your Google Account is essential to you using Google Workspace effectively. You can use the Google Account app to configure your account. Be aware that your organization's Google Workspace administrator may let you configure only some settings.

This section gives you an overview of the many configuration settings the Google Account app offers. A good starting point is to review your personal information and decide which parts of it to share with your colleagues, but it is a good idea to also run the Security Checkup tool to resolve any security issues that Google has identified.

Open the Management Screen for Your Google Account

In Google Drive or another Google Workspace app, click **Google Account** (such as M) to open the Google Account panel, and then click **Manage your Google Account.**

The Google Account management screen appears in a new browser tab. This screen contains seven tabs: Home ( ), Personal Info ( ), Data & Personalization ( ), Security ( ), People & Sharing ( ), Payments & Subscriptions ( ), and About ( ). The Home tab normally appears at first.

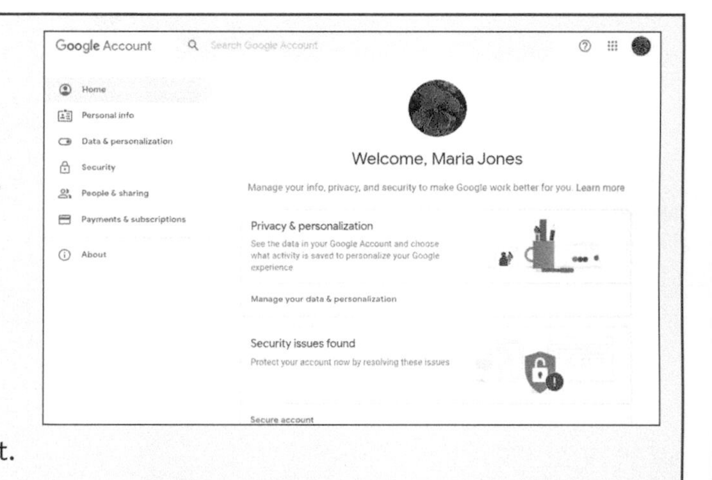

Take Actions on the Home Tab

The Home tab of the Google Account screen provides links to other areas.

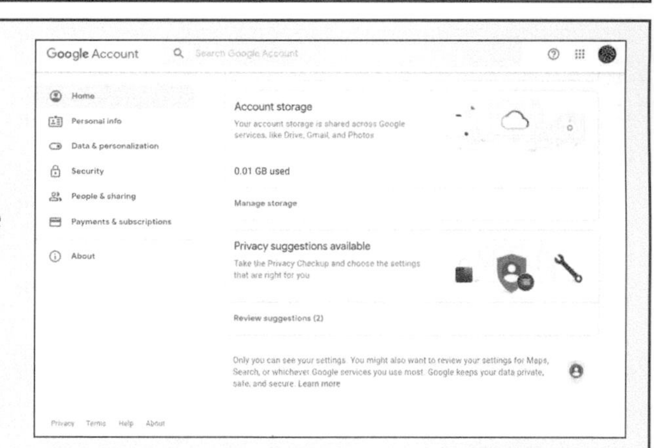

- In the Privacy & Personalization box, you can click **Manage your data & personalization** to display the Data & Personalization tab.
- If the Security Issues Found box appears, you can click **Secure** to launch the Security Checkup tool.
- In the Account Storage box, you can see how much storage you have used, and you can click **Manage storage** to display the Drive Storage screen, which shows details of your usage. Normally, an administrator manages storage, so you cannot make changes here.
- If the Privacy Suggestions Available box appears, you can click **Review suggestions** to display the Privacy Checkup screen.

Review and Amend Your Personal Information

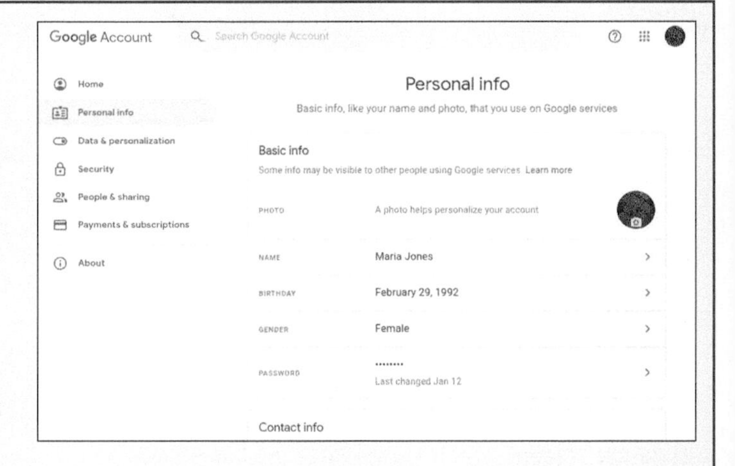

Click **Personal info** (▤) in the left pane to display the Personal Info tab. Here, you can review the personal information that Google services use for you. Depending on how your organization's administrator has configured Google Workspace, you may be able to edit some information.

The Basic Info box shows your photo, your name, your birthday, your gender, and when you last changed your password.

The Contact Info box contains your email address or addresses and your recovery phone number for your account.

The Choose What Others See box gives you access to the About Me screen, on which you can choose which pieces of information are available to whom.

Choose Data & Personalization Options

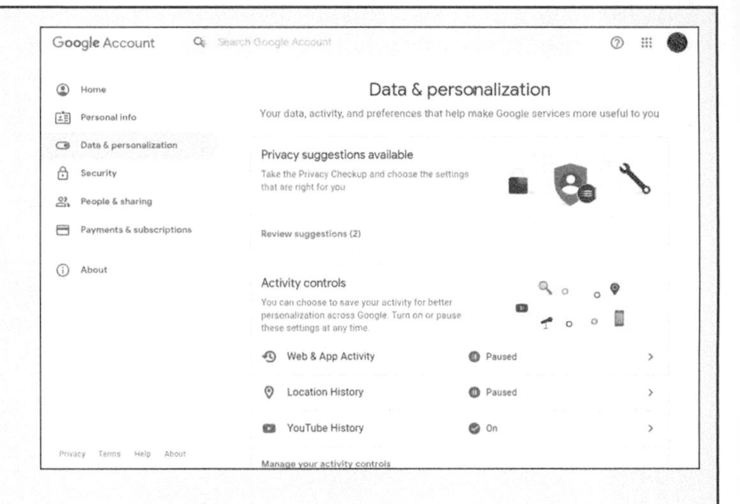

Click **Data & personalization** (⊂⊃) in the left pane to display the Data & Personalization tab, which provides controls for specifying how Google handles your data and activities.

If the Privacy Suggestions Available box appears, you can click **Review suggestions** to display the Privacy Checkup screen.

The Activity Controls box shows your current settings for Web & App Activity, Location History, and YouTube History. Each of these can be On (✔) or Paused (⏸). To change these settings, click **Manage your activity controls**, and then work on the Activity Control screen.

continued ►

The Google Account app includes settings for controlling which of your online activities — Web & App Activity, Location History, and YouTube History — Google tracks. You can also choose to enable or disable ad personalization.

To protect your Google Account, you will likely want to turn on 2-Step Verification, which adds a second authentication step to sign-ins on computers or devices you have not designated as trusted. You can turn on 2-Step Verification on the Security tab in the Google Account app.

Choose Data & Personalization Options (continued)

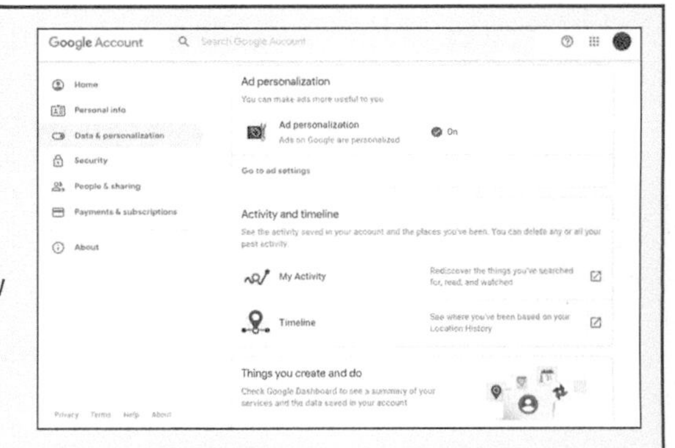

The Ad Personalization box shows whether ad personalization is on or off. You can click **Go to ad settings** to display the Ad Personalization screen, where you can change the setting.

In the Activity and Timeline box, you can click **My Activity** to display the My Google Activity screen, on which you can review your Web & App Activity, your Location History, and your YouTube History. Alternatively, click **Timeline** to display the Timeline screen, which shows your movements.

The lower parts of the Data & Personalization screen enable you to visit Google Dashboard, review your account storage, download or delete your data, and set general preferences for Google services on the web.

Review Security Settings and Recommendations

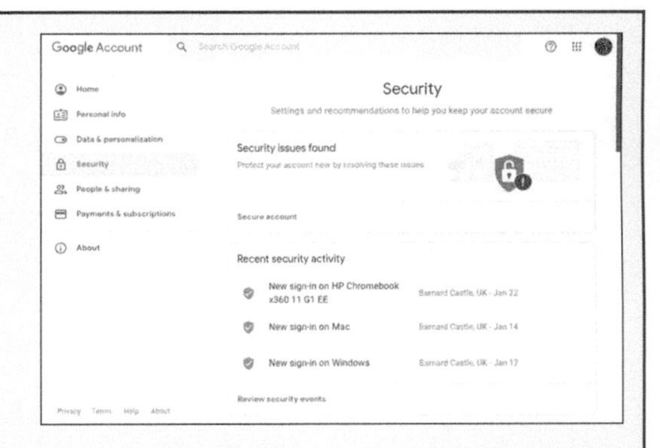

Click **Security** (🔒) in the left pane to display the Security tab, where you can review security issues and recommendations and adjust your settings.

If the Security Issues Found box appears, click **Secure account** to display the Security Checkup screen, and then work through the issues it identifies. For example, you may need to add means of verification or authentication.

The Recent Security Activity box shows recent security events, such as sign-ins from different locations or devices. You can click **Review security events** to see more.

In the Signing In to Google box, you can click **Password** to change your password, and you can click **2-Step Verification** to enable or disable the 2-Step Verification security mechanism. (An administrator may prevent you from changing these settings.)

In the Ways We Can Verify It's You box, you can set or change your recovery phone numbers and recovery email addresses.

Review People & Sharing Settings

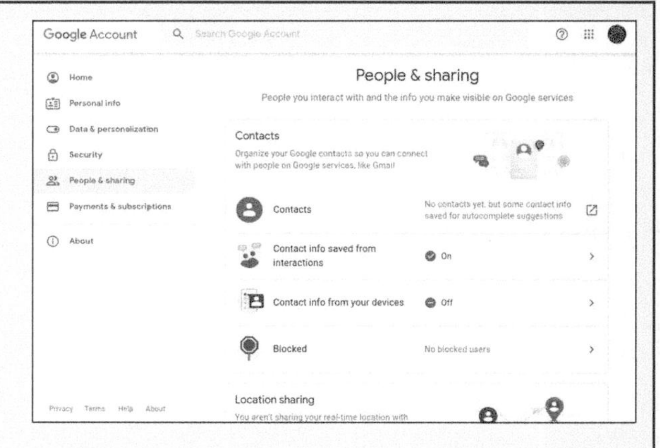

Click **People & sharing** in the left pane to display the People & Sharing tab. On this tab, the Contacts box provides options for saving contact information from interactions, such as messages, and for gathering contact information from your devices. You can also review and prune your list of blocked users.

The Location Sharing box shows whether you are sharing your real-time location with anyone on Google. You can click **Manage location sharing** to display the Location Sharing screen for more details.

The Choose What Others See box gives you access to the personal information you make visible to other people via Google services.

Review Payments and Subscriptions Settings

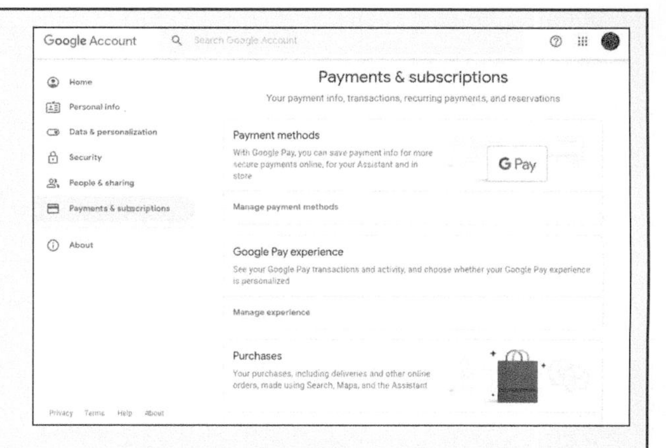

Click **Payments & subscriptions** in the left pane to display the Payments & Subscriptions tab. Here, you can click **Manage payment methods** in the Payment Methods box to display the Google Pay screen. You can click **Manage experience** in the Google Pay Experience box to display the Manage Your Google Pay Experience page, which lets you view your transactions and configure your Google Pay settings. You can click **Manage purchases** to visit the Purchases screen, where you can review purchases made using Search, Maps, and the Google Assistant. You can click **Manage subscriptions** to display the Subscriptions page, which lists your subscriptions. And you can click **Manage reservations** to go to the Reservations page, which shows reservations made using Search, Maps, and the Google Assistant.

Navigate the Google Calendar Interface

Google Calendar is a web-based calendaring service that enables you to manage multiple calendars and create events, reminders, and tasks.

Google Calendar packs a large amount of data into its interface. You can choose what period of time to display — 1 day, 4 days, 1 week, 1 month, or 1 year — or instead, display a straightforward list of events. You can choose whether to show weekend days or hide them to reduce the amount of information displayed. You can also choose whether to show events you have declined or to hide them.

Navigate the Google Calendar Interface

1. From Google Drive, or from any app that displays the Google Apps icon (⠿), click **Google Apps** (⠿).

   The Google Apps panel opens.

2. Click **Calendar** (31).

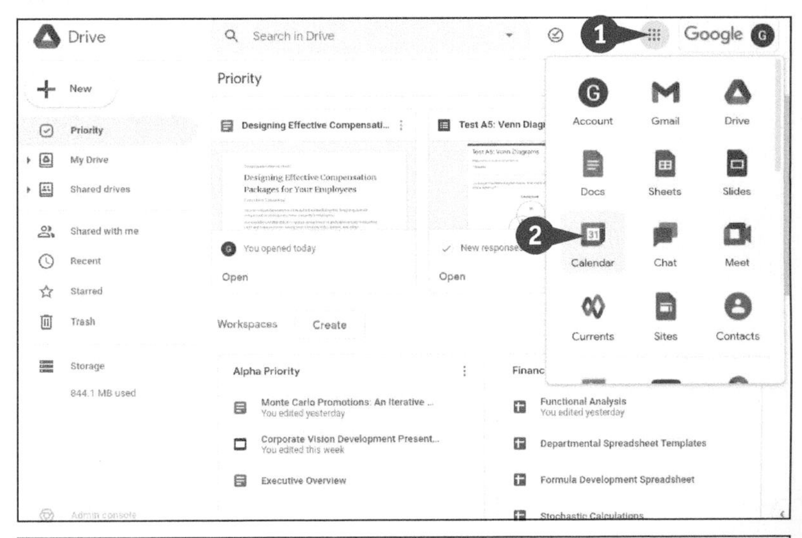

Google Calendar opens.

A The panel on the left is the Main Menu.

B The calendar control enables you to navigate by date.

C The Search for People (👥) box enables you to search your calendar by people.

D The My Calendars list and Other Calendars list let you control which calendars appear.

E Your calendar entries for the selected date range appear.

3. Click **Main menu** (≡).

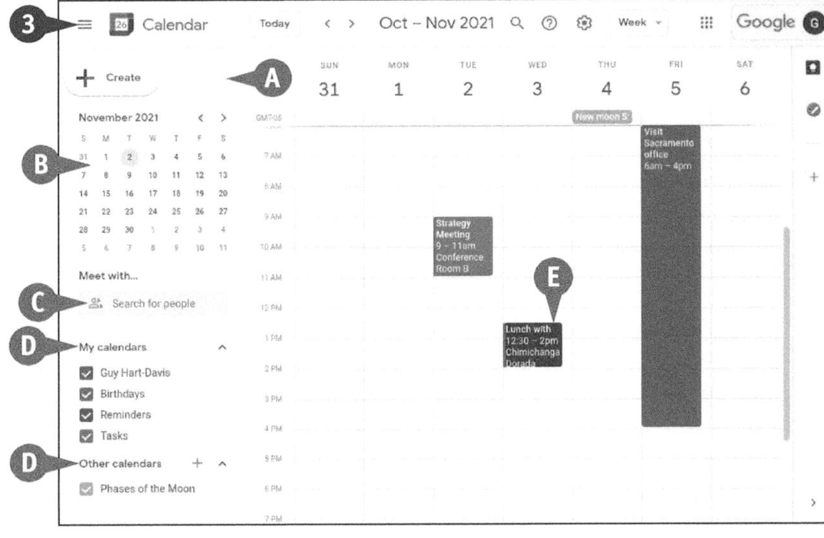

The Main Menu closes, giving more space for the calendar entries.

F You can click **Hide side panel** (>) to hide the side panel, if needed.

4 Click **Show** (▾).

The Show pop-up menu opens.

5 Click **Day**, **Week**, **Month**, **Year**, **Schedule**, or **4 days**, as appropriate.

Note: Click **Schedule** to display a list of your upcoming events in date order.

G You can click **Show weekends** to display or hide weekend days.

H You can click **Show declined events** to display or hide events you have declined.

Google Calendar shows the time period you chose.

I You can click **Today** to display the current date.

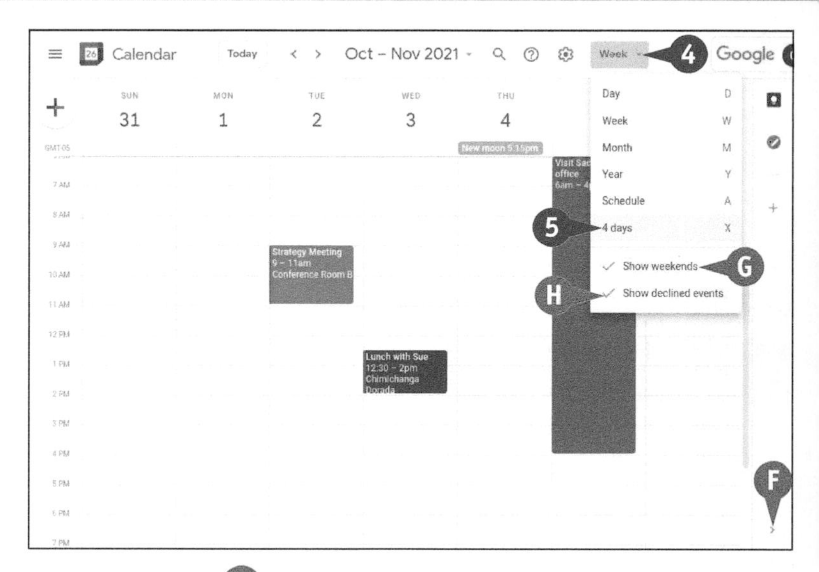

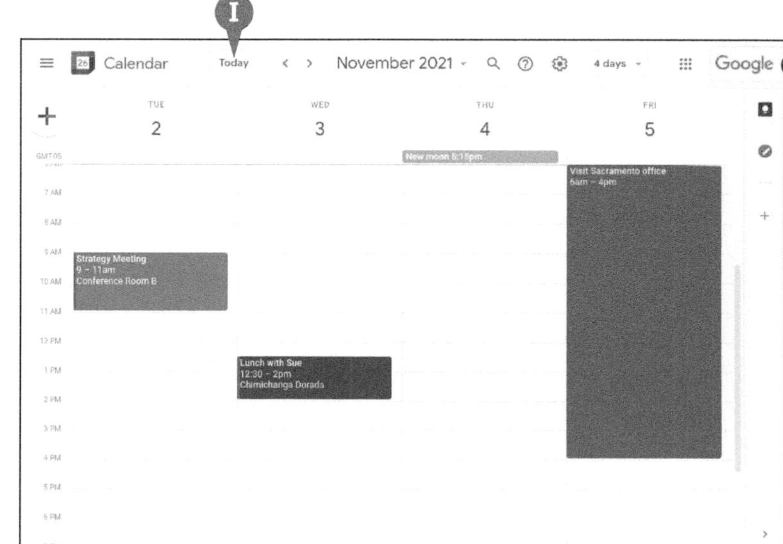

TIPS

What other way can I use Google Calendar?
In Gmail, Google Drive, and other apps that display the side panel, you can click **Calendar** (31) to display the Today list in the side panel, giving you quick access to your events. You can click **Open in new tab** (↗) to open Google Calendar in a separate tab so that you can use it fully.

Should I allow Google Calendar to give me "better" notifications?
Better notifications contain more data, so they are usually helpful. If Google Calendar displays the Want to Get Better Notifications? dialog box, asking your permission to display notifications through the browser, click **Continue**. In the calendar.google.com Wants to Show Notifications dialog box that opens, click **Allow**.

Create a New Calendar

Google Calendar enables you to create as many calendars as you need to separate your events into logical categories. Google Calendar starts you off with four default calendars: a calendar that bears your name, a Birthdays calendar, a Reminders calendar, and a Tasks calendar. These calendars appear in the My Calendars list in the Main Menu in Google Calendar by default.

You can create other calendars as needed. For example, you may want to create separate calendars for work events, home events, and other categories of commitments that you will track in Google Calendar.

Create a New Calendar

Note: If the Main Menu is not displayed on the left of the Google Calendar window, click **Main menu** (☰) to display it.

1. Click **Add other calendars** (+).

   The pop-up menu opens.

2. Click **Create new calendar**.

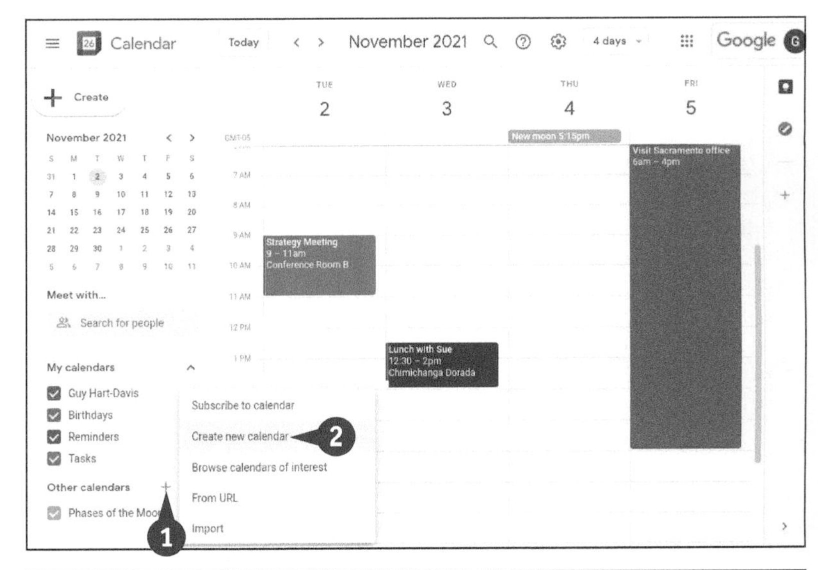

The Settings screen appears, showing the Create New Calendar screen in the Add Calendar section.

3. Click **Name** and type the name for the calendar.

4. Click **Description** and type a description that will help you — and anyone with whom you share the calendar — grasp the calendar's contents.

5. Verify the time zone is correct. If not, click **Time zone** (▾), and then click the appropriate time zone.

6. Click **Create calendar**.

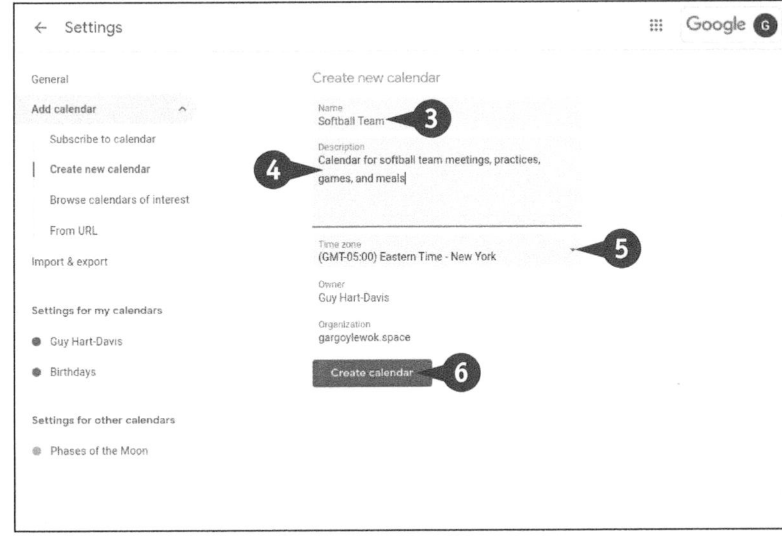

A pop-up message appears, confirming the creation of the calendar.

A You can click **Configure** to configure further settings on the calendar.

7 Click **Back** (←).

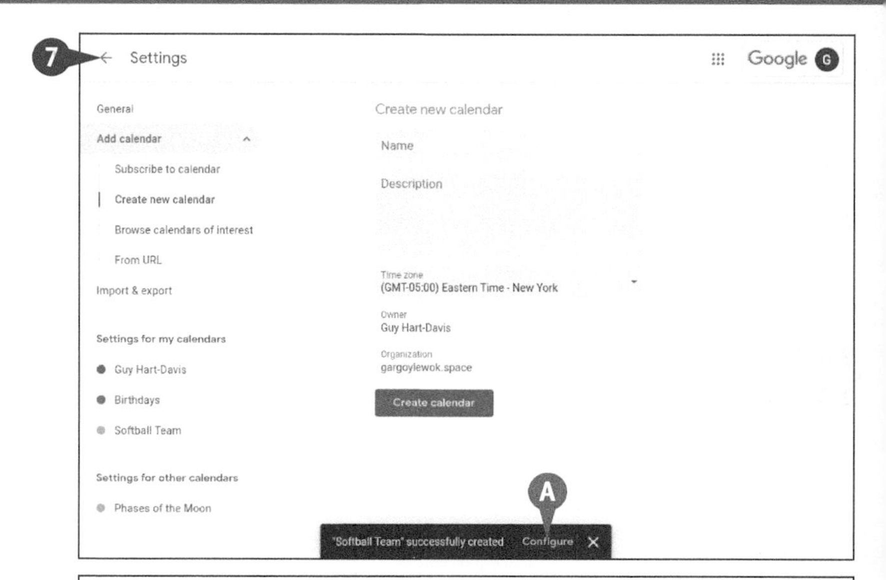

The Calendar interface appears again.

B The new calendar appears in the My Calendars list.

C You can toggle the display of a calendar's events by clicking its check box (such as ☑ or ☑).

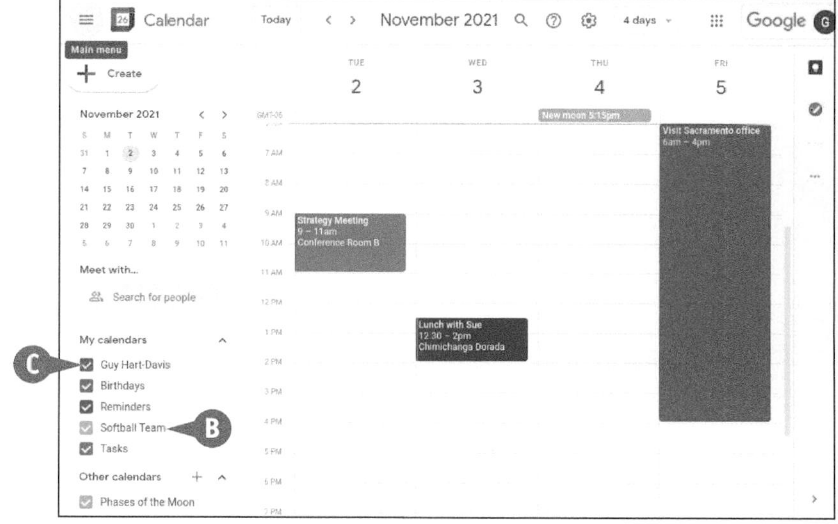

TIP

How do I import a calendar I have exported from another calendaring app?

You can import calendar files in Apple's iCal format or CSV — comma-separated values — format. Start by exporting the calendar to one of these formats.

Click **Add other calendars** (+) to open the pop-up menu, and then click **Import.** The Settings screen appears, showing the Import screen in the Import & Export section. Click **Select file from your computer** (⬆) to display the Select a File to Open dialog box, click the calendar file, and then click **Open.** Click **Add to calendar** (▾), and then click the calendar into which you want to import the events. Click **Import.**

Create an Event in Google Calendar

Google Calendar enables you to create events for your time commitments, such as appointments, meetings, or trips. Your events appear as separate items on the grid, so you can see what you are supposed to do when.

You can create an event either for a specific length of time, such as 30 minutes or 2 hours, or for an entire day. You can create an event that occurs only once or an event that repeats one or more times on a schedule.

Create an Event in Google Calendar

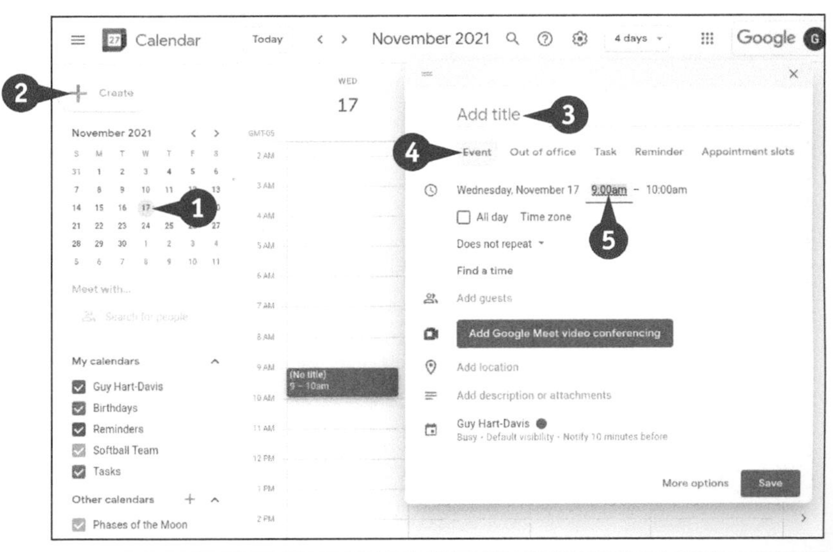

1. In Google Calendar, click the date for the event.
2. Click **Create** (+).

   The New Event dialog box opens.
3. Click **Add title** and type the title for the event.
4. On the tab bar, make sure Event is selected. If not, click **Event.**
5. In the time readout, click the start time.

   The time controls appear.

Note: Google Calendar sets the new event's length to the default duration. See the tip for how to change the default duration.

A. You can select **All day** (☑) to create an all-day event.

6. Click the start time.

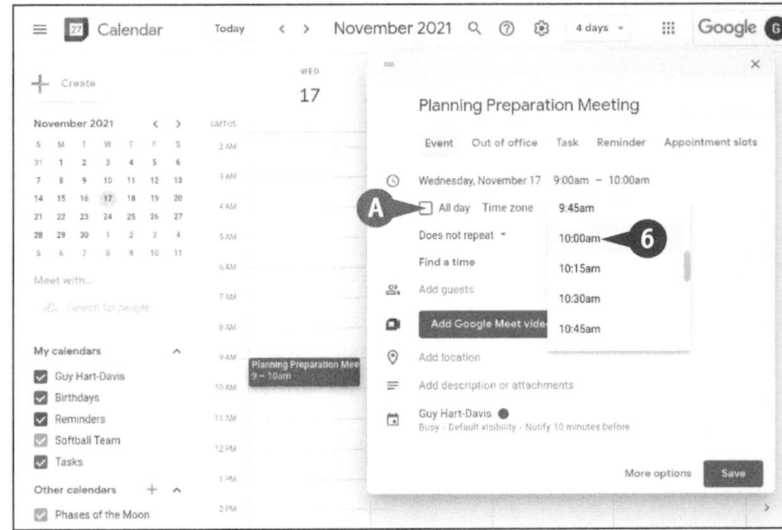

Google Calendar enters the new start time and updates the end time based on the default duration.

B You can click the end time and change it, if needed.

7 Click **Add location** and type the location.

Note: As you type the location, Google Calendar suggests matching locations from Google Maps. You can click a location to enter it.

8 Click **Save**.

The New Event dialog box closes.

C The new event appears on your calendar.

D A pop-up message saying *Event saved* appears for a few seconds.

E You can click **Undo** to delete the event.

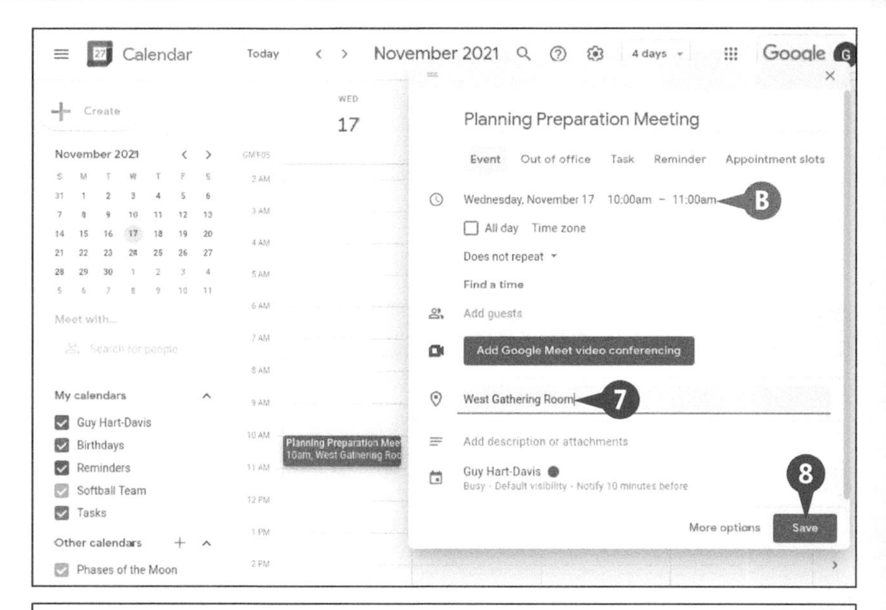

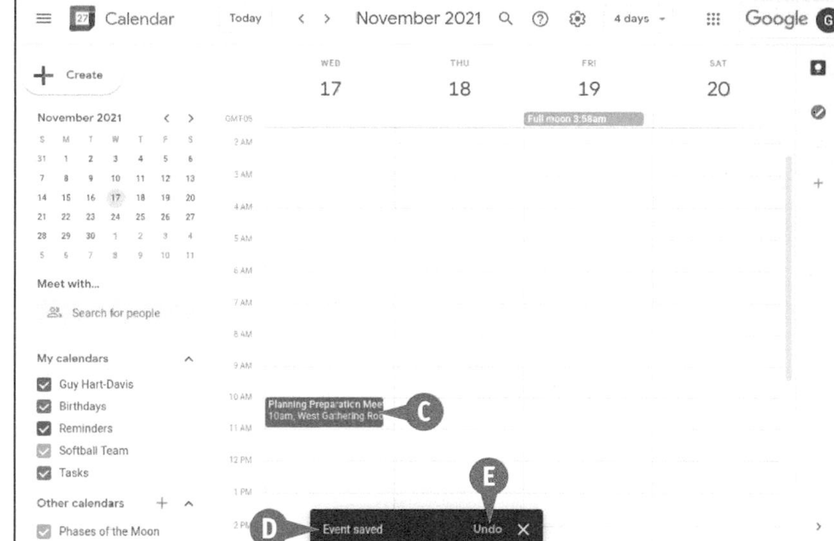

TIP

How do I change the default duration for new events?

In Google Calendar, click **Settings** (⚙) to open the Settings menu, and then click **Settings** to display the Settings screen. In the General section of the sidebar on the left, click **Event settings** to display the Event Settings section. Click **Default duration** (▾) to open the pop-up menu, and then click **15 minutes**, **20 minutes**, **30 minutes**, **45 minutes**, **60 minutes**, **90 minutes**, or **120 minutes**, as appropriate. Select **Speedy meetings** (☑) to trim 5 minutes off meetings of 45 minutes or shorter and to trim 10 minutes off longer meetings. Click **Back** (←) to return to the Calendar interface.

Share a Calendar with Other People

Google Calendar enables you to share your main calendar, or a calendar you have created, with other people so that they can view its contents. The people you specify can then access the shared calendar by subscribing to it, as explained in the following section, "Subscribe to a Shared Calendar."

You can choose what level of access other people have to your shared calendar. For example, you can specify that one person can see all the details of events in a calendar, whereas another person can see only that you are busy during those events.

Share a Calendar with Other People

Note: If the Main Menu is not displayed on the left of the Google Calendar window, click **Main menu** (≡) to display it.

Note: If the My Calendars list is collapsed, click **My calendars** (⌄ changes to ⌃).

1. Move the cursor over the calendar you want to share.

   Pop-up controls for that calendar appear.

2. Click **Menu** (⋮).

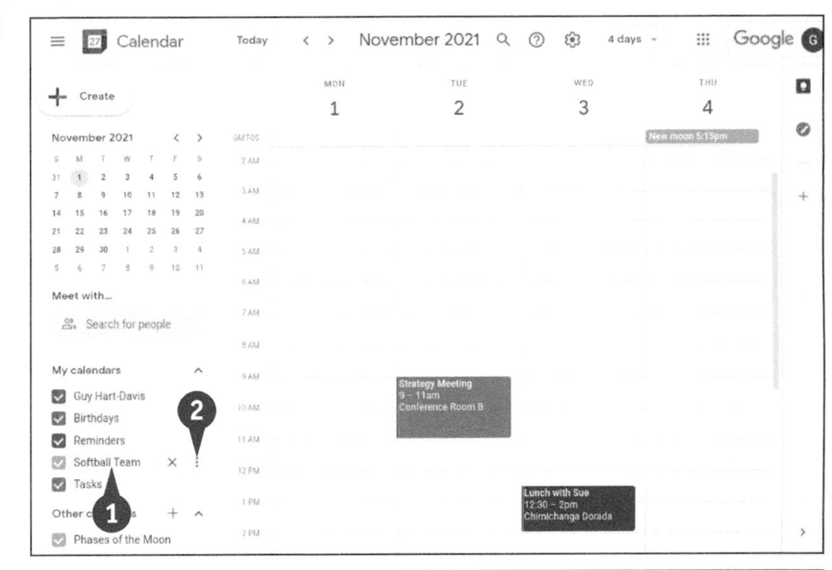

   The menu opens.

3. Click **Settings and sharing**.

Ⓐ You can click a color button to change the color assigned to the calendar.

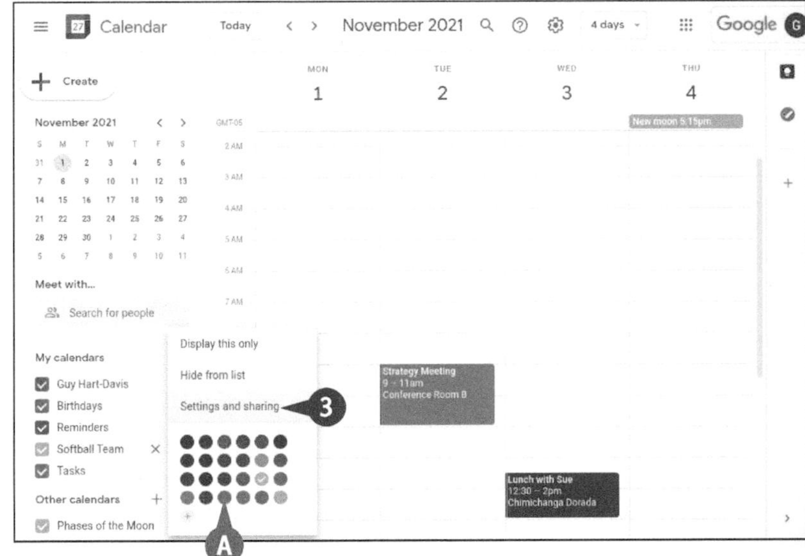

The Settings screen appears, showing the Calendar Settings screen for the calendar.

4 Click **Share with specific people**.

The Share with Specific People screen appears.

Note: You cannot share your Birthdays calendar, your Reminders calendar, or your Tasks calendar.

5 Click **Add people** (+).

The Share with Specific People dialog box opens.

6 Click **Add email or name**, and then click the person with whom you want to share the calendar.

B A button shows the person's name.

7 Click **Permissions** (▼), and then click the appropriate permission. See the tip for advice.

8 Click **Send**.

The Share with Specific People dialog box closes.

9 Click **Back** (←).

The calendar interface appears again.

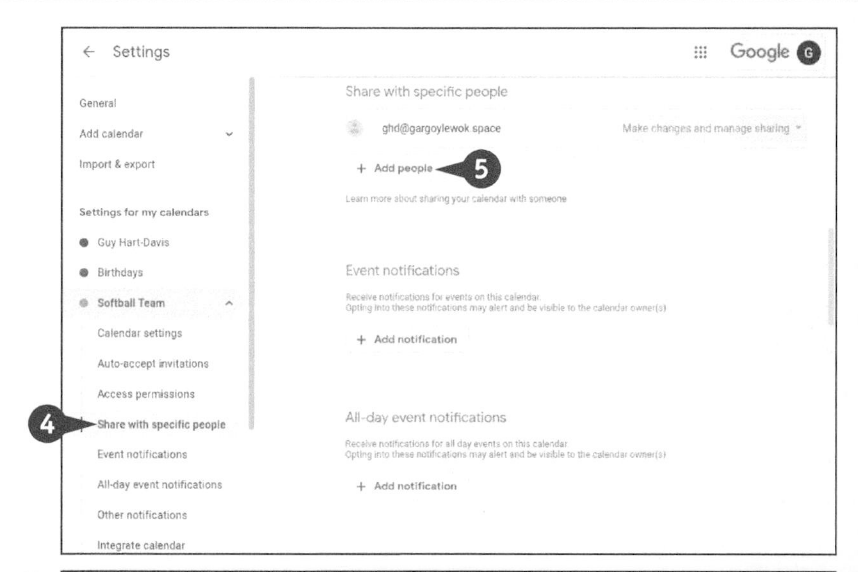

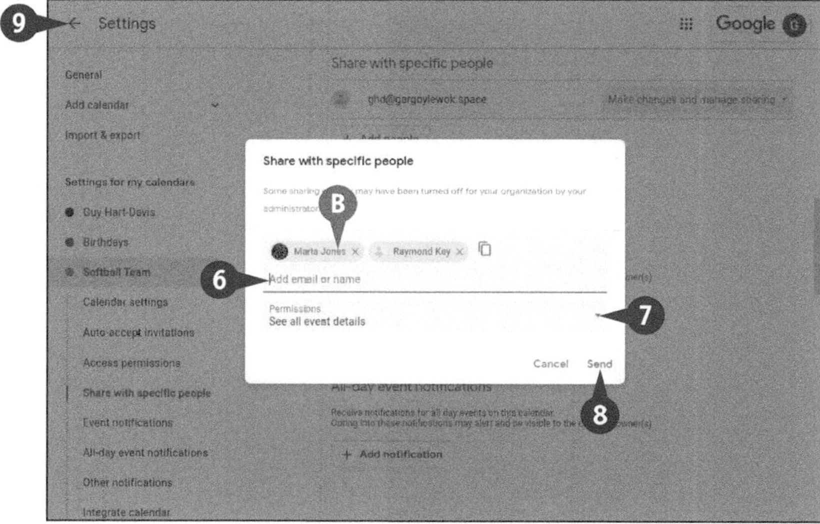

TIP

Which permissions should I assign when I share a calendar?

Normally, you would assign the See All Event Details permission, enabling the person to see each event's details but not change them. If you are sharing the calendar only so that the person can see whether you are free or busy at a particular time, assign the See Only Free/Busy (Hide Details) permission instead.

If the person will help you manage your calendar, assign the Make Changes to Events permission. If you want to let the person not only make changes but also share the calendar with others, assign the Make Changes and Manage Sharing permission.

Subscribe to a Shared Calendar

Just as you can share a calendar with others, you can subscribe to a calendar that one of your contacts has shared with you on Google Calendar. Your contact gets to control the level of access you receive, from being able to see only when the contact is free or busy to being able to see all the details of events, making changes to events, or even making changes and managing sharing.

Google Calendar also enables you to add published calendars, such as those for sports teams or public bodies.

Subscribe to a Shared Calendar

Note: If the Main Menu is not displayed on the left of the Google Calendar window, click **Main menu** (☰) to display it.

1. In Google Calendar, click **Add other calendars** (+).

   The pop-up menu opens.

2. Click **Subscribe to calendar**.

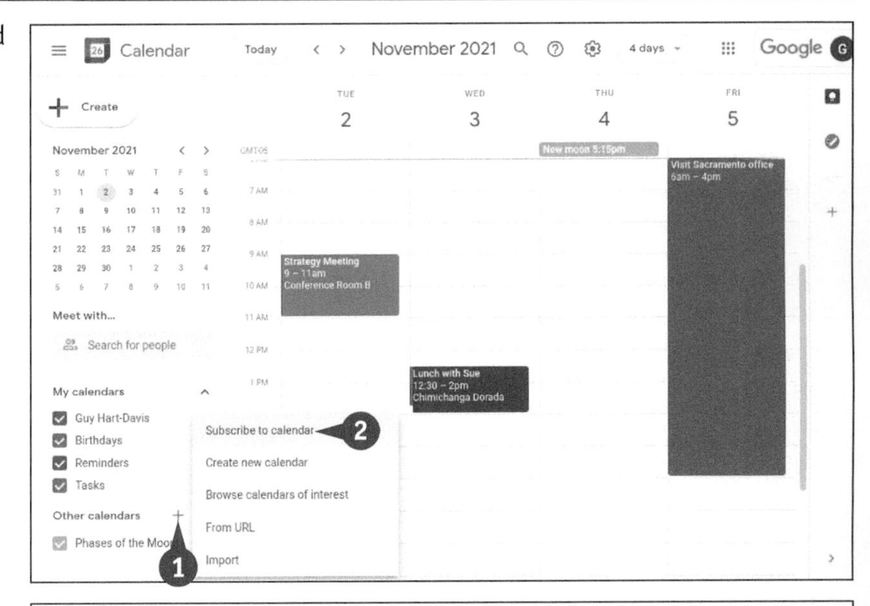

   The Settings screen appears, showing the Subscribe to Calendar screen in the Add Calendar section.

3. Click **Add calendar**.

   A pop-up menu opens showing available contacts.

4. Click the contact who is sharing the calendar.

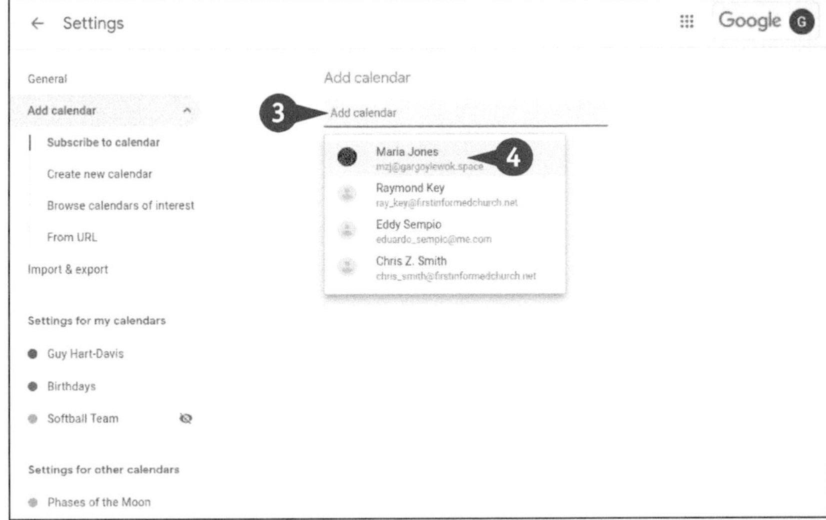

The contact's email address appears in the Name box.

5. Optionally, edit the default name for clarity.

6. Optionally, type a description of the calendar to make it easier to identify.

A. In the Access Permissions area, you can select **Make available to public** (☑) if you want to make the calendar available to the public. If you do this, click the pop-up menu button (▾), and then click **See only free/busy (hide details)** or **See all event details**, as needed.

B. If you do not want to make the calendar available to the public, you can select **Make Available for [Your Organization]** (☑) to make the calendar available to everyone in your organization. If you do this, click the pop-up menu button (▾), and then click **See only free/busy (hide details)**, **See all event details**, **Make changes to events**, or **Make changes and manage sharing**, as needed.

C. You can select **Show calendar info in other Google apps, limited by access permissions** (☑) to allow the calendar's information to be displayed in other apps.

7. Click **Back** (←).

The calendar interface appears again.

The calendar you added appears in the Other Calendars list in the Main Menu.

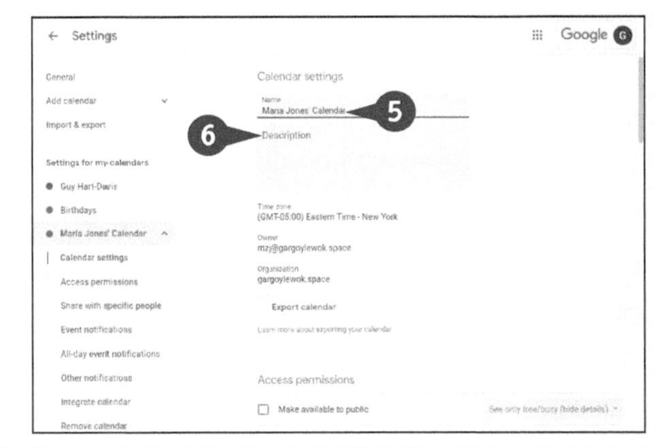

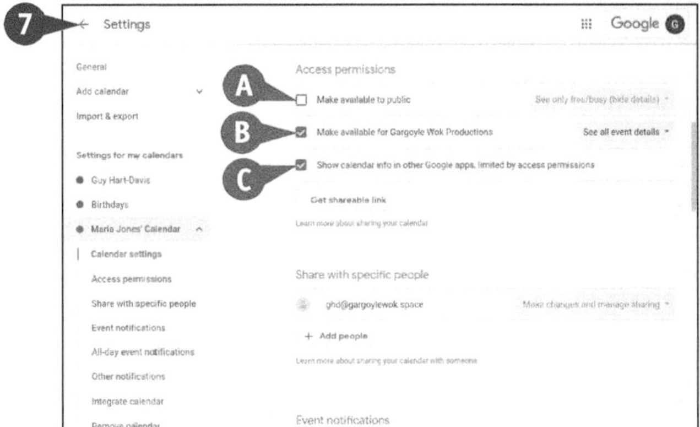

TIP

How do I add a sports team's calendar to Google Calendar?

You can add a published calendar, such as a sports team's calendar or a holidays calendar, by using the Browse Calendars of Interest feature. In the Main Menu, click **Add other calendars** (+) to open the pop-up menu, and then click **Browse calendars of interest**. The Browse Calendars of Interest screen in the Add Calendar category of Settings appears. Go to the Holidays list, the Sports list, or the Other list; locate the calendar; and then select its check box (☑). The calendar then appears in your Other Calendars list.

Add Someone to Your Contacts

Google Contacts is a web-based database that enables you to store information about your contacts. Google Contacts stores the data for each contact in a contact record that contains storage slots for many different items of information, from the person's names and phone numbers to their email addresses and photo.

To add a contact, you create a new contact record and enter the person's data on it.

Add Someone to Your Contacts

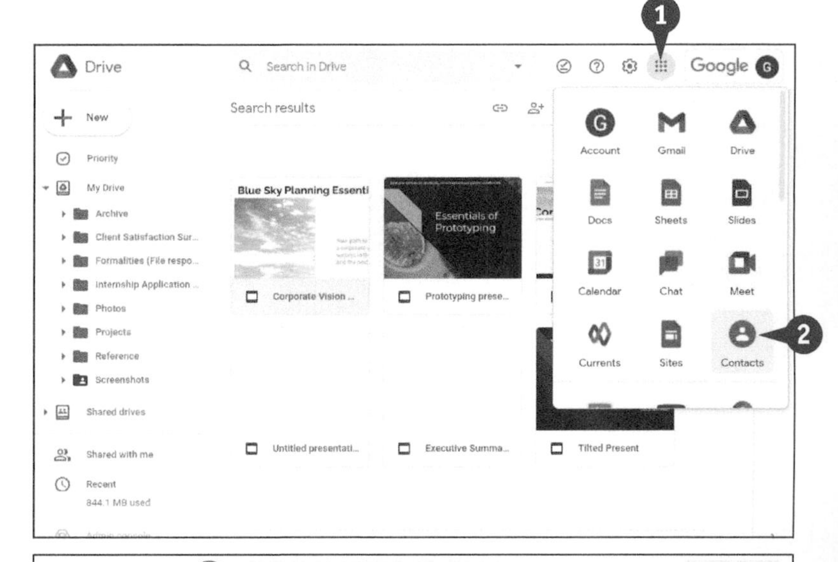

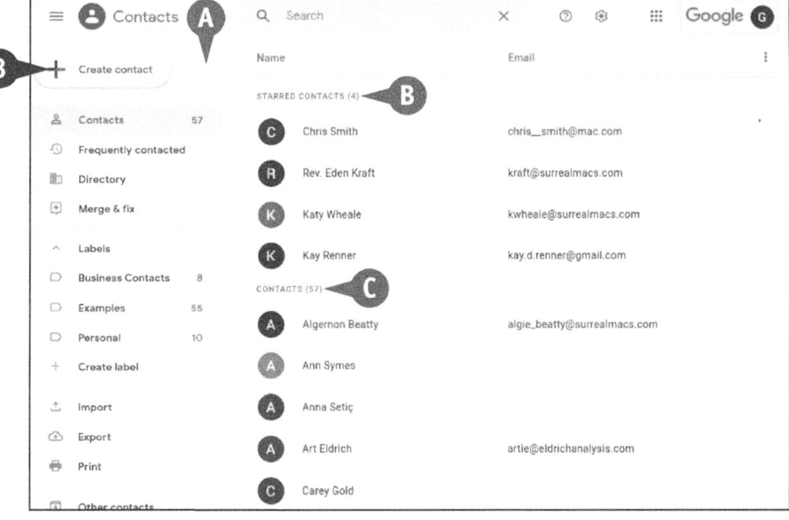

1. From Google Drive, or from any app that displays the Google Apps icon (⠿), click **Google Apps** (⠿).

   The Google Apps panel opens.

2. Click **Contacts** (👤).

   Google Contacts opens.

   A The Main Menu area appears on the left side of the window when the window is wide enough. This menu provides navigation links, labels, and commands.

   B The Starred Contacts list contains contacts you have marked with a star — for example, to designate them as being important.

   C The Contacts list contains all your contacts, including starred contacts.

3. Click **Create contact** (+) to open the Create Contact pop-up menu, and then click **Create a contact** (👤).

Note: You can create multiple contacts in a single move by clicking **Create contact** (+) and then clicking **Create multiple contacts** (👥).

The Create New Contact dialog box opens with the First Name field selected.

4. Enter the contact's first name.
5. Click **Last name** and enter the contact's last name.

Note: You can press Tab to move from one field to another in the Create New Contact dialog box. Press Shift+Tab to move backward.

6. Enter other information, as needed.
7. To assign the contact to one or more labels, click **Label** (🏷).

Note: The Label button shows No Label when no label is assigned to the contact.

The Add to Label pop-up panel opens.

8. Click each label to which you want to add the contact.
9. Click outside the Add to Label panel.

The Add to Label panel closes.

10. Click **Save**.

The Create New Contact dialog box closes.

The contact appears in the Contacts list.

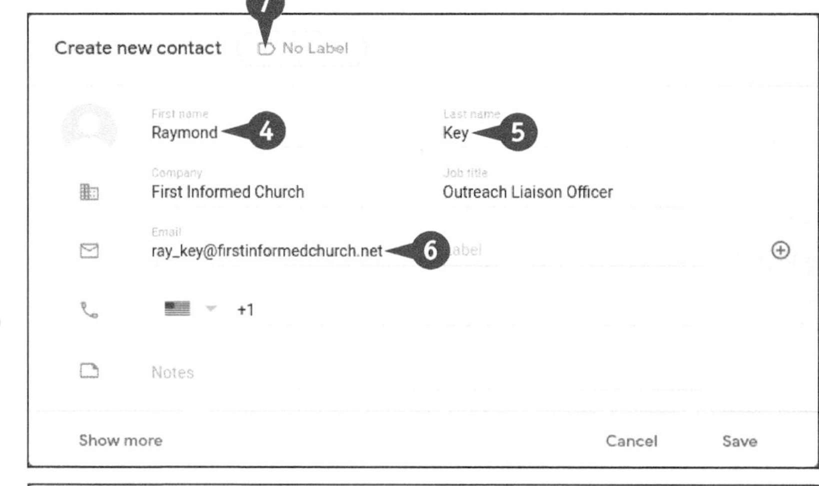

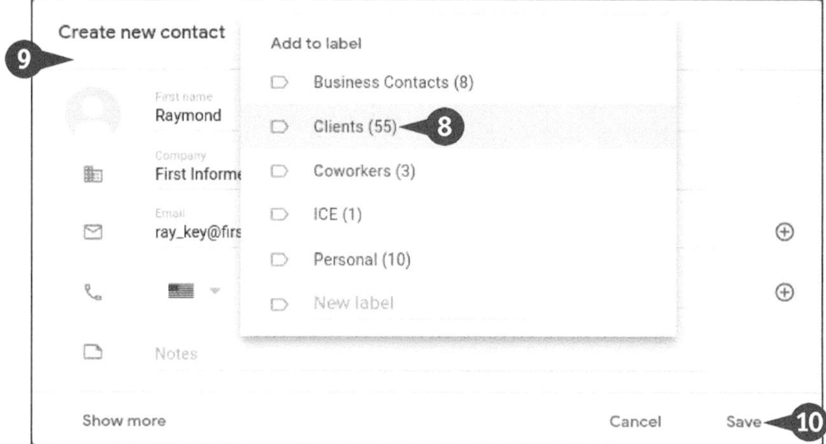

TIP

What other way can I start adding a contact?
In Gmail, open a message from a sender who you want to add to your contacts, and then move the cursor over the sender name. In the pop-up panel that appears, click **Add to Contacts**. Gmail adds the contact information to Google Contacts. The Edit Contact button replaces the Add to Contacts button. You can click **Edit contact** to open the Edit Contact dialog box in Google Contacts. The Edit Contact dialog box is essentially the Create New Contact dialog box with a different title.

Change a Contact's Information

Google Contacts enables you to easily edit the information for a contact. So, when you learn that a contact's details have changed, or you learn new information you want to add, you can open the contact record and make the changes needed.

You can edit any of the contact record's fields, which provide prebuilt storage for information from the contact's birthday to their website. If you need to add information that does not fit neatly in any of the existing fields, you can put it either in the custom field or in the notes field.

Change a Contact's Information

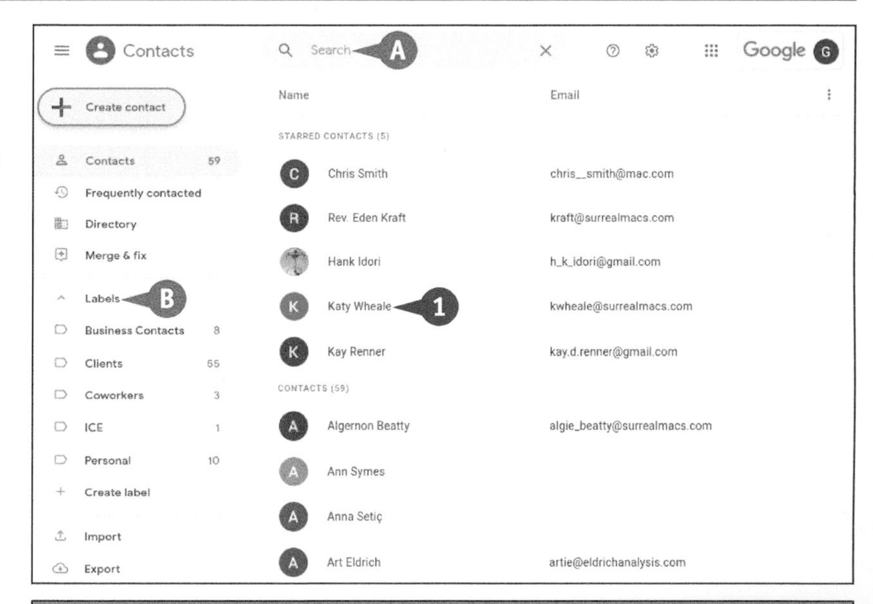

1. In Google Contacts, click the contact you want to edit.

A You can locate a contact by clicking **Search** (🔍) and starting to type the contact's name or other identifying information.

B You can click a label in the Labels section of the Main Menu to display only the contacts assigned to that label.

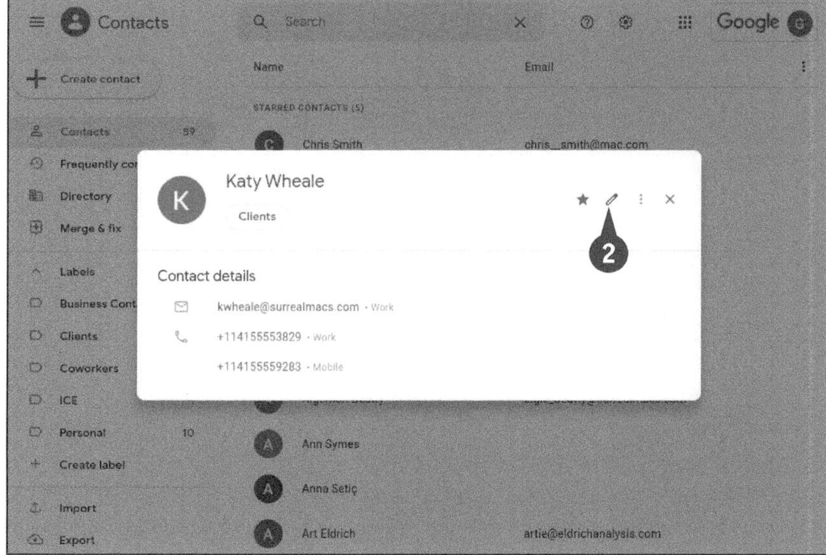

The contact record opens.

2. Click **Edit Contact** (✏).

The Edit Contact dialog box opens.

3 Edit the contact data, as needed.

C The name of the active field appears in blue.

D You can click **Add** (⊕) at the right side of a line to add another item of the same type.

E To delete the information in a field, move the cursor over the field, and then click **Remove** (✕).

4 To display the full set of fields in the contact record, click **Show more**.

The Edit Contact dialog box displays the remaining fields.

F You can scroll down to display other fields.

5 Enter additional information, as needed.

6 Click **Save.**

Google Contacts saves your changes.

The Edit Contact dialog box closes.

The contact record appears, showing the updated information.

7 Click **Close** (✕) in the upper-right corner of the contact record.

The contact record closes.

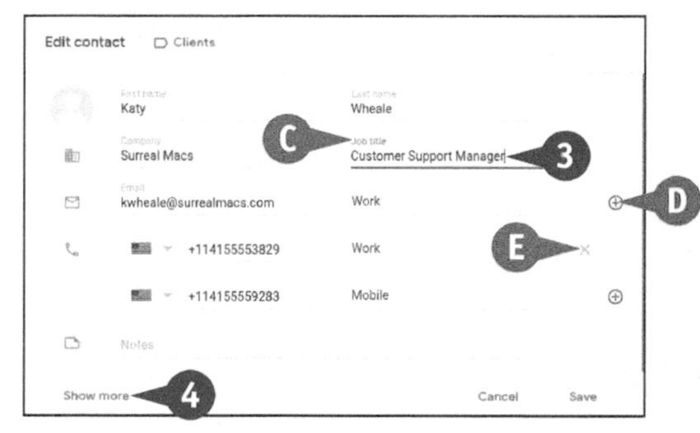

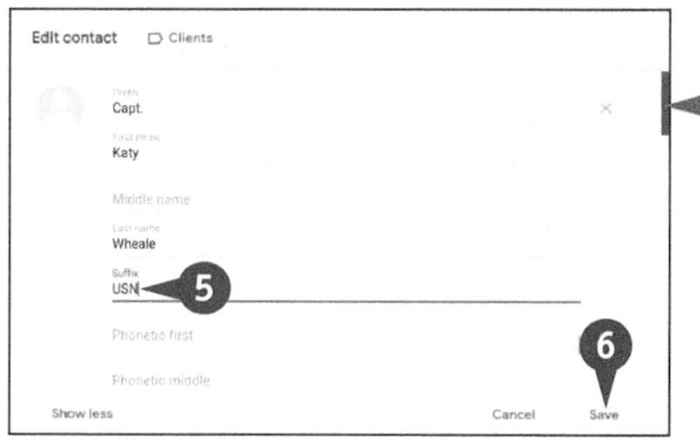

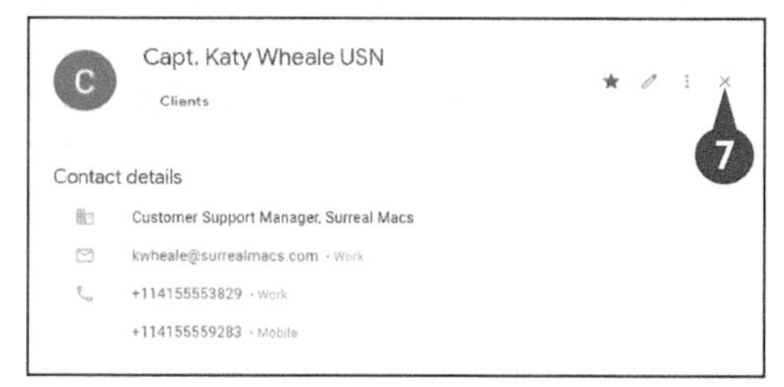

TIP

How do I delete a contact?

Move the cursor over the contact's record so that it becomes highlighted and the Edit button (✏) and Menu button (⋮) appear at its right side. Click **Menu** (⋮) to open the menu, and then click **Delete** (🗑). In the Delete This Contact? confirmation dialog box, click **Delete**.

Organize Your Contacts into Groups with Labels

Google Contacts enables you to organize your contacts into separate groups by applying labels to them. Creating groups makes it easier to find the contacts you need. For example, you might apply a label called Clients to your clients so that you can quickly identify all your clients or send them a group email.

After applying labels, you can view a single label at a time or search within a label.

Organize Your Contacts into Groups with Labels

1. In Google Contacts, move the cursor over the first contact to which you want to apply the label.

A check box (☑) replaces the contact's picture or letter circle.

2. Select the check box (☑).
3. Continue selecting contacts by moving the cursor over a contact, and then selecting the check box (☑).

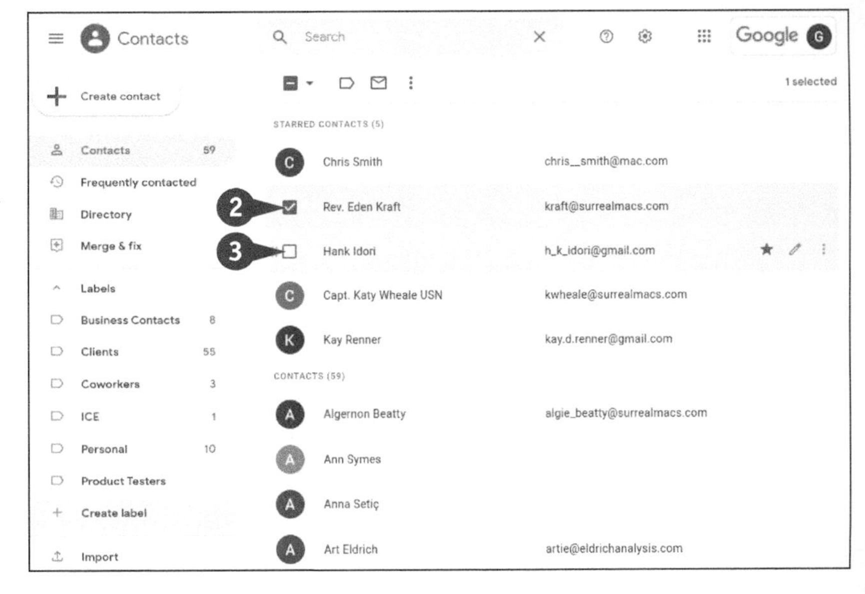

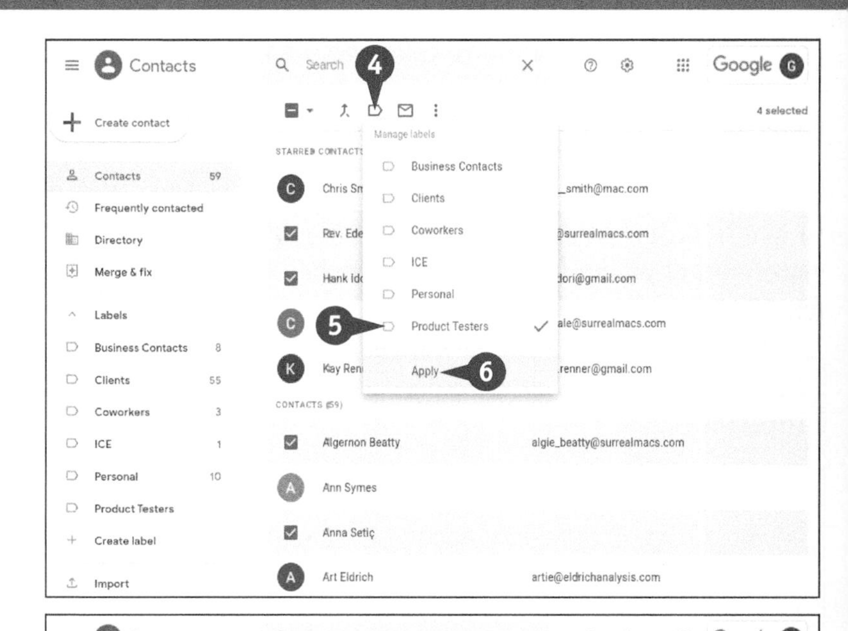

4. When you have selected all the contacts you want to label, click **Label** (▷).

   The Manage Labels pop-up panel opens.

5. Click each label (▷) you want to apply.

6. Click **Apply**.

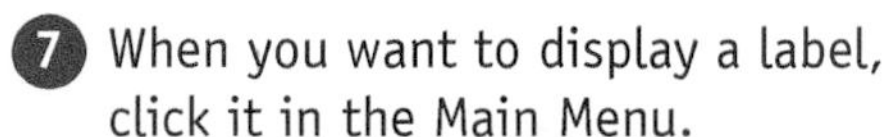

7. When you want to display a label, click it in the Main Menu.

Note: If the Main Menu is hidden, click **Main menu** (≡) to display it.

Note: If the Labels section of the Main Menu is collapsed, click **Labels** (⌄ changes to ⌃) to expand it.

   The contacts in the label appear.

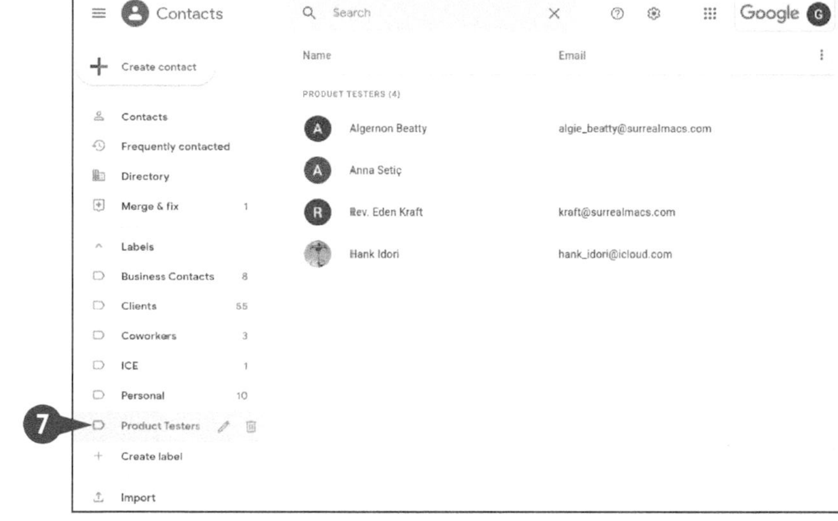

TIPS

How many labels can I apply to a contact?

You can apply as many labels to your contacts as you need to be able to sort the contacts the way you wish.

How do I make Google Contacts display more contacts in its window or tab?

In Google Contacts, click **Menu** (⋮), and then click **Display density** to open the Display Density dialog box. On the tab bar at the bottom, click **Compact** to switch to the Compact View from Comfortable View, which is more spacious. Then click **Done** to close the Display Density dialog box.

Create Notes Using Google Keep

Google Keep enables you to take and organize notes. You can create text notes, notes with images, notes with drawings, and lists; you can create reminders from notes; and you can use labels to sort and group your notes.

Google Keep syncs your notes through your Google Account, so you can access them from any device. In addition, Google provides mobile versions of Google Keep. You can install the Google Keep app on your Android phone or tablet from the Play Store or on your iPhone, iPad, or iPod touch from the iOS App Store.

Open Google Keep and Navigate the Interface

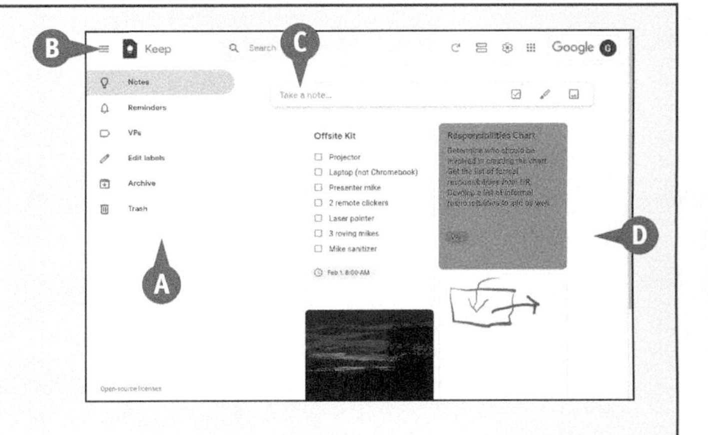

You can open Google Keep from any app that displays the Google Apps icon (⠿), such as Google Drive or Gmail. Click **Google Apps** (⠿) to open the Google Apps pop-up panel, and then click **Keep** (▣). Google Keep opens in a new tab.

The Main Menu (A) appears on the left side of the Google Keep screen, providing commands and navigation links. You can click **Main menu** (☰, B) to toggle the Main Menu between showing icons only and showing icons and text.

The Take a Note box (C) appears at the top of the document area, ready for you to enter data or start a new list (☑), a note with drawing (✎), or a note with image (🖼). Below this box appear the notes (D) included in the current view; in this example, the Notes view shows all notes.

Create a Text Note

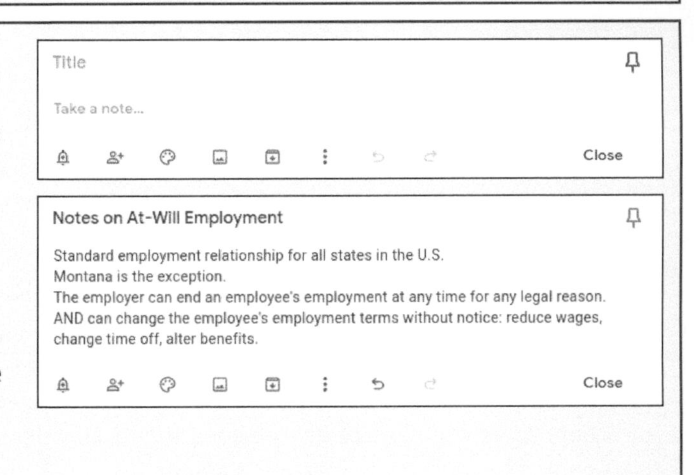

To create a text note, click **Take a note.** The Take a Note box expands to show a Title field at the top and a row of buttons at the bottom.

Type or paste the text of the note. To give the note a title, click **Title** and type the title.

You can click **Remind me** (🔔) to add a reminder to the note; click **Collaborator** (👤+) to add a collaborator; click **Change color** (🎨) to change the note's background color; click **Add image** (🖼) to add an image to the note; and click **Archive** (🗃) to archive the note.

Click **Close** when you are ready to close the note.

Create a Note with a Drawing

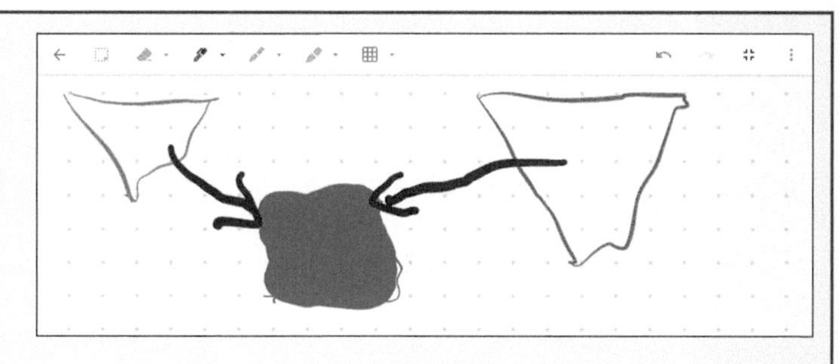

To create a note with a drawing, click **New note with drawing** ( ). Google Keep displays a blank page for you to work on. Click **Pen** ( ) to select the Pen tool for drawing thin lines. Click **Marker** ( ) to select the Marker tool for drawing thick lines. Click **Highlighter** ( ) to select the Highlighter tool for applying highlight color. Click the same button again, or click the pop-up button ( ), to display the pop-up panel of colors and sizes. Click **Grid** ( ) to open the Grid pop-up panel and apply a grid of squares, dots, or rules. Click **Eraser** ( ) to select the Eraser tool for erasing content; to erase all, click the pop-up button, and then click **Clear page** on the pop-up menu. Click **Select** ( ) to activate the Select tool, which you use to select items you have drawn.

Click **Back** (←) to display the note in a note window, and then click **Close** to close it.

Create a Note Based on an Image

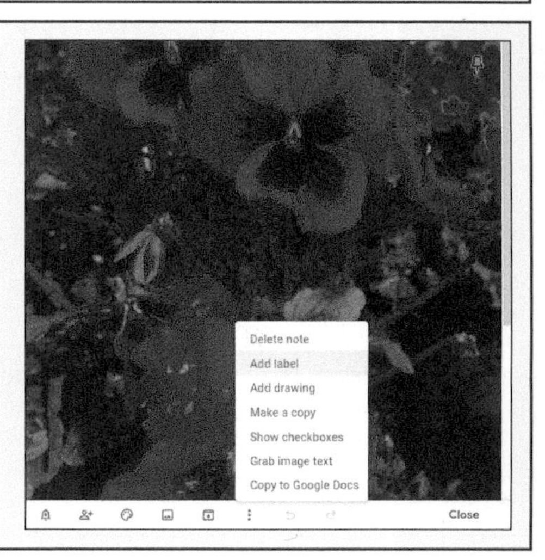

To create a note based on an image, click **New note with image** ( ). In the Select One or More Files dialog box that opens, navigate to and select the image file, and then click **Open**. Google Keep creates a note based on the image. You can click **Menu** (⋮) and then click **Add label** to add a label to the image. Click **Close** when you are ready to close the note.

continued ►

Google Keep gives you several ways to share and use the notes you take. First, you can quickly share a note with a collaborator by clicking **Collaborator** (👤+) and entering the person's name or email address in the Collaborators dialog box. Second, you can copy a note's contents into a new Google Docs document and then open that document straight from Google Keep. Third, you can open Google Keep in the side panel of Google Docs and simply drag notes into a document.

Create a List

To create a list, click **New list** (☑). Google Keep expands the Take a Note box, and you can type the first list item. Press Enter or Return to create each subsequent item. Click **Title** and type the title for the list. Click **Close** when you are ready to close the note containing the list.

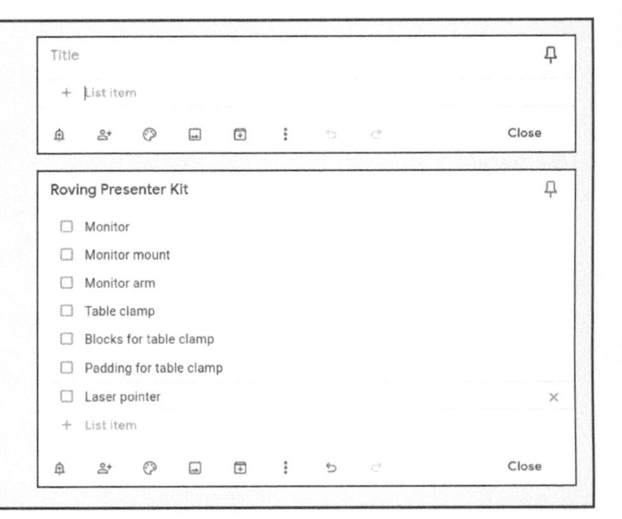

Organize Your Notes with Labels

Google Keep enables you to apply labels to your notes so that you can organize them into groups. The labels appear in the Main Menu, where you can click a label to display the notes to which you have applied it.

To edit your list of labels, click **Edit labels** (✏) in the Main Menu, and then work in the Edit Labels dialog box that opens.

To apply a label to a note, click the note, click **Menu** (⋮), and then click **Add label**. In the Label Note panel that opens, select each label (☑) you want to apply. You can also create a new label by clicking **Enter label name**, typing the label, and then pressing Enter or Return.

Copy a Note to Google Docs

Google Keep provides the Copy to Google Docs command, which lets you instantly create a new Google Docs document containing the contents of a note.

In Google Keep, click the note to open it. Click **Menu** (⋮) to open the menu, and then click **Copy to Google Docs**. Google Keep displays the *Copied to Google Docs* message when the operation is complete. You can click **Open Doc** (E) to open the document immediately in Google Docs so that you can start work on it.

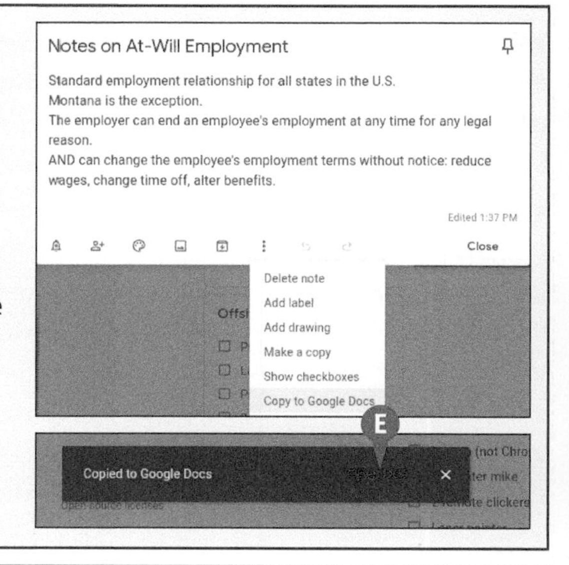

Add Multiple Notes to a Google Docs Document

Google Workspace also enables you to include multiple notes in a Google Docs document. In Google Docs, click **Keep** (◘) to open Google Keep in the side panel. You can then drag a note from Google Keep to where you want to place it in the document (F).

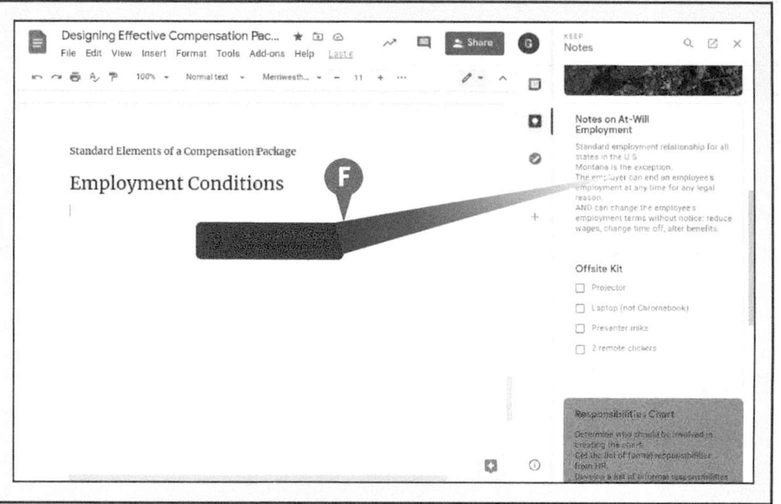

Track Your Commitments with Google Tasks

To help you keep track of your commitments, Google provides the Google Tasks service. Google Tasks runs in the side panel within Google Drive, Gmail, Google Calendar, and some other apps, giving you quick access to your tasks while you are working with email or your schedule.

You can create various lists to sort your tasks into different categories. For example, you might create a Work list, a Home list, a Family list, and an Errands list. After creating the lists you need, you can assign your tasks to lists, as appropriate.

Track Your Commitments with Google Tasks

Display Google Tasks in the Side Pane

1. In Google Drive, click **Tasks** (✓).

Note: If the side panel is hidden, click **Show side panel** (<) to show the side panel.

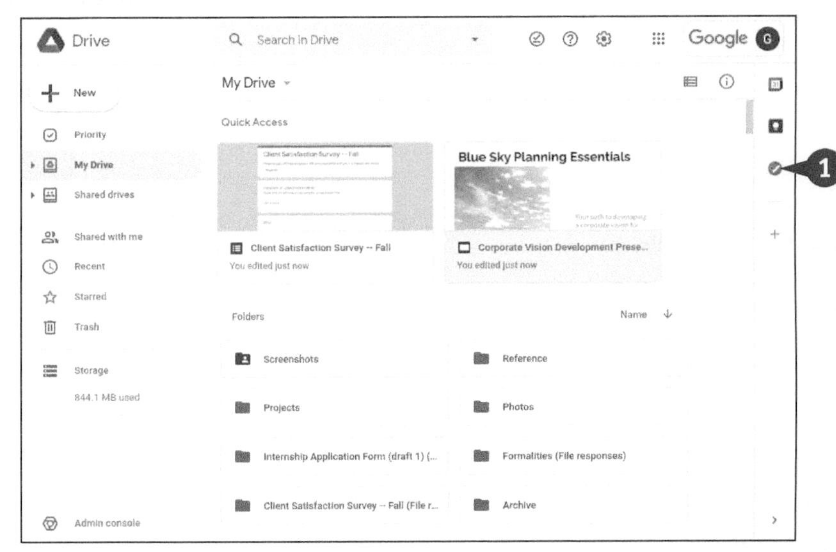

The side panel expands and shows Google Tasks.

- **A** The Lists button shows your current list of tasks.
- **B** You can click **Lists** (▾) to access other lists.
- **C** The tasks in the current list appear.
- **D** When you finish working in the side panel, you can click **Close Tasks** (✕) to close the Google Tasks pane.

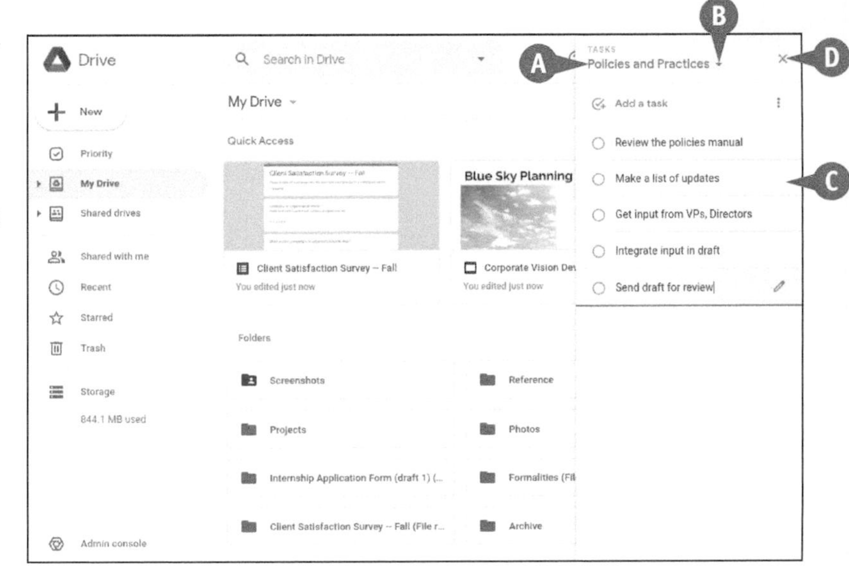

Set Up Your Task Lists

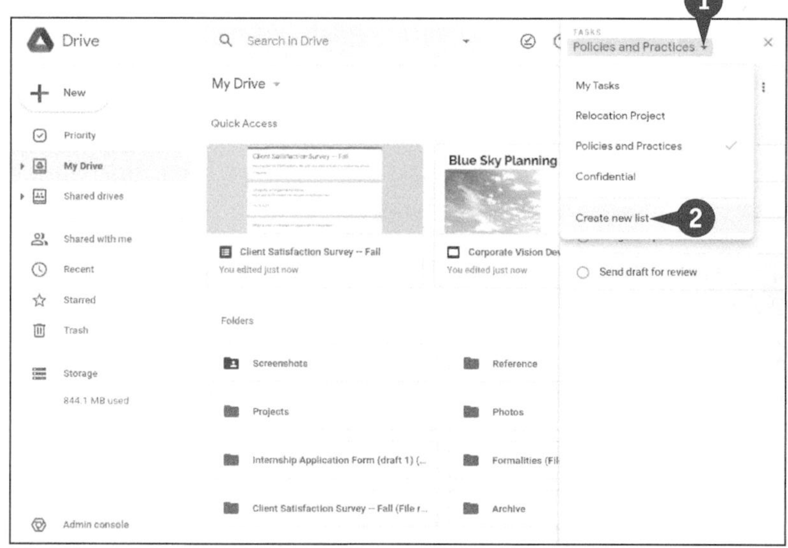

1. Click **Lists** (▾).

   The Lists pop-up menu opens.

2. Click **Create new list.**

   The Create New List dialog box opens.

3. Type the name for the new list.

4. Click **Done**.

   The Create New List dialog box closes.

   Google Tasks creates the new list and displays it in the task pane.

   As the list contains no tasks yet, the pane contains a cartoon prompting you to add a task.

   You can now set up the other lists you need by repeating steps **1** through **4**.

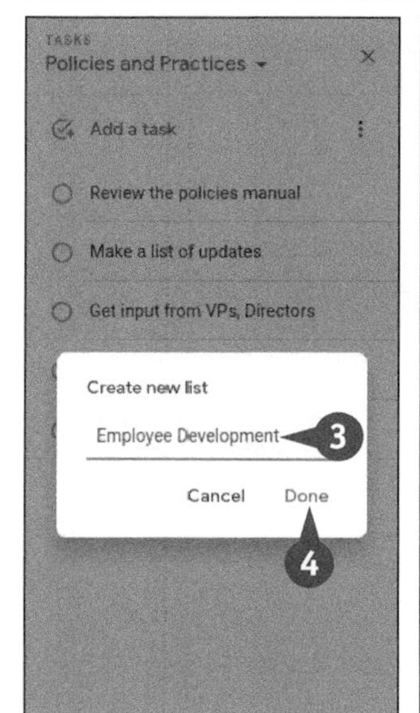

TIP

How do I change the order of my task lists?
Click **Lists** (▾) to open the Lists pop-up menu. Move the cursor over the list you want to move so that the handle (⁝⁝) appears. Click the handle (⁝⁝), and then drag the list to where you want it on the Lists pop-up menu.

continued ►

When you create a task, you can enter just the task name, or you can enter any details you have. You can assign a due date, which can include a due time, to the task. You can also add subtasks to a task, effectively dividing up the task into a series of steps that are easier — or perhaps just faster — to complete.

After adding tasks to your lists, you can sort them into your preferred order. And once you finish a task, you can mark it as complete.

Track Your Commitments with Google Tasks (continued)

Create a Task

1. Click **Lists** (▼).

   The Lists pop-up menu opens.

2. Click the list in which you want to create the new task.

   The list you clicked appears.

3. Click **Add a task** (⊘).

   A blank line appears for the new task.

4. Type the task name.

Note: If you do not want to add details beyond the task name, you can press Enter to enter the task and start creating another task in the same list.

5. Click **Edit details** (⋮).

   The Details pane for the task appears.

6. Click **Add details** and type or paste any text details needed.

7. If needed, you can click **List** (▼), and then click a different list.

8. To schedule the task, click **Add date/time**.

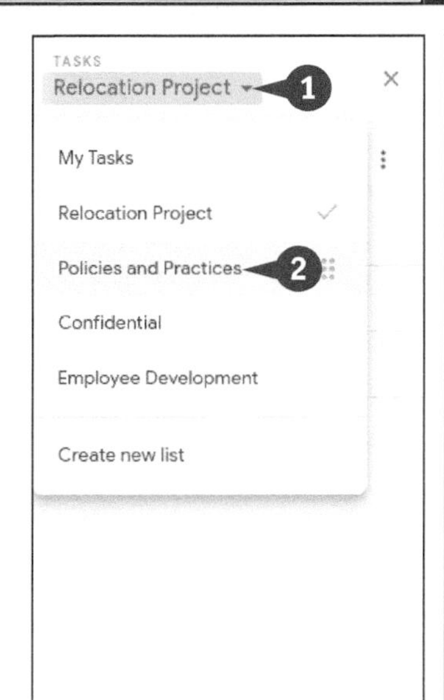

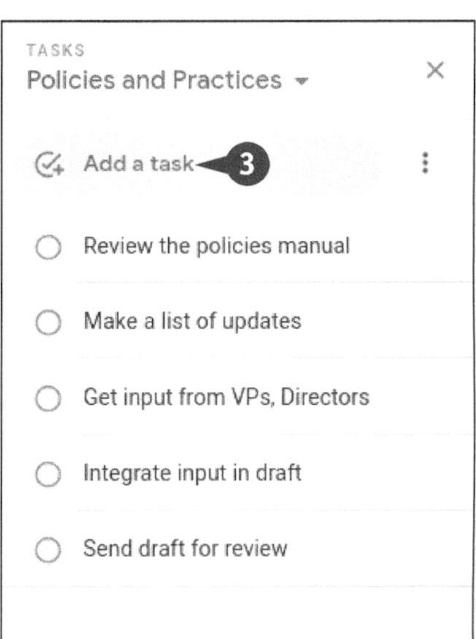

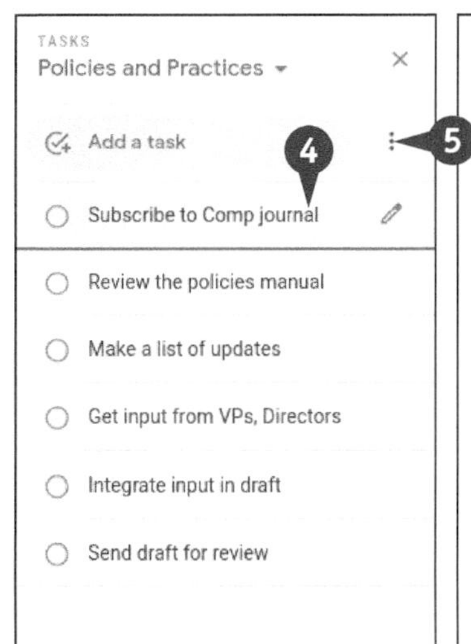

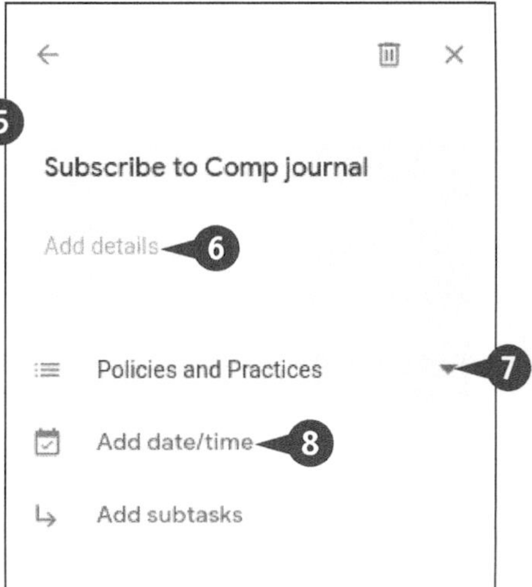

The date and time pane opens.

9. Click the date.
10. To assign a time, click **Set time** (🕓).

    The pop-up menu opens.

11. Click the appropriate time.

    E. If you need to create a repeating task, click **Repeat** (🔁), and then specify the details in the Repeat dialog box that opens.

12. Click **OK**.

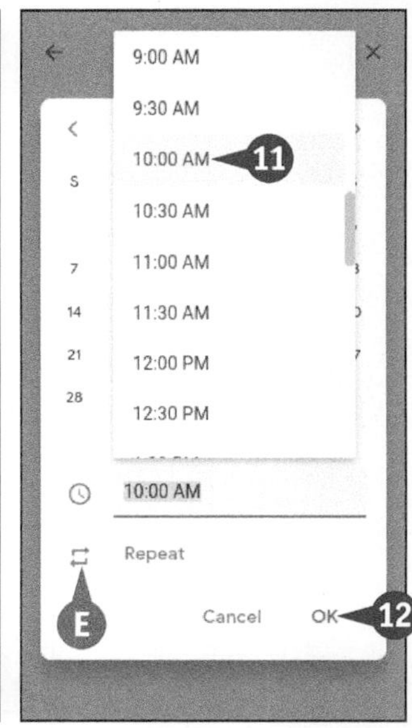

The date and time pane closes.

F. You can click **Add subtasks** (↳) to start adding subtasks to the task.

13. Click **Back** (←).

    The task appears in your task list.

    G. When you complete a task, click **Mark complete** (○ changes to ◉).

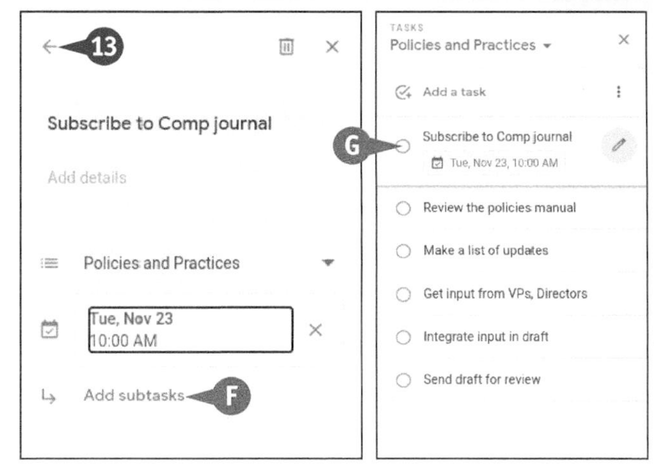

TIP

How do I change the order of the tasks?

You can display the tasks either in what Google Tasks calls My Order — in other words, the order you choose — or by date. To choose the order, click **Menu** (⋮) to open the menu, and then click **My order** or **Date** in the Sort By section of the menu.

If you use My Order, you can click a task and drag it up or down the task list to where you want it to appear.

CHAPTER 12

Creating Forms with Google Forms

In this chapter, you learn how to use the Google Forms app to create online forms for gathering information. After a quick overview of what Google Forms enables you to do, you open the app, create a new form, and add content to it. You learn how to import questions, add multiple sections and collaborators to a form, and preview and test the form. You also learn how to send a form to its respondents and how to view their responses to it.

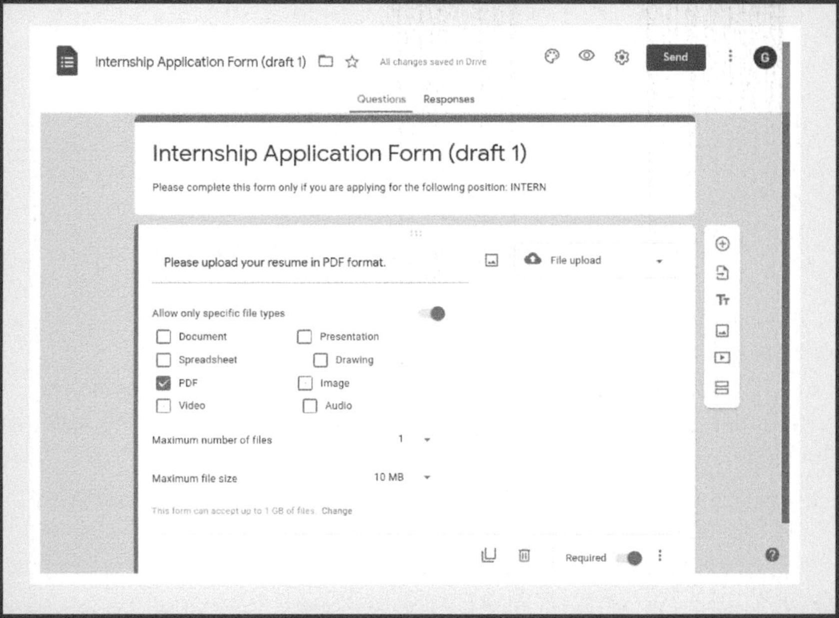

Understanding What You Can Do with Google Forms

Google Forms enables you to create a wide range of forms using a straightforward and user-friendly interface. This section briefly outlines the key stages involved in creating forms. The rest of this chapter covers these essentials in detail, taking you step by step through what you need to know to produce flexible and effective forms.

Start a New Form Either from Scratch or Based on a Template

Google Forms lets you create a new, blank form that gives you a clean slate on which to work, but the app also provides an extensive selection of templates to give you a jump start on creating various types of forms. The Google Forms Template Gallery divides its templates up into three sections: Work, Personal, and Education. The Work section offers templates such as an order form, a job application, and a work request; the Personal section includes templates for contact-information and event-registration forms; and the Education section includes templates for assessment and course-evaluation forms.

Add Questions to a Form

After creating a form, you populate it with questions that ask either literal questions of the respondents or put other demands to them. Google Forms provides 11 different forms of questions, including multiple-choice questions and check boxes, short text answers and paragraph-length text answers, drop-down menus, and date and time pickers.

You can add one or more images to a question, either as an integral part of the question or as decoration; alternatively, you can add a single video from YouTube. You can choose whether any given question is required or optional.

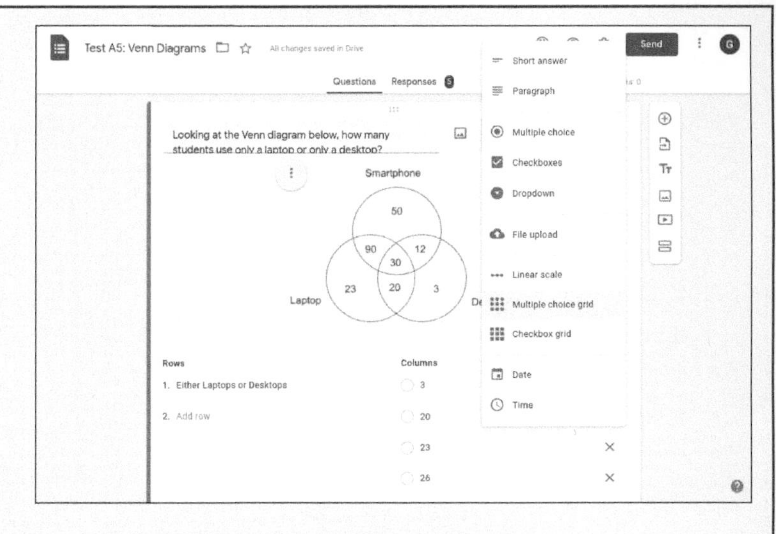

CHAPTER 12

Creating Forms with Google Forms

Create a Multi-Section Form and Control Progression Through It

In Google Forms, a form can consist of a single section that contains all its questions, but you can also create multi-section forms. You might use multiple sections either to break a form down into more manageable chunks or to customize the user's progression through the form based on their answers to specific questions.

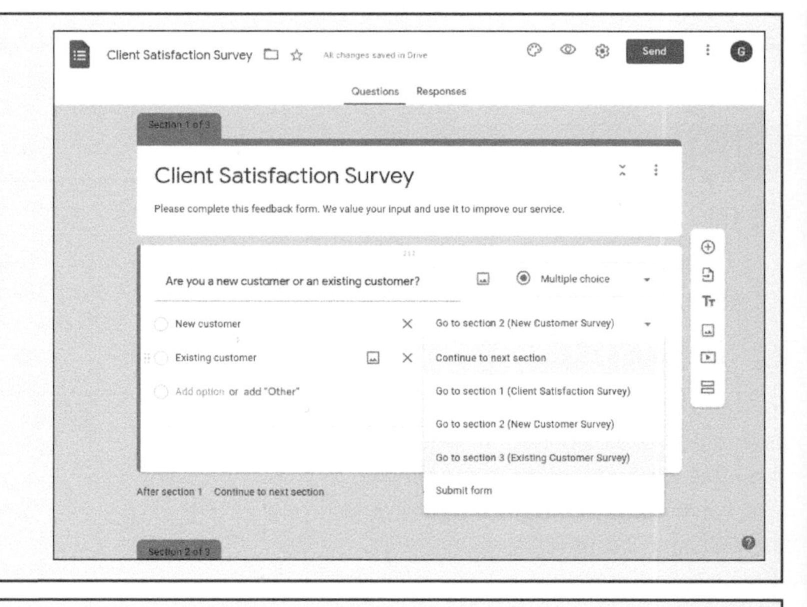

Preview and Test a Form

Once you have added some questions, and perhaps some sections, to a form, you can preview the form to make sure it looks and behaves the way you intend it to. While previewing the form, you can fill it in just as a respondent would, and you can submit your response to generate sample data.

Send the Form to Its Respondents and View Their Responses

When your form is ready for use, you can send it to its respondents via email, share it with them by sending a link via instant messaging or other means, or post the form on your website.

When respondents submit their responses, Google Forms collects the data. You can then access it by displaying the form's Responses screen, which enables you to view the response data as a summary, by individual questions, or by individual respondents.

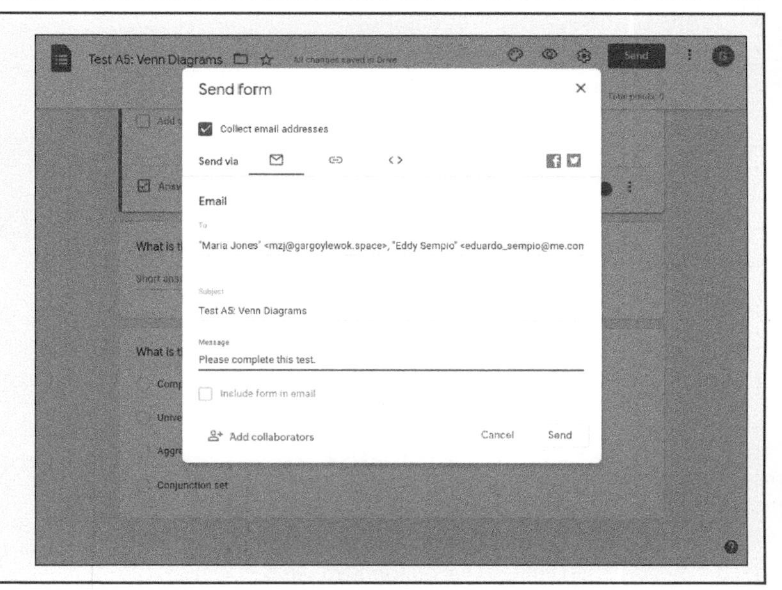

Start Creating a Form

Google Forms enables you to create forms for all types of purposes. You can start by creating a blank form and then populating it with the text and controls you need, as explained in this section. Alternatively, you can browse the available form templates to find one that will provide a suitable basis for the type of form you want to create.

Start Creating a Form

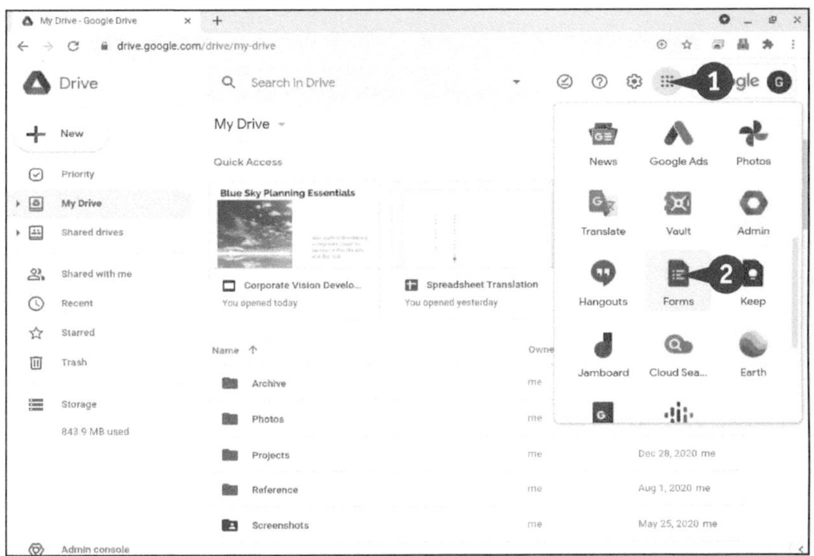

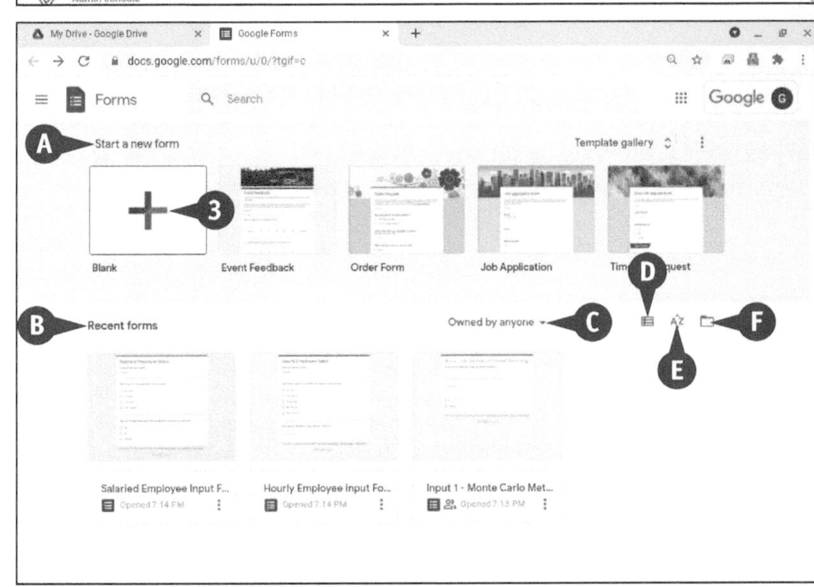

1. From another Google app, such as Google Drive, click **Google apps** (⠿).

   The Google Apps panel opens.

2. Click **Forms** (▤).

Note: From various Google apps, such as Google Docs or Google Sheets, you can start a new blank form by clicking **File**, clicking or highlighting **New**, and then clicking **Form** (▤).

   The Google Forms app opens.

- **A** In the Start a New Form area, you can start either a new blank form or one based on a template.
- **B** The Recent Forms section shows forms that have been opened or modified recently. You can click a form to open it.
- **C** You can click **Owned by** (▾) and then click **Owned by anyone**, **Owned by me**, or **Not owned by me**, as needed.
- **D** You can click **List view** (▤ changes to ⊞) to switch to List view. Click **Grid view** (⊞ changes to ▤) to switch back to Grid view.
- **E** You can click **Sort options** (A↕Z) to change the sort order.
- **F** You can click **Open file picker** (🗀) to display the Open a File dialog box.

3. Click **Blank** (+).

Google Forms creates a new blank form.

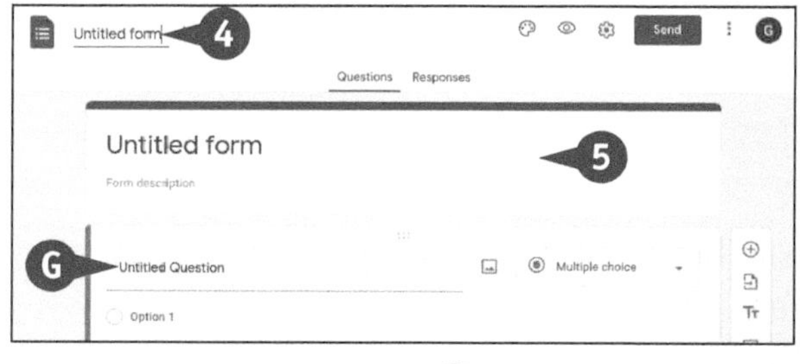

G The form contains one multiple-choice question, which you can change to a different type.

4 Click **name** and type the name under which to save the file.

5 Click outside the Name field or press Enter or Return.

Google Forms saves the form under the filename.

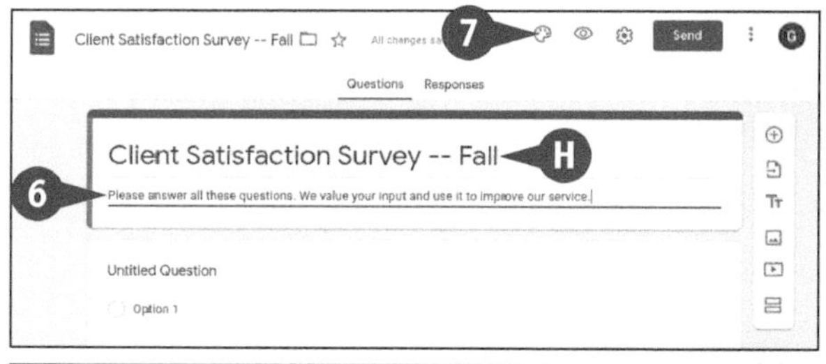

H The Title field automatically takes on the filename. If you want to change the title, click **Title** and type the new title.

6 Click **Form description** and type the description for the form.

7 Click **Customize Theme** (🎨).

The Theme Options pane opens.

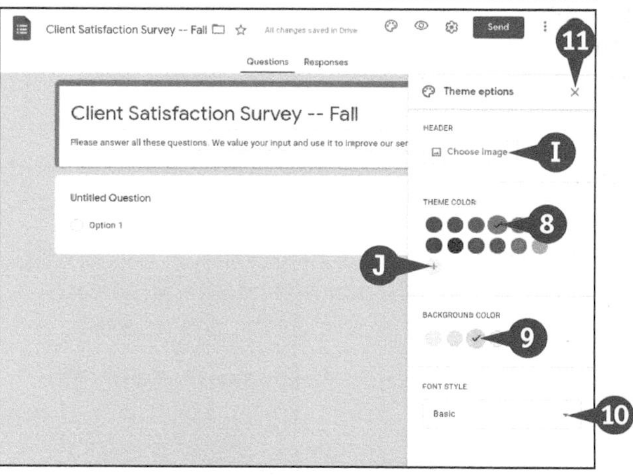

I You can click **Choose image** (🖼) to open the Select Header dialog box, which enables you to add a heading image to the form.

8 In the Theme Color area, click the theme color to apply.

J You can click **Add custom color** (+) to create a custom theme color.

9 In the Background Color area, click the background color.

10 Click **FONT STYLE** (▾), and then click **Basic**, **Decorative**, **Formal**, or **Playful**, as needed.

11 Click **Close** (▾).

The Theme Options pane closes.

TIP

What is the Template Gallery in Google Forms?

Click **Template gallery** (⇕) to display the Template Gallery screen. For a Google Workspace account, this screen has two tabs: the General tab and a tab for your organization. Click **General** to display the General tab, which includes three categories of templates: Work, Personal, and Education. Click the tab for your organization to display your organization's templates. Locate the template you want to use, and then click it.

For a personal Google account, no tabs appear, just a list of the templates that would appear on the General tab.

Choose Settings for a Form

After creating a new form, take a minute to choose suitable form settings on the three tabs of the Settings dialog box. The General tab contains settings for collecting email addresses, sending response receipts, requiring respondents to sign in to Google Accounts, allowing respondents to edit their submitted responses, and letting them see summary charts and text responses.

The Presentation tab lets you display a progress bar, shuffle the question order, and display a confirmation message for responses. The Quizzes tab enables you to turn the form into a quiz, assigning point values to questions and allowing automatic grading.

Choose Settings for a Form

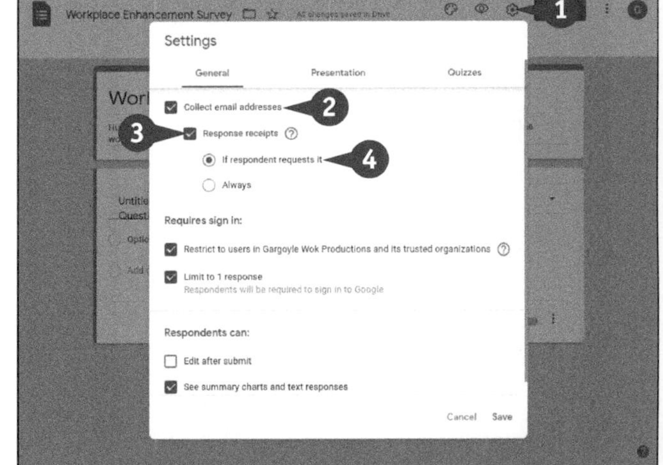

1. With the form open, click **Settings** (⚙).

   The Settings dialog box opens.

   The General tab appears at first.

Note: The color of the check boxes and option buttons in the Settings dialog box varies depending on the form's theme color.

2. Select **Collect email addresses** (☑) if you want the form to collect respondents' email addresses.
3. Assuming you select **Collect email addresses** (☑), you can select **Response receipts** (☑) to have Google Forms send receipts for form responses.
4. Assuming you select **Response receipts** (☑), specify which receipts to send by clicking **If respondent requests it** (○ changes to ◉) or **Always** (○ changes to ◉), as appropriate.

5. In the Requires Sign In area, select **Restrict to users in *Organization* and its trusted organizations** (☑) to restrict use of the form to your organization and those it trusts.
6. Select **Limit to 1 response** (☑) to limit each respondent to a single response. Google enforces this restriction by making each respondent sign in to a Google Account.
7. In the Respondents Can area, select **Edit after submit** (☑) to allow respondents to edit their submitted responses.
8. Select **See summary charts and text responses** (☑) to let respondents view summary charts and text responses from other respondents.
9. Click **Presentation**.

The Presentation tab appears.

10. Select **Show progress bar** (☑) to have the form display a progress bar showing the respondent how much of the form they have completed.

11. Select **Shuffle question order** (☑) to randomize the question order.

12. Select **Show link to submit another response** (☑) to display a link from which the respondent can start another response. This check box is not available if you selected **Limit to 1 response** (☑) on the General tab.

13. In the Confirmation Message area, type the message to send for each form response.

14. Click **Quizzes**.

    The Quizzes tab appears.

15. To turn the form into a quiz, set the **Make this a quiz** switch to On (●).

    The other settings become active.

16. In the Release Grade area, click **Immediately after each submission** (○ changes to ◉) or **Later, after manual review** (○ changes to ◉), as needed.

17. In the Respondent Can See area, select **Missed questions** (☑) to let respondents see questions they answered incorrectly.

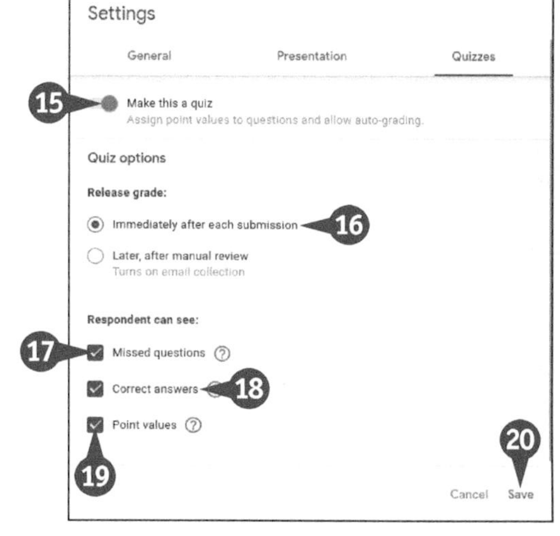

18. Select **Correct answers** (☑) to let respondents see correct answers.

19. Select **Point values** (☑) to let respondents see their total points and the points they scored for each question.

20. Click **Save**.

    The Settings dialog box closes.

Why is the Show Link to Submit Another Response check box not available?

If the Show Link to Submit Another Response check box on the Presentation tab of the Settings dialog box is dimmed and unavailable, it is likely because the form is limited to a single response per respondent. Click **General** to display the General tab, and then deselect **Limit to 1 response** (☐).

Add Questions to a Form

After creating a form and choosing settings for it, your next move is to add questions to the form. Google Forms enables you to add a wide variety of types of questions, including multiple-choice questions and check boxes, short text answers and paragraph-length text answers, drop-down menus, and date and time pickers.

If you are working in a new form you have just created, the form may contain a new, default question. You need not delete this question; instead, you can change it to whichever type of question you need.

Add Questions to a Form

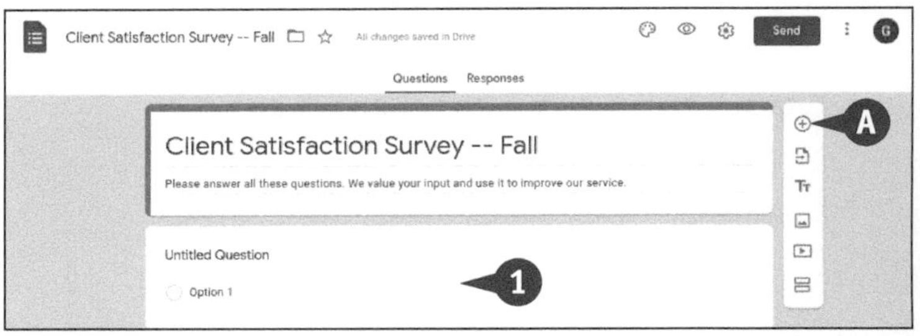

Ⓐ If your form does not contain a new, default question, click **Add question** (⊕) to add one.

❶ If the question is collapsed, showing only the default title — *Untitled Question* — and an option button, click anywhere in the question.

The question expands.

❷ Click **Question type** (▾).

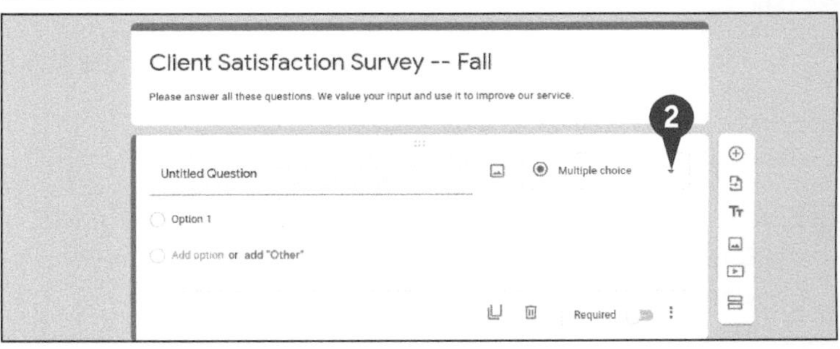

The Question Type pop-up menu opens.

Ⓑ The File Upload (☁) question type enables the respondent to upload one or more files. See the following section, "Request the Respondent Upload Files," for instructions on using this question type.

❸ Click the question type you want to add. This example uses **Short answer** (═).

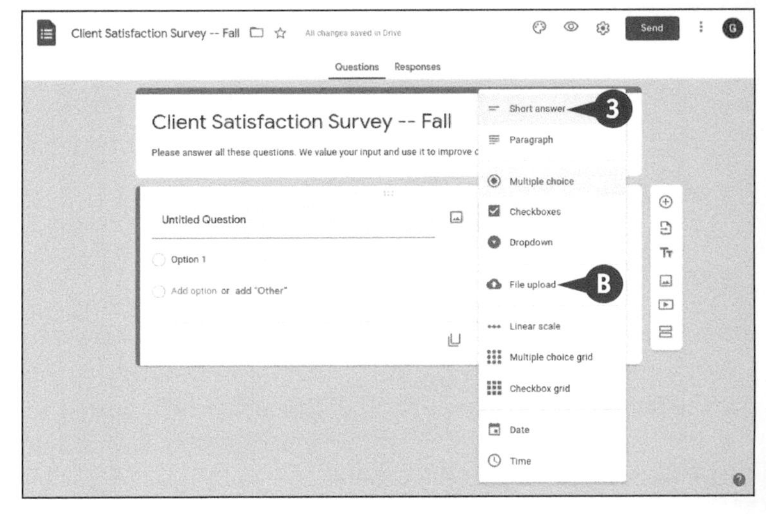

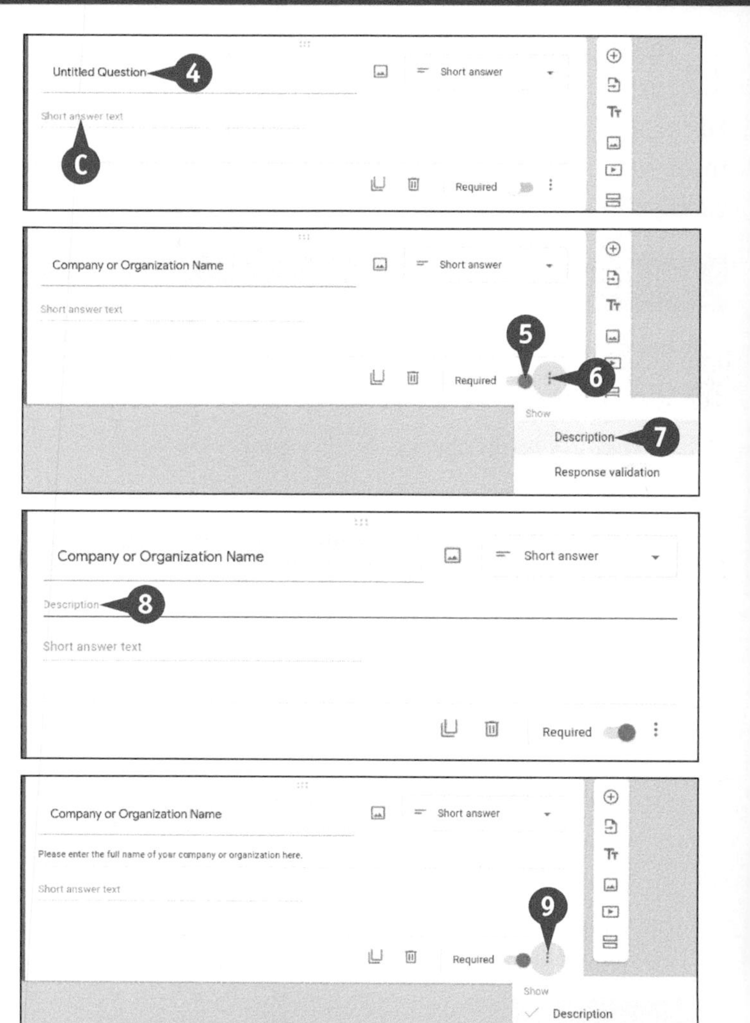

C Google Forms changes the question to the type you chose — in this case, the short-answer type.

4 Click **Untitled Question** and type the title of the question. This is the text that tells the respondent what to do.

5 Set the **Required** switch to On (●) if you want to require the respondent to answer the question.

6 Click **Menu** (⋮).

The menu opens.

7 Click **Description** if you want to add a description field to the form.

Google Forms adds the Description field and positions the cursor in it.

8 Type the description text. For example, you might spell out in more detail the information the question requests.

9 Click **Menu** (⋮).

The menu opens.

10 Click **Response validation** if you want to add response validation to the question.

TIP

How can I make each question required by default?

Click **Menu** (⋮) in the upper-right corner of the Google Forms screen, between the Send button and your Google Account icon. On the menu, click **Preferences** (⚙) to open the Default Settings dialog box. In the Questions area, select **Make questions required** (☑). Also in the Questions area, you can assign a default point value for quiz questions by selecting **Default quiz point value** (☑) and typing the value in the text box. In the Forms section of the dialog box, you can select **Collect email addresses** (☑) to collect email addresses by default. Click **Save** to close the Default Settings dialog box.

continued ►

Add Questions to a Form (continued)

Google Forms enables you to add data validation to some question types. *Data validation* means checking the respondent's input to make sure it conforms to the criterion that you specify. For example, if you use a short-answer field to request an email address, you can specify that the response passes validation as an email address; if you request a number, you can specify boundaries, such as that it must be between 50 and 100 or that it must be an integer.

Add Questions to a Form (continued)

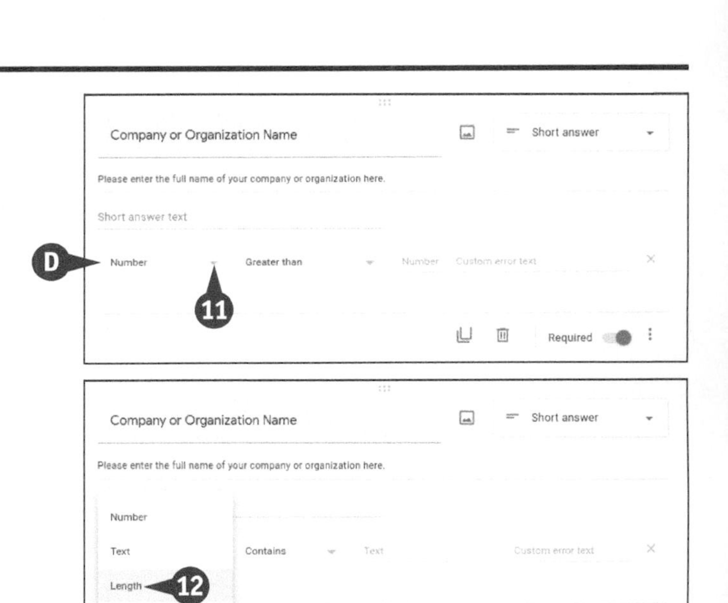

D The Response Validation controls appear.

11 Click the leftmost pop-up menu (▾).

The pop-up menu opens.

12 Click the validation type you want: **Number**, **Text**, **Length**, or **Regular expression**. This example uses **Length**.

The controls to the right of the leftmost pop-up menu change to display fields suitable for your selection.

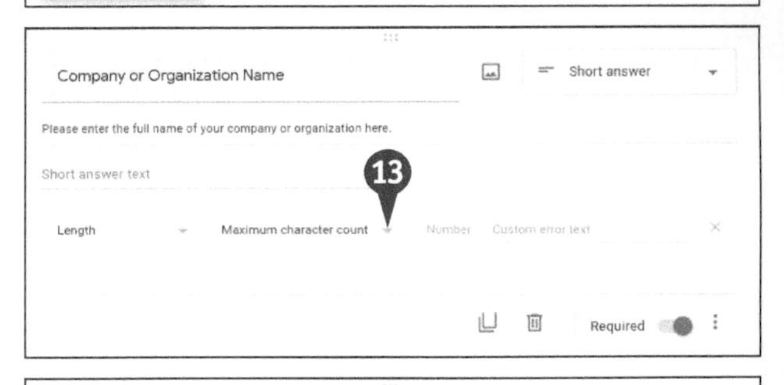

13 Click the second pop-up menu.

The pop-up menu opens.

14 Click the appropriate menu item for your criterion. For this example, you would click **Minimum character count**.

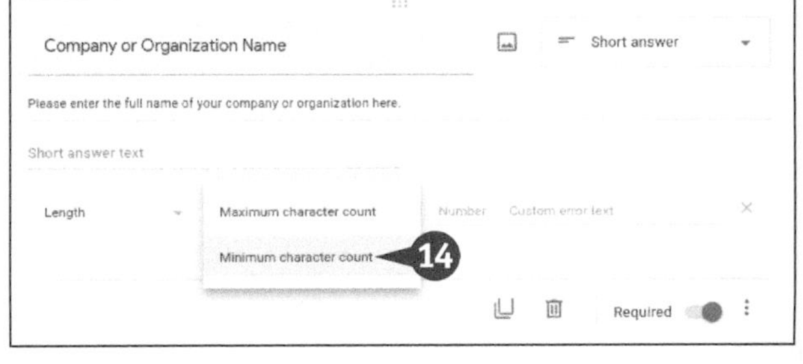

15 Fill in the remaining field or fields to complete the criterion. For this example, click **Number** and type the number for the minimum character count.

16 Click **Custom error text** and type the error text for the form to display when the input fails validation.

E You can click **Duplicate** (⧉) to create a duplicate of this question. Duplicating a question can save you time when a form requires similar questions.

17 Click **Add question** (⊕).

F Google Forms collapses the completed question so that it takes up less space.

Google Forms adds a new question after the question you completed.

You can now choose the question type and specify its details as explained in this section.

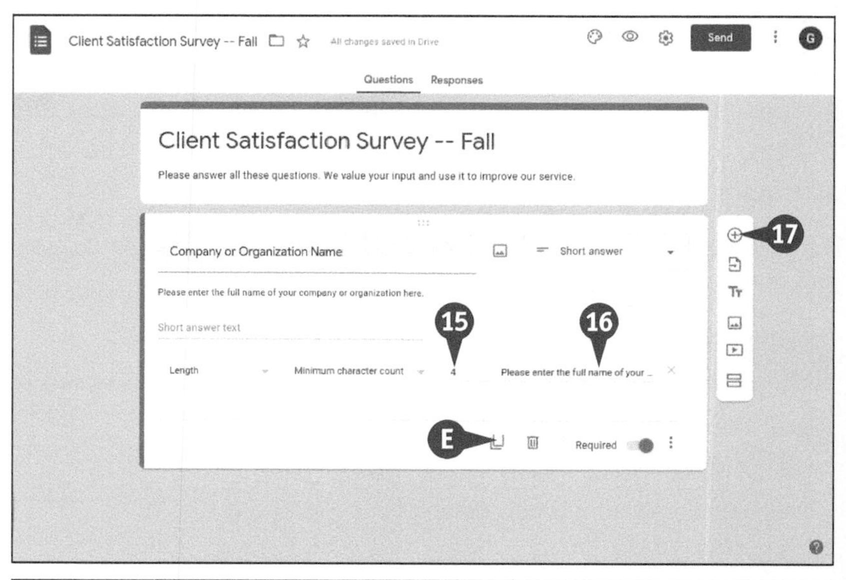

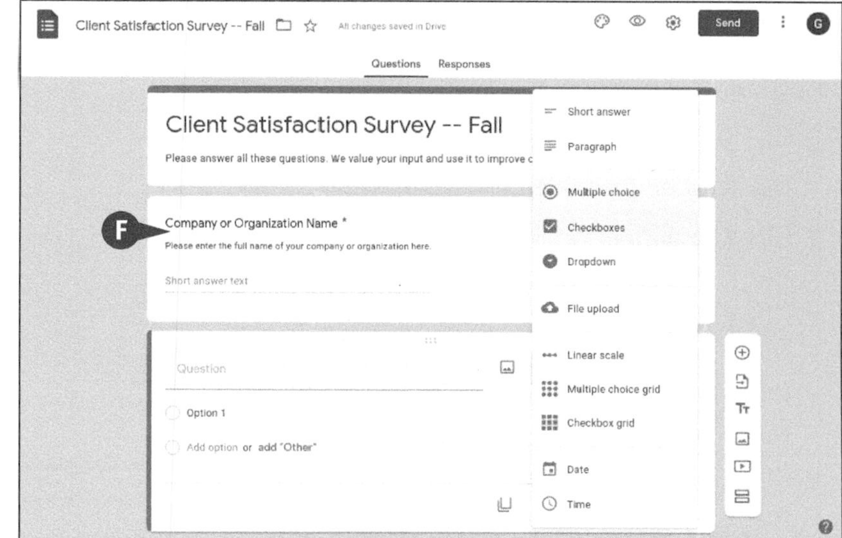

TIP

For which question types can I use response validation?

You can use response validation for short-answer questions, paragraph questions, and check box questions. For a short-answer question, you can validate by number, by text content, by text length, or using regular expressions; see the section "Using Regular Expressions for Advanced Searching" in Chapter 3. For a paragraph question, you can validate by text length or using regular expressions. For a check box question, you can require that the respondent select at least, select at most, or select exactly a specific number of check boxes. Other questions types restrict the answers a respondent can give, which works as a form of self-validation. For example, a linear-scale question does not let the respondent enter a "wrong" value.

Request the Respondent Upload Files

Google Forms enables you to request form respondents to upload a file to Google Drive. For example, in a job application form, you might request respondents to upload a résumé. You can choose to allow only specific file types, such as Document or PDF; you can set the maximum number of files; and you can set the maximum size for any file. You can also specify whether the file upload is required.

To upload a file, any respondent to the form must sign in to Google. The files that respondents upload go to the form owner's Google Drive.

Request the Respondent Upload Files

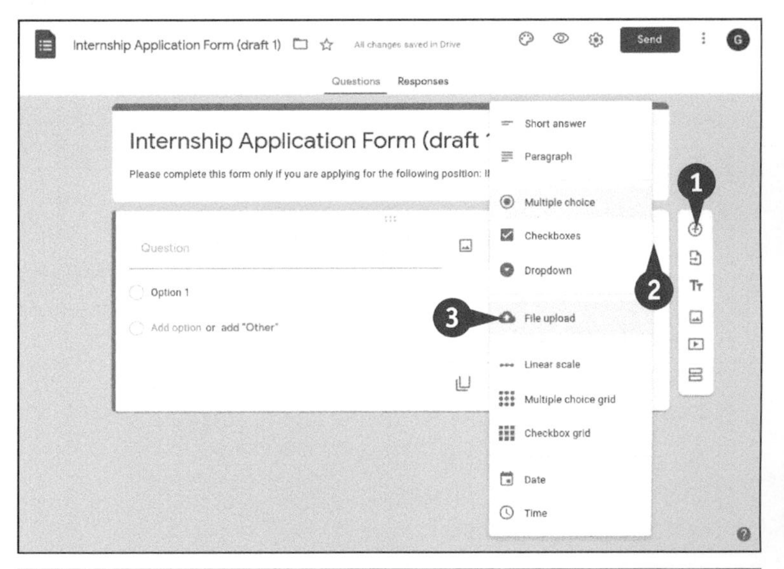

1. At the appropriate point in the form, click **Add question** (⊕).

   Google Forms adds a new default question to the form.

Note: If your form currently has an unused question at the appropriate point, you can simply use that question.

2. Click **Question type** (▾).

   The Question Type pop-up menu opens.

3. Click **File upload** (☁).

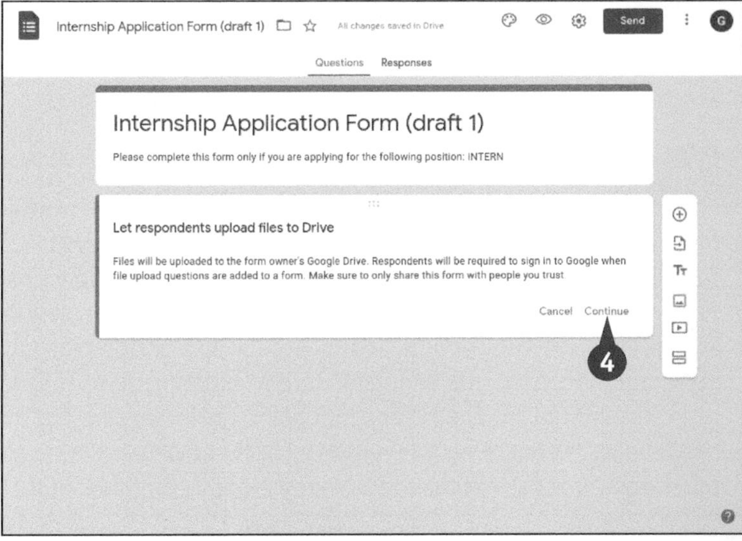

   The Let Respondents Upload Files to Drive dialog box opens.

4. Click **Continue**.

Note: By default, a form can accept up to 1 GB of files. To increase this limit, click **Change** in the lower middle part of the question to display the Settings dialog box. In the Maximum Size of All Files Uploaded section, click the pop-up menu (▾), and then click **10 GB**, **100 GB**, or **1 TB**, as needed. Click **Save** to close the Settings dialog box.

The Let Respondents Upload Files to Drive dialog box closes.

5 Click **Question** and type the question, such as a prompt explaining what type of file to upload.

6 If you want to accept only specific file types, click **Allow only specific file types** (changes to).

Note: In Google Forms, a switch appears in the theme color.

The Allow Only Specific File Types area expands.

7 Click each file type you want to allow (☐ changes to ☑).

Note: A selected check box appears in the theme color.

8 Click **Maximum number of files** (▼), and then click **1**, **5**, or **10**, as appropriate.

9 Click **Maximum file size** (▼), and then click **1 MB**, **10 MB**, **100 MB**, **1 GB**, or **10 GB**, as appropriate.

A You can click **Change** to change the maximum total file size the form can accept.

10 Set the **Required** switch to On () if you want to make the file upload a requirement for completing the form.

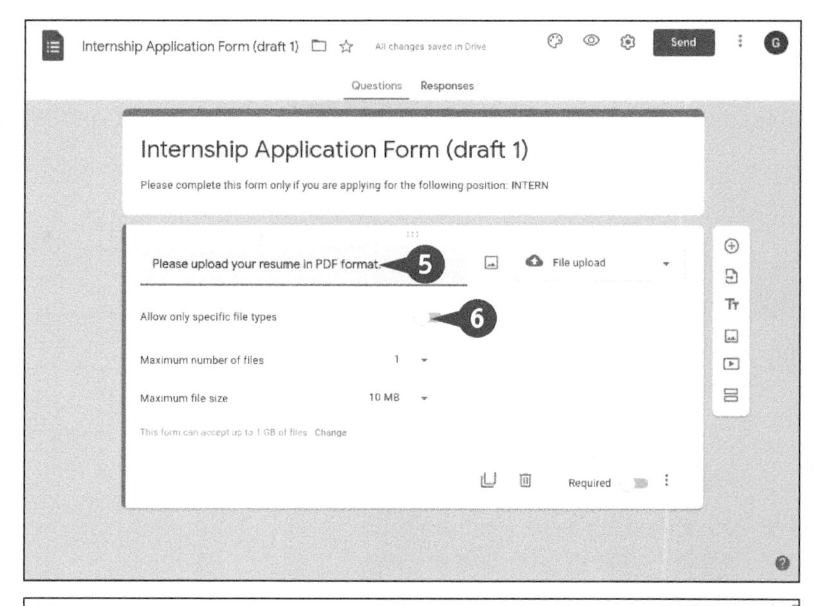

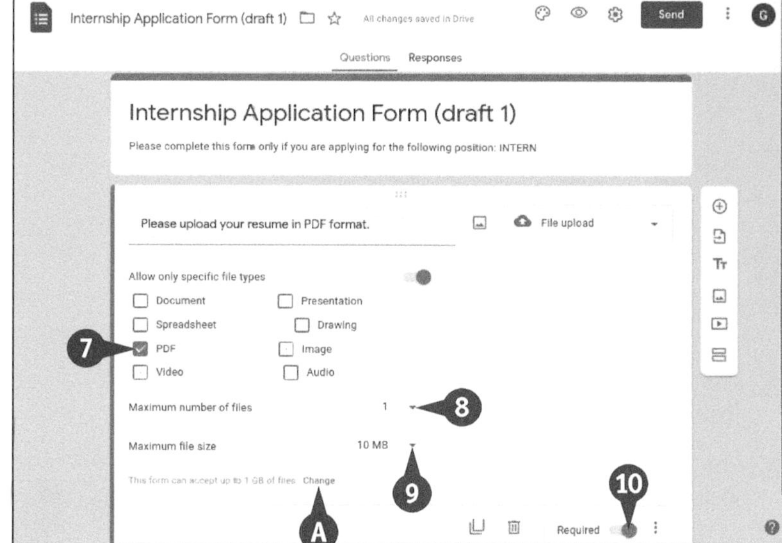

TIP

What maximum file size should I set for a question?

That depends on what type of files you are requesting. 1 MB is often enough for a spreadsheet file or a document file, but a PDF file, image file, or drawing file may need 10 MB. A presentation file or audio file may need 100 MB, a short video may need 1 GB, and a long video may need 10 GB.

Add Images to a Question

Google Forms enables you to enhance your questions by adding images to them. For example, for a Paragraph question, you could add an image for the respondent to describe or analyze. Alternatively, you could simply add an image to provide visual interest and break up a monotonous form.

For multiple-choice questions and check box questions, you can add an image for each answer. For all other question types, you can add only a single image.

Add Images to a Question

1. At the appropriate point in the form, click **Add question** (⊕).

   Google Forms adds a new default question to the form.

2. Click **Question type** (▾), and then click the appropriate question type. This example uses **Multiple choice** (◉).

3. Click **Untitled Question** and type the text for the question.

4. Click **Add image** (▣).

   The Insert Image dialog box opens.

5. Navigate to the location of the image. For example, click **GOOGLE DRIVE** to add an image from Google Drive.

   A. You can click **UPLOAD** to upload an image from your computer.

   B. You can click **CAMERA** to take a photo with your device's camera.

   C. You can click **BY URL** to specify the web address for the image.

   D. You can click **PHOTOS** to use a photo from Google Photos.

   E. You can click **GOOGLE IMAGE SEARCH** to search for an image.

6. Click the image.

7. Click **INSERT**.

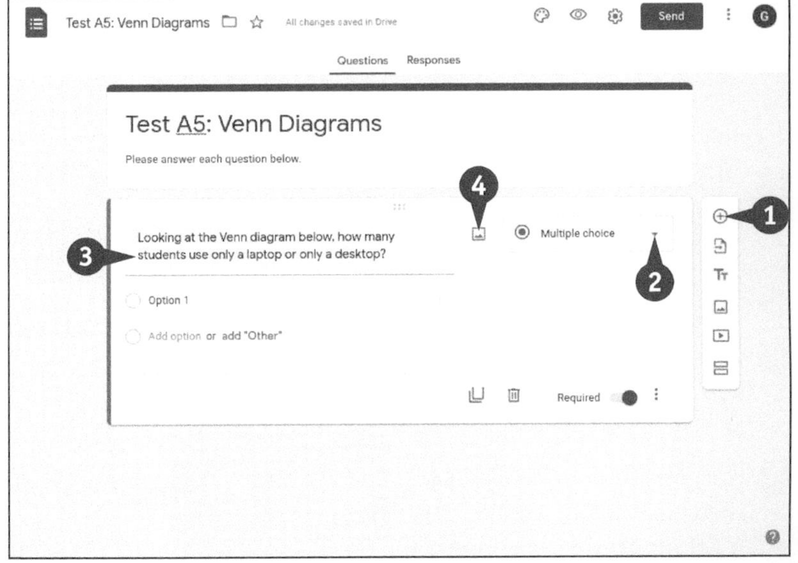

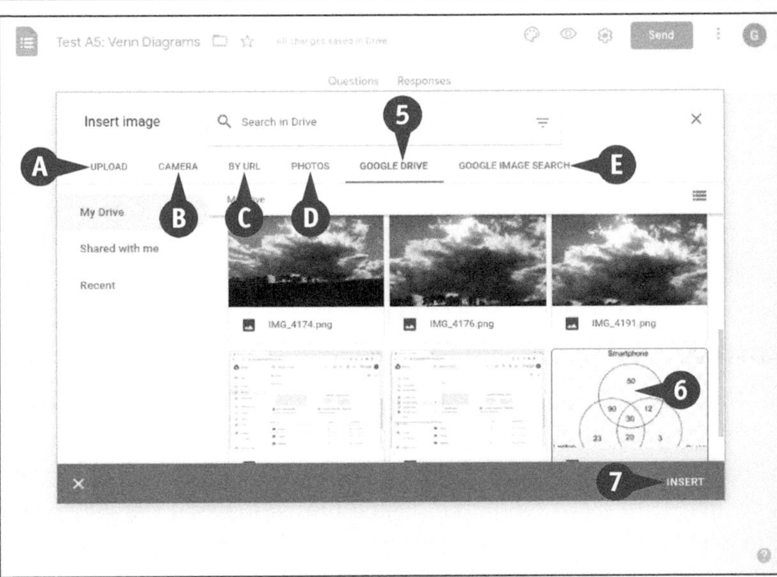

The image appears in the question.

8. Click **Menu** (⋮).

   The pop-up menu opens.

   F You can click **Change** (🖼) to replace the image with another image.

   G You can click **Remove** (🗑) to remove the image.

   H You can click **Add a caption** to add a caption under the image.

9. Click **Left align** (≡), **Center align** (≡), or **Right align** (≡) to specify the alignment. This example uses **Center align** (≡).

   Google Forms applies the alignment to the image.

10. Click the image.

    A blue outline appears around the image, with square sizing handles (■) at the corners.

11. Drag a sizing handle (■) to resize the image, as needed.

12. Click the answer and type its content. If there are multiple answers, click each answer in turn, and then type its content.

    You can then enter other answers, as needed.

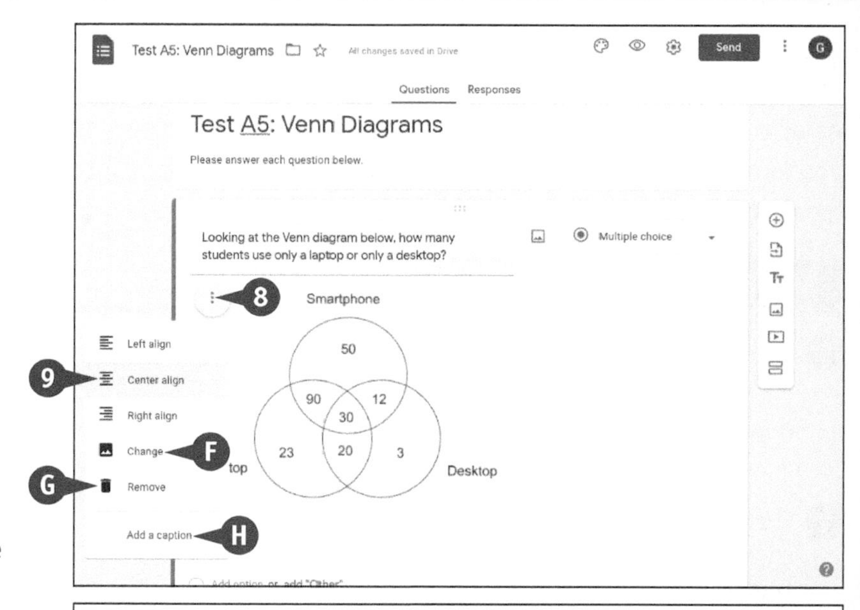

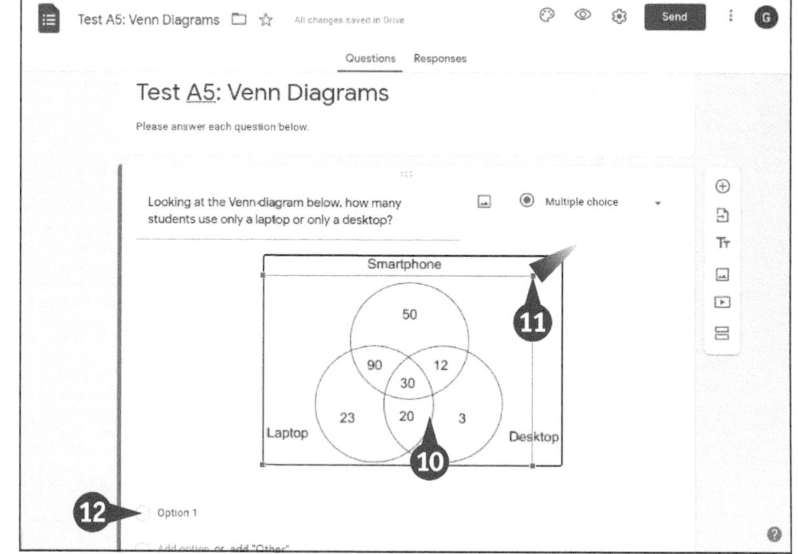

TIP

How do I use multiple images for multiple-choice questions?

Create the question by clicking **Add question** (⊕) to open the Add Question pop-up menu, and then clicking **Multiple choice** (◉). Type the text for the answers. Move the cursor over the answer to which you want to add an image. The Add Image button (🖼) appears on the right side of the answer's row. Click **Add image** (🖼) to open the Insert Image dialog box. You can then select and insert an image as described in the main text of this section.

Add a Video to a Question

Google Forms enables you to add a video to a question. Adding a video lets you not only tap into a rich vein of online content, but also create varied and challenging questions in your forms.

As of this writing, you can add a video only from YouTube, not from other video sites or websites. If you know the video's web address on YouTube, you can simply paste it in; if not, you can search to locate the video.

Add a Video to a Question

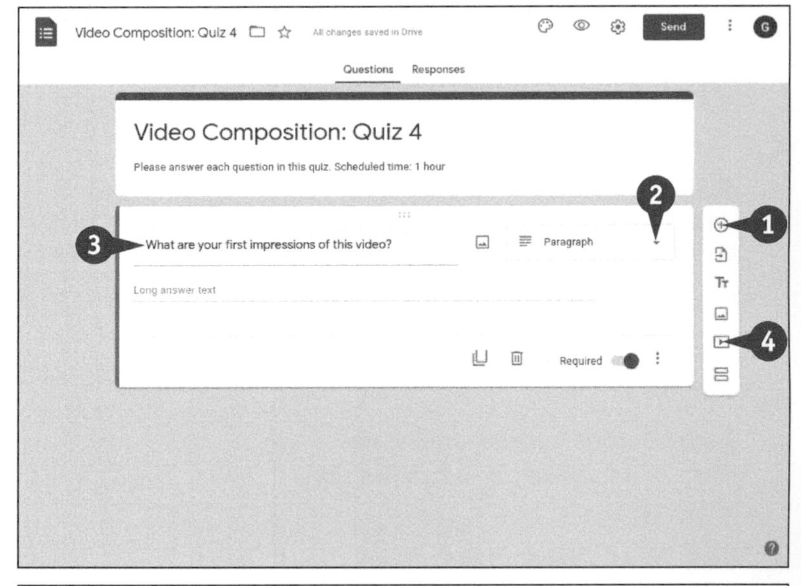

1. At the appropriate point in the form, click **Add question** (⊕).

   Google Forms adds a new default question to the form.

2. Click **Question type** (▾), and then click the appropriate question type. This example uses **Paragraph** (≡).

3. Click **Untitled Question** and type the text for the question.

4. Click **Add video** (▶).

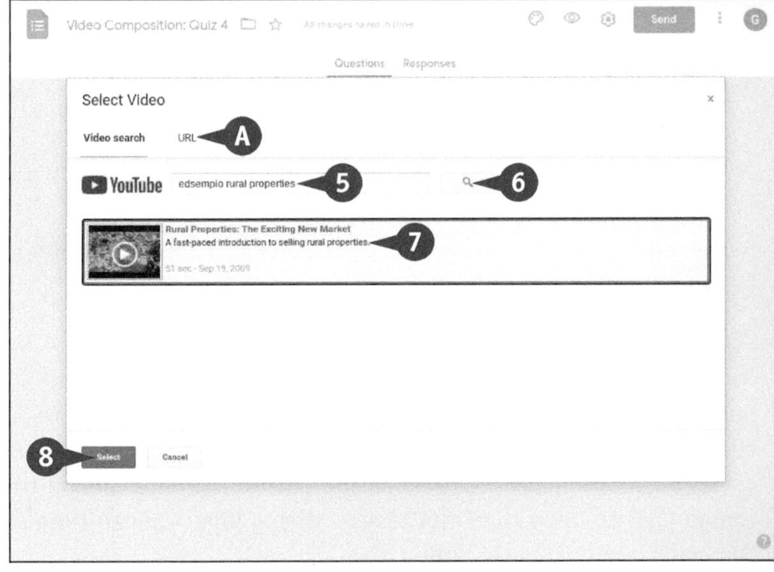

The Select Video dialog box opens.

The Video Search tab appears at first.

Ⓐ You can click **URL** to display the URL tab, on which you want paste the URL of the YouTube video you want to add.

5. Type your search term or terms.

6. Click **Search** (🔍).

   Any matching search results appear.

7. Click the video you want to insert.

8. Click **Select**.

The Select Video dialog box closes.

The video appears in the form.

9 Click **Untitled Video** and type the caption for the video.

10 Click **More options** (⋮).

The More Options pop-up menu opens.

B You can click **Change** (▣) to replace the video with another video.

C You can click **Remove** (🗑) to remove the video.

11 Click **Left align** (≡), **Center align** (≡), or **Right align** (≡) to specify the alignment. This example uses **Center align** (≡).

Google Forms applies the alignment to the video.

12 Click the video.

A blue outline appears around the video, with square sizing handles (■) at the corners.

13 Drag a sizing handle (■) to resize the video, as needed.

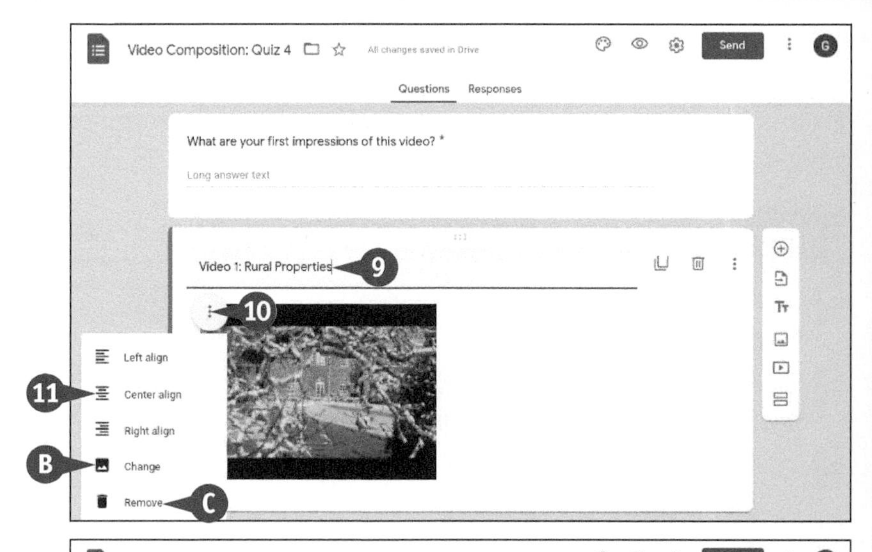

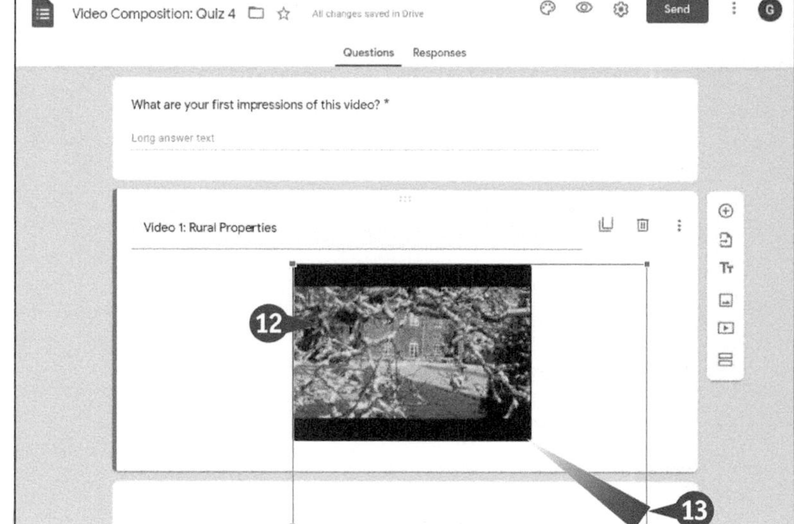

TIP

Can I use a video from a source other than YouTube in a form?

As of this writing, you cannot use video from another source directly. The best workaround is to insert a link to the video and to include instructions telling respondents that the video will open in a separate tab and that they will need to return to the form after viewing the video.

If you own the rights to the video, consider posting the video on YouTube as a private listing, one that is not publicly accessible. You could then use the video on a form.

Import Questions from an Existing Form

Google Forms gives you two ways to get a jump start on creating a form whose contents resemble those of a form you have already created. First, you can duplicate an entire form by using the Make a Copy command; see the tip for details. Second, you can import some or all of the questions from an existing form into another form, as explained in the main text of this section.

Import Questions from an Existing Form

1. Open the form into which you want to import questions.
2. Select the question after which you want to insert the imported questions.
3. Click **Import questions** (⇥).

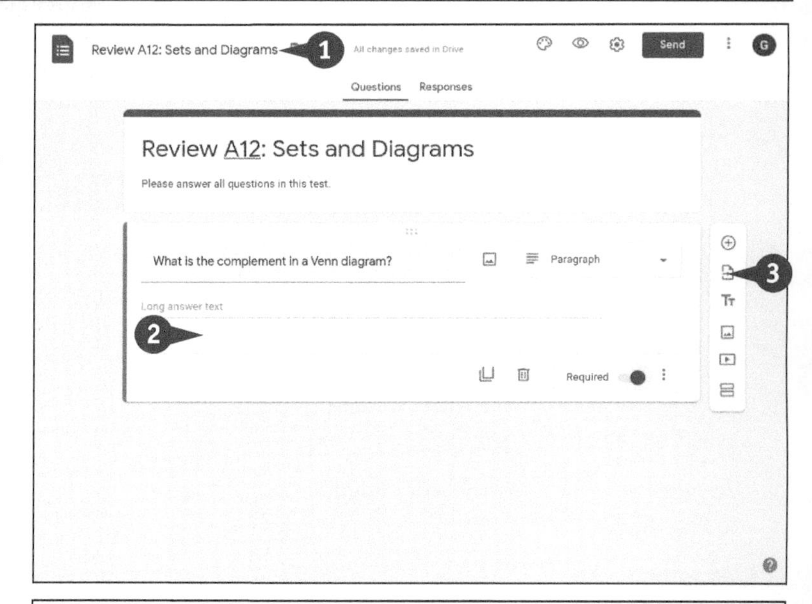

The Select Form dialog box opens.

The Forms tab appears at first.

A. You can click **Previously selected** to display the Previously Selected tab, which lists forms from which you have previously imported questions.

4. Click the form from which you want to import questions.
5. Click **Select**.

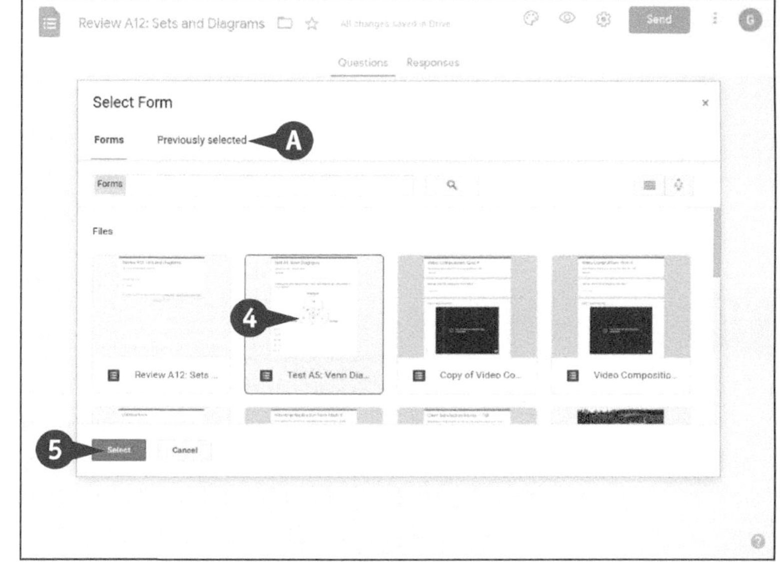

The Select Form dialog box closes.

The Import Questions pane appears on the right side of the window.

B If you chose the wrong form, click **Change form** to open the Select Form dialog box again.

C You can click **Select all** (☐ changes to ☑) to select the check box for each question.

6 Click each question you want to import (☐ changes to ☑).

7 Click **Import questions**.

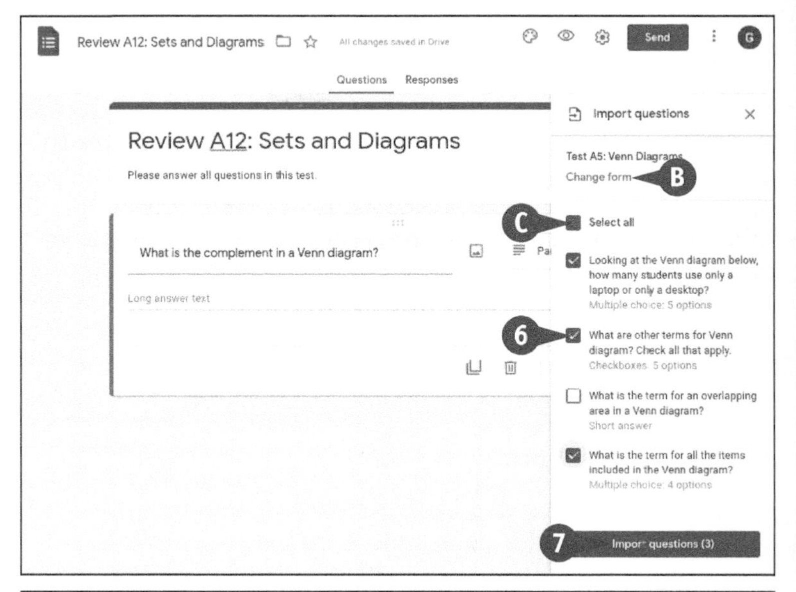

The Import Questions pane closes.

Google Forms imports the questions.

D A pop-up message shows the number of questions imported. This message closes after a few seconds.

E You can click **UNDO** to undo the import.

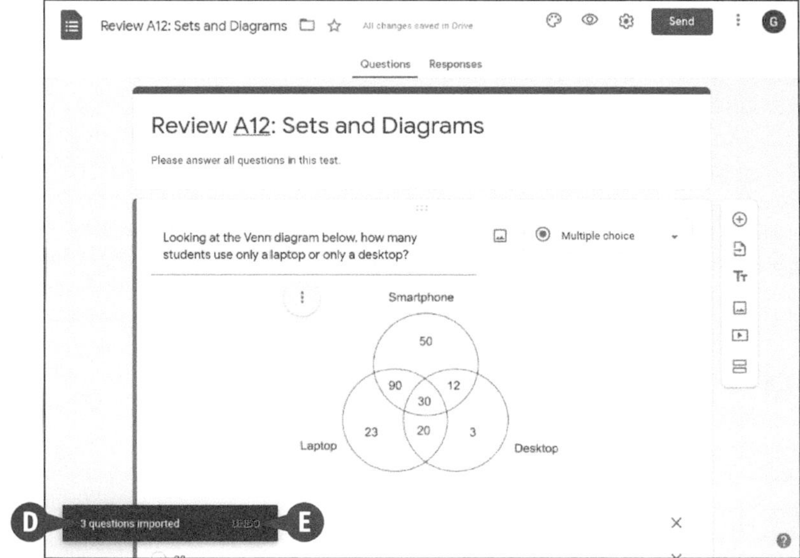

TIP

How do I duplicate an existing form?

Open the existing form in Google Forms, click **Menu** (⋮) to open the menu, and then click **Make a copy** (⧉) to display the Copy Document dialog box. The Name box shows *Copy of* and the name of the existing form; edit the name as needed. In the Folder area, click the current location, such as My Drive, to open the Select a File dialog box; navigate to the new location; and then click **Select**. The Select a File dialog box closes. Click **Share it with the same people** (☐ changes to ☑) if you want to share the duplicated form with the same people. Then click **OK**. The new form opens, and you can edit it as needed.

Create a Form with Multiple Sections

Many forms require only a single section through which all respondents must work from start to finish, but other forms benefit from being divided into sections — for two reasons. First, sections can make a form less daunting for respondents. Second, you can configure the form to control progression from section to section based on the respondent's answers, allowing the respondent to skip inapplicable questions.

This section shows you how to create a form with multiple sections. The following section, "Control Progression Based on Answers," explains how to use the respondent's answers to decide which subsequent sections confront them.

Create a Form with Multiple Sections

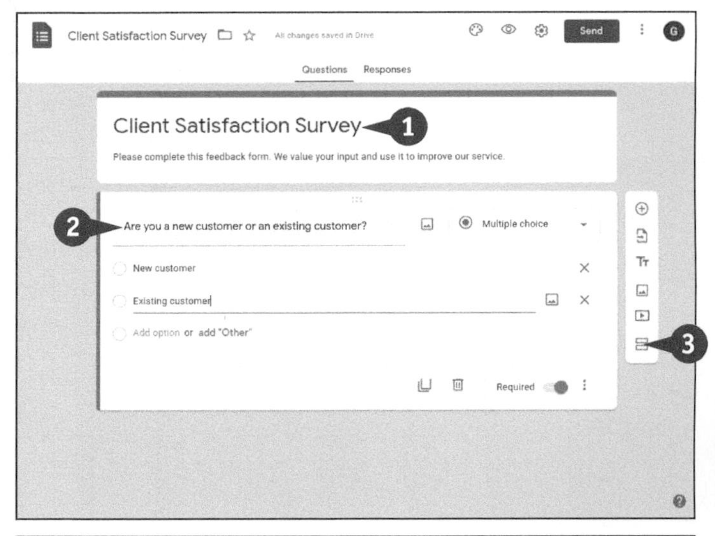

1. Start a form as usual.
2. Add the questions for what will become the first section. At this point, this is the only section.

   The example form's first section contains a single multiple-choice question, which asks whether the respondent is a new customer or an existing customer. The answer to this question determines which section the respondent sees next.
3. Click **Add section** (☰).

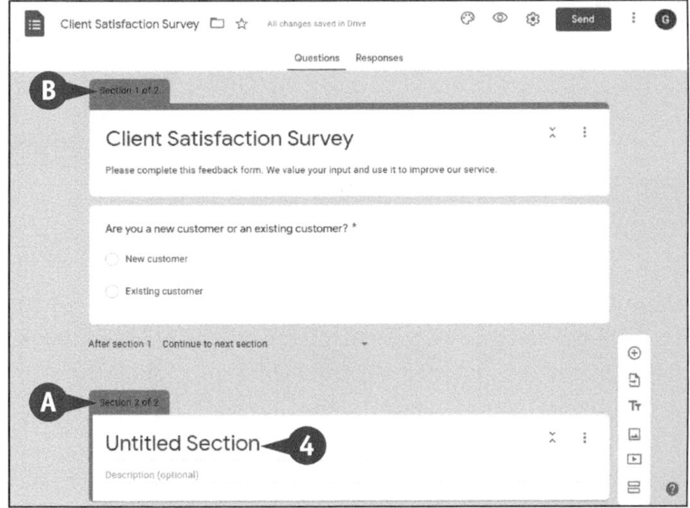

- **A** Google Forms adds a new section to the form.
- **B** The first part of the form becomes Section 1.

4. Click **Untitled Section**.

5 Type the section name.

6 Optionally, click **Description (optional)** and type a description.

7 Click **Add section** (☰).

C Google Forms adds a third section to the form.

8 Type the section name.

9 Optionally, click **Description (optional)** and type a description.

D The After Section pop-up menu below the end of each section except the last enables you to specify which section the respondent will see next.

E The default choice in each After Section pop-up menu is Continue to Next Section.

F You can click **Go to section** to specify a different section.

Note: Alternatively, you can use the respondent's answer to a question to decide which section to show next. See the next section, "Control Progression Based on Answers."

G You can click **Submit form** to submit the form instead of continuing.

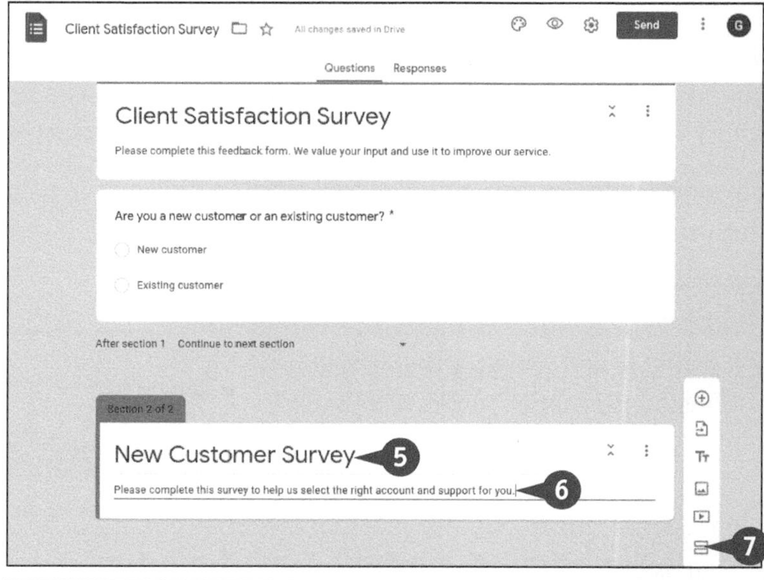

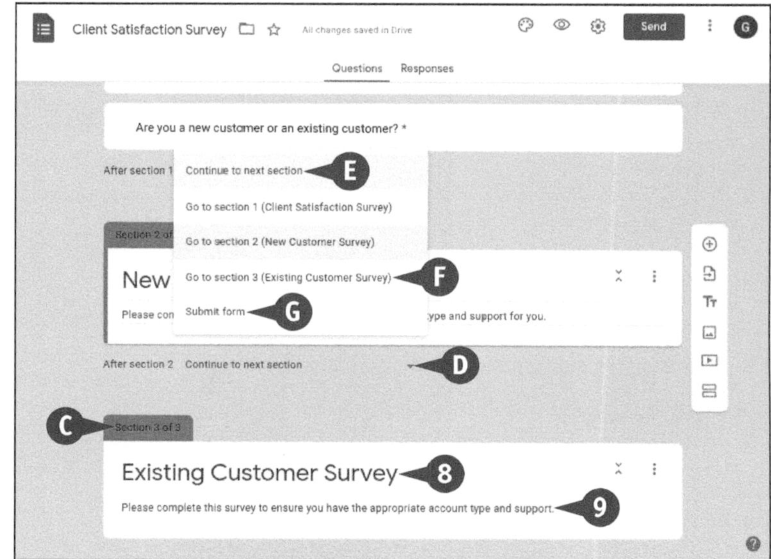

TIP

How can I rearrange the sections in a form?

Click **Menu** (⋮) to display the pop-up menu. You can then click **Merge with above** to merge the section with the preceding section; click **Move section** to display the Reorder Sections dialog box, in which you can shuffle the order of the sections, and then click **Save**; or click **Delete** to delete the section.

The pop-up menu also includes the Duplicate Section command, which creates a duplicate of the section immediately after it.

Control Progression Based on Answers

After creating multiple sections in a form, you can configure the form to automatically display the appropriate next section based on the respondent's answer to a particular question. For example, you might use a question that asks if the respondent is a new customer or an existing customer to direct new customers to one section of the form and existing customers to another section.

To control progression, you can use either a multiple-choice question or a drop-down question, but not other question types.

Control Progression Based on Answers

1. In the form, click the question that you will use to control progression through the form.

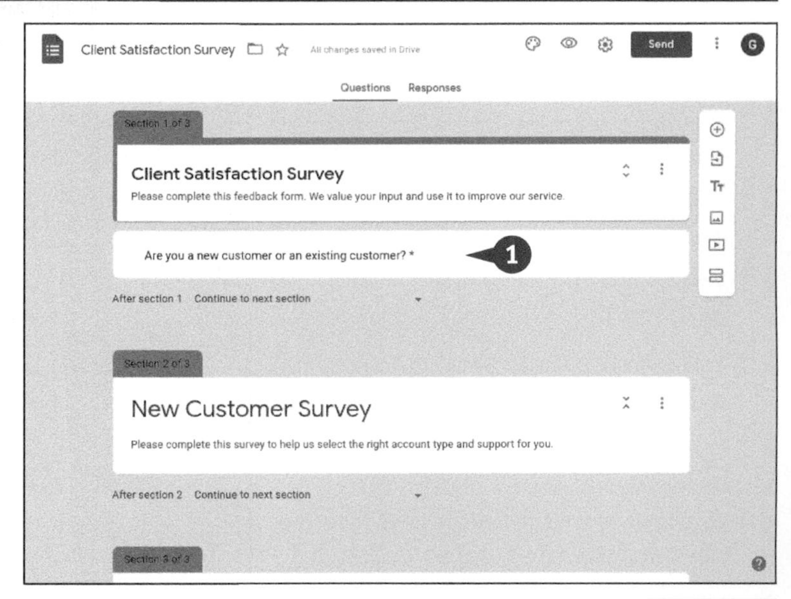

The question expands if it is collapsed.

2. Click **Menu** (⋮).

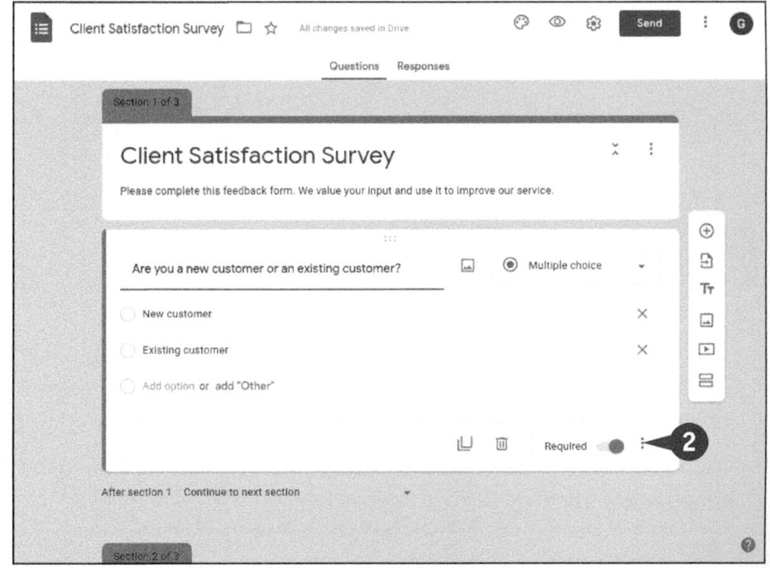

The menu opens.

3. Click **Go to section based on answer.**

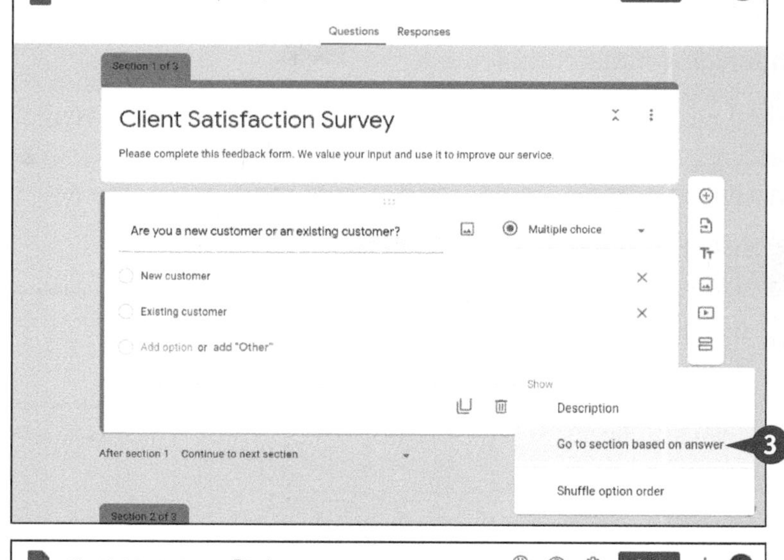

Ⓐ A Go to Section pop-up menu appears to the right of each option button or to the right of the drop-down menu.

4. Click **Go to section** (▾).

The Go to Section pop-up menu opens.

5. For the drop-down menu or for each option button, click the action you want the form to take if the respondent selects this answer. For example, click **Go to section** and the appropriate section number and name.

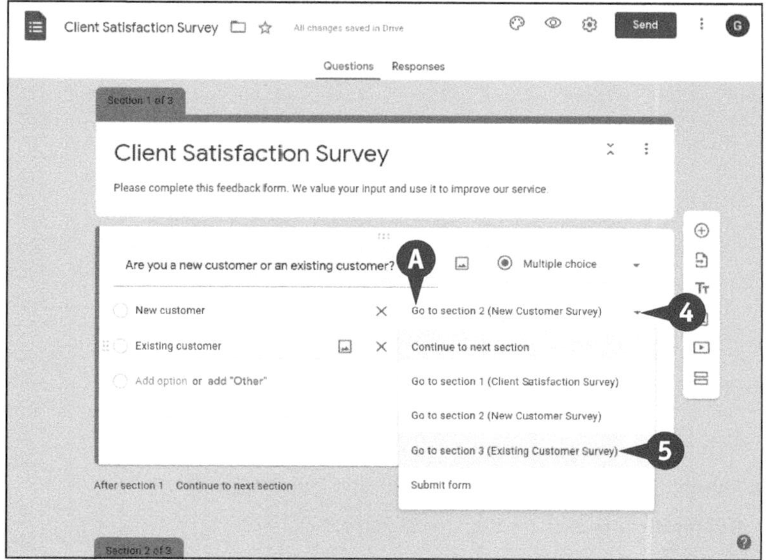

TIP

Why can I use only a multiple-choice question or a drop-down question to control progression?
These two question types offer a set of predefined answers from which the respondent can pick only one answer, so these types are suitable for making a flow decision. For example, selecting one option button in a multiple-choice question deselects whichever other option button was previously selected, if any. By contrast, a check box question allows the respondent to select either a single check box or multiple check boxes, so a check box question is not suitable for making a flow decision.

Add Collaborators to a Form

Google Forms enables you to share a form with one or more collaborators, people with whom you are working. Collaborating on a form can be a great way to avoid omissions and test a form thoroughly before deploying it.

When adding collaborators, you may need to configure your sharing settings in the Share with People Settings dialog box. Here, you can control whether editors can change permissions on the form and share it as well as whether viewers and commenters can download, print, and copy files.

Add Collaborators to a Form

1. Open the form you want to share.
2. Click **Menu** (⋮).

   The menu opens.
3. Click **Add collaborators** (👥).

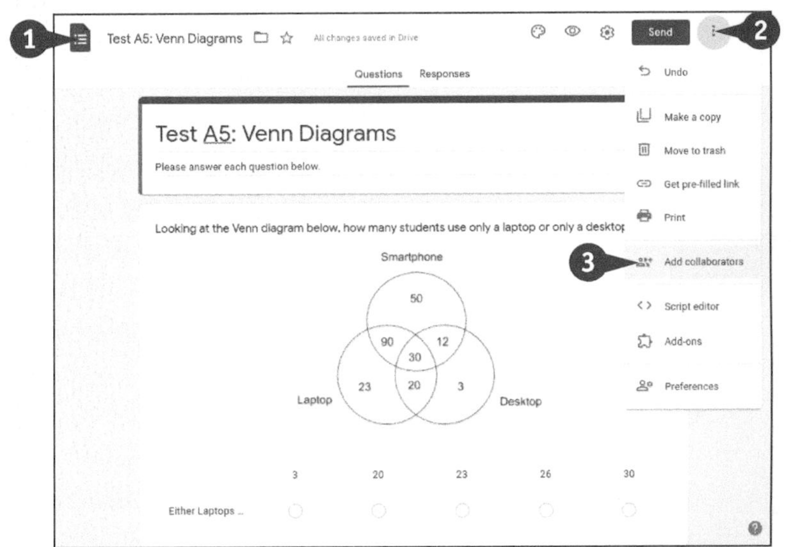

The Add Editors dialog box opens.

4. Click **Settings** (⚙).

   The Share with People Settings dialog box opens.
5. Select (☑) or deselect (☐) **Editors can change permissions and share**, as needed.
6. Select (☑) or deselect (☐) **Viewers and commenters can see the option to download, print, and copy**, as needed.
7. Click **Back** (←).

   The Add Editors dialog box opens again.

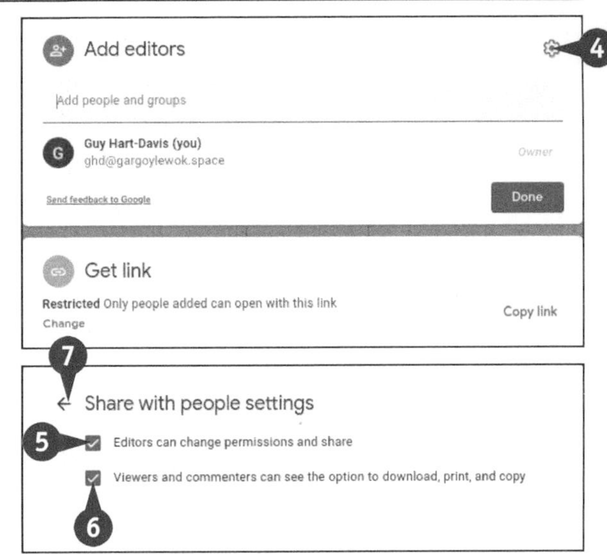

8 Start typing the first collaborator's name.

A list of matches appears.

9 Click the appropriate match.

The collaborator's name appears as a button.

You can now add other collaborators if you need to.

A You can click **Remove** (✕) to remove the name.

10 Select **Notify people** (☑) if you want the collaborator to receive a message telling them you have added them.

11 To add a custom note to the message, click **Message** and type the text.

12 Click **Send**.

The Add Editors dialog box closes.

Google Forms sends the message.

A *Person added* notification appears for a few seconds near the top of the Google Forms window.

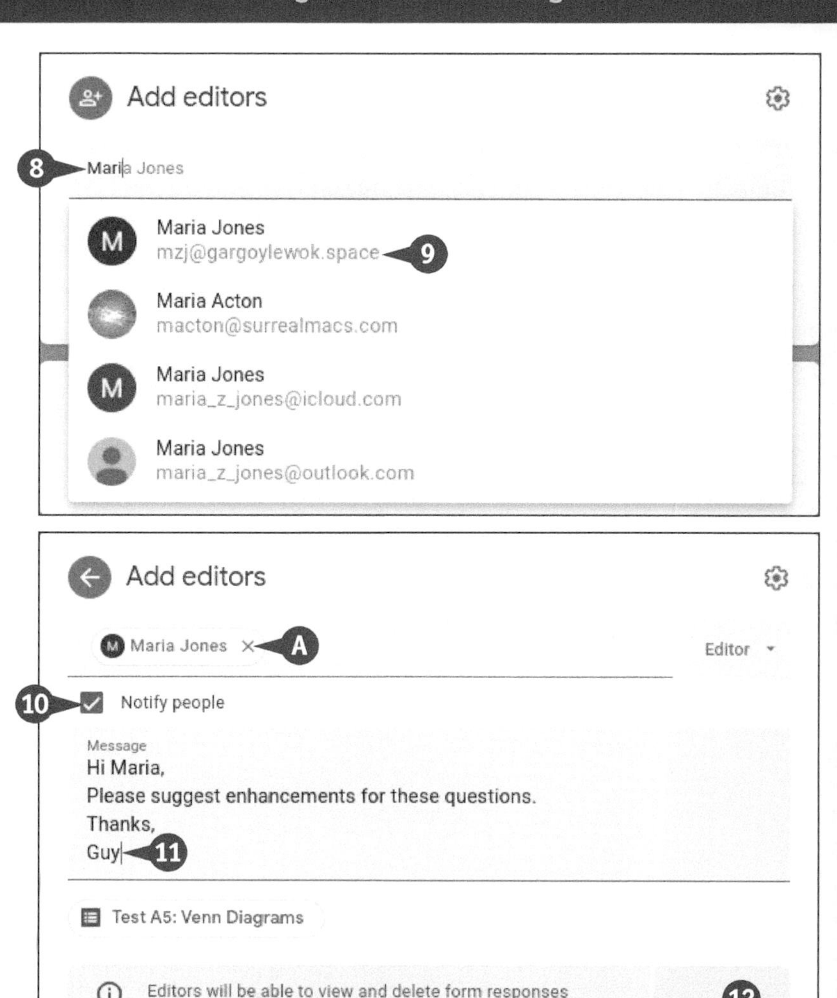

TIP

How do I remove a collaborator from a form?
With the form open, click **Menu** (⋮) to open the menu, and then click **Add collaborators** (👥+) to open the Add Editors dialog box. On the right side of the row for the collaborator, click the pop-up menu button (▼), which shows their current role, such as Editor. On the pop-up menu, click **Remove**.

Preview and Test a Form

After you have added some questions to a form, and perhaps divided it up into sections that you configure to control the flow of the form, you should preview and test the form to make sure it looks and works as planned. You may also want to have your collaborators preview and test the form to help identify any problems you miss.

When you preview the form, you can fill it in and submit your response just as a respondent would.

Preview and Test a Form

1. Open the form you want to preview and test.
2. Click **Preview** (◎).

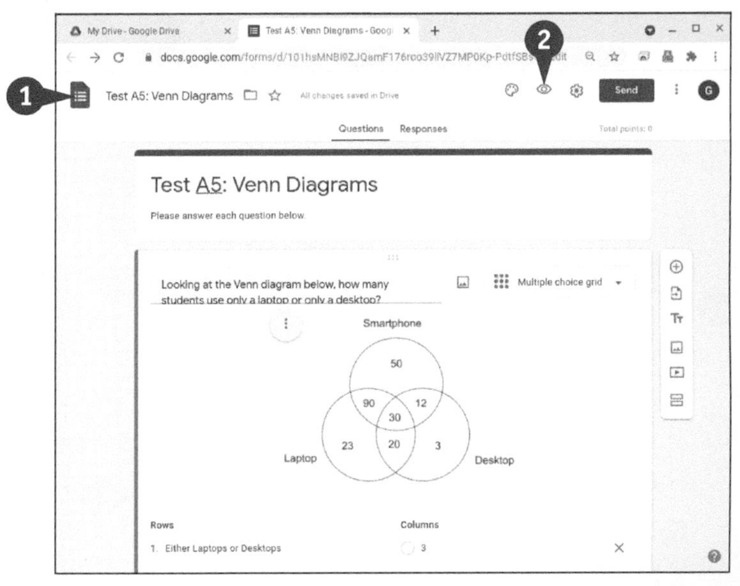

- **A** The form's preview opens in a new browser tab.
- **B** The Required legend shows that the red asterisk indicates a required question.

3. Verify that the red asterisk appears for each required question.
4. Check the size, position, and readability of any images or videos you have included.
5. Use the controls to answer each question. For example, for a multiple-choice question, click the appropriate option button (◯ changes to ◉).

Note: Scroll down to reach other questions.

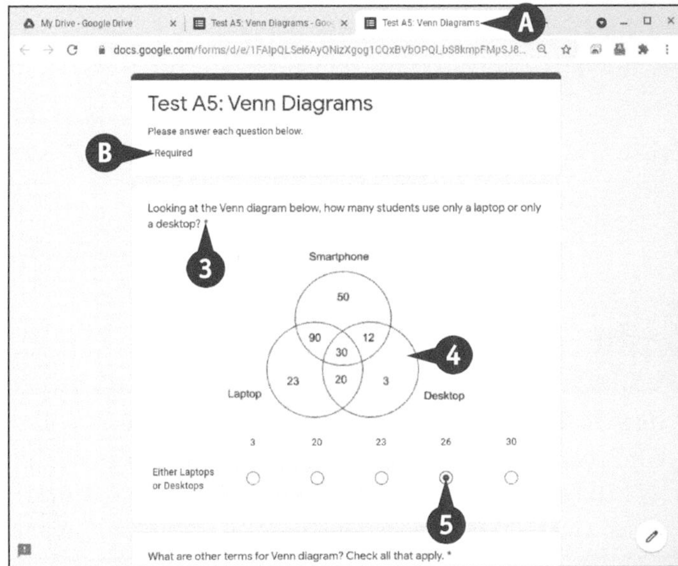

- **C** For a check box question, you can select (☑) one or more check boxes.
- **D** For a short-answer question, you can type your response.
- **E** For a multiple-choice question, you can select a single option button (○ changes to ◉).
- **F** You can click **Clear selection** to clear your choice in a multiple-choice question.
- **G** You can click **Edit this form** (✎) to switch to editing the form.

6. When you reach the end of the form, click **Submit**.

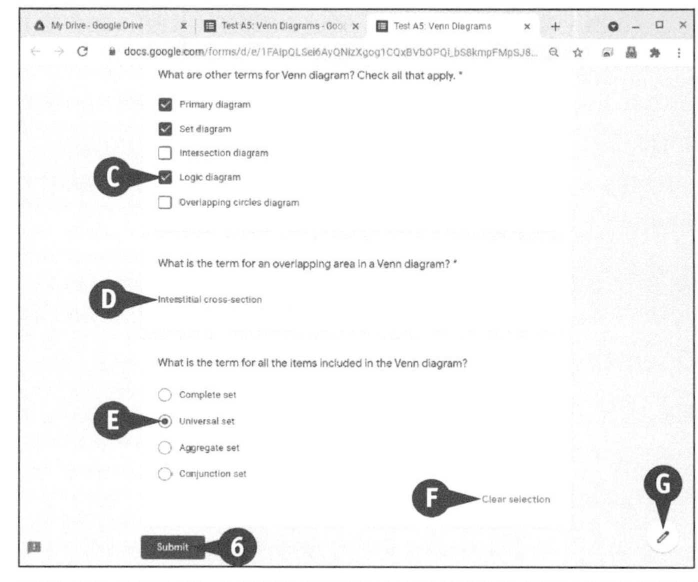

Google Forms submits the form.

A screen appears, showing you the form's message confirming that your response has been received.

- **H** If the View Score button appears, you can click **View score** to view your score for the form.
- **I** If the Submit Another Response link appears, you can click **Submit another response** to start another response.

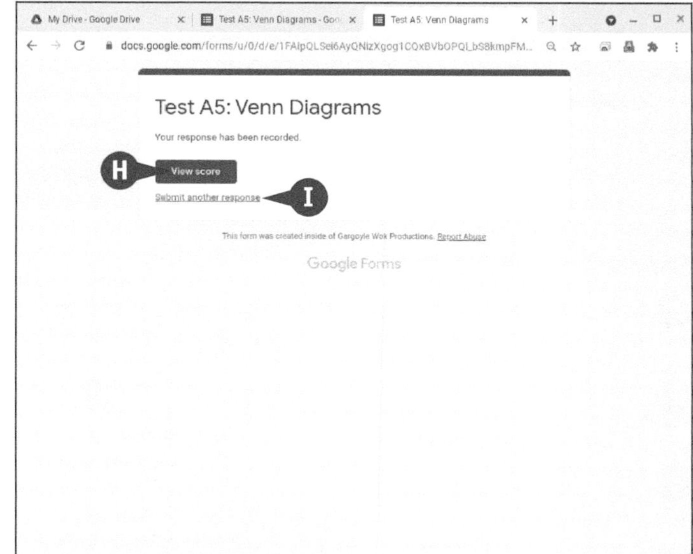

TIP

Why does the Leave Site? dialog box open when I click Edit This Form?

The Leave Site? dialog box opens to warn you that changes you have made to the form may not be saved — in other words, the answers you have chosen on the form will be lost. Given that you are previewing and testing the form, this is not a problem the way it would be if you were using the form for real. Simply click **Leave** in the Leave Site? dialog box to leave the form so that you can edit it.

Send a Form to Its Respondents

When your form is ready for use, you can send it to its respondents so they can fill it out. Google Forms enables you to send a form in three main ways. First, you can send a form via email, either including the form itself in the body of the email message or simply including a link to the form. Second, you can create a link to the form and then share the link via your preferred means, such as in an instant message. Third, you can share the form on a website by creating the HTML code needed to embed the form in a web page.

Send a Form to Its Respondents

Open the Send Form Dialog Box

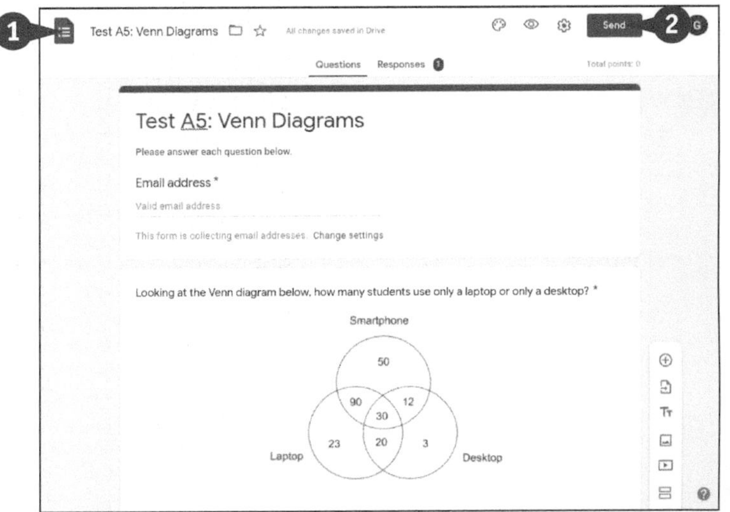

1. Open the form you want to send.
2. Click **Send**.

   The Send Form dialog box opens. You can send the form via email, as explained in the first subsection; send a link to the form via email or another means, as discussed in the second subsection; or copy HTML code for embedding the form in a web page, as covered in the third subsection, so that you can share it via a website.

Send a Form via Email

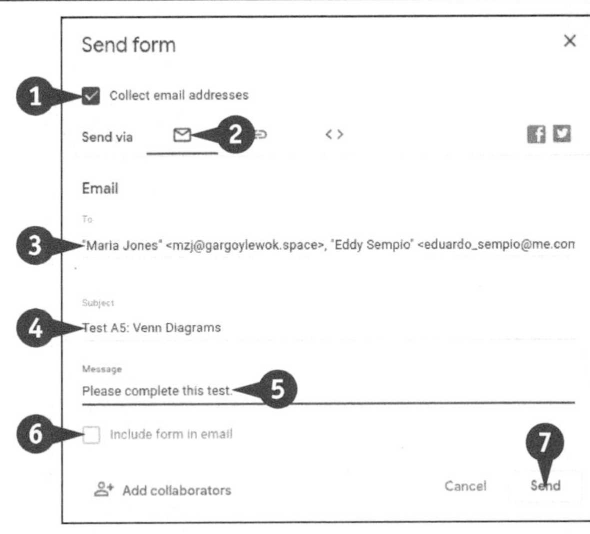

1. Select **Collect email addresses** (☑) if you want the form to collect respondents' email addresses.
2. If the Email tab (✉) is not selected, click **Email** (✉) to display its contents.
3. Click **To** and enter the email addresses of the recipients.
4. If necessary, edit the default subject, which is the form name.
5. Customize the default message, as needed.
6. If the Include Form in Email check box is available, select **Include form in email** (☑) to include the form in the message rather than sending only a link.
7. Click **Send**.

   Google Forms sends the form.

Send a Link to a Form

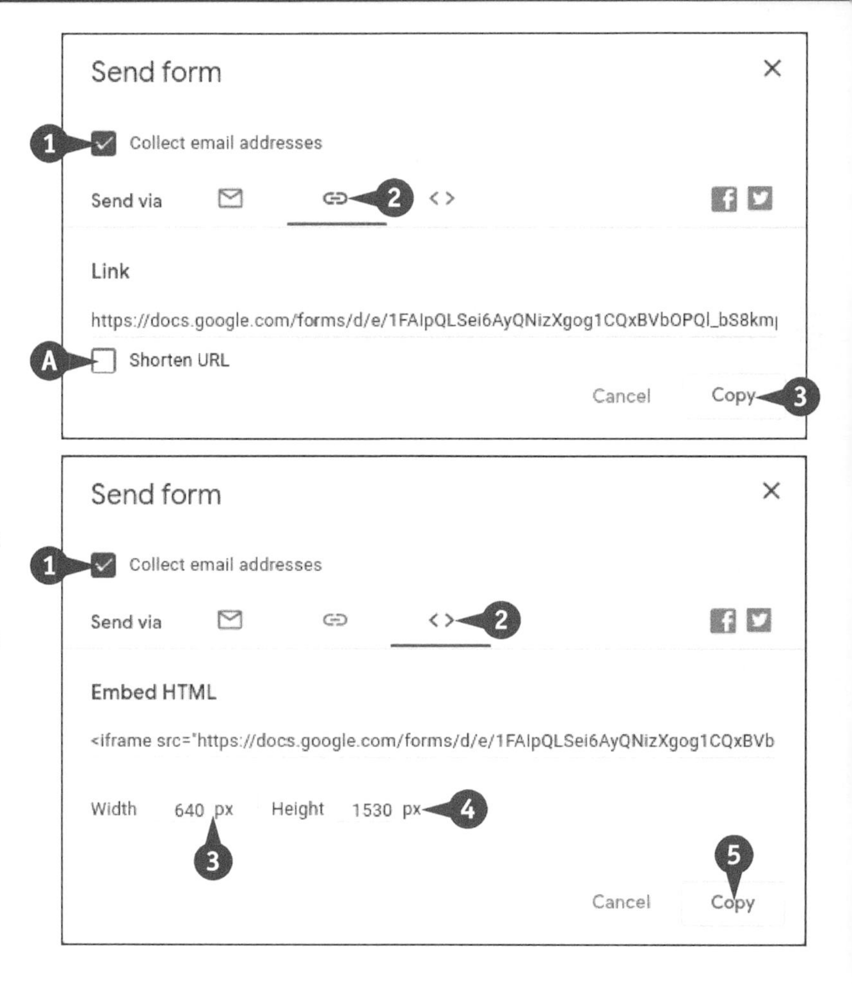

1. Select **Collect email addresses** (☑) if you want the form to collect respondents' email addresses.
2. If the Link tab (🔗) is not selected, click **Link** (🔗) to display its contents.

   A. You can select **Shorten URL** (☑) to create a shorter version of the URL.
3. Click **Copy**.

   Google Forms copies the link to your computer's clipboard. You can then paste the link into whichever app you are using to share it.

Get HTML to Embed the Form in a Web Page

1. Select **Collect email addresses** (☑) if you want the form to collect respondents' email addresses.
2. If the Embed HTML tab (< >) is not selected, click **Embed HTML** (< >) to display its contents.
3. Click **Width** and adjust the width measurement, in pixels, if needed.
4. Click **Height** and adjust the height measurement, again in pixels, if needed.
5. Click **Copy**.

   Google Forms copies the HTML to your computer's clipboard. From there, you can paste it into the appropriate web page in a web-page editor.

TIP

In what other ways can I share a form?

You can share a Google Forms form on Facebook or on Twitter. Open the form, and then click **Send** to open the Send Form dialog box. Select **Collect email addresses** (☑) if you want the form to collect respondents' email addresses. Then click **Share form via Facebook** (f) or **Share form via Twitter** (🐦), sign in to the service, and follow the prompts.

View the Responses to a Form

After you send a form to its respondents, or share the form with them via other means, Google Forms automatically tracks the responses sent to the form. Starting from the form itself, you can quickly access the responses, which you can view in three ways: as a summary of all responses, by questions, and by individual responses.

Google Forms enables you to send the form's responses to a Google Sheets spreadsheet so that you can tabulate and analyze them. You can either create a new spreadsheet or use an existing one.

View the Responses to a Form

1. Open the form whose response you want to view.

   A. The Responses tab button shows the number of responses received.

2. Click **Responses**.

   The Responses screen appears.

   B. You can set the **Accepting responses** switch to Off ( ) to stop accepting responses to the form.

3. Click **Summary**.

   The Summary tab appears.

   C. You can view the summary of results for each question.

Note: Scroll down to see further questions.

4. Click **Question**.

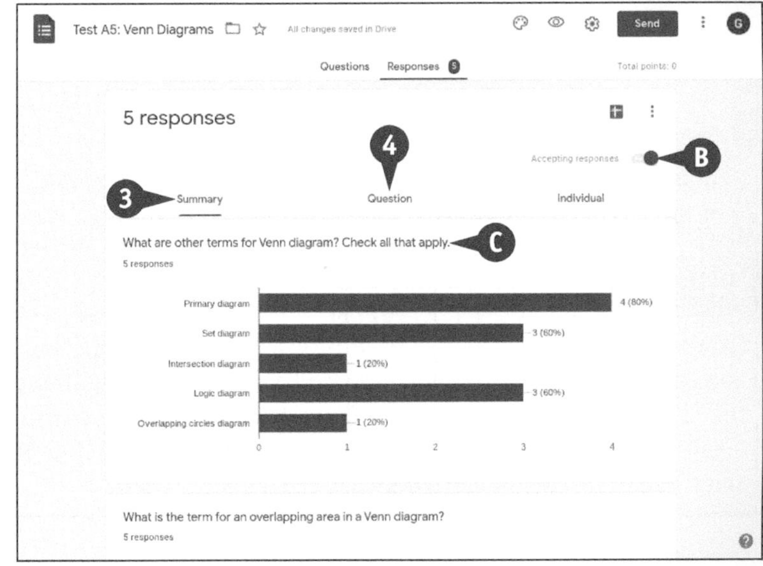

The Question tab appears.

D You can click **Question** (▾) to display the list of questions, and then click the question you want to see.

E You can click **Previous** (<) to display the previous question.

F You can click **Next** (>) to display the next question.

G You can see respondents' answers to the questions.

5 Click **Individual**.

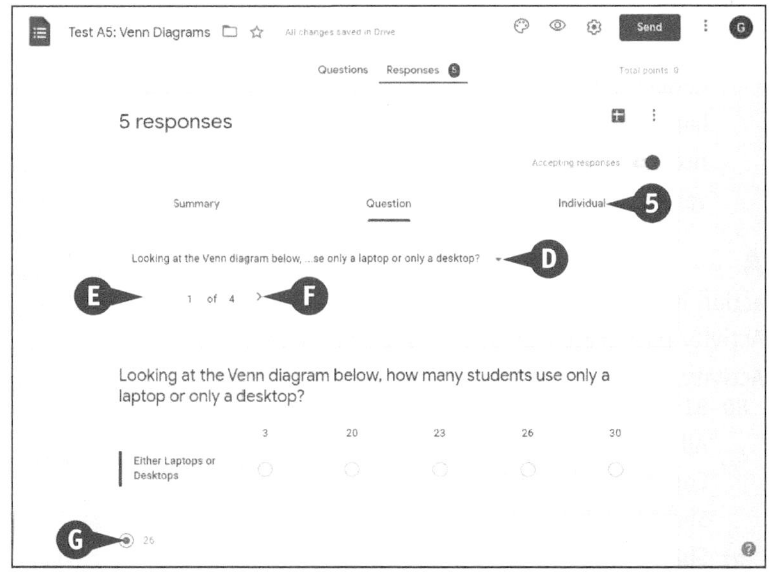

The Individual tab appears, showing the responses for one individual respondent at a time.

H You can click **Previous** (<) to display the previous respondent's responses.

I You can click **Next** (>) to display the next respondent's responses.

J You can see the respondent's answers to each question.

6 When you finish viewing responses, click **Questions**.

The Questions screen appears again.

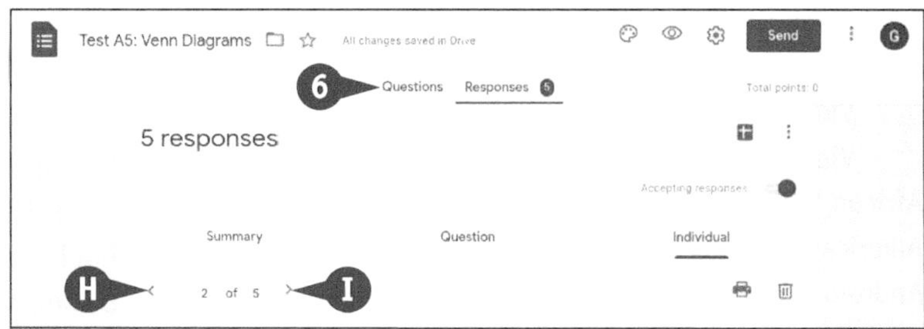

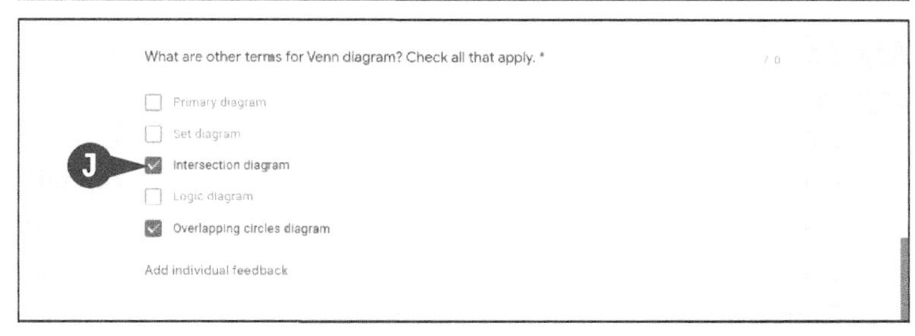

TIP

How do I send a form's responses to a spreadsheet?

With the form open, click **Responses** to display the Responses screen, and then click **Create Spreadsheet** (⊞) to the left of the Menu button (⋮); alternatively, click **Menu** (⋮), and then click **Select response destination.** The Select Response Destination dialog box opens. To create a new spreadsheet, click **Create a new spreadsheet** (○ changes to ◉); edit the suggested name as needed; and then click **Create.** To use an existing spreadsheet, click **Select existing spreadsheet** (○ changes to ◉) and then click **Select**; in the Choose a Spreadsheet Where We'll Copy Responses to Your Form dialog box, click the spreadsheet, and then click **Select.**

E

F

G

H

I

K

L

M

N

O

T

U

V

W

Z